Katharine of Aragon

ABOUT THE AUTHOR

PATRICK WILLIAMS is Emeritus Professor of Spanish History at the University of Portsmouth and is a Fellow of the Royal Historical Society. He has written extensively on Spanish history, notably in his studies of Philip II and the Duke of Lerma, first minister and favourite of Philip III. He is completing two volumes on Spanish government in the Early Modern period. He lives in Southsea.

Praise for Patrick Williams

Armada
'Absorbing, intelligent... an original, wide-ranging narrative'
BBC HISTORY MAGAZINE

Philip II
'Up-to-date and sound'
GEOFFREY PARKER

Katharine *of* Aragon

Henry VIII's Lawful Wife?

PATRICK WILLIAMS

Emeritus Professor of Spanish History
at the University of Portsmouth

AMBERLEY

First published 2013

Amberley Publishing
The Hill, Stroud
Gloucestershire, GL5 4EP

www.amberley-books.com

British Library Cataloguing in Publication Data.
A catalogue record for this book is available from the British Library.

ISBN 978-1-84868-325-9 [HARDBACK]
ISBN 978-1-4456-1923-1 [PAPERBACK]
ISBN 978-1-4456-1880-7 [EBOOK]

Typesetting and Origination by Amberley Publishing
Printed in Great Britain

CONTENTS

PROLOGUE
THE LIFETIME OF KATHARINE OF ARAGON (1485–1536)

Every year the clergy and congregation of Peterborough Cathedral pay homage to the memory of Katharine 'of Aragon', who is buried in the cathedral. It is remarkable that an Anglican cathedral should render such honour to a Roman Catholic queen, the more so since it was Katharine's 'divorce' from Henry VIII that was in effect the signal for the separation of the Church in England from the Roman communion, but it is a powerful and moving tribute to the memory of a woman who, although a Spaniard by birth, became – and remains – one of the best-loved and most admired of English queens.

Katharine married twice into the English royal family that we know as 'the Tudors'. Both marriages proved to be of momentous historical importance. Her first marriage, to Prince Arthur, lasted only for months before Arthur died in 1502 but the question of whether it had been consummated came to have an extraordinary – and bitterly divisive – importance in the development of English history: until her dying day Katharine maintained with unflinching determination that it had not been consummated. This study will suggest that she was telling the full truth: drained by illness, Arthur was impotent.

Katharine is of course chiefly known to history for her second marriage, when she became the first of the six wives of Henry VIII, loved with real intensity and then abandoned with fulminating ruthlessness by a man who was transformed from a brilliant (and tender) young king into one of the most brutal of English monarchs. She knew Henry VIII better than anyone, for she was married to him for longer – much, much longer – than any of his other wives. She was, indeed, the only one of Henry's wives who could intimidate him: it was his rage at her refusal year after year to bend her principles – religious, dynastic and personal – before his tempestuous will that explained the unremitting vindictiveness with which he treated her (and their daughter Mary) in her later years. There was genuine nobility in Katharine's resistance to Henry, and there was, too, a triumph over him after both of their deaths: in 1553 Mary became the first regnant Queen of England, as Mary I.

Katharine's story is, however, more than merely the account of her marriages, for she was among the best-connected people of her age and her story involved some of the great powers of Europe at a formative time in the development of the Continent's political, economic and religious structures, when the 'nation-states' of Western Europe were coming into being. Her parents and her second husband were emblematic figures among the great state-founders (or refounders) of this generation. Katharine's parents – Isabella I, Queen of Castile, and Ferdinand II, King of Aragon – have left an imprint on history which is even greater than Henry VIII's. The 'Catholic Kings', as they were known, unified the Crowns of Aragon and Castile and so created the country that we know as 'Spain'. They then set their new country on the road to political and military pre-eminence in European politics and to the establishment of a truly world-wide empire across the seas in 'the Indies' which has left a defining mark on the world in which we live today.

It was to be central to Katharine's fate that she was also the aunt of Charles V, Holy Roman Emperor (1519–58) and King of Spain (as Charles I, 1516–56). By temperament and background, Charles faced backwards, to a Christendom that had been unified – if often only in theory – under Pope and Emperor and he sought with quixotic singlemindedness to re-establish the old order and to withstand the growth of the national powers. The central dynamic of this extraordinary man's life was his obsession with preserving and expanding the power of his own family, the Habsburgs: Charles V was the supreme dynast. Paradoxically, this man of the medieval past was also the first European to rule over an empire on which the sun never set: as the result of an unforeseeable sequence of deaths he became the inheritor of the new Spain that Ferdinand and Isabella had created. It was during his reign that Spain acquired the two cornerstones of its empire in the Americas – Mexico was conquered in 1519–21 and Peru in the mid-1530s. Accordingly, Charles became, in a very real sense, the first 'globaliser'. But his power developed less dramatically in Europe than it did in the Americas; it was not until the mid- to late 1520s that he acquired the military and financial power to enable him to compete with the King of France for supremacy in Europe. It was Charles's triumph in Italy in the years 1525–7 that ultimately cost Henry VIII his chance of winning an annulment or a divorce and led in turn to the dreadful bitterness of the fate suffered by Katharine.

It is more than probable that if Katharine had provided Henry with a male heir their marriage would have survived until death parted them; Katharine was wise enough in the ways of kings to understand that they took mistresses with whom they lived parallel lives, and she was discreet enough, on the whole, to turn a blind eye to Henry's serial infidelities. But within a decade or so of his accession in 1509 it was becoming evident that Katharine would not be able to present Henry with a prince who could succeed to his throne. Like Charles V, Henry VIII was a dynast: the transmission of his throne to a male heir was *everything* to him. Katharine became pregnant with easy facility but was repeatedly unable to carry her children to term. Six times she carried Henry's children but only twice did she give birth to live children – in 1511 to Prince Henry, who survived for fifty-three days, and in 1516 to Princess Mary, who alone lived to adulthood, dying at the age of forty-two. Katharine's failure to provide Henry with a male heir broke the king's love for her, and perhaps too it contributed to the dramatic changes that came over him as a man and as a king. Henry threw Katharine into internal exile in England and, as she refused to facilitate his search for an annulment or divorce, so he treated her ever more vindictively. For the last five years of her life Katharine was denied contact with her daughter: even as she lay dying, Henry refused to let Mary visit her. Then, on hearing of Katharine's death, he dressed himself in celebratory yellow and danced and feasted to celebrate the end of the life of the 'harridan' whom he had once loved. The young gallant with whom Katharine had fallen in love so long ago was turning into a monster.

As the daughter and wife of such monarchs as Ferdinand and Isabella and Henry VIII, as the aunt of Charles V and as the mother of Mary I, Katharine stood at the centre of many of the tumultuous developments of a crucial half-century in the development of Europe and of its place in the world. Her marriages in England helped to reinforce the status and prestige of England and 'the Spanish Monarchy' as two of the emergent nation-states of Western Europe. Henry's determination to end his marriage to her also made of her, in time, an emblematic figure in the titanic struggle of the 1520s and 1530s that is known as 'the Reformation' and which led within a few years of her death to the division of Western Europe between a (broadly) Protestant north and a Catholic south. She was left afloat – barely – as history roared around and past her, but she did not drown.

It is ironic that Katharine, whose chief claim on history was her failure to produce a male heir to succeed to the throne, was part of the generation that lived through what has been called 'the Population Revolution', which led to a doubling of the number of Europeans in the first two-thirds of the sixteenth century (despite horrific statistics of infant mortality). But this was a revolution which did leave Katharine behind; her failure to carry children to term and to produce a boy to outlive her husband was not untypical of the fate of many women, but few suffered so cruelly for it as she did.

It is also ironic that Katharine has been mistitled by history: she was born in Castile and has no claim on the title 'of Aragon'. The point is not merely semantic: as a Princess of Castile Katharine was legally entitled to succeed to the throne of Castile if her elder brother and sisters failed to provide for the succession but because she was not born in Aragon she was legally disbarred from succeeding to that throne. The title 'of Aragon' is therefore incorrect and misleading. Nevertheless, it has been so universally applied to her that it is now too late to change it and so its usage will continue in this book; there is, after all, only one 'Katharine of Aragon'.

Intellectually, Katharine was very much a woman of 'the Renaissance'. It was curiously appropriate that she had been born at Alcalá de Henares, where in 1499 the most advanced university in Spain was established (La Universidad Complutense). In the years 1502–22, the university produced the celebrated 'Polyglot Bible', in which the Old Testament was printed in Caldean, Hebrew, Greek and Latin and the New Testament in Greek and Latin; it was one of the emblematic works of what was called 'the New Learning', the rediscovery of the culture and values of classical antiquity and their application to the contemporary world. Katharine knew Cardinal Francisco Jiménez de Cisneros, who had supervised the project – indeed, she had been born in his palace – and came in time to form friendships with some of the leading members of the great generation of humanist scholars who were transforming European letters – Antonio de Nebrija and Juan Luis Vives among the Spaniards; Thomas

More and John Colet among the Englishmen. Indeed, Katharine was part of a generation in Spain which was learning to value women in quite a new way; as an expression of this, the University of Alcalá (like that of Salamanca) even appointed women to professorial chairs. Truly, the world was changing at an astonishing rate.

The production of Alcalá's great Bible was itself an expression of the intellectual revolution that was coming about as a result of the invention and rapid establishment of the printing press. Johannes Gutenberg had constructed the first wooden press using movable type in 1440, and it has been estimated that by 1500 as many as 20 million books may already have been printed in Western Europe. Half of these were religious tomes but they also included a wide range of political and even scientific volumes. The first printing presses in Spain were established in 1468 in Barcelona and Valencia; in France, in Paris in 1470. In 1476 William Caxton published Geoffrey Chaucer's *Canterbury Tales* as the first book to be produced in England; he was to follow this with a hundred or so other titles before he died in 1492. The presses played their role in the development of the new monarchies and also in the consolidation of the new religions and sects that appeared during the Reformation. Of course, most people could not read, but as cheap books began to circulate around Europe it became possible for educated people to read to all. Katharine's generation lived through a technological revolution that is comparable to that which we are nowadays experiencing with the spread of computer and mobile technology – and the disputes in which she became a central figure inspired a Europe-wide controversy in which polemicists, propagandists, scholars and universities used the printing press to churn out thousands of treatises, pamphlets and books. One great man, John Fisher, produced so many books in defence of Katharine against Henry that he could not remember how many he had written. Books became the currency of political and religious discourse, but they could carry danger to those who produced them: Fisher went to the scaffold for his contumacy and courage.

The circulation of printed books stimulated the development of languages, which in turn encouraged the growth of national consciousness. We should not exaggerate: many people thought of themselves as natives of a town, village or district rather than as belonging to a national unit. But there is no doubt that a sense of national identity was developing and that it was being fostered by contacts with 'abroad' and by the growing self-confidence of national languages. It was a paradox that the monarchies that were so self-consciously attempting to develop a sense of national identity were sometimes led by people who were not natives of the lands over which they ruled. Henry VII of England was a Welshman, while Charles I of Spain was born in Ghent. Moreover, several monarchs did not have easy familiarity with the language of their new lands; Isabella of Castile may well have spoken Portuguese as her first language and it is amusing – if fruitless – to speculate whether Henry VII's long years in Wales and in France cost him any familiarity with the English language. Certainly, there was nothing amusing to Castilians about Charles of Habsburg's inability to speak their language: it contributed to the alienation that led to a great revolt against him in 1520–21 (the revolt of the *comuneros*) that very nearly cost him his Spanish inheritance.

Katharine's lifetime saw Europe's view of itself re-shaped by two events of the most profound and enduring historical importance – the conquest of Constantinople by the Ottoman Turks in 1453 and the 'discovery' of the Americas by Christopher Columbus in 1492. Ottoman Turkey had an enormous population and was ruled with iron control by its sultans, and in this generation it turned its forces on Christendom. The fall of Constantinople on 29 May 1453 effectively marked the end of the Roman Empire and announced the establishment of an Islamic empire of apparently limitless power: with the conquest of Persia (1514), Syria (1516) and Egypt (1517), the Eastern Mediterranean became an Islamic lake. The new empire then turned against western Christendom – in 1521, Belgrade fell; in 1522, Rhodes; in 1526, the Kingdom of Hungary was dismembered and in 1529 imperial Vienna itself was placed under siege. The wave of apparently irresistible attacks terrified Europe, not least because the long history of Islamic conquests since the seventh century demonstrated that only the Iberian countries had ever regained their liberties once they had been overrun. Conquest by Islam bade fair, therefore, to be permanent. Was Italy – the cultural and religious core of Europe – to be next?

The terrifying, and apparently unremitting, Turkish advance levered the concept of the 'crusade' back into the vocabulary of western Christendom. Pope Pius II (1458–64) meant it sincerely when he urged Christian princes to unite against 'the Turk' in the wake of the loss of Constantinople but others – including popes – made cynical use of it for their own reasons. The responsibility for leading the resistance of Christendom fell to the House of Austria and to the Holy Roman Emperor; in Charles V, the ideal of the Christian crusade against the power of the infidel found its very personification. In this sense at least, the Burgundian prince inherited the mantle of Ferdinand and Isabella, who had earned their title of 'the Catholic Monarchs' by reconquering Islamic Granada for Christianity. Katharine's nephew, like her parents, was a noted 'crusader' and he pursued his destiny with heroic determination, personally leading campaigns against Tunis (1535) and Algiers (1541).

With the 'discovery' of the Americas in 1492 – land was first sighted on 12 October – there came about a reappraisal of the centrality of Europe and of Christianity in the world: was Europe at the core of the world? What were the rights of people who had never heard of Jesus Christ? It happens that a great *mappa mundi* has survived which paints the old and new worlds exactly as they were known in 1500 (the year before Katharine left Spain for England): Juan de la Cosa confidently placed Europe and the Mediterranean at the centre of the world and briefly sketched the Americas. But geographical knowledge was growing at an astonishing rate: by 1513 the Spanish knew that they had discovered not only a new world in the Americas but a great new ocean, 'the Pacific', and in 1519–22 the epic voyage named after Ferdinand Magellan circumnavigated the globe, bringing even newer and more challenging perspectives to Europe. Even now, the rate of change accelerated; in 1519, exactly as Magellan left Spain, Hernán Cortes began the conquest of Mexico that would bring untold riches to Spain and change all European attitudes to discovery and expansion overseas. The 'discovery' of the Americas, like the Ottoman conquest of Constantinople, was only the beginning of a long process of tumultuous change, of an enduring reassessment of Europe's place in the world.

Katharine had close contacts with both of these epochal events; she was present as a small child when her parents received the keys of the city of Granada from the Moorish king in 1492 and she sat alongside them in Barcelona when in 1493 Columbus brought them the first reports of 'the New World'. He also presented them with the first 'Indians' from the New World, dressed in their garish costumes and dancing for their new sovereigns. How the young Katharine must have gawped at these strange men! She could never have understood that these few men would one day stand as symbols of one of the very greatest of recorded human tragedies – the enslavement and transportation of millions of men, women and children to serve the imperatives of Europe's colonial empires. But if Katharine could not have guessed at this, she was most certainly, even at the age of seven, aware of the imperatives of 'crusade' and 'discovery'.

The conquests of Constantinople and Granada and the 'discovery' of 'the Indies' formed crucial parts of her education in the ways of the world that was changing with such extraordinary speed in front of her.

What did not change – it never changed! – was Katharine's religious faith. She was born, lived and died as a devoted member of the 'One, Holy, Roman, Catholic and Apostolic Church' (to give it its formal title). There is no evidence that even in her darkest moments of abandonment and despair she ever doubted her faith or the Church which organised and administered it for her. Certainly, as the daughter of 'the Catholic Monarchs' she must have had an Erastian appreciation of how scornful her parents could be about the lack of moral fibre in some of the popes with whom they had dealings: Katharine would most certainly have appreciated that grave tensions could arise between monarchs and popes. But her faith in the papacy never wavered, and it was tribute to the depth of her religious faith that it did not do so, for few loyal Catholics suffered so much at the hands of the popes of the 'High Renaissance' as did Katharine, and it was her sad destiny to have her fate decided by three of the most egregious of them – Alexander VI (1492–1503), Julius II (1503–13) and Clement VII (1523–34).

1

EUROPE & ITS WORLD, 1500: RECOVERY & EXPANSION

Europe Expanding: The Great Discoveries & the Population Revolution
In 1500, Juan de la Cosa produced and signed a *mappa mundi* which showed the world as it was known to be at one of the defining conjunctures in its history. De la Cosa was a distinguished sailor and cartographer; not only had he sailed with Columbus in 1492 but he owned the Admiral's flagship, the *Santa María*. Despite the loss of his treasured ship after it ran aground in Haiti on Christmas Day 1492, de la Cosa sailed on Columbus's second voyage (1493–6) and then accompanied Americo Vespucci on the voyage in 1499 that led to the naming of 'America'. His map incorporated his discoveries on these great journeys and also those of Bartolomeu Dias, the Portuguese sailor who had rounded the 'Cape of Good Hope' in 1488. He even squeezed in references to Vasco da Gama's arrival in India in 1498 and to John Cabot's voyages for the English Crown in 1496–98. De la Cosa's map was therefore very much a 'state of the art' production but even as the map went to press it was already out of date, for it did not incorporate the discoveries that had been made by Columbus on his third voyage (1498–1500).[1]

De la Cosa's map proudly reflected the pioneering discoveries of which he had been part: he mapped the islands of the Caribbean fairly accurately and drew the northern coast of South America with some precision. He also permitted himself to conjecture that South America encircled the Caribbean and continued northwards into the area that we know as North America. His great map is, accordingly, not merely very beautiful but very accurate: in it we can see exactly how the world appeared to a man on the cutting edge of knowledge and discovery in 1500.

Even as the sailors of Portugal and Spain reached out into the Indian and Atlantic Oceans (and in 1521 they would sail into the Pacific Ocean) de la Cosa resolutely centred his map on the Mediterranean, the cultural, commercial and religious centre of the world as he knew it. At the epicentre of his map lay Italy, the focal point of much of European culture and religion. De la Cosa's map of the Mediterranean was informed by the deep practical knowledge accumulated by sailors over centuries, and its contours and distances are so accurate that they might almost have been taken from a modern satellite photograph. However, the farther away from the Mediterranean that the map moved, the more it blurred – and sometimes even distorted – geographical realities. For instance, on the northern periphery of Europe, de la Cosa's image of the British Isles was little more than a sketch that was only tolerably competent; London and the trading towns of the south coast were well known and scientifically mapped but Scotland and the coast of Ireland were largely *terra incognita* – or perhaps we might say that they were lands in which Continental Europe had little interest. The British Isles seemed largely indeed to consist (not for the last time) of Southern England and the great capital city.

The 'great discoveries' being made by Columbus, Dias and their fellows paralleled another historical revolution, for the population of Europe (and indeed of much of the world) virtually doubled during the century after 1450: historians refer to this tumultuous change as 'the population revolution'. In the first instance, this revolution represented a recovery by Europe's people from what may properly be described as the most profoundly important catastrophe in their history, the 'Great Plague' or 'Black Death' of 1348–52, when over one-half of the population died as bubonic plague spread from Southern Europe, reaching as far north as Yorkshire.[2] The proportionate importance of the disaster has been most graphically expressed by Professor Samuel Cohn, who bravely reminds us that the human losses in the two world wars of the twentieth century were 'minor in comparison' with those resulting from the Great Plague, for they resulted in the deaths of about 3 per cent of European people while the plague killed over 50 per cent (and in some places even up to 80 per cent).[3]

Recovery came about slowly, as the result of the (comparative) absences of virulent and large-scale plagues and the small-scale losses in warfare.

By 1500 the population of Europe had just about regained the levels of 1348 – about 85–100 million people. Fernand Braudel, a historian touched by genius, wrote of the range of political, social and economic consequences that flowed from 'the population revolution', reminding us that the dynamic energy that it unleashed had the most enormous and wide-ranging consequences in every sphere of life:

> The very striking, and indeed revolutionary advance of the first sixteenth century (1450–1550) on the whole slowed down during the second (1550–1650) ... this increase was universal ... it was common to both rich regions and poor, the populations of the plains, the mountains, and the steppes, to all towns, whatever their size, and all rural districts. [The reader] will be prepared to accept that this biological revolution was the major factor in all the other revolutions with which we are concerned, more important than the Turkish conquest, the discovery and colonization of America, or the imperial vocation of Spain. Had it not been for the increase in the number of men, would any of these glorious chapters ever have been written? ... This increase lay behind all the triumphs and catastrophes of a century during which man was first a useful worker and then, as the century wore on, a growing burden. By 1550 the turning-point had been reached. There were too many people for comfort.[4]

It is ironic that historical demographers should speak of the population revolution as having come about during a 'healthy' period, for the statistics of life and death were truly ghastly – so much so indeed that it seems remarkable that population levels even grew, let alone doubled. To properly understand this revolution we have to rid ourselves of some misconceptions. Most notable among them is the belief that sixteenth-century people had life expectancies of thirty-five years or so. This is simplistic, for longevity depended upon passing a series of critical hurdles. The most important of these were those of gestation and birth and the first two years of life: barely half of the children who were born alive survived past their second birthday. For the mother herself, childbirth was a traumatic and dangerous ordeal and many women made wills before they went into labour.[5] Katharine herself had a dreadful experience of childbirth; over the years 1510–18 four of her babies either were either stillborn or died prematurely. Only two survived the hazards of gestation and birth (and one of them only lived for fifty-three days).

Political Structures: A Primogeniture
The national monarchies of Western Europe passed ordinarily through the male line. Certainly, in some countries – England and Castile among them – girls could succeed if there was not a male heir, but monarchy remained in essence a male institution. In France, 'the Salic Law' expressly prohibited female succession. In other states and countries, women were not officially debarred from succeeding but it was held impracticable for them to exercise power and it was generally assumed that they would marry so that their husband could govern in their stead. England came into this category: in practice, although not strictly in legal theory, it was axiomatic that to maintain domestic peace the throne had to be transmitted in the male line, preferably from the king to his eldest son.

It therefore became the first responsibility of kings and queens to secure the succession by producing at least one male child – preferably more – and girls who could be used for marital alliances. Some families managed this without apparent difficulties but for others it proved to be tantalisingly difficult to secure the succession in the male line. Often, it seemed as if it was monarchs who found it hardest of all to provide for a masculine succession: Henry VIII famously married six times but produced only three children who survived into their teens, and only one of them was a male. Similarly, in France, Charles VIII (1483–98) and Louis XI (1498–1515) both died without leaving heirs, and so Francis I (1515–47) became the first King of France since Louis XI in 1483 to produce a male heir who lived to succeed him (Henry II, 1547–59).

Failure to produce a male heir who would succeed, unchallenged, to the throne was the source of much of the political disturbance that marked Western Europe in the late fifteenth century. Indeed, few thrones had suffered as much as the monarchies that form the subject of this study, the English and the Spanish. The English throne was struck time and again by violence: Henry VI was murdered in 1471 and in 1483 Richard of Gloucester almost certainly killed King Edward IV's two sons – 'the Princes in the Tower' – so that he himself could succeed to the throne. It was a dangerous thing to be King of England, more so to be an aspirant to the throne. Monarchs in Spain did not have to fear for their lives in the fifteenth century but in the Kingdom of Castile the manifest impotence of Henry IV (1454–74) created almost insoluble problems within the body politic – problems that were resolved when on Henry's death in 1474 his half-sister Isabella seized the throne for herself.

In both England and Spain the long decades of political turbulence were brought to an end by monarchs who won their thrones in battle – Henry VII in 1485 in England and Isabella in Castile after the civil war of 1474–79. Both monarchs then made deeply considered marriages to unite their realms and legitimise their own power: Henry VII virtually brought 'the Wars of the Roses' to an end by marrying Elizabeth of York in 1486, while Isabella married Ferdinand, heir to the thrones of Aragon in 1469, thereby effectively uniting the Crowns of Castile and Aragon.

But marriage was only the first step and would probably prove to be meaningless if male children did not follow from it. The pressure on wives to produce at least one male heir who outlived his father – and who preferably was by that time an adult – was enormous and unrelenting. The business of royal marriage was to produce boys. And it *was* a business: wives who did not present their husbands with sons faced hazardous futures across the monarchies of Western Europe, for the failure to produce a male heir in turn imposed unsustainable pressures upon the kings themselves. Nowhere was this to prove to be more true than of the marriage of Henry VIII and Katharine.

Universalist Claims: The Papacy & the 'Holy Roman Empire'

The titular leadership of Europe lay jointly with the papacy and the 'Holy Roman Empire', which between them claimed religious and secular supremacy over all Christians. In both cases, ancestry legitimised these elevated claims: the papacy insisted that it lay in direct 'Apostolic succession' to St Peter while the Emperor grandly boasted that he was the heir not just of Charlemagne but of the Roman emperors, the Caesars.

Papal claims to authority over all Christians had most recently been restated in 1439 by the General Council of the Church in Florence, which used several Biblical texts to underpin the Pope's authority, the most important of them being from Matthew 16:17–19:

> Simon Peter answered Jesus, 'You are the Christ, the Son of the living God.' Jesus replied, 'Blessed are you, Simon son of Jonah, for this was not revealed to you by man, but by my Father in heaven. And I tell you that you are Peter, and on this rock I will build my church, and the gates of Hell will not overcome it. I will give you the keys of the kingdom of heaven; whatever you bind on earth will be bound in heaven, and whatever you loose on earth will be loosed in heaven.'

The last sentence of Christ's injunction to Peter provided the papacy with the power that brought it into conflict with secular rulers, for the papacy interpreted it to mean that Christ had conferred upon St Peter and his successors the ultimate authority in disputes between Christians over matters of scripture, dogma and practice – that the Pope could, for example, 'bind' or 'loose' subjects from their allegiance to their monarchs or 'bind' or 'loose' individuals from their marriages. Papal claims of absolutism in matters religious would be tested to destruction by Henry VIII over his 'Great Matter', and in this the king was part of a historic generation for it was in the 1520s and 1530s that much of Europe broke with the papacy, rejecting its claims of primacy among Christians.

Popes were elected by cardinals voting in conclave: the rank of cardinal had existed from the fourth century and conferred the right to act as a senior adviser to the Pope. The 'College of Cardinals' was instituted in 1150 and given responsibility for the management of elections to the papacy: the Pope was chosen by a majority vote among those cardinals who were able to present themselves in Rome for the conclave. A papal conclave became proverbially a place where political and personal calculations carried weight but the Church believed – despite, it must be said, a fair amount of evidence to the contrary – that the cardinals were guided by the Holy Spirit in making their choice. The choice of Pope was in effect, therefore, a divine choice.[6]

The universalist claims of the papacy were profoundly weakened by a series of disasters and scandals that struck the Holy See during the fourteenth and fifteenth centuries. The rising power of the French monarchy found expression in the removal of the papacy from Rome to Avignon (1309–77) when six prelates, all of whom were born in the south of France, were elected Pope. When Gregory XI returned the papacy to Rome in 1377 he and his successors had to begin the formidable task of re-establishing the prestige and authority of the institution. In the first instance, the popes had to recover their authority over the 'Papal States'; to do so, they were obliged to engage in political and even military struggles in the turbulence that was contemporary Italy. More importantly still, the papacy had to lead Europe in its resistance to the sustained assaults mounted by the Ottoman Turks on the borderlands of Southeastern Europe and the Mediterranean, assaults which reached a fulminating point with the capture of Constantinople in 1453.

The papacy had precious few resources with which to carry out its obligations. Rome itself had a population of only about 50,000 people[7] and Eamon Duffy has reminded us that the city 'had no industries except pilgrimage, no function except as the Pope's capital'.[8] But the popes of the late fifteenth century were ambitious and imaginative and as they struggled to restore their patristic, territorial and political power they yet found the resources to indulge themselves as great patrons of art, reconstructing Rome and decorating its churches with great works of painting and sculpture. For instance, Sixtus IV (1471–84) brought new standards of display to Rome: he patronised great painters – Botticelli and Raphael chief among them – and began the rebuilding of St Peter's, where he employed Alberti, Bramante, Michelangelo and Bernini for the chapel that was named after him (the 'Sistine Chapel'). It was often difficult for contemporaries to understand the balance of priorities – papal, personal and familial – which underlay such apparently unbridled self-indulgence.

The secularism of the Church led to growing criticism. Anti-clericalism was of course a staple of European life and in a real sense it bespoke the certainties that underpinned the authority of the Church; it was easier to attack clerical behaviour because so few people questioned clerical authority. But so widespread were the criticisms that even some popes accepted their legitimacy: Pius II (1458–64) – himself a scholar of European renown – complained that it was the misconduct of clerics themselves that justified any and every attack on them:

> On every single thing we do the people put the worst interpretation. We are in the position of insolvent bankers. We have no credit. The priesthood is an object of scorn. People say that we live in luxury, amass wealth, are slaves to ambition, ride on the fattest mules and the most spirited horses, wear trailing fringes on our robes and walk the streets with puffed-out cheeks under red hats and full hoods, breed hunting dogs, lavish much on actors and parasites and nothing on the defence of the Faith. And they are not entirely wrong. There are many among the cardinals and the other members of the Curia who do these things and, if we are telling the truth, the luxury and pride of our Curia is excessive. This makes us so hateful to the people that we are not listened to even when we speak the truth.[9]

Pius's strictures fell upon a papacy that had yet to enter the most secular (and corrupting) phase in its history. Certainly, many Catholics were increasingly receptive to the idea that it was necessary to have limitations placed upon the power of the papacy by making use of General Councils of the Church. Indeed, some Catholics – prominent bishops and laity among them – went so far as to argue that a General Council of the Church had equality or even precedence of authority over the Pope.[10]

By the time of Henry VIII's accession there had been sixteen General Councils since the first of them, at Nicaea in 325, had written the Creed and fixed the date of Easter. It had become customary for these councils to meet in Rome and the first council of Henry's reign ('the fifth Lateran Council', 1512–17) came in retrospect to mark the end of the centuries during which the papacy held unquestioned power over the Church and over the Christian peoples of Europe. By coincidence, 'Lateran V' closed almost exactly as Martin Luther nailed his ninety-five theses to the door of the castle church in Wittemberg; the strains of the Reformation brought the conflict between papalists and conciliarists within the Church to a head in the twenty years or so after the point at which Henry VIII decided that he had to separate himself from Katharine (*c.* 1524–27); the king's struggle for a divorce became enveloped by the great struggle within the Church to restrict the power of the papacy and to reshape the very nature of the Church.

Chief among the secular institutions competing with the papacy for the titular leadership of Europe was the most anachronistic of them all, the 'Holy Roman Empire'. This strange entity had come into being on Christmas Day 800 when Pope Leo III crowned Charlemagne as 'august emperor' (*'imperator augustus'*), raising him to pre-eminence among the monarchs of Europe and implying that he was the heir to the Caesars. The coronation of the Emperor by the Pope came in time to be profoundly symbolic for both parties: for the Emperor, it acknowledged the sanctity of his office as much as its unique authority among the crowned heads of Europe while for the Pope it confirmed his primacy over the Emperor, for he had conferred the title upon him. In truth, the lands of the Empire did not form a coherent political unit; they incorporated 365 or so states, some of them very large and important but others no more than independent cities. Accordingly, the resources that the title provided for its holder were in splendidly inverse proportion to the prestige that it endowed upon him: the Holy Roman Emperor had few secure tax revenues and exercised little real political power.

Like the papacy, the imperial dignity was also – in theory, at least – an elective office. The 'Imperial College' consisted of seven Electors, three of whom were ecclesiastics and four were secular princes.[11] These dignitaries pondered long and hard before voting – but then normally chose whoever had paid them the most. Their votes did not come cheap; indeed, the fiercer the contest for election so the more expensive the votes of the Electors became. The victor then had to seek coronation by the Pope, for until he did so he remained in constitutional theory only 'Emperor-elect'. For this reason the practice developed by which emperors had their eldest son elected as 'King of the Romans' so that they would in turn succeed automatically to the title of 'Emperor-elect'. The Austrian House of Habsburg had held the imperial title since 1452, when Frederick III had been crowned. On Frederick's death in 1493 his son Maximilian succeeded him, but since he was never crowned by a Pope he remained only 'Holy Roman Emperor-elect'. It bitterly grieved Maximilian that he did not have the full dignity of his office.[12] Equally, Charles V deeply resented that the hiatus between his election in 1519 and his coronation in 1530 denied him the fullness of the imperial title: after his coronation he compensated himself by styling himself 'Caesar' so that there could be no question but that he enjoyed power and status of a thoroughly different order from that of mere kings and princes.

The Nation-States of Western Europe

While the papacy and the Empire claimed pre-eminence over the peoples of Christendom, real power lay with the nation-states of Western Europe. The restoration of monarchical authority was a crucial feature of the lifetime of Katharine. The key developments were four – the re-establishment of French primacy in Europe; the consolidation of monarchical authority in the countries of Western Europe; the development of a new country in Spain with the unification of the Crowns of Castile and Aragon and its projection onto the world stage as a great colonial power; and the challenge to French power by the growth of a Burgundian–Habsburg conglomerate which, in the years after 1500, underwent one of the most astonishing growths in European history.

In turn, these four developments morphed into three when in the years after 1516 the Burgundian–Habsburg conglomerate absorbed the Spanish Monarchy and its overseas territories. Slowly, a new superpower came into being and it was invested with the authority of the Holy Roman Emperor when Charles of Habsburg won the imperial election of 1519. By the late 1520s it was beginning to be funded by treasure from the Spanish New World. This astounding union of Burgundian–Habsburg–Spanish suddenly presented a realistic and tangible opposition to the power of the French monarchy. By the mid-1520s, the existence of two superpowers and their struggle for political hegemony in Europe forced the other nation-states to choose between them. Henry VIII and his ministers had to calculate long and hard before deciding which side to support.

Power: The French Monarchy

In 1500, France was by far the largest political unit or country in Europe, covering an area of 450,000 square kilometres (nowadays the country is one-fifth or so larger, at 551,000 square kilometres). Her population had fallen from 20 million before the Great Plague to about 16 million by 1500, but even this diminished figure represented about one-fifth of the population of the continent of Europe.[13] Demographically, France was a dynamic and expanding country.

France also enjoyed substantial geographical advantages which allowed her to exert her influence throughout Europe. The centrality of her geographical position enabled her to exercise her power in Northern and Central Europe and in Italy. Moreover, internal communications were normally excellent; although the Alps and the Pyrenees separated France from Italy and Spain, the mountain ranges within France did not pose serious physical obstacles (as they did, for instance, in Spain); the *massif central* is highest at the Puy de Sances (1,855 metres). Moreover, the rivers greatly facilitated the movement of produce, people and animals. Broad, long and (normally) deep, the great rivers of France – notably the Seine, Rhône, Sâone, Loire and Garonne – enabled producers to move their goods in industrial amounts and people to travel in large numbers. Of course, the soil of France was proverbially fertile and its mountains were rich in minerals. We should not forget that France was a great maritime power: she had extensive coasts on the Mediterranean, the Atlantic and the (English) Channel and had long developed strong trading interests throughout Northern and Western Europe, the Mediterranean and the Middle and Far East.

During the second half of the fifteenth century, France made use of her natural advantages to re-establish her power in Europe, regaining lost provinces and dramatically rounding out her frontiers. In 1453, she recovered Gascony from England in what became the last battle of the Hundred Years' War and in 1477 Louis XI destroyed the power of Burgundy and annexed the towns of the Somme, Picardy and the northern territories of the historic Duchy of Burgundy. By 1481, Anjou, Maine and Provence were subsumed into the monarchy and Brittany followed suit in 1492. In 1498 when Louis XII succeeded to the throne he annexed his family estates of Valois, Blois, Orleans and the county of Commines into the royal domain. These acquisitions of territories in the years 1453–98 had profound importance for the political realities of Europe. Heavily peopled, centrally placed, dynamically reasserting her power: France was in 1500 pre-eminent among the powers of Europe, strong, vibrant – and militarily aggressive.

'The True Seat and Sceptre to Dominate the Whole World': Italy[14]

If France was the political centre of Europe, Italy was – as Juan de la Cosa's map reminds us – the Continent's real fulcrum. Italy lay at the heart of Christendom, with the throne of St Peter as its focal point. It was the cradle of Roman civilisation and during the Renaissance reaffirmed the cultural leadership that had belonged to Rome under the Caesars. Italy was prodigiously rich; with 10 million or so inhabitants it was one of the most densely populated parts of Europe and its wealth (and most especially that of its great cities) attracted admiration and envy from the rest of Europe.[15] Italy was also a great trading and commercial centre, linking the eastern and western sectors of the Mediterranean and bringing Europe into contact with Asia, the 'Middle East' and Africa. Five major states dominated the peninsula – the Papal States in the centre; Milan, Florence and Venice in the north; and 'the two Sicilies' – the island of Sicily and the Kingdom of Naples – in the south.

The popes of the 'High Renaissance' were obliged to look to their political power, both externally against enemies such as the Republic of Venice who chiselled away at their territories, and internally against fractious families such as the Orsini and the Colonna, who conspired to undermine the Papal States from within. The papacy became corrupted by this, and in particular by the behaviour of two pontiffs who ruled for a decade each. Alexander VI (1493–1503), a masterly politician whose chief concern often appeared to be to provide for his many children, tried to carve out a territory for his son, Cesare. By contrast, Julius II (1503–13) – who had been the most bitter enemy of Alexander – was determined to regain the lands lost from the Papal States in order to restore the power and prestige of the institution. Both of these men fascinated and terrified their contemporaries and it was a tragic irony for Katharine that it should have been them who facilitated her two marriages – and it proved tragic for her that the Pope who was ultimately charged with resolving the her marital difficulties should have been Clement VII (1523–34), who was congenitally incapable of making difficult choices and of then holding to a decision. Katharine was devoted to the papacy, and she was systematically betrayed by it – but so, in his very different way, was Henry

VIII, who for many years trusted it to resolve his marital problem for him as it had conveniently solved those of, for example, the kings of France.

In the north of Italy, the Duchy of Milan and the Republic of Venice competed for power and influence. Both were very wealthy – Milan from its command of the riches of the Plain of Lombardy, Venice from its fabled trading empire in the Eastern Mediterranean. Milan was a vitally important strategic and communications centre; it controlled mountain passes into Austria and Northern Europe, and if it acted as a bulwark against the French (and the Swiss) it also provided its ruler with the base from which to threaten Provence. It was of defining significance that it was not an independent state, for it was an imperial fief that was in the gift of the Emperor.[16] In 1450 Francesco Sforza, a famous *condottieri*, won control of the duchy and although he was unable to persuade the Emperor to invest him formally with the dukedom he succeeded in founding a dynasty which ruled the duchy – with some important interruptions – until 1535. But the powers of Europe were determined to control Milan, for it was the key to northern Italy and, more importantly, to dominance over the papacy: most especially, the Emperor claimed suzerainty over it while successive kings of France were obsessed by the need to conquer it so that they could control it. Accordingly, Milan became a focal point of the politics of Europe during Katharine's lifetime, and the wars fought in and over the duchy consistently impinged upon her life.

The 'Most Serene Republic' of Venice gained its wealth by serving as a trading entrepôt between Asia and Europe. Isolated and remote in its lagoon, Venice lived a life of fantasy that was justified by its geopolitical uniqueness and by its fabled wealth. Its claims were indeed fully as extravagant as its riches: so widespread were its trade and influence that it proclaimed that it was an 'empire' and in celebration of its magnificence it celebrated once a year its 'marriage with the Sea'. But Venice never felt secure in its land frontier and during the fifteenth century it insistently sought to expand into the *terrafirme*. This brought it into conflict with Milan to the west, the House of Austria to the north and the papacy to the south. The 'Most Serene Republic' was a dangerous neighbour.

Florence was less powerful than either Milan or Venice; it was a financial and cultural centre and for sixty years until 1494 the great banking family of the Medici family ruled the republic, providing stability, wealth and prestige to the state and its citizens. The leadership of Lorenzo the Magnificent (1469–92) allowed both the Medici family and the city of Florence to carry weight out of proportion to their real strength. Lorenzo saw himself – and was seen by many contemporaries – as a man who could be a mediator or leader precisely because he seemed to be above politics. Notwithstanding his carefully cultivated reputation, Lorenzo was the most political of men and his family were the most obsessively (and enduringly) self-interested of all the great families of Italy. After Lorenzo's death the Medici were overthrown and Florence once again declared itself a Republic. This revolution had enormous consequences, facilitating the French invasion of 1494 which changed the face of European politics by introducing the era of 'the Italian Wars' and which (as one of its lesser consequences) resulted in the exiling of the Medici from Florence. The power and ambitions of the Medici family also had their points of contact with Katharine, for it was part of her tragedy that the Medici Pope Clement VII was often more concerned with re-establishing the power of his family in Florence than he was with fulfilling his duties as pontiff.

The Kingdom of Naples had an importance in the south that neatly paralleled that of Milan in the north, and it was no coincidence that the destinies of both states interacted consistently with each other. Naples, too, was a fief – but of the papacy rather than of the Empire – and by 1500 the monarchies of Spain and of France each had strong claims to rule it.[17] Since the papacy – firmly placed between Milan and Naples – was equally fearful of both powers it became a central precept of papal policy never to allow Naples and Milan to be ruled by the same ruler or dynasty, for to do so would have substantially degraded the independence of the Holy See. Katharine's father won Naples for Spain in 1504 and it proved to be a historic triumph – Naples remained under Spanish sovereignty for 200 years. However, it may justifiably be suggested that Ferdinand's concentration on winning Naples distracted him from applying himself to resolving the dreadful problems faced by his daughter in England after the death of Prince Arthur in 1502.

'The Promised Land': The Duchy of Burgundy

The 'Duchy of Burgundy' was an extraordinarily complex and attenuated conglomerate of territories, stretching some 800 kilometres from the Channel to Provence. Its political importance was enhanced by its being adjacent to both France and the Empire. It had access to some of the major rivers of Western Europe, connecting the Rhine–Moselle–Meuse and the Saône–Rhône. Indeed, its geographical advantages made it a focal point of the trading systems of Northern Europe. It population was about 2.5 million people and it was heavily urbanised, incorporating over 250 towns and cities, among them some of the most important and cosmopolitan cities of northern Europe – Brussels, Amsterdam and Dijon. But above all, the duchy ruled the city of Antwerp, the most vibrant trading, banking and commercial city in Northern Europe. It also controlled some leading seaports on the Channel coast (Ostend, Calais, Boulogne). Its languages were chiefly French, German and Dutch.

From 880, Burgundy was a fief of the Crown of France but in 1363 John II of France endowed it upon his son Philip 'the Bold' as a fief.[18] It was to be of historic importance that the dukes of Burgundy were thus obliged to pay homage to the King of France for possession of their territories; in time this led to the anomalous position that the Emperor Charles V held some of the most important of his family lands as a vassal of Francis I – a situation which aggravated the deep personal and dynastic bitterness between the two men. This, too, had its implications for Katharine.

The dukes of Burgundy were painfully conscious that their duchy had its unity only in their persons and that they did not enjoy royal status. They therefore systematically set themselves to outstrip the kings of Europe in both wealth and in courtly dignity and they deliberately became the great innovators and upholders of courtly etiquette – formal, extravagant and chivalric. The ostentation and sophistication of display, whether it be in courtly ceremonial or in the magnificence of the palaces that the dukes built, was a political weapon of the first order, emphasising power and majesty, wealth and sophistication. Indeed, so wealthy was the duchy and so pre-eminent was its court among those of Europe that Philippe de Commynes wrote of Burgundy in the middle of the fifteenth century that it was 'the Promised Land, more so than any other on earth'.[19]

The culture of the Burgundian court reached its zenith during the reign of Philip III 'the Good' (1396–1467). It was as an expression of the courtly and chivalric values of his dukedom that on his wedding day (11 January 1430) Philip established the Order of the Golden Fleece. The new order took its symbol from the fleece of the Argonauts; it ostensibly celebrated an unquenchable search for military glory but in reality it was little more than a ceremonial order that existed in the first instance as the bodyguard of the duke himself. Deeply anachronistic as the new Order was as Europe moved away from the 'Age of Chivalry', it struck a chord among the social and ruling elite of Europe, who yearned to be invited to join it.

In 1454 – the year after the Fall of Constantinople – Philip instituted a magnificent series of festivals to inspire and spread the values of

Burgundian chivalry by concentrating them on a war against the Turk (the '*Fêtes du Faisan*'). Moreover, the duke gallantly vowed to challenge the Sultan to single combat for the great city. Nothing happened of course, but the series of festivals reaffirmed the cultural leadership of the dukes of Burgundy and were widely imitated in the other courts of Europe. In reality, like much else at the Burgundian court, the festivals were narcissistic and otherworldly, an excuse to celebrate the greatness of the dukes of Burgundy: Karl Brandi referred to 'the impressive, sumptuous and yet wholly meaningless shell within which the duke and his family lived out their lives'.[20] But the culture had widespread impact among contemporary monarchs: Charles V clutched the culture of Burgundy to himself (and never allowed himself to be portrayed without the necklace of the Order of the Golden Fleece) and among the other monarchs who were proud to be invited to join the Order and proclaimed that they would live by its values were Edward IV and Henry VIII of England. Indeed, many of the festivals that illuminated English courtly life while Katharine was married to Henry VIII – and in which they took part together as an expression of their unity – were Burgundian in origin and inspiration.

Nemesis awaited. For Charles 'the Bold' (1467–77), chivalric greatness was not enough. True, he organised one of the most splendid courtly events of his time when he married Margaret of York, sister of Edward IV, in 1468. But his political and military judgement were clouded by the unbridled ambition that earned him his sobriquet and he engaged in a war against France that led to the destruction of the Duchy of Burgundy and to his own death. Charles was determined to establish Burgundy as a great middle kingdom between France and the Empire, stretching from the North Sea to the Mediterranean, and his decision to go to war with Louis XI proved to be a catastrophic error; on 5 January 1477 he was killed in front of the city of Nancy. With his death the ancient and proud Duchy of Burgundy was subsumed into the French monarchy; only the free county (Franche-Comté) remained outside the control of Louis XI and his successors.

Among his failings, Charles had neglected to properly secure the succession to his duchy: marriage came second to war. When he was widowed in 1465 by the death of Isabelle of Bourbon after eleven years of marriage he had only one child, Mary. He then strengthened his alliance with England by marrying Margaret of York. Since they were cousins of the fourth degree they needed a papal dispensation but this was readily acquired. The exchange of chivalric honours accompanied

the wedding; Edward IV was named as a Knight of the Golden Fleece
(14 May 1468) and Charles received the Order of the Garter (13 May
1469).[21] However, the marriage produced no children, probably because
Charles was too busy waging war to spend time with his wife: in the
first seven years of their marriage the couple spent the equivalent of
only one year together.[22]

The succession to the Duchy of Burgundy lay now with Mary, who was
nineteen years of age. She chose Maximilian of Austria, son of Frederick
III, as her husband. Maximilian was one of the most interesting – and
eccentric – men of his time. He was a few months older than Mary, born
in 1459. He carried the blood of Europe in his veins: among his thirty-
two immediate ancestors three were German, two French, four Italian,
ten Portuguese and Spanish, three English, three Polish, one Lithuanian
and four Russian; two others cannot be identified. He spoke seven
languages.[23] It was fitting that Maximilian should have felt obliged to
come to Mary's court for the wedding even though he was King of the
Romans and heir to the Holy Roman Empire: Burgundy was worth a
pilgrimage and the couple were married in Ghent on 18 August 1477.[24]

Mary gave birth to two children – Philip (22 July 1478) and Margaret
(10 January 1480) – but then died after a riding accident on 27 March
1482. Maximilian became guardian and regent for his children. Because
he was a foreigner he was given only very limited rights within the
duchy and his access to his children was restricted.[25] A regency council
governed for the young prince, who was sent to Malines and brought
up by Margaret of York. In December 1482 Maximilian was obliged to
accept the (second) Treaty of Arras, by which France absorbed much of
Burgundy, and to agree to marry Margaret with the Dauphin; she was
handed over to the French in April 1483. The disintegration of the great
duchy seemed to be complete and the cities now divided fractiously
to pursue their own interests. Inevitably, civil war ensued; it took
Maximilian two years of fighting to defeat the rebels and be reunited
with his son. In April 1486 Maximilian was elected King of the Romans
but even this grand title did not protect him from his fractious subjects;
when in 1488 he returned to Ghent the citizens seized and imprisoned
him. Commynes, who had so admired Burgundy as 'the Promised Land'
a generation earlier, now lamented its fate: 'Today I do not know in this
world a people so desolate.'[26]

When Maximilian succeeded to the imperial title in August 1493 he
casually handed the government of Burgundy and the Low Countries to

Philip, who was fifteen years old. The transition of authority was blurred but from June 1495 official documents carried Philip's name alone and in September 1494 the young archduke formally opened his government with a *joyeuse entrée* into Louvain.[27] He was sixteen years of age.

Periphery: The Spanish & English Crowns

While the Pope and Emperor claimed pre-eminence in Europe and France, Italy and Burgundy formed the political core of Western Europe, Spain and England lay, relatively isolated, on its peripheries. In 1500, both were emerging from long periods of political turbulence in which their power and reputation had diminished and both urgently needed to make good these deficiencies so that they could exercise their power and influence in Europe.

Spain was divided by great mountain ranges and – largely as a result of this – consisted by 1500 of two distinct countries, the Kingdom of Castile and the 'Crown of Aragon'. Castile was the major territorial power, holding about two-thirds of the lands of Iberia and three-quarters of the population – about 4.3 million people by 1500. It was a mountainous and often barren land; except for the rich valley of the Guadalquivir River – Andalusia – its soil was often of poor quality. But Castile was rich in its political, cultural and economic connections for it faced in three directions – northwards to the Bay of Biscay and the Channel, with the markets of England and the Low Countries for its wool; south-east to the Mediterranean and south-west to the Atlantic and the Canary Islands. By contrast, 'the Crown of Aragon' was a composite monarchy which consisted of the kingdoms of Aragon, Valencia and Sicily, the Principality of Catalonia and the islands of Cerdagne and Sardinia: its concerns lay almost entirely in the Mediterranean and with North Africa. Its population in 1500 was probably just under 1 million. Ferdinand and Isabella united their two kingdoms in marriage in 1469 and although each crown retained its separate identity in law, so effectively did the couple work together that within a few years – certainly by 1480 or so – their right to rule had become recognised as unchallenged at home and abroad. In 1492 they rounded out their achievements by conquering the Islamic Kingdom of Granada; to celebrate their great triumph they expelled the unconverted Jews of Spain and sent Christopher Columbus across 'the Ocean Sea' (as the Spanish called the Atlantic). Spain was now united under its joint monarchs; monotheistic and monocultural in its religious practice; and about to undertake one of the transforming achievements of world history in 'discovering' the Americas. Spain had become a player of rank and substance on the European stage, worthy of respect – and worthy of being wooed for the hands of its children in marriage (below, chapter 2).

The English crown had also suffered half a century or more of weakness by 1500, and the chief concern of Henry VII (1485–1509) was to survive on his throne and to pass it on, unchallenged, to a male heir. He succeeded brilliantly in this (below, chapter 3). England's concerns were more parochial than those of the Spanish Monarchy and by 1500 the country and its rulers had little interest in the New World across the Atlantic. True, in 1497 John Cabot discovered 'Newfoundland' and in 1508–09 his son Sebastian reached Hudson's Bay, but the English did not follow this up; the difficulties of reaching the summer trade winds inhibited their southward oceanic ventures and in any event the kings of England were much more concerned with re-establishing their power in France. England's political and economic vision was still fixed across the Channel that it called its own to France and the Low Countries. And of course England looked warily north, always anxious about the ability of the kings of Scotland to create trouble.

England's defining foreign relationship was indeed with France: the two countries had interacted since the Norman Conquest of England in 1066. The dynastic connection had led in part to the Hundred Years' War (1337–1453) in which England had won some brilliant military victories – notably at Crécy (1346) and Poitiers (1356) – but by the end of the fourteenth century most of the gains had been lost. Then Henry V, in a short but brilliant reign (1413–22), re-established English claims on the French throne, most notably with his victory at Agincourt (1415), which led to the highpoint of English intervention in France when Charles VI of France recognised Henry in 1420 as his heir. Henry died suddenly in 1422 and from the 1430s the French once again pushed the English back; Charles VII (1422–61) drove them out of Normandy and reconquered Gascony (1450–53).

Although Henry VIII could never have brought himself to acknowledge it, the loss of the English empire in France was ultimately of benefit to the English crown. England had to settle for playing a role within a European world that was increasingly divided between the great powers of France and the Habsburg–Burgundian–Spanish conglomerate. England could seek to balance the powers, or more correctly to back the winner in the ceaseless wars between them. She would simultaneously develop her commercial interests and edge her way to becoming a naval power. In practice, this generally meant being in a positive relationship with the House of Habsburg, which controlled the Low Countries, for they were becoming increasingly central to England's commercial and trading prosperity.

England, in fine, was useful to the two great powers who were emerging on Mainland Europe. Perhaps this applied essentially in a negative sense. The Habsburgs feared that if England allied with France its fleet could obstruct the sea route from Spain to the Low Countries while France recognised that English military and commercial power might tilt the balance towards the Habsburgs at key moments by distracting kings of France from their fundamental obsession with Italy. But in general, France and the Habsburgs were not positively worried about England; they never forgot that England was vulnerable to interference in Ireland and Scotland, and that indeed the English succession was itself far from secure. It is premature to think in terms of England holding a 'balance of power' in Europe. In reality, England was a makeweight in European affairs: France and the Habsburgs sought to make use of England and most certainly did not regard the country as their equal.

Focal Point: The Italian Wars

The power of France and the weakness of her rivals in Western Europe created the opportunity for the military adventurism in Italy that led to 'the Italian Wars': for a generation from 1494 the political history of Western Europe was normally focussed on the wars that arose from a succession of French expeditions into Italy: Charles VIII (1494); Louis XII (1499, 1500, 1509, 1512) and Francis I (1515, 1521, 1524 and 1536) all sent or led such invasions. There were solid dynastic reasons for their actions: Charles VIII had a dynastic claim on Naples and Louis XII on Milan. But in reality the ambitions of these French kings were political: they sought to balance the growing power of the Habsburg–Burgundian conglomerate by winning a controlling interest in Italy. There were, it is true, also more mundane, or personal, motives: invading Italy became a rite of passage for new kings of France – they were the new Hannibals, crossing the Alps to win *gloire* for themselves, to impose their power on Italy and demonstrate their pre-eminence in European politics.

Experience failed to teach these kings that it was easier to invade Italy than to maintain an army there: repeatedly, enormous French armies marched triumphantly into and through Italy but then had to retreat in disarray because the Crown could not maintain them financially and support their provisions and supplies. Dysentery and cholera also did much to frustrate French military ambitions in Italy. There was a second reason why French triumphs tended to be short-lived, for they inevitably obliged European powers who were fearful of France to form leagues against her; the states system of Western Europe did not allow for one state to become overmighty and alliances sprang up against any power that seemed likely to be gaining a hegemonic position.

The magnetic attraction that drew successive kings of France into Italy proved to be a profoundly important (and repeated) strategic error, for in the aftermath of the disintegration of the Duchy of Burgundy, France should have bolstered her defences on her north-eastern frontiers rather than indulging in the pursuit of *gloire* in Italy. In failing to do so, France allowed the House of Habsburg to consolidate its power in the remnants of the Burgundian territories, most especially in the rich and strategically important 'Low Countries'. Even more importantly, France lost the struggle for Italy. Ultimately, the regular invasions by the French Crown led to the pre-eminence of its great rival in the peninsula.

It was in the wars in Italy that Henry VIII and his ministers lost their chance to resolve the difficulties created by his determination to end his marriage to Katharine. It was from the mid-1520s, exactly as Henry VIII sought to separate himself from Katharine, that Charles of Habsburg – Katharine's nephew – secured a dominant position in Italy and exercised increasing control over Pope Clement VII. Henry VIII would be unable to find a satisfactory settlement of his marital difficulties not merely because he could not persuade or force Pope Clement VII to grant him an annulment or divorce, but because he never had a realistic chance of doing so while Katharine's nephew dominated Italy and intimidated the Pope.

2

SPAIN: THE CATHOLIC KINGS: A QUESTION OF LEGITIMACY?

The Impotent King: Henry IV of Castile (1454–74)
It is a curiosity that Ferdinand and Isabella were both the children of
kings named Juan II – respectively, of Juan II of Aragon (1458–79) and
of Juan II of Castile (1405–54). Both kings married twice but while the
succession to the Castilian throne became subsumed in doubt, that to
Aragon proved to be comparatively straightforward. The confused
(and confusing) history of these marriages needs to be understood as it
became the central point of reference for the dynastic policies pursued
by Ferdinand and Isabella and for the familial and psychological
development of their children.

Juan II of Castile's first wife, María of Aragon, gave birth to Henry
(1425) and lived for another twenty years without producing any more
children. Her successor, Isabella of Portugal, then presented Juan with
Isabella (22 April 1451) and Alfonso (17 December 1453). When Juan
II died in 1454, therefore, Henry succeeded him by right of being his
eldest son, as Henry IV, and Alfonso became second-in-line until Henry
produced an heir. Isabella lay third in succession behind her half-brother
and brother. It happened that both of Isabella's brothers predeceased her
without leaving children, and so the throne eventually became hers – but
only after she had won it in war.

Ferdinand's route to the thrones of Aragon was much simpler but it
also followed on the death of a half-brother. Juan II of Aragon's first wife,
Blanche of Navarre, presented him with one son, Charles, Prince of Viana

34

and two daughters, Blanche II of Navarre and Eleanor of Navarre, and his second wife, Juana Enríquez, gave birth to Ferdinand and to Juana of Aragon. Prince Charles died in 1461 and so Ferdinand succeeded him as heir to the throne.

Henry IV proved to be a feeble king; he was controlled by strong personalities and incapable of providing protection for his subjects in the face of an increasingly undisciplined nobility. But above all else, Henry IV's kingship was weakened – devastated, indeed – by doubts about his sexual potency and, consequently, by the question of the legitimacy of the daughter whom he proclaimed as his own.

Suspicions had arisen about Henry's virility long before he succeeded to the throne. In 1440 he had married Blanche of Aragon but after thirteen years of marriage the couple had not conceived any children. In such circumstances it was inevitably decided that the reproductive failure lay with the woman rather than the man but Blanche determinedly refused to accept the blame: she announced that her husband was incapable of procreation. Blanche's accusation had devastating implications for the king and his dynasty, especially when she submitted to an examination which proved (to the satisfaction of her doctors) that she could have children. Henry and his advisers did the best they could do in the circumstances: they found two prostitutes in Segovia who were prepared to swear that the king had had intercourse with them. It was not much of a testimonial but it satisfied the papacy: Pope Nicholas V declared that the reason why the couple had never had sexual intercourse was because their marriage had been bewitched and was, in consequence, canonically invalid; he therefore issued a dispensation which freed both parties to remarry.[1] The dispensation was designed to save Henry's manly honour and to salvage what it could from his dignity as king but it stimulated a dreadful nickname for him – 'Henry the Impotent' ('Enrique el Impotente'). When in 1454 he succeeded to the throne he was already a figure of derision, openly mocked by his people and by many of his great nobles.

This made it all the more urgent that Henry secure the throne by producing an heir. He promptly married Juana, Princess of Portugal (1455). It was the custom in Castile for royal couples to display their nuptial bedsheets on the morning after their marriage to prove that intercourse had taken place. When Henry ordered that the tradition should not be observed he inevitably provoked much sarcastic comment about his virility. As the years passed without the production of a royal child, these comments increased in frequency and acerbity. There was, therefore, widespread bemusement when after seven years of marriage Queen Juana gave birth to a daughter, who was named after her (28 February 1462).

Speculation as to the identity of the child's father ran riot: the unfortunate princess became known as 'the daughter of the queen' before an even more humiliating nickname was endowed upon her – 'Juana la Beltraneja', in acknowledgement of the widespread conviction that she was the child of Don Beltrán de la Cueva, Duke of Alburquerque, a favourite of both Henry IV and his queen. Fernando del Pulgar, Isabella's Chronicler Royal, subsequently told the story with relish:

> After five years of marriage, Queen Juana conceived a child; the idea that she had done so created great scandal throughout the kingdom because the impotence of the king was well known as the result of many experiences. It was believed that the child that the queen had conceived was by another man and not by the king, and [people] affirmed that it was one of his favourites, who was called Don Beltrán de la Cueva, Duke of Alburquerque, a man whom the king loved greatly ...[2]

The truthfulness or otherwise of the matter cannot be established, at least until DNA tests are carried out. Still, Juana was a royal child and was duly sworn in as heiress of Castile in May–July 1462. The king's position was insupportable, and Henry's kingship reached a dreadful first low point when a faction of noblemen and churchmen publicly degraded his effigy and deprived him of his crown, conferring it instead upon his half-brother Alfonso ('the Farce of Avila', 5 June 1465). With two claimants to the throne, civil war inevitably broke out.

The sudden death of Alfonso on 5 July 1468 dramatically transformed the political situation, for the succession to Henry IV now lay between two women – Juana la Beltraneja, whose legitimacy was widely scorned; and Isabella, the king's half-sister, who seemed to many to be no more than the leader of a grasping faction but who was at least unquestionably the daughter of a king by his lawful queen.

Queen Juana shortly provided her husband's enemies with unarguable justification for rebelling against him by giving birth to the children of two men: even Henry IV was obliged to accept that he was not the father of these children. He therefore met with Isabella at the primeval statues of bulls at Toros de Guisando in Avila and formally recognised her as the legitimate heiress to his throne. He declared his marriage to Juana at an end because of her adultery – 'Queen Juana has not used her person cleanly' – and announced that he was once again a single man (Agreement of Toros de Guisando, 18/19 September 1468).[3] Accordingly, Isabella assumed the title of 'Princess of the Asturias', the acknowledged heiress to the throne of Castile. She was seventeen years old.

As such, Isabella immediately became a figure of European importance, and the question of her marriage became an urgent one.[4] She decided to marry Ferdinand, Prince of Aragon and, as was her custom when she had made a major decision, she acted on it at once: on 1 November 1468 Juan II of Aragon – who had pushed strenuously for the marriage – was informed that Isabella had decided to marry his son and heir. The agreement was made on 3 February 1469; four days later Ferdinand solemnly swore to accept it. After the arrangements had been formalised, Ferdinand travelled across northern Castile to join Isabella, arriving at Dueñas, just outside Valladolid on 9 October. Three days later, Isabella wrote to Henry IV to inform him that her future husband had arrived for their wedding; she seems not to have identified Ferdinand by name but was presumably content that she had performed her homage to her king in advising him that she was about to marry. Her letter could not disguise her contempt for the king – or her determination to succeed him on the throne.

Although Isabella deigned to inform her sovereign of her actions she did not find the time to extend the same courtesy to her pontiff; since she and Ferdinand were second cousins – they were both great-grandchildren of Juan I of Castile (1358–90) – they required a papal dispensation from the impediment of affinity to validate their marriage.[5] They evidently decided that they could not spare the time for an appeal to Rome but nevertheless contrived to produce a papal dispensation: the document that was read out at the marriage seems to have been drawn up not by the Pope but by Juan Arias, Bishop of Segovia (and it seems to have suffered an unfortunate error in misidentifying the Pope who had issued it, naming Pius II instead of Paul II). In short, the papal dispensation under which the future Catholic Kings married was a forgery, and not a very good one; it was probably nothing more than a glib recycling of an older document. But it had authority enough to satisfy the Castilian Church, for no less a figure than Alfonso Carrillo de Acuña, Archbishop of Toledo and Primate of the Church in Spain, validated it and stood approvingly – next to the papal nuncio in Spain! – while it was read out. Ferdinand and Isabella would not be the last couple to rush down the aisle but there were not many who had both the nerve and the ability to involve a Primate of Spain and a papal nuncio in forging a papal dispensation to enable them to do so.[6]

The ceremony during which the documents that validated the marriage were read took place in the small palace of Juan de Vivero, a noble supporter of Isabella. There, in the evening of 18 October, Ferdinand swore to observe all the laws and privileges of Castile and he and Isabella took the vows of marriage in front of witnesses. By candlelight, Archbishop Carrillo read the papal dispensation and the nuptial agreements were duly signed. The marriage ceremonies took place on the following day in the church of Santa María la Mayor (on the site of the modern cathedral) and they were conducted not by the Primate of Spain but by a humble parish priest, Pero López de Alcalá. By not performing the ceremony Archbishop Carrillo presumably protected himself against any disciplinary action by king or Pope. In marrying each other, Ferdinand and Isabella had broken pretty much every rule in the book but they preserved the most important ones of all: they were formally bedded in front of a host of witnesses and on the following morning their stained bedsheet was processed through the streets to the sound of trumpets to verify that the marriage had been consummated. On 20 October, Ferdinand and Isabella sent a messenger to Henry IV to inform him of their marriage and to assure him that they remained his most loyal and obedient subjects.

The Seizure of the Crown of Castile, 1474[7]

Within weeks, Isabella was pregnant and on 2 October 1470 gave birth to a daughter, who was named after her and styled 'Princess of Castile and Aragon', expressing the hope (which was far from certain of accomplishment) that she would inherit both kingdoms. Even Henry IV could not endure that humiliation and on 26 October 1470, at Val de Lozoya, he disinherited the new princess (and her daughter) and once again recognised Juana as his heiress:

> Having regard to the little respect [that Isabella] has shown for law and seeing the little obedience that she has given me in marrying on her own authority, without [my] agreement and licence, and for many other things that she has done, by this present letter I disinherit her and cancel the right that I formerly gave her ever to

succeed to the throne as hereditary princess. I order that from this moment on my much beloved daughter Juana is to be taken to be the princess and legitimate heiress, and that the oaths should be taken to her with customary solemnity...[8]

Ferdinand and Isabella rejoined by insisting that Juana was not the child of the king (21 March 1471).

The newly-weds were fortunate in their Pope. Francesco della Rovere was elected as Sixtus IV on 9 August 1471. He needed Spanish support in Italy and correctly calculated that Isabella would be much more likely to provide this than would Henry IV. He promptly issued a bull (*Oblatae nobis*, 1 November 1471) which recognised the validity of the marriage even though it had taken place without a legitimate papal dispensation. Three weeks later, Sixtus despatched his vice-chancellor, Cardinal Rodrigo Borgia, to Spain ostensibly to preach the Crusade and to establish whether the Church was to recognise the agreement at Toros de Guisando or the decree from Val de Lozoya as the legitimate decision in determining the succession to the Crown of Castile. In reality, the decision had already been made: Borgia was given authority to produce the dispensation recognising the legitimacy of the marriage of Ferdinand and Isabella when he saw fit.

Rodrigo Borgia was to become one of the great figures of the age and since he was to play a crucial role in the development of the reign of Ferdinand and Isabella (and indeed to become a major figure in Church history) we should introduce ourselves to him.[9] He was born in Játiva in the Kingdom of Valencia in 1431 and during his childhood he was known by his family name of 'Borja'. However, his ambitions lay in Italy and he Italianised his name to 'Borgia' to further his career. He earned a doctorate in Law from Rome University. As the nephew of Pope Calixtus III (1455–58) he rose effortlessly to a cardinalate in 1456 at the age of twenty-five and became Vice-Chancellor of the Church in 1457; in this capacity he effectively managed the bureaucratic and financial apparatus of the Church and displayed for the first time his superb gifts as an administrator.

Among his many other dignities Cardinal Borgia was Bishop of Valencia and it proved to be a happy chance for him that his visit to Spain enabled him to collect his rents as archbishop. He arrived in the city of Valencia on 21 June 1472 and his discussions with Juan II and Prince Ferdinand convinced him that the papacy should confirm its support for Ferdinand's marriage to Isabella; he therefore had the papal dispensation supplied to them. He then travelled to the court of Henry IV and persuaded many Castilian aristocrats to accept the marriage of Ferdinand and Isabella, at least tacitly. He spent three weeks at Alcalá de Henares, where he lodged in Cardinal Jiménez de Cisneros's palace while he negotiated with Isabella. When he returned to Rome in September 1473 he confirmed Sixtus IV in his support for Ferdinand and Isabella and on 19 July 1474 the Pope despatched a brief to Isabella assuring her that he would always hold her in his affection and confidence; it was his recognition of the lawfulness of her succession to the throne and by implication of that of her heirs.[10] Isabella's negotiations with Borgia had been successful but they had left her with an intense dislike of the man; presumably she disguised this, and if she did so it was as well, for in 1492 the cardinal rose to the throne of St Peter as Pope Alexander VI.

Henry IV died on the night of 12 December 1474. On the following day in Segovia Isabella proclaimed herself to be his lawful successor. The people of the city joyously cheered, 'Castile, Castile, Castile for the queen our lady, Queen Isabella, and for King Ferdinand as her lawful husband.'[11] Unlike England and many other countries, Castile did not have a ceremony of coronation to mark the transference of the throne from the dead monarch to his successor: rather, the transition took place when the senior representatives of the kingdom (ecclesiastical and secular) publicly pledged their loyalty.[12] Normally this transference took place at the Cortes of Castile but Isabella – with characteristic decisiveness – insisted that in her case this had already occurred after the agreement at Toros de Guisando. Accordingly, she now proclaimed herself queen, effectively seizing the throne: she was twenty-three years of age.[13]

The exclamation that was shouted in Segovia was in effect a declaration of war against the followers of Juana la Beltraneja. In May 1475 Juana duly married Alfonso V of Portugal; they described themselves as 'Kings of Castile' and immediately took up the gauntlet that Isabella had thrown down. The war was bitter and lasted until September 1479, when it was brought to an end with the Treaty of Alcaçovas-Toledo which recognised Isabella as the Queen of Castile. Defeated, la Beltraneja entered a convent and stayed there until her death (28 July 1530). Isabella was now the unquestioned Queen of Castile – and it was evident that the alliance that would henceforth dominate Iberia would be between Castile and Aragon rather than between Castile and Portugal. Ferdinand and Isabella had learned a lesson that they never forgot: the security of Castile's border with Portugal would always take precedence over other needs. Accordingly, securing and maintaining their alliance with Portugal became the first priority of their foreign policy.

The Union of the Crowns

Juan II of Aragon died in 1479 and it therefore happened that Ferdinand succeeded to the thrones of the Crown of Aragon exactly as his wife secured her position on the throne of Castile. The two monarchs then began to unite their countries in all but name: together, Ferdinand and Isabella created 'Spain' and made her a major European power and they set her, too, on the way to becoming a global power after the discovery of 'the Indies' in 1492. But there was a darker side to their achievement: they established the Spanish Inquisition in 1478 and their persecution of the religious and cultural minorities within Spain led to a process of ethnic cleansing in the decade 1492–1502 which brought to an end the long tradition of toleration (*convivencia*) whereby Spain had generally lived throughout the Middle Ages as a country of 'the three faiths' – Christianity, Islam and Judaism. In 1492 they expelled all unconverted Jews from Spain, and in 1502 followed suit with the Muslims. Ferdinand and Isabella regarded this cleansing process as being among their greatest achievements and they gloried in the title conferred upon them (and their successors) in 1494 by Alexander VI as 'the Catholic Kings'. History has been less admiring.

The court of Isabella was ceaselessly on the move; she travelled unremittingly, even when she was pregnant, to whichever part of Castile required her immediate attention.[14] Ferdinand loyally accompanied her, recognising that he was obliged in practice to subordinate the needs of Aragon to those of Castile. The ceaseless royal travels meant that a 'court' did not develop in anything like the fullness that characterised, for example, those in France or England. Indeed, Isabella did not even have a capital city in which her court could theoretically reside: the court was wherever she was. A strictly selected group of courtiers, administrators, noblemen and clerics travelled with her to manage business, while Ferdinand was accompanied by a much smaller coterie of his own. This meant that the affairs of court and government were in a very real sense conducted in a spirit of organised chaos on the road by monarchs working with an intimate circle of senior advisers. But there was one advantage, for the system – if it can be called that – allowed Ferdinand and Isabella to keep the closest eye on the activities of these advisers and to travel quickly to wherever the need for their presence was most urgent.

If the first key to the achievement of the Catholic Kings was the harmony with which they worked with each other, the second was the explosive energy which they applied to their kingship and – above all – to their re-establishment of control over Castile.

The central problem facing Ferdinand and Isabella was indeed the dramatic contraction in the authority of the Crown of Castile in recent years – what Joseph Pérez has called 'the degradation of the royal patrimony and the prerogatives of the Crown'.[15] Law and order had substantially broken down as the great nobles had taken advantage of the Crown's weakness under Juan II and Henry IV to extend their own power and, increasingly, to dominate the towns and cities. Isabella re-established the authority of the Crown over the nobles, recovering alienated royal lands and depriving the nobility of a primary role in government, preferring instead to use lawyers (*letrados*) who were entirely dependent on her. She also secured control over the Grand Masterships of the three Military Orders – Santiago (1476), Calatrava (1487) and Alcántara (1494).

Isabella reinvigorated the Council of Castile as the central tool of her government, and so successful was the council that other bodies were established in imitation of it for other areas of responsibility, notably the Council of Aragon (1494). Most famous (or infamous) of all the new councils was that of the Inquisition (1481) which addressed itself in theory with the problems created for the Crown by those converted Jews (*conversos*) who were reneging on their conversion to Catholicism and continuing to practice their original faith; in practice the Inquisition ruthlessly broadened its own scope so that it could attack irregularities in religious practice however it chose to define them.[16]

The councils lay at the heart of Isabella's reforms of government and she supplemented them by having two chancelleries administer law in Castile – Valladolid for the north and Granada for the south. She used *corregidores* as a key instrument of re-establishing law in the towns and cities; these officers were appointed for three-year periods to prevent them from developing their power. Isabella ruthlessly reclaimed many of the lands seized by the aristocracy during the fifteenth century and reincorporated many cities into the royal demesne. In a symbolic crowning of her own work, Isabella published a codification of the laws of Castile in 1503. When she died in 1504 the Crown enjoyed an income of 314 million *maravedies*, twice as much as it had had in 1480.[17] The rule of law and the freedom of a large income: Isabella had been dazzlingly successful.

Isabella was similarly ambitious in reorganising the Church and in extending the Crown's control over it. She secured *patronatos* from the papacy that enabled her to appoint to the episcopal bench and to senior positions in the religious orders. She made effective – if cynical – use of Rodrigo Borgia, who was elected as Pope Alexander VI on 11 August 1492. In 1494, Alexander conferred upon Ferdinand and herself the extraordinary privilege of being entitled to reform all religious communities in Spain. The monarchs entrusted the task to the redoubtable – and ruthless – Cardinal Jiménez de Cisneros, who duly imposed a new discipline on the great orders (the Franciscans, Dominicans, Benedictines, etc.) that meant that Spanish monastic life was purified and reinvigorated a generation before the Reformation. In fine, Ferdinand and Isabella established power over the Church in Castile that was the envy of many of her fellow monarchs (notably perhaps those in England).

Isabella therefore renewed the power of the monarchy in Castile to such purpose as to create in effect a new state; so powerful were the institutions of government that she revitalised or invented in the decade after her triumph over la Beltraneja in 1479 that she was able to resume the war against 'the Moors' of the Kingdom of Granada in 1482. During the next ten years, the queen's artillery pounded the ramparts of the 'Moorish' cities of the south: the most unrelenting (and brutal) onslaught was that on the great port of Málaga in 1487.[18] The campaign was crowned with dazzling success when Granada surrendered on 2 January, bringing to an end centuries of Moorish occupation of southern Spain. Isabella guaranteed her defeated foes the right to continue practising their religion, culture and costume.[19]

By legend, the *reconquista* was a war that had lasted since 711 when the Islamic invaders had crossed into Spain from Africa. In practice it was no such thing, for the different cultures had often co-existed with each other and indeed the 'reconquest' was abandoned for decades or more at a time. However, the conquest of Granada was undoubtedly a great event in European history: to many it compensated for the loss of Constantinople in 1453.

The completion of the *reconquista* had two consequences of historic significance. In the first instance, it led directly to the expulsion of the Jews; in March 1492, the Crown decreed that un-converted or falsely converted Jews should leave the country; about 150,000 left Spain in the next months. At the same time, Isabella freed Christopher Columbus to sail west across 'the Ocean Sea' to find a route which would not only take him to Asia but also provide a means by which the Islamic world could be attacked from the rear. He sailed on 3 August 1492 and when he returned in 1493 was warmly welcomed by Ferdinand and Isabella and their children. Pope Alexander VI again proved obliging to his royal countrymen, issuing papal bulls to validate their discoveries and dividing the unknown world between Castile and Portugal (*Inter caetera* and *Eximiae devotionis*, 3–4 May 1493). In 1494 the Treaty of Tordesillas between Castile and Portugal ratified the papal generosity to them. In 1494 Alexander also conferred the title of 'the Catholic Monarchs' upon Ferdinand and Isabella, helping to consecrate their monarchy (at least in their own eyes).[20] Again, the other monarchs of Western Europe must have noted admiringly the favours conferred upon the Spanish monarchs by the Spanish Pope.

The Royal Couple

Ferdinand and Isabella did indeed fascinate their contemporaries and there are many descriptions of them. Among the most revealing is that of Jerónimo Münzer, who visited Spain in 1494–95. Perhaps because he was a foreigner (and almost certainly because he was a man) Münzer naturally believed that it was Ferdinand who was the dominant partner in the marriage – that, for instance, it was he who made the decision to conquer Granada and then pushed it through. As we will see, he was wrong in this. Nevertheless, despite his confusion Münzer portrayed Isabella as a woman of extraordinary vigour and achievement; indeed, he admitted that he found it difficult to credit that a woman could possess so many admirable qualities:

> The queen is forty-eight years old and so is older than the King, but she appears to be no more than thirty-six. She is tall, somewhat chubby and of agreeable countenance. Such is her knowledge of the arts of peace, such is her wisdom in the arts of war that it appears unbelievable that a woman should understand so many matters [so well].
>
> She is devout ... and spends great amounts of money on ornaments for churches. She respects religious people and establishes houses for them.
>
> During the war of Granada, she was constantly at the side of her husband although he listened to her advice and warnings.
>
> She and the king sit together to administer justice; they listen to lawsuits and resolve them, either through conciliation or by issuing judgements against which no appeal can be made.

It is said that the Almighty, seeing that Spain was languishing, sent this exceptional woman so that – in union with her husband – she could save her country from ruin.

Finally, she is so devout, so pious, of such a sweet disposition that one would struggle in vain to sing the praises that her virtues deserve.[21]

Hernando del Pulgar knew the royal couple at much closer range than did Münzer and he produced unforgettably intimate and unique portraits of them. As Isabella's secretary and Chronicler Royal, Pulgar was of course an apologist for the queen; it was his responsibility to put the most favourable gloss on all her actions. He duly performed this function, but he did much more than this, providing us with realistic and vibrant portraits of the royal couple. We need to remember two other facts about Pulgar when reading his portraits of Ferdinand and Isabella – that as a *converso* he had reason to fear and resent the manner in which they had persecuted the Jews and that as an author he was acutely conscious of the difference between reading the printed word privately and having it read in public. It is impossible to escape the conclusion that Pulgar constructed some of his sentences to allow a reader to emphasise his text in a manner that gave a completely different interpretation from that given by a formal reading.[22] In the following excerpts, the italicised emphases give an indication of how the emphasis might have been changed in a public reading:

[Ferdinand] was *by nature* inclined to do justice, and he was also merciful and took pity on the unfortunates whom he observed in difficulties. And he had an unusual charm, *so that anyone who spoke with him at once loved him and desired to serve him, for he had a friendly manner. His counsel was also sought, especially by the queen his wife, because she knew his great ability.*

It was of course an obligation of a monarch 'to do justice' and to indicate that Ferdinand was merely 'inclined' to do so was powerfully suggestive of his informed self-interest. But even more startling was Pulgar's reference to the king's notorious unfaithfulness and to Isabella's awareness that she had to be constantly vigilant about it; courtiers would have known well enough that Isabella had very good reason to keep a close eye on his whereabouts and activities – and the point is confirmed by the punning nature of the Spanish verb 'to serve', which has a sexual connotation.

Pulgar concluded by alluding to two qualities of Ferdinand's that were also notorious – his meanness with money and his ability to bend truth as far as his circumstances required at any time. He then returned to the king's serial infidelity:

Since he spent all his income on affairs of war and was always in need of money, we cannot describe him as being generous. He was a man of truth, notwithstanding that the great difficulties into which the wars placed him *occasionally caused him to equivocate ... Notwithstanding that he loved the queen, his wife, very much, he also gave himself to other women ...*

Pulgar's riotous description of Ferdinand concluded with what he knew to be an untruth of his own: 'This king conquered and won the Kingdom of Granada.' Everybody knew that it was Isabella who was the driving force behind the attack on the Moorish kingdom and that (as Pulgar shortly made clear) she ensured that her husband stuck to the task that she had set him of conquering the kingdom.

When Pulgar turned to Queen Isabella he excelled himself. He reminded his audience of her iron self-control and then returned to the theme of her vigilance where her husband was concerned: 'She possessed such self-control that even at the time of her deliveries in childbed she concealed her pain, forcing herself not to reveal or show the pain which at that time women feel and show. *She loved the king her husband very dearly and watched over him exceedingly.*'

Like Münzer, Pulgar found it difficult to understand that a woman could possess all the qualities that Isabella demonstrated:

She was a very intelligent and discreet woman, which qualities we rarely see combined in one person; she spoke very well and had such an excellent mind that, although she was busy with such arduous duties as she undertook in governing her kingdom, she committed herself to learning Latin, and in the space of one year succeeded in learning it so well that she understood anything spoken or written in Latin.

Pulgar then once again emphasised that Isabella was a woman of unshakeable willpower; he made it clear that it was she who had ended the civil disorder in Castile and then made it chillingly explicit that it was Isabella who launched the assault on the *conversos*, explicitly stating that only a minority of them were returning to the practice of their Judaic faith and that therefore Isabella was punishing the whole community for the transgressions of a few. This was a deeply bitter denunciation of the queen by her Jewish Chronicler Royal:

> She was *disposed to doing justice*, so much so that it was understood that she pursued the path of sternness rather than that of mercy, and this helped to remedy the great criminal corruption that she found in the realm when she ascended to the throne ...
>
> This queen is the one who extirpated and eliminated the heresy that existed in the kingdoms of Castile and Aragon, where *some* Christians of Jewish lineage were returning to Jewish customs *and made them live like good Christians* ...

The bit now fully in his teeth, Pulgar scornfully brushed aside the idea that it had been Ferdinand who had determined to conquer Granada. His drumbeat reached a heavy and irresistible crescendo as he drove home his theme that it was the work of Queen Isabella:

> Through the solicitude of *this queen* there was begun and *through her diligence continued* the war against the Moors, until the entire Kingdom of Granada was conquered. And we swear that we learned of and knew certain great lords and captains of her kingdoms who, tiring of [the effort] abandoned all hope of being able to win, considering the great difficulty of continuing the struggle, *and through the great perseverance of this queen* and *through her work* and diligence *which she continually made* in the provisions, and through the efforts *which she made with great expense of energy,* she brought to a conclusion this conquest, which by divine will *she seemed to have undertaken* ...

The Royal Children

Isabella gave birth to six children, of whom five survived and lived into adulthood. The dynasty seemed to be solidly entrenched. However, the marriage proved in time to be a classic case-study in the dangers and difficulties of royal regeneration and state-formation. Although Ferdinand and Isabella produced a large family, their reproductive history was curiously uneven and was distinguished by a dreadfully important gender imbalance: of their five children, only one was a boy. Their first child, Isabella, was born within a year of their marriage, in 1470, but the queen probably did not conceive again for seven years (although rumours circulated that she had miscarried in 1474). Certainly, Isabella became sufficiently anxious about her fertility to take on a Jewish doctor, Lorenzo Badoz, to help her conceive.[23]

These were dangerous years, for if the *infanta* Isabella died the future of the dual monarchy would be at risk and in any event it was far from certain that the princess would be allowed to succeed to the thrones of the Crown of Aragon because she had not been born in the country. Pulgar recorded that Isabella underwent 'great penances, prayers and sacrifices and [patronised] holy works, praying to God that she should conceive'. When she did so, and then gave birth to a son on 29 June 1478, there were celebrations throughout the kingdoms of Castile and Aragon because the royal couple now had a male heir who could inherit all of their realms, uniting them together for all time.[24] The child was named Juan (after both of his grandfathers) and celebrations spread around Castile and Aragon. Juan was duly carried around Spain to be sworn in as heir to the thrones of Castile (Cortes of Toledo, 1 April 1480); to those of Aragon (Calatayud, 12 May 1481); the Principality of Catalonia (Barcelona, 14 July 1481), and to the Kingdom of Valencia in the capital city (20 March 1483).[25]

The birth of Prince Juan in 1479 appears to have triggered Isabella's fertility and in the following year she gave birth to Juana (6 November 1479). She then conceived twins, but was delivered of only one child (Maria, 29 June 1482); her unnamed twin sister was stillborn.[26] The birth of Katharine on 16 December 1485 brought the queen's childbearing to an end: she was thirty-four years old. She and Ferdinand must have been disappointed to have had a fourth daughter rather than a second son but they did not allow themselves to question their fate and duly celebrated the birth with tournaments and courtly celebrations. Cardinal Jiménez de Cisneros, in whose palace the *infanta* was born, gave a splendid meal for the royal couple and their households.[27] With five live children, it seemed that the thrones of Castile and Aragon were secure.

Juan was given every preparation for kingship; his formal education began at the age of six. He was taught by distinguished teachers, among them Pedro Martir de Angleria, Fray Diego Deza and Gonzalo Fernández de Oviedo. Under their guidance, Juan read classical authors and developed a commitment to musical forms, both sacred and profane. He was instructed in the arts of war and the equestrian pursuits that were held to be the perfect metaphor for them.[28]

While Juan was educated for kingship, his sisters were prepared for their roles as wives and queens. Castile was indeed at the forefront of educating women in the later fifteenth century and at least two of its universities had even allowed women to rise to professorships – Beatriz Galindo and Lucía de Medrano in Salamanca and Francisca de Lebrija in Alcalá de Henares. Isabella was deeply aware that her own education had been neglected and found such time as she could to improve herself; she studied Latin under Beatriz Galindo ('La Latina') and was successful enough to be able to converse in the language. She also developed a special interest in the study of the Castilian language; she was a generous patron to the great linguist Antonio de Nebrija, who in 1492 published the first European grammar to be written in a vernacular language, dedicating it to Isabella herself. Nebrija took a special interest in the education of the four princesses and was joined by other distinguished tutors – La Latina herself and the Italian brothers Alessandro and Antonio Giraldini, who supervised their patristic and classical studies. The girls also studied music and learned to play the clavichord and other instruments.[29] Katharine seems to have had a special interest in the Church Fathers and in music. She was not adept at languages, and although she could read Italian and French she spoke them poorly and struggled badly with English when the time came for her to learn it. Nevertheless, she persevered with her Latin and became tolerably competent in it. Katharine was a practical student, adept at the traditional feminine arts and crafts of lacework and embroidery.

We have a beguiling description of the royal children in 1494–95 by Jerónimo Münzer, a German scholar who spent five months in Spain. Juan was now seventeen years old; he was fluent in Latin but although an impediment in his lower lip restricted the clarity of his speaking, he was cordial and benevolent. Isabella, the eldest at twenty-four years of age, was already a widow after four months of marriage and was living the life of a religious, making ornaments for churches. Juana, fourteen, was 'for her age and sex' very learned, accomplished in reciting and composing verses. The third daughter, María (whom Münzer wrongly named as Leonor), was nine and the youngest was Katharine, of whom he unfortunately recorded no more than that she was seven years old.[30]

The education of the children went beyond book-learning and the courtly arts. They were taught, consciously and deliberately, about their obligations as children of great monarchs and came to understand that the needs and demands of their dynasty had priority over any of their own wishes or ambitions: their marriages – and if necessary their remarriages – would be arranged for them. They were the son and daughters of monarchs and they would behave – and be used – as such. The children of Ferdinand and Isabella learned about *realpolitik* and, most especially, about the nature and purposes of the marriages for which their parents destined them. They studied, too, the Catholic doctrine of marriage by which marriage was solemnised not in the Church before a priest but in the marital bedroom when the couple physically consummated their union. It was no accident that the children of Ferdinand and Isabella all enjoyed vigorous sex lives – with the exception of Katharine in the first of her marriages – for it had been inculcated in them that it was their solemn and binding obligation before God and their parents to consummate their marriages – and to produce children (below, chapters 5 and 6).

This was because they would play a central role in developing and reinforcing the status and permanence of the new dynasty. Isabella herself certainly needed no reminding of the nature of marriage-inheritance and she had the perfect partner in Ferdinand, who had an intuitive understanding of the needs of diplomacy and of the strengths and weaknesses of the states of Europe. By the mid-1490s Ferdinand had begun to create a series of diplomatic alliances that would place the newly created dual monarchy on the European stage. The central dynamic of his foreign policy was brilliantly economical: he would serve Castile's interests by neutralising Portugal by marital alliance with a Castilian princess and Aragon's by securing Naples. Above all, he would oppose the power of France across the face of Europe by marrying his children with the royal families of Burgundy and England to create an anti-French power bloc in Northern Europe. Ferdinand's children were, indeed, the essential constituent parts of his brilliant project. So, too, was the Spanish Pope: in 1493 he and Isabella secured a promise from Alexander VI that he would grant dispensations for any marriages that they arranged for their children which fell within the second degree of consanguinity. In time they went even beyond this, securing dispensations from Alexander for two of their girls to marry the widowers of their sisters – one of whom had given birth to a child.[31] Isabella despised Alexander VI but she was never above using him for her own purposes.

Nothing, indeed, symbolised an alliance between two states more fully and enduringly than a marriage between their children.[32] Such marriages confirmed the enduring friendship between monarchs (and their subjects) and could have long-term political importance; we have seen how, for example, the competing claims on the throne of Naples and the Duchy of Milan went back for centuries. Indeed, such significance was attached to royal marriages that the negotiations for them could last for many years. It could even happen that children became the subjects of such discussions as soon as they were born – and in rare cases, even before they were born. The minimum age for marriage was defined by canon law as being twelve years of age but agreements normally made allowance for the consummation of the marriage to take place a year or two later.

There were of course differences between the uses to which boys and girls could be put. Because inheritance to thrones normally went by primogeniture, European monarchs kept their eldest boy at home and only married their younger sons abroad. Girls, however, were most certainly to be married abroad – to secure alliances and perhaps even win thrones for Spain in succeeding generations.

The first priority of Ferdinand and Isabella was to resolve the tensions with Portugal and to neutralise the threat that la Beltraneja (or in the future, her children) could be used as a claimant on the throne of Castile. The birth of Prince Juan enabled the monarchs to arrange a marriage for their first-born child, and at Alcaçovas in 1490 it was agreed that Princess Isabella would marry Prince Alfonso, heir to the throne of Portugal. The wedding took place in Seville on 18 April 1490. Ferdinand and Isabella were exultant and celebrated what they took to be a new era in relations within the Iberian peninsula with a fortnight of lavish *fiestas*. Their daughter and her bridegroom were equally joyous: rumour had it that the young couple were so eager to consummate their marriage immediately after the ceremony that they did so within a monastery.[33]

Tragedy followed: on 12 July 1491 Alfonso died after a riding accident. In her distress, his widow cut her hair and returned to her mother's court determined to enter religious life; in her view she had fulfilled her obligations to her parents by marrying and she now wished to devote herself to the salvation of her soul. Ferdinand and Isabella were also distraught and could not bring themselves to attend the memorial service for Alfonso but they had no intention of agreeing to their daughter's insistence that she would not marry again, even though they had promised her this before she married Alfonso: parental *realpolitik* was about to face its first challenge. Meanwhile, the succession to the throne of Portugal devolved upon Prince Manuel, son of the Duke of Braganza.

3

ENGLAND: A 'KING TO BE OBEYED': HENRY VII

The Conquest of the Throne & Establishment of the Dynasty, 1485–87
The Wars of the Roses were brought to a first conclusion by the victory of
Henry, Earl of Richmond, at the Battle of Bosworth Field on 22 August
1485. There seemed little reason to believe that Henry's victory would
be of more than transient importance for the instability of the English
throne had become truly proverbial: in 1488 the Spanish commissioners
negotiating for the marriage of Katharine with Henry's son Arthur
presumed to remind the new king of the insecurities that attached to
his throne – 'bearing in mind what happens every day to the kings of
England'.[1] But Henry Richmond broke the cycle: when he died in 1509
few doubted that his son had the unchallenged right to succeed him, and
the throne stayed in his house until the extinction of his line with the
death of his granddaughter, Elizabeth I, in 1603. The dynasty that the
Earl of Richmond founded proved to be the most successful in English
history.

The fragility of the English crown long antedated the Wars of the
Roses. Many of the characteristics of that weakness had become evident
during the long (and interrupted) reign of Henry VI (1422–71). Henry
was only one year old when he succeeded his father Henry V, the victor
of Agincourt, and his reign seemed to begin well enough; in 1429 he
was crowned as King of England and in the following year as King of
France. But he was manifestly unequal to the legacy he had inherited, and

nowhere was this more evident than in the loss of England's territories in France: in the 1430s and 1440s France reconquered the old Plantagenet territories in Normandy and by 1453 had completed the conquest of Gascony. By 1461 only Calais remained of the Plantagenet empire in France.

Under the stress of this and many other failures, Henry VI suffered a mental breakdown in 1453: his incapacity triggered the Wars of the Roses between the white rose of York and the red rose of Lancaster. Both houses were descended from the Plantagenets, from Edward III's third and fourth sons, John of Gaunt and Edmund of Langley. As they took advantage of the weakness of the Crown, leading magnates sought to win advantage for themselves; the Wars of the Roses were characterised by the belligerence of the overmighty noblemen and their families. Henry VI was deposed in 1461 by Edward of York (who became Edward IV) and was imprisoned in the Tower of London for five years. In 1470 he was restored to power by the Earl of Warwick ('the Kingmaker') but was then deposed for a second time in 1471 when Edward IV returned from exile. This time there was no restoration: he was murdered in the Tower of London, in all probability on Edward IV's orders. The Lancastrian line was now extinct. When Edward IV died in 1483 his two sons, Edward (V) and Richard, Duke of York, were duly imprisoned in the Tower and murdered; few doubted that Edward IV's brother Richard, Protector of the young princes, was responsible and he did little to enhance his reputation when he then declared that he was the legitimate monarch, taking the name of Richard III.

The Earl of Richmond was Welsh by birth, born in Pembroke Castle on 28 January 1457. His family name was variously spelt – 'Tudor', 'Tudr' and so on – but neither he nor his descendants used it willingly for they were embarrassed by both their ancestry and name: the founder of the 'House of Tudor', Owen Tudor (*c.* 1400–61), was probably of illegitimate birth and was certainly descended from a Welsh prince, Rhys ap Gruffud.[2] His own children were then born out of wedlock; Owen lived with Catherine, the widow of Henry V of England (and daughter of Charles VI of France) and she presented him with five children, including Edmund and Jasper Tudor. In 1453 Henry VI legitimated his two half-brothers and raised them to earldoms – Edmund to that of Richmond and Jasper to that of Pembroke. Owen Tudor fared less well: he was beheaded in 1461.

But if the future Henry VII carried no royal blood on his father's side he could claim kinship with the royal family through his mother, Margaret

Beaufort. In 1455 Henry VI arranged a marriage for Jasper Tudor (now Earl of Richmond) with Margaret Beaufort, the daughter of John, 1st Duke of Somerset.[3] Margaret was the great-great-granddaughter of Edward III (1327–77) but like her husband she was of illegitimate stock: she was a granddaughter of John of Gaunt and his mistress Katherine Swynford. John and Katherine lived together for a quarter of a century before marrying in 1369; their four children (including Margaret's father) were also legitimated by Act of Parliament. However, in 1407 another Act debarred their descendants from inheriting the throne of England. Further complication was added to Margaret's status by her marriage to John de la Pole, son of the 1st Duke of Suffolk, in 1450 (when she was only about seven years of age) but this marriage was readily dissolved by the papacy in 1453 on the grounds that she was underage and that the marriage had never been consummated.

Edmund Tudor did not wait for his young bride to grow up before commencing sexual relations with her; she conceived immediately and gave birth to the future Henry VII in 1457 after a horrendous delivery which nearly killed both her and the child. And, a mother at thirteen, Margaret was already a widow, for Edmund died a few months before Henry was born. Margaret was unable to have any more children and probably suffered the consequences of her first and only labour for the rest of her life. She would take proper care of young girls who needed her protection, including Katharine (to whom she formed a close attachment). But it was to her son that Margaret was most devoted; she undertook responsibility for bringing him up and played the major role in protecting him as he grew to manhood. Henry always remained close to her, and it is surely not fanciful to see Margaret Beaufort's influence on him in the single-mindedness and resilience that characterised his life.

Henry Richmond's claim to the throne of England thus had to take account of the illegitimacy of both sides of his family and of the successive debarments and legitimations that each had endured. But fragile though his claim was, it was yet proximate enough to oblige him to spend his formative years in real danger. When Henry VI was murdered in 1471, Jasper Tudor fled to Brittany and took Henry with him. Now fourteen years of age, Henry was placed under the care of Duke Francis II of Brittany. It remained a precarious existence: in 1476 he was nearly handed over to Edward IV.

Henry's situation was resolved by the strength of his mother. Margaret had married for a third time in 1472, to Sir Thomas Stanley, 1st Earl of

Derby, and her new status enabled her to bring Henry back to court in 1482. It was hoped that he would be restored to his father's title and perhaps even marry the king's eldest daughter, Elizabeth of York. But when Edward IV died on 9 April 1483 and his brother seized the throne, Henry once again felt obliged to flee to France. He attempted to invade England but was ignominiously driven back by hostile winds. Guided by his formidable mother, he courted Yorkists, aware how many of them had been repelled by Richard III's brutal seizure of power. On Christmas Day 1483, in Rennes Cathedral, Henry swore an oath that he would unite the houses of Lancaster and York by marrying Elizabeth of York, the eldest of Edward IV's ten children by Elizabeth Woodville: it was a decisive move in broadening the support available to him.

Henry launched his second invasion from Honfleur on 1 August 1485, with a force of less than 1,000 men. He landed near Milford Haven on 7 August and marched through Wales into England. On 22 August he gave battle to Richard III near Market Bosworth. He probably owed his victory to the late intervention of William Stanley, who waited to see how the conflict was progressing before deciding which side to join. Richard died courageously; his crown was placed on Henry's head and his soldiers acclaimed him as king. Henry VII (as he now became) carefully dated his accession to the throne to the day before the battle so that anyone who fought against him was guilty of treason: it gave him a crucial hold over these men.

Henry's first priority was to secure the capital and to be crowned as lawful monarch.[4] On 3 September he entered London in triumph and proceeded to St Paul's Cathedral where he placed three standards as proof of his victory in battle – a victory that was of course itself a manifestation of divine favour. A *Te Deum* was celebrated as the Church validated his right to the throne. These acts, following on the acclamation of him as king at Bosworth Field, were part of a carefully choreographed legitimation of Henry's rule which reached its climax with his coronation on Sunday 30 October. Henry had a profound understanding of the power of symbol and of display and his coronation ceremony was conducted at Westminster Abbey in the traditional manner but with an extravagance that emphasised that he now enjoyed the full resources of majesty, and that these had been conferred upon him as the lawful sovereign by God, Church and people:

With great pomp he was conveyed to Westminster and there, on the thirtieth day of October, was with all accustomed ceremonies anointed and crowned king by the full assent of the Commons as well as of the nobility, and was named King Henry the Seventh of that name ... He obtained this kingdom and enjoyed it as a thing decided upon and provided by God ...

The coronation ceremony was a highly formalised reciprocal bonding between the new king and his subjects, for Henry not only received the fealty of the leading dignitaries of court, church and state but bound himself in return to observe the laws and privileges of the kingdom and of the Church.[5] He was anointed and crowned by the Archbishop of Canterbury; the sacral power of majesty was confirmed by the Church in the authority of its Primate. But it was not merely as 'King of England' that Henry was crowned: his full title was as 'rightful and undoubted inheritor of the Crowns of England and France' and explicit reference was made to 'the king's two duchies of Gascony and Normandy'.[6]

Henry now exercised his right as king to convene a meeting of Parliament to consolidate his authority. In November, the Parliament duly passed an Act proclaiming that the Crowns of England and of France belonged legally to Henry and his heirs. Before closing the assembly, on 10 December Henry graciously accepted a petition from the House of Commons that he should marry Elizabeth of York and unite the houses of York and Lancaster.[7]

It was now two years since Henry had reached out to his Yorkist opponents by solemnly swearing that he would marry Elizabeth. Of course, as a daughter of Edward IV, Elizabeth had a strong claim on the throne in her own right but Henry was determined that he should in no way appear to owe his crown to her and therefore delayed their marriage until he had been crowned as the lawful king. Since he and Elizabeth were distantly related, it was evident that a papal dispensation from the impediment of affinity was needed. However – like Ferdinand and Isabella in 1469 – Henry decided that he could not wait on the delays that would inevitably arise with a request to Rome and so he secured a dispensation from the papal legate in England, James, Bishop of Imola. The marriage took place on 18 January 1486, and on 27 March Pope Innocent VIII ratified the decision of his legate. To symbolise the union of the houses of York and Lancaster, Henry's propagandists invented a rose that was red and white.

It was traditional for a new king to make a formal and wide-ranging progress at the beginning of his reign to show himself to his subjects and extract their commitment of loyalty to him. Henry particularly needed to secure the North and he set out in March for a progress which took him through Lincoln and Nottingham to York, and then south-west to Worcester, Gloucester and Bristol, returning to London on 5 June. Both Lincoln and York had especial need to impress their new monarch with their loyalty for they had supported Richard III; indeed, the City of York had recorded that Richard III 'later mercifully reigning upon us was through great treason ... piteously slain and murdered to the great heaviness of this City'.[8] No whit abashed, the city now eagerly demonstrated its loyalty with civic and religious pageants for the new king. In return, Henry accorded York the singular honour of holding a Chapter of the Order of the Garter within its walls; normally this only took place at Winchester and Henry added point to his gesture by holding the Chapter on St George's Day (23 April). He also recognised York's financial difficulties by reducing its tax burden. Reconciliation was accompanied by threats: in Nottingham, Henry established a commission of loyalists to enquire into treasons and conspiracies in the Midlands. Among the great magnates who rushed to pledge their loyalty to the new king was the Earl of Northumberland.[9]

By happy chance, the papal bulls of dispensation for Henry's marriage to Elizabeth arrived during his progress and they were duly read out in the cathedrals in Worcester and Gloucester to emphasise that the papacy had recognised his legitimacy as king.[10]

Even greater satisfaction came when Elizabeth conceived almost immediately. Henry decided that the child would be born in Winchester, the ancient capital of Wessex, where according to chivalric legend the court of Camelot had been situated. In taking Elizabeth to Winchester for her delivery, Henry was validating his family's historical importance back deep into the days of the Arthurian legend. When Elizabeth presented him with a son on the night of 19–20 September 1486, there was a certain inevitability about the choice of the name of Arthur. In reality, King Arthur had no more existed than had the wizard Merlin, and it may well have been that Henry VII chose the name precisely because it was unique: there had never been a King Arthur of England. More practically, he conferred the title of Duke of Cornwall upon his son.

Arthur was baptised in Winchester on 24 September.[11] He was given a small household and the honours that were appropriate to his dignity as heir to the throne cascaded onto his little head: he was invested as

Prince of Wales and Earl of Chester and created a Knight of the Order of the Bath (30 November 1489) and a Knight of the Garter (8 May 1491); when, in his sixth year, his father left England to invade France, the little prince was named as 'Guardian of England' (October 1492). It appears likely that he first visited Wales in 1494 and Chester in 1498.[12] As he passed out of infancy, Arthur was given a more formally structured household; his education was entrusted to John Rede, who had previously been Headmaster of Winchester College (1484–90). Henry established a council to guide him as Prince of Wales and placed it under his uncle Jasper Tudor. In November 1493 Henry conferred upon his son and heir the estates of the Earldom of March.

The First Pretender: Lambert Simnel (1487)

Henry VII was fortunate that he was able to concentrate on domestic affairs during the first two years of his reign. His three most proximate neighbouring rulers were all minors: Charles VIII was thirteen when he succeeded to the throne of France in 1483; James IV of Scotland was fifteen in 1488 and Philip of Burgundy was ten when in the same year he succeeded to his dukedom. Only the Emperor-elect, Maximilian, was already a mature and tested ruler among the leaders in Northwestern Europe.

Henry dealt easily enough with the first Yorkist challenge to his rule. In February 1487, a young man claiming to be Edward, Earl of Warwick, son of Edward IV's brother the Duke of Clarence, landed in Ireland and proclaimed that he was the lawful King of England. The Pretender's real name was Lambert Simnel and he was probably the son of an artisan in Oxford, but he found ready support from Yorkist leaders: John de la Pole, Earl of Lincoln, joined him and Margaret of York, Dowager Archduchess of Burgundy, provided him with 2,000 mercenaries. Simnel also found ready recognition from those Irish lords who favoured the House of York, and on 24 May was crowned in Dublin Cathedral as King Edward VI of England. Much of Ireland supported the Pretender and within weeks he led an invasion of England to claim the throne, landing in Cumbria on 4 June.

Henry VII responded with his customary vigour and on 16 June defeated Simnel's army at the Battle of Stoke, near Newark. Simnel was captured, Lincoln was killed and Lovell disappeared, probably to Burgundy. Although there would be other alarms for Henry in the years to come, the Battle of Stoke marked the real end of the Wars of the

Roses. The king demonstrated his disdain for Simnel by employing him in his kitchens. He took the precaution of making another progress to the Yorkist North – to York, Pontefract, Durham and Newcastle – and when on 3 November he made a second triumphal entry into London he commemorated his victory at Stoke with a *Te Deum* at St Paul's. Now, Henry was ready to have his queen crowned. The festivities began on 23 November and Elizabeth's coronation took place at Westminster Abbey two days later. In time, Henry became deeply attached to his queen.

It was fully three years after Henry's own coronation before he had to deal with a major crisis in foreign affairs; it centred upon the Duchy of Brittany. When Louis XI of France died in 1483 his daughter Anne of Beaujeu assumed the regency for her teenage brother Charles VIII. She had to confront an Orleanist conspiracy against the Crown which was supported by Duke Francis II of Brittany (The Foolish War, 1485–88); in July 1488 the royal army crushed the forces of Brittany and Francis II was obliged to acknowledge that he held his duchy as a vassal of the King of France. It happened that Francis then died in September after a riding accident and Anne of Beaujeu duly claimed the wardship of his heiress, a twelve-year-old girl who was also named Anne.

The extinction of the male line of the duchy thereby raised the very real prospect that the crown of France would gain control of Brittany. This was deeply alarming to Henry VII, for if France acquired the Breton ports she would control the whole of the southern coast of the Channel except for Calais. Henry certainly needed no reminding of how the Channel ports could facilitate an invasion of England. Accordingly, early in 1489 he agreed to protect the Duchy of Brittany against France (Treaty of Redon, 8–14 February 1489). He secured from Parliament the right to levy a tax to provide £100,000 to pay for 6,000 men to fight in the duchy: the small army sailed to France in April. Henry also agreed to help Maximilian against rebels who were supported by France (Treaty of Dordrecht, February 1489) and sent 1800 troops under Giles Daubeney to support him.[13] These were small-scale operations but were nevertheless significant, for when his two little forces landed on Continental soil so Henry himself stepped metaphorically onto the stage of European politics. Much more significant was the agreement that Henry began to pursue in the spring of 1488 with the Catholic Kings of Spain for an alliance between their two houses.

Spanish Match?

There were many antecedents when in the late 1480s the Crowns of England and Spain began to edge towards an alliance with each other. Castile and England had well-established trading and commercial contacts; the ports of Southern England such as Portsmouth, Plymouth and Bristol had traded for generations with Santander, Bilbao and San Sebastián and had even established significant colonies as far south as Seville. Indeed, it was now over a century since the two countries had come together in a double marital alliance; in 1371–2 Pedro I ('the Cruel') of Castile had married two daughters to sons of Edward III – Constanza to John of Gaunt, Duke of Lancaster (1371) and Isabella to Edmund of Langley, Earl of Cambridge (1372).

These two marriages led in time to the creation of the houses of Lancaster and York and also to the families from which Ferdinand and Isabella were descendants. In 1372, Constanza gave birth to a daughter who became known as Katharine of Lancaster (Catalina de Lancaster) and in 1388 Katharine married Henry, the son of Juan I of Castile. Henry succeeded to the throne of Castile in 1392 as Henry III and in 1405 Katharine gave birth to the child who would become Juan II of Castile, grandfather of Isabella the Catholic.

Ferdinand of Aragon was the grandson of Ferdinand I of Aragon who was the brother of Henry III of Castile. It was because of his affinity with Isabella as second cousins that they required the papal dispensation that they forged in 1469.[14] The affinity of the English and Castilian royal houses, distant though it was, also had implications for the discussions that now began about a marriage between the children of the English and Spanish crowns.

It is probable that it was Henry's success at the Battle of Stoke that encouraged Ferdinand of Aragon to think seriously about an alliance with him. Certainly, Ferdinand had no intention of becoming involved in the political and military struggles of Northern Europe but he realised that he might well be able to profit from a revival of England's traditional hostility to France. In the mid-1480s, Ferdinand's primary ambition in foreign affairs was to regain the strategically important Pyrenean frontier counties of Rousillon and Cerdaña which had been seized by France in 1462. Retention of the two counties by France would greatly facilitate the passage of a French army into Catalonia while their reacquisition by the Crown of Aragon would substantially strengthen Spanish defences against France. It was essentially to explore the possibility of forming an alliance against France that Ferdinand persuaded Isabella to send Dr Rodrigo González de Puebla to London in 1487 to assess the new king and to sound him out about an alliance between them.

González de Puebla was a man of comparatively low social rank and had the disadvantage of being of *converso* blood but Ferdinand evidently trusted him. This was to prove a rare error of judgement by the king, for González de Puebla proved to be an inept and bungling ambassador who created difficulty after difficulty for his sovereigns and who became deeply disliked by their daughter Katharine. But Henry VII liked him very much – almost certainly because he could manipulate him so easily.[15]

While an alliance with England was currently low on Ferdinand's priorities, for Henry VII such an agreement represented something akin to the holy grail of diplomacy, for it would confer unquestioned legitimacy upon him and his house to be allied with one of the most prestigious of western monarchies. On 10 March 1488, Henry therefore commissioned John Weston and Thomas Savage to lead a delegation to Spain to conclude a treaty of alliance with Ferdinand and Isabella. The ambassadors were instructed to settle all areas of dispute between the Crowns and to seek ways in which they could co-operate together in future. There was no explicit mention of any marriage negotiations, presumably because Henry VII dared not risk the embarrassment that would follow on being rejected by Ferdinand and Isabella. In all probability, however, secret instructions made allowance for such a topic to be raised.[16]

The Spanish response to the English embassy staggered Henry VII: Isabella sent Juan de Sepúlveda to London to join González de Puebla and on 30 April she and Ferdinand despatched powers to the two men authorising them to negotiate a marriage between Katharine and Arthur. The two ambassadors were also to bring all agreements and treaties between England and Castile up to date.[17] When Henry VII realised what was being offered to him he became literally wide-eyed with amazement: on reading the powers that González de Puebla presented to him he 'opened his eyes with joy' and immediately entered into the discussion of details, insisting that he wanted Katharine to be sent to England as soon as possible, if practical even before she reached puberty. Indeed, so thrilled was the normally undemonstrative king that when speaking of the projected marital alliance 'he broke out into a *Te Deum Laudamus*' and it came to be his practice – at least at this early stage of the negotiations – of touching his hat with respect every time that he mentioned Ferdinand and Isabella. It was as if Henry could not believe his good fortune.

The Spanish ambassadors ungenerously – and most undiplomatically – reminded him of the value of such an alliance with their monarchs: they confided in Henry that 'bearing in mind what happens every day to the kings of England, it is surprising that [Ferdinand and Isabella] should dare to give their daughter at all' and they assured him that 'the greatness and prosperity of Spain would contribute much to make that impossible which has happened so often and which still happens to kings of England'. González de Puebla assured Ferdinand and Isabella that these observations had been made 'with great courtesy, in order that they might not feel displeasure or be enraged'. Henry seems to have been too enraptured by the prospect of negotiating a Spanish match to have taken offence at Spanish arrogance.[18]

He therefore wasted no time: by 7 July an agreement had been reached in principle between the two Spanish ambassadors and the English commissioners (Richard Foxe, Bishop of Exeter, and Giles Daubeney) on the terms of the marriage agreement; the details were deliberately kept vague but the outline of the contract was beginning to be defined. It was agreed that Ferdinand and Isabella would send Katharine to England in 1500 when she was, at fifteen, old enough to consummate the marriage. They would pay the expenses for her journey and clothe her appropriately. The dowry (or marriage portion) was fixed at 200,000 escudos; one half of this was to be paid when Katharine arrived in England and the other half on the day when the marriage was solemnised in church. The subjects of the kings of Spain in London would stand surety for this. In return, Henry VII was to endow Katharine with one-third of the revenues of Wales, Cornwall and Chester; it was calculated that these would amount to 80,000 gold crowns. Katharine retained her rights of inheritance to the Crowns of Spain (which in practice meant to that of Castile, for women who had not been born in Aragon could not succeed there).

The marriage agreement was to be only one part of a more wide-ranging treaty. All treaties of peace, commerce and alliance were to be restored to the condition that they had held in 1458 and England and the Spanish crowns were to assist each other if attacked and were not to allow rebels of one party to live in the other's country. If one party made an alliance the other was to be included. Henry agreed to send ambassadors to Spain to hammer out the details with Ferdinand and Isabella.[19]

As the last of their duties, González de Puebla and Sepúlveda were allowed to see Arthur. The prince was – by accident or otherwise – naked and asleep when they arrived to inspect him; they duly confirmed that his qualities were 'quite incredible' without entering into specifics.[20]

It was only now that a first, provisional, agreement had been made that the real negotiations began over the details. In a cynical attempt to save money, Ferdinand and Isabella decided that they would provide Katharine with a dowry of 100,000 escudos rather than the 200,000 that had been agreed upon and they insisted that this should be calculated in Castilian gold coin rather than in English coin so as to allow fewer errors (and cheating). They raised questions about the increased monies and rents that would be presented to Katharine when in due course she became Queen of England. It was entirely characteristic of Ferdinand to renegotiate an agreement upon which the ink was barely dry and when González de Puebla received the new demands he dared not even put them to Henry VII. Ferdinand's real position was made clear: it was a condition of the treaty that Henry VII would actively support Ferdinand's claims to the counties of Rousillon and Cerdagne. Indeed, Ferdinand believed that the 'principal reason' for which he had signed the treaty with Henry VII was to recover the two counties.[21]

Like a fisherman reeling in his catch, Ferdinand now encouraged Henry to join openly in an alliance against France. On 17 December 1488 he instructed González de Puebla to emphasise to Henry VII that all the opponents of France should unite to regain their lands in France – Rousillon and Cerdagne for Catalonia; Gascony and Normandy for England. Ferdinand thus foreshadowed the creation of the 'triple alliance' of Spain, England and the Low Countries against France.[22] But Henry was already hooked: within days he had appointed Thomas Savage and Richard Nanfan to travel to Spain to negotiate the terms of the marriage and a diplomatic alliance.[23]

The English Embassy to Spain & the Treaty of Medina del Campo (27 March 1489)[24]

González de Puebla and Sepúlveda accompanied Savage and Nanfan on their journey to Spain so that they could report directly to Ferdinand and Isabella and join in the negotiations. The journey of the four ambassadors proved to be especially fraught. They sailed from Southampton on 19 January 1489 in two Spanish ships but a change in the wind obliged them to take refuge in Plymouth on the following day. They set sail again on 1 February but two days later powerful winds forced them into Falmouth; not until 12 February did the weather relent sufficiently to allow them to embark for the third time. Three days later, in the Bay of Biscay, they ran into 'a great storm of wind and rain' that convinced them they were about to die – 'and all the ambassadors cried to God, and to all the Saints of Paradise and not only they but all who were on board the ship'. Against all their fears they made it safely to Laredo (16 February). Still, their troubles persisted: it was only with difficulty that lodgings were found for them and then a violent snowstorm obliged them to remain in Laredo for seven days. They left on 23 February and arrived in Burgos on 26th, where they stayed eight days. They travelled on to Valladolid, where they spent a further three days before hearing that Ferdinand and Isabella were ready to receive them in the market town of Medina del Campo. When they entered the royal presence on 14 March it was after two months during which they had endured terror on the seas and acute discomfort on land.

Medina del Campo lay in the heart of Old Castile and served two functions: it was a financial and banking centre and a favoured residence of Isabella. The town was a focal point of Castile's wool and textile trades and the trade fairs that it held in May and October reflected its growing importance as an international banking and financial centre and attracted merchants and financiers from much of Western Europe. It had a population of about 15,000 and so it was of a size with better-known cities such as Segovia or Salamanca. But over the long winter months it was bitterly cold: the Castilians still say that the wind that blows down from the mountains that encircle the *meseta* of Castile 'cannot blow out a candle but can kill a man'. The ambassadors were now safe: but they were freezing.

The palace was small and did not compare in grandeur with those in, for example, Segovia, Toledo or Seville, but it sat on a corner of the enormous *plaza mayor* where the fairs took place, enabling Isabella to keep a watchful eye on proceedings. Befitting its status as a great trading centre, Medina del Campo had one of the largest castles in Castile; La Mota had been built over the last two centuries as one of the major strongpoints of the kingdom, with a moat and a prodigious tower and it held 120 pieces of artillery with which to defend itself. It also held some dreadful dungeons in which important prisoners were held.

Notwithstanding any doubts that they entertained about Henry VII's ability to remain in power in England, Ferdinand and Isabella went to great lengths to impress his envoys with the luxury of their surroundings and the extravagance of their own dress and jewellery; Savage and Nanfan – and, through them, their master – were left in no doubt about the wealth and power of the Spanish monarchs. Isabella was normally known for the austerity of her dress but for the interview with the English envoys she presented herself as a queen of wealth and power:

> It was about 7 o'clock in the evening when the ambassadors were summoned, and daylight was falling. They were accompanied by a great number of torchbearers, and on arriving in the palace they found the king and Queen in a hall seated beneath a rich cloth of gold; in the middle of this great cloth was a shield quartered with the arms of Castile and Aragon.
>
> The king was dressed in a rich robe of cloth of gold, which was woven entirely of gold and was edged with a rich trimming of fine sable.
>
> The queen was seated beside him. She wore a rich robe of the same woven cloth of gold, which was shaped in the Spanish fashion … On top of the robe she had a riding hood of black velvet which was slashed so as to display the cloth of gold which she wore underneath. The hood had a lining of solid gold, shaped into oblong pieces that were as long as a finger and half as wide; each oblong was decorated with jewels that were so valuable that no one has seen their like. Around her waist the queen had a girdle of white leather which had a pocket which was studded with a great ruby the size of a tennis ball, and this in turn was surrounded by five rich diamonds. Moreover, a number of precious stones highlighted the rest of the girdle. Around her neck, the queen wore a rich gold necklace of red and white roses, and each rose was itself decorated with a large jewel. Two ribbons hung down across her chest, each of them adorned with large diamonds and rubies, pearls and other jewels – perhaps in all there were a hundred or so of these.
>
> The queen wore a short cloak of crimson satin which was edged with ermine over her dress; it hung almost casually over her left shoulder. Her head was uncovered …
>
> I calculate that the dress that she wore must have been worth over 200,000 crowns of gold.[25]

Katharine herself made her first appearances just over a week later, on 24–25 March 1489. Once again, Ferdinand and Isabella displayed their wealth, and the English ambassadors freely admitted that they were dazzled by this as well as by the warmth of the reception given to them:

On the 24th day of March the king and queen sent for the ambassadors. It was the eve of Lady Day in March, and they went to hear Compline. Afterwards, they accompanied the king and queen into a gallery which was hung with fine tapestries. There they found the young princesses, Doña Maria and Doña Katharine, Princess of England. The king and queen entered and sat down. The prince [Juan] sat on the ground in front of his parents and his sisters in turn sat in front of him. I must say that the queen and her daughters were very richly dressed. Both princesses – María and Katharine – had fourteen ladies-in-waiting in attendance upon them; all of these were ladies of noble lineage, and they were dressed in cloth of gold; it was a beautiful thing to see the richness of their dresses.

The ladies-in-waiting danced with each other in pairs, and then the king and queen commanded Princess María to take to the floor and dance; she selected a young lady of the court who was about her own age and led her to dance.

People speak of the honour done to ambassadors in England: certainly it cannot be compared to the honour which is done to ambassadors in the Kingdom of Castile, and especially so in the time of this great king and queen...

And on the 25th day of this same month of March the said monarchs provided another festival in honour of these ambassadors, to wit, a bull-fight. And afterwards there came out about a hundred knights and other noblemen who were well mounted on fine jennets who skirmished and ran with dogs in the way they fought with the Saracens: it was a fine sight. The king and the queen, the prince and three of the princesses watched from a scaffolding; the ambassadors sat beside them. And it was beautiful to see how the queen held up her youngest daughter, Katharine, Princess of Wales, who was three years of age. After the festivities were concluded, the king and queen retired into a large room and took the ambassadors with them, and there the ladies of the court began to dance with the gentlemen who had performed in the sports of the bulls and the dogs.

The king was dressed at this time in a gown of black cloth with open sleeves. And the left sleeve of the gown was edged with great rubies and pearls ... The queen wore a rich robe of green satin which was decorated with lozenges embroidered and worked very skilfully with the needle. And round the collar of the queen's robe, in the style of a necklace, was a border which was as wide as two fingers; it was made up of large jewels and pearls. The border of the robe and its sleeves hung down to the ground; they were made of crimson velvet. The queen's motto was sewn upon it in large letters of beaten gold, a quarter of a yard in length, and each letter was decorated with large pearls. It was the richest thing that has ever been seen.

The prince was dressed in a short robe down to the breech, and with black lower garments and shoes with long points in the old fashion. His robe was bordered with the same motif as was the queen's, and in similar letters of beaten gold. He wore a cap of black velvet made in a roll, again in the old fashion.

Princess Isabella was dressed in a robe of green cloth of gold with a beautiful rich necklace of gold; and she wore a great number of large jewels.

The third daughter, Princess María, who is married or betrothed to the Archduke Philip of Austria, was dressed in a rich grey cloth of gold. And she, too, wore clothes that were lavishly decorated with precious jewels.

And as for the dresses and the wealth of the ladies of the court, I could not put it into writing for you, for it would take me a year to do them justice, and however much I wrote, there would still be a great deal more to be said of them ...[26]

The treaty was signed by the Spanish commissioners and the English ambassadors on 27 March and was ratified by Ferdinand and Isabella on the following day.[27] It incorporated the three agreements – military and political; commercial; and marital – upon which Ferdinand had always insisted. The two countries agreed to assist each other in defending their present and future dominions against any enemy and to provide help within three months if any aggressor turned on one of them. If either ally went to war with France the other would be obliged to join them, but because Henry had concluded a peace with France until 17 January 1490 Ferdinand would not be able to call upon him for support before that date. Nevertheless, both parties specifically guaranteed not to make peace with France without the approval of the other partner, save in the unlikely event that France restored Normandy and Aquitaine to Henry or Rousillon and Cerdagne to Ferdinand; in such circumstances the benefitting party could make peace without reference to the other. Neither was to favour or accommodate rebels against the other. The subjects of each crown would be entitled to travel in the country of the other without passports and would have the same rights as the natives of that kingdom. Free trade was to exist between their subjects and customs were to revert to those which had been in operation thirty years before. The trading provisions were especially favourable to English merchants; Professor Wernham wryly remarked that 'the Spanish councillors who negotiated these clauses must have been nodding badly'.[28] The most important provisions were simply stated: the marriage of their children would strengthen the alliance and was to be contracted by proxy (*per verba de futuro*) as soon as practical and then to be sworn to by Arthur and Katharine in person (*per verba de praesenti*) and consummated as soon as they reached the appropriate age.[29]

Ferdinand and Isabella had to admit failure in their attempt to reduce the marriage portion, which remained at 200,000 escudos, to be calculated as 4s 2d sterling; one-half of this was to be paid when Katharine arrived in England, the other half within two years thereafter. They had also to accept that their own goods as well as those of their subjects in England would stand surety for the dowry. The other provisions remained substantially as agreed in London except for one major confusion created by González de Puebla, who insisted that Henry's commissioners had accepted that the king would accept one-quarter of the dowry in jewels, ornaments and furnishings. Savage and Nanfan resolutely denied that this had been agreed and it was decided that the question would be put under oath to the individuals concerned. The problem resulted in almost endless ill feeling between the two monarchs over many years. Ferdinand and Isabella promised to send Katharine properly clothed with ornaments and jewels befitting her rank but it was not clearly specified whether she was to retain these for her own use or to surrender them to Henry as part of her dowry. The point was to prove of substantial importance and to have widespread implications: was Katharine to lose her jewels and valuables and be obliged to rely on her husband and father-in-law to replace them? Was Henry VII to accept valuable items as part of the dowry which were in effect second-hand? The problems created by the vagueness of phrasing festered for years and helped to make Katharine's life in England a misery as the issue was still not resolved when Arthur died.

The partners to the agreement fenced over the question of when Katharine would travel to England. Although Ferdinand and Isabella agreed that Katharine's marriage would take place within one month of her arrival they refused to be specific about when she would travel, merely recording that this would be decided upon in the future. In one sense, the date chose itself: Arthur would reach his fourteenth birthday in September 1500 and would then be old enough in the eyes of the Church to consummate the marriage. Katharine, on the other hand, would reach the age at which she could be lawfully married in December 1497 when she celebrated her twelfth birthday. Evidently, Ferdinand and Isabella intended to keep her in Spain at the very least until Arthur reached lawful adulthood in 1500.

The Family of Henry VII & Elizabeth

When Henry VII agreed to the marriage of Arthur and Katharine he could not be certain that his own line of succession was secure but his anxieties eased when over the next two years Elizabeth presented him with two more children: on 29 November 1489 she gave birth to a daughter who was named Margaret and on 28 June 1491 she was triumphantly delivered of a second son at Greenwich Palace; the infant was given his father's name and was baptised by Bishop Foxe of Exeter in the church of the Observant Friars at Greenwich.

A torrent of honours marked the early years of the life of Prince Henry: by the age of three he had become Warden of the Cinq Ports, Constable of Dover Castle, Earl Marshal of England and Lord Lieutenant of Ireland and invested with the Order of the Bath. On 1 November 1494 he was created Duke of York to make the point very publicly that the previous holder of the title – Richard, one of the two princes who had been murdered in the Tower of London – was dead. So important was this political and public statement that Henry VII celebrated it by mounting the greatest festivities of his reign thus far. In May 1495, the four-year-old prince was invested as a Knight of the Order of the Garter.[30]

War with France – and the Conspiracy of Perkin Warbeck

In September 1490, Henry engaged in a flurry of diplomatic activity. On 11–12 September he reached agreement with Maximilian that they would fight the French in support of Anne of Brittany, and five days later joined a league with Spain and Maximilian for mutual defence against France. On 23 September Henry ratified the Treaty of Medina del Campo. Maximilian was the first to act: on 19 December he married Anne of Brittany by proxy.[31]

It was not a moment too soon for Henry to wrap himself in foreign support, for a new pretender appeared in 1491 and he was to present much greater and more persistent trouble for Henry than Simnel had done.[32] Perkin Warbeck was probably the son of a customs official in Tournai, and although he could not speak English fluently he claimed to be Richard,

Duke of York, the younger of Edward IV's murdered sons. In November 1491 he landed in Ireland and was well received; Maurice Fitzgerald, Earl of Desmond, recognised him as Richard of York. Once again, Irish disaffection with English rule threatened Henry VII's security on the throne.

Charles VIII invaded Brittany in 1491 with an army of 30,000 that easily overwhelmed the Breton forces. The price of his victory was simple enough: he obliged Duchess Anne to marry him (6 December). The Duchy of Brittany was now for all practical purposes subsumed into the French monarchy. In marrying Anne, Charles inflicted a double humiliation upon Maximilian, for not only had he been engaged to Anne but his daughter Margaret had been pledged to Charles VIII himself. The French king now sent Margaret back to her father with the promise that he would return to him the Franche-Comté and Artois.

Henry VII was even more aggrieved than Maximilian by events in Brittany. Perhaps, indeed, he had lost more than Maximilian, for France now controlled the whole of the southern coastline of the Channel except for Calais. But he was perhaps more angered by Charles VIII's support of Perkin Warbeck and set himself to go to war with him. In October he summoned Parliament to vote the subsidies with which to fight the campaign; with real reluctance, it did so. In November he proposed to Ferdinand that they should jointly declare war on France before 15 April 1492 and launch simultaneous invasions in the summer.[33] Ferdinand strung him along: he now agreed that Katharine would be sent to England as soon as she had reached her twelfth birthday, which would be in December 1497 (Treaty of Westminster, 8 March 1492).[34] But of course he – and more especially his wife – had no intention of letting Katharine leave Spain at such an early age. Much less would Ferdinand fight against France for the advantage of Henry VII: his eyes were fixed on his northern frontier and on Italy.

The English war effort in France was still small-scale – in mid-June the English navy engaged briefly with some French ships – but when Charles VIII welcomed Perkin Warbeck as 'a kinsman and friend' Henry VII was provoked beyond endurance: early in August 1492 he declared war on France. On 2 October he led an army of 20,000 men across the Channel and three weeks later laid siege to Boulogne. It was too late in the year for him to achieve any military victory but in invading France Henry had re-emphasised that he was both king and soldier and had made the clearest statement to all – at home and abroad – of his confidence in his security on the throne. Henry proved to be a lucky general: though late and small his war-effort was well timed, for Charles VIII had much more urgent priorities and so – to Henry's surprise – it was the King of France who sued for peace.

Peace was signed at Étaples on 3 November 1492. Henry recognised Charles VIII's claim to the Duchy of Brittany and won three major gains for doing so – most important (and enduring) of all, he was recognised by France as the lawful King of England; Charles promised not to aid any rebels against Henry and expelled Warbeck and his supporters from France; finally, Charles agreed to pay an annual pension to compensate Henry for his expenses in the war in Brittany in effect in return for putting his claim to the throne of France into abeyance. Henry VII always liked others to pay him and he would now receive the generous indemnity of £159,000 in half-yearly instalments of £2,500. On 12 November, Henry returned to Calais, deeply content that he had been successful in his first war against France. Ferdinand might well have reflected – for the first time? – that the King of England had more mettle than he had thought.

Expelled from the French court, Perkin Warbeck turned to the House of Habsburg. He fled first to the Low Countries, where Margaret acknowledged him as her nephew, and then travelled on to Vienna where Maximilian recognised him as the lawful King of England and promised to provide him with support to win his throne.[35] Two English rebels intrigued against Henry; on 14 March 1493, Sir William Stanley involved himself in a Yorkist conspiracy and about the same time Sir Robert Clifford fled to Margaret's court. But although Philip of Burgundy agreed not to help Warbeck, Margaret continued to do so. Henry therefore ordered an embargo on trade with the Low Countries from 18 September 1493, forbidding the Merchant Adventurers to trade with Antwerp or with any other ports in the Low Countries. The measure was deeply unpopular and on 15 October there were riots in London. In May 1494 Maximilian responded with a counter-embargo and seized the goods of English traders but the hostility of his merchants and traders meant that the measure was unsustainable and he had to relent. Once again, the King of England had shown a mastery of the mechanics of European politics, a perception of how he could use and profit from them.

It soon became evident that Charles VIII's settlement with Henry VII at Étaples was merely a prelude to a more widespread settlement that would free his hands for his invasion of Italy. Charles made treaties with Ferdinand and Maximilian in which he gave them major concessions in return for tacitly accepting his assault on Italy. In January 1493, Ferdinand of Aragon duly promised not to oppose the invasion on condition that Charles returned Rousillon and Cerdagne to the Crown of Aragon and even agreed with Charles that neither of them would marry any of their children with the English house or with that of the King of the Romans without the express consent of the other (Treaty of Narbonne-Barcelona, 8–19 January 1493).[36] Henry now realised how Ferdinand had duped him – and perhaps that the marriage of Arthur and Katharine would never take place. It was a salutary lesson for the new king in the hazards of dealing with 'the Fox of Aragon'.

Four months after making the Treaty of Barcelona, Charles agreed with Maximilian to return Artois and the Franche-Comté to the House of Burgundy as his price for not opposing the invasion (Treaty of Senlis, 23 May 1493). French generosity seemed truly to be without limits. It was certainly without strategic sense for the key frontier territories that Charles alienated in 1493 were not recovered by France for well over a century and a half. Europe held its breath and waited now for the King of France to invade Italy.

4

BETROTHAL, 1494–1497:
THE PROMISE OF A MARRIAGE:
FRENCH WAR, SPANISH DIPLOMACY

The First French Invasion of Italy & the 'Holy League' (1494–5)
The crisis in Italy had been years in the making, for the French crown
had long determined to reassert its claim on the Crown of Naples as
soon as the opportunity presented itself, and the death of Ferdinand I
('Ferrante') in January 1494 did precisely that.[1] Charles VIII wasted no
time: on 3 September he led an army of more than 15,000 men into the
Alps and when he reached northern Italy his force was doubled in size
by the mercenaries who were awaiting him. Charles grandly justified his
invasion by announcing that his campaign was merely the prelude to
his leading a European crusade against the infidel: the English were told
that 'the king is taking up arms to repossess his Kingdom of Naples in
order to use it as a base for a crusade in Greece. He will use his troops to
overthrow the Ottoman Empire.'[2]

Indulgent rhetoric apart, the French irruption into Italy in 1494 proved
to be a landmark event in European history, opening half a century of
intense warfare between France and Spain. 'The Italian Wars' (as these
conflicts became known) were not brought to an end until 1559 but they
were much more than a military conflict: they came to subsume many
of the pivotal issues in international politics during the first half of the
sixteenth century and acted as the focal point for many of the tensions
between the emerging nation-states of Western Europe – and above all
else for the welling conflict between France and Spain. Katharine's life

would be insistently influenced by them, and she was far from alone in this.[3]

Charles's march cowed Italy into submission and led directly to regime change in Florence, Milan and Naples. The Medici were replaced in Florence by a pro-French republic which was dominated, if only briefly, by the radical friar Girolamo Savonarola, while in Milan Lodovico Sforza was restored to power as a reward for allowing Charles's army to march across the duchy.

Most apprehensive of all were the Pope and the King of Naples. As the French army approached Rome Alexander VI genuinely feared for his own life, and the enthusiastic welcome that Charles received from the people of Rome in the last days of 1494 did little to assuage his terror. Alexander encouraged Charles to move southward by promising to invest him with the Crown of Naples if he took his army peacefully through the Papal States. He then fled with his cardinals into the security of the Castel Sant'Angelo (6 January 1495) while Charles enjoyed the delights of Rome for a month.[4] Alfonso II of Naples (who had succeeded his father in 1493) did not dare to confront the invader: he abdicated in favour of his son, Ferdinand II ('Ferrantino'). Charles entered the city of Naples on 22 February: he had not had to fight a single battle since leaving France. Francesco Guicciardini, an Italian patriot who was ashamed of his countrymen, contemptuously compared Charles's triumph with that of Julius Caesar in Gaul: 'Thus Charles, in a remarkable succession of incredible good fortune, even more than Julius Caesar, conquered before he saw.'[5]

Charles VIII's tumultuous success was, however, both short-lived and counter-productive. He alienated many supporters in Naples by the preferential treatment he gave to his French followers and he soon realised that it was one thing to find the resources to take a great army into Italy, quite another to maintain it as it settled down there as an occupying force. Most importantly of all, Charles dared not absent himself long from France, and when he left Naples on 20 May 1495 to return home the great city was seething at his misrule. He again passed through Rome (1–3 June 1495) even though he had promised not to do so: Pope Alexander fled to Orvieto and then on to Perugia as Charles tried vainly to catch up with him to force him to invest him with the Crown of Naples.

The diplomatic triumphs that Charles had won in 1493 by buying off the powers who might have opposed his invasion proved as ephemeral as his military success. Alexander VI, Maximilian and Ferdinand were not men to keep their promises once they had secured their objectives and even while Charles marched south they joined together in an alliance against him: on 31 March 1495, Alexander VI united the enemies of France – the Papacy, the Empire, Spain, Venice and Milan and some smaller Italian states – into what he shamelessly named 'the Holy League'. Ostensibly, the purpose of the League was to defend Christendom against the Turk but in reality it was designed to drive the invader out of Italy and to restore the political balances within the peninsula: the unholy Pope would lead a crusade against the Most Christian King. Naturally, once Charles was safely out of Italy, Alexander promptly forgot his promise to invest him with the Kingdom of Naples, securing Ferdinand of Aragon's loyalty by promising to grant it to him instead.[6] The Holy League was formally proclaimed on 10 April 1495 while Charles VIII and his army were ensconced in Naples: much of Western Europe was now allied against the King of France – exactly as Ferdinand had calculated would prove to be the case.

Ferdinand of Aragon's Diplomatic System: The Marriages of 1495–8

It was, indeed, Ferdinand who gained most from Charles VIII's folly.[7] By the Treaty of Barcelona in 1493 he had secured his north-eastern border with the recovery of the counties of Rossellon and Cerdaña, including the splendid fortresses of Perpignan and Salces, and his support for the Holy League won him Alexander VI's promise – for what it was worth – that he would be invested with the Kingdom of Naples. A further gain was not immediately evident: Ferdinand entrusted his army in Italy to Gonzalo Fernández de Córdoba, a younger son of an Andalusian noble family who had won renown during the war in Granada. Fernández de Córdoba's first campaigns against the French were not successful – he was defeated at Seminara in Calabria (28 June 1495) – but he began then to apply himself to developing methods which would defeat French cavalry and Swiss infantry by massed squares of pikemen supported by artillery fire; a first victory, at Atella, in July 1496 convinced him that he had both understood the problem confronting him and provided the answer to it. Over the next few years he would revolutionise the nature of warfare: Ferdinand of Aragon would reap the benefits.[8]

Ferdinand never thought of the Holy League as anything more than a short-term solution: he attached much more enduring importance to creating a solid and permanent league against France. Indeed, in this central construct of his foreign policy he faithfully followed the example of his father, Juan II of Aragon, who had sought to create a 'triple alliance' against France between the Crown of Aragon, the Duchy of Burgundy and the Kingdom of England. In his five children Ferdinand had the perfect agents for his policy, for they were now all of an age at which marriages could be reasonably arranged for them: in 1494 the eldest of them (Isabella, already a widow) was twenty-four while the youngest (Katharine) was eight. During 1495–98 Ferdinand negotiated marriages for them which created the triple alliance against France. But Ferdinand's brilliance proved to be counter-productive, for as the result of a catastrophic series of deaths in 1497–1500 these marriages led in time to the absorption of the united crowns of Spain into the hands of a foreign dynasty.

Portugal

It will be recalled that Ferdinand and Isabella placed their relationship with Portugal above all others in foreign affairs since it provided them with an essential part of their domestic security as well as the hope that their dynasty would one day unite the whole Iberian peninsula under its leadership. Accordingly, between 1490 and 1498 they arranged no fewer than three marriages for (two) daughters with the scions of the Portuguese royal house. They started by marrying their eldest child, Isabella, to Crown Prince Alfonso of Portugal in 1490. When Alfonso died after a riding accident in 1491 they offered María in marriage to Crown Prince Manuel. However, when Manuel rejected the proposal because he needed a bride who would be able to secure the succession with some immediacy Ferdinand and Isabella decided that Princess Isabella (who was now twenty years old) would have to marry Manuel to reaffirm the alliance.

Unfortunately, the princess adamantly refused to agree, reminding her parents that they had promised before she married Alfonso that if she was widowed she would be free to retire into a life of religious contemplation and not be obliged to marry again. It took Ferdinand and Isabella until November 1496 to persuade her that it was her familial duty to marry the heir to the throne of Portugal and the marriage was celebrated in 1497. Tragically, Isabella died in childbirth in 1498. Her parents were devastated by her loss, coming as it did a year after Juan's death and in circumstances for which they may well have blamed themselves. Manuel then reluctantly agreed to marry María (who was now sixteen years old). The diriment impediment of affinity was easily brushed aside: anxious to oblige Ferdinand and Isabella so that they would support his ambitions for his own son, Cesare, in Italy, Pope Alexander readily issued the appropriate dispensations: granting such dispensations came easily to this Pope. The third Castilian–Portuguese marriage was brilliantly successful: María presented Manuel with ten children, including Isabella, who became the wife and Empress of Charles V and the mother of Philip II. In 1580 Philip brought the plans of his great-grandparents to fruition when he absorbed Portugal into his realms and thereby united all the Crowns of Iberia under his rule.

The Habsburg–Burgundian Conglomerate: 'The Most Remarkable Marriage Contract in the History of Modern Europe'

The core of Ferdinand's anti-French alliance lay with the double marriage that he made with the Habsburg–Burgundian conglomerate: by the Treaty of Antwerp (20 June 1495) he and Isabella agreed to a double marriage with the children of Maximilian of Austria and Mary of Burgundy – Juan to Margaret of Austria and Juana to the Archduke Philip, heir to the Dukedom of Burgundy and prospective heir to the imperial title.[9] The marriages would provide both the Spanish Monarchy and the Habsburg–Burgundian dynasty with protection against France. They proved to have such momentous historical significance as to fully justify Karl Brandi's description of them as 'the most remarkable marriage contract in the history of modern Europe'.[10]

Both parties attached sufficient importance to the marriages to dispense with the exchange of dowries on the grounds that they were making equal commitments to each other. More importantly, they determined that the exchange of brides would take place as soon as possible: the fleet which took Juana to the Low Countries would return immediately with Margaret. Unfortunately, Juana's departure was delayed because of the war with France and perhaps also because Ferdinand and Isabella were beginning to worry about her mental stability. Certainly, her parents were sufficiently concerned that she should be safely conveyed to the Low Countries to have Christopher Columbus himself advise on the composition of her fleet. No fewer than twenty-two ships – and 4,610 people – weighed anchor at Santona on 21 August 1496 but storms forced them to take shelter in Portland in England and it was not until 8 September that Juana disembarked in the Low Countries, at Bergen-op-Zoom.[11] There was no one of importance to greet her and it was three weeks before Margaret of Austria met her in Brussels (1 October). Margaret then accompanied Juana to Lille where on 12 October she was belatedly welcomed by Philip; he was eighteen and Juana was one month short of her seventeenth birthday. But if the reception of the *infanta* was disparagingly chaotic her marriage was promptly carried out: Philip found a priest to perform the marriage ceremony that very day and within hours of their meeting the young couple consummated their marriage.[12] Juana fell almost instantly in love with her husband but Philip never reciprocated: for him – even before Juana's mental collapse – this was a marriage of convenience, and nothing more.

It was now too late in the year for the fleet to return to Spain and so Margaret stayed in the Low Countries while the winter storms passed. She sailed at the turn of February–March 1497 but her fleet was hit by a violent storm in Biscay; terrified that she was about to die – and strapped to a mast – Margaret scribbled a few lines of poetry for her own tombstone:

> Here lies Margaret
> Unhappy woman!
> For she was twice married
> And died a virgin.[13]

Against all her fears, the fleet reached Santander, berthing on 6–8 March. Margaret arrived in Burgos on Palm Sunday (19 March) and since a marriage could not be celebrated during Holy Week, she and Juan had to content themselves with taking their vows in the great cathedral and waiting for the religious festivities to end before the marriage ceremony at the beginning of April. The young couple immediately entered into their marital relations with such ardour that stories soon began to circulate that Juan was wearing himself out in his endeavours.[14] Within weeks, Margaret was pregnant. The alliance between Spain and the House of Habsburg was now doubly secure – and doubly consummated. Four of the children of Ferdinand and Isabella were now married: it was time to arrange for the youngest child to join them in the married state.

England

Although Ferdinand and Isabella had agreed in 1489 to marry Katharine to Arthur, it was not until 1495–96 that they began to seriously commit themselves to bringing the marriage about. There were two reasons for their delay – the tender ages of the children; and the doubts that Ferdinand and Isabella had about the survival of Henry VII on his throne. Ferdinand was probably the most perceptive of contemporary political observers and it was during 1494–95 – while Italy was convulsed by the French invasion – that he recognised that Henry VII had effectively consolidated his authority and that he could probably be relied upon sufficiently to entrust a daughter to his care. In those years, Sir Edward Poynings stabilised the power of the English crown in Ireland (at least for the moment) and Henry demonstrated his ruthlessness and his self-confidence by sending no less a figure than Sir William Stanley to the block for treasonable intrigue against him (16 February 1495). Indeed, Henry was proving to be a king who was blessed by good fortune, for he even benefited from an incompetent invasion by Perkin Warbeck, who landed 300 men at Deal on 3 July 1495.[15] Warbeck himself wisely stayed on board ship while his supporters were slaughtered, and he fled to Ireland, joining Desmond in the Siege of Waterford. Poynings lifted the siege in August. Henry VII was now a king with whom Ferdinand of Aragon could do serious business.

There remained much to do, for the marriage negotiations had stagnated since 1489. In November 1494 Ferdinand named Jofre de Sasiola as ambassador to England but he evaded the appointment, ostensibly on grounds of ill-health.[16] On 25 February 1495 Sasiola was replaced by González de Puebla, who was sent back to England with a three-part brief – to persuade Henry to join the Holy League; to negotiate the details of the agreement for the marriage of Arthur with Katharine; and to resolve the difficulties in commercial relations between the two countries.[17] González de Puebla arrived in May. Henry greeted him coolly, noting the tardiness with which Spain had distanced herself from Warbeck and threatening that his council favoured a French alliance rather than a Spanish one.[18] González de Puebla insisted that Ferdinand genuinely intended to reach an agreement for the marriage by the spring of 1496 and conveyed Ferdinand's characteristically mischievous assurance to Henry that he should not trust Charles VIII 'because he keeps his promises so badly, even to friends'.[19]

On 30 January 1496 Ferdinand and Isabella issued their definitive instructions to González de Puebla to negotiate the marriage: it was the critical moment. Again they emphasised that Katharine's marriage was only to be arranged within a tripartite agreement that would be marital, military and commercial.[20] They understood full well that Henry did not want to go to war with France but insisted that since the Pope was under attack it was incumbent on 'all Christian princes' to help him. Moreover, it was in Henry's best interests to be part of the Europe-wide effort to put a break on French ambition, since England itself would be vulnerable if

France increased her power.[21] They also insisted that an accommodation had to include Philip of Burgundy and encouraged Henry to resolve the trading disputes with the Low Countries and thereby to cut off the support given to Warbeck ('the so-called Duke of York') by Burgundy.[22] Only after González de Puebla had offered all these arguments and inducements was he to negotiate the details of the dowry that Katharine would bring with her.[23]

Henry did not need any encouragement from Spain to resolve his dispute with Philip; the trade embargo was bitterly resented by his merchants and – a much more pertinent consideration for the king – was costing him revenue in taxes. Accordingly, he negotiated a wide-ranging agreement with Philip by the treaty of 24 February 1496 that became known in the Low Countries as the *Magnus Intercursus*. Philip granted preferential trading terms to English merchants but Henry doubtless attached even greater importance to the pledge that both governments made not to assist rebels against the other: the Low Countries were closed to Warbeck.

Warbeck had fled to Scotland, where on 20 November 1495 James IV provocatively received him as 'Prince Richard' and then married him to a distant relative, Lady Katherine Gordon. Ferdinand hoped that a reconciliation between England and Scotland would deprive France of Scottish assistance and Warbeck of Scottish support. There was already a Spanish agent in Scotland – Martin de Ferreira – and Ferdinand invited James to send ambassadors to Spain to negotiate for a marriage with a Spanish princess, quite neglecting to mention that since all their daughters were spoken for the daughter whom they might offer to Scotland would have to be one of Ferdinand's illegitimate offspring. They also sent Pedro de Ayala to Scotland in the summer of 1496 to undermine Warbeck's relationship with James IV by offering a Spanish bride.[24] In September James IV and Perkin Warbeck crossed into England at the head of a small army but they failed to raise the North and after three days – and having marched a puny 4 miles into English territory – they had to beat a humiliating retreat back into Scotland. James IV would be unable to do anything of substance for Warbeck: the Pretender's options were fast running out and James was being forced to recognise that he needed an alliance with England.

On 26 April 1496 Ferdinand and Isabella ordered González de Puebla to press ahead with the marriage. They insisted that the dowry be as small as possible and still hoped that Henry could be persuaded to join the League.[25] But since they wanted to smooth relations with James IV they ordered the ambassador not to publish the marriage of Katharine until negotiations with Scotland had been concluded.[26]

Henry abandoned his neutrality in the summer of 1496: on 18 July, he finally joined the 'Holy League'. He did so very much on his own terms; he resolutely refused to go to war with France but looked forward optimistically to being party to the settlement at the end of the conflict. Certainly, the first dividend was evident enough: the papal nuncio presented Henry with the papal cap and sword of maintenance – the symbols of his status as defender of the Church.[27]

It was a measure of the seriousness of Ferdinand and Isabella about the negotiations with England that Isabella herself now became deeply involved in the them. On 12 and 15 September 1496 she authorised González de Puebla to conclude the marriage negotiations; she urged Henry to invade France in order to distract Charles VIII but recognised that his anxieties about the vulnerability of his Scottish frontier might prevent him from doing so. She also made a point of insisting that Katharine should be allowed to bring no fewer than 150 people with her to England: her daughter would travel in the style befitting her dignity as a Princess of Castile.[28] A point of tension would develop with Henry VII here, who was anxious that Katharine should not have a large Spanish household and who considered that she should bring about twenty or thirty people with her.

The revised agreement for the marriage of Arthur and Katharine was signed in London on 1 October 1496 by Thomas Savage, now Bishop of London, and González de Puebla. The wedding vows would be taken verbally when Arthur reached his twelfth birthday in 1498 and the consummation would take place when he attained his majority in 1500; if, however, it was decided to celebrate the marriage before Arthur's fourteenth birthday the Pope would be asked to issue a dispensation for his being underage. The dowry was fixed at 200,000 escudos of four *chelines* and two *peniques* each: half of this was to be paid in cash within ten days of the celebration of the marriage and a further 50,000 escudos within one year thereafter and the final 50,000 within the second year. When Katharine became Queen of England her dowry would be increased in an appropriate manner.

On 1 January 1497 Ferdinand and Isabella ratified the agreement and Katharine signed her authorisation for González de Puebla to celebrate her betrothal (*esponsales*) to Arthur.[29] At about the same time, Henry VII sent a signed decree promising Ferdinand and Isabella that the first-born son of Katharine and Arthur would become the heir to the throne of England if Arthur predeceased him.[30]

The Betrothal of Katharine & Arthur, Woodstock, 15 August 1497

Within weeks, the marriage agreement between Spain and England that had been brought about with such difficulty was tested to the point of destruction by two dramatic (and contrasting) events: in February, Ferdinand agreed to a truce with France which effectively marked the end of the Holy League (Truce of Lyons, 25 February 1497)[31] and in the spring Henry VII was confronted with the gravest crisis of his reign when a revolt erupted in Cornwall against his fiscal demands and a force of 15,000 peasants crossed the Tamar and headed resolutely for London. Both monarchs were now faced with defining choices: could Henry trust Ferdinand, who had so consistently tried to persuade him to go to war with France and had now made peace with France without consulting him? Could Ferdinand continue to place serious reliance upon a monarch whose security on his throne could be threatened by a horde of peasants from the perimeter of his kingdom? Both kings – each of them cynical and cold in their calculations – decided that what held them together was of more enduring importance than the suspicions that threatened to drive them apart. The marriage agreement of 1 October 1496 held, just.

Ferdinand was no whit embarrassed by having made peace with France without informing Henry and he happily instructed González de Puebla to remind Henry of the enduring importance to him of the alliance with Spain.[32]

Henry VII dealt with the Cornish rebels with savage precision: on 17 June, his army slaughtered 2,000 of the peasant 'army' at Blackheath. At the end of the month the leaders who had survived were executed and Henry then punished thousands of others by imposing fines on them. Strengthened by his victory, Henry VII settled his relations with James IV. Perhaps it was to save face that James invaded England and began a siege of Norham Castle. Once again, it was no more than a token effort, lasting this time for ten days before James abandoned the siege and made a truce with the Earl of Surrey. In September this was formally extended to a truce of seven years (Treaty of Ayton).[33]

Warbeck was now in desperate straits. He landed at Cork in July 1497, and, hearing of the revolt in Cornwall (and unaware that it had already been crushed) headed there in September. His forces – once again, they could not be called an army – dissolved in the face of Henry's army.

Warbeck claimed sanctuary and then abjectly surrendered on promise of his life. The king marched westwards in triumph, and on 5 October Warbeck was brought before him at Taunton and publicly acknowledged that he was an imposter. Henry took him back on his triumphant return to London. His throne was now all but secure, and he disdainfully allowed Warbeck – like Simnel before him – to stay at court.

The crushing of the Cornish rebellion cleared the way for the formal betrothal by proxy of Katharine to Arthur; it took place on 15 August 1497 in the royal manor of Woodstock near Oxford. González de Puebla proudly stood proxy for Katharine; physically stunted, despised by so many for his appearance, poverty and Jewish blood, the ambassador stood proudly as the representative of his monarchs. Arthur made a favourable impression on observers: the Ambassador of Milan noted that he was 'taller than his years would warrant, of remarkable beauty and grace, and very ready in speaking Latin'. A recently rediscovered painting shows him about this time as a serious and self-assured young man; he is holding a 'gillyflower', the symbol of purity and betrothal or marriage.[34]

For the Catholic Church the act of betrothal was no mere formality. Since at least the twelfth century the Church had regarded the betrothal as being so binding on the parties who committed themselves to it that it had created the diriment impediment of 'public honesty' (*publicae honestatis*) to emphasise that their action took the form in canon law of a public act, assuring each other and the community of which they were part that they had undertaken the fullest and most solemn vow to commit themselves in marriage until death parted them. Of course, since Arthur and Katharine were children they would have to take the oaths of marriage for themselves when they reached adulthood. The oaths of 1497 were taken *per verba de futuro*; that is to say, they were a promise for the future. But in that future Arthur and Katharine would have to take the oaths *per verba de praesenti*, committing themselves *in the present tense* to their marriage; they could do this either in person or through deputies. Once that had been done, a true marriage would exist. Fr Thomas Doyle O. P. has summarised the enduring significance of a ruling by Pope Alexander III (1159–81) on the nature of the promise to marry:

> Once consent had been freely exchanged by the parties who were baptised, a true sacramental marriage existed. The attribute of absolute indissolubility was added when the marriage was consummated by sexual intercourse. This understanding of when

marriage came into being has remained the teaching of the Church to the present day.[35]

Two consequences followed: the agreement created an affinity in canon law between the two families involved and the individuals concerned were not free to commit themselves to marry anyone else unless the betrothal was formally brought to an end either by mutual agreement or by a decision of the Church. In fine, in the eyes of the Church the act of betrothal formed a mutually binding commitment. If one of the partners subsequently even cavorted with a member of the opposite sex the action was regarded as having caused grave scandal in two respects – in offending against the sanctity of marriage itself (even though the vows of marriage had not yet been taken) and in disavowing and dishonouring the partner to whom he or she had so publicly committed. In consequence, the act of betrothal came to have significance that was almost comparable in canon law with the vows that were taken in Church on the day of the formal wedding. But after all the vows were taken – be they *per verba de futuro* or *per verba de praesenti* – the marriage still had to be consummated to be full and complete: until it was so there still existed the possibility that it could be dissolved – a course of action that could be recommended by a bishop but only authorised by the Pope himself.

5

1497–1501: THE RENEGOTIATION OF A MARRIAGE – AND THE CONDITION OF PRINCE ARTHUR

'Three Daggers of Pain': The End of the Male Line of the Trástamara Dynasty, 1497–1500

The honeymoon of Prince Juan of Castile and Margaret of Austria lasted barely a month before, on 13 June 1497, Juan developed a fever. It was said that Juan's tutors had warned his parents that he was expending his energies in his sexual activities but that Isabella rejected their advice that she urge restraint on the prince, insisting on the Biblical injunction that those who had been joined together by God could only be separated by Him.[1] Juan's condition deteriorated in the autumn and on 1 October news reached Ferdinand and Isabella (who were celebrating the wedding of Isabella and Manuel in Seville) that their beloved son was dying. The prince was in Salamanca: Ferdinand rode furiously and arrived in time to comfort him when he died on the night of 3–4 October. Isabella was shattered by Juan's death but absorbed the news with her customary fortitude and faith, proclaiming that 'God gave him to me. He has taken him from me. Blessed be His will.' But in Isabella's desolation, there was still hope for the dynasty, for Juan had left his wife with child. Tragically, Margaret miscarried of a boy in November.

The double loss meant that the succession to the throne of Castile passed once again to Queen Isabella of Portugal, the first-born child of Ferdinand and Isabella; she was summoned from Portugal and sworn in as heiress at the Cortes of Toledo (29 April–14 May 1498): her husband, Manuel I, took the oath as her prince-consort.[2]

Ferdinand was unable to persuade the Cortes of Aragon to accept his daughter as heiress to the Crown of Aragon. On 14 June 1498, the Cortes insisted that only princesses who had been born within the kingdom were entitled to rule it in their own right, and this of course excluded Isabella, who had been born in Castile. But once again there remained hope that the Union of the Crowns of Castile and Aragon could be preserved and indeed that Portugal could be added to them: Isabella of Portugal was pregnant and if she gave birth to a boy the child would inherit the Crowns of Castile and Aragon and Portugal. The golden prizes that lay at the heart of the domestic ambitions of Ferdinand and Isabella – that the Union of their Crowns would endure in the male line and that Portugal could be subsumed into the family inheritance – still lay within their reach. Isabella was hurriedly taken to Zaragoza and there, on 23 August 1498, she duly gave birth to a boy, who was named Miguel. Yet again tragedy devoured the hopes of the Catholic Kings, for the delivery cost Isabella her life: she was twenty-eight years old.

Queen Isabella was devastated by the loss of her two eldest children within ten months and she collapsed into a decline from which she was never to recover. The indomitable queen who had controlled national life, who had overcome every obstacle confronting her by the force of her willpower, was no more. But still tragedy had not run its course, for on 20 July 1500, Miguel died: he was one month short of his second birthday.

With Miguel's death, the projected union of the Crowns of Iberia crashed down with apparently dreadful finality: each of the three crowns would now devolve upon a separate heritor. The contemporary historian Andrés Bernáldez wrote eloquently of the 'three daggers' that had pierced the heart of the great queen between 1497 and 1500:

> The first dagger of pain that struck the soul of Queen Isabella was the death of Prince Juan. The second was the death of Doña Isabella, Queen of Portugal, her eldest child. The third dagger of pain was the death of Don Miguel, her grandson, with whom she was already consoling herself. And from that time the queen lived without happiness … and this damaged her health and cut her life short.[3]

Worse: the death of Juan meant that the Crown of Castile would pass to Juana, whose mental health was a source of deepening anxiety to her parents. Ferdinand and Isabella had no doubt that Philip of Burgundy intended to govern Castile in his wife's name: would the Crown of Castile be exercised in effect by a king-consort who was not only a foreigner but who owed his loyalty to France? Would Philip not only succeed in practice to the kingship of Castile but in time inherit the Holy Roman Empire after his father's death and then subsume Castile into a new Burgundian–Habsburg monolith in which its principles and values would count for little or nothing? Ferdinand and Isabella had not only lost two of their beloved children: they were now, it appeared, certain to lose everything for which they had striven with such unremitting willpower and brilliance. And still more dreadful news arrived for them: reports from Brussels suggested that, under the stress of her mental collapse, Juana was wavering in the practices of her religious faith. As Isabella crumbled it fell to Ferdinand to salvage whatever he could from the wreckage.

Chief among Ferdinand's problems was the breakdown in his relationship with Philip of Burgundy. It was evident that Philip was sufficiently confident that Juana would secure the succession to the throne of Castile to believe that he no longer had real need of Ferdinand and Isabella: in August 1498 he pledged his fealty to Louis XII in return for the counties of Flanders and Artois (Peace of Paris, 2 August 1498) and formally swore allegiance as the vassal of the King of France (15 August). Philip's actions made the English alliance even more important for Ferdinand: that Katharine should marry Prince Arthur now became an essential priority for him.

Hope: The Confirmation of the English Marriage

In the last weeks of 1497 González de Puebla found that his task was gravely undermined by the unexpected return to London of the ubiquitous Don Pedro de Ayala. When Perkin Warbeck fled from Scotland, Ayala decided – apparently on his own initiative – that his work in the kingdom was completed and travelled to London where he set himself up as 'Spanish ambassador to Scotland in London on business'.[4] Arrogant and abrasive, Ayala despised the low-born González de Puebla and set out to make his life a misery. He was the more able to do so because Henry VII happily played the two men off against each other.

It was therefore with good reason that Ferdinand became anxious about the turn of events in both London and Brussels, and in the spring of 1498 he named two emissaries to travel north to investigate how his affairs were being conducted in the two cities and to reassure Henry VII of the commitment of his wife and himself to the marriage. The men he chose were a decidedly odd couple: Sancho de Londoño was a Knight Commander of the Order of Santiago while Tomás de Matienzo was a Dominican friar who was close to Inquisitor-General Torquemada. The knight and the friar-inquisitor were instructed to travel to London to convince Henry VII to proceed with the marriage and to resolve the tensions between González de Puebla and Ayala; then they were to cross to the Low Countries to report on the condition of Juana and to make it unambiguously clear to Philip that he had no claim on the Castilian throne.[5]

The two men arrived in London on 2 July 1498. Henry was sufficiently apprehensive about the purposes behind their visit to rush back from a hunting trip to meet them. Aggressively, he complained that he had not received any letters from Ferdinand and Isabella for one year and eleven days. His mood was transformed when he understood that the emissaries had come not to re-negotiate the marriage but to confirm it.[6] Londoño and Matienzo made a point of humiliating González de Puebla by refusing to allow him to join them for their first discussions with the king. Henry would have none of it, making it clear that he expected to conduct negotiations through González de Puebla: pointedly, he gave the ambassador four hours of his time and allowed his own wife and mother to attend at least part of the discussions.[7]

González de Puebla duly informed Ferdinand and Isabella how gratified he had been to hear Henry, his queen and his Queen Mother speak so admiringly of them and of Katharine.[8] When he handed Queen Elizabeth two letters from Ferdinand and Isabella and two from Katharine, Henry joyously insisted that he should be given one of the letters from the princess so that he could carry it around with him. Coquettishly, his wife refused: she had already sent one to Prince Arthur and resolutely refused to give up the second one. The delightful little charade seemed to gratify the three royal actors and the Spanish ambassador in equal measure.

As further proof of English goodwill, González de Puebla reported a few days later that the Queen Mother and Queen Elizabeth had suggested that Katharine should practise speaking French with Margaret so that she should be able to converse in the language when she arrived in England: evidently they had little optimism that Katharine would master English. Curiously, they also urged that Katharine should start drinking wine because the water in England was not safe. Henry responded by insisting to González de Puebla that he report to Ferdinand and Isabella just how delighted he was with the progress in negotiations. The marriage had been saved.[9]

This was more than could be said for the reputation of González de Puebla, which was eviscerated by the report sent back by Londoño and Matienzo. They informed Ferdinand and Isabella that the ambassador was despised by the English for his low rank – (*sc.* his Jewishness?) – and that he lived indecorously in a house of ill repute. Moreover, his diplomatic activities had consistently been more favourable to Henry VII than to his own monarchs and he had exploited his position to secure bribes from courtiers and merchants. By contrast, the emissaries praised Ayala as a nobleman of rank who had spent his own money to maintain himself even though they admitted that he was a very aggressive personality.[10] Londoño and Matienzo left London on 15 July and arrived in Brussels a fortnight later. The only good news that they could then send to Ferdinand was Matienzo's assurance that there were no grounds for concern about Juana's religious orthodoxy but that her mental fragility was being undermined by tensions within her marriage.[11] Philip's hostility to Juana was probably not lessened when on 16 November she presented him with another daughter; the child was named Leonor.

European politics were transformed by the death of Charles VIII on 7 April: the warrior king struck his head on a doorframe in his château at Amboise after a game of tennis. Since his only child – a son – had predeceased him his direct line came to an end and he was succeeded by his cousin Louis, Duke of Orleans, who became Louis XII. It is not clear how old the new king was since apparently his birth had been regarded as of such little consequence that no record had been made of it: informed opinion was that he was about thirty-eight. What was not in doubt was that Louis XII was an experienced politician: he had rebelled against Charles VIII (in 'The Foolish War',) and lived to tell the tale. Guicciardini (who had despised Charles VIII) thought highly of him – 'mature in years, experienced in many wars, moderate in spending, and incomparably more self-reliant than his predecessor had been'.[12] On succeeding to the throne Louis proclaimed that he was not only 'King of France' but also the legitimate heir to the Duchy of Milan. He summoned the Spanish ambassador to inform him that he intended to reclaim the duchy by conquest.

When Ferdinand learned this he responded in his own inimitable way – by making an agreement with Louis XII (as he had done with Charles

VIII in 1493) in which he agreed not to oppose the French invasion in return for a settlement of all outstanding differences between France and Spain (Treaty of Marcoussis, 5 August 1498). It was of course nothing more than a holding operation: Ferdinand had not the slightest intention of allowing Louis to conquer Milan.[13]

As in 1493, Ferdinand looked to build bridges with England to oppose the power of France. Henry understood full well how much Ferdinand needed his alliance and recognised that the power of France was so great that the rest of Christendom could scarcely resist it and he would not commit an army to assist Spain in a war with France. Moreover, he demonstrated how secure he was on his throne by having González de Puebla attend an interview with Perkin Warbeck in which the erstwhile 'Duke of York' accepted that he was an imposter and that Margaret of York had always known he was not the son of Edward IV. What Henry would do was to proceed with the marriage of Arthur and Katharine, and he urged Ferdinand and Isabella to send the princess to England as soon as possible. He added that Queen Elizabeth had been overjoyed to receive their letter and would write back to them and that he hoped that Arthur would follow suit.[14] Spain and England would have a marital alliance if not a military one.

The First Wedding By Proxy of Katharine & Arthur: Tickenhill Manor, Bewdley, 19 May 1499
Arthur seems to have spent the second half of the 1490s living in Ludlow and Tickenhill. Ludlow Castle was a fine example of a Norman castle and although it was no longer a major military centre its position on the border between England and Wales made it a natural focal point from which the English government could supervise affairs in Wales. Henry provided his son with a Council in the Marches comprised of senior men whom he trusted to guide him; chief among them were Jasper Tudor, Henry's uncle; Bishop William Smyth of Lincoln, who served as President of the Council; and Sir Richard Pole, who was Chamberlain to the Prince. The other councillors included a number of men who had served Henry VII in his exile in Brittany. Arthur's education was entrusted to a number of distinguished scholars. Initially, Dr John Argentine, who had spent some years in Italy, and then John Rede and Bernard André became his tutors. André (who was blind) was an Augustinian friar from Toulouse who taught Arthur a range of classical authors. The prince studied French under Giles Dewes and

Latin and was probably taught Greek by Thomas Linacre, one of the most eminent scholars of the age.[15]

On Whit Sunday, 19 May 1499, the wedding by proxy (*per verba de praesenti*) of Arthur and Katharine was celebrated at Tickenhill Manor, near Bewdley, 22 miles from Ludlow.[16] William Smyth, Bishop of Lincoln, and John Arundel, Bishop of Coventry and Lichfield, led the English party into the chapel. The latter then proclaimed to the prince that King Henry wished his marriage to Katharine to be contracted *per verba de praesenti* so that it should be indissoluble. Arthur replied that he rejoiced to contract the marriage in obedience to the Pope and to his father but also because he had a deep and sincere love for the princess. González de Puebla then affirmed that he was authorised to conclude an indissoluble marriage in Katharine's name and handed over his powers of authorisation to the bishop; they were read 'in a loud voice' by Dr Richard Nic. The prince and the ambassador joined their right hands together and Richard Peel, Lord Chamberlain of the prince, held both of their left hands. Arthur declared that he accepted Dr González de Puebla's right to act as proxy for Katharine. The ambassador then swore on behalf of the princess that she took Arthur as her lawful husband. Arthur and Katharine were now man and wife in the eyes of the Church – and of the monarchs of England and Spain. In October, Arthur wrote from Ludlow Castle to his new wife of his earnest desire to meet her and of the grief that he felt at the delay in her arrival, describing her as 'my most entirely beloved spouse'.[17]

González de Puebla's triumph was short-lived, for Ferdinand and Isabella evidently decided that they required another ambassador to negotiate the treaty of alliance that followed on the betrothal. They despatched Juan Manuel from Brussels as extraordinary ambassador and agreement was reached on 10 July which drew together the agreements that England and Spain had made with each other since the Treaty of Medina del Campo in 1489 and committed both powers to supporting each other against France.[18] Ferdinand had not been able to persuade Henry to join him in war but the two kings had agreed that if one of them was attacked the other would come to his defence. In the circumstances it was a treaty of nominal importance rather than of any military substance. And both crowns had fudged the vexed question of what would happen to the jewels and other valuable possessions that Katharine would bring with her: most especially, were they to be her property or Henry VII's?

The Unholy Alliance: Louis XII & Alexander VI & the Second French Invasion of Italy

Like Charles VIII in 1494, Louis made meticulous preparations for his invasion of Italy. Happily, he could count on the generous support of the Pope. Alexander VI had been the great loser by the Truce of Lyons of 1497 and was so infuriated that France and Spain had brought his 'Holy League' to a precipitate end by making peace without him that he punished them both by investing the Crown of Naples in Frederick, son of Ferdinand I of Naples (11 June 1497). He thereby deprived both Ferdinand of Aragon and Louis of France of the hope of succeeding to Naples in the immediate future.[19]

Only three days later, the Pope's rage turned to grief, for on the night of 14–15 June 1497, his beloved son Giovanni, 2nd Duke of Gandia, was stabbed to death by unknown assassins and his body was flung into the Tiber. Inconsolable, Alexander announced that he would abdicate.[20] Immediately, rumours circulated that it was Giovanni's brother, Cesare, who had organised the murder – and perhaps, indeed, even committed it himself. Brilliant and violent, devoid of moral principles and settled only on his own advancement, Cesare was the model of the Renaissance prince: Machiavelli paid him the supreme tribute of recognising him as the outstanding example of such princes.[21] Alexander probably did not suspect him of involvement in Giovanni's death and now decided that he would facilitate Cesare's rise to power to replace Giovanni as the de facto head of the Borgia family in the secular world.

There was a difficulty: Cesare Borgia was a cardinal. As a younger son, he had followed an ecclesiastical career while Giovanni (who was two years older, born in 1474) had carried the secular ambitions of the family. When Alexander was elected to the papacy he had blithely named Cesare to succeed him as Archbishop of Valencia, notwithstanding that he was not even a priest. He had then raised him to the cardinalate, at the age of eighteen (20 September 1493). But Giovanni's death meant that the secular leadership of the family had to devolve upon Cesare. Of course, Alexander had no need of support from anyone in securing Cesare's laicisation and duly brought this about by himself. However, he needed the compliance of the King of France to raise Cesare's status in the European political world by granting him a ducal title (and a favourable marriage). Even for this most corrupt and manipulative of popes, the quid pro quo was outrageous: so that Louis XII should name Cesare to the Dukedom of Valentinois, Alexander VI agreed to dissolve the king's marriage to Jeanne de Valois.

Louis had been obliged to marry Jeanne as a young man at the insistence of Charles VIII and found her repulsive; she was a cripple and could not have children. In her saintly way – Jeanne was canonised by the Catholic Church in 1950 – the queen gave as good as she received, claiming that the king had been incapable of sexual intercourse.

On 18 August 1497 Cesare Borgia became the first cardinal in the history of the Catholic Church to renounce the dignity, and on that singular day was presented with the title to his dukedom by the French ambassador in Rome. Within a further month, Alexander issued two bulls which ended Louis XII's marriage to Jeanne and freed him to marry Anne, Duchess of Brittany, by absolving him from the diriment impediment of affinity: Anne had, of course, been married to Charles VIII. Louis's new marriage led directly to the absorption of the Duchy of Brittany into the patrimony of the French royal house (although the arrangement was not formalised for another thirty years). And still, Pope Alexander's ecclesiastical horse-trading had not finished: on 17 September 1498, George d'Amboise, Bishop of Rouen and chief minister of Louis XII, was raised to the cardinalate in recognition of his services.

On 1 October 1498, the new Duke of Valentinois left Rome to carry the marital dispensations to Louis XII and the red hat to the Bishop of Rouen. In gratitude, Louis presented Cesare with the hand of his niece Charlotte d'Albret, the sister of the King of Navarre: the Borgias had joined the ranks of royalty – and the authority and reputation of the sovereign pontiff had reached its nadir.[22] The lesson for the other crowned heads of Europe was as simple as it was stark: papal favour, and more especially, papal dispensations from the sacred vows of marriage, could be bought from this Pope:

A Papal Dispensation: The Politics of Pope Alexander VI, 1499

14 January 1497	murder of Giovanni de Borgia, II Duke of Gandia
18 August 1497	Cesare Borgia renounces cardinalate and is named Duke of Valentinois
September 1497	Alexander VI annuls marriage of Louis XII and Jeanne de France
17 September 1498	George d'Amboise raised to cardinalate
1 October 1498	Cesare Borgia leaves Rome with papal dispensation
8 January 1499	marriage of Louis XII and Anne of Brittany
10 May 1499	Cesare Borgia marries Charlotte d'Albret
8 October 1499	Cesare Borgia enters Milan with Louis XII

Alexander's conduct disgusted the Catholic Kings of Spain. They invited the kings of England, Portugal and France to join them in having their ambassadors in Rome protest against Alexander's behaviour and demand a reform of the Church: only Manuel I supported them. When the complaints of Spain's resident ambassadors were contemptuously dismissed by Alexander (27 November 1498), Ferdinand and Isabella sent two extraordinary ambassadors to demand of the Pope that he reform his conduct: Alexander listened to them with undisguised fury and when they made explicit reference to his simony and to the punishment that God had inflicted upon him with the murder of his eldest son the pontiff responded with brutal directness – 'God had punished your kings more since they do not have any (male) descent'.[23] The Spanish Pope had all but broken with the Catholic Kings of Spain.

In preparing his invasion of Italy Louis XII studiously followed the formula established by Charles VIII in 1494; he reached agreements with the papacy, Empire, Spain, Portugal, England and Burgundy to give him a free hand. Once again, leading Italian powers were complicit: driven by its hatred of Lodovico Sforza, Venice provided soldiers in return for the town of Cremona (Treaty of Blois, April 1499) while Florence welcomed the invasion in the hope that it would facilitate the recovery of Pisa. When the French army approached Milan Sforza fled and the duchy resisted for only twenty days: Louis XII entered the city on 8 October 1499. But Louis then miscalculated badly by returning promptly to France: Milan rebelled against French rule and Sforza was restored. In April 1500 Louis sent another large army into Italy and extracted revenge: Sforza was taken prisoner and carried off to France (where he was kept a prisoner until he died in 1508).

As always, Ferdinand held his nerve: calculating that a King of France would once again overreach himself in Italy he cynically negotiated with Louis XII to divide the Kingdom of Naples between them on the grounds that Frederick V had forfeited his right to the kingdom by negotiating to bring the Turk into Italy.[24] Agreement was reached by the Treaty of Chambord-Granada (October–November 1500): Louis XII would enjoy the title of King of Naples and control the capital city while Ferdinand (who was already King of Sicily) would assume the title of Duke of Calabria and Apulia. When Louis pressed on to Naples, Frederick tamely submitted to him as his vassal and he too was sent off to France to live out his days as a French pensionary. Louis now secured from Maximilian his investiture as Duke of Milan. France had won Milan: would she now gain Naples?

The Birth of Charles of Habsburg, 25 February 1500 & the Succession to the Throne of Castile

Juana, Archduchess of Burgundy and heiress to the Crown of Castile, was delivered of her first son (and third child) on 24 February 1500. The birth of an heir to the Duke of Burgundy was in itself a significant but fairly unremarkable event; the child would inherit the remnants of the Duchy of Burgundy and might even one day succeed to the imperial title. However, Juana's mental incapacity meant that the infant would succeed – probably very soon – to the throne of Castile. So it proved: by an extraordinary succession of deaths and genetic accidents, Charles became one of the most important and influential figures in European history and a figure of global importance.

Charles was baptised on 6 March under the painting by the Van Eyck brothers of *la adoración del cordero místico*. As with his grandfather Maximilian, the blood of Europe coursed through his veins: he had German, Portuguese, Castilian, Burgundian, French and Italian blood. But above all else he was a Burgundian. Within weeks of his birth he was invested with membership of the Order of the Golden Fleece: it would be the most cherished, and the most defining, of the sixty or so titles that he would hold and it adorns every portrait and statue of him. As he grew up, Charles revelled in the elaborate ceremonies of the royal household and in time he named his first-born legitimate son for his own father, Philip. Charles has been called 'the father of Europe' and has even been appropriated as an honorary Spaniard by some Spanish historians but to understand him we must always – *always!* – remember that he regarded himself first and foremost as a Burgundian and then as a Habsburg. His other titles were of distinctly subsidiary importance to him. The news of Prince Miguel's death reached Brussels on the night of 10–11 August 1500: Juana and Philip were now princes of the Asturias and it was imperative that they leave at once for Castile so that Juana could be recognised as heiress and receive the oaths of loyalty from the Castilian estates.

Because of Juana's incapacity Margaret of Austria assumed the role of foster mother to the prince and his two sisters.[25] She brought them up at her celebrated court in Malines. They spoke French as their first language and their lives were regulated by Burgundian etiquette and guided by Burgundian ministers and courtiers. Naturally, Margaret gave the central roles in Charles's education to two Burgundians – Guillaume de Croy, Lord of Chièvres, who became his Grand Chamberlain in 1509, and

Adrian Florenszoon ('Adrian of Utrecht') who was named as his chief tutor in 1511. Both men left enduring marks upon the young prince. Chièvres raised the prince as a Burgundian nobleman, imbued with the values of chivalry that were embodied by the Knights of the Order of the Golden Fleece and committed to the theory and practice of war. Chièvres insisted that in his early years – at the very least until he had secured his various inheritances, and most especially the throne of Castile – Charles had at all costs to remain at peace with France. Adrian was a cleric of humble origins who had begun his career as a parish priest and risen to academic excellence as a Doctor of Divinity, Professor of Theology and Vice-Chancellor of Louvain University. Deeply influenced by the teaching of the Brethren of the Common Life, Adrian had a profound influence upon Charles's piety. By extraordinary coincidence, Adrian would become Pope in 1521, in an election that Charles took as proof of his own providential mission.

Marriage proposals came rapidly for the future Duke of Burgundy. In the summer of 1501 – when he was not yet eighteen months old – he was engaged to Claudia, daughter of Louis XII: it was a first success for Chièvres's pro-French policy. The anxieties that Ferdinand and Isabella felt about Philip of Burgundy's movement towards a French alliance were confirmed by the news, for it raised the horrendous possibility that at some time in the future the throne of Castile might be united with that of France. Nevertheless, they felt obliged to acknowledge that they would not oppose the marriage of Charles and Claudia as long as Juana and Philip travelled to Spain to secure the throne of Castile by receiving the fealty of their subjects. But neither was ready to make the journey: Juana was pregnant while Philip loudly proclaimed that he would rather go to hell than travel to Spain.[26] The lesser obstacle was cleared when on 15 July Juana gave birth to a daughter; she was named Isabella.

The Portuguese Marriage: Manuel I & María

Ferdinand and Isabella saved the alliance with Portugal by persuading Manuel I to marry María, the sister of his dead wife Isabella; María was now eighteen years of age. The agreements were signed on 20 May 1500. Because Manuel and María were cousins, and – more especially – because he had been married with her sister and had a child by her, a papal dispensation was necessary. The price exacted by Alexander VI for granting the dispensation was that his great-nephew Pedro Luis de Borja should become Archbishop of Valencia; on 29 July he was appointed to the archbishopric. He was the sixth Borja to have ruled the archdiocese in succession.[27] The Catholic Kings may have been repelled by the conduct of Alexander VI: but they continued to trade favours with him.

María crossed into Portugal on 20 October 1500. Her husband was waiting for her; they took their vows and immediately consummated the marriage. Maria was the most fortunate of the children of the Catholic Kings.[28] She proved also to be the most fertile of them: between 1500 and 1516 she gave birth to ten children. The eldest, born on 6 June 1502, was to become King Juan III of Portugal and a year later, on 24 October 1503, María was delivered of Isabella, who married Charles V and became the mother of Philip II. It would be under Philip II that the dream of Ferdinand and Isabella of uniting their crowns with that of Portugal would finally be realised (1580).

A Young – and Fragile – Prince

The wedding by proxy of Arthur and Katharine at Bewdley in May 1499 and the treaty with Spain in July left one loose end for Henry to cut before Ferdinand and Isabella could allow their daughter to leave Spain, and in the autumn he duly did so. In August, in the dank confines of the Tower of London, the Earl of Warwick and Perkin Warbeck conspired to overthrow Henry. The king knew well enough what they were planning and in November they were executed – Warbeck on the gallows and Warwick on the block. At the beginning of January 1500, González de Puebla reported to Ferdinand and Isabella that England had never been as peaceful as it now was and that there did not remain 'a drop of doubtful royal blood' in the realm.[29]

By the summer, González de Puebla was optimistic that 'the glorious marriage' of Arthur and Katharine would shortly take place. Henry had received Katharine's ratification of her marriage and the ambassador reported that the whole of England was excited at her imminent arrival. He assured Ferdinand and Isabella that the king was preparing 'festivities such as had never before been seen in England'. Henry wanted detailed information about who would be accompanying Katharine and requested (without attempting to put a diplomatic gloss on it) that the ladies who travelled with her should be beautiful as well as of noble birth – or 'at least that none of them should be ugly'. Certainly, Henry was anxious to restrict the number of courtiers and servants who would come to England but made it clear that he would welcome as many persons of high rank as Ferdinand and Isabella should send with her as long as they returned to Spain after the wedding.[30]

Ferdinand, by contrast, was deeply anxious about the terms agreed by González de Puebla and decided for the second time in two years that he needed to send another ambassador to discuss with Henry VII all the details of the agreements made and establish what remained to be negotiated. He had sent Gutierre Gómez de Fuensalida to Brussels as ambassador to the Archduke Philip and he now despatched him on a temporary mission to London. Gómez de Fuensalida proved to be by far the most capable ambassador of the Catholic Kings in London, although on this first visit he remained in England only for two months; in 1508 he returned briefly as ambassador in his own right.[31] His instructions ordered him 'to inform himself of everything that is going on there'; he did so with brilliance and relish.[32]

Ferdinand had reason enough to be anxious about González de Puebla's competence; on 6 June he had written to him fiercely criticising him for not having improved upon the terms originally negotiated at Medina del Campo in 1489. Ferdinand therefore itemised all the changes and modifications that he required, remorselessly reworking every detail so that he should have to pay less (or later) than had been agreed.

In the midst of Ferdinand's anger with González de Puebla it emerged that he and Isabella were for the first time picking up doubts as to whether Prince Arthur would be capable of consummating the marriage with Katharine. The prince – it must be remembered – would not even reach his fourteenth birthday until 22 September 1500. Although he may have been tall for his age he was certainly not healthy and it was entirely reasonable that doubts should have arisen as to his capacity to consummate the marriage. Nothing is known of the state of his sexual development: had he even reached puberty in 1500?

In his letter of 6 June 1500 to González de Puebla, Ferdinand contented himself with expressing this most delicate of matters in financial terms: was the dowry to be paid after the marriage – or after it was consummated? He insisted that the provision which stated that the first instalment of Katharine's portion was to be paid 'ten days after the solemnisation' of the marriage should be changed to 'ten days after the consummation of the marriage' since *he now understood that some time might intervene between the solemnisation of the marriage and its consummation*. At all events, one-half of the first instalment was to be paid only after the consummation.[33] A marker had been laid down: a thunderously important question had been discreetly posed.

It is evident that speculation about the condition of the prince was circulating in political society in both England and Spain, for before González de Puebla received Ferdinand's letter, on 27 June he informed his sovereigns that Henry VII had determined that Arthur and Katharine should live at court during the first year of their marriage.[34] Might this imply that they would not necessarily live together as man and wife? It most certainly implied that they would be beginning their married life under the watchful eyes of their father and mother-in-law.

Gómez de Fuensalida was not helped in establishing what was going on in England by González de Puebla.[35] Indeed he complained to Ferdinand and Isabella that no matter how many times he asked the resident ambassador for information it was never forthcoming. He had therefore to find things out for himself. He began inauspiciously; when on Sunday 5 July he was received by Henry VII and his council he asked the craven question of when Arthur would reach his fifteenth birthday. This of course was the key date in all calculations to be made about the wedding of Arthur and Katharine and it is difficult to believe that Gómez de Fuensalida's ignorance was feigned. Henry patiently affirmed that the birthday would be on 22 September (give or take a day). Gómez de Fuensalida then asked whether, as soon as that date had passed, Henry would be prepared to despatch ambassadors to Spain with Arthur's authority as an adult to celebrate the marriage *per verba de praesenti*. Henry refused, no doubt believing that the ambassador was attempting to push back the date for Katharine's departure for England: if his own ambassadors could not leave England until after 22 September they would not reach the Spanish court (wherever that might be at that time) before mid-October and it would then be too dangerous for Katharine to travel by sea to England. Henry insisted that Katharine should be in England when Arthur celebrated his birthday, adding that this would ensure that she could cross Biscay in relative safety.[36]

A couple of days or so later, Gómez de Fuensalida was received by a number of bishops who were members of the King's Council. Led by the Archbishop of Canterbury, they were scathing about the changes that he had requested, noting that the ink was 'barely dry' on the letters from Ferdinand and Isabella assuring Henry that Katharine would travel at the end of summer 1500 and that the words of González de Puebla confirming this to them were still 'ringing in their ears'. Wanfully, Gómez de Fuensalida insisted that there had been misunderstandings in translation. The bishops were unimpressed, insisting that a delay would be gravely damaging to Henry VII's standing abroad, especially because he had invited guests from the leading courts of Europe to the wedding: there would be 'great infamy everywhere' for the King of England's reputation if the princess's arrival was deferred.[37]

Henry VII summoned Gómez de Fuensalida on Sunday 12 July and together they spent hours poring over every detail of the agreements covering the marriage: it was an education for the ambassador and since he returned to Brussels immediately after the interview it was not until 25 July that he wrote his report to Ferdinand and Isabella. His long letter was electrifying. Certainly, there had been much for him to digest and his report was as detailed as it was comprehensive – and it shattered whatever was left of the reputation of González de Puebla with his sovereigns. It also provided the most extraordinary – and tantalising – report of Henry's fears about the physical condition of Prince Arthur.

Henry's opening gambit astounded the ambassador by effectively rewriting all the arrangements for the marriage. He welcomed Gómez de Fuensalida by itemising all the reasons why he should not allow Katharine's departure to be delayed. He then informed him that because of the great love that he had for Ferdinand and Isabella and the acute fears that he held about having the princess sail in the winter he was prepared to do precisely that: he assured Gómez de Fuensalida that it was acceptable to him that Katharine should delay her departure for England until the spring of 1501. Henry emphasised that the decision was his and that his council was set against his course of action – and reiterated that he was able to agree to it because the marriage of Arthur and Katharine was already an accomplished fact and was indissoluble in the eyes of the Church. Henry informed Gómez de Fuensalida that he would send an amended agreement for Ferdinand and Isabella to sign agreeing to the delay. But it was evident that he was playing for time: why should he have done this? It will be suggested that the answer is as simple as it is historically important: Henry VII was anxious about the physical well-being of his eldest son and wanted to hold him close to him so that he could protect him in his vulnerability. This most calculating of men was acting as a father rather than as a king.

Gómez de Fuensalida had started his investigations by asking González de Puebla for information about Prince Arthur's rentable income but was unsuccessful:

I have never been able to learn anything about affairs here from the doctor although many times I have asked him that he should inform me of them. In particular, I asked him to let me know what rents the Prince of Wales had because it seemed to me in the agreements of marriage that the princess would have each year for her own sustenance and maintenance the third-part of the Prince's rents, and he never replied to me...

Gómez de Fuensalida's researches had led him to understand that the prince's income did not exceed £27,000–28,000 of rent per annum, a derisory amount that was no greater than that enjoyed by many 'Welsh barons'. The importance of his discovery was simple enough: Katharine would therefore enjoy only £6,000–7,000 of rent annually. The ambassador's powers of arithmetical division were faulty but there was nothing wrong with his political and diplomatic calculation and he now put an alarming – and alarmingly prescient – question to Ferdinand and Isabella: 'I write this to Your Majesties so that you should understand and see what could be left for the princess to live off if God should make any disposition of the prince and she was left without children (which God forbid).'

The phrase 'if God should make any disposition of the prince' was tautologous but simply understood: it meant 'if Arthur died'. Gómez de Fuensalida did not presume to answer his own question but he was clearly letting Ferdinand and Isabella know that there were concerns about Arthur's health. Having prepared the ground, he now made an astonishing declaration:

I have understood from a reliable source that the king has decided that the prince will know his wife sexually on the day of the wedding and then separate himself from her for two or three years because it is said that in some way the prince is frail, and the king told me that he wanted to have them [Arthur and Katharine] with him for the first three years [of their marriage] so that the prince should mature in strength.

I have also learned from a reliable source that they will do with the princess what is done with the archduke [Philip], which is that the prince will fulfil everything that is necessary and will not [subsequently] have a separate household [from Katharine]...[38]

No one made any reference to the tragic death of Katharine's elder brother, Juan, who had died as recently as 1497 from what was believed to be surfeit of sexual activity at an early age (eighteen): probably no one needed to. What was now incontrovertibly evident – in both England and Spain – was that the King of England was worried about the physical well-being of his son and heir.

Henry VII and the ambassador also discussed the jewels and valuables that Katharine would bring with her. Again, Gómez de Fuensalida was appalled by what the king revealed to him. He prefaced his account by relating that González de Puebla was deeply hostile to his even discussing the matter with Henry VII. González de Puebla claimed that that Ferdinand and Isabella had promised to give a dowry of 200,000 escudos with their daughter's hand and that this amount was to be paid in cash. Up to 35,000 escudos were to be given in plate, jewels, pearls and precious stones and it had been agreed that when Katharine arrived in England these possessions were not to be taken from her but were to be valued and a receipt obtained stating what they were worth. When their value had been assessed (and agreed) they were to be included in the final payment of the 200,000 escudos of the dowry and were to be given to the king. If, however, Ferdinand and Isabella wanted Katharine to retain them they should freely present her with them and not give them to her on a temporary basis as part of her dowry. They would then have to provide Henry VII with the equivalent amount of money. Henry now repeated this formulation to Gómez de Fuensalida – as the ambassador noted without a single variant on González de Puebla's rationale – and stated emphatically that he would not be prepared to take Katharine's jewels from her. Indeed, he emphasised that he would rather give her jewels to this value himself rather than deprive her of her own precious possessions.

Henry also presented Gómez de Fuensalida with a memorial about the office-holders in Katharine's household which the ambassador understood to have been written by González de Puebla. He insisted on a much smaller entourage than Ferdinand and Isabella had wanted and specifically excluded a number of offices which he believed would create confusion in England – *mayordomo mayor*; *capellan mayor*; secretary; Master of the Horse. Gómez de Fuensalida retorted that a simple gentleman in Spain would expect his wife to bring such office-holders with her when she left her father's house to live in marriage. Henry replied by drawing attention to the difficulties that had followed in the Low Countries when Juana had brought a surplus of Spanish women and men with her. He insisted that he would not have comparable confusion introduced into his own court. Moreover, since Katharine did not speak any English it would hinder her becoming familiar with the language – and with the English people – if she was surrounded by Spaniards and spoke Spanish all the time in her own household. Henry declared that he was immovable on this point and gave Gómez de Fuensalida a list of twenty offices which would be acceptable to him:

> a noble matron, who would be a widow, with one servant
> three ladies of noble rank who were virgins, with one servant
> a lady to act as porter
> a child to serve in the Chamber
> two chaplains, one to double as confessor and the other as secretary, with two servants and two stablemates
> a doctor with a servant and a stablemate
> a cook with a servant
> two child-stablemates

Faced with this stark list and the intractability of the king, Gómez de Fuensalida suggested that Henry would find a household of twenty-five people acceptable.[39] Doubtless – given the remarkable volte-face that Henry had performed over the scheduling of Katharine's arrival – the ambassador was more than satisfied with what he was reporting to his sovereigns.

Because Katharine would now be coming to England in 1501 Henry now accepted a further prorogation in the payment of the money owed to him until the Feast of San Juan 1501 (24 June) on condition that Ferdinand and Isabella should by Christmas return to him, signed and sealed, the paper which he now sent them listing the changes to which he had agreed in Katharine's schedule.[40]

It is not known when Gómez de Fuensalida's momentous letter reached Ferdinand and Isabella, who were in Granada, and during July–August they continued to write with their own plans and problems. Essentially they were trying to delay Katharine's departure, for like Henry VII they were anxious to push the date of the wedding back for personal and familial reasons. While Henry was fearful of his son's strength and maturity, Ferdinand and (much more especially) Isabella were eager to delay Katharine's departure, for she would be the last of their children to leave home. It will be recalled that the agreement for María's marriage to Manuel I of Portugal had been signed on 20 May 1500 and she was now preparing for her departure. When she left court in October only Katharine would then remain with her parents.

On 25 July 1500 Ferdinand and Isabella wrote to Henry assuring him that they intended to send Katharine as soon as possible and that they would not 'for all the riches of the world' break their agreement with him. Indeed, the fleet was being prepared to carry her to England. There was, however, a problem: although the marriage was already binding since it had been conducted *per verba de praesenti*, they nevertheless required that it should again be formally celebrated after Arthur had reached his fourteenth birthday in September. It may have been a measure of Ferdinand and Isabella's determination to delay their daughter's departure that it took them nearly two weeks to complete this letter (5 August).[41] On 13 August they once again wrote to Henry promising that they would send Katharine to England as soon as Arthur had taken his vows as an adult.[42]

It was probably within days of sending this latest letter that Ferdinand and Isabella received the news from Gómez de Fuensalida that Henry had, quite independently of their pleas, given them permission to delay Katharine's departure; nothing is known of their response, but still they continued to insist that Arthur should take his vows *in verba de praesenti* as an adult precisely so that it could never be subsequently claimed that when he had taken his wedding vows he had been a minor and that in consequence the wedding itself could be declared null and void.[43] The punctiliousness with which Ferdinand and Isabella insisted that every theological and ecclesiastical contingency should be foreseen and dealt with did them great credit, as sovereigns and as parents. How differently they would behave when negotiating Katharine's second marriage!

Katharine signed her powers authorising González de Puebla to ratify the marriage by proxy that had taken place at Bewdley on 19 May and empowered him to act once again as her proxy when Arthur took his vows *per verba de praesenti* as an adult; she signed the authorisation in Granada on 20 December 1500, unaware that the ceremony that she was now approving had already taken place.[44]

The Second Wedding By Proxy of Katharine & Arthur: Ludlow, 22 November 1500

González de Puebla ungenerously ascribed the delay in sending Katharine's authorisation for the second wedding by proxy to the machinations of Pedro de Ayala and Gutierre Gómez de Fuensalida. Fearing that the marriage was now in serious danger, he decided on his own authority to present Henry with the letter from Ferdinand and Isabella of 3 October and a previous (apparently undated) authorisation from Katharine allowing him to stand proxy for her. It was an extraordinary risk for him to take and Henry initially refused to countenance yet another ceremony. However – in González de Puebla's account – when the ambassador pointed out that this was the procedure that had been followed in Flanders with the marriage of Philip and Juana, Henry's opposition melted; he consulted with his council and agreed that the marriage should be celebrated yet again. In truth, the king was delighted: the marriage could be further secured in canon law and he would not yet have to part with his beloved son.

Anxious that Henry should change his mind, González de Puebla suggested ('with great haste') which officers of the English court were needed for the ceremony – again, the account is his own – and immediately headed off with them for Wales. On 22 November 1500, the marriage of Arthur and Katharine was celebrated once again in Ludlow Castle, in recognition of the fact that Arthur could now take his vows in person as an adult. The service was conducted by William Smyth, President of the Council of Wales and Bishop of Lincoln, and he made no effort to disguise his lack of enthusiasm for the task; he claimed to believe that a secular officer should officiate because the marriage was a clandestine one and he as a prelate would incur the danger of being suspended from his position for some years if he conducted it. González de Puebla reassured him that the wedding had already taken place twice and that the Pope, the king and Queen of Spain and the King of England had approved of it; accordingly, he would incur no danger if he performed the service – but the implication was clearly that he would most certainly be in trouble if he did not do so. Once again, González de Puebla held the prince's hand as the vows were exchanged. At the wedding banquet, the ambassador was honoured almost beyond his comprehension, sitting at the right hand of the Prince of Wales: all the dishes were served to him first 'and in general more respect was paid to him than he had ever received before in his life'.

Two notaries had been present to record the details of the service and they prepared authenticated accounts of what had happened for both crowns. González de Puebla immediately sent a messenger to the port of Bristol to take ship for Spain with the copy for Ferdinand and Isabella.

Still, the negotiations went on. Henry was now confident enough of Katharine's departure for England to authorise a list of the Spanish servants who could remain with her in England. Nevertheless, Henry insisted that Katharine would be better and more respectfully attended by English ladies and gentlemen 'than ever princess has been served before'. González de Puebla urged that specific job descriptions be provided for each of Katharine's ladies and requested that he be given twenty-five days notice of her departure from Spain. He recommended that the princess's fleet should sail to Southampton, which was the most convenient port from which to progress to London.

And still there was the problem of the jewels: González de Puebla had not dared to speak to Henry about them and the situation now remained as had been agreed in the treaty of 10 July 1499 – that, *two years after the marriage had been consummated*, their value was to be discounted from the last instalment of the dowry paid by Ferdinand and Isabella. It is not clear when González de Puebla had found out about this provision and it may be that he had only just uncovered it. At all events, he now begged his sovereigns 'to release him from the nightmare that overwhelms him' and give him permission to return to Spain. There, he assured them, he would be the most diligent servant to them.[45]

Not for three months did Isabella reply to the ambassador's letter; probably, winter storms had delayed its passage, and it was certainly a long way – in midwinter! – from Abingdon to Granada. The queen professed herself profoundly satisfied with the preparations being made by Henry and urged him not to commit himself and his subjects to unnecessary expense on her daughter's behalf, reminding him that Katharine and her party would stay in inns and in small villages during their journey to the Spanish coast. She had added a few names to the list of ladies who were to stay with Katharine in England, delicately insisting that she would be happy for her daughter to be served by English courtiers as long as she had Spaniards about her person. Interestingly, Isabella did not agree to a specific number of servants for her daughter – but she would send three times as many as Henry had stipulated.[46]

Ferdinand and Isabella and their household (including Katharine) left Granada at the end of March and headed north. However, they were promptly obliged to return to Granada by a revolt among 'the Moors' of Ronda; Isabella informed González de Puebla on 8 April that it would be a month or two at most before Katharine could leave and promised that she would send her as soon as possible.[47] On the same day, the queen wrote to Henry VII expressing her pleasure that the solemnisation of the marriage had been repeated and affirming that the marriage was legally binding and indissoluble. Isabella apologised that Katharine was not ready to depart and asked Henry to grant a further short delay: she pledged her word as a queen that her daughter would sail for England as soon as possible.[48]

Ferdinand returned to Granada on 15 May and spent a week with his wife and daughter. After what must have been very painful farewells from her parents, Katharine began her long and arduous journey to A Coruña. Low in spirit and in health – she was still suffering the after-effects of her fever – Katharine left Granada on 21 May 1501.[49] She was fifteen years and five months of age: she would never see her parents again.

6

1501–1502: MARRIAGE TO THE FRAIL PRINCE

Arrival in England

The journey from Granada to A Coruña on the Atlantic coast took three months. Katharine and her entourage had to cross the mountains of Granada to reach the valley of the Guadalquivir and then traverse the Sierra Morena into Extremadura. She turned her long journey into a pilgrimage as she bade farewell to Spain, paying homage at the shrine of the Virgin of Guadalupe and then gaining the jubilee of a pilgrim in the Cathedral of Santiago de Compostela. Ferdinand and Isabella had anticipated that Katharine would reach the coast in mid-July but so arduous was the journey that it took her a further month to do so.[1]

Katharine embarked at A Coruña on 25 August but a violent storm forced the fleet back towards the northern coast of Spain and it found refuge in Laredo 40 kilometres or so to the east of Santander on 2 September. It remained there for over three weeks as repairs were carried out. On 27 September – very late in the year to risk sailing the Bay of Biscay – the expedition set sail again and duly ran into a dreadful storm as it rounded the Isle of Ushant off the Brittany coast; even modern sailors are extremely wary of the rocks off Ushant and Katharine and her company must have been truly terrified as they fought their way away from the sprawling rocks. They survived both storm and rocks and when on 1 October they gained the safety of Plymouth harbour it was decided – not unnaturally – to complete the journey to London by land. It took them over a month to do so but if it was cold and wet their feet were at least on dry land.

The welcome given to Katharine in Plymouth justified the decision to take refuge there, for it was reported to Isabella that her daughter 'could not have been received with greater rejoicings if she had been the Saviour of the world'. To give thanks for their safe arrival, the princess and her party went to a local church; prayers were said there that Katharine would provide the Kingdom of England with the heirs that it needed.[2]

Notwithstanding that Henry VII had insisted that only twenty or so servants should travel with Katharine, about sixty people disembarked at Plymouth: Isabella would compromise her daughter's dignity for no one.[3] They were led jointly by Alonso de Fonseca y Acevedo, Archbishop of Santiago, and Diego Fernández de Córdoba, 3rd Count of Cabra and Admiral of Castile, who would be responsible for handing over Katharine to Henry VII and then return home after the marriage was completed. Cabra was accompanied by his wife Francisca de Zúñiga y de la Cerda. Chief among the other dignitaries were Antonio de Rojas, Bishop of Majorca (who would also return to Spain) and Don Pedro de Ayala, Protonotary of Spain and Ambassador in England.

The people who would be staying with Katharine in England were led by a brother and sister, Don Pedro Manuel and Doña Elvira Manrique, who held the leading positions in the princess's household; Pedro, as *mayordomo mayor* [Lord High Steward] of Katharine was the senior male member of her household but Elvira Manrique, as *camarera mayor* [Lady Chamberlain] exercised much fuller control over the daily life of the household. Elvira was a formidable personality and she would impose herself upon the young and impressionable princess rather than encouraging her to gain independence. She had her own little household, which consisted of a maid of honour (Doña Martina Mudarra) and two female servants and two male squires whose names have not survived. Doña Catalina Cárdenas was maid of honour in Katharine's apartments and may have been in charge of the other six ladies-in-waiting.

Seven male office-holders worked under Pedro Manrique. Juan de Cuero, as Master of the Wardrobe, had responsibility for Katharine's private chambers and for the safeguarding of her jewels and plate; he was accompanied by his wife (whose name is not recorded). Alonso de Esquivel served as Master of the Hall and Francisco de Merueña as Clerk of the Household. The names of the Comptroller of the household, Quartermaster and the Keeper of the Plate are not recorded while Katharine's secretary is recorded only as Pasamonte. She also had a purser, butler, six pages and four equerries.

Katharine's chapel was led by her confessor, Alessandro Giraldini, and had a second chaplain in Pedro de Morales. An unidentified Englishman served as her almoner. She had three gentlemen-in-waiting. She brought her own cook (who had two assistants) and baker. To serve at table she had a chief waiter and a cupbearer. She also had two servants who attended on her in her private rooms, and a laundress and a sweeper.

For Henry VII, the arrival of Katharine was the fullest recognition on the international stage of the legitimacy of his dynasty as rulers of England. So excited was he that he summoned Arthur (who was in Wales) to join him and together they rushed to meet the princess on the road. On 6 November, king and prince encountered the Spanish party at Dogmersfield in Hampshire, midway between Basingstoke and Aldershot.[4] When Henry was told that he would not be allowed to see Katharine because she was resting he insisted that he would do so 'even if she was in bed': unstated was his determination that in his realm there would be no foreign customs restricting his conduct. When he was introduced to Katharine it was with 'great joy and gladness'. He talked with her and her advisers in Latin, changed out of his riding clothes and went off to enjoy his supper. He subsequently brought Arthur to meet Katharine: music was played in her chamber and the young couple danced together – to the displeasure of Doña Elvira.[5]

Henry was deeply satisfied that Katharine met his expectations: she was young and pretty and presumably she was fertile. He hurried back to London, determined to celebrate her arrival and marriage in the most sumptuous manner; for once, he would not count the cost (although he would diligently ensure that most of it would fall on the City and guilds of London). Katharine and her entourage travelled at a more leisurely pace: on the outskirts of the capital she was greeted by Henry, Duke of York, who led her into the city.[6]

London, 12 November: 'The Most Original ... Pageant ... Ever Presented in England'

The City of London had been anticipating Katharine's arrival for a year now and when she arrived on Friday 12 November it gave the freest rein to its joy: 'Every lord both spiritual and temporal was keeping open house with right great royalty of food and drink.' Katharine dined at Lambeth Palace and proceeded to St George's Field where the churchmen, aristocracy and knights of England were assembled to greet her. These dignitaries then led her in the most splendid procession as she made her formal entry into the City.

It is not known who devised the pageants with which the City welcomed Katharine but Sydney Anglo has described them in his thrilling study of Tudor pageantry as 'perhaps the most original and complex essay in the pageant medium ever presented in England ... the supreme masterpiece of English civic pageantry'.[7] While they were quintessentially English, due deference was of course paid in the pageants to Burgundian ceremonial: they drew inspiration from Jean Molinet's *Le Trosne d'Honneur*, an elegy composed on the death of Philip the Good in 1467 for his son Charles the Bold.[8]

Six pageants welcomed Katharine as she journeyed from London Bridge to Cheapside, all of which celebrated the theme of 'Honour' and elevated the royal marriage in religious, chivalric and cultural terms. For instance, the first pageant, at London Bridge, celebrated the two husbands to whom Katharine was committing herself – Jesus Christ and Arthur. Two lady saints then welcomed her – Katharine herself and Ursula, who as a British saint reminded Katharine of her descent from John of Gaunt. In the second pageant, at Gracechurch Street, the 'union rose' greeted Katharine in the name of the united families of York and Lancaster; since Katharine was the embodiment of Nobility and Virtue she would worthily exercise power and influence in the realm and be an example to all. At the Conduit in Guildhall, 'the Sphere of the Moon' predicted the success of the marriage in terms of love and the production of children: happily, King Alfonso the Wise of Castile made an appearance to predict that the marriage would be fecund. The fourth pageant, at the Great Conduit in Cheapside presented Arthur as the Sun King, the fount of justice and the illumination of the earth and emphasised his many virtues. The fifth pageant ('The Temple of God') celebrated the sacred nature of marriage and the 'Catholic Church shining in front of my face/With light of faith, wisdom, doctrine and grace': in emulation of the 'Hail Mary', it enjoined of Katharine that 'blessed be the fruit of your belly' while Henry VII was the described as the 'most Christian king and most steadfast in the faith'. The concluding pageant, at the far end of Cheapside, returned to the central theme of the six displays that the marriage of Arthur and Katharine was not an end in itself but was a means whereby both of them, through living a life of Virtue, should reach Honour for themselves.

On the following day, Saturday 13 November, Henry VII formally received the Spanish party at Barnard's Castle. The king was accompanied by his family and nobility; his two sons sat on either side of him, Arthur on the right. The Spanish party showed their documents of authorisation, including the paper which solemnly passed on Ferdinand's assurance that Katharine was a virgin.[9] Katharine then rode to Barnard's Castle for her formal introduction to Queen Elizabeth. She then returned to spend the eve of her wedding day at the Bishop of London's palace.

Marriage to Arthur, St Paul's, 14 November 1501

The marriage took place on Sunday 14 November at St Paul's Cathedral.[10] The cathedral was hung with the richest tapestries and a raised timber pathway had been built from the choir door to a stage in front of the altar where the young couple would take their vows; for safety's sake, the pathway had handrails on either side. A closet had been constructed for Henry and Margaret so that they could watch the ceremony without being seen by the congregation.

At 9 o'clock in the morning John de Vere, 13th Earl of Oxford and Great Chamberlain of England, led a party of noblemen to collect Arthur and conduct him to the cathedral: on arrival, the prince went into a private room to change into his wedding clothes and was then taken back into the cathedral. Katharine now made her entrance. Like Arthur, she was dressed in white satin but her dress – like those of her ladies-in-waiting – was Spanish in design, with wide supportive hoops. Her face was covered by a veil of white silk which had a golden border and her hair hung loose over her shoulders, symbolising her chastity.

Katharine was led from the palace to St Paul's by the Duke of York and the Count of Cabra and at the entrance to the cathedral she was greeted by the civic and ecclesiastical dignitaries of England, led by Henry Deane, Archbishop of Canterbury:

> The ... princess [was] accompanied by the estates of England and Spain – a good number of lords, knights, gentlemen and ladies ... – and was herself led by two honourable persons of high rank, the Duke of York and the Earl [of Cabra] that came with her from Spain. Lady Cecil carried her train.
>
> She made her progress from the Palace where she had lodged towards the centre of the Church of [St] Paul's by the west door until she came to the spot where she was to be married. The [Arch]bishop

111

of Canterbury was waiting there for her with eighteen more bishops and honourable abbots, who were mitred full solemnly...[11]

Before proceeding into the cathedral there was business of state to be done: the Count of Cabra handed over to English ministers the documents from Ferdinand and Isabella that authorised the marriage and agreed on its terms; among them was the king's solemn assurance that his daughter was a virgin. The archbishop guided the couple through their marriage vows and then Arthur triumphantly led his bride along and around the walkway so that they could acknowledge the congregation in every part of the cathedral: they received a tumultuous welcome, some people shouting 'King Henry', and others 'Prince Arthur'. There followed the pontifical High Mass of the Trinity and the solemn blessing of the couple. Again there was business of state to be done: at the altar itself Katharine was endowed with the titles to the lands and rents that the King of England had endowed upon her as her settlement.

Arthur and Katharine then led the procession out of the cathedral. They were raucously greeted by the crowd, whose joy in the wedding was doubtless heightened by the pleasures of fountains running freely with wine. To loud – and drunken? – acclamation, Arthur and Katharine were taken to the palace of the Bishop of London for the wedding feast. Once again, they were led by Henry, Duke of York and the Count of Cabra. The feast surpassed anything thus far in the celebrations: its theme was 'all the meats of England'.

In the evening the bedding of the newly-weds took place. Again, there was riotous goodwill and joy. It fell to the Earl of Oxford in his capacity as Lord Chamberlain of England to test 'the bed of state' by lying down first on one side and then on the other to check that nothing protruded from the mattress that could do harm to the prince and his bride. Katharine herself was then laid to bed before Henry VII led his son and a somewhat rowdy party of wellwishers into the chamber. Bishops then blessed the bed and room with oils, and wine and spices were handed round. Then the order was given – it is not clear by whom – for the guests to leave and they did so, bringing the day to an end 'with joy, mirth and gladness'.[12] Of what happened when the door closed there is no record.

Katharine spent Monday resting and received only one visitor: the Earl of Oxford brought her a 'special token' from the king and the warmest message: 'and joyously saluted her with words of most favour and reverence, saying that his Highness wished above all things to be of good comfort [to her] and that he waited impatiently for the time when he might see her to his great joy and gladness'.[13]

During the week after the marriage ceremony the court gave itself over to a series of highly structured celebrations and courtly entertainments in the form of jousts and tournaments, 'disguisings' and dances. The court enjoyed at least one great banquet daily: the king himself provided four of them. While the influence of Burgundian ceremonial was much in evidence in the etiquette of the court these celebrations were characteristic of the vitality of the English court – noisy, extravagant and strongly competitive. The 'disguisings' allowed members of the royal family and leading courtiers and noblemen and women to appear, ostensibly in disguise, in pageants and theatrical productions. The only Spanish contribution appears to have been the performance of a tumbler who amazed the court with his acrobatics. The procession of knights into the tilt-gallery provided opportunities for mechanical and chivalric ingenuity; for instance, on 18 November, the Duke of Buckingham once again displayed his power and wealth, entering on a moving pavilion that was complete with turrets while William Courtenay arrived in a dragon led by a giant. On Wednesday 24 November the men who were to be involved in foot combat arrived in an enormous ship which fired salvoes with 'a huge noise'. No expense or ingenuity was spared.[14]

On Tuesday 16 November, Henry VII met his nobles at 6.00 a.m. and they rode to St Paul's to give thanks for the wedding. Later that day, Katharine was brought privately to meet the king. They greeted each other joyously with 'right pleasant and favourable words, greetings and communications'. When the princess returned to eat, she did so not in the Spanish fashion but in the English: it was a significant rite of passage for her. She and her entourage then travelled on the Thames to join the king and queen at Barnard's Castle. It took more than forty barges to transport the royal party to Westminster – 'so as heretofore have not been seen so many barges so well accompanied upon the Thames at one time'. The day ended with the ceremonial preparations and vigil of the seventy-six men who were to be invested into the Order of the Bath on the following day: that such an unprecedentedly large number of men were knighted at once was explicit recognition of the importance of the occasion for Henry VII ('whereof so great a number and multitude have not been seen heretofore in England knighted at one time').[15]

The first jousts took place on Thursday in front of Westminster Hall.[16] The ground was gravelled and sanded and a tilt-yard was built. Stands were erected – on the south side for the party of the king and queen, on the north for the Lord Mayor of London and his party, and around the edges of the field for 'the honest and common people' who thronged to see the jousts. Henry's generosity did not extend to letting these people in free of charge; apparently they had to pay steeply for the privilege. But they were evidently content to do so; the crowd was packed so tightly that only the faces of the spectators could be seen. The nobility of England made their entrance in splendid style, none more so – of course – than the Duke of Buckingham:

> In his pavilion of white and green silk, four-square with proper turrets and towers of curious construction, set full of red roses of the king's crests – the pavilion was carried and upheld and conveyed with many of his servants on foot in jackets of black and red silk … and the said lord's servants and gentlemen were well-mounted, with their horses trapped and hung with spangles of gold and bells, that their uniform, marching ahead of their horses and courageous demeanour gave great pleasure and gladness to the king's grace and to the whole realm of England that was present there…[17]

Once again, it was agreed that the joust was unprecedented: 'that such a field and royal jousts so noble and so valiantly performed have not been seen nor heard of…'[18]

On Friday 19 November, the 'disguisings' and banquet were held in Westminster Hall. The occasion was notable for the energetic and joyous commitment of the Duke of York to the festivities. He danced with his sister Margaret with such vigour that he threw off his gown – a performance that gave his parents 'right great and singular pleasure'.[19]

The next four days were given up to banquets and jousts and courtly celebrations. Henry took the party hunting in the grounds of Richmond Palace and there was 'great slaughter' of the deer. The king gave the meat to the Spanish party to eat as they wished; not all of them were pleased to accept and eat it.

After eight days of celebration, the Spaniards prepared to leave. They enjoyed a last meal, which was served on splendid plates of gold and silver: the Archbishop of Santiago's alone was worth £600–700. On Monday 22 November they took leave of Henry VII, Queen Elizabeth and the Queen Mother and the newly-weds. Katharine became distraught at bidding farewell to people who had supported and encouraged her

– 'whereupon she was partly annoyed and pensive' at their departure. Henry was more than equal to the moment: he summoned the princess and her ladies to his library and after he had – teasingly? – shown them some of his books he commanded a jeweller to display some jewels:

> Yet over this, to augment and increase gladness, mitigate sorrow and refresh and comfort her spirits, his prudent Highness had provided a jeweller there with many rings with precious stones and huge diamonds and jewels of most goodly fashion, every one of them being of great richness and treasure. He asked her to look over them and to behold them carefully, and then to choose one of them that she most liked. And after she had chosen at her pleasure, every lady of Spain who was with her made their own choices and the remaining jewels were given to the English ladies. And thus with the pleasure and other diversions and gifts [Katharine] somewhat allayed her heaviness and drew herself into the manner, guise and customs of England with her most dear and loving husband the noble Prince Arthur [and] with her revered and well-beloved father-in-law Henry the Seventh...[20]

Henry VII's sensitivity and generosity betokened his deep contentment and pride at the marriage and at the manner in which he, his court and nation had celebrated it; he subsequently wrote to Ferdinand and Isabella – although not until 28 November did he find time to do so – how much he had admired Katharine's beauty and poise and that she had been welcomed into his capital city 'with the acclamation of such masses of people as never before had been seen in England'. For his own part, he promised Ferdinand and Isabella that Katharine 'has found a second father who will ever watch over her happiness and never permit her to want anything that he can procure for her'.[21] Arthur, too, was enchanted with Katharine: he joyously wrote to Ferdinand and Isabella (on 30 November) that no woman in the world could be more agreeable to him than his new bride.[22]

Man & Wife: To Live Together?
Henry's generosity was the better-judged for he had been deeply embarrassed by a dispute that he had had with Juan de Cuero, Katharine's Keeper of the Wardrobe, over the vexed question of the jewels, gold and silver that were to form part of the payment of the third instalment

of the dowry. The details of the dispute are contained in a splendidly malevolent letter from Pedro de Ayala to Ferdinand and Isabella at the end of December. Ayala set out to do everything he could to damage the reputation of González de Puebla but he also provided – incidentally to this main purpose – evidence which makes it very clear that Henry had very deep anxieties about allowing his son to live with Katharine in full married state.

Ayala recalled that when the marital festivities were over Henry asked for the delivery of the jewels and precious items that he believed he was now entitled to but Cuero refused to hand them over, stating that under the marriage treaty he was obliged to retain them for Katharine's use. Henry believed that he had been insulted and after negotiations continued fruitlessly for a fortnight he went to see Katharine and Elvira Manrique. Ayala claimed to have been present at the interview. Henry explained that before he had met Katharine at Dogmersfield González de Puebla had told him that 35,000 ducats' worth of pearls, jewels, gold, silver and tapestry were to be delivered to him without delay and had read to him the letter from Ferdinand and Isabella in which this was stipulated. When the marital festivities were concluded, González de Puebla suggested that Henry ask for the treasures and he duly summoned Cuero, who insisted that they were to remain in his possession and that he was to be given a receipt for them. Henry was astonished to be asked for a receipt for something that he had never been given and questioned González de Puebla about it. According to Ayala's account, González de Puebla urged Henry to keep secret what he was about to tell him and suggested that if Katharine retained the jewels Henry could refuse to accept them as they would have been used and therefore become second-hand. If he did so, Ferdinand and Isabella would then be shamed into paying Henry their value: Katharine could keep her jewels and Henry could get his money. González de Puebla insisted that Katharine had agreed to this stratagem.

Henry rejected the idea out of hand, saying that it was fraudulent and demeaning to his majesty; he apologised for having asked for the jewels and begged Katharine to write to her parents explaining why he had erroneously done so. When González de Puebla re-read the letter from Ferdinand and Isabella he understood – Ayala claimed – that they had insisted that the jewels remain in Cuero's safekeeping. Henry claimed that González de Puebla had deceived him as much as his own sovereigns and urged Katharine, Elvira and Ayala himself to inform them of the truth, insisting that he would be ashamed to be known as a person who asked for what was due to him before he was legally entitled to it. Indeed, he boasted to Katharine that he was so rich that he could spend a million ducats in gold without falling into debt. He then left the princess.

An even larger question now loomed: on the day after the shaming argument about the jewels, Henry summoned Ayala to discuss with him whether Katharine should accompany Arthur to Wales. It will be recalled that in the summer of 1500 Gutierre Gómez de Fuensalida had reported to Ferdinand and Isabella the rumours that he had picked up about the frailty of Prince Arthur – that he had been informed on good authority that Henry VII wanted his son and daughter-in-law to consummate their marriage on their wedding night and then live apart for two or three years; and that the king himself had told him that he wanted Arthur and Katharine to live with him for three years so that the prince could grow in strength.[23] Ayala now confirmed that the separation of the newly-weds remained a priority for Henry and indeed for his wife. He reported that on the day after Henry had his discussion with Katharine, Elvira Manrique and himself about the jewels he was summoned separately to the royal presence:

> On the following day he summoned me and told me that he was deeply anxious because it was necessary to send the Prince to Wales and both in his council and in that of the prince there had been different opinions – some saying that it would be good for the princess to go to Wales and others saying that she should not. Each of these had given good reasons for their views and he himself did not know how to decide. He asked me for my view. I said that there would be many advantages if she remained, notably that both the princess and the prince would be better able to tolerate separation if she was in [Henry VII's] company and that of the queen because they could compensate her for the great pain that she would be suffering as a result of her separation from the prince – [a separation] that she would not be easily able to tolerate if she was in his house in Wales.
>
> I gave many other reasons that the king himself had put to me only a few days earlier for deciding that the princess should remain in his company for the next two years.
>
> The following day the king spoke with the princess and told her the same things that he had told me – that it was necessary that the prince should go to Wales and that there were diverse opinions among his councillors but he himself would not decide one way or

the other except in accordance with her wishes, declaring that he would not decide anything other than what she wanted.

Her reply was that neither in this matter nor in any other did she have any wishes other than what His Highness had and that she would be content with whatever he decided. He replied asking her not to leave the decision to him because it might be that his decision would cause her anger. She repeated her first answer.

This indecision continued for four days, during which the king had the prince work on the princess to persuade her to say that she preferred to go [to Wales] rather than stay. She refused to say and so the king, making a great display of his sadness, declared that it would be convenient for her to go to Wales although this was the thing that he most regretted in the world...

The decision having been made that Katharine would travel to Wales with Arthur and live with him as his wife, discussions turned now to the size of her household and the provisions and wages that would be provided for it. Again, Ayala let it be known how badly González de Puebla had negotiated, reporting that Henry VII claimed that he had never even discussed the matter with him. It was agreed that the young couple would live off the prince's rents. Clearly, Henry was furious that he had not been given the jewels and valuables. Ayala recommended that Ferdinand and Isabella should promptly pay him their cash value. He reported that Henry had not given Arthur anything with which to furnish his own house – not even table utensils – and that no payments had been assigned for the members of the household. Arthur would have to use the possessions that Katharine brought with her.

And still, the question of sexual relations would not go away:

I on my part and Doña Elvira on hers have said to the king that we believe that Your Highnesses, knowing the very tender age of the prince, would be pleased rather than displeased if they did not live together for some time. He replied that he was astonished to hear this because one of the reasons that had persuaded him to decide [that they should do so] was that one of the principal people that your Highnesses had placed near the princess had talked to him at great length about this and the conclusion that he had put forward on the part of your Highnesses – and he was speaking as a man who knew your wishes – was that [Henry] should be asked that under no circumstances in the world should he separate them but must send her with her husband, and if this was not done your Highnesses would be badly contented and [the princess herself] would be in despair.

On being questioned very hard he declared that it had been Alessandro [Giraldini] who had given him this view and that he had done so with the support and advice of the doctor [*sc.* González de Puebla].[24]

Henry VII was the most self-contained of kings. He was always prepared to take advice widely but he resolutely kept his own counsel, making it a point of principle never to let anyone know what he was thinking. And yet, when it came to deciding whether or not to allow his son and heir to live in wedlock with his new bride he shared his doubts with at least five Spaniards over a period of at least four days – with Katharine herself; Elvira Manrique; ambassadors González de Puebla and Ayala and Alessandro Geraldini. This break with Henry VII's personal and regnal custom is intriguing, the more so since it revolved around a matter which had such overwhelming importance to his kingly majesty as the security of the succession to his own throne. It is evident – unarguable, indeed – that Henry had grave doubts about Arthur's physical well-being and that he did the best he could to create a situation in which others persuaded him that Arthur should be given two or three years to grow in strength before living with Katharine as man and wife. Did his worries stem from the fate of Katharine's own brother Juan, who had died within months of marrying as a result – it was believed – of over-exerting himself in sexual pleasures? But Juan had been eighteen when he married: Arthur was fifteen.

Tragedy: The Death of Arthur, 2 April 1502
Arthur and Katharine remained at court from their marriage on 14 November until they departed for Wales on 21 December: nothing is known of their living arrangements during these weeks. Is it reasonable to assume, in view of Henry's repeatedly stated anxieties about his son, that they lived apart? At all events, when they arrived in Ludlow at the end of the year they settled down – as everyone assumed – to enjoy conjugal bliss. Again, nothing is known of their arrangements. The two Spanish ambassadors remained in London so that they could be close to the king – and no doubt so that they could keep a vigilant eye on each other – and so there are no extant reports

from them about the life of the young couple in Wales. Nor have any letters from Katharine's household survived. Of their life together in Ludlow we know nothing that is strictly contemporaneous.

Of course, it was cut tragically short. The anonymous chronicler of Katharine's marriage recorded that Arthur's renewed rule in Wales lasted only between the feasts of Christmas and Easter before he was consumed by a disease which devoured his body:

> He ruled from the feast of the Nativity of Christ in the previous year until the solemn feast of the Resurrection, at which time there grew and increased upon his body, whether it was as a result of excessive eating or as a result of natural causes, a lamentable and – ... most pitiful disease and sickness, which he with such painful and violence battled against [but] it was driven into the inner parts of him; that cruel and fervent enemy of nature, the deadly corruption, did utterly vanquish and overcome the pure and friendly blood, without the relief of a doctor or physical help and remedy. Thus the lively spirits of this noble Prince finally died, to the agony, sorrow and great discomfort of our Realm of England and all of Christendom.[25]

His illness was described as the 'sweating sickness' but it may have been pulmonary tuberculosis. Arthur died on 2 April 1502.

Arthur's body was disembowelled and embalmed. It was then wrapped in a cloth of wax and placed in a coffin.[26] It remained in the chamber of Ludlow Castle until 23 April, when it was taken into the hall by yeomen of Arthur's chamber. Either that day or the following day, the coffin was carried in procession to Ludlow parish church. On 25 April it left Ludlow in a specially constructed and upholstered wagon; it travelled through Bewdley and reached Worcester Cathedral on 26 April. On 3 May a splendid burial service was held in the cathedral.[27]

It fell to Sir Richard Pole as Arthur's Grand Chamberlain to write the letters informing Henry VII of the death of his son and heir. When his terrible letters arrived at court, Henry's courtiers were reluctant to take the responsibility for showing them to the king and persuaded Henry's confessor to hand them over to him. The confessor went to the king's chamber and insisted that all the king's attendants and courtiers should leave before he informed Henry of the death of his son and heir. The king – so austere and imposing in his public life – responded as a father would to the dreadful news:

And when His Grace understood that sorrowful and heavy tidings, [he] sent for the queen, saying that he and his queen would take the painful sorrow together. And after she came and saw the king her lord and husband in that natural and painful sorrow – as I heard say – that with full, great and constant comfortable words [she] besought His Grace that he should first, after God, remember the wealth of his own noble person, the comfort of his realm and of herself, and how that my Lady his mother had never had more children but himself alone, and that God's Grace had always protected him and brought him where he was [*sc.* the throne]. In addition, God had lent them a fair, goodly and young prince and two fair princesses, and that ... [they were] both young enough [to have more children]. And that the prudence and wisdom of His Grace spread over the whole of Christendom so that it should please him to accept this.

Then the king thanked her for her good comfort and after she had gone back to her own chamber the natural and motherly remembrance of her great loss hit her so sorrowfully in the heart that those who were near her were obliged to send for the king to comfort her. And then His Grace in true, gentle and faithful love came to her in haste and relieved her and told her what wise advise she had given him earlier, and he for his part would thank God for his sons, and he wished that she would do likewise.[28]

On 9 April a requiem Mass was celebrated for the prince in St Paul's Cathedral but no members of the royal family attended for they were not allowed to be in the proximity of death. Katharine's health collapsed under the strain of Arthur's death and she was slowly taken back to London in a carriage masked in black.

Arthur's death was a profound regnal loss to Henry VII as well as a personal catastrophe, for he now had good reason to fear that his own death might be followed by a royal minority. He had lost two of his three sons in two years – Edmund had died in June 1500 – and the survival of the dynasty hung on the life of Henry, Duke of York, who was only eleven years of age. Henry acted ruthlessly to provide such protection for his family as he could: Sir James Tyrrell was executed in May 1502, ostensibly because he had confessed (under torture) to murdering 'the Princes in the Tower' but in reality because he was a supporter of the de la Pole family.[29] Within months of having so many hopes raised by the marriage of Arthur and Katharine, Henry VII was now plunged into uncertainty and dismay about the prospects of his new dynasty: would it survive?

7

WIDOWHOOD – AND THE PAPAL DISPENSATION TO REMARRY

Sisters in Despair: The Duchess of Burgundy & the Princess of Wales
Ferdinand was in Toledo when on 3 May 1502 he heard of Arthur's death. It was the beginning of a tumultuous week. Isabella was in very poor health and Ferdinand did not break the news to her for six days.[1] But the king could not shield his wife from even darker news for Philip and Juana arrived at court on 7 May and it was immediately evident that Juana was in a state of mental collapse. As always, Ferdinand held his nerve: on 10 May, he commissioned Fernán Duque de Estrada to travel to England as an extraordinary ambassador to put the astounding proposal to Henry VII that Katharine should marry Henry, Duke of York.[2]

While Ferdinand acted, Isabella mourned: she could not bring herself to attend the memorial service for Arthur for it was too painful a reminder of the death of Juan and she contented herself with offering a *novena* of prayers and masses for the soul of the dead prince.[3] But in the midst of grief there came further anxiety, for Philip made no attempt to disguise either his determination to secure control of the Crown of Castile for himself or his readiness to forge an alliance with the King of France to do so. Not only was Ferdinand's triple alliance against France collapsing but it seemed probable now that the Crown of Castile would pass in practice into the hands of a foreign (and hostile) prince. It was no doubt after intense discussion that Ferdinand and Isabella decided that they had to preserve the union of their crowns even if Philip was to be the ultimate beneficiary. They therefore had the Cortes of Castile pledge its fealty to

Juana as the lawful heiress of the Crown and to Philip as her legitimate consort (22 May 1502).[4]

Once again, the Cortes of Aragon proved intractable. Isabella was too ill to travel to Zaragoza and so Ferdinand rode there alone. He opened the Cortes on 23 July but was no more successful in persuading the procurators to pledge their fealty to a princess than he had been in 1497. The Cortes would only agree to take the oath to Juana when she produced a second male child who could ensure the succession in the masculine line: Juana's first son, Charles, would inherit Castile while a second son – as yet unborn – would succeed Ferdinand in Aragon. Moreover, the Cortes had the prescience to insist that if in the future Ferdinand remarried and had a son then that child would have precedence in the succession to the Crown of Aragon over any son of Juana's and Philip's. Ferdinand had failed to ensure that the Union of the Crowns would continue in the next generation.

Juana and Philip themselves travelled the long and hard road to Zaragoza in mid-October to receive this deeply unsatisfactory fealty (26–27 October). However, on the day after the oaths had been taken Ferdinand learned that Isabella's condition had deteriorated and immediately rushed back to her. He instructed Juana and Philip to replace him at the Cortes but neither was prepared to do so: Philip feared that Isabella might die before she could confer upon him the right to govern Castile in Juana's name and rode in hot pursuit of his father-in-law, leaving his wife in Zaragoza. Juana's emotions were more complex: certainly, she was anxious to be reunited with her mother in case she was dying but she was also distraught that her husband had abandoned her: she too left for Madrid (24 November). The Cortes of the Kingdom of Aragon were simply abandoned.

Isabella curtly rejected Philip's insistence that he should rule Castile in Juana's name: furious, the archduke let it be known that he was 'burning' to leave Spain. When Isabella refused to allow Juana to travel with him because of her pregnancy, Philip left without her (19 December). Juana was devastated: she sank into mourning as if her husband had died.[5] When Isabella tried to mollify her by promising that she could return to the Low Countries after her delivery Juana flew into such a fierce rage that Isabella was obliged to recognise that her daughter was on the brink of a mental breakdown.[6] Isabella had lost two children since 1497 and now had to confront the probability that her eldest child – the heiress to her crown – was disintegrating mentally. As for Philip, he stopped off at

Lyons to sign an agreement with Louis XII that France would support him in his struggle to win the Crown of Castile for himself (Treaty of Lyons, 5 April 1503). He had broken with Ferdinand and Isabella.

Juana gave birth to a second son on 10 March 1503; he was named Ferdinand. Isabella attended the baptism: it was to be her last appearance in public. Juana now endured another excruciatingly painful meeting with her parents when they refused to allow her to return to Brussels, ostensibly because they were at war with Louis XII but in practice because they were so alarmed by her mental condition (18 June). Instead, Ferdinand and Isabella took the dreadful decision to incarcerate their daughter in La Mota, for her own protection. In her prison Juana furiously refused all food, neglected her personal hygiene and appearance and became increasingly violent towards her servants. Ferdinand and Isabella could now have no doubt that their daughter was unfit to succeed to the Crown of Castile.[7]

When Duque de Estrada arrived in England he found that the first precondition for his mission was in place; after Arthur's death, Katharine had been isolated in her chambers until it became certain that she was not carrying her dead husband's child, and only when it had become evident that she was not pregnant had Henry VII been able to allow his last son to assume the title of Prince of Wales.[8] Henry VII and Duque de Estrada now entered upon a complex game of bluff as they edged their way into the fraught negotiations, and they did so unencumbered by the involvement of González de Puebla, who was left unaware of the real purpose of his new colleague's mission.[9] The opening gambit was simple enough; when, in June, Duque de Estrada informed Henry that he intended to take Katharine back to Spain, the king brusquely informed him that he was not obliged by the agreement with Ferdinand and Isabella to return the dowry or (by implication) the princess herself.[10] The situation of the two crowns was simple enough: Ferdinand and Isabella desperately needed to retain the English alliance (and would not have wished to have their daughter returned to them as a dishonoured woman) while Henry was never a man to voluntarily give up money and much less to hand back a Princess of Spain who was now of major value to him as a tool in negotiations. Katharine – although she probably did not know it – was destined to remain in England.

While Ferdinand and Henry VII played at bluff, Isabella acted. There can be no doubt that the queen loved Katharine – the same cannot be said of Ferdinand with any conviction – and that she was determined to see her settled before she herself died, as she knew that she would shortly do. But Isabella was every whit as calculating as her husband and she shared with Ferdinand the conviction that their alliance with England had to be preserved: between 12 July and 25 August she therefore wrote five letters to Duque de Estrada and González de Puebla ordering them to do everything that they could to reinforce friendship with England.[11] Like her husband, Isabella sent the key letters to Duque de Estrada. Indeed, in her letter to him of 12 July, Isabella expressly linked Katharine's remarriage with the French threat in Italy and with the possibility that Henry VII might marry his son to a French princess:

> You will know that the King of France is on the road to Milan with an army ... You will understand how important it is to us not to delay the agreement for the marriage of the Princess of Wales, our daughter, with the Prince of Wales, especially because it is said that the King of France is working to obstruct this (and is) seeking the marriage of the Prince of Wales with his own daughter or with the daughter of M. Angoulême...

But was Katharine a virgin? Isabella knew well enough that Henry VII would find it much easier to accept the proposed remarriage if he was convinced (or pretended to be) that he was presenting a virgin bride to his last son. Equally, the queen understood perfectly well how absolutely imperative it was that there should be no doubts about the legitimacy of the children born to a royal marriage: her marriage to Ferdinand in circumstances of secrecy and danger in 1469 and her seizure of the throne of Castile in 1474 had been based upon that premise.

In the chaos that followed Arthur's death no one had thought to investigate properly whether the prince had consummated his marriage; witnesses in the households of Arthur and Katharine had not been interviewed and no professional diplomatic assessment had been made either in England or in Spain as to whether sexual intercourse had taken place. We have seen that Ferdinand did not even pause to consider the question in May before despatching Duque de Estrada to England. But a document did subsequently arrive in Spain insisting that Arthur had consummated the marriage and it came from no less a figure than Alessandro Giraldini, Katharine's confessor, who wrote to Isabella to this effect.

Giraldini's letter has not apparently survived, but when Katharine learned what he had written she was outraged and had Elvira Manrique write at once to Isabella to affirm that she remained a virgin. It cannot have been easy for the princess to admit to her mother that she had failed in the defining purpose of her marriage; given the history of her family – siblings and parents – she would have regarded this as a shaming secret. Certainly, the declaration that Elvira now despatched to Spain was to envelop and haunt Katharine for the rest of her life.

Isabella, however, was greatly relieved by the news and in her letter to Duque de Estrada of 12 July threw her weight behind her daughter: 'It is now known for certain that the Princess of Wales, our daughter, remains as she was, for Doña Elvira has written this.' Accordingly, Isabella instructed the ambassador to negotiate Katharine's marriage to the new Prince of Wales with such urgency that he was not even to take the time to consult with Ferdinand and herself before committing them to an agreement: 'You are to work to have the arrangements made for the marriage without consulting us because any delay whatsoever would be damaging and so therefore you are to make the new agreement, sign it and take the oath (to observe it).'[12]

A bitter lesson had been learned: Isabella informed the ambassador that she would only 'pay the remainder of the dowry when the marriage is consummated'. She also demanded that he ensure that Henry VII provide Katharine with the means with which to support herself. But while Ferdinand and Isabella pushed urgently for the new marriage they continued to instruct Duque de Estrada to give Henry the impression that he was preparing the plans for Katharine's return to Spain: they would not appear as supplicants to the King of England.[13]

The reality of Ferdinand's position was set out in a letter to Duque de Estrada on 1 September 1502 when – exactly as Isabella had done – he drew a defining connection between the French invasion of Italy and Katharine's remarriage. Ferdinand was deeply anxious that Louis was now preparing in Milan an army with which he would march south and conquer Naples (and perhaps even Sicily). He therefore instructed Duque de Estrada to urge Henry VII to join with him in resisting the growth of French power by launching a joint assault on France. Ferdinand was – he assured his ambassador – confident that such a campaign would result in England regaining Gascony and Normandy and France being driven out of Italy. In a second letter to the ambassador on the same day, Ferdinand again specifically linked the war against France with the betrothal of Katharine to Prince Henry by insisting that the marriage would not take place if Henry VII did not support him against Louis

XII.[14] Katharine would marry Prince Henry to help secure Spain's power in Italy.

Bedsheets & Canon Law: Marriage, Public Honesty – and Papal Dispensations

It was the custom in the Castilian royal house to display bedsheets on the morning after a wedding to prove that intercourse had taken place and that a virgin bride had been deflowered. It will be recalled that Ferdinand and Isabella themselves had their wedding sheet displayed round Valladolid in 1469 to the sound of trumpets and timbals – literally, they made a song and dance of their marital triumph – and they did so to make a brutally stark contrast with the inability of Henry IV to consummate his marriages. Their children understood the need to follow suit and did not temporise about seizing their marital pleasures. We have seen, indeed, that Katharine's siblings – Isabella, Juan, Juana and María – entered enthusiastically upon the physical celebrations of their marriages. Evidently they enjoyed sexual activity as much as they understood dynastic needs – and (as we will see) the theological nature of marriage as defined by the Roman Catholic Church.[15]

Katharine never displayed bedsheets. It might be conjectured that she did not do so because it was not the custom of the English royal house to mark and celebrate a marriage in this way but it is not unreasonable to assume that in the case of her marriage to Arthur she did not do so because nothing had taken place.[16] It is probable that the question did not even arise when she married Henry VIII in 1509, for this marriage – unlike that of 1501 – was celebrated in conditions of strict privacy within a royal palace and so the possibility of displaying bedsheets did not arise. In any event, we may reasonably assume that it would have been a very bold spirit who presumed to require evidence of Henry VIII that he had been successful in consummating his marriage.

The display of the marital bedsheets by the Catholic Kings and their children was much more than a political ploy designed to protect themselves against the accusation of impotence that Ferdinand and Isabella (and others) had levelled against Henry IV of Castile: it betokened a profound understanding of the realities of Catholic theology and – above all else – a recognition that the rite of marriage took place not in a church but in the marital bed.

In Catholic canon law, marriage was one of seven 'sacraments', the core practices of Catholic religious life which had been instituted, the Church

127

believed, by Jesus Christ himself.[17] These were defined as 'outward signs of inward grace'. The sacraments of confirmation and holy orders could be administered only by a bishop while those of confession, communion and the last rites ('extreme unction') were the preserve of priests. Baptism was also normally restricted to the priesthood but in cases where it was feared a child might die before a priest could arrive to perform the rite a layperson could lawfully perform the sacrament in his place. Six of the seven sacraments were therefore in practice performed by ordained priests or bishops (who were of course also priests).

Marriage was the exception: although a couple took their vows in church in the presence of a priest and signed the record of marriage under his supervision, it was – and is – they themselves who performed the rite of marriage when they committed themselves physically to each other. In other words, the act of sexual intercourse between the couple was *in and of itself* the act of marriage. In ancillary fashion, the sexual act also created a new family bond ('affinity') in drawing the blood relatives of the couple into their kinship: having had intercourse made a man a blood relative of the woman's family (and vice versa). This was true for all manner of folk, but of course was especially relevant when the marriage of a monarch (or his heir) was involved: indeed, it may be said to have been the *purpose* of diplomatic marital alliances.

The Catholic Church did not acknowledge that a marriage which had been freely and properly entered into could ever be unmade. The injunction of Matthew 19:4–6 was unalterable: 'The two [the man and his wife] shall be in one flesh. Therefore now they are not two but one flesh. What therefore God has joined together, let no man put asunder.' Not even the Pope had the right to unmake a marriage that had been freely entered into, celebrated in public and consummated.

The Pope had full authority to dispense from all human and ecclesiastical laws but since the laws which operated in the case of matrimony were held to be of divine origin he was only entitled to 'dispense' with them by using the derived power which he held as Vicar of Christ. Popes had exercised this power for 300 years or so but (as we have seen) by the early sixteenth century the religious and ethical standards under which they did so had fallen badly into disrepair; time after time, Renaissance popes – and, above all, Alexander VI – showed themselves willing to issue dispensations to monarchs and members of their families on grounds that were partisan or even trivial. Increasingly, the perception spread among the rulers of Europe that the grant of such dispensations was negotiable, governed more by political expediency than theological rectitude.

It will be recalled that the Church attached great importance to the act of betrothal, recognising that when a couple publicly pledged to marry each other they created a bond between themselves (and their families) that was so strong as to be more than quasi-sacramental: certainly, it was held to be canonically binding on them (above, chapter 4). It was unarguable that Arthur and Katharine had been formally – indeed, repeatedly – betrothed and had themselves undergone a marriage ceremony witnessed by thousands of people in Westminster Abbey.[18] On the night of the marriage they had also been bedded in Westminster in front of many witnesses. Moreover, they had then lived together (after a fashion) for four months before Arthur died. Whether intercourse had taken place then or subsequently became in one sense an irrelevance: there was no possible room for doubt that Arthur and Katharine had repeatedly and publicly committed themselves to each other – and that they had done so latterly *as adults, per verba de praesenti.* Accordingly, under the precepts of *publicae honestatis,* Katharine was automatically and explicitly prohibited from marrying Arthur's brother. The question then arose whether the Pope himself could dispense with the impediment of *publicae honestatis.*

However, if Arthur and Katharine *had* consummated their marriage they had become fully and lawfully man and wife in the eyes of the Church and had thereby created a 'diriment impediment' of marriage in the collateral line of the fourth degree and in the direct line. No one – not even the Pope – could dispense from the divine law: Katharine could not *under any circumstances* lawfully marry Prince Henry.[19]

But Ferdinand and Isabella were in a hurry: the French invasion of Italy obliged them to consolidate their alliance with England. Accordingly, they decided to appeal to Rome for a dispensation on the grounds – which they knew to be false – that the marriage of Arthur and Katharine *had* been consummated; they therefore sought release from the impediment of affinity. Foolishly, they did not back this up by asking also for a dispensation from the impediment of 'public honesty' just in case intercourse had not taken place. In August 1503 the request was sent to Rome. The approach of the Catholic Kings had little to do with theology – Katharine had, after all, insisted to them on her most solemn word that she remained a virgin and they would not have doubted her word for one moment – and everything to do with diplomacy and war:

the alliance with England had to be preserved. Ferdinand and Isabella gave no thought to theological niceties – or to the implications for their daughter if they had misjudged the situation.

Isabelline Diplomacy: The Betrothal of Katharine to Prince Henry, 23 June 1503

So, too, with Henry VII, who now had profound anxieties about the succession to his own throne, for Queen Elizabeth had died on 11 February 1503, nine days after being delivered of a daughter. The queen was thirty-seven years old and had given birth to seven children in just under fifteen years: her child was named Catherine but she lived only a few days. Henry was distraught, for he had come to love his wife deeply. And of course he was deeply worried about the succession to his throne for he now only had three children – Margaret (born 1489); Henry (1491) and Mary (1492) – and although the girls could succeed to the throne, in practice the endurance of the dynasty depended on the life of Prince Henry.

As he slowly recovered his health, Henry VII decided that he needed to marry to produce at least one more son to secure the succession. At forty-five years of age he was – he was convinced – an attractive match. No doubt, too, he was anxious to secure a rich dowry. Since Henry's fellow monarchs seem to have been as convinced of his desirability as a spouse as he was himself, offers flooded in for his hand: Philip of Burgundy proposed that Henry should marry his sister Margaret, Dowager Duchess of Savoy; Louis XII put forward his cousin, Margaret of Angoulême, be it for Henry himself or for his heir; and Ferdinand enticed him with his niece (and widow of Ferdinand II of Naples), Juana, Queen of Naples. None of the marriages came about, for each of the three ladies refused even to contemplate marrying the ageing King of England: none of them shared his own generous assessment of his desirability. In his desperation, Henry even allowed it to be known in England that he was prepared to marry Katharine.

Isabella was incandescent. It may have been as a furious response to Henry's suggestion that she now took charge of the negotiations for Katharine's remarriage. On 11 April 1503 she wrote to her two ambassadors in England, and again the letters were intriguingly different in style and substance.

Isabella reminded González de Puebla that she had trusted him to make agreements that would be binding on Henry VII because he was a lawyer: she was deeply angry to learn that Henry did not regard himself as being obliged either to return Katharine to her or refund the downpayment on the dowry. Isabella professed herself 'unable to believe' that the ambassador had allowed a situation to arise in which she and her daughter were humiliated and told the ambassador in the bluntest terms that unless these matters were remedied she would hold him personally responsible: Katharine was to be returned to her without delay and González de Puebla clearly understood that he could remain in England only in order to accomplish this but that if he was unable to do so he was to return to Spain and face the queen's wrath.[20]

While Isabella terrified González de Puebla, she entrusted Duque de Estrada with her principal business. He was to convey to Henry both her condolences on the death of Elizabeth and her rage for what she took as the indecent suggestion that he might marry Katharine: 'This would be something that is very grave and never seen, that merely to have spoken of it is offensive to the ears and we will not agree to it for anything in the world.'[21] Isabella instructed Duque de Estrada that the death of the Queen Mother (who had acted as a mother to Katharine) and the shameful conduct of the king obliged her to insist on the return of her daughter to her, at least during the minority of Prince Henry. However, this state of affairs would alter if the new marriage was promptly agreed:

How more it will be necessary that she be returned if her marriage to the Prince of Wales is not concluded at once. For this reason the king, my lord, and myself have agreed that the said princess, our daughter, is to leave at once for here, with the guide and help of Our Lord. But before she leaves you are to endeavour by all means and manners that you can devise to conclude and formalise the said marriage of the Princess of Wales with the Prince of Wales...[22]

It certainly appears to us to be a very serious and strange matter that we have conducted ourselves [in our dealings] with the King of England with such love and openness ... and with such a good desire to preserve and extend the relationship and friendship between ourselves and himself and his successors that he should now conduct negotiations in the manner that he does. [His conduct] is not what is ought to be, nor is it appropriate between such princes, nor should our honour and that of the Princess of Wales our daughter endure that he should make use of such devices in these negotiations. And certainly, if it happened that a princess who was a daughter of the

King of England found herself in our realms in similar circumstances
... we would protect her honour more than we would our own.[23]

Because of the love that we have for the King of England and
[his] kingdom we gave the Princess of Wales [to him] with a very
good heart so that she should marry the Prince of Wales, and God
having taken [the prince] to him before they consummated the
marriage, we have seen from letters [from England] that the King of
England wishes that the said princess should marry the new Prince
of Wales. We have wished that on both our parts we could cleanse
and overcome the loss [of Prince Arthur] and that with this renewal
[of our relationship] the love and friendship between the two royal
houses and their subjects should be increased...[24]

Isabella insisted that Katharine's dowry for a marriage to Prince Henry
would remain the same as it had been for her first marriage and that the
second instalment would only be paid 'when the Prince of Wales and the
princess have celebrated and consummated the marriage'.[25] She would
allow Katharine to remain in England if Henry VII agreed promptly to her
conditions for the remarriage but if not she was to be returned to Spain
immediately, without even waiting for the return of the 100,000 escudos.
Isabella could hardly contemplate the possibility that Henry would keep
Katharine's jewels, plate and money for himself: 'it would be the most
inhuman and dishonest thing and the most contrary to virtue that has
ever been seen or heard of'.[26] She offered a commercial inducement,
suggesting that if an agreement was promptly reached she would allow
English merchants to use Castilian ports as if they were their own. As for
Henry's remarriage, she and Ferdinand judged that the Dowager Queen
of Naples would be an appropriate bride and offered to use their good
offices to advance his suit. But Doña Elvira was to prepare Katharine's
goods for her return and Duque de Estrada was to arrange for her to sail
home in a fleet of merchant ships that would shortly be leaving the Low
Countries for Spain.

Isabella's blunt diplomacy cut through all the difficulties, and Duque
de Estrada's negotiations with a trio of English commissioners – William
Warham, Bishop of London and Keeper of the Great Seal; Richard Foxe,
Bishop of Winchester, Keeper of the Privy Seal, and Dr William Barons,
Master of the Rolls – promptly resolved the outstanding difficulties. At
Richmond Palace on 23 June 1503 the treaty was signed for the marriage
of Prince Henry with Katharine. Two days later the marriage was

formally celebrated by proxy at the Bishop of Salisbury's palace in Fleet Street: it would take place on 28 June 1505 when Prince Henry reached his fourteenth birthday.[27]

Both crowns now undertook to use all their influence to secure a dispensation from Pope Alexander to allow the marriage expressly on the grounds that the princess had consummated her marriage with Arthur. Once the treaty had been ratified the marriage would take place within two months *per verba de praesenti* and would then be celebrated as soon as Prince Henry reached his fifteenth year in 1505. Henry's negotiators stipulated that it was also a precondition of the marriage that Ferdinand and Isabella could demonstrate that the whole of the marriage portion was in London, ready for delivery to him. Ferdinand and Isabella renounced the right to reclaim the down-payment of 100,000 escudos and would provide a marriage portion of 200,000 escudos (at 4s 2d) when the marriage was agreed; since Henry had already received 100,000 escudos they would only pay the same amount as the second instalment. Two-thirds of this (65,000 escudos) was to be paid in coined gold; 15,000 in plate and vessels of silver and gold and 20,000 escudos were to take the form of Katharine's jewels, pearls and ornaments; in each case, the valuation was to be made in London. Katharine was to return all the titles to the rents and revenues that Arthur had settled upon her in Wales, Cornwall and Chester and on the day of the wedding Henry would provide her with a new dowry which would be at least as great as Arthur's had been. If Katharine became Queen of England she was to enjoy a second dowry, which would consist of one-third of the revenues of the Crown of England. She would hold both dowries for life. If Prince Henry died before his father and left a son or sons born to Katharine, Henry VII would promise to make the first of these sons the Prince of Wales and to secure the succession to the Crown of England for him. The treaty was to be ratified within six months.

The Quest for a Papal Dispensation, 28 August 1503

When Louis XII mustered an army on the Catalan border in the summer of 1503 Ferdinand rode to Barcelona to take charge of the defences, and it may well have been for this reason that it was not until 23 August – two months after the agreement had been signed at Richmond – that he issued his instructions to Francisco de Rojas, Ambassador in Rome to seek a dispensation from Alexander VI for Katharine's marriage to Prince Henry.

Ferdinand instructed Rojas to impress upon the Pope that although Katharine remained a virgin he was obliged *for political reasons within England* to request a dispensation which stated that her marriage with Arthur had been consummated. At the core of Ferdinand's request lay a legal difficulty: one of the clauses in his treaty with Henry VII had expressly stated that Katharine and Arthur had enjoyed full sexual relations and although it was now recognised that this was mistaken the affirmation that the marriage had been consummated had potentially the most profound implications for the English royal family. In fine, English lawyers had raised the possibility that at some time in the future doubts could be raised retrospectively about the legitimacy of any children born to Henry and Katharine *if they married without a papal dispensation which specifically absolved her from the diriment impediment that would have arisen from her having consummated her marriage to Arthur*. So, although Arthur and Katharine had not consummated their marriage, the Pope was to be asked to absolve them from having done precisely this so that at some future date the legitimacy of any children born to Henry and Katharine could not be questioned:

> And although in the said clause it says that the marriage of the said princess our daughter with Arthur, Prince of Wales (who is now dead – and may he be in Glory) was consummated the truth is that it was not consummated and that the said princess our daughter remains as intact as she was before she married.
>
> However, the lawyers in England have decided that because people in England might have scruples and doubts about the matter, that although it is true that the said princess, our daughter, remains a virgin and although she was married to Prince Arthur they did not consummate the marriage and so, in order to dispel all doubts in the future about the right of succession of any children who – God being pleased – should be born of this marriage that has now been agreed it may be said in the dispensation that they consummated the marriage and so His Holiness is issuing a dispensation in accordance with the clause of the treaty so that this second marriage can be made.

Ferdinand recognised that even Alexander VI would take pause when confronted with such a request and so he instructed Rojas to impress upon him that the alliance between England and Spain was very much designed to be in his own interests: 'We are certain that the union between ourselves and the King of England, our brother, will always appear very advantageous to his Holiness for the good that can be expected to devolve from it for Christianity, for His Holiness and for the Apostolic See, for it is principally in the favour of the Apostolic See...'[28]

It was too late: Alexander VI had died on 18 August, five days before Ferdinand wrote his letter.

The 'Terrifying Pope': Julius II (1503–13)

Alexander was succeeded by Francesco Piccolomini, who took the name of Pius III but lived for only twenty-six days as pontiff. He was replaced by Giuliano della Rovere, who became Julius II. The new Pope had risen to prominence under his uncle, Sixtus IV (1471–84), who created him a cardinal at the age of twenty-eight (1471) and then raised him to the Archbishopric of Avignon in 1474; he retained the position until he was elected Pope, together with eight other bishoprics, the most important of them being that of Bologna (1483–1502).[29] Della Rovere was a bitter enemy of Rodrigo Borgia and fled to France when Borgia was elected as Alexander VI in 1493. He returned to Italy with the army of Charles VIII and when the invasion failed he returned to France, staying there in safety until Alexander VI's death.

Della Rovere had been a candidate at every conclave since 1484 and – knowing how papal elections worked – he now energetically scattered concessions, bribes and threats among the cardinals in Rome: he would continue the war against the Turk, convene a General Council of the Church within two years and refuse to commit the Holy See to any war without the approval of two-thirds of the cardinals. So successful was he that the conclave which elected him proved to be the shortest in recorded papal history, lasting only for a few hours (31 October 1503).[30] The new Pope promptly forgot every promise that he had made to secure his election.

Della Rovere's character was marked by extraordinary and unyielding physical energy and ambition. It did not take him long to earn the sobriquet 'the terrifying Pope'. Julius II was, above all else, a soldier who was determined to regain control of the lands of the Papal States. He had at least three children – all of them daughters – but simony was not his abiding sin and he never advanced his family as Alexander VI had done. Rather, he used the great wealth that he amassed to become one of the greatest patrons of art in history: we owe – among other great works

– Michelangelo's ceiling of the Sistine Chapel to Julius II's generous (but unremittingly demanding) patronage.

It was into Julius's robust hands that the fate of the proposed marriage of Prince Henry of England and Katharine fell. But if Julius could not be bribed (as Alexander VI could be) he was not a man to be hurried and it soon became evident that the marital situation of the heir to the English throne was low on his priorities. It was as an expression of this that when Julius and his advisers cobbled up a dispensation which seemed to suit all the various purposes demanded of it the document was distinguished by the sloppiness with which it was structured and the lack of precision of the canonical language in which it was phrased. So important was the production of the document that no one noticed – or indeed, even seemed to care – how inadequate it was. The consequences would be truly monumental. For all the major parties concerned – Ferdinand and Isabella, Henry VII, Julius II – the papal bull was designed to facilitate an essentially political act. The lesser parties – Prince Henry and Princess Katharine – would have to live with the consequences.

Ferdinand wrote to Henry VII from Barcelona on 24 September 1503 ratifying the Treaty of Richmond but within hours of doing so learned that the French had taken the fortress of Salces, and so he immediately penned another letter to Henry requiring that he provide him with the military support that the treaty demanded of him.[31] Isabella added her authority, writing on 3 October to Duque de Estrada that he urge Henry to meet his treaty obligations and send her 2,000 high-quality infantry to defend the frontier. So desperate was the queen for these reinforcements that she gave permission for Henry to avail himself of Katharine's jewels as surety for them.[32]

While Ferdinand and Isabella hoped – unavailingly as it turned out – for help from England their own 'Great Captain' began to secure Naples for them. The division of Naples between France and Aragon that had been agreed in 1501 was destined to be a short-lived compromise and war duly broke out in the spring of 1502. Within a year, Gonzalo Fernández de Córdoba began a historic campaign; his victories at the Battles of Cerignola (28 April 1503) and Garigliano (6 October–7 November 1503) secured control of the Kingdom of Naples for Spain, and when on 1 January 1504 Gaeta became the last French stronghold to surrender to him the conquest of Naples was complete. The triumph of 'the Great Captain' proved to be of enduring importance in European affairs, for Naples remained a Spanish possession for 200 years.[33] It also made Ferdinand of Aragon once again into a major figure in European politics. He returned to join Isabella in Medina del Campo for the last stages of her long, slow death.

Isabella allowed Juana to leave for the Low Countries in March 1504, in all probability because she wanted her daughter out of Castile when she herself died. Philip was horrified by Juana's condition and considered having her locked up for her own protection.[34] But when he tried to persuade Juana to sign a document granting all her powers in Castile to him she refused to do so: Juana was broken but – as always – she would not betray her parents, not even at the insistence of her adored husband.[35]

The Papal Dispensation, 23 December 1503

Julius II issued his much-delayed dispensation on 23 December 1503.[36] But he did so not in writing but in an oral statement: it would take him a further six months or so to get around to producing a written version. Ferdinand and Isabella – but not Henry VII – knew what the Pope had done: on 26 June 1504 they wrote to Duque de Estrada that Julius had granted the dispensation verbally but that he was waiting for the arrival of an ambassador from Henry VII before issuing it in writing.[37] Most certainly, Pope Julius was a man to do things in his own time.

At the turn of July–August 1504 Duque de Estrada went to pay his respects to Henry prior to departing for home at the end of his mission. The king was profoundly alarmed, suspecting that the ambassador's departure was an indication that the dispensation would not be arriving and insisted that he remain in England until it did so. With the greatest reluctance, Duque de Estrada agreed to stay until the end of August.

On 10 August 1504 Duque de Estrada was writing a lengthy letter to Isabella when the papal dispensation arrived; he seems to have carried on with his letter as he absorbed the implications of the document on his desk. Duque de Estrada's letter was updating Isabella on the care that Henry VII was taking of both Katharine and Prince Henry. Katharine had been unwell and Henry VII had taken her to Richmond and on to Windsor, where they had spent nearly a fortnight hunting. They then returned to Richmond for a week and the king made a brief visit to Westminster before going on to Greenwich. The ambassador reported that Katharine's health had worsened recently; she had lost her appetite and her complexion had dramatically worsened. Her doctors had twice bled her but when this proved unsuccessful they then administered an enema to purge her. Notwithstanding the evidence to the contrary, the physicians pronounced themselves confident that Katharine would recover completely. Certainly, Henry VII was sufficiently worried to keep her close to him. At the same time – intriguingly – the king was evidently growing much closer to his last son and took him with him when he left court, presumably to spend time hunting:

> He has taken the prince with him for this journey, something that he has not done in recent years because [the prince] was studying. I believe that he does so in order to enjoy his company, and this seems to be a marvellous thing because, not only does the prince deserve this but there is probably no better school in the world that would be of so much profit to him as to travel with his father, who is so wise and so diligent in everything; nothing escapes him. Certainly, the prince has in [his father] such a good teacher and steward that if [the king] lives for another ten years the prince will be left so well educated and so richly provided for as any man in the world could be.

Duque de Estrada was puzzling on these accounts of Henry VII's loving care of Katharine and Prince Henry when he recorded – almost absent-mindedly – that the papal dispensation had arrived: 'On leaving Greenwich ... the papal brief arrived and on the same day it was sent on to me so that it could be shown to the Lady Princess.' What had in fact arrived seems to have been a summary made in Spain of the document sent by Julius II to Isabella: Duque de Estrada was most certainly not entrusted with possession of the original document.[38]

Henry VII was delighted to learn of the arrival of the dispensation and – no doubt to the horror of the ambassador – let it be known that he would publish the document to all the 'principal persons' of the kingdom on 1 November. On 24 November 1504 – the day of Queen Isabella's death – Ferdinand sent a copy of the dispensation to Henry VII.[39] When, a few months later, the Vatican learned that a copy of the bull had been sent from Spain to England it was deeply grieved because Julius II had expressly sent it to Isabella under vow of secrecy to comfort her in her last agony.[40]

The preamble of the dispensation noted that the marriage of Arthur and Katharine had 'probably' been consummated (*'forsan consummatum'*).[41] It then dispensed them from the diriment impediment of affinity. This ruling gave the monarchs of England and Castile the authorisation they required to carry through the marriage of Henry and Katharine, but it was – as time was to make only too clear – grotesquely defective. In his definitive discussion of the dispensation, Professor Scarisbrick pointed out that the dispensation freed the young couple from the impediment of affinity *if the marriage of Arthur and Katharine had been consummated* and in doing so it released them – but only implicitly – from the impediment of 'public honesty' created by Katharine's betrothal, marriage and public bedding with Arthur. However, if Katharine's marriage with Arthur had not been consummated – as Katharine was always to insist – then no question of affinity arose between Henry and Katharine and between their separate families. In this eventuality, the Pope should have *explicitly* dispensed them from the impediment of public honesty. He failed to do so, perhaps because of the pressure under which the new marriage was being pushed through, more probably for the simple reason that no one advised him to do so: perhaps Julius II was so preoccupied with what he regarded as more important business that he simply was not bothered to have his experts in canon law think the process through. In terms of Roman Catholic canon law, the wedding of Henry and Katharine proved to be a shotgun marriage, organised hurriedly and dispensed with only after unimaginable agony. Professor Scarisbrick suggested that since Julius's bull had not explicitly dispensed with the impediment of public honesty, Katharine's second marriage was not valid: in this (as in so much else) he was perfectly correct.[42] In 1504 none of the parties gave a thought to this possibility: they had all got what they needed and – like Pope Julius – moved on to more important matters. And on 26 November 1504 Queen Isabella died, and everything changed.

8

1504–1509: THE END OF THE ANGLO-SPANISH ALLIANCE?

The Death of Queen Isabella & the Collapse of Anglo-Spanish Amity
It is not known if Julius's flawed bull was seen by Isabella, much less whether she derived any comfort from it, for she died on 26 November 1504 in Medina del Campo. Isabella had modified her will on 23 November with a codicil in which she named Juana as her heiress in Castile but effectively made it a condition that Ferdinand should serve as Governor for her at least until Juana's eldest son reached twenty years of age; if Charles lived, that would be in 1520. The clause was intended both to facilitate Ferdinand's control over Juana and Castile and to place Philip in a painful dilemma, for if he acknowledged that his wife was incapacitated he had to recognise that by Isabella's testament it was Ferdinand who was to govern Castile and not him.[1]

Isabella was widely mourned: Montigny described her death as 'a loss to all Christendom', and recalled, as so many did, that Isabella had been a monarch of extraordinary ability who had been obeyed throughout her realm.[2] Bernáldez agreed:

> During the time of their marriage the king and herself were very much feared, obeyed and served, both by the grandees of their kingdoms as by the people of royal and seigneurial lands. Accordingly, they held all their realms and lordships throughout this time in peace, concord and justice: bands of thieves were crushed, the roads were secured, gaming boards were confiscated, ruffians were whipped and exiled

and thieves were executed with arrows. The poorest received justice as did the gentlemen, and they were protected.[3]

The death of the great queen led to twenty years of uncertainty and growing turbulence in Castile which threatened to undo all her work in re-establishing and consolidating the authority of the Crown. Katharine was the first victim of the changed situation. Because Castile was likely to pass out of the control of her family her marriage to Prince Henry might no longer bring significant advantage to England: there would surely be a much better marriage to be made now for the Prince of Wales.[4] Indeed, Henry VII had to restructure the whole of his foreign policy now that his two allies against France – Spain and Burgundy – were being driven apart by the crisis in Spain. Since Henry recognised that Philip would in all probability become the de facto ruler of Castile, he determined to ally with him while he also took the precaution of moving closer to France, fearful that Louis XII would now become the dominant player in Europe. Certainly, Henry found that the mutual detestation that he and Philip shared for the King of Aragon greatly facilitated the negotiations for an alliance. As for Katharine herself: she was increasingly treated with indifference and harshness by her father-in-law while she was virtually ignored by her father, who seemed to be so preoccupied with his problems in Spain and Italy as to pay no heed to her predicament. Indeed, it often seemed (not least to Katharine herself) that Ferdinand had forgotten about her.

Within hours of Isabella's death, Ferdinand had Juana proclaimed as Queen of Castile and summoned the Cortes of Castile so that she could receive the oaths of loyalty of her subjects and he himself be named as Governor of the kingdom in her stead. The Cortes met in Toro (January–February 1505) and duly recognised Juana as Queen of Castile and Ferdinand as the 'legitimate guardian, administrator and governor' of the kingdom because her mental condition made it impossible for her to rule.[5] The Cortes sent *procuradores* to Brussels to inform Juana that they had taken these decisions and to remind Philip that if his wife proved incapable of ruling her rights passed not to him but to her father. Ferdinand also despatched Lope de Conchillos, one of his Principal Secretaries, with a document for Juana to sign in which she accepted the provisions of the Cortes of Toro. Juana signed the paper but when Philip learned what she had done he confiscated Conchillos's dossier and had him imprisoned and tortured; the unfortunate secretary gave up all the details of Ferdinand's plans.[6]

Juana's mental condition fascinated contemporaries and has continued to exercise historians. She had been an intelligent and alert child, talented in the performing arts, but it may be that she had suffered from a depressive illness even before she had married Philip of Burgundy in 1496. Joseph Pérez has suggested that she had inherited such an illness from her maternal grandmother, Isabella of Portugal, which deprived her of the will or energy to govern in her own right and increasingly focussed her vision on her obsession with earning the love of her husband.[7] Certainly, Philip's treatment of her was dismissive and cruel, almost from the beginning of their marriage and it worsened progressively over the years: he was embarrassed by her increasingly neurotic devotion to him and would have locked her up as a madwoman by about 1503–04 had it not been for her claim on the Crown of Castile.[8]

Philip was advised on Castilian affairs by Don Juan Manuel, the brother of Elvira Manrique. Don Juan was a born conspirator and his intrigues came to have serious consequences for Katharine. He encouraged Philip to cultivate senior Castilian noblemen and churchmen, recognising that the deep resentment of many members of the Castilian elite to the confiscations that they had suffered under Isabella was compounded by their hostility to Ferdinand as a foreigner. Philip followed the advice and sent Chièvres to Spain to rally support among the nobility. He also carried with him a letter signed by Juana on 8 May 1505 in which she denied that she had lost her reason but made it tacitly evident that she would entrust the government of Castile to Philip: the Castilian elite were to be obliged to choose between Philip and Ferdinand.[9] As news trickled through to Ferdinand of what was happening in Brussels he finally realised how badly – and how consistently – Manuel had deceived him and he understood, too, that Doña Elvira was closely involved in London in his duplicity; by June 1505 Ferdinand was warning Henry VII against confiding in Elvira.[10]

Philip mounted a sumptuous funerary service for Isabella and promptly announced that he and Juana had formally assumed the title of King and Queen of Castile.[11] He also declared that on arriving in Spain Juana would proclaim that the Cortes of Toro had been unlawful and summon a new body to confirm his right to rule in her name. Unfortunately, Philip was unable to leave at once for Castile because he was involved in a war with the Duke of Guelders and because Juana was pregnant: the way was cleared for his departure by a truce with Guelders in the summer and when Juana gave birth to Maria (the future Queen of Hungary) on 18

September Philip could at last make plans to travel to Castile to claim the throne.[12]

As Isabella lay dying, Louis XII and the leaders of the House of Habsburg – Maximilian and Philip – came together in an alliance that was designed to secure substantial advantages for each of them – the Crown of Castile for Philip; the Duchy of Milan for Louis XII; and a fortune of 100,000 crowns for Maximilian. In the autumn of 1504 the three men signed a series of agreements which became known – not altogether correctly – as the 'First Treaty of Blois' (22 September 1504). Maximilian agreed to invest Louis XII with the Duchy of Milan in return for a grant of 100,000 crowns and the return of the Duchy of Burgundy to Philip. Maximilian and Louis undertook to support Philip's right to rule in Castile in his wife's name. The alliance was to be sealed by the marriage of the Archduke Charles to Claudia of Angoulême: the Kingdom of Naples would form the dowry. Ferdinand was confronted with a triple alliance determined to destroy his power in Spain and Italy. This made his need of the English alliance greater than ever.[13]

Katharine, 1504–05

Katharine's grief at her mother's death must have compounded every insecurity and fear that confronted her in her widowhood. She was in poor health and could still only speak English stutteringly. Moreover, Henry VII's kindness towards her evaporated with Isabella's death and with Ferdinand's resolute refusal to settle her dowry. Katharine became increasingly despondent at Henry's hostility and at her own penury: in March 1505 she had González de Puebla inform Ferdinand that she had sold or pawned some of her possessions to buy food for herself and her household and she had the ambassador urge her father 'on pain of his honour' not to abandon her.[14] Apparently she continued to sell property; in the autumn, González de Puebla reported to Ferdinand that at least five pieces of silver were missing.[15] Ferdinand was indifferent to the news, and did no more than encourage his daughter to rely upon the generosity of Henry VII.[16]

Infuriated by Ferdinand's intransigence over the dowry, Henry had his son register on 27 June 1505 a formal protest in front of Bishop Foxe against his proposed marriage to his brother's widow. The date was carefully chosen: it was the day before the prince's fourteenth birthday – the day on which, according to the treaty of June 1503, his marriage to Katharine should have been solemnised. Henry VII also let it be known that he was thinking of having Prince Henry engaged to marry Margaret of Angoulême.[17]

Being caught in the middle of the conflict between the two unyielding kings was torment enough for Katharine but she had further cause for anxiety with the growing instability in her own household; to her hatred of González de Puebla she added in the autumn of 1505 a complete loss of confidence in Elvira Manrique. The crisis was probably initiated by Katharine's sale of some of property: González de Puebla informed Ferdinand and Isabella that Katharine's generosity needed to be circumscribed and that Elvira was the person to do this.[18] Henry was aware of the growing tensions within Katharine's household and on 27 August wrote to the princess expressing his displeasure that her servants seemed unable to live at peace with each other, bluntly refusing her request to intercede on her behalf.[19]

The crux of the problem lay in the treachery of Doña Elvira, who was persistently encouraging Katharine to facilitate a meeting between Henry VII and Philip of Burgundy; Elvira even arranged for letters to be sent to Katharine from Juana and Philip in which they emphasised how eager they were to meet Henry VII. Naively, Katharine was only too receptive to these blandishments for such a meeting held out the delectable prospect that she would see her beloved sister Juana again.[20] She therefore informed González de Puebla that she intended to write to Henry VII to encourage him to arrange the interview. The ambassador was appalled and sought to defuse the situation by offering to personally give Katharine's letter to Henry VII; Katharine doubted that he would do this and resolutely refused to hand the letter over to him. Desperate, González de Puebla then confronted Elvira Manuel and let her know that he was aware of the treachery of her brother and herself. But Elvira did not buckle; González de Puebla returned to his lodgings but had barely sat down to dinner when he learned that Elvira had herself forwarded Katharine's letter to Henry. He rushed to Katharine and, swearing her to secrecy, explained that the proposed interview with Henry was being engineered by the Manuels to damage the interests of her father by forging an alliance between England and Burgundy against Spain. Horrified, Katharine agreed to write another letter and the ambassador sent it to Henry VII with a messenger whom he ordered to ride so hard at to overtake Elvira's courier.[21] For Elvira, it was the end: when Ferdinand heard of what she had done he had her leave England, ostensibly so that she could go to the Low Countries to undergo an eye operation. She never returned.

Worn out, Katharine sank into deep despair and sought consolation in a rigorous programme of fasting and prayer. Her health suffered so badly that those close to her became deeply alarmed and they evidently ensured that their anxieties reached the very highest levels for in October 1505 no less a figure than Pope Julius II wrote to Prince Henry urging him to restrict the severity of Katharine's new religious practices lest they damage her health – and (by implication, no doubt) her fertility.[22]

In her desperation, on 11 December 1505, Katharine wrote to her father. It was probably not coincidence that after the departure of Doña Elvira Henry had negotiated a deal with González de Puebla whereby the princess would be moved into one of his own houses, almost certainly Durham House. This meant that Katharine and her servants would be better-fed but also that she had lost control over her own household; she bitterly resented this and naturally vented her spleen on the ambassador, whom she blamed for all her troubles. Having done so, she then wrote a postscript in which she rebuked her father for his parsimony in not ensuring that Henry VII was properly paid what was owing to him:

Most high and most powerful lord,

Until now I have not wished to let your Highness know how bad things are here so as not to anger you, and also in the hope that they would improve. But it is rather to the contrary and my troubles multiply every day. This is all because of Dr [González de] Puebla, who has not only been guilty of a thousand lies and untruths against the service of your Highness but who has now caused me new pain. In the hope that your Highness will not think that I am complaining without reason I wish to tell you about everything that has gone on.

Your Highness already knows how many times I have written to him that since I came to England I have not received a single *maravedí* other than for food and it was because of this that I have run up many debts in London. What is even more painful to me is to see my servants and ladies-in-waiting suffering and not being able to dress themselves [decently]. All this has been because of the actions of the Doctor, who despite the orders given him by your Highness to negotiate on my behalf with the King of England, my lord, to provide for my needs has not troubled to do so for fear of angering him. He has neglected the service of your Highness.

Now, in addition, a few days ago, Doña Elvira Manrique asked my permission to go to Flanders for an operation on an eye condition;

145

she has lost the use of one eye and there is a doctor in Flanders who cured Princess Isabella of the same disease with which she is affected. She tried to have him brought here so that she would not have to leave me but was unable to do so. Since she would not be able to serve me if she became blind I have not opposed her departure. I begged the King of England, my lord, either to give me an elderly English noblewoman as a companion until Doña Elvira returned or to take me into his own court. I charged the Doctor to see to this, thinking to make an honest man of the scoundrel, but the best he could do was merely to have me brought to court. This pleased me because it was something that I had already asked the king to agree to but [the doctor] negotiated an agreement whereby I would dismiss my own household and lose the furniture of my chamber and then have to live in one of the king's houses in which I could not exercise authority myself. This weighed heavily on me, not only for my own sake but because it is against the service of your Highness: it is the very opposite of what should be.

I beg your Highness to remember that I am your daughter and to see to it that I should not suffer such pain because of the doctor. Rather, that you will send another ambassador here who will be a real servant of your Highness and who will under no circumstances fail to pursue your Highness's service. And if your Highness does not believe me, send another ambassador here who will inform him of the true state of affairs and then [your Highness] can take the appropriate actions...

As for myself, I have suffered so much pain and discomfort that I have largely lost my good health; for two months I have suffered from severe tertian fevers and this is the reason why I have improved so little.

I beg your Highness to forgive me for presuming to ask your Highness for such a great favour as that this doctor should not stay here because he certainly does not fulfil the service of your Highness...

May our Lord guard the life and royal estate of your Highness and ever increase it as I wish.

From Richmond, 11 December.

My lord, I had forgotten to remind your Highness that it was agreed that your Highness was to give the plate and jewels that I brought with me to England as part of my dowry. I am certain that since I have already used these the King of England will not accept any of the plate or jewels. Indeed, he himself told me that he was indignant that it should be said of him in his own kingdom that he might take my ornaments from me. Nor should your Highness expect that he will calculate their value and return them to me because I am convinced that he will not do this, not least because such a thing is not the custom here. Similarly, the king would not value the jewels that I brought here at half of their true worth because here things are valued at much lower rates. In any event, the king has so many jewels that he values money rather than jewels. I presume to write this to your Highness because I know that there will be great embarrassment caused for your Highness if the king refused to accept the jewels, except at a much lower price. It seems to me that it would be better if your Highness kept [the plate and jewels] for yourself and gave money to the King of England.

Your Highness will see what is best to your service, and with this I will be most content.

The humble servant of your highness, who kisses your hands.[23]

A fortnight later Katharine again urged her father to replace González de Puebla, whom she described as a lying incompetent. Wistfully, she noted that her marriage to the Prince of Wales would secure the peace of Christendom.[24]

Ferdinand's central preoccupation in 1505–06, however, lay not in the north of Europe but in the south, with maintaining his control over Naples. The alliance of Louis XII, Maximilian and Philip in the 'First Treaty of Blois' drove Ferdinand to return to his invariable practice when threatened by a King of France – to make an alliance with him. On 12 October 1505 Ferdinand's agents signed the 'Second Treaty of Blois', by which Louis XII formally renounced his claim on the throne of Naples on condition that Ferdinand paid him 1 million ducats in ten years and married his eighteen-year-old niece, Germaine de Foix. Any child born of the marriage would inherit the Kingdom of Naples (notwithstanding Louis XII's commitment of 1504 to having a child born of the projected marriage of Charles of Habsburg and Margaret of Angoulême succeed to the throne). Ferdinand agreed to help Louis XII against all his enemies, including Philip of Burgundy, and the marriage with Germaine took place *per verba de praesenti* in Dueñas (where Ferdinand had stayed on the nights before his marriage to Isabella) one week later and was consummated in July 1506.

There were, of course, never any certainties involved when Ferdinand of Aragon signed an agreement but the two treaties of Blois in 1504–05 did make it probable that Italy was now to be divided between a French north (Milan) and an Aragonese south (Naples and Sicily). Luis Suárez, a distinguished historian of Ferdinand's foreign policy, described the Second Treaty of Blois as his 'masterwork', and so it was for it confirmed that Naples was now legally and completely the possession of the Crown of Aragon and that it was recognised as such by the Crown of France.[25] Exactly as Castile seemed about to slip irrevocably away from him, Ferdinand secured the power and authority of the Crown of Aragon over 'the two Sicilies' and began to separate Philip of Burgundy from Louis XII: it was a dazzling tour de force.

Magisterial though Ferdinand's duplicity was, there is some evidence that he was – for the only time in his life? – ashamed of one of his own actions, for he secretly disavowed his new marriage, swearing in front of three notaries that he had only agreed to marry Germaine because of the need to secure control of the Kingdom of Naples. He stipulated that when he died the kingdom was to revert to whoever succeeded him on the thrones of Aragon and not to Germaine and her descendants or family: Naples would remain Aragonese. Once again, 'the Fox of Aragon' reneged on a solemn treaty obligation before the ink was dry on the paper.

Many nobles in Castile judged that Ferdinand's remarriage was a betrayal of Isabella's memory and accordingly found it easier to accommodate themselves to Juana and to Philip: at the turn of 1505–06 leading figures began to abandon Ferdinand and turn to Philip for their futures. Certainly, the archduke appreciated that he needed to hurry to Castile and announced that he would travel by sea and meet with Henry VIII en route. Henry had already lent Philip £108,000 in April 1505 and now and in September added a further £30,000 to help fund his journey to Spain.[26]

Once again, Ferdinand sought to protect himself by making a treaty with an avowed enemy. Recognising that Juana and Philip would shortly claim the throne of Castile and that Philip would exercise de facto sovereignty, he agreed to recognise their sovereignty in return for confirmation of his position as Governor of the kingdom (Treaty of Salamanca, 24 November 1505). Although, therefore, Ferdinand retained the title of Governor he had effectively abandoned Castile to Juana and Philip. This had serious implications for Katharine in England, re-emphasising to Henry VII – if he needed it – that there was little point in marrying his heir to Katharine. The three principals now prepared for urgent journeys – Philip and Juana would travel to Castile to claim their throne, while Ferdinand would leave – abandon? – Spain to consolidate his authority in Naples.

Bouleversement: The Enforced Stay of Juana & Philip in England (16 January–22 April 1506) & the Death of Philip (25 September 1506)

Philip was so desperate to reach Castile that he took the foolhardy risk of sailing in midwinter.[27] Indeed, the foul weather that repeatedly delayed his departure should have forewarned him but on 7 January 1506 he and Juana sailed from the Low Countries in a grand fleet of thirty-six to forty ships, accompanied by over 2,000 people. Almost inevitably, they ran into a violent storm at the entrance to the Bay of Biscay; it blew for thirty-six hours and scattered the convoy. Philip was among those who in their terror vowed that if they were saved they would go on pilgrimage to Santiago de Compostela or to Guadalupe: Juana prayed only that she might die with her husband. Many ships were lost (including the one carrying the royal treasure) but over half of the fleet made safety in the harbours of Cornwall and Dorset. The royal galleon reached Melcombe Regis on 16 January: relieved, Philip sent a messenger to Henry VII to inform him of his arrival and of his intention to visit him. He would not travel Biscay again in the winter.

Henry could hardly believe his good fortune and on 30 January despatched his son to Winchester to greet his guests and escort them to Windsor. He entertained Philip and his entourage with unstinting generosity for a month (31 January–2 March). On 9 February, Henry VII conferred the Order of the Garter upon Philip, reciprocating his own investiture into the Order of the Golden Fleece in 1491. Henry secured from Philip the promise that he would hand the Earl of Suffolk over to him on guarantee of his life and in return agreed to recognise Philip as King of Castile and to support him in his efforts to win the throne. The two rulers also settled the commercial disputes which had dislocated the cloth trade between their territories on terms that were very favourable to English merchants. The treaty replaced the *Intercursus Magnus* of 1496 and so was much resented by merchants and traders in the Low Countries that they dubbed it the *Intercursus Malus*. Henry was so gratified by the deals that he had struck that he agreed to lend Philip yet more money: by 1509 the Duchy of Burgundy would owe Henry more than one-third of a million pounds.[28]

It was as a sign of Henry's deep contentment that he and Philip signed their treaty while seated in chivalric splendour in their stalls of the Order of the Garter. Montigny, who was an expert on courtly entertainments, believed that the pageantry in the ceremony was of a lavishness such as had not been seen in a royal household for a century.[29] Detailed discussions for a marriage between Henry VII and Margaret of Savoy broke down over Margaret's steadfast refusal to countenance the proposal.[30] Undismayed, Philip opened negotiations with Henry to marry his daughter, Mary, to Philip's son, Prince Charles. Henry VII's commitment to this marriage was intriguing. Certainly, Charles was a great catch; he would in all probability inherit the throne of Castile when the unfitness of his mother to rule was legally recognised and it was still possible – if at this stage unlikely – that an arrangement might be made whereby he would inherit the thrones of the Crown of Aragon. Most certainly, he could expect (in the distant future) to succeed to the imperial title, which was currently held by his grandfather Maximilian and would surely pass on his death to Philip and subsequently to Charles himself. If Charles and Mary had a son it was possible, therefore, that a grandson of Henry VII would himself become Holy Roman Emperor. Certainly, in the unending round of marital negotiations it appeared daily more certain that Prince Henry would never marry Katharine. Indeed, a strong part of the motivation of both Henry VII and Philip of Burgundy in seeking a marital alliance was to spite Ferdinand of Aragon.

Philip did not wish to expose his wife to the view of the English and Juana spent just one night at Windsor, on 10 February. She met Katharine only for a few hours and under close supervision: both sisters long remembered their agony in being so constrained. Katharine was sent back to Richmond on the next day while Juana travelled to Falmouth on 14 February to wait for Philip.

Philip and Henry said their farewells on 2 March. Although Henry had spent lavishly on hospitality and entertainments he had profited greatly from the enforced visit of the archduke: he had re-established England's traditional friendship with Burgundy, secured the promise of the repatriation of Suffolk and won advantageous trading terms for his merchants in the Low Countries. With very good reason he ordered his son to value Philip's interests more than his own. Perhaps, indeed, Henry's mind was turning to his own mortality for when he left Philip he urged him (as was reported) to be 'the father, guardian, protector and friend of my son the Prince of Wales'.[31]

Remarkably, Philip did not leave for Spain for nearly two months. The first of several delays came about when he developed a fever and was obliged to rest for ten days in Reading. With fulsome generosity, Henry continued to meet his expenses: Montigny observed that Philip found it impossible to spend any of his own money.[32] On 25 March Philip was reunited with Juana near Penryn and on the following day the English courtiers departed. But even now bad weather forced him to repeatedly postpone his departure and not until 22 April did his fleet set sail: it was eighty-two days since Philip had been driven ashore and fifty-one since he had parted from Henry. Happily, the Bay of Biscay was calm and the fleet arrived in A Coruña on 26 April.

Philip's journey over the mountains of Galicia to Valladolid was grimly uncomfortable and took nearly two months but he must have been reassured by the number and the seniority of the Castilian aristocrats who flocked to assure him of their loyalty, the dukes of Infantado, Béjar and Nájera, the Count of Benavente and the Marquis of Ceñete chief among them.[33] The Castilian nobility was abandoning Ferdinand in a headlong rush; only the Duke of Alba and the Count of Cifuentes remained loyal among the leading nobles. But it was to be more important still that the agèd Cardinal Jiménez de Cisneros did so.

Philip did not find the time to meet Ferdinand until 20 June, when he greeted him briefly in the small village of Remesal near Sanabria. Arrogantly, Philip ordered Ferdinand to go to the tiny town of Villafáfila while he himself stayed in the palace in Benavente as their agents negotiated with each other. There was, in truth, not much to discuss for Ferdinand had little to offer and the agreement was quickly made: Ferdinand signed on 27 June and Philip on the following day ('Treaty of Villafáfila-Benavente', 27–28 June 1506). With characteristic insouciance, Ferdinand insisted that he had decided when Isabella died that he would allow the transference of the kingdom to Juana and Philip to avoid civil war in Castile; accordingly, he agreed to the annulment of Isabella's testament and accepted that Philip could rule in Juana's place if her illness continued. But even in his weakness, Ferdinand did not go without recompense, for as his price for the concessions he secured half of the income from the Indies for his lifetime and retained the lucrative masterships of the Military Orders of Santiago, Alcántara and Calatrava. He therefore had access in his own right to substantial sums of cash in Castile – but he would make none of it available to help his daughter in her penury in England.[34] As always, Ferdinand was playing for time.

Everything changed with dramatic suddenness within a few weeks. Philip continued on a slow triumphal journey round Old Castile but when he reached Burgos on 1 September he became ill with a pulmonary infection. His condition worsened progressively for three weeks, and on 25 September he died. Inevitably there were those who suggested that he had been poisoned but in all probability a weak physique had not been equal to the cumulative demands made on it by the arduous journeys of the previous nine months.[35]

The implications of Philip's death rippled across Western Europe. In Spain, it seemed to confirm that the Union of the Crowns was ruptured and that Castile would probably disintegrate under the rule of its distraught queen and as it awaited the growth to adulthood of a prince who was currently only six years of age. In the Low Countries, too, it seemed likely that Charles's minority would inevitably presage years of weakness; Margaret of Austria assumed the governorship. The continued retention by the House of Habsburg of the imperial title was now also at risk: would the electors be prepared to choose Charles – a mere child – to succeed his ageing grandfather?

The situation in Castile was saved by the relentless energy of Cardinal Jiménez de Cisneros, who faced down rebels and obliged leading nobles to involve themselves in government. The Flemish councillors could not summon enough support to risk rebelling against the regency government and many of them returned home. Juan Manuel attempted to flee from Castile but was captured and imprisoned.[36]

Juana collapsed physically and mentally. Initially, her distress manifested itself in going for days without food and in refusing to wash or to change her clothes. But soon she descended into a madness that justified Montigny's horrified description of her as 'a woman without sense'.[37] More obsessed than ever by her love for Philip, on 20 December Juana ordered that his corpse should be exhumed so that she could take it for burial in the royal catafalque in the Cathedral of Granada. Juana set off on her long journey across Castile with a few trusted followers but would only travel by night – and by candlelight – so that no one should know that her husband had died. She opened the coffin every day so that she could lovingly kiss Philip's feet and assure him of her continuing love for him. She refused to let the coffin leave her sight and would not even take shelter in convents since she did not want Philip's body to be in the presence of other women. In time, the spectral nightly procession towards Granada would become part of Castilian folklore. But Juana was obliged to stop for one unalterable schedule: on 10 January 1507, she gave birth in Torquemada to a daughter whom she named Katharine.[38]

The Return of Ferdinand to Spain & the Revival of the English Marriage
Ferdinand learned of Philip's death in Portofino in Naples on 6 October 1506. He understood at once that Isabella's testament was again effective and that he had the right to act as Governor in Castile. He recognised, too, that the future of the Crown of Castile lay now with Charles of Habsburg–Burgundy and that if he preserved the authority of the Crown it would only be so that it could be passed on to Charles. Doubtless, too, he understood that if he could regain control over Castile he might well be able to resurrect the alliance with England: both Juana and Katharine therefore had much to hope for from Ferdinand's return to Castile.

But Naples came first. Ferdinand resisted Juana's urging that he return to Castile by arguing that if he left Naples without fully securing his authority there the Pope might take the kingdom back into his jurisdiction and then bestow it upon whomsoever he chose – perhaps even upon the King of France. Castile therefore came second: Ferdinand established a *troika* of Cardinal Cisneros, the Constable of Castile and the Duke of Alba to govern Castile until he returned. The Parliament of Naples duly recognised Ferdinand as king and acknowledged that the kingdom was a possession of the Crown of Aragon and that the succession to Ferdinand would remain in his direct line and not pass to Germaine or to any children or grandchildren of her marriage to Ferdinand. But still Pope Julius demurred: much as he now needed Ferdinand's support he was not yet ready to invest him with the Crown of Naples. Recognising that he had gained all that he could, at least for the moment, Ferdinand left for Spain on 4 June 1507. He met Louis XII at Savona and they agreed to maintain the status quo, with France ruling Milan and Aragon controlling Naples.[39] Both monarchs fully understood that they had once again only patched up a truce with each other.

Ferdinand arrived in Valencia on 20 July.[40] Still he did not hurry back to Castile: on that day he wrote to González de Puebla ordering him to ask Henry for a further postponement in the payment of Katharine's dowry since he would be detained in Valencia for a month or so.[41] Not until 29 August did Ferdinand meet Juana, who was accompanied by two of her children, Ferdinand and Katharine. Juana was radiantly happy at the reunification but Ferdinand was deeply shaken by her condition: he halted her macabre pilgrimage to Granada and had her confined under secure control in the small town of Arcos, south of Burgos. She lived there for nearly eighteen months until she was transferred to the royal palace at Tordesillas, where she remained – with one poignantly brief interlude – until her death in 1555.[42]

The death of Philip of Burgundy shattered some of the most important of Henry VII's diplomatic plans and he responded with the most extraordinary of his quests for a second bride, letting it be known now that he might be interested in marrying Juana, Queen of Castile. Of course Henry had briefly met Juana early in 1506 and he seems to have been sufficiently impressed by her to doubt whether the stories of her madness were authentic. The most decisive factor in his proposal was that he knew that Juana was fertile and that she was young enough to have more children: she could present him a second son. Juana was still only twenty-eight years old and had given birth to six children in the years 1498–1507; all of her children were still alive and – as Henry noted – none of them appeared to have inherited her mental condition. By marrying Juana, Henry would perhaps bolster the security of his own family on the throne of England and could revivify England's alliances with the Low Countries and Castile. Perhaps Henry hoped for nothing more than to be able to play a role in resolving the crisis of the Castilian succession – but it is nonetheless difficult to escape the conclusion that he was genuinely interested in marrying the mad queen. And of course, Juana would bring a splendid dowry.

Whatever his intentions, Henry was determined to secure the Burgundian–Habsburg alliance and so while he pursued Juana's hand – or pretended to do so? – he also sought that of her son Charles for his daughter Mary. In 1502 Henry had married his elder daughter, Margaret, to James IV of Scotland; they formed a curious couple – the bride was twelve years old while her husband was thirty-five – but the alliance promised to bring substantial political advantages in securing the safety of England's border with Scotland.[43] Henry could no longer delay in securing a husband for his younger daughter and in December 1507 he and Maximilian agreed that Charles would marry Mary and that the Kingdom of Castile would be their marriage portion: quite how this was to be managed was not immediately evident. What was, however, clear was that the English royal family would be allied with the House of Habsburg–Burgundy, holders of the imperial title. In December 1508 the last of the major courtly celebrations of Henry's reign took place in St Paul's to celebrate the marriage by proxy and the chronicler of the event recorded that the 'flourishing red roses [*sc.* of England] be so planted and spread in the highest imperial gardens and houses of power and honour'.[44] For a king who knew that he had not long to live, it was a tempting – perhaps irresistible – prospect. One way or another, Henry would have a Habsburg–Burgundian marriage: did he even now hope that his own marriage to Juana would make it a double alliance? And it is evident that Henry still hoped to marry his son and heir to Katharine. Certainly, it is remarkable that for all the difficulties that Henry encountered in dealing with Ferdinand of Aragon – and they were in reality only just beginning – he never cancelled the projected marriage of Prince Henry with Princess Katharine.

Katharine: The Years of Abandonment, 1505–09

On 22 April 1506 – the day after Philip and Juana sailed for Spain – Katharine wrote a letter to her father which was a startling and sustained rebuke to him for his neglect of her. She began by noting that he had not replied to any of her letters complaining about her 'extreme needs' and begged him to remember that she was his daughter and could look to no one else but him for support. Henry fed her only out of charity and she was so impoverished that since her arrival in England she had only been able to afford two new dresses. Katharine assured her father that she remained his 'humble servant' but she had left him in no doubt as to her poverty, degradation – and anger.[45]

Katharine's predicament was indeed raising profound concerns in Castile: on 28 August 1506 Juan López, one of the trustees of Isabella's testament, wrote scathingly to Ferdinand (who was still in Naples) that Isabella would never have tolerated the treatment that Katharine was receiving.[46] Ferdinand wanly blamed the trustees themselves and Philip for not allowing him access to the Castilian funds so that he could send the marriage portion to England, quite ignoring the fact that he controlled the fabled resources of the Military Orders: everything had to wait on his return to Castile![47] In April, after an unpleasant interview with González de Puebla, Henry agreed to postpone the payment until the feast of the Archangel (29 September); Henry understood only too well the strength of his position and informed the ambassador that he would determine the rates of exchange for the gold and silver. González de Puebla took the point and urged Ferdinand not to try to drive a hard bargain.[48]

On 15 April 1507 Katharine reported to Ferdinand that the promise of a new date of payment had led to an abatement in Henry's fury with him. She added a new complaint to the familiar litany of her hardship, pointing out that she had not seen the Prince of Wales for four months and 'hoping to God' that Ferdinand would not worsen her predicament by requesting any further delays in his payments to Henry. But even as Katharine poured out her heart to her father her situation worsened: later that very day she wrote again to Ferdinand with the devastating news that Henry had told her 'very positively' that he no longer regarded himself and his son as bound by the agreement to marry her because the marriage portion had not been paid.[49]

Katharine's spirits lifted considerably when early in August she heard that her father had returned to Spain: it was the first good news that she had received in years.[50] Henry's mood seems to have lightened at the same time, and probably for the same reason: he informed González de Puebla that the marriage of Prince Henry and Katharine would take place as soon as the money was paid, and since three Italian merchants had agreed to provide the bills of exchange there was at least a real possibility of this actually happening. Again, the marriage with Juana was enticing Henry.[51] Henry agreed to another postponement and when on 7 September Katharine conveyed the good news to Ferdinand she felt obliged to point out that Henry was not making any substantive concession since he was not committed to keeping the contract: Katharine suspected that Henry's unwonted generosity was stimulated by his impatience to hear a positive answer about his proposal to marry Juana rather than to facilitate her own marriage.[52]

Katharine became so animated by the new turn of events that she threw herself into her correspondence. On 4 October 1507 she wrote to Ferdinand urging him – yet again! – to replace González de Puebla, insisting that she only told the ambassador what she wanted Henry to know.[53] Three weeks later she did her best to persuade her sister of the attractiveness of Henry VII as a prospective husband, emphasising that he was a powerful and rich prince who was 'endowed with the greatest virtues'.[54] Dared Katharine now hope that her sister might come to live in England as queen? It was probably to humour Katharine that Ferdinand ordered González de Puebla in January 1508 to let it be known that if Juana was to marry again it would only be with the King of England. Unfortunately, he added the rider that Juana was so stricken with grief that she was determined to remain a widow and that she was fixated on the corpse of her late husband, refusing to bury it. Ferdinand promised that he would do all he could to persuade Juana to bury Philip so that all parties could then move on, but he had to insist that he felt there was no real prospect of this happening.[55]

The Rumbustious Diplomat: The Return of Gutierre Gómez de Fuensalida

Ferdinand did at least oblige Katharine by sending a new ambassador to England, and it was a man in whom he had the fullest confidence and who was well known to both Katharine and Henry VII: in January 1508 Ferdinand appointed Gutierre Gómez de Fuensalida as ambassador to England to urge Henry to have the wedding ceremony of Katharine and Prince Henry take place immediately and he gave him letters of credit to settle the monies that were outstanding from the dowry: the 100,000 escudos remaining from the dowry for Katharine's marriage was to be paid ten days before or after the celebration of the marriage in church and its consummation. Ferdinand explained that he had been unable to pay these monies because of the deaths of Isabella and Philip and his own absence from Spain. He insisted that it was his 'absolute priority' to ensure that the marriage was now celebrated and consummated and urged his new ambassador to make all speed to England.[56]

Gómez de Fuensalida did so, arriving in London on 22 February. Unfortunately, Henry VII could not see him immediately because he was suffering from gout[57] and when he was granted audience on 4 March he was warned that because the king was still weak the meeting was to be a short one. Henry insisted that he did not want to change the agreement to marry his son to Katharine and the two men agreed that Katharine was a young woman of exceptional character and aired a few banal generalities. Mindful of his promise not to weary the king, Gómez de Fuensalida then prepared to leave when Henry ordered him to pull up a chair, and they briefly discussed other matters. The meeting seems to have been conducted in a courteous spirit and Henry ordered the ambassador to discuss the detailed arrangements with the members of his council. When he then did so, Gómez de Fuensalida revealed for the first time that the money to make good the payments on the dowry was already in England and that two-thirds of it (65,000 escudos) would be paid in cash, 15,000 in gold and silver and 20,000 in precious stones and pearls. The ambassador was surprised and angered to learn that Katharine had sold valuables that were worth about 35,000 ducats, and was even more disturbed when he understood that the princess had only received about 20,000 ducats for them. That money would have to be made up.

Gómez de Fuensalida reported to Ferdinand that Henry had aged since he had met him in 1500 and that his doctors did not want him to conduct any business; over subsequent weeks he had to content himself with dealing with the members of the Privy Council. He also effectively freed himself from having to work with González de Puebla by sending Ferdinand a devastating analysis of his untrustworthiness: 'I find that he is truly a servant of the King of England, and although there cannot be two opposites in one man in this individual there are: his heart is English and his tongue is Castilian.'[58]

As for Katharine: the princess was, the ambassador reported, 'so ill and disconsolate' that he could barely find the words to describe her condition. He proceeded to deliver a pointed rebuke to Ferdinand for his treatment of her, wishing 'to God' that he himself was rich enough to help her with money. Katharine, he informed his sovereign, had lost faith in the parents who had let her waste away in England; for want of 30,000–35,000 ducats they had put her honour and their own at risk. He averred that he did not know anyone who had been as badly treated as Katharine and begged Ferdinand not to allow the treatment of his daughter to continue. And her situation continued to worsen: on 26 March Gómez de Fuensalida was summoned by the king's councillors to be told that Henry would under no circumstances accept any of the precious objects and jewels that Katharine had brought with her as part-payment of the dowry.[59]

While Henry insisted that he would not accept the jewels he most certainly wanted to see them and Gómez de Fuensalida agreed to mount a display of them. Henry brought his mother with him to inspect them. He subsequently professed that he was impressed by them but would not take even one of them because to do so would be a thing of 'much inhumanity' that would darken his reputation throughout Europe. Gómez de Fuensalida was not allowed to meet Henry and found himself increasingly contemptuous of the men with whom he was dealing: 'The council of this king are all women, I mean the Privy Council.'

For the real woman who was at the heart of the conflict, the ambassador had nothing but admiration and tenderness; he warned Ferdinand that 'I have great fear that she will fall into some great illness, because [she] is not healthy but is weak and very discoloured and her complexion is much damaged'. In summarising Katharine's condition Gómez de Fuensalida conjured a powerfully emotive metaphor to damn both of the monarchs who had treated her so badly: 'Never was such cruelty inflicted on a

158

captive in the lands of the Moors as the princess is subjected to here.'[60] The ambassador was as eloquent as he was fearless.

Replying to the ambassador's letters of early March, Ferdinand insisted that he had the fullest trust in Henry VII's integrity and therefore expected him to keep the agreements that he had made with him: 'I consider him to be a very virtuous and truthful prince who for nothing in the world would act against his word and treaty.' He forwarded a banker's draft for 10,000 ducats to make up the shortfall in the dowry. He ordered Gómez de Fuensalida to bring the negotiations for Katharine's marriage to a speedy conclusion and again insisted that he would do everything in his power to persuade Juana to look favourably upon Henry's suit once she had buried her husband. However, he made it clear that to force the issue with Juana would 'destroy all her health'. He affected to be well disposed to the marriage of Charles and Mary but insisted that it could not be linked to the agreement binding Prince Henry to Katharine. As for Katharine, he felt obliged to insist that 'I have such love for the Princess of Wales and hold her person and honour [equal] ... to my own ...': it is interesting that Ferdinand should have felt obliged to have made this observation to his ambassador even before he received the shuddering rebuke that Gómez de Fuensalida had sent to him, as it happened, on the very previous day.[61]

Henry did not receive Gómez de Fuensalida for several weeks but when at Easter he met Katharine she complained bluntly to him that in the forty days of Lent she had not had access to him. Henry – accompanied again by his mother – excused himself on the grounds of illness and raged at Ferdinand's conduct, lambasting him as 'a poor prince' who did not pay his debts and who had cruelly incarcerated her sister. The king did nothing to discount rumours that Katharine was to be sent back to Spain.[62]

Gómez de Fuensalida was infuriated equally that Henry would not receive him and that the Privy Councillors did so. At the turn of April–May, he tried to force the issue by writing to the king that he had received letters from Ferdinand of such importance that they justified him asking for an audience that very day. He received no reply. Since he was evidently not going to be summoned to the palace, he presented himself there and sent word to the Privy Council that he was waiting for audience; after more than three hours he was told that there was no possibility of his meeting the king and that since all the members of the council were not yet present he would have to wait on the arrival of the absent members before being summoned. Inevitably, Gómez de Fuensalida exploded with rage: he sent a message to the councillors rebuking them for 'playing with me as if I were a man of no importance'. Eventually – unfortunately he does not say how long he had to wait – he was summoned to meet the council. It was to be an acrid meeting. Richard Foxe, Bishop of Exeter and Lord Privy Seal, insisted that Henry was not well enough to conduct business and suggested that the ambassador write a summary of what he had to convey to the king so that it could be passed on to him. Gómez de Fuensalida rejected the offer. He argued vigorously – he knew no other way – with the council, over the evaluation of the jewels; whether they could be given and accepted as part of the dowry; over the money that Katharine had to live off; how badly Katharine was served at table, and so on. The exchange was robust on both sides: at one moment the Privy Seal angrily shouted, 'Ridiculous!' at one of the assertions of the ambassador.

Gómez de Fuensalida added a new complaint – that Katharine had not been allowed to see the Prince of Wales, to whom after all she was lawfully married. Scathingly, he noted that young Henry was surrounded only by men 'as if he was a woman' and normally lived in a chamber which could only be approached through the king's own quarters – 'and he is so subjugated that he does not utter a word except in reply to what the king asks him'. As for Katharine, she was now so weak that it would be a kindness to take her away from England.

On 8 May, Gómez de Fuensalida was again summoned to meet the Privy Council. He was told that Henry had proclaimed that 'even if he was the lord of the whole world' he would not accept any of Katharine's jewels or stones as part of the dowry. It was a negotiating ploy: the Lord Privy Seal urged the ambassador to be patient in the hope that things would turn out better. Naturally enough, Gómez de Fuensalida replied that he 'could not suffer this with patience' and was told that he might only have to wait eight days but with the rider that it might be two months before he heard anything. The English were indeed toying with the ambassador. But once again, Henry had not closed the door on the marriage of his heir to the Princess of Wales.[63]

Still, Henry would not meet the Spanish ambassador. Gómez de Fuensalida tried 'everything possible' to secure an audience to discuss the marriage of Henry with Juana but was fobbed off with the reply that if Ferdinand was serious about the marriage he would see to it that Philip was properly buried. For his own part, Henry let it be known that he had never heard of anything 'so infamous' as a widow carrying around the corpse of her dead husband. More to the point: if Gómez de Fuensalida produced 100,000 escudos proper discussions could begin. The ambassador was at his wits' end, once again referring contemptuously to the members of the Privy Council as women ('las consejeras del Rey'): it was the only riposte that satisfied him. He protested, too, that Katharine's living quarters had been downgraded and that she was now living over the royal stables.[64]

At last, on the feast day of St John the Baptist (24 June) Henry summoned Gómez de Fuensalida to an audience. They retailed the familiar arguments about the marriage with Juana – Henry insisting that Philip should be buried at once; Gómez de Fuensalida that Ferdinand could not take the risk of destroying what remained of Juana's mental well-being. Henry remembered that when he met Juana (in 1506) he had thought that she was in good health and that he believed that she remained so. He made the revealing suggestion that if he married Juana he would not leave England to do so. He dismissed as 'a joke' the suggestion that he should contribute his own property towards Katharine's dowry. The discussion concluded bluntly enough – Henry arguing that he and his son were free of the commitment to marry Katharine; Gómez de Fuensalida emphasising that nothing could alter the married state to which Prince Henry had been committed *per verba de praesenti*.

But still, Henry persisted with the negotiations for the marriage. On 28 June the Privy Council once again met Gómez de Fuensalida and both parties conducted their business seriously. The English stated that the marriage of Prince Henry and Katharine could go ahead when the 100,000 escudos were deposited and the arrangements for the marriage of Prince Charles and Princess Mary were confirmed. Gómez de Fuensalida retorted by asking for a valuation of the rents of the Principality of Wales, the Duchy of Cornwall and the County of Chester so that there could be no misunderstanding of what Katharine was entitled to. It was suggestive of the seriousness with which the English were now negotiating that they tightened the screws on Katharine's living conditions; they stopped the food allowances for her confessor and physician and reduced the amounts given to other members of her household. When Gómez de Fuensalida met Katharine on 1 July he found that she was so ill that she could barely talk, insisting that unless she and her ladies were given better food they would go on hunger strike. The ambassador duly reported to Ferdinand that his own servants ate better food than the princess. He gave a detailed account of his dealings with González de Puebla, which he had concluded by handing him his letter of dismissal with the bitter remark that 'you have been a better servant to the King of England than to the king, our lord'. As for himself, he was desperate to leave England.[65] At the end of July, the ambassador reported that Katharine was 'dangerously ill'.[66]

On Spain's national day of St James (25 July) Henry again granted audience to Gómez de Fuensalida to inform him that he was dropping his pursuit of Juana's hand. He did not believe that she was mad: 'Although some say her illness is feigned, others [say] that it is not, I am inclined to the first view.' But he would wait no longer and declared that while he was being urged by many people within his kingdom to marry again he would not pursue the marriage with Juana.[67] Katharine's chances were improving.

Ferdinand learned at the beginning of August that Henry insisted that the whole of the 100,000 escudos had to be paid in cash without any part-payment in plate or jewels and that he wanted confirmation of Ferdinand's support for the marriage of Prince Charles and Lady Mary. He turned witheringly on him. He noted – at last! – how badly Henry had treated Katharine and how dishonourable his conduct had been: indeed, he averred that he would willingly have broken with Henry had he not been determined to bring about the marriage of his beloved daughter. Ferdinand's actions spoke less fluently than his words; since Henry had insisted that the 200,000 escudos of Katharine's portion for her marriage to Prince Henry should be settled upon himself and the Prince of Wales and must never be reclaimed by the Spanish crown regardless of circumstances, Ferdinand raged that the demand was unjust but that it was Katharine's money and she could do what she wanted with it. Ferdinand was passing to his impressionable and fragile daughter the responsibility for negotiating this with Henry VII and his son. Ferdinand insisted that he could not understand why Henry VII was so hostile to him: 'All this I say, because, in treating with people of no honour and indifferent character, it is necessary to take care that we receive no injury and that we ourselves are not cheated.' He therefore made a gift to his daughter of all of the jewels and precious objects that she had been given before leaving Spain. It was for her to decide what to do with them. He agreed to pay the outstanding 100,000 escudos in cash and to look favourably upon the proposal that Charles should marry Mary – but only if the marriage of the Prince of Wales and Katharine took place immediately. For good measure, he threatened to have the princess brought back to Spain.[68] The 'Fox of Aragon' never lost his nerve – or his utter shamelessness.

At the beginning of September, Gómez de Fuensalida reported that Katharine was beyond comforting:

> The princess is so despairing that neither reason nor excuses can comfort her, because on the one side she resents what is happening [to her] and on the other she believes that your Highness has forgotten about her. She cannot credit anything else because it has been such a long time since your Highness informed her of what was happening in her cause, nor has he written anything at all to give her hope of what might happen in the future. And for certain, very powerful lord, I myself can only marvel in view of what life has dealt her in the past and the present that she is not more ill than she has been.[69]

While Katharine's health deteriorated, Henry's seemed to improve; he was well enough to hunt for three or four days and on his return summoned Gómez de Fuensalida for what proved to be the most tumultuous of their meetings. It started with a groundbreaking concession by Henry, who insisted that while he would not accept any of Katharine's treasure or jewels as part of the dowry he would take the best of the plate, but only at prices that were valued by London assayers. After years of haggling, the vexed question of the jewels and plate had been settled in a trice.

This success did not, however, soothe the nerves of the two adversaries. Gómez de Fuensalida now suggested that Henry should waive his right to a dowry for Katharine's second marriage: the king became so angry at this suggestion that the ambassador thought that 'he might catch fire' and as the discussion continued Henry 'turned brighter yellow than a candle'. So enraged was Henry that Gómez de Fuensalida found it impossible to get a word in edgewise, but when he did he contrived to suggest that Henry should be grateful enough to have Katharine married to his son to forget about the marriage of Charles and Mary. When the ambassador left he gave Katharine an expurgated account of the interview because he did not want to make her angry or depressed. Henry VII had no such compunction; bumping into Gómez de Fuensalida as he came out of Katharine's chambers he insisted that they should visit the princess together and then in a loud voice told her:

> My daughter: I, for the great love that I have had for you have given you my two sons, both of them my heirs ... and I have turned down

other women who were offered to me for my son, women who were as good as you ... In order to keep my word I have not wanted anything other than to have you as my daughter and have persevered in this even though I and my son are free because your father broke his word and did not fulfil with me what he had promised within the time that was stipulated. Even now he has not fulfilled this but he wants me to accept in part-payment of the dowry some of the plate that you brought with you. Your father has [also] not wished to sign a declaration that I sent to him confirming the marriage of the prince [*sc.* Charles], his grandson, and the Lady Mary, my daughter...

Gómez de Fuensalida was not a man to allow even the King of England to speak thus in his presence and told Katharine that Henry had no justification for delaying her marriage. At this – the ambassador recorded – Henry 'jumped up like a cat'. After a further angry exchange Gómez de Fuensalida informed Henry that his demands were unreasonable. The mutual abuse mounted; when Gómez de Fuensalida retailed the kingdoms that Ferdinand ruled as testament to his greatness, Henry exploded: 'Certainly, you do great honour to your king with so many kingdoms and yet he does not have the 100,000 escudos with which to pay the dowry of his daughter!' The king stormed out. Katharine thanked the ambassador for finding the words that she could never have found for herself. It was announced at court that because Ferdinand had not paid the dowry the marriage would not now be celebrated. When he heard this, Gómez de Fuensalida wrote furiously to Henry denying that this was the case.[70]

The war of words between the King of England and the Spanish ambassador took place against an eruption of real war in Italy when Julius II opened hostilities with the Republic of Venice. The details of the conflict need not concern us, but so angry was Julius with Venice's contumacy in seizing some papal lands in its war with Cesare Borgia and in refusing to allow Julius to exercise his right of veto over an ecclesiastical appointment that he declared holy war on the Republic, excommunicating every one of its citizens. He offered to crown Maximilian as Emperor if on his journey to Rome he destroyed the Venetian army. Beguiled by the prospect, Maximilian duly set off with an army of sorts but the Venetians easily defeated him: he would not be crowned at Rome in 1508.

Julius then made offers to the kings of France and Spain that they could not refuse: Louis XII could hardly believe that the Pope was inviting him to invade Italy and promptly raised an army with which to do so while

Ferdinand extracted from Julius the promise that in return for his military support he would invest him with the Kingdom of Naples. Maximilian remained loyal to the Pope, and in December 1508 the four powers – Julius II, Louis XII, Ferdinand and Maximilian – joined together in the 'League of Cambrai' to attack and destroy Venetian possessions in the *terrafirme*. The 'terrifying Pope' donned his armour.[71]

While Julius had some successes, it was Louis XII who gained most from the war. Once again, a French army crossed the Alps, and to brilliant purpose: Louis XII destroyed the Venetian army at Agnadello (14 May 1509) and opened the way to the lagoon itself. French power in northern Italy seemed irresistible. Anxious – too late – about French intentions, Julius promised to invest Ferdinand with the Kingdom of Naples (July 1509). To pursue his vendetta against the Republic of Venice, the Pope had substantially enhanced the power of France and Spain but he had also effectively ensured that war would continue between them in the peninsula. He soon recognised his mistake and decided to drive the French out of northern Italy. To do so, he would seek the support of the rulers of Western Europe. In England a young prince who was no doubt waiting impatiently for his father to die could not have dared to imagine that he would be invited to satisfy all his military dreams by going to war against the King of France in support of the Pope.

On 9 March 1509 Katharine wrote again to her father insisting that he send a new ambassador; Gómez de Fuensalida had been a great disappointment to her, and his unremitting belligerence hindered her cause – not least because Henry VII refused even to meet him – while González de Puebla was in effect an agent of Henry VII. The agreement to marry Mary to Charles had weakened her position and meant that Henry no longer had need of Ferdinand or of another Spanish match. She did not know how she would be able to sustain herself, especially now that her household goods had been sold. Only a few days ago, Henry had told her that he was not obliged to provide for her and her household but would do so out of love for her: even her food was given to her as a charity.

In reality, Katharine's disenchantment with Gómez de Fuensalida arose not from his attitude to Henry VII but from his welling hostility to the conduct of her confessor, Fray Diego Fernández. Katharine regarded Fray Diego as the 'best confessor a woman could want' but in truth he appears to have been a meddlesome intriguer who had become involved in a power struggle with Francisca de Cáceres, one of Katharine's ladies-in-waiting. The details were petty enough. It seems that after the dismissal of Elvira Manrique in 1505 Francisca had developed a leading position within Katharine's household, and since it appears that she was every bit as domineering a character as Elvira, Katharine came to resent both her authority and her personality. The princess was presented with the opportunity to dismiss Francisca when she announced that she had decided to marry the Italian banker Francesco Grimaldi despite Katharine's strong objections. The princess dismissed her and she went to live in the house of Gómez de Fuensalida. The ambassador despaired: 'there was not such confusion in Babylon' as there was in Katharine's household.[72] Less than a fortnight later Katharine wrote again to her father, expressing her total confidence in her confessor and her fears that she would collapse and die under the strain of her life in England.[73]

Henry VII: Decline & Death (21 April 1509)

Henry VII had suffered badly from bronchial illness in the winters of 1507–08 and 1508–09 by the end of March 1509 it was evident that he was dying. He signed his testament on 31 March and died as midnight approached on 21 April. His councillors were so anxious at the possibility of unrest that they did not announce until 23 April that the king had died. Henry was laid to rest in his splendid new chapel in Westminster Abbey alongside his queen on 11 May.[74]

Henry VII, crabby and mean-spirited as he was in his last years, was one of the greatest of English monarchs. He ended the Wars of the Roses and revived the reputation of the Crown of England at home and abroad, and it was as the most enduring recognition of his achievement that his throne now passed to his son without dispute. Moreover, Henry had made the Crown solvent and left great riches to his heir which enabled him to enter upon years of extraordinary extravagance that defined his own kingship, court and government (at least until the money ran out). Essentially, Henry VII had reinvigorated late-medieval institutions of government and made them work more efficiently to the advantage of the Crown. He had been careful not to fritter his financial resources on unnecessary display but had been prepared to finance the most extravagant celebrations and festivities when the occasion warranted it, most notably in the prodigious welcome that he had mounted for his daughter-in-law in 1501 and in the magnificence of the tomb that he had created for his beloved wife and himself in Westminster Abbey. He was wary of Parliament but he used it to validate his actions and to make (and remake) laws; he convened six meetings of Parliament in twenty-three years, but so secure was he on the throne in his last years that only one of these (1504) was summoned after 1497. He had increased trade, not least so that he could increase his own revenues. He had brought about improvements in the navy, beginning the development of naval bases at Portsmouth, Greenwich and Woolwich, and passed on five great ships to his son, including two powerful warships, the *Regent* and the *Sovereign*, both of which had been completed in 1490–91: he thereby laid the foundation for the creation of a royal navy that would be one of the great achievements of Henry VIII.

Henry VII's achievement has generally been seen as a secular one. But it is well to remember that he was always clearly focussed on his obligations to the Church, to which he was profoundly loyal. The most approachable image of himself that he has left to us makes this abundantly evident: in the façade of Bath and Wells Cathedral we see Henry placed at the very core of religious life as the central character in a façade which examines the Path to Heaven by way of Jacob's Ladder. The centrality of the image was a metaphor for the role of the Crown in the life of the Church. Henry stands inscrutably in the middle of the facade looking down on his subjects milling below him with the quizzical gaze so characteristic of him. This extraordinary conjuncture of Church and Crown reminds us that Henry invariably maintained good relations with the papacy but does not make it expressly clear that – as was his wont – he benefited from them. Henry twice received the papal sword and cap – in 1489 from Innocent VIII and in 1496 from Alexander VI.[75] Few of his contemporaries doubted that Henry VII had been the most formidable of kings: none doubted the sincerity of his religious beliefs and – it was not always quite the same thing – his devotion to the Roman Catholic Church. The image of him at Bath and Wells is stunning confirmation of this, and it is ironic that the building was the last great abbey to be built in England before Henry's son dissolved the monasteries.

The news of Henry's death travelled slowly and only indirectly to Spain. When Ferdinand received the first unconfirmed reports that Henry had died and wrote to Gómez de Fuensalida ordering him to do everything in his power to persuade the new king to marry Katharine without delay. He promised that the dowry would be promptly paid and sent bills of 100,000 escudos drawn on merchants in England. Ferdinand's keenness to persuade Henry to marry Katharine knew no bounds: he even authorised the ambassador to ratify a treaty for the marriage of Charles and Mary.[76]

More even than this; when Ferdinand heard officially that Henry VII had died he sent Henry VIII his condolences and suggested that if anyone rebelled against him he himself would personally lead a powerful army to England to help him secure the throne.[77]

Evidently someone in his court raised with Ferdinand the possibility that opposition might be made in England on theological grounds to Katharine's remarriage and so he instructed Gómez de Fuensalida to remind Henry VIII that he was already married to Katharine and that he would commit grave sin if he abandoned her. He also expressly noted that the Pope had given the necessary dispensation for the marriage and brought two further points to the notice of the new king – that the marriage of Charles and Mary depended upon him marrying Katharine; and to persuade him that the marriage would be fecund permitted himself to recall that Manuel I of Portugal had married two sisters and been blessed with numerous offspring. Ferdinand professed himself confident that the same happiness would follow for Henry and Katharine.[78]

9

WIFE TO BLUFF KING HAL: THE CHILDBEARING YEARS

Accession & Coronation
'A Perfect Model of Manly Beauty … in Favour with Both God and Man':
Henry VIII, King of England

The new king was eighteen years old but was little known to even close observers of life at court.[1] It was doubtless because Henry VII had been scarred by the losses of Arthur and Edmund that he maintained the strictest control over the last of his sons, not allowing him far from his sight and restricting the circle of people who were allowed to have dealings with him. He worried overmuch, for young Henry was the very picture of health – 6 feet 2 inches or more in height, and every bit as burly as he was tall – and he was possessed of an innate and enormous physical energy. He towered over those around him and indeed might well have seemed to have been a son of the giant Edward IV rather than of Henry VII (who was not especially tall).[2] His stature and his ebullient energy substantially moulded his character: he was an imposing man, and as he grew into his kingship he came to dominate all around him. He gloried in the name with which he had been christened, consciously identifying himself with Henry V, the great conqueror of the French. Henry wanted – yearned – to go to war with France, to become the new Henry V; true to himself, he would spend about one-quarter of his long reign at war with France.[3] Perhaps, indeed, Henry would have settled for being the new Edward IV, who as recently as 1475 had invaded France with a force that was so enormous that it took three weeks to cross the Channel.[4]

It was a particularly fortunate circumstance that Henry's miserly father had left him an overflowing treasury with which to accomplish his destiny of going to war with France. Within days of his accession he had confidently declared that he would attack the King of France and then he strode contemptuously out of an audience with a French ambassador so that he could go to the tilt-yard. In the summer of 1509 he arrogantly insulted the ambassador, who had suggested he might seek peace with France, rhetorically declaiming that 'I ask peace of the King of France, who dare not look at me, let alone make war.'[5]

Henry excelled at the equestrian and courtly arts; for such a big man he was surprisingly nimble and adroit. However, descriptions of him insistently emphasised the range of his intellectual qualities. He was widely read and an accomplished linguist; he had been taught the classics and spoke French fluently and had passable Italian (and, later, Spanish). He came to regard himself as an authority of European standing on theology – with disastrous results – and dabbled in modern sciences. He had a special interest in composing music, both secular and religious; indeed, while the chronicler Edmund Hall admired his energy he was careful to note his musical abilities in both secular and religious genres:

> Exercising himself daily in shooting, singing, dancing, wrestling, casting of the bar, playing at the recorders, flute, virginals, and in setting of songs, making of dances, & did set two goodly masses, every [one] of them of five parts, which were often sung in his chapel, and afterwards in diverse other places.[6]

The descriptions of Henry by Venetian ambassadors and the Apostolic Nuncio, in 1515, 1517 and 1519 are well known but deserve to be restated, for they all emphasised his intellectual as well as his physical qualities:

> King Henry was not only very expert in arms, and of great valour, and most excellent in his personal endowments, but was likewise so gifted and adorned with mental accomplishments that they believed him to have few equals in the world. He spoke English, French, and Latin; understood Italian very well; played almost on every instrument; sang and composed freely; was prudent, sage, and free from every vice... [1515].[7]

This most invincible king, whose acquirements and qualities are so many and excellent that I consider him to excel all who ever wore a crown; and blessed and happy may this country call itself in having as its lord so worthy and eminent a sovereign... [1517][8]

King Henry was twenty-nine years old [in 1519], and much handsomer than any other Sovereign in Christendom – a great deal handsomer than the King of France. He was very fair, and his whole frame admirably proportioned. Hearing that King Francis wore a beard, he allowed his own to grow, and as it was reddish, he had then got a beard which looked like gold. He was very accomplished and a good musician; composed well; was a capital horseman, and a fine jouster; spoke good French, Latin, and Spanish; was very religious; heard three masses daily when he hunted, and sometimes five on other days, besides hearing the office daily in the queen's chamber, that is to say, vespers and compline. He was extremely fond of hunting, and never took that diversion without tiring eight or ten horses, which he caused to be stationed beforehand along the line of country he meant to take. He was also fond of tennis, at which game it was the prettiest thing in the world to see him play; his fair skin glowing through a shirt of the finest texture. He gambled with the French hostages to the amount, occasionally, it was said, of from 6,000 to 8,000 ducats in a day.

He was affable and gracious; harmed no one; did not covet his neighbour's goods, and was satisfied with his own dominions, having often said to the ambassador, '*Domine, Orator*, we want all potentates to content themselves with their own territories; we are satisfied with this island of ours.' He seemed extremely desirous of peace. [1519][9]

The Venetian ambassadors (and their staff) were highly professional observers of political and courtly life, not given to hyperbole and most certainly not taken in by appearances or beguiled by courtly glamour: when they reported to their fearsome employers, the Doge and Senate, they fully realised that they had to provide information and judgements that were based on the keenest and most impartial observation. It is useful therefore to recall that a decade or so later the secretary of another Venetian ambassador in London wrote even more admiringly of the king as 'a perfect model of manly beauty in these times':

He (Moriano) having nothing else to do, remained contemplating the physical beauty and perfection of his Majesty, for he can declare that never in his days did he see any – he will not say sovereign, the number of whom is small, but – man handsomer, more elegant, and better proportioned than this king, who is pink and white, fair, tall, agile, well formed, and graceful in all his movements and gestures. [He] chooses to believe that nature, in producing this prince, did her utmost to create a perfect model of manly beauty in these times ... [Henry was] so glorious and admirable a sovereign, in favour both with God and man. [1529][10]

The contrast with Henry VII could hardly be more manifest, and Henry VIII fully intended that it should be so: he had waited with a patience that could not have come readily to him to come to the throne and he was determined now to stamp his personality on court and country – and on Europe. On 24 April in the first act of his reign he dramatically separated himself from his father's government and announced a new beginning for himself by having Empson and Dudley imprisoned in the Tower of London.

The Royal Couple: Marriage & Coronations

Henry made an even more decisive a break with the past by deciding that he would marry Katharine. Gómez de Fuensalida was invited to the council and was almost speechless when told that Henry had decided to proceed with the marriage.[11] Henry let it be known that he was doing so in order to satisfy his father's dying request to him but this was spurious: Henry VIII was – we may be confident of this, surely! – a king to choose his own bride, and most especially so at the outset of his reign. He knew Katharine well, and indeed had become close enough to her to have worried his father into separating them from each other. Katharine was young and attractive and – the most important consideration for Henry VIII – she was from a proverbially fertile family; her mother had given birth to five children who lived to adulthood (1470–85), her sister Juana to five (1498–1507) and another sister, María, had already had six children since 1502 and would have another four by 1516. Moreover, each of Katharine's four siblings had – like her parents – been successful in regeneration within a year of marriage (although of course the child of Juan had died). Henry could therefore be reasonably confident that the marriage would lead to the birth of children, including – and especially – at least one boy. But the marriage also made manifest Henry's determination to pursue the friendship with Spain that was so fundamental to his anti-French policy. Henry VIII therefore began his reign by culling his father's ministers and by choosing his own wife. Shortly, he would choose his own war, happily aligning himself with the Pope so that he could do so.

Henry and Katharine were married without public ceremony in the friary church at Greenwich on 11 June.[12] It was strange that such an ebullient and extraverted king should have chosen to marry privately rather than in a great public service in St Paul's or Westminster Abbey. Indeed, even his austere father had made his own wedding into a great ceremony of state. It has been suggested that it was a mark of the new king's confidence in his right to the throne that he did not feel obliged to make such a grand public statement as his father had done. More probably, Henry wished to push through the marriage before any objections could be made to it on theological or political grounds: he knew well enough that there were those who believed that his marriage to his brother's widow was canonically indefensible and so he had it conducted it in private (and in effect in secrecy) precisely so that no opportunity might be given to anyone who wished to speak out against it.

Once Henry and Katharine were married there was no need for secrecy or subterfuge and no such inhibitions operated for their double coronation on Midsummer's Day, Sunday 24 June.[13] Now Henry could glory publicly in the security of his throne: Henry VII had been crowned alone so that no one could think that he owed his crown to his wife (who, it will be recalled, had a better claim to it than did Henry himself; above, chapter 3). But the double coronation of 1509 proclaimed glorious new certainties, at once opening and celebrating a new Golden Age: a courtier wrote that 'our king's heart is set not upon gold or jewels or mines of ore but upon virtue, reputation and eternal fame'.[14]

For all that the coronations of Henry and Katharine marked a dramatic new beginning they were organised under the precepts of a venerable old book; since at least 1307–08 the coronations of kings of England had been based upon the *Liber Regalis* and Henry rigorously followed its requirements.[15] The ceremonies were designed to emphasise that the royal couple were being crowned in accordance with hallowed traditions both secular and religious, and they were careful, too, to associate the leading dignitaries of court, church and state with them. There was a further purpose: like his father, Henry VIII was crowned not just as 'King of England' but also as 'King of France'.

The formal preparations for the coronation began on 20 June when the 'Coronation Claims Court' met to decide which dignitaries would be assigned the leading roles at the coronations and at the subsequent courtly revels. The decisions were of substantial political significance for they established priorities and pre-eminences that would endure well beyond the day of the coronations itself. It was decided that Edward Stafford, Duke of Buckingham, would serve as Constable for the day before the coronation and as Lord High Steward for the day itself and that Thomas Howard, Earl of Surrey, would act as Earl Marshal. These men thus set down markers for leadership at court under the new king, and it was no idle competition in which they now engaged: their rivalry would end with Buckingham mounting the scaffold in 1521 for treason.[16]

On 21 June the king moved to the Tower of London and there paid tribute to a tradition that had begun in 1399 of creating new Knights of the Bath in celebration of his coronation. Among the men who received this singular mark of royal favour was a comparatively unknown courtier whose name would come to resonate at court: Thomas Boleyn.

On Saturday 23 June, Henry and Katharine left the Tower of London for their formal procession into Westminster. Henry rode on horseback while Katharine was carried in a horse-drawn litter covered with a splendid canopy and she sat 'upon a cushion of white damask cloth of gold, bareheaded and wearing a round circle of gold set with pearls and precious stones'. Holinshed described her 'with hair hanging down to her back of very great length, beautiful and goodlie to behold'.[17] Like her husband, Katharine wore gold and jewels in abundance. The streets were hung with tapestries and cloth of gold and the dignitaries of the City of London consciously displayed their most lavish clothes; no doubt many of them ran up debts to do so. The barons of the Cinque Ports held canopies over the royal couple and the guilds and liveried companies of the City competed with each other in the welcome they gave to Henry and Katharine. The people of London played their role in their thousands, raucously cheering the young couple.

The procession halted as it approached the Grand Conduit and Thomas More, a young lawyer, welcomed Henry and Katharine on behalf of the Mercer's Company. More was a distinguished intellectual who had known Henry for a decade; in 1499, when the prince was only eight years old he had presented him with some verses and introduced him to his friend the great Dutch humanist Desiderius Erasmus. Now, in elegant Latin, More eulogised the new king's physical and intellectual abilities, his learning and his respect for the law. It was remarkable that More should have dared to criticise the king's father, if only obliquely, by praising Henry VIII for having 'banished fear and oppression': he must surely must have cleared this remark with senior figures at court for time would show that he was the most discreet of men. Less controversial was his welcome to Katharine, the future 'mother of kings' who 'fecund in male offspring will … render your dynasty stable and enduring for all time'.[18]

Unfortunately, no sooner had More's eulogy concluded than a violent storm shattered the elegance and splendour of the parade. Katharine's canopy collapsed under the weight of water and she was soaked; she took refuge under a tradesman's awning and waited for the downpour to cease. When she proceeded on her way, her beautiful hair and clothing were bedraggled.

At daybreak on coronation day, Sunday 24 June 1509, Henry and Katharine were led in procession from Whitehall to Westminster Hall accompanied by the lords temporal; in the great hall Henry took his place on the 'King's Bench' in recognition of his role as lawgiver while Katharine sat on a slightly lower throne.

The 900 yards from Westminster Hall to the abbey were covered in blue ray-cloth and the royal procession was led along it by the newly invested knights of the Bath and the senior dignitaries of Court and Church. Henry Bourchier, Earl of Essex, carried the king's sword while three earls carried the secular insignia – Buckingham as Lord High Steward of the coronation carried St Edward's crown; on his right, the Earl of Surrey, as Earl Marshal, held the sceptre and on his left, William Fitzalan, Earl of Arundel, carried the orb. The archbishops of Canterbury and York (William Warham and Christopher Bainbridge) were dressed in pontifical vestments and the Abbot of Westminster (John Islip) carried the regalia to the altar: tradition had it that these had belonged to Edward the Confessor, patron saint of English kingship – the stone chalice, paten, staff and crown, the sceptre with the cross, the rod with the dove, three swords and the spurs. Henry processed after the archbishops; he was accompanied by the bishops of Exeter and Ely, while the barons of the Cinque Ports held a golden canopy over him throughout the ceremony. Katharine and her attendants followed her husband. The queen's regalia consisted of a crown, 'a sceptre of gold with a dove in the top' and a 'rod …[which] also had a dove in the top'.

The ceremonies in the abbey were rigidly structured and compartmentalised.[19] The first of these was 'the Recognition'. A stage had been constructed in front of the high altar and Henry and Katharine were led to their thrones on it. Archbishop Warham then accompanied Henry to the four corners of the abbey, proclaiming that by the laws of God and of man he was the legitimate heir to the throne, and asking the assembled people whether they accepted him as such: loudly, they affirmed that they did. In that moment, Henry became King of England, the 'rightful and undoubted inheritor by the Laws of God'.

The coronation service took place within the Mass itself. Henry was accompanied to the altar and was offered a pall and a pound of gold. He then reverently prostrated himself on the floor (as a priest would do at the beginning of his ordination Mass). On rising, he took the oath to observe the laws and privileges of the kingdom, including the freedom of the clergy and people. He solemnly swore on the Gospels that 'with good will and devout soul I promise and perfectly grant to each and every one of you and to all the Churches which are committed to you that I will maintain the privileges of canon law and of holy Church'. Having sworn that he would be a good and faithful son of the Church, Henry was anointed as king by the supreme representative of that Church in England, the Archbishop of Canterbury – on his hands, breast, back, shoulders, elbows and head.

Recognised now as monarch by both the Church and his loyal subjects and dressed in his coronation robes and spurs, Henry sat in front of the high altar. His sword was blessed in recognition that he was the defender of the realm and St Edward's crown was then censed and blessed and placed on his head and he was invested with all the regalia of monarchy. As the lawful King of England, Henry VIII now received the homage of the clergy and peers. Katharine was then anointed on her forehead and chest and invested with a ring, crown, sceptre and rod; she was now the lawful Queen of England. At the climax of the Mass, Henry and Katharine received communion in private behind a silken cloth. After the Mass had concluded they were taken to St Edward's shrine behind the high altar to disrobe of their garments of state in preparation for the procession back to Westminster Hall.

Now the people of London again saluted the royal couple. A house had been constructed in Westminster Hall, covered with tapestries and crowned with an imperial crown – the first indication that Henry was to be regarded as an Emperor within his own realm. The Lord Marshal ushered each person to his or her appointed seat. The trumpets were sounded for the banquet to begin and the Duke of Buckingham and the

Lord Steward, both mounted on horses that were lavishly covered with embroidered trappings, led in the 'truly sumptuous' banquet.

On the following day a tournament was held. In one gruesome spectacle a number of men ('Lady Pallass's Scholars') dressed as foresters or gamekeepers in green cloth arranged a paddock into which young deer were brought; dogs were then set loose on them and as the deer were killed they were presented to Queen Katharine and her ladies. Another group of men now entered ('Crocheman and his Knights') who declared that they were the servants of the goddess Diana and had heard that the Lady Pallass's knights had come into these parts to perform feats of arms. They therefore challenged the knights to combat and Crocheman proclaimed that if Lady Pallass's knights defeated them they would be given the greyhounds and the corpses of the deer but that if Diana's knights were successful they themselves were to be given the swords of the knights whom they had defeated. Katharine and her ladies duly asked Henry for advice and he ruled that because the conflict was fraught with danger each party would be allowed only a restricted number of thrusts at each other and that the prizes would go on the merits of individual soldiers. Henry's decision was duly admired as representing a first proof of his wisdom.[20]

Not until 17 July did Henry write to Ferdinand to inform him that he had buried his father and had married Katharine. Henry assured Ferdinand that the marriage ceremonies had been splendid and that they had been 'most enthusiastically' welcomed by enormous crowds of his subjects. Notwithstanding the discourtesy involved in the delay in writing, Henry assured his father-in-law that although the festivities had been of exceptional quality he himself was not neglecting affairs of state.[21] Katharine also wrote to Ferdinand of her happiness and of her deep love for her husband. Ferdinand replied that he hoped that their joy would last for their lifetimes for 'to be well married is the greatest blessing in the world' and that 'a good marriage is not only an excellent thing in itself but creates all other kinds of contentment'. For once, we may assume that Ferdinand was speaking from the heart.[22]

The Court of Henry VIII

The celebrations for the coronations of Henry and Katharine set the tone for the court life of the early years of the reign. Henry's view of kingship was delightfully uncomplicated – in that it was defined by its magnificence. He certainly shared Edward IV's taste for splendid display and for the rituals and glory of chivalry.[23] The examples of the

Burgundian and French courts – which Henry only knew of course by reputation – were paramount for him. And of course he had his father's treasure to spend.

The court of the early modern nation-states was the focal point of national life.[24] This meant that the royal household was not merely composed of the nobles and courtiers – men and women – who served the king and his queen but also incorporated the noblemen and women who added lustre to to it by their presence and liberality; the administrators who found the money to pay for it; the judges who administered the laws; the churchmen who managed the consciences of king, court and political nation.

In the early sixteenth century kings did not spend the whole of their year in the capital city; indeed, Spain did not even have a capital city while the King of France might spend only days or weeks at a time in Paris.[25] Henry VIII did not like to spend the heat of summer in London and especially so when there was the merest hint of illness. In particular, Henry was fearful of 'the sweating sickness' which seems to have first appeared in 1486; death could come within hours although 'it was an easy death'. A particularly savage outbreak hit London in August 1517 and was still virulent a year later. It caused an immense number of deaths and severely dislocated the work of court and government since Henry fled to the country, leaving ministers and courtiers behind him.[26]

The City of London had a disproportionate influence on national life. It still had much of its medieval walling and although it only had about 50,000 inhabitants it was a vibrant capital, at once the centre of the court and judiciary. Although it had two great churches in which the major ceremonies of the Church took place (Westminster Abbey and St Paul's Cathedral) it was not the ecclesiastical capital – that privilege belonged to the archiepiscopal see of Canterbury – but its 100 or so parishes were an expression of the deep-rooted Catholicism of its people. Like Paris it had the advantage of being inland on a great navigable river; the Thames enabled London to become a major commercial and trading centre (and also allowed the monarch to gain ready access by water to his palaces within the metropolis and those as far afield as Windsor Castle.

London is the capital of the kingdom and the residence of the ambassadors and merchants; it is a very notable city situated on the Thames, a magnificent river, navigable for vessels of any burden, 60 miles from the sea, and with a very strong tide. This river is convenient for trade, embellishing the city, and rendering it cheerful, and over it is a very large stone bridge.

London contains many houses on either side of the river, and two large churches of extreme beauty [*sc.* St. Paul's and Westminster Abbey], in one of which the present king's father is buried. In various parts of the city there are many palaces of divers citizens and merchants, but the larger ones and the most superb are on the river, the owners being the chief personages of the kingdom. Besides the two belonging to the king and one to the queen, the three dukes (*sc.* Norfolk, Suffolk and Richmond), the two marquises (*sc.* Dorset and Exeter), and several bishops have mansions there, each of them worth 12,000 crowns, with very delightful gardens.

The population of London is immense, and comprises many artificers. The houses are in very great number, but ugly, and half the materials are of wood, nor are the streets wide. In short, I am of the opinion, all things considered, that it is a very rich, populous and mercantile city, but not beautiful.[27]

Henry VII had not turned his attention to improving his network of palaces in London until the later 1490s, probably because only then did he feel secure on his throne.[28] His first major building project had followed on the destruction by fire of much of the royal property in Sheen in Richmond in 1497; he rebuilt it and renamed it as Richmond Palace to commemorate his own Earldom of Richmond. He introduced galleries built on the Burgundian model but the palace remained a reconstruction of a medieval building rather than a contemporary one. It was used for the celebrations of the marriage of Arthur and Katharine. In 1502 Henry extended the palace by founding the house of the Friars Observant next to it.

Henry VII's most significant building was the riverside palace at Greenwich, which he completed by 1504. It was built around a courtyard and provided lodgings for the king and queen. It too was built as a Burgundian palace and had a gallery connecting it with the Church of the Friars Observant. Henry also built new towers and galleries at the Tower of London and Windsor Castle. In 1501 or so he began rebuilding Baynard's Castle as a town house.

Henry VIII did not become really interested in building projects until about 1530 or so and his commitment thereafter justified Simon Thurley's description of him as 'certainly the most prolific, talented and innovative builder to sit on the English throne'. In the early years of his reign he used the palaces that he had inherited from his father and allowed Thomas Wolsey freedom to develop his buildings at York Place and Hampton Court. In time Henry would demonstrate how much he had learned from his first minister.[29]

Henry VIII's court was a great national stage on which the young king could demonstrate his chivalric and physical qualities. Accordingly, the court became the centre of an apparently unending series of festivities, tournaments and pageants, whether for the traditional feast-days (such as Christmas and New Year, Easter, May Day and Midsummer) or for special occasions such as the birth of a royal infant or the welcoming of foreign rulers or their ambassadors. He was particularly concerned to have music of excellence and in 1516 persuaded Friar Dionisius Memmo, the celebrated organist of St Mark's Cathedral in Venice, to move to London and become his chaplain and director of music.[30]

Henry threw himself with the fullest energy into tournaments; Sydney Anglo has shown how during the years to 1524 or so Henry participated as the central figure in these tournaments, sometimes even at risk of serious injury. Although the king was ostensibly disguised so that he could win the tournament without being recognised, no one could fail to identify his burly figure or indeed his splendid energy. Henry delighted in his physical prowess and took special pleasure in displaying himself to his new bride.[31] In May 1510, Luis Caroz, the new Spanish ambassador, wrote a report of the tournaments to which Henry gave himself with such zest:

> The King of England amuses himself almost every day of the week with running the ring, and with jousts and tournaments on foot, in which one single person fights with an appointed adversary. Two days in the week are dedicated to this kind of tournament, which is to continue till the Feast of St John, and which is instituted in imitation of Amadis and Lancelot and other knights of olden times, of whom so much is written in books.
>
> The combatants are clad in breast plates and wear a special kind of helmet. They use lances of fourteen hands breadth long with blunted iron points. They throw these lances at one another and fight afterwards with two-handed swords, each of the combatants dealing twelve strokes. They are separated from one another by a barrier which reaches up to the waist in order to prevent them from seizing one another and wrestling.

There are many young men who excel in this kind of warfare but the most conspicuous among them all, the most assiduous and the most committed in the combats is the king himself, who never omits being present at them.[32]

Katharine greatly admired her husband's prowess on the tournament field and from the time of the coronation attended as often as she could; in one miniature painting she can be seen in a central position. She enjoyed the less rumbustious entertainments at court and played her part in all of them, enjoying the dances and laughing at Henry's enthusiasm and tomfoolery.

As queen, Katharine had a household of nearly 200 people. Her household was controlled by William, Lord Mountjoy, as Chamberlain. She had eight ladies-in-waiting, led by two sisters of the Duke of Buckingham, Elizabeth and Anne Stafford.

Katharine seems to have developed her closest friendship with Margaret Pole. Margaret's family had a claim on the throne and had suffered dreadfully for it; her father had been executed by Edward IV (his brother) and her brother Edward by Henry VII in 1499 to prepare the way for Katharine's arrival in England. For this reason, the relationship between the two women may well have initially been fraught. They knew each other briefly in Ludlow, where Margaret's husband, Sir Richard, was Prince Arthur's Chamberlain but seem to have lost touch until Margaret returned to court at the accession of Henry VIII and became a lady-in-waiting to the queen. They then became close friends. Indeed, Katharine may well have influenced her husband to favour Margaret; the restoration to her of her brother's lands in 1512 was followed in 1513 by the grant to her of the Earldom of Salisbury. Henry also paid for her son Reginald to study at Oxford University. When Katharine gave birth to Mary in 1516, Margaret was named as her governess. The relationship between the two women deepened over subsequent years and Margaret remained loyal to her mistress. Indeed in 1541 she went to the block in imitation of her father and brother and in tribute to her friendship with Katharine; the execution was horribly botched and the axeman needed ten (or more) strokes to despatch her.

The Childbearing Years: 1509–1518
Childbed, 1509–18

The dazzling success of the coronation (and its subsequent tournaments and festivities) was soon eclipsed, for Katharine became pregnant almost immediately. On 1 November 1509 Henry joyously wrote to Ferdinand that 'the queen is pregnant, and the child in her womb is alive'.[33] Ferdinand's joy on receiving the news was tempered with the calculation that came so naturally to him; he urged Katharine to avoid all exertions during her pregnancy. Indeed, she was not even to write in her own hand! He added, 'With the first child it is necessary for women to take greater care of themselves than [they have to] with subsequent deliveries.'[34]

Katharine now became subject to a highly structured routine as preparation for her delivery.[35] It is probable that she made a will, mindful of the hazards that she was about to endure, but no record of this has survived. At the end of January she 'took the chamber', passing from the world of the court which was dominated by men into a chamber peopled entirely by the women who would look after her. She stood beneath her cloth of state and shared wines and spices with members of the court and Lord Mountjoy, her Chamberlain, called on all present to pray that God would protect her ('give her the good hour') in the perils that she was about to undergo. She then entered the birthing room; no men were allowed to enter, although they could bring provisions and supplies to the door.[36]

Tragically, on 31 January 1510 – thirty-three weeks after the wedding – Katharine was delivered of a stillborn daughter. She and Henry were devastated and they determined to keep the tragedy quiet: Katharine remained in her confinement and it was given out at court that her pregnancy was continuing. The truth was known to only four people other than the couple themselves.

It seems certain that Henry and Katharine immediately resumed sexual relations in the desperate hope that Katharine could conceive again and spare both of them from having to admit to her failure to carry her child to term. As the weeks dragged on, talk began at court of a 'phantom pregnancy'. But by the end of May Katharine was indeed once again pregnant. Only now did she and Henry inform Ferdinand that she had miscarried four months earlier: on 25 May, Diego Fernández wrote to Ferdinand that Katharine was pregnant, adding that on 'the last day of January in the morning her Highness brought forth a daughter ... this affair was so secret that no one knew it until now except the king my lord, two Spanish women, a physician and I'.[37] Katharine wrote to her father two days later that she had been delivered of a still-born daughter 'some days ago' – even now she could not bring herself to give her father the full details, much less to explain how she had remained silent on the matter for four months. She had, she informed Ferdinand, 'miscarried a dead daughter and because it was considered here an ill omen I did not write before to tell your Highness'; she begged her father 'not to be angry with her for it was the will of God' and assured him that she thanked God for having given her such a gentle and understanding husband.[38] The secret of the stillbirth had been so well kept that not even the new Spanish ambassador, Luis Caroz, knew of it.

Historians have puzzled over the mystery of Katharine's second pregnancy following so immediately (and secretively) upon the failure of her first. They have not been helped by Caroz, who was evidently furious that he had not been informed of the stillbirth in January; scathingly, he wrote that the queen was continuing in her confinement even though it was known (in April–May) that she was menstruating. He did not understand the depth of the embarrassment that Henry and Katharine felt at her failure to bring her first child to term, and perhaps too he could not comprehend the crushing sense of shame that consumed the queen. Nor, too, did Caroz – and those who have followed him – understand that midwives in the early sixteenth century recognised – quite correctly – that a woman could continue to menstruate during early pregnancy.[39]

The gamble taken by Henry and Katharine in having the queen continue in her confinement was triumphantly vindicated: on 1 January 1511 Katharine was delivered of a boy. Naturally, the day was held to be a portent: what could be more indicative of God's favour than to produce the heir to the throne on New Year's Day! The child was named after his father and was baptised on 5 January.[40] Exultant, Henry made a pilgrimage to Walsingham to give thanks. The 'churching' of Katharine took place in February and to celebrate her reintegration into court life Henry held what was claimed to have been the most expensive tournament ever held in England.[41] The new Golden Age had truly begun. But it came to a shuddering halt when, on 22 February, Prince Henry died, probably of a bronchial failure: he was fifty-two days old. Henry and Katharine were beyond grief. But as he collected himself, Henry displayed his most ebullient and generous qualities: he was extremely solicitous of his wife. For her part, Katharine professed herself to be very proud of her husband.[42]

It would be two years before Katharine became pregnant again. The tragedy then repeated itself; on 17 September 1513 the queen was delivered of a male child but he lived if at all only for a few hours.[43]

And again: in November 1514 Katharine gave birth to a prince who survived at most for a very short time, possibly because he was slightly premature: 'The queen has been delivered of a stillborn male child of eight months to the very great grief of the whole court,' reported the Venetian ambassador.[44] On 18 February 1516 Katharine was at last delivered of a child who lived, and although Henry was disappointed that it was a girl he once again gallantly supported his wife, proclaiming that 'we are both young; if it was a daughter this time, by the grace of God, the sons will follow'.[45] On 9–10 November 1518 Katharine gave birth to a stillborn daughter, and again it may have been a premature delivery: 'The queen has been delivered in her eighth month of a stillborn daughter to the great sorrow of the nation at large.'[46] It was a crushing disappointment: 'Never had the kingdom so anxiously desired anything as it did a prince,' wrote the Venetian ambassador.[47] It was Katharine's last delivery.

Katharine in Childbed, 1509–18

31 January 1510	Unnamed girl	Stillborn (33 weeks?)
1 January 1511	Prince Henry	Died 22 February 1511
17 September 1513	Unnamed boy	Premature? Stillborn?
November 1514	Unnamed boy	Premature? Lived for a few hours?
18 February 1516	Princess Mary	Died 17 November 1558
10 November 1518	Unnamed girl	Premature? Stillborn?

Katharine's six verifiable pregnancies therefore resulted in the birth of only two children who lived more than a few hours – Prince Henry (1511), who survived less than two months and Princess Mary (1516) who lived for forty-two years. Two children (in 1510 and 1518) were certainly stillborn and two others may well have been but certainly did not live more than a few hours (1513, 1514). In four of her pregnancies, therefore, the difficulty that Katharine experienced was in carrying her children to term (of thirty-nine weeks) and delivering them safely.

Much has been made of Katharine's 'miscarriages' but Professor John Dewhurst, a distinguished gynaecologist, has urged historians to be very cautious in their use of this term: in modern scientific parlance, the definition of miscarriage should be 'the expulsion of the child from the womb before twenty-eight weeks of pregnancy'. It is far from clear that any of Katharine's deliveries can be thus categorised. We need to remember that not every pregnancy would be known to observers at court, but it seems likely that only in the thirty-two or so months between her deliveries in 1511 and 1513 and perhaps in the years after the disappointment of 1518 could Katharine have miscarried according to this definition. There is no reliable record of her having done so: the probability is that the list above represents the full record of her pregnancies.[48]

The King & the Queen

Henry took great pride in his queen in the early years of their marriage. He treated her with great tenderness, most especially during her pregnancies; for instance, he ensured that when she was about to give birth at the beginning of 1516 no one told her that her father had died.[49] She accompanied him to courtly and political occasions – to the May Day celebrations in 1515[50] or to the launching of the *Henry Grâce á Dieu* in the same year.[51] Most notably of all, when he left in 1513 to wage war on the King of France he entrusted Katharine with the responsibility of being his Regent. Theirs was evidently a happy marriage.

Some of their interaction was indeed playful, suggesting an easy familiarity with each other. The great rivalry that blossomed between Henry and Francis I after the latter's accession in January 1515 led to a lighthearted competition over the luxuriance of their beards: Henry announced that he would not shave until he had met Francis, who reciprocated by promising that he, too, would grow a beard until he met Henry. As the hairs on the kingly chin sprouted, Katharine took exception and persuaded Henry to cut his beard off. Diplomatically, it was given out that the love between the two kings lay in their hearts, not on their chins.[52]

The most public demonstration of Katharine's influence over Henry came after the 'Apprentices Riots' of May 1517. On May Day, hundreds of apprentices rioted in London, protesting against the privileged position of foreign traders and merchants. Ordinary Londoners readily joined in, attacking not only artisans and merchants but even some ambassadors, among them the Spanish and Portuguese. The rioters even threatened Wolsey himself and the Lord Mayor of London. There was, in truth, more sound than fury involved and the riot largely burned itself out by the evening, by which time effective action by the authorities had led to hundreds of arrests. For the first time in the reign Henry showed his ability to respond with savagery to crisis; a score or so leaders were hanged at the gates of the city and their bodies were quartered and publicly displayed. But having dealt with the ringleaders, Henry clearly wanted to draw a line under the incident and so he organised a highly elaborate charade on 14 May in Westminster Hall that enabled him to demonstrate his magnanimity to young men who had clearly been led astray. Paraded in front of the king were 400 rioters with halters around their necks to indicate the fate that awaited them. Henry was accompanied by Katharine and, with tears in her eyes, she threw herself on to her knees and begged her husband to pardon the culprits. Her example stimulated Wolsey and some leading noblemen to implore the king for mercy. Persuaded, Henry ordered that they be released. Henry's popularity soared but so too did Katharine's: Henry would one day come to regret just how popular Katharine was with the citizens of his capital city.[53]

The First War with France

The growth of French power in Italy that was symbolised by the great victory at Agnadello in May 1509 led Pope Julius to reverse his policies in the peninsula; fearful now of the power of France, he made peace with Venice (February) and hired 6,000 Swiss infantrymen (March); he then formally invested Ferdinand with the Crown of Naples (July) so that he could be sure of his support against France.[54]

Henry yearned to become involved in the war but was not able to do so, perhaps because he felt the need to balance the factions in his council; in March 1510 he signed a peace with France and on 24 May with Spain.[55] He had to content himself in 1511 by sending two small expeditions on to the European mainland as an expression of his power. He despatched Lord Thomas Darcy with 1,500 archers to Spain to help in the crusade against 'the Moors' but when Darcy arrived at Cadiz in the middle of June he found that Ferdinand had lost interest in the campaign and returned home: it was a first warning to the young king of the hazards of dealing with his father-in-law. Henry then sent Sir Edward Poynings with 1,000 archers to help Margaret of Savoy in her war with the Duke of Guelders; these were more successful.[56]

On 4 October 1511 Julius formed 'the Holy League' with Spain and Venice to drive the French out of Italy. When Julius excommunicated Louis XII, Henry VIII enthusiastically joined the League (13 November) and agreed with Ferdinand that he would attack France during 1512 (Treaty of Westminster, November 1511): how better to show his mettle than by fighting a holy war with powerful allies in support of the Pope against France?[57]

Some senior English councillors were troubled that England was set upon provoking France and insisted that Henry should maintain his father's policy of peace with France, insisting that Louis XII was anxious to remain on friendly terms with Henry and that England had no vital interests in northern Italy. They also argued that war with France would very probably damage England's relations with Scotland. However, a group of younger councillors argued enthusiastically in favour of the war. Most notable among them were young men who were contemporaries of the king and could be counted as friends – Charles Brandon, Richard Neville, Thomas Howard and Thomas Grey.

Chief among the advisers who urged Henry VIII to go to war with France was Katharine. She begged him to support her father in war, insisting that he should win martial glory for himself at the outset of his reign. Her arguments found support from the Duke of Buckingham and Lord Edward Howard and even from Archbishop Warham, who urged Parliament to support the Pope in his war against France.[58] Julius II proved evermore accommodating to the young king: in March 1512 he agreed to transfer Louis XII's realms and titles – including even that of Most Christian King – to Henry VIII. This was not to be published until Louis had been defeated, but it would be a delectable triumph over the King of France for Henry to assume his most cherished title.

As a loyal son of the Church Henry probably paid little heed when Louis XII demonstrated the damage that a king could inflict upon the papacy but in time to come he must have remembered the King of France's strategies. Louis XII encouraged his cardinals to send out invitations for a General Council of the Church which would meet in Pisa in September and suspend the Pope from the exercise of his office. Only a few cardinals turned up but in April 1512 the renegade council declared that 'the Pope has incurred the penalties laid down by the holy decrees of the Councils of Constance and Basle; we therefore declare that he is suspended from his papal office and that his authority lawfully devolves on to this present assembly'.[59]

The threat was chilling reminder of the papacy's imprisonment at Avignon and Julius responded by convening an authentic General Council: the fifth 'Lateran Council' opened in April 1512, but its primary purpose was not to reform the Church so much as to unite Christendom in a war against the King of France.

Henry's preparations were thorough. Parliament readily voted him a tax for war on France. In April 1512, Admiral Howard swept the Channel and the Western Approaches with a fleet of eighteen ships. He landed some men who pillaged villages in Brittany but when he engaged a French fleet the *Regent* grappled with an enemy ship and went to the bottom when an explosion ripped through the magazine of the French ship; only 180 men were saved out of 600. Howard's next engagement with a French fleet cost him his life when he foolishly tried to assault some galleys in harbour in Brittany (April 1513).[60]

Louis XII entrusted his army in Italy to his brilliant young nephew Gaston de Foix. Initially, Foix won dazzling victories over the armies of the Holy League but after he was killed at the Battle of Ravenna in April 1512 the morale of his army disintegrated. When – at Pope Julius's prompting – the Swiss invaded Milan, the French retreated homeward and Massimiliano de Sforza was established as Duke of Milan.[61] The French had lost their powerbase in northern Italy. As a lesser consequence of the French collapse, the Medici were restored to power in Florence.

Ferdinand's immediate priority in 1512 was to secure Spain's Pyrenean frontier by conquering Navarre and when he suggested that Henry could take advantage of his attack on Navarre to reconquer Gascony Henry jumped gleefully at the opportunity. In the summer of 1512 he sent 12,000 men to Spain under Thomas Grey, 2nd Marquis of Dorset; they carried a papal indulgence forgiving the sins of all who died in battle. The campaign was an unmitigated fiasco. Ferdinand wanted the English force merely to cover his campaign against Navarre and Dorset and his men spent months at Fuenterrabía waiting to be summoned to war while Ferdinand conquered Navarre. Since they were not properly provisioned for a long campaign their food supplies soon proved to be inadequate. Worse, their supplies of beer soon ran out; when the soldiery attempted to compensate for this by drinking local wine both their digestive systems and their discipline were wrecked. By the autumn the English force was little better than a drunken and angry mob and it pillaged local villages. In October, in defiance of their commander, the men returned home. It was profoundly humiliating for Henry; instead of reclaiming former glories in France he had been deceived and manipulated by his ally and deeply embarrassed by the incompetence and drunkenness of his own troops.[62]

In November 1512, Maximilian joined the Holy League. Plans were now made for a fourfold onslaught on France which would – it was confidently hoped – lead to the break-up of the country. Julius II and Massimiliano Sforza would invade from Italy; Maximilian from the Low Countries; Henry VIII from Calais, and Ferdinand through Gascony and Languedoc. France would be dismembered. In November Parliament voted the necessary taxes. Henry would revenge himself in person for the humiliations that his armed forces had suffered in 1511-12.

The tumultuous pontificate of Julius II came to an end with his death on 12 February 1513. In February he was succeeded by Cardinal Giovanni de' Medici, who took the name of Leo X. The new Pope was a patron of the arts and a man who loved the pleasures of life but most of all he loved his own family: it would be the central precept of his papacy that he would advance the power and prestige of the Medici family. Although Leo was much less obviously corrupt than Alexander VI and less abrasive than Julius II, his tenure of the papacy was, in its very different way, to be deeply corrosive of its public morality and damaging to its reputation.

The death of Julius II encouraged Louis XII to re-establish his power in northern Italy. In March 1513, Louis XII allied with Venice and in May a French army once again crossed the Alps to attack Milan. For the first time they suffered a major defeat in battle when the Swiss crushed them at Novara (6 June). Massimiliano was recognised by the Holy League as Duke of Milan. The Swiss invaded France and besieged Dijon; they lifted the siege only when the French commander agreed to abandon French claims to Milan. Louis promptly renounced the agreement.[63] For the second campaign in succession the military power of France had been humiliated. On 18 April, Henry and Ferdinand joined in an alliance against France.[64]

But for Ferdinand, there was triumph; on 23 March 1513 the Cortes of Navarre formally acknowledged the absorption of the kingdom into the Crown of Castile.[65] Ferdinand lambasted the English as contemptible soldiers and made peace with France. He justified his treachery by claiming that his greatest concern was for the good of the Church and that the best service that he and Henry could perform for Christianity would be to pursue the reform of the Church. He also claimed that he wanted to postpone the Anglo-Spanish war against France until it had a more realistic chance of success.[66] He doubtless enjoyed Henry's humiliation but was no whit distressed by it, for he had secured his northern frontier, rounding out his achievement of reacquiring Roussillon and Cerdaña in 1493 with the conquest of Navarre.

The Campaigns of 1513: Thérouanne, Tournai & Flodden Field

On 25 April 1513 the parties to the Holy League swore at St Paul's Cathedral that they would go to war against the excommunicated King of France. Henry prepared the way for his departure for France by ordering the execution of Edmund de la Pole, Earl of Suffolk, imprisoned in the Tower of London since 1506; he dared not risk having de la Pole serve as a focal point for dissent and the long-delayed sentence was carried out on 30 April. Henry demonstrated his confidence in Katharine by naming her as his Regent during his absence: the queen would be responsible for the government of England while he was away.

On 30 June 1513, Henry led an army of 30,000–40,000 men in magnificent splendour from Dover to Calais.[67] Once again, an ally failed to deliver on his promises: early in August, Maximilian arrived with only 2,000 men. If this was a derisory force, Henry accepted with alacrity Maximilian's offer to serve him as a footsoldier: what, after all, could add more lustre to his own reputation (and generalship) than having the Holy Roman Emperor-elect as one of his soldiers! He allowed Maximilian to tag along. Certainly, Katharine was immensely proud of Henry's martial fervour, regarding him as a crusader against the 'schismatical' King of France; as Henry prepared his campaign, in September 1512 she described his motives to the English ambassador in Rome so that he could represent them to the Pope:

Her consort is so bent on war against the French, the foes of the Church, that he is determined never to rest or desist until their king be utterly destroyed; having said openly to all hearers a few days previously that he firmly believed that neither the Pope nor his very dear father [King Ferdinand] would ever desert him, though if by any chance they should happen thus to do, yet he would never withdraw from this war until that schismatical sovereign be made an end of.[68]

Katharine constantly urged Wolsey to do all that he could to keep Henry out of harms way. The campaign was satisfactorily brief.[69] On 16 August, a French attempt to relieve Thérouanne was fought off and so rapidly did the French cavalry flee the field – and the English chase joyously after them – that the engagement became derisively known as 'the Battle of the Spurs'. Thérouanne surrendered on 23 August. The prizes were great: some 240 French noblemen and ten or so banners and standards were taken. On 24 August Henry entered Thérouanne in splendid triumph. Katharine was as exultant as her husband: 'The victory hath been so great that I think none such hath been seen before. All England hath cause to thank God for it, and I specially, seeing that the king beginneth so well.'[70]

Henry was little more than irritated when a Scottish herald arrived at Thérouanne to declare that if he did not withdraw from France James IV would invade England in support of his ally Louis XII. Henry would not be deterred and proceeded to besiege Tournai; the town surrendered on 23 September and two days later Henry enjoyed an even more splendid 'joyous entry' at Tournai than he had at Thérouanne. It was especially satisfying to him that he received the keys in his capacity as King of France. He was now truly a conqueror of the French, a worthy successor to Henry V and Edward IV.

And, without knowing it, he had gained an even greater victory at home James IV had indeed supported his French ally by crossing into England but on 9 September, Surrey comprehensively destroyed his forces at Flodden Field. James was killed, skewered by two pikes, many of his senior nobles were killed or taken prisoner and perhaps 10,000 of his soldiers died with him. Katharine wrote to Henry that 'to my thinking, this battle hath been to your Grace and all your realm the greatest honour that could be, and more than you should win all the Crown of France'. She reminded him to thank God for the victory: 'I am sure that your Grace forgets not to do this, which shall be the cause of sending you many more such great victories, as I trust He shall do.' Katharine had originally intended to send James IV's corpse to Henry but was dissuaded from doing so by her advisers – 'our Englishmens' hearts would not suffer it'. She prayed that God would send Henry home safely to her promptly and undertook to make a pilgrimage to Walsingham to give thanks for the great victory. She signed herself 'your humble wife and true servant, Katharine'.[71]

As Katharine almost implied, the triumph at Flodden was in truth much greater than Henry's in France and it had long-term consequences: Scotland was left without the capacity to defend itself and the regency for James V passed into the hands of his mother, Margaret, sister of Henry VIII. It would be a long time before a Scottish army would dare engage an English army again. Both successes, therefore, confirmed Henry in his conviction that he had gained important and prestigious victories.

In reality, Henry's triumphs at Thérouanne and Tournai proved to be extraordinarily expensive. It was said that he had taken with him fourteen wagons full of gold and another four of silver. All this had been spent and for no great purpose, for the acquisition of the two towns proved to be inordinately expensive since they had now had to be garrisoned and defended against the King of France. The real beneficiary was Maximilian, who without contributing anything of substance to the campaign had been protected against the uses that Louis could have made of the two towns against his territories. One of the king's servants benefited substantially, too: Thomas Wolsey, who had organised the campaign, was raised to the Bishopric of Tournai.[72]

In October, Henry returned home in triumph and promptly agreed a new league against France.[73] During the next few months he rewarded the friends who had helped him win military glory – Surrey was created 2nd Duke of Norfolk and his son Thomas became 1st Earl of Surrey, and Charles Brandon was raised to the Dukedom of Suffolk. This cohort of young men would exercise enhanced influence in the aftermath of triumph. But so, too, would the little-known churchman who was raised to the Bishopric of Lincoln, for Henry recognised that the true architect of his great victories of 1513 was Thomas Wolsey.

The Rise of Thomas Wolsey, Cardinal & Lord Chancellor

Thomas Wolsey had entered royal service in the last days of Henry VII. He rose with astonishing suddenness under Henry VIII so that, having been an unknown royal almoner in 1509, by 1515 he stood at the head of Church, government and judiciary. He retained his power until he fell from favour with Henry in 1529. Wolsey fascinated his contemporaries and his spell has endured with historians but the verdicts passed on him have been subject to the most dramatic (and even violent) swings. In the nineteenth and early twentieth centuries, serious historians caricatured him as the emblematic figure of all that was wrong with the Catholic Church in England. He was dismissed as having helped through his own cupidity and vanity to fostering the anti-clericalism that was so fundamental in preparing the ground for the success of the Reformation in England.

Historians began to reappraise Wolsey from the middle or so of the twentieth century. Professors Elton and Scarisbrick both discerned in him a statesman of substance who had many positive achievements to his name and in recent years he has come to be seen as an innovative statesman and lawyer; most notably has this been evident in the splendid biography by Peter Gwynn.[74] At the same time, Henry's contribution to government in his early years has been reappraised. In particular, Professor George W. Bernard has demonstrated that Henry never kept less than the most vigilant eye on the development of his government's policies on major matters and that while he continued to enjoy the hunt, the joust, the banquets and the dances he was always aware of what was being done in his name. The king who was once seen as a dilettante in his early years is now viewed as a deeply vigilant and committed monarch, able to reconcile his kingly pleasures with his obligations: in his magnificent study, Bernard reminds us of the ever-present power and authority of Henry VIII, even as a young man.

All have been agreed that Wolsey had an extraordinary capacity for sustained hard work and that he developed a remarkably close working relationship with Henry VIII. Certainly, Henry was determined always to keep a close eye on the general drift of policy but he had no intention of committing himself on a daily basis to studying correspondence and balance-sheets as his father had done. He much preferred to enjoy the delights of court life and of his equestrian pursuits, especially in the summer when he loathed being in London. Wolsey – tireless and imaginative – was the ideal minister for him, able at once to take the burden of government off the king's shoulders while anticipating his every wish. Wolsey's first biographer was George Cavendish, who published a life of him in the middle of the sixteenth century; Cavendish rightly noted that 'the king committed all his will and pleasure unto [Wolsey's] disposition and order ... [because] all his endeavour was only to satisfy the king's mind'.[75] Like most people who observed Henry at work, Cavendish was impressed by the king's self-confident authority. Henry trusted Wolsey – but he watched him intently.

While Wolsey often appeared to be the king's alter ego in reality he was probably Henry's best teacher. It is now recognised that by the mid-1520s Henry was able to intervene very effectively in governmental affairs when he chose to do so. Despite appearances to the contrary, Henry had a close knowledge of the details of government and of administration. He owed this to Wolsey – and to his own ability, while Wolsey worked, to watch carefully what he was doing (and sometimes what he was not doing). Thomas Wolsey never forgot that the king was watching him – and neither should we.

It is likely that Wolsey's rise to power was facilitated by his being a churchman; the noblemen and courtiers who served Henry did not see him as a threat while senior churchmen who had risen under Henry VII such as Archbishop Warham of Canterbury and Bishop Fox of Winchester – respectively Lord Chancellor and Lord Privy Seal – stepped aside for him, probably with genuine enthusiasm to be rid of the burdens of secular office.[76] Certainly, Wolsey's consolidation of power in the years 1513–15 enabled Henry to dispense with his father's ministers, men who were a generation older than him and whom he found crusty in their personal manner and conservative in their policies.

Wolsey's rise in the Church was dizzying. He started the reign as Dean of Lincoln and in February 1513 became Dean of York. Later in 1513 he was presented to the Bishopric of Tournai in recognition of his role in organising the army that conquered the town and in March 1514 rose to the Bishopric of Lincoln. He did not have time to visit his bishopric

– something that became familiar to him – before in September he was raised to the Archbishopric of York. He held a number of other bishoprics simultaneously.[77] Still he had hardly begun; in September 1515 the Pope raised him to the cardinalate: he now stood at the apex of the Church in England. And still his rise had only just begun: on Christmas Eve 1515 Henry VIII conferred upon him the position of Lord Chancellor and thereby made him responsible for administering the law and controlling the judiciary throughout England. But despite his unique array of offices Wolsey remained only the second churchman in England after Archbishop Warham of Canterbury: he resolved this as best he could in January 1524 by having the Pope appoint him as legate *a latere* for life. He was now the first minister of the Crown and the leading churchman.

Wolsey's energy was matched by a pride that was never far removed from arrogance; it could be very difficult to gain access to him and he was often brusque in his treatment of leading men at court and even with foreign ambassadors. Wolsey loved display and wealth, justifying it on the grounds that he was the senior minister of a great king. Again, we can turn to a Venetian witness, who described the cardinal as a man of high achievement and – sometimes – of high ideals but also as a statesman who (in the contemporary fashion) expected to profit from the offices that he held and who did so to excess precisely because so many of his positions were especially lucrative:

> He was of low origin, and had two brothers, one of whom held an untitled benefice, and the other was pushing his fortune. He ruled both the king and the entire kingdom. On Giustinian's first arrival in England he used to say to him, 'His Majesty will do so and so.' Subsequently, by degrees, he went forgetting himself, and commenced saying, 'We shall do so and so.' He had then reached such a pitch that he used to say, 'I shall do so and so.'
>
> He was about forty-six years old, very handsome, learned, extremely eloquent, of vast ability, and indefatigable. He transacted alone the same business as that which occupied all the magistrates, offices, and councils of Venice, both civil and criminal; and all state affairs were managed by him.
>
> He was pensive, and had the reputation of being extremely just. He favoured the people exceedingly, and especially the poor, hearing their suits, and seeking to despatch them instantly. He also made the lawyers plead gratis for all poor men.

He was in very great repute; seven times more so than if he were Pope. He had a very fine palace, where one traversed eight rooms before reaching his audience chamber. They were all hung with tapestry, which was changed once a week. Wherever he was, he always had a sideboard of plate worth 25,000 ducats. His silver was estimated at 150,000 ducats. In his own chamber there was always a cupboard with vessels to the amount of 30,000 ducats, as was customary with the English nobility. He was supposed to be very rich indeed in money, plate, and household stuff.

The Archbishopric of York yielded him about 14,000 ducats, and the Bishopric of Bath 8,000. One-third of the fees derived from the Great Seal were his; the other two were divided between the king and the Chancellor. The cardinal's share amounted to about 5,000 ducats. By new year's gifts he made about 15,000 ducats.[78]

Nor did Wolsey ever forget just how expensive war was and that military greatness came at a prohibitive price; it was a paradox that the ministers who made his name and secured his place in the royal affections by his management of war ardently desired peace. Between 1509 and 12 June 1513 the Chamber had paid out just over £1 million, two-thirds of it on war and nearly half in the single week of 5–12 June 1513.[79] At a time when Henry's annual income was about £150,000 the campaigns of 1512 and 1513 had cost at least £922,000 (of which no less than £650,000 had been spent in 1513). Henry had in these two years spent most of the treasure that his miserly father had bequeathed him.[80] Future wars would have to be paid for out of his own current income.

The Lull Before the Storm: The Marriage Alliances of 1514

Emperor-elect Maximilian had been humiliated repeatedly in the wars he had fought (or tried to fight) in the Low Countries and Italy but during the course of 1514 Maximilian – brilliant and eccentric, disorganised and undisciplined as he was – arranged marriages for two of the daughters of Philip and Juana that rounded out the Spanish–Burgundian marriages of 1496–97 and helped construct the greatest dynasty in European history. Maximilian would win by diplomacy what he could not win in war: Mary was engaged to Louis II of Hungary and Isabella to Christian II of Denmark. Maximilian also opened negotiations for a French bride for his grandson Charles (who of course was engaged to Princess Mary of England); he did not even consult with Margaret of Austria and there was general disgust in the Low Countries when news leaked of his proposal, for Charles's projected English was popular there.

Maximilian's duplicity added to Henry VIII's problems in foreign affairs but in an important sense also simplified them. Henry had learned during 1511–12 to distrust Ferdinand of Aragon and he had begun to think about allying with France to take Navarre from Ferdinand and even to pursuing his wife's claim to the throne of Castile.[81] In the spring of 1514 Henry opened secret negotiations with France and a treaty was agreed in July–August; Henry retained Tournai and Thérouanne while his pension was increased to a total of 1 million crowns to be paid in instalments of 26,315 crowns on 1 May and 1 November each year.[82] It was agreed that Louis XII would marry Mary Tudor; the marriage by proxy took place at Greenwich Palace on 13 August 1514.[83] Mary was eighteen years old and was as repelled by the idea of marrying Louis (who was ugly and, at fifty-two, nearly three times as old as herself) as she was enchanted by the prospect of becoming Queen of France. She drove a hard bargain with her brother, agreeing to marry Louis only on the condition that after his death – which she very much hoped would be proximate – she could marry whomsoever she chose. Beguiled as he was by his sister, Henry readily agreed. Mary married Louis on 8 October and on 5 November was crowned Queen of France in the Abbey of St. Denis.[84] The re-establishment of friendly relations between England and France meant that Henry had strengthened his position, apparently as the result of a successful war. But a significant turning-point had been reached, for Henry's resentment of Ferdinand had helped drive him into a French alliance. Like Maximilian, Henry now had a dynastic web, if a comparatively humble one: his sisters were Queen Regent of Scotland and Queen of France. But for Katharine there was a sadness in Mary's departure, for she lost her closest friend at court.

Unfortunately, Margaret soon forfeited her authority in Scotland; James IV's will stipulated that she could only remain as regent for her infant son as long as she retained her widowed state but on 6 August she married Archibald Douglas, 6th Earl of Angus. Some Scottish lords were so angered by the marriage that they invited John Stewart, 2nd Duke of Albany and heir-presumptive to the throne, to return from France to serve as regent.[85] Turbulence had returned to Scottish politics.

With the accession of Henry VIII and his marriage to Katharine, the work of Gutierre Gómez de Fuensalida came to an end and he was replaced by Luis Caroz de Villaragut. Don Luis has claims to have been the worst and most uninformed Spanish ambassador in London during Katharine's lifetime and by December 1514 he had had enough, writing a scathing report to a friend at court of his profound discontentment with every aspect of his work and life in London, asking that his concerns be placed directly before Ferdinand. Caroz protested that he was treated by the English not as an ambassador but like 'a bull at whom everyone throws darts'. He was severely critical of Katharine herself, insisting that Ferdinand should appoint a 'discreet and intelligent person' to repair the serious disorders in her household. Caroz laid the blame for these squarely at the door of Friar Diego Fernández, Katharine's confessor, 'who has told her that she ought to forget Spain and everything Spanish in order to gain the love of the King of England and the English'. He also criticised María de Salinas whom Katharine loved 'more than any mortal'. More significantly he warned Ferdinand against the influence of Juan Manuel, 'who is able to dictate to the Queen of England how she must behave'. Caroz was contemptuous of Henry who 'behaves in the most offensive and discourteous manner' whenever Spanish affairs were discussed. Caroz urged Ferdinand to 'put a bridle on this colt', insisting that he should teach Henry to behave properly and with due respect to Spain. Not surprisingly, the ambassador concluded by begging for permission to return home.[86]

10

THE GREAT RIVALS, 1515–1521: CHARLES OF HABSBURG & FRANCIS OF VALOIS

Charles of Habsburg & Francis of Valois

During the first five days of 1515 the shape of European politics underwent changes that were to prove to be of profound and enduring importance. On 1 January, Louis XII of France died and was succeeded by Francis, Count of Angoulême and Duke of Valois, who was both his cousin and his son-in-law: he became Francis I.[1] The new king was twenty years old. Four days later, in the Parliament Hall of Brussels, Charles of Habsburg announced his coming-of-age and his acquisition of power as Duke of Luxembourg and Burgundy and ruler of the Low Countries: he was a month shy of his fifteenth birthday.

It was curiously appropriate that Francis and Charles should have entered upon their power within days of each other for they committed themselves – most especially after Charles's election as Holy Roman Emperor in 1519 – to a rivalry that lasted until Francis's death in 1547. Indeed, rarely has a rivalry between two men had such profound and long-lasting effects in European history as this one. Charles and Francis fought over high ideals and with low methods; they consistently gave solemn commitments to each other which they broke with abandon. Above all, they fought in Italy, which now became – much more fully even than it had been after the invasion by Charles VIII in 1494 – the bearpit of Europe. Francis disdained Charles and in time Charles more than fully reciprocated with a deep and growing distaste. At its core, the rivalry of the two men was dynastic, political and military but it was leavened by an intense – and ever-deepening – mutual rancour. They came to truly hate each other, and their hostility became an important factor in the rivalry between their power-blocs that dominated Western European politics during the first half of the sixteenth century.

In 1515 there seemed little immediate possibility of them becoming rivals, for Francis was king of the most powerful country in Europe while Charles was merely Duke of Luxembourg and Burgundy. By physique and temperament, too, they were very different. Francis, who was well over 6 feet tall, cut a magnificent figure (although his enemies pointed out that he had rather spindly legs and an over-long nose). Francis was ebullient and energetic, enormously ambitious. He loved all the equestrian arts but was not content with merely jousting and hunting, although it has been said that he was 'addicted' to these pursuits: Francis was determined to announce himself in 1515 by winning military glory in Italy at the head of his army. He had two other passions, for women and for the arts, but much as he gave himself to both of these with unstinted commitment, his deepest love was for war, his essential motive to seek personal glory on the battlefield. And he had yet another obsession: with his mother, Louise of Savoy. A Venetian summed up the curious mixture of energy and indolence that characterised Francis as he began his reign:

> He is inexpressibly handsome and generous ... The king's mode of life was as follows: He rose at 11, heard Mass, dined, then remained for two or three hours with his mother, and afterwards visited his girlfriends or went out hunting, then during the whole night visited here and there; so that by day it was impossible to obtain audience of him.[2]

Charles was physically unimpressive. His bones were weak and in time he suffered from severe arthritis. His jaws did not meet, with the result that his speech was slurred and he ate noisily.[3] Indeed, his table manners were atrocious: he ate and drank far too much, emulating the Caesars (in this as in so much else) by making himself vomit so that he could continue to gorge on his food; it is probable that the severe gout that afflicted him in later years was exacerbated by his self-indulgence. His hanging jaw and his slurred speech convinced many that he was unintelligent but he was deeply reflective, slow to speak and even slower to act. When the need arose he could operate decisively (and on occasions with brutal ruthlessness). Charles was not only very perceptive but he was possessed (at least until the beginning of the 1540s) of an almost unbreakable will. He had a high ideal of ruling but it was one which was founded in the rights that were due to him as a ruler. He demanded loyalty from his subjects as a precondition of his princely generosity; when he took his oath in the States General of the Low Countries he promised that if his subjects were loyal to him 'I will be a good prince for you'.[4] Despite the weakness of his body, he displayed prodigious energy: when he made an inaugural royal progress through the Low Countries to receive the pledges of loyalty from his new subjects it was a first suggestion of that physical robustness and resilience that belied the apparent frailty of his physique. It would one day be calculated that over the thirty-nine years of his emperorship (1519–58) he had spent one day in four on the road and slept in over 3,200 beds; in a lifetime of fifty-eight years he lived in the Low Countries for approximately twenty-eight years; in Spain for nearly eighteen; in the Empire for eight and in Italy for two and a half.[5] His mind was always focussed on his twin duties, to God and the House of Habsburg: in truth, he generally regarded their interests as being identical. Like Francis I he avidly sought military glory and spent much of his reign marching – and even sailing – with his armies, often leading them into battle. A man of action, Charles was also a man of letters with a profound and informed interest in contemporary scholarship and – as the great Titian could testify – he was a generous patron of the arts. And he was a prodigiously prolific letter writer; the correspondence by which he communicated with his ministers and agents across the face of Europe was a wonder of the age.[6]

Charles declined Francis's invitation to attend his coronation and sent Henry of Nassau to represent him and to negotiate the legal basis of his relationship with the new king. On Chiévres's advice, Charles was prepared to swear that he was Francis's vassal for Flanders, Artois and Burgundy and to agree to marry Renée, younger daughter of Louis XII, with Milan as the dowry; in truth, Renée was not much of a catch since she was no longer the daughter of a reigning monarch. Ever practical, Charles recognised that he had to placate Francis until he had secured the thrones of Spain; he freely confessed that 'a dishonourable peace is worth more to me than a just war'.[7] It was most unfortunate that the grandiose plans were not matched by basic competence: the ambassadors arrived too late for the coronation. Francis agreed to the marriage of Renée and Charles and guaranteed that if he himself broke the treaty the towns of the Somme were to be forfeited to Charles (Treaty of Paris, 24 March 1515).[8] In Nôtre-Dame Cathedral on Palm Sunday, 2 April 1515, the oaths of commitment were taken for the marriage and Charles acknowledged that he was Francis's vassal and would remain under his tutelage until he was nineteen.

Francis was determined to announce himself to his countrymen and to Europe by avenging the humiliations that France had suffered under his predecessor in 1513 at Novara, Thérouanne and Tournai. He would do so on the very grandest stage, in Italy: as the first act of his reign, Francis would regain Milan. Certainly, money seemed to be no object: he bought off Henry VIII with the promise of a pension of 1 million écus over the next ten years.[9] Francis raised an army of nearly 35,000 men and provided it with more than forty large cannons. With daring innovation, he led his great army across the 3,514-metre-high Col d'Argentière into Italy, often crossing in single file over the most hazardous of passes. The parallel with Hannibal was not lost on Francis (and his publicists). A force of about 30,000 men was waiting to confront him, the fruit of the alliance between the papacy, Spain and the Swiss Confederation, and they were astounded by the sudden arrival of the French army.

Francis and his great army descended into the Lombard Plain and at Marignano, 16 kilometres outside the city of Milan, crushed the imperial army (13–15 September 1515). So complete was Francis's triumph that to this day the French still refer to Marignano as 'The Battle'. The king received his laurels on the battlefield, being knighted by the chevalier Bayard. He also acknowledged the outstanding service of his childhood friend, Charles Bourbon, who had commanded the advance guard, by conferring upon him the dignity of Grand Constable of France: it was the last occasion on which Francis would display generosity of spirit to a man whom he came to regard as a rival for military *gloire*.

Coming as it did one day after Francis's twenty-first birthday, the stunning victory proclaimed both the power and the military brilliance of the new king: exultant, Francis had a medal struck in which he proclaimed, 'I have conquered those whom only Caesar had defeated.' No contemporary king had made such a dramatic opening to a reign as Francis I had done in 1515; he had indeed struck terror into Europe and reaffirmed the power and ambition of France. He had dramatically outstripped the achievements of Charles VIII and Louis XII, neither of whom had won victories in Italy that could be remotely compared with that at Marignano. The Pope, Venice, Genoa and a majority of the thirteen Swiss cantons recognised the new realities by making an alliance with Francis.[10] He returned to France an immeasurably strengthened monarch, undoubtedly the major figure in Europe.

Henry VIII took note. He seethed with envy of his young contemporary but although he recognised that Francis was a worthy adversary he still dismissed him for his French-ness – 'this King of France was indeed a worthy and honest sovereign, but nevertheless a Frenchman, and not to be trusted'.[11] Francis would also develop an intense – and deeply personal – rivalry with the King of England, for the two men were very similar – in their physical excellence and vigour; in their transcendent egoism; and in their deeply competitive natures. Francis I and Henry VIII were born to go to war with each other but Francis never forgot that Charles of Habsburg was his real rival. Henry VIII was a lesser opponent – and how it hurt the King of England's pride that this was manifestly so! Henry did the best he could in the circumstances, agreeing with Ferdinand and Juana to an alliance which was ostensibly aimed at France while expressly agreeing that neither would go to war with Francis (Treaty of Westminster, 19 October 1515).[12] It was a token effort of no real substance, not least because Ferdinand was at death's door.

Henry had a more immediate difficulty within his own family and court, for when Louis XII's death left his sister Mary a widow he despatched Charles Brandon, Duke of Suffolk, to bring her home. But before he did so Suffolk had the nerveless temerity to marry Mary in Paris in mid-February. The circumstances under which the marriage came about are shrouded in mystery – it seems likely that Henry had promised Mary that if she married Louis XII she could subsequently choose her own husband if she was widowed. Certainly, Henry was enraged but he melted in front of Mary's curious insistence that she alone was responsible for the marriage. Probably, too, his anger was moderated by Wolsey's securing a lavish payment to him from the newly-weds. At all events, on 13 May 1521 Mary and Suffolk were married again, at court in Greenwich, and both Henry and Katharine attended. For Katharine, the return of her old friend must have been a most agreeable turn of events.[13]

The Accession of Charles to the Thrones of the Spanish Monarchy
Ferdinand died on 23 January 1516. Not until the very previous day could he bring himself to recognise Charles as his successor to the thrones of Aragon and Naples. He also urged his grandson to take loving care of his 'beloved wife', Germaine de Foix: in this at least, Charles more

than followed his grandfather's advice, if not quite in the manner that Ferdinand had intended, for he adopted Germaine as the first of his long-term mistresses and had at least one child by her.[14]

On 13 March 1516, splendid obsequies were celebrated for Ferdinand in Brussels Cathedral. After the royal standard of Aragon was lowered to the ground, Charles stood on a dais: he was already Duke of Burgundy, ruler of the Low Countries and King of Aragon and Naples and he now raised a dagger towards heaven and pronounced himself King of Castile 'jointly with the Catholic Queen, my lady'. Joseph Pérez has written of 'an authentic coup d'état' whereby Charles and his advisers effectively wrested the Crown of Castile from Juana's enfeebled hands while allowing her to retain the dignity of the title.[15] A formula was devised which gave Charles parity with his mother and conferred the crown upon him: 'Juana and Charles, her son, by the grace of God kings of Castile, León and Aragon'. Juana remained 'the proprietary queen' and Charles her 'co-ruler'. Legally, this situation remained operative until Juana's death in 1555.

Now that Charles was king of the thrones of Spain, the treaty of 1515 with France had to be renegotiated. In the Treaty of Noyon (13 August 1516) Charles agreed that France would retain control of Milan while Francis recognised Charles's sovereignty over Naples. Charles also acknowledged the legitimacy of Francis's lordship of Navarre and affirmed that he was Francis I's vassal for Flanders and Artois.

The treaty was to be sealed with Charles's marriage to Francis's daughter Louise (born 19 August 1515) and since the infant was the third French princess to whom Charles had been engaged it might be useful to recall the details of the commitments that he had thus far made to them. Charles's first French fiancée, Claudia, had been taken away from him to marry the future Francis I in 1514 and in the early weeks of Francis's reign Charles was given Claudia's younger sister Renée as compensation. However, this was only a holding operation and when Louise was born Francis had the opportunity to bind Charles closer to him by giving him his own daughter rather than that of his predecessor. At Noyon, therefore, it was agreed that Charles would marry Louise. Since Louise was only one year old, Charles's commitment to marry her was an aspiration rather than a commitment – in its way, this was another holding operation.

The treaty therefore secured Naples for Spain but in giving away Milan and Navarre undid much of the work of Ferdinand. For Charles and his Flemish advisers this was a price worth paying so that he could buy the time to take control of the Spanish thrones, and as soon as Charles reached Spain he informed Francis that he would not return Navarre to him.[16] The promise to cede Navarre to France had been yet another holding operation on Charles's part and it is well to remember that in what became a fraught personal relationship between Charles and Francis, it was Charles who first broke his word.

Francis I rounded out his victory at Marignano by making favourable agreements with the Swiss Confederation and the papacy. He agreed to pay the Swiss 1.7 million écus in cash and an annual pension of 2,000 livres in return for their promise that they would henceforth serve only the French crown (Treaty of Fribourg, 29 November 1516). A fortnight later, Francis renegotiated with the Pope the terms under which the Gallican Church was governed: by the 'Concordat of Bologna' (11–15 December) Francis and Leo agreed that the kings of France would henceforth nominate to all episcopal sees, major abbacies and priories in their realms. This represented a significant diminution of papal authority in France: although the papacy retained a right of veto over appointments in practice this was largely theoretical and clerical rights of appeal to the Roman Curia were severely restricted. It should be noted that Ferdinand and Isabella had secured similar powers (*patronatos*) in the years after 1483 which entitled them to nominate to all bishoprics in their kingdoms, and of course with the establishment of the Inquisition in 1478 they acquired enormous control over the spiritual lives of their subjects. In England, Henry VIII could only envy the power over the Church that the monarchs of France and Spain enjoyed.

Desperate as Charles was to travel to Spain to claim his new inheritance he did not have the money with which to do so. In July 1517, therefore, he negotiated a loan of 40,000 English crowns from Henry VIII for three years.[17] Nor was this the sum of Charles's indebtedness to Henry, for when Henry sent his little force to fight with the Archduke Margaret's army against the Duke of Guelders he lent Margaret 35,000 escudos to pay for them; Charles agreed to repay this at 10,000 escudos annually as soon as he had paid off the first loan.[18] Henry had both demonstrated his wealth and his determination to maintain friendly relations with the House of Habsburg; it would not be the last time that he would pay for Charles to travel from England to Spain – and he was moving perceptibly towards an alliance with Charles against France.

Charles sailed for Spain on 8 September 1517. On arriving, he travelled to Tordesillas, 22 kilometres south of Valladolid, to meet his mother in her palace-prison. He was horrified by the squalor that confronted him: Juana and his sister Catalina were unkempt and dressed in ragged clothes and of course his father – dead now for eleven years – remained unburied. He brooked no argument from his mother in insisting that Philip be decently laid to rest; Juana reluctantly interred him in the convent of Santa Clara. Juana more readily agreed to relinquish her sovereign authority to Charles, thereby legitimising his government in her eyes and in those of the world. In return, Charles agreed that Juana could retain all her titles. He was now truly King of Castile, if only by default of his mother's incapacity.[19]

Cardinal Jiménez de Cisneros died on 8 November as he travelled to meet his new sovereign. It is unlikely that Charles's advisers would have allowed the venerable cardinal to play any role in government. Charles remained totally dependent upon 'the Flemings'; still only seventeen years of age, he had neither the will nor the self-confidence to assume control of government himself and in any event could not speak any Spanish. Three men formed the inner core of his circle – Guillaume de Croy, Lord of Chièvres; Juan de Sauvage, Chancellor; and Antoine de Lalaing, Lord of Montigny. Chièvres remained the leader, and it was doubtless under his guidance that Charles showered wealth and dignities upon his countrymen: Chièvres had already taken control of Castile's finances by having had himself appointed in 20 April 1516 as chief finance officer of Castile (*contador mayor de Castilla*) and was shortly named as Captain-General of the Sea for the Crown of Aragon and Admiral of Aragon. Nor did church positions escape the newcomers: for instance, Adrian of Utrecht was named as Bishop of Tortosa. But the most scandalous of all the appointments – and the one that became most deeply symbolic for Spaniards of the priorities of their new king – was the appointment of Guillaume de Croy to succeed Cisneros as Archbishop of Toledo: the new Primate of Spain was sixteen years old.[20]

When the Cortes of Castile opened in Valladolid on 7 February 1518 the scene was set for a bitter confrontation.[21] But Charles could not even spare the time to remain in Castile: on 22 March 1518 he left Valladolid to travel to the east so that he could secure his control over the kingdoms of the Crown of Aragon. As a precautionary measure he despatched his brother Ferdinand away from Spain; until Charles married and had a child Ferdinand was next in line to the throne and it was feared that he might provide a focal point for opposition to Charles. On 23 May, Ferdinand sailed to the Low Countries, never to return to Spain.[22] Charles was obliged to remain in Zaragoza, the capital city of Aragon, for eight months while he negotiated with the Cortes for their oath of loyalty and their money.[23]

Jean de Sauvage died in Zaragoza and was replaced as Charles's Chancellor by Mercurino Arborio di Gattinara. Born in Savoy in 1465, Gattinara was thirty-five years older than Charles and their relationship was one of master and tutee. Gattinara was a Doctor of Law and had become the legal adviser of Charles's aunt, Margaret, when she married the Duke of Savoy. When Margaret returned to Brussels after being widowed, Gattinara accompanied her and served as her legal adviser as she assumed the governorship of the Low Countries after the death of Philip the Fair in 1506. Margaret also served as foster mother to Juana's children and as Charles grew into his teenage years Gattinara began to tutor him, inspiring him with the ambition of reaching in time for the political, cultural and ideological leadership of Europe. But all that lay in the future: what Charles needed above all else in the years immediately after 1516 was a respite from war or from the threat of war while he secured his power in Spain and prepared to win the imperial title, which because of the declining health of Maximilian would surely soon become vacant.

The Universal Peace of Christendom: The Treaty of London, October 1518

Within this context, England had a particular relevance for Charles and his ministers: in the years after 1516 they came to set an alliance with England among their chief and most enduring priorities in foreign policy. They recognised that Henry VIII's inveterate hostility to France made him a natural ally and they understood, too, the identity of commercial interests that bound England to the Low Countries. Dynastic interests complemented political identities; Charles appreciated very clearly the importance to the House of Habsburg of forming a marital alliance with England; indeed, he eventually attached quite as much significance to achieving this alliance as had Ferdinand and Isabella. He began his pursuit of an English match soon after the birth of Princess Mary in 1516 and persevered in it – through many vicissitudes – until in 1544 Mary married his own son, the future Philip II of Spain. Charles was always a man to take the long view.

Katharine and her daughter thereby came to be of central and enduring importance to Charles as he developed his dynastic and political strategies;

it is important to understand that this was less because of their Spanish-ness than because they were close relatives who could be deployed in the development of the Emperor-elect's dynastic policies. To Charles of Habsburg, family was everything: he spent his life rushing across Europe and the Mediterranean from crisis to crisis but his plans were invariably underscored by the dynastic ambitions that he held for his family – and by the completely unsentimental way in which he made use of his blood relatives to further his purposes.

Three landmark developments underscored the evolution of this policy by Charles and his advisers – his adherence to the Treaty of London (1518); his compliance in the tedious 'Conference at Calais' (1521) and – above all – his extraordinary and unprecedented visit to England in 1522, when he committed himself to an alliance with England and a war with France. Certainly, the three events were part of a short-term programme designed to buy Charles time before he confronted the power of France but they also came to form the bedrock of his determination to pursue a marital alliance with England.

It was a particularly happy circumstance that Charles's plans chimed in with the policies of Henry VIII and Cardinal Wolsey.[24] Certainly, there were differences between king and minister: Henry yearned to go to war with France while Wolsey – although he was always eager to satisfy his monarch's wishes – was much more cautious, aware that it would fall to him to find the resources for war, and enduringly conscious, too, that his own fortunes might always decline with the vagaries of war. Like most ministers of finance, Wolsey abhorred war. However, it also seems clear that Wolsey was committed to a peaceful policy on ideological grounds. What Charles offered now proved irresistible to him: Charles was content – eager, even – to allow London to become the diplomatic centre of Europe if in doing so he could buy time in which to consolidate and extend his power in the Low Countries and Spain and win the imperial throne. Equally, he knew that he would shortly have to go to war with Francis I and that when he did so it would be to fight wars on a new scale of intensity for which Francis had the resources and he did not. If Charles had needed any reminding on this point, his failure even to be able to fund his own journey to Spain in 1517 without a loan from the King of England would have served as a painful (and embarrassing) *aide-memoire*. Peace – the buying of time – was his central policy at the turn of the 1510s–1520s, and Henry VIII and Wolsey proved to be his staunchest allies in pursuing it.

Henry VIII never lost his taste for war with France. Political and financial realities regularly obliged him to deny himself the pleasure of going to war with France and indeed on occasions even forced him to ally with Francis I against Charles, but Henry was never happier than when fighting the French. However, he fully recognised that he needed a period of financial retrenchment after the expenditures on war in 1512–14 (which Richard Hoyle has calculated at about £1 million).[25] When therefore Wolsey was able to offer Henry the prospect of playing the role of arbiter of Europe rather than of the conqueror of the French, it doubtless appealed to his vanity as much as to his growing sense of financial realities. Never a man to do things by half, Henry threw himself into his new role with his accustomed energy. Wolsey, too, was deeply gratified to position himself at the centre of the European stage. Indeed, until 1523–24, Henry and Wolsey played their roles with ebullient brilliance as they hosted peace conferences, mounted tournaments, provided the most splendid meals and the most lavish courtly and chivalric entertainments for foreign ambassadors and guests. But at the end of the day, their roles were temporary, illusory and self-serving: the great issues that divided Charles V (as he became in 1519) and Francis I could not be solved by dancing and dining in staterooms or by parading in the tilt-yard. They would be resolved on the battlefield, and when the time came for the two monarchs to go to full and open war, Henry VIII and Wolsey would have to decide with whom England would ally. In the event, the choices that they made proved to be consistently wrong and it cost them dearly by the later 1520s – in Henry's case, the chance of resolving his marital difficulties in Rome; in Wolsey's, the possibility of surviving in office once he had failed to secure a settlement of Henry's 'Great Matter'. By 1529 – probably, indeed, by 1527 – the die had been cast: the arbiters of Europe had become victims of the new political realities. Katharine, Queen of England, was the first to fall.

The first fruit of the new English policy was a meeting of the leading Christian powers which Wolsey convened in London in the autumn of 1518. On 6 March 1518 Pope Leo X proclaimed a five-year truce in Western Europe so that he could organise the monarchs of Christendom in a crusade against the infidel. He found a ready response among the intellectual elite; indeed, the European humanists of the early sixteenth century found that the threat from the Turk provided them with the perfect tool with which to remonstrate with their own monarchs for shedding Christian blood in pursuit of their secular interests.[26] The monarchs themselves were less convinced of the need for peace between them and had no intention of fighting against the Turk but for their own purposes went along with the papal project. Leo X despatched legates to European capitals to secure support for his great crusade and in October the representatives of twenty European nations met in London to agree to a non-aggression treaty between them so that they could turn their energies against the Turk. For Henry and Wolsey it was a high moment: they were the loyal servants of the papacy and the convenors of a great European peace conference.

Cardinal Lorenzo Campeggio travelled to England as legate *a latere* and since he would subsequently play a pivotal role in the attempt to prevent the collapse of the marriage of Henry VIII and Katharine, we should say something about him.[27] In truth, Campeggio had an especially interesting career. He had been born in Milan in 1474 and had entered academic life, earning a doctorate in Canon and Civil Law in Bologna University and teaching there. He married Francesca Vastevillani and had three sons by her. Since he also sired at least two illegitimate daughters by other women, it may reasonably be observed of him that he understood the temptations of the flesh.

Francesca died in 1509 and Lorenzo decided to enter the religious life. He proved to be brilliantly successful. Indeed, he enjoyed a meteoric rise in the Roman Curia and was sufficiently trusted by Julius II to be appointed as papal ambassador (nuncio), first to the Emperor Maximilian and then to the Duchy of Milan (1512). He was named cardinal-priest on 1 July 1517 because (it was said) of his learning, but it may well have been that his gift of 27,000 ducats to the papal treasury had as much to do with it as his academic laurels.

When, therefore, Campeggio was charged with his mission in England, he was an experienced papal diplomat and a Vatican insider. But he was in poor health and it was only when Leo X insisted that he depart for England that he dragged himself away from Rome (18 April 1518). Unfortunately, Henry VIII and Wolsey insisted that the Pope should raise Wolsey to the dignity of legate *a latere* so that he could have parity with Campeggio in England. For six weeks, Campeggio kicked his heels in Calais until papal confirmation of Wolsey's elevation was announced in Rome (17 May). It took time for the news to reach Henry and so it was not until 23 July that Campeggio was allowed to cross to England. On 29 July he made his formal entry into London and was warmly welcomed by Henry and Wolsey.

It happened, therefore, that Campeggio was in England when on 3 October, the General Peace of Christendom was proclaimed at St Paul's. Wolsey celebrated an especially splendid pontifical High Mass but when Henry and his guests swore at the high altar to observe the articles of peace the terms were read in such low voices that few realised that the promise to send an expedition against the Turks had been discreetly abandoned. Notwithstanding this deception, the banquet at Durham House was beyond compare: the Venetian ambassador noted that 'the like ... was never given either by Cleopatra or Caligula'. Henry was in his element.[28]

To oblige the Pope, Henry would even make peace with the French and on 4 October the treaty of peace was signed. Henry was pleased to rid himself of the expense of maintaining his garrison in Tournai and was even happier to accept a gift from Francis of 600,000 crowns, to be paid in annual instalments of £5,000 in addition to the £10,000 that Louis XII had committed to pay him. If Henry could not go to war with France, he could at least have French money to compensate him for his loss.

The treaty was sealed with the engagement of Princess Mary, who was not yet three years of age, with Francis, Dauphin of France, who had been born in February. Neither Henry VIII nor Francis I could have taken the engagement too seriously but it was celebrated in splendid style at Greenwich Palace on 5 October; Admiral Bonnivet stood proxy for the Dauphin. Henry had to make one major concession: the French insisted that he should formally recognise Mary as his successor, and it was probably because Katharine was in the last stages of a pregnancy that he agreed to the demand in the hope that she would produce a boy and thereby nullify his promise. In return, Francis forbade the Duke of Albany to return to Scotland to stir up trouble against England. Henry's precocious infant daughter played her role to perfection. At the celebrations for her engagement Mary approached the Admiral and asked him, 'Are you the Dauphin of France? If you are, I wish to kiss you.'[29] On 7 October, Henry gave a yet another magnificent banquet to celebrate the General Peace of Christendom and the new amity with France. Henry – and his chief minister – stood, as appeared, at the very core of European politics.[30]

The Treaty of London of 1518 proved to be a brilliant but beguiling illusion. Henry VIII and Wolsey were *not* the central figures in European diplomacy and the primary reality of European politics was not to be found in treaties, banquets and jousts. It lay in the power of France and in the unrelenting determination of Francis I to maintain his control of Milan and the mastery of northern Italy. To a lesser extent, it lay also in the determination of Charles to play for time until he had secured his Spanish inheritance and won the imperial throne. Henry VIII and Wolsey played a brilliant hand – and indeed satiated both of their enormous egos – but the realities of power would be decided in three focal points of power and influence – in battle on the Plain of Lombardy; in the banking houses in Augsburg where the credit would be negotiated with which the imperial electors would be bribed; and in Aachen itself, where the imperial election would take place and where the victor would be crowned.[31] And when those decisions were reached, Henry and Wolsey would have to stop play-acting and commit themselves to either Charles or to Francis. The question of whom Mary married would then have to be dealt with seriously.

The Imperial Election: Aachen, 28 June 1519

Maximilian died on 12 January 1519. He bequeathed his family titles as Archduke of Austria to his grandson Charles but since the imperial title was elective the stage was now set for the first great contest – and the defining one – between Charles and Francis. Francis had already established his reputation as a brilliant soldier and had the riches of France behind him. Charles did not have comparable wealth but he had access to credit, most notably through the support of the Fugger family of bankers of Augsburg, whose control over the silver and copper mines of the Tyrol provided them with legendary riches. The contest was to be about money – in fine, about bribery – and the fighting was dirty: for instance, the French negotiators happily drew the attention of the electors to Juana's mental instability, leaving it to them to wonder whether Charles had inherited it. Charles and his negotiators talked the language of high idealism but recognised realities by unashamedly putting their faith in the corruptibility of the electors. They were not misguided: it was said that it cost Charles 2 tonnes of gold to buy the election. Jacob Fugger provided two-thirds or so of it and in years to come would remind Charles, 'It is well known that Your Majesty without me might not have acquired the Imperial Crown...'[32]

Charles was duly elected on 28 June. He heard of his triumph in Barcelona on 6 July 1519. Six days later, Gattinara sent a memorial to him insisting that he should see himself as the new Charlemagne, charged by the Almighty to construct a 'universal monarchy', in which as the pre-eminent secular ruler in Europe he guided his fellow monarchs and rulers towards a peaceful future: he assured Charles that God 'has raised you above all the kings and princes of Christendom ... He has set you on the way towards a world monarchy, towards the uniting of all Christendom under a single shepherd.'[33] Although he was only nineteen years of age, Charles could not have known that he would have an extended opportunity to fulfil Gattinara's prophecy, for he became the longest-serving of the Holy Roman Emperors, reigning until his death in 1558.

In terms of the geographical extent of his power, Charles could indeed now reasonably pose as the heir of Charlemagne. He had titular authority over the Holy Roman Empire and ruled the remnants of the Duchy of Burgundy and the Low Countries, Spain and its possessions in the Mediterranean. He also had the lands in 'the Indies' that Christopher Columbus had discovered for Castile: thus far, these had proved to be of disappointing value but by extraordinary coincidence it was in the year in which Charles became Holy Roman Emperor-elect that Hernán Cortes and his handful of warriors began the conquest of Mexico that would bring unparalleled mineral wealth to Charles as King of Spain. By the late 1520s, that wealth was beginning to be an important factor in Charles's struggle with Francis I – and it was redoubled when in the mid-1530s Francisco Pizarro and his brothers conquered the Kingdom of Peru.

From the moment of his election Charles styled himself as 'Caesar'. However, in law, he could only claim the titles of 'King-elect of the Romans, future Emperor ... King of Castile' and so on. Resonant as the imperial title was, it conferred little real power on him, for the 365 or so states of the 'Holy Roman Empire' created more problems for the Emperor-elect than they provided him with resources. Within the Empire, the competing jurisdictions of the great princes, archbishops and free cities made it very difficult for Charles to govern without their tacit agreement. Further restrictions on the power of the Emperor-elect were added by the gathering momentum of the Reformation within the Empire and by the thrust of the Ottoman Turk against the imperial borders in the south and east: Hungary and the ancestral lands of the Habsburgs in Austria were particularly vulnerable and in February 1522 Charles agreed to renounce to Ferdinand those parts of the five Austrian duchies that he had hitherto retained and gave him regency powers over the Tyrol and Wurttemberg. Ferdinand would have to resist the Turk on Charles's behalf.[34]

The election as Emperor-elect also had serious implications for Charles's dealings with the papacy, reviving the tensions that had characterised the relationship between popes and emperors in the High Middle Ages. The papacy had traditionally feared the junction of Naples and Sicily and Milan under a single ruler and throughout the years of Charles's tenure of the imperial dignity successive popes were insistent that they often had more to fear from the Holy Roman Emperor than they did from the King of France or even from the Turk. Time was to prove that they were correct in this judgement.

The Departure of Charles from Spain: Castile in Revolt

When Charles learned of his election as Emperor it became his first priority to return to Northern Europe to be crowned as King of the Romans. It would have been much more convenient for him to leave for the Empire from Barcelona but he was obliged to convene a Cortes of Castile, both to calm the growing anxieties of his Castilian subjects about their subordinate place in his polity and also to acquire the resources for his journey: once again he had no money for a journey that was vitally important to him. Already, dissent was reaching dangerous levels; on 7 November 1519 the great city of Toledo wrote to the other Castilian cities insisting that the king should neither leave Castile nor be allowed to dispose of the resources of the kingdom to the advantage of his foreign servants.[35]

Charles left Barcelona on 21 January and arrived in Valladolid on 1 March. He visited his mother in Tordesillas to assure her that he would promptly return, and headed for A Coruña on the north-west coast to embark.[36] Outrageously, he convened a meeting of the Cortes of Castile for Santiago de Compostela on 31 March 1520.[37] When Bishop Pedro Ruiz de la Mota of Badajoz, speaking on behalf of the king, insisted that Charles's election to the imperial dignity was a divine command for him to pursue peace within Christendom so that he could lead a war against the Turk, Charles interjected to guarantee that he would return within three years at the latest.[38] But in his anxiety to depart he made commitments without deliberating on what he was doing; having promised not to appoint foreigners to office he promptly named Adrian of Utrecht as Regent of Castile. It took five votes before the *servicio* was voted and even then it was only approved by a small majority. When Charles sailed on 20 May 1520 Castile was on the point of revolt: on 30 July the cities of Salamanca, Toledo, Toro and Ávila formed a junta to coordinate action against their sovereign.[39] Charles left the government in the hands of a foreign bishop who could not speak Castilian and who always found it very difficult to take even straightforward decisions.

In these circumstances, it was truly extraordinary that Charles should have broken his voyage to the Low Countries to negotiate with Henry VIII for his support. Charles knew that Henry was about to meet Francis I and was determined to deal with him before his rival did so.[40] Charles arrived at Dover on 26 May: he welcomed many English noblemen on board his galleon before he set foot on English soil. Wolsey formally greeted him and escorted him to Dover Castle, where Henry VIII was waiting. On the following day the two monarchs and the cardinal rode to Canterbury where the most lavish celebrations were laid on to rejoice at Charles's presence in England – banquets, revels and dancing. Mass was celebrated to mark Whitsunday. Wolsey rejoiced in his new dignity as legate *a latere* by allowing dukes and earls to wait on him at table. Katharine met her nephew and as a mark of generosity to Charles and herself, Henry allowed her to take part in the negotiations.[41] It is not clear what, if anything, the two monarchs decided but it was significant that they agreed to meet again after Henry's encounter with Francis I. On 31 May, Henry and Charles took their leave of each other a few miles outside Canterbury. Wolsey accompanied Charles to Sandwich, where he sailed for the Low Countries while Henry travelled to Dover to take ship for France; Wolsey hurried to catch up with him.

Anglo-French Whimsy: The Field of the Cloth of Gold, June 1520
While the meeting with Charles V had been an urgent and businesslike one, that with Francis I was extravagant and self-indulgent almost beyond belief. It took place in a fairly rustic setting in some open fields near Guisnes and became known as 'The Field of the Cloth of Gold' after one of the pavilions that was dressed in that fabric. Certainly, there were important political advances to be made. Above all, Francis I wanted to secure English neutrality in his imminent war with Charles. But – as was always to be the case with Henry VIII and Francis I – both kings wanted to measure themselves against each other, as chivalric figures who were possessed of unlimited resources, even as magnificent physical specimens of kingly virility.

For this reason, neither king counted the cost.[42] They lived in artificially constructed castles and conducted their meetings and banquets in pavilions adorned with the most expensive fabrics. A detailed record exists of Henry's party, which consisted of 5,832 people and 3,217 horses.

Naturally, he was accompanied by his queen and also took with him his sister Mary, formerly Queen of France and now Duchess of Suffolk. At least 114 nobles travelled and the Church was represented by the archbishops of York and Canterbury and other bishops. Wolsey himself had about 300 people in his suite. There are no reliable figures for the size of the French contingent but it is reasonable to assume that since Francis would not be prepared to be outshone by Henry it matched the English party in both size and quality; certainly, it included the King of Navarre, several dukes, three Marshals of France and four cardinals.

Henry was clearly determined to honour his wife in the great festivities. Katharine travelled with a suite of no fewer than 1,175 people and was allocated three chambers for herself and her servants. Henry thereby made it manifest that Katharine was his honoured and beloved wife and at the festivities at the Field of the Cloth of Gold did public honour to her. It would not be the last time that he placed Katharine at the very centre of his courtly and diplomatic affairs.

The first interview between the monarchs took place at the Val Doré (in English territory) on 7 June, the feast of Corpus Christi. They dismounted to greet each other and embraced (as was said) a score of times in their delight at meeting. They deftly circumvented the difficulties created by Henry's claim to be King of France by tacitly ignoring it. On 9 June they met again and proclaimed that they were bringing about an 'age of peace'.

If this was so, an intense competitiveness was to inform the new age. It reached its height in the banquets that Henry and Francis provided for each other's queens (10 June) and the tournaments and jousts (11–22 June). So carried away were the kings that they undertook an impromptu wrestle: neither of them ever forgot that Francis threw Henry to the ground. When they parted on 24 June, Henry and Francis vowed to erect a church on the site of the Field of the Cloth of Gold to commemorate their meeting. Of course, the vow proved as ephemeral as the events that had taken place on the field: the church was never built.[43]

Henry returned to more serious business by meeting Charles again, at Gravelines and Calais (10–14 July). Although the hospitality that Henry provided was worthy of Charles's status, the discussions took place as brisk business meetings. They reiterated their commitment not to make peace with France within two years and to holding a conference at Calais to resolve the issues between the nations. But it was indicative of Henry's increasingly serious commitment to an alliance with Charles that he agreed in principle to marry his daughter to him, notwithstanding that for two years Mary had been engaged to the Dauphin of France. Of course both Henry and Charles knew that engagements between infants could be readily broken but if the marriage of Charles and Mary did take place it would have profoundly important consequences for it would bind England to the House of Habsburg and any children born of the marriage would have claims on the English throne, and perhaps even on the thrones of Spain: England would therefore become part of the Habsburg–Burgundian conglomerate monarchy. And of course the fusion of England with Charles's *imperium* would enable Henry to go to war with the King of France to his heart's content. For Katharine, the marriage of her daughter to her nephew would crown her life's work in bringing Spain and England together into permanent alliance. So that the two monarchs could develop their understanding, they agreed to maintain permanent embassies at each other's courts.[44]

As Charles planned for war he learned that he was in danger of losing his Kingdom of Castile, which in the summer of 1520 duly collapsed into 'the revolt of the communes' (*comuneros*). What began as a nationalist and political rebellion against a foreign and abusive dynasty was rapidly transformed into a social rebellion. Inevitably, the nobility of Castile sided with the monarchy and their army crushed the *comuneros* at the Battle of Villalar (23 April 1521); the battle was to prove to be one of the landmark events in the development of Spanish history for it confirmed the alliance between the foreign dynasty and the Castilian nobility.[45] The revolt of the *comuneros* was the most important rebellion in Spain in the sixteenth century and Charles and his successors never forgot how close the House of Habsburg had come to losing Castile. Charles recognised at once that he had to return to Castile to re-establish the authority of the Crown, and his conviction that he had to do so was doubtless reinforced by the irruption of a revolt against his authority in the Kingdom of Valencia, but this was a lesser revolt than that of the *comuneros*.

Even now, Charles had an even more important appointment: on 23 October, in the Cathedral at Aachen, he was crowned as King of the Romans and Emperor-elect: seated on the throne of Charlemagne he received the sword, ring and sceptre that had belonged to the great Emperor. Although Charles had not yet been crowned by the Pope he was now recognised as Holy Roman Emperor-elect.[46] Impoverished and politically weak as he was, Charles was undoubtedly pre-eminent in rank among the crowned heads of Europe.

The Commitment to the Imperial Alliance, 1521–22

During the summer and autumn of 1521, Charles V and Francis I tested each other in skirmishes in Italy, the Low Countries and on the Pyrenean border between France and Spain. It is not clear that these activities properly justify the use of the term 'war' but by the end of the year the combatants had truly reached that stage. It was significant that neither power formally declared war. Postures were being struck but there was a dangerous reality beneath the posing: both Charles and Francis knew that their real conflict would take place in Lombardy.

Charles's immediate priority was to demonstrate his commitment to his new dignity as Holy Roman Emperor-elect. The most important issue confronting him here was the religious crisis in Germany, and Charles summoned and then attended the Diet of Worms (28 January–25 May 1521). The celebrated meetings with Martin Luther took place on 17–19 April. Luther refused to recant and, having failed to dissuade him from what was now open rebellion against the Church, Charles allowed him to leave Worms safely. To the end of his days Charles regretted that in adhering to his word of honour to give Luther safe passage from Worms he had allowed the great heretic to escape.

Henry had no need to compromise with Luther and in the summer of 1521 demonstrated the depths of his loyalty to the Catholic Church (and to the papacy) by attacking the German friar. On 12 May, outside St Paul's Cathedral, the works of Luther were publicly burned and Bishop John Fisher preached – for two hours! – against his heresy. Henry then let it be known that he was himself writing a tract that would demonstrate the error of Luther's ways – his *Assertio Septem Sacramentorum*. On 2 October the tract was formally presented to Leo X and nine days later the Pope conferred the title of 'Defender of the Faith' (*Defensor Fidei*) on Henry.[47]

While Charles wrestled with religious dissent in Germany, Francis went to war with him by proxy, providing the money and men for invasions of Charles's territories in Navarre and Luxembourg. Both were defeated but the danger of all-out war was very real – on 22 October 1521 the armies of Charles and Francis came within shouting distance of each other on the border of the Low Countries. Both monarchs held back: they were not yet ready for real war.

Chièvres died in May 1521. Gattinara seized the moment, bidding now to become Charles's senior minister: at the end of July he set out a detailed programme for Charles that would lead him to the establishment of the 'Universal Monarchy'. He proposed that Charles should follow what he termed his 'ten commandments'. Chief among these was that the Emperor should maintain his alliance with the Pope and that he should demonstrate his high principles and his practicality by not wasting the resources granted him by his subjects. Gattinara assured Charles that if he behaved thus God would support the justness of his cause. He insisted powerfully on the pre-eminence of Italy within the imperial vision and urged Charles to vigorously pursue his military campaigns against France in the peninsula.[48]

Certainly in the twelve months or so after Gattinara urged Charles to establish the 'Universal Monarchy' events seemed to conspire to convince Charles that he was indeed being favoured by the Almighty. In May 1521 Charles signed a treaty with Leo in which he effectively bought the Pope's support by making a number of concessions to the Medici family: Charles undertook to guarantee Medici power in Florence, to restore Parma and Piacenza to the Pope and to allow the re-establishment of Francesco Sforza in Milan. In return, Leo gave permission for Spanish troops to march through the Papal States from Naples to Lombardy. Most important of all, Leo agreed to crown Charles as Emperor and to invest him with the Kingdom of Naples, drawing up the bull of investiture on 28 June.[49] The Pope was in the Emperor-elect's hands.

The Conference of Calais opened in August 1521, ostensibly to resolve the tensions between Charles and Francis and to lead to the peace among Christians that Leo X had proclaimed. The leading powers gave every appearance of taking it seriously: Charles and Francis both sent their Chancellors (Gattinara and Antoine de Praet). Wolsey arrived in Calais on 2 August: under the terms of the Treaty of London he would chair the meetings and (hopefully) reconcile the enmities. He could not have been surprised when his invitation to Charles and Francis to submit to his arbitration was refused. He then informed the French that he needed to consult with Charles V but when he travelled to Bruges it was almost certainly with the intention of agreeing an alliance with Charles against France. The broker of peace among the nations was about to commit his king to war.[50]

The alignment of England with the imperial power of Charles V was confirmed when on 25 August 1521 Henry and Charles concluded a treaty in which they agreed to invade France in 1523.[51] Once again, Charles promised to seal the alliance by marrying Princess Mary; the marriage would take place when Mary reached twelve years of age in

1528. Charles agreed to pay Henry nearly £30,000 to compensate him for the loss of his French pension but the agreement was to be kept secret until November so that another instalment of Wolsey's pension would be paid by Francis. If – or more realistically, when – Francis refused to make peace with Charles, Henry and Charles would declare war on him and in 1523 launch invasions against him of armies of 40,000 men, Charles from Spain and Henry from Calais. Charles also undertook to use his best efforts to secure the papacy for Wolsey. Henry had abandoned his position as arbiter between the great powers and committed himself to a war on France that would be on a vastly greater scale than that of 1513.[52] By 28 August, Wolsey was back in Calais, still working – to all outward appearances – at reconciling Charles and Francis.

Charles's promise to marry Mary was an aspiration rather than a promise, for Henry had acknowledged that the Emperor-elect might subsequently decide to take another wife 'and he will only be bound to take her if he is then at liberty' to do so. Henry also promised that Mary was to be regarded as his 'sole heir' and that she would succeed to the throne if he had no legitimate son in the future.[53] In fact, since Katharine's last pregnancy had been in 1518 Henry had now to recognise that in all probability Mary would be his only child unless Katharine died and he himself remarried. The whole tenor of Henry's negotiations with Charles was therefore underscored by his tacit acknowledgement that – barring a miracle – he would not now have a son by his wife and that he had to make alternative arrangements to secure the succession.

The imperial alliance with England was almost immediately absorbed into a pan-European alliance against France when on 24 November 1521 a secret treaty was agreed between Charles, Leo and Henry VIII. They extended a cordial welcome to the kings of Portugal, Poland, Hungary and Denmark (all of whom were married to Habsburgs) and to the Duke of Savoy. When Wolsey returned to England in December 1521 he knew that war was scheduled to begin in March 1523. Francis I understood readily enough that Henry VIII had deceived him and at the end of 1521 sent Albany to Scotland to foment trouble against England.

An Imperial Pope? The Election of Adrian VI (9 January 1522)
Charles's grand diplomacy suffered an apparent setback when Leo X died on 1 December 1521. Marino Sanudo – one of the shrewdest of political commentators – wryly commented that no Pope had ever more closely resembled the Trinity than Leo X because he had spent the funds of three

popes – the surplus left to him by his predecessor, his own income and that of his successor.[54] Charles and his advisers looked now to reinforce the alliance with England by promising to support Wolsey's candidature in the new conclave. Bernard de Mezza, Charles's ambassador in England, suggested that although it was not probable that Wolsey could win the papal election Charles should pursue his candidature 'with such zeal and lively interest as to show yourself in earnest'.[55] Charles was certainly prepared to do this, for it would cost him nothing; he ordered Mezza to remind Wolsey that 'we have never failed to have his advancement and elevation in view and that we most willingly hold to the promise made to him at Bruges respecting the papal dignity'. Accordingly, Charles assured Wolsey that he would 'use in this affair and in every other which concerns his interest all the power and influence without any reserve which we can command.'[56] The English alliance might justify an English Pope.

Wolsey's advice was practical enough: the imperial troops should march on Rome to intimidate the cardinals in his favour and against a French candidature:

> Nothing would more contribute towards determining the result of the election in my favour than the march of the Imperial troops now in Italy towards Rome: and in case neither presents nor good words have their effect on the College of Cardinals, they should be compelled by main force to the choice which his Majesty approves: so that in no case they be suffered to elect a dependant on the French, the result of which would be the destruction of Naples and Sicily, involving that of all Christendom: this would be avoided by my election.

The cardinal concluded by insisting that he was ready to spend 100,000 ducats to secure his election.[57] Before he received Mezza's despatch, Charles wrote to Henry VIII ('my good uncle, brother and father') insisting that Wolsey's 'prudence, learning, integrity, experience, as well as other virtues and accomplishments for which he is distinguished, render him eminently worthy of such a dignity'.[58] On the same day, he wrote to Wolsey, 'No effort on my part will be wanting for the desired result, and that my favour in this affair will be confined to you alone.'[59]

There seems no real reason to doubt that Charles would have been tolerably pleased to have helped secure the papacy for Wolsey. However he seems not to have pushed for any candidate and was as astonished as anyone when news reached him of the election on 9 January 1522 of Adrian of Utrecht.[60] Charles admitted that he had never anticipated his old tutor's elevation to the papal see: 'The choice, which fell upon one who was never even contemplated by any party, appears to have been the choice of God [rather] than of man.'[61] Certainly, he must have reflected on Gattinara's insistence that he should now seek to create a Universal Monarchy: the Pope who had been born in Utrecht would surely work closely with his former tutee, who of course had been born in Ghent.

Charles shortly had even more reason at the turn of 1521–22 to be astounded by the favours being showered upon him by the Almighty, for in November 1521 his general Prospero Colonna recaptured the city of Milan and on 27 April 1522 destroyed the French army at La Bicocca, 6 miles outside Milan. In truth, both triumphs owed much to the incompetence of the French commander, Odet de Foix, Viscount of Lautrec, but the victory at La Bicocca proved to be a historic moment in the development of warfare, marking the end of the pre-eminence of the Swiss pikeman and the beginning of that of the Spanish infantry and artillery: Colonna had rounded out the work of 'the Great Captain', confirming the pre-eminence of Spanish arms in European warfare. Lautrec had to abandon most of the towns that France had controlled in Lombardy and on 30 May Colonna captured Genoa after the briefest of sieges. French power in northern Italy had been broken: Marignano had been undone.

Charles's conquest of Milan (and his acquisition of Genoa) was as defining a moment for the new politics in Europe as Francis's had been in 1515: there could be now be no doubt that there were two great military powers in Europe, and the stage was set for a conflict between them that would dwarf everything that had happened since the French invasion of Italy in 1494. In the early summer of 1522 Henry VIII and Wolsey might well have congratulated themselves on having had the prescience to ally England with the House of Habsburg. For her part, Katharine must have recognised that although her childbearing years had come to an end she retained the centrality of her position in all of the political, courtly and familial ambitions of her husband. Henry continued to share her bed.

11

KATHARINE'S SALVATION? 1522–1523: THE EMPEROR'S VISIT & THE SEALING OF THE IMPERIAL ALLIANCE

The Visit of Charles V to England (26 May–7 July 1522)[1]
Charles was as fully committed to the alliance as was Henry VIII and on 26 May 1522 he arrived in England to pledge himself personally and publicly to it: he stayed for six weeks. The significance of this visit has not always been fully appreciated. It was a matter of the deepest principle to Charles that since he was Holy Roman Emperor-elect he had no equal among the princes of Europe: he was – and by a very long way in his view – the first among the rulers of Europe. He therefore always gave his time very sparingly to his fellow monarchs, anxious that they should not think that they had any parity with him. In years to come he would spend months negotiating with members of his own family about the legacies that he would leave them but he would never again spend weeks on end with a monarch who was not a member of his dynasty.[2] In 1520 he had met Henry VIII twice, on both occasions for five days – 26–31 May in England and 10–14 July in Calais and Gravelines. By contrast, in 1522 he spent thirty-six days in Henry's company (28 May–3 July). The visit to England in 1522, therefore, was as unique as it was extraordinary and it was so because its purposes were fundamental to the whole polity of the Emperor-elect. It was the expression of a long-term strategy that Charles pursued throughout his reign – to form an alliance with the King of England against France and to ensure that England was locked into his political system, hopefully

even by being absorbed into his dynasty. Katharine and her daughter were central to this strategy.

The context within which the visit took place was every bit as extraordinary as its duration. Charles's presence was urgently needed in Castile to restore the authority of the Crown after the revolt of the *comuneros*. To delay was to risk the loss of Spain: and yet Charles spent six weeks in England! Moreover, to ensure that he could reimpose his control over Castile Charles was taking 4,000 German mercenaries and an enormous artillery train with him to Spain; he clearly could not enter England with an army and so the troops had to be left in the Low Countries – and paid for – while he was in England. And Charles could not afford to pay even for his journey back to Spain, let alone find the resources to fund an extended stay in England. It is doubtful whether it ever occurred to Henry that Charles would stay for six weeks but that he should have agreed to pay the expenses for his visit and then lend him the money for his journey to Castile was testament to the importance that he attached to the visit and to the creation of the alliance with Charles. Certainly, Henry did the best he could to hive as much of the expenses off to the towns and cities in which Charles stayed and most especially to the Lord Mayor and the guilds of the City of London.

This was well judged, for when Charles and his advisers drew up the initial list of the imperial entourage they included no fewer than 2,044 people and 1,126 horses.[3] On reflection, Charles decided that it would be impolitic to impose such a burden on his hosts and reduced the numbers to 1,000 people and about 500 horses; he ordered that the others should remain in Zeeland and join him in Southampton for the voyage to Spain.[4] But even these lesser numbers would still impose dreadful financial and logistical burdens on their hosts, for they (and their horses) would all have to be lodged and fed throughout the stay, and it was a matter of honour for Henry that his imperial guests should live in England to the splendid standards to which they were accustomed. Further negotiations reduced the numbers to 397 men 'of rank' and about as many servants and provisioners.

The composition of the imperial party made it evident exactly how much importance Charles attached to the visit. He would bring with him leading noblemen, churchmen and administrators from Spain and the Low Countries. The Spanish nobility was led by the Duke of Alba and the Marquis of Villafranca, the Dutch by the Prince of Orange, the Count of Egmont and the Duke of Cleves. A host of lesser nobles and a swathe of bishops were also included in the entourage. Charles's intention of staying in England for some time was implicit in the list of Spanish administrators who accompanied him, making it clear that he intended to carry on with his correspondence with Spain while in England; his two chief Secretaries of State (Francisco de los Cobos and Francisco de Vargas), six members of the Council of Castile and eight from the Council of Aragon sailed with him. Four members of his Council of Flanders also travelled with him. Charles was a celebrated gourmet and while he intended to pay due respect to the delights of English cooking he also took the precaution of bringing his cooks and fruiterers with him as well as his surgeons and a barber. He was also accompanied by a corps of musicians, including eight trumpeters for state occasions.[5] But while Charles arrived with every intention of carrying on his governmental work in England the evidence is that he so enjoyed the ceaseless round of festivities that Henry provided for him that he quite failed to keep up with his government business.

The logistical problems in provisioning the imperial party consumed a great deal of energy on the part of English administrators. While they did their best to identify at each stop on the road the 397 rooms in which the senior men would sleep they did not record where the lesser men would be lodged.[6] Detailed thought was given to the amount of meat, fruit and fish to be provided for each man, from the Emperor-elect downwards. It was decided to draw up a list of meals that would be required on a daily basis and the requirements were highly personalised, depending on the status of the guest: for the senior men, individual menus were produced.[7]

Imperial noblemen and courtiers did not live by bread alone and a remarkable effort went into providing wine and beer for them. The royal provisioners again allocated a daily allowance for senior men and did their best to guess what would be required at each stop. Naturally, this would vary with the length of time that the royal parties would spend at individual locations and the provisioners took refuge in broad figures; they calculated, for instance, that at Richmond there would be ten main meals and that they would require 'plenty' of wine while at Dover (where only two days would be spent) they could get by with three casks of Gascon wine and a vat of Rhenish wine. The greatest problems lay of course at court in London and they therefore carried out a survey on 26 March of how much wine was stored in the cellars of the eleven wine merchants and in the twenty-eight principal taverns in the capital; they calculated that there were 809 pipes of wine.[8] They then allocated wine and beer to the lodgings in the city where their guests were staying; to

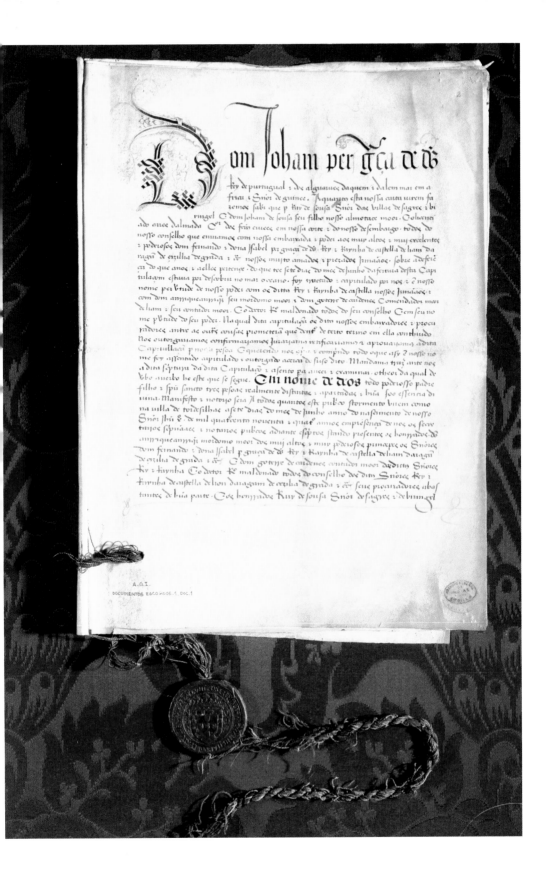

Dom Joham per g̃ca de d̃s

Rey de purtugual ꞇ de algarues daquem ꞇ dalem mar em a
frica ꞇ Snõr de guinee. Aquantos esta nossa carta virem fa
zemos sabj que p̃ Ruy de sousa Snõr das villas de sagres ꞇ bi
ringel ꞇ dom Joham de sousa seu filho nosso almotace moor ꞇ o luenei
ado onꞇꞇ dalmada c̃or ꞇ dos frrɥ euuꞇꞇ em nossa corte ꞇ do nosso desembargo todos do
nosso conselho que euuiamos com nossa embaixada ꞇ poder aos muy altos ꞇ muy excelentes
ꞇ poderosos dom fernando ꞇ dona ffabel pꞇ gr̃ca de d̃s Rey ꞇ Rynha de castella d̃ ham da
ragõ de ezilla degrnda ꞇ c̃ nossos muyto amados ꞇ prezados Jrmããos. sobre a deferē
ci do que anos ꞇ aelles pteuce do que tre sete dias do mes de Junho da feitua desta Capi
tulacem estaua por descubrir no mar oceano. foy mouetado ꞇ capitulado por nos ꞇ e nosso
nome per Vtude de nosso poder com os ditos Rey ꞇ Rynha de castella nossos Jrmããos ꞇ
com dom anrryqueannrigi seu moordomo moor ꞇ dom gutere de caidenes Comendador mor
de ham ꞇ seu contador moor. Co dotor t̃o maldonado todos do seu conselho Cem seu no
me pꞇ Vtude do seu poder. Naqual dita capitulacõ os dita nossos embaixadores ꞇ procu
radores antre as outras cousas prometeia que d̃n̄f de certo retino em ella contiuodo
nos outorguiamos confirmayamos Juarjama ꞇrificaijamos ꞇ aprouayamos, a dita
Capitulacõ p̃ nosa pesoa Cqueredo nos ꞇsj ꞇ comprido todo oque esf ꞇ nosso no
me for assenado capitulado ꞇ outorgado acerca d̃ suso dito Mandamos trazi ante nos
a dita scptura da dita Capitulacõ ꞇ a sento pa auec ꞇ examinar otheor da qual de
Vbo auerbo he este que se segue. **Em nome de d̃os** todo poderosso padre
filho ꞇ spũ sancto tres pesoas reaalmente disjntue ꞇ apartadas ꞇ hũa soo essenria di
uina. Manifesto ꞇ notoryo seia At todos quantos este pubco stormento birem como
na uilla de toidesilhas a sete dias do mes de Junho anno do nascemento de nosso
Snõr Jhũ x̃o de mil quatrcento nouenta ꞇ quatṙo annos em presenca de nos os secre
tarjos scpuããcs ꞇ no tanos pubcos adiante escptos standos presentes os honrrados d̃o
anrryqueannrigi moordomo moor dos muj altos ꞇ muj poderosos primcepes os Snõres
dom fernando ꞇ dona ffabel pꞇ gr̃ca de d̃s Rey ꞇ Raynha de castella de ham daragõ
de ezilla degrnda ꞇ c̃ ꞇ dom gutere de caidenes contador moor dos ditos Snõres
Rey ꞇ Raynha ꞇ o dotor t̃o maldonado todos do conselho dos ditos Snõres Rey ꞇ
Raynha de castella de liõ daragam de ezilla de grnda ꞇ c̃ seus procuradores abas
tantes de hũa parte. Cos honrrados Ruy de sousa Snõr de sagres ꞇ de bringel

Previous page & this page: 1, 2 & 3. The Treaty of Tordesillas (illustration 1), 7 June 1494. In 1494 the kings of Portugal and Castile divided the unknown world between them in the Treaty of Tordesillas, a small town (illustration 2) chosen because it was on the road from Castile to Portugal. The plaque (illustration 3) on the small palace in which the treaty was signed commemorates the 500th anniversary and shows Tordesillas as it spreads out above the River Duero. ((1) © Archivo General de Indias, Seville. (2) and (3) Author's collection)

4. Ferdinand II of Aragon
(b. 1452; reigned 1479–1516).
Katharine's parents were
commemorated in Granada
Cathedral by these splendid
statues of Felipe Vigarny in 1520–
22, which idealise them as 'the
Catholic Monarchs'. (Courtesy of
Royal Chapel, Granada, 1520–22)

5. Isabella I of Castile (b. 1451;
reigned 1474–1504). (Courtesy of
Royal Chapel, Granada, 1520–22)

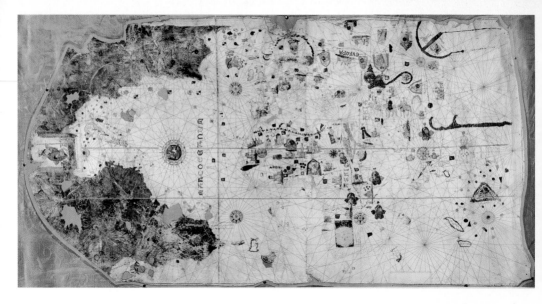

6. Juan de la Cosa, map of the world in 1500. The map records the world as it was known to Europeans in 1500. (Courtesy of Museo Naval, Madrid)

Left: 7. The palace of Juan de Vivero, Valladolid. The marriage of Ferdinand and Isabella took place in this small palace in circumstances of secrecy and danger. (Author's collection)

Above: 8. The Archbishop's Palace, Alcalá de Henares. Katharine was born here on 16 December 1485. The palace was also the location for the first interview between Isabella and Christopher Columbus (1486). (Author's collection)

Opposite: 9. Statue of Katharine of Aragon in front of Archbishop's Palace, Alcalá de Henares, by Manuel González Muñoz (2007). Katharine is shown with a book in recognition of her learning – and in tribute to her being a daughter of the great university town of Alcalá de Henares. (Author's collection)

Left & above: 10. & 11. The Alhambra, Granada, and the Royal Palace ('Alcázar'), Seville. Katharine spent much of her early years travelling with the itinerant household of her parents. She became familiar with the great cities of Granada and Seville – and with the civilisation of Islamic Spain. (Courtesy of Elizabeth Norton)

Above & right: 12. & 13. The castle at Medina del Campo ('La Mota'). The initial agreement to marry Katharine with Prince Arthur was negotiated in Medina del Campo in 1489. Medina was a favoured residence of Queen Isabella and had international significance for the fairs that were held there twice yearly. The extraordinary castle held a commanding view over the great plain and was known as 'the Moat' because of the large moat which surrounded it. (Both author's collection)

Left: 14. Henry VII (b. 1457; reigned 1485–1509). Henry was an austere and practical man who ended the Wars of the Roses. The marriages of his sons to Katharine of Aragon vindicated his success in restoring English power and prestige in Europe. (Courtesy of Elizabeth Norton)

Above left, above right & opposite: 15, 16, & 17. Bath Abbey was begun in 1499 and was the last great abbey built before the Reformation. Henry VII is portrayed on the façade between the ladders of 'Jacob's dream' – a remarkable statement about the closeness of Church and Monarchy on the eve of the Reformation. The abbey was dissolved in 1539. (Photographs by Andrew Desmond, Bath Abbey Trustees)

ELIZABETHA VXOR HENRICI.S VII.

Above left: 18. Lady Margaret Beaufort (1443–1509), Countess of Richmond and Derby, mother of Henry VII. Henry VII's mother was of royal blood. She became a great patron of learning, founding two colleges at Cambridge and endowing chairs of Divinity at Oxford and Cambridge. (Courtesy of Ripon Cathedral)

Above right: 19. Elizabeth of York (1465–1503), wife of Henry VII. As a daughter of Edward IV, Elizabeth carried royal blood in her veins. She presented Henry with eight children, but only three reached adulthood. It is surely not fanciful to see the genes of Edward IV in the physique (and personality?) of Henry VIII. (Courtesy of Ripon Cathedral)

Left: 20. Perkin Warbeck (*c.* 1474–99). The imposter. Warbeck caused Henry VII untold trouble because he was useful to the king's opponents as the focal point for rebellion against Henry. He variously impersonated the Earl of Warwick, an illegitimate son of Richard III, and then Richard, the younger of the 'Princes in the Tower'. He was clearly possessed of some energy, landing in Ireland, Scotland, Kent and Cornwall to lead revolts or uprisings against the king. Henry was surprisingly tolerant of him until he was provoked once too often by a second attempt to escape from the Tower of London. (Courtesy of Jonathan Reeve JRCD3b20p795)

Above: 21. Woodcut, 'The coronations of Henry VIII and Katharine' (1509), Stephen Hawes (c. 1474–1529), printed by Wynkyn de Worde in *A Joyfull Medytacyonh to All Englonde of the Coronacyon of Our Moost Natural Soureayne Lorde Kynge Henry the Eight*, 1509. Henry and Katharine gaze lovingly at each other as they are crowned beneath their symbols of the Tudor Rose and the Granada Pomegranate. Intriguingly, Henry is beardless, and it may be that this was at Katharine's request, for she disliked his beard. (Courtesy of Cambridge University Library, Sel. 5–55)

Right: 22. Katharine of Aragon as a young woman. Katharine is painted here in the English style, with a freshness and vitality that dates the picture to the mid- to late 1510s. (Courtesy of Ripon Cathedral)

KATHERINA VXOR HENRICI . . viii.

23. Henry VIII (b. 1491; reigned 1509–47), Lucas Horenbout (c. 1505–44), c. 1526–27. Horenbout produced six miniature watercolour portraits of Henry in 1526–27 – at about the time that he began to develop anxieties about the legitimacy of his marriage to Katharine – and his lust for Anne Boleyn. (The Royal Collection © 2011. Her Majesty the Queen [RCIN 420640])

24. Katharine harangued by Cardinals Campeggio and Wolsey at the Legatine Court, 1529. This woodcarving from Canterbury Cathedral continues the great medieval tradition of the satirical gargoyle as the two cardinals urge Katharine to give Henry his freedom to remarry by herself entering a convent. (Courtesy of Jonathan Reeve JR977oldpc 15001600)

25. Katharine admires Henry's skill in the joust. Henry was skilled in the chivalric arts and here Katharine admires his performance at the joust. Henry jousted enthusiastically until the early 1520s. (Courtesy of Jonathan Reeve JR1098b2fp204 15001550)

Above left: 26. Philip 'the Good', Duke of Burgundy (b. 1396; reigned 1419–67). After Rogier van der Weyden (*c.* 1399–1464), *c.* 1445. Duke Philip is wearing the Order of the Golden Fleece that he founded in 1430 and which became the symbol of Burgundy's cultural and chivalric leadership of Europe. (The Royal Collection © 2011. Her Majesty Queen Elizabeth II [RCIN 403440])

Above right: 27. Philip 'the Handsome' (1478–1506), Archduke of Austria and Duke of Burgundy, after Rogier van der Weyden (*c.* 1399–1464), *c.* 1500. Philip was proverbially unfaithful to Juana, whom he married in 1496. When her mental health broke down he made no secret of his intention to rule Castile in her stead but he died suddenly in 1506. He is wearing the emblem of the Order of the Golden Fleece. (The Royal Collection © 2011. Her Majesty Queen Elizabeth II [RCIN 403438])

28. Juana I (b. 1479; queen regnant 1504–55), sculptor unknown, Tordesillas. Juana broke down completely in 1506 and from 1507 until her death in 1555 was incarcerated in the palace at Tordesillas. Her son Charles ruled in her place, officially as co-monarch with her. Juana carries the globe in tribute to the importance that Tordesillas had acquired when in 1494 the Crowns of Castile and Portugal signed a treaty there which divided the undiscovered world between them. (Author's collection)

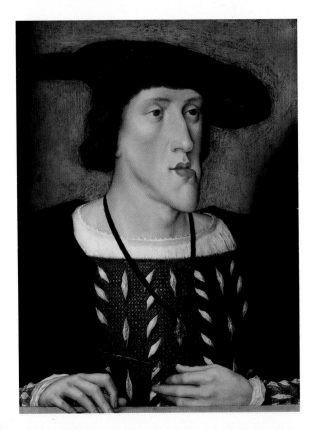

29. Charles V (b. 1500; King of Spain 1516–56, Holy Roman Emperor 1519–58), Flemish School, 1514–16. Charles became King of Spain in 1516 due to his mother's unfitness to rule. Like his father, he is wearing the Order of the Golden Fleece – a reminder that he was always a foreigner in Spain. The portrait may have been sent to England when he was engaged to marry Henry VIII's sister Mary. (The Royal Collection © 2011. Her Majesty Queen Elizabeth II [RCIN 403439])

30. Louis XII of France (b. 1462; reigned 1498–1515), Workshop of Jean Perreal (c. 1455–1530), c. 1510–14. Louis's invasion of Italy in 1499 brought England and Spain closer together. He is wearing the Order of St Michel. (The Royal Collection © 2011. Her Majesty Queen Elizabeth II [RCIN 403431])

31. Francis I of France (b. 1494; reigned 1515–47). After Joose van Cleve (d. 1520–21), c. 1530. Francis I began his reign in 1515 with the dazzling triumph at Marignano that re-opened 'the Italian Wars' – and which confirmed Henry VIII in his resentment of him. (The Royal Collection © 2011. Her Majesty Queen Elizabeth II [RCIN 403433])

32. Brothers and emperors: Charles V and Ferdinand I, anonymous sketch, Flemish sixteenth century. The brothers had not known each other as children but came to develop a begrudging confidence in each other. Ferdinand succeeded Charles as Emperor in 1558. (Author's collection)

33. *The Field of the Cloth of Gold*, 1520, British School, *c.* 1545. The extraordinary meetings between Henry VIII and Francis I near Calais (7–24 June 1520) set the tone for their deeply competitive relationship. However, the meeting brought no political benefits (other, perhaps, than disguising Henry's movement to an imperial alliance to which he committed himself in 1522, when Charles V visited England). Henry is accompanied by Cardinal Wolsey and the leading noblemen of his court. The queen's tent is probably on the extreme right and Katharine herself may well be in the litter behind the tent. (The Royal Collection © 2011. Her Majesty Queen Elizabeth II [RCIN 405794])

34. The Archivo General, Simancas. Simancas became the central archive of the Spanish crown in the 1540s. Until that date its holdings tend to be uneven but it remains extraordinarily rich as the examples here demonstrate. (Author's collection)

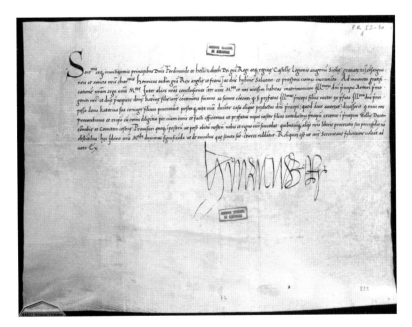

35. Letter of Henry VII to Ferdinand and Isabella promising that any son born to Katharine and Arthur will be named as Prince of Wales. (Courtesy of the Archivo General, Simancas AGS Patronato Real 53, No. 10)

36. Ratification by Henry VII on 3 March 1504 of the marriage agreement between Henry VIII and Katharine of Aragon dated Richmond, 23 June 1503. The splendid first page of the document is decorated with the royal arms and with the red rose of Lancaster. Henry himself secretly renounced it, no doubt with the knowledge of his father. (Courtesy of the Archivo General, Simancas AGS Patronato Real 53, doc. 1)

Above: 37. Pope Julius II, brief of dispensation for marriage of Katharine and Prince Henry, 26 December 1503, AGS Patronato Real, 61 no. 116. The dispensation was sloppily prepared but so anxious were the two crowns to organise the marriage that neither examined it properly – with disastrous consequences in the 1530s. (Courtesy of Archivo General de Simancas, Patronato Real)

Above right: 38. The last will and testament of Isabella the Catholic, Medina del Campo, 12 October 1504. Isabella's will and testament recognised that her daughter Juana would succeed her as Queen of Castile and granted King Ferdinand administrative rights over the kingdom. Isabella died on 26 November 1504. (Courtesy of the Archivo General de Simancas, Patronato Real 30, no. 2)

39. On her journey from Plymouth to London Katharine saw her first great English cathedral, that of Exeter. (Author's collection)

Above and below left: 40. & 41. As Princess of Wales, Katharine spent a few weeks with Arthur in the forbidding (and cold) castle at Ludlow. (Author's collection)

Above right: 42. Thomas Wolsey, Lord Chancellor of England. (Courtesy of Jonathan Reeve JR1169b2p7 15001550)

43. Prince Arthur, Katharine's first husband and Henry VIII's older brother. (Courtesy of David Baldwin)

Above: 44. Bath and Wells Cathedral. Thomas Wolsey held this see between 1518 and 1522. (Author's collection)

Left: 45. Desiderius Erasmus 'of Rotterdam' (1466–1536), Quintin Massys (1465/6–1530), 1517. A scholar of European eminence but a shameless flatterer of kings and princes. The picture was a gift for Sir Thomas More, a close friend and admirer. (The Royal Collection © 2011. Her Majesty Queen Elizabeth II [RCIN 405759])

Opposite: 46. Sir Thomas More (1478–1535), Hans Holbein the Younger, *c.* 1526–27. An early portrait as he approached the years of crisis. A reluctant Lord Chancellor in 1529, More resigned in 1532, knowing that he could not support the king over the 'divorce' and the Royal Supremacy. He was executed in July 1535 and canonised in 1935. (The Royal Collection © 2011. Her Majesty Queen Elizabeth II [RL 12225])

Above left: 47. John Colet, Dean of St Paul's (1466/7–1519), Hans Holbein the Younger (1497/8–1543), *c.* 1535 (posthumous). A leading humanist who attacked abuses within the Church but who also rebuked Henry VIII for going to war. He died before he had to confront the issues of the Reformation. (The Royal Collection © 2011. Her Majesty Queen Elizabeth II [RL 12199])

Above right: 48. John Fisher, Bishop of Rochester (*c.* 1469–1535), Hans Holbein the Younger, *c.* 1532–34. An austere churchman and scholar, Fisher wrote several books against the divorce and opposed the Royal Supremacy. Executed in 1535: he was so weak that he had to be almost carried to the scaffold. Canonised in 1935 with More. (The Royal Collection © 2011. Her Majesty Queen Elizabeth II [RL 12205])

Left: 49. Henry Howard, Earl of Surrey (1516/17–1547), Hans Holbein the Younger, *c.* 1533–36. A poet and scholar, who was close to Henry and to Anne Boleyn. He was executed for treason only a few days before Henry died in 1547 but the king's death saved his father (who was to have died a few hours later). (The Royal Collection © 2011. Her Majesty Queen Elizabeth II [RL 12216])

Anna Bollein Queen.

50. Anne Boleyn (b. *c.* 1500; Queen of England 1533–36), Hans Holbein the Younger, *c.* 1533–36. Henry was infatuated by Anne, who was ebullient rather than beautiful but may have abstained from full sexual relations so that she could become his queen. He married her in 1533, shortly before she gave birth to the future Elizabeth I. Anne's failure to provide a male heir rather than her alleged adultery – with, among others, her brother – led her to the scaffold. (The Royal Collection © 2011. Her Majesty Queen Elizabeth II [RL 12189])

Above: 51. William Warham (*c.* 1450–1532), Archbishop of Canterbury (1503–32), Hans Holbein the Younger, 1527. Warham was the senior churchman at the eye of the storm over Henry VIII's divorce. He had crowned Henry and Katharine in 1509 and with Wolsey had endeavoured to find a way of ending the marriage in 1529. He did not bring himself to state his outright opposition to the divorce until he was himself at the point of death in 1532. (The Royal Collection © 2011. Her Majesty Queen Elizabeth II [RL 12272])

Opposite: 52. Clement VII's bull, 23 March 1534. Pope Clement VII (1523–34) was the master of the politics of dissimulation but he was repeatedly overtaken by events; he did not issue this bull confirming that Henry's marriage to Katharine was valid until after Henry had married Anne Boleyn and had a child by her. (Archivo General de Simancas, Patronato Real 53, f. 117 (1))

Anglici Matrimonij.

Sententia diffinitiua

Lata per sanctissimum Dñm Nostrum D. Clementem Papā vij. in sacro Consistorio de Reuerendissimorum Dominorum S. R. E. Cardinalium consilio super Validitate e Matrimonij inter Serenissimos Henricum VIII. e Catherinam Angliæ Reges contracti.

PRO.

Eadem Serenissima Catherina Angliæ Regina,

CONTRA.

Serenissimum Henricum VIII. Angliæ Regem.

Clemens Papa. vij.

Hristi nomine inuocato in Throno iustitiæ pro tribunali sedentes, & solum Deum præ oculis habentes, Per hanc nostram diffinitiuam sententiam quam de Venerabilium Fratrum nostrorum Sanctæ Ro. Ec. Car. Consistorialiter coram nobis congregatorum Consilio, & assensu ferimus in his scriptis, pronunciamus, decernimus, & declaramus, in causa, & causis ad nos, per Sedem Apostolicam per appellationem, per charissimam in christo filium Catherinam Angliæ Reginam illustrem a nostris, & Sedis Apostolicæ Legatis in Regno Angliæ deputatis interpositi tam legitime deuolutis, & aduocatis, inter prædictam Catherinam Reginam, & Charissimum in christo filium Henricum VIII. Angliæ Regem Illustrem, super Validitate, & inualiditate matrimonij inter eosdem Reges contracti, & consormati reboque aliis in actis, causæ & causarum huiusmodi latius deductis, & dilecto filio Paulo Capissucho causarum sacri palatij tunc decano & pro ipsius Pauli absentiam Venerabili Fratri nostro Iacobo Simonete Episcopo Pisauren. vnius ex actis palatij causarum Auditoribus locumtenenti, audiendis instruendis, & in Consistorio nostro Secreto referendis commissis, & per eos nobis, & eisdem Cardinalibus Relatis, & mature discussis, coram nobis pendentibus, Matrimonium inter prædictos Catherinam, & Henricum Angliæ Reges contractum, & inde secuta quærunq fuisse, & esse validum, & canonicum validuq, & Canonica, suoque debitus de buisse, & debere sortiri effectus, prolemque exinde susceptam, & suscependam fuisse, & fore legitimam, & præfatum Henricum Angliæ Regem teneri, & obligatum fuisse, et fore ad cohabitandum cum dicta Catherina Regina eius legitima coniuge, illamq maritali affectione, & Regio honore tractandum & eundem Henricum Angliæ Regem ad præmissa omnia, & singula cum effectu adimplendum condemnandum omnibusq iuris Remedijs cogendum, & compellendum fore, prout condemnamus, cogimus, & compellimus, Molestationesq, & deuocationes Per eundem Henricum Regem eidem Catherinæ Reginæ super inualiditate, ac super dicti Matrimonij quomodolibet factas, & præstitas fuisse, & esse illicitas, & inustas, & eidem Henrico Regi super illas ac inualidatate matrimonij huiusmodi perpetuum Silentium imponendum fore, & imponimus, eundemq Henricum Angliæ Regem in expensis in huiusmodi causa pro parte dictæ Catherinæ Reginæ coram nobis, & dictis omnibus legitime factis condemnandum fore, & condemnamus, quarum expensarum taxationem nobis imposterum reseruamus.

Ita pronunciauimus .I.

Lata suit Romæ in Palatio Apostolico publicatis Consistorio die. XXIII. Martij. M. D. XXXIIII.

Blosius.

53. Tomb of Katharine of Aragon, Peterborough Cathedral. Katharine's tomb is now the centrepiece for an annual celebration of her life. (Courtesy of Elizabeth Norton)

Above left: 54. Mary Tudor. Katharine triumphed posthumously over Henry when their daughter Mary succeeded to the throne. It was a disastrous reign and she has gone down in history as 'Bloody Mary'. (Courtesy of Ripon Cathedral)

Above right: 55. Philip II of Spain (b. 1527; reigned 1556–98). Charles V's son married Katharine's daughter and was briefly king-consort of England. Better known to English history as the man who sent 'the armada' of 1588 against Elizabeth. (Author's collection)

Left: 56. The Emperor Maximilian. (Author's collection)

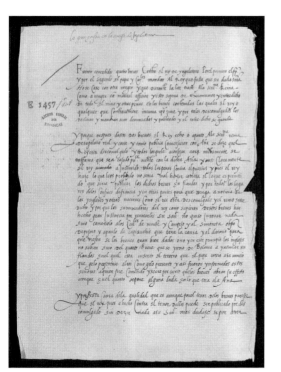

Above left: 57. Understanding Pope Clement. The Spanish government found it difficult to keep track of whether Pope Clement intended to excommunicate Henry VIII or not: in this document it analyses the various bulls that he had issued on the subject. (Courtesy of Archivo General de Simancas)

Top right & above: 58. & 59. West front of Winchester Cathedral. (Courtesy of the Chapter of Winchester)

60. Map of Europe.
(Author's collection)

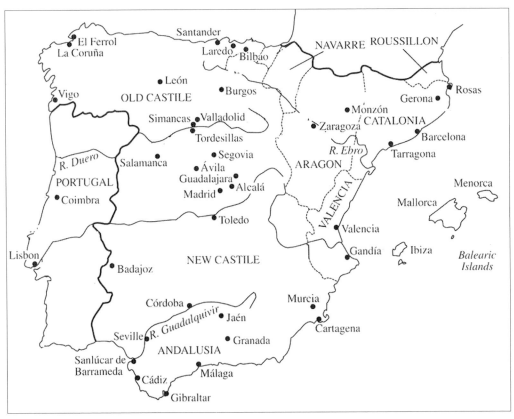

61. Map of Spain. (Author's collection)

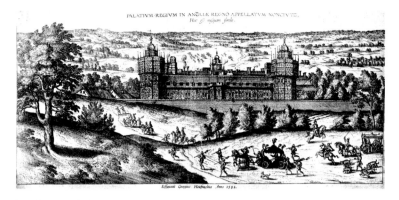

62. Nonsuch Palace. Built by Henry from scratch 1538–47 as a palace designed to express his wealth and power – thus its name as a palace unlike any other. It also served as a hunting-lodge adjacent to the lands of Hampton Court. Henry designed it as a place of recreation for himself and his close circle but he himself was too ill to make much use of it (although some of its architectural features expressly reflected his immobility). Nothing survives of the palace except its place in legend, but in reality Henry was vainly trying in Nonsuch to recreate the glories of his youth. It stayed in the royal family for 150 years until Charles II presented it in 1670 to the Duchess of Cleveland, one of his mistresses. (Courtesy of Jonathan Reeve JR1018b5fp204 15001550)

63. York Place/Whitehall Palace. Wolsey held York Place as Archbishop of York from 1514 and used it as a town house and place of business. Henry acquired it in 1529–30 and renamed it 'Whitehall Palace'. He turned Wolsey's lodgings into quarters for Queen Anne. He built a celebrated tiltyard here, together with tennis courts and a cockpit. In 1536 he designated the building as 'Whitehall Palace'. By 1547, when Henry died, the palace's grounds covered 23 acres: it was the largest royal palace in contemporary Europe. Charles I (1625–49) used it as a favoured residence: ironically, he was executed there in January 1649. (Courtesy of Jonathan Reeve JR779b46fp192 14501500)

64. Greenwich Palace. The friary church on the left of van Wyngaerde's sketch of 1558 was greatly favoured by the royal family. Henry VIII was born in the palace; he was baptised in its church and married Katharine there in 1509. He also had both of his daughters christened there. He enjoyed the extensive grounds and the facilities on the river that the palace gave him and visited it more frequently than he did any other of his palaces. But he turned on the friars of the house when they opposed him for replacing Katharine with Anne: several suffered gruesome martyrdoms as traitors. (Courtesy of Jonathan Reeve JR944b46fp180 14501500)

Left: 65. Richmond Palace. Henry VII built Richmond Palace on the site of the palace of Sheen, which was largely destroyed by a fire in 1497. The name was significant, for it reflected Henry's status as Duke of Richmond (a title which he used in a vain attempt to disguise his Welsh origins). He died in the palace in 1509. Henry VIII appreciated its proximity to London and its extensive hunting-grounds; the palace also had an early example in England of a Renaissance garden. In 1510 Katharine gave birth to the ill-fated Prince Henry there: he lived only fifty-three days. Katharine and her daughter lived there during their exile from court and before they were sent away from London. In 1540 Henry VIII presented the palace to Anne of Cleves as part of her divorce settlement. Elizabeth I died there on 24 March 1603. (Courtesy of Jonathan Reeve JR945b20p788 15001550)

Below left: : 66. Tower of London. Begun by William the Conqueror, the impregnable Tower served as a prison for the most important prisoners of the crown: John Fisher, Thomas More and Thomas Cromwell were among those who were imprisoned and executed here. So, too, were two of Henry VIII's queens, Anne Boleyn and Catherine Howard. But the Tower also served as a royal palace, notably when queens stayed there on the night before their coronation: Katharine and Anne Boleyn both did so. (Courtesy of Stephen Porter)

67. Hampton Court Palace. Thomas Wolsey created at Hampton Court the most opulent expression of his greatness, wealth and patronage of the arts. He used it as a country house from which he had ready access to London by water and hosted many important diplomatic occasions here. While many admired Hampton Court, Henry coveted it and took it over after Wolsey's fall in 1529. He enjoyed its extensive hunting facilities and (as with Greenwich, Whitehall and Nonsuch) used it for riverside sports and entertainments, building a new courtyard and extending the Great Hall. All of his queens had apartments here. (Courtesy of Jonathan Reeve JR1091b20p884 15001550)

take one example, Dr Dolman (who was to provide twelve 'featherbeds' for his guests)[9] was provided with two hogs of wine and two barrels of beer.[10]

While their provisioners were struggling with these problems of supply, Henry and Wolsey prepared for Charles's arrival by giving serious offence to the French ambassador. When news conveniently reached court that some English merchants in Bordeaux had been imprisoned and their goods confiscated, Wolsey summoned the French ambassador and demanded angrily whether the arrests were the acts of friendship that Francis I had sworn to observe at the Treaty of London. Indeed, he even went so far as to explicitly – and very publicly – question the integrity of Francis: 'Is this the word of a king?' The ambassador's protests that the reports were false were swept aside: Wolsey rejoined that the King of England's council did not deal in 'fables'. Severe reprisals were imposed; the ambassador was placed effectively under house arrest and the lord mayor was instructed to imprison all Frenchmen in the capital during the king's pleasure and to sequestrate their goods. As an even more explicit gesture, Henry sent his navy to scour the Channel to attack French ships. But still he had not declared war on Francis: a chronicler recorded sombrely that 'there was neither peace between England and France nor open warfare'.[11] When war was shortly declared it would be done in the very grandest of styles.

The Visit of Charles V to England, 1522

26–29 May	Dover
30 May	Canterbury
31 May	Sittingbourne
1 June	Rochester
2 June	Gravesend and by barge to Greenwich
2–6 June	Greenwich
6–8 June	London
9 June	Richmond
10 June	Hampton Court
11–20 June	Windsor Castle
21–22 June	Farnham
23 June	Alresford
24–26 June	Winchester
26 June–3 July	Bishops Waltham
4–6 July	Southampton
16 July	Santander

On 20 May, Wolsey set the tone of untempered extravagance that would distinguish the visit when he rode through London on his way to Dover to greet the Emperor-elect; he was accompanied by two earls, thirty-six knights, one hundred or so gentlemen, eight bishops, ten abbots and thirty chaplains. About 700 servants trailed behind him. The cardinal and his entourage travelled with stately ease: it took six days to reach Dover. Charles arrived at Gravelines on 25 May and was welcomed by the Marquis of Dorset and the Bishop of Chichester. He then rode with them to Calais where he made a splendid 'joyous entrance'. On the following day he sailed to Dover, arriving at four in the afternoon. Wolsey was waiting for him on the sands with an entourage of 300; the two men embraced and the cardinal took the Emperor-elect by the arm and rode with him to Dover Castle, side-by-side. Unfortunately, Charles had to make himself at home in the castle for three days because the irruption of foul weather prevented the bulk of his party from sailing to join him for that amount of time.

Henry arrived at Canterbury on 27 May and on the next day rode to Dover where he met Charles, as Hall tells us, 'with much joy and gladness'. Since it was the feast of the Ascension they spent the night in Dover. On the following day, Henry proudly took his guest on board the *Henry Grâce à Dieu* so that he could admire the great ship itself and proceed to view the royal fleet in the harbour; Charles and his lords 'much praised the making of the ships, and especially the artillery, they said [that] they never saw ships so armed'. Charles's generous response probably encouraged Henry to take him on a guided inspection of the *Mary Rose*.[12] In demonstrating England's naval power to his guest Henry was consciously showing Charles what an important ally he could be against the King of France. Martín de Salinas, ambassador of Archduke Ferdinand at Charles's court, noted admiringly that the English fleet could carry 10,000 men.[13]

In the afternoon of 28 May, Henry led his guests to Canterbury. They were greeted outside the city by the mayor and aldermen and then processed inside, riding side by side with their naked swords of state carried before them. Although Charles rode on the right of Henry, indicating that he was both an honoured guest and of superior rank to him, the fact that Henry rode next to him must have been deeply satisfying to him as an expression of the prestige that the Emperor-elect's visit conferred upon him.

Over the following days the royal parties rode to Sittingbourne and Rochester (where they were welcomed by Bishop John Fisher) and on to

Gravesend, where thirty barges were waiting to carry them to Greenwich. Progress was slow because Henry had not been able to provide the 600 horses that he had promised; Salinas – who grumbled ceaselessly throughout the visit – complained that for this reason the journey to London was 'extremely tiring'.

Henry went on to Greenwich ahead of Charles to prepare the reception for him. At 6 o'clock in the evening of 2 June Charles disembarked at the palace and was formally welcomed on the waterfront by Henry and then at the 'hall door' by Katharine and Princess Mary: in the Spanish custom, Charles asked his aunt for her blessing and Katharine joyously gave it to him. She must have been deeply moved to meet Charles again, the more so because he was now the fiancé of her daughter; in their encounter, the Anglo-Spanish alliance to which Katharine had dedicated her life was renewed and revivified. The implications were momentous, for it was now four years since Katharine had last been pregnant and it was evident that – barring a miracle – she would not be providing Henry with a male heir: in making the arrangements, therefore, to marry Charles to Princess Mary, Henry was accommodating himself to the failure of his marriage to provide directly for the succession and looking to resolving his difficulties by anticipating the birth of a male heir in the next generation – to his daughter.

On Wednesday, 4 June Henry entertained Charles with a jousting tournament and naturally he took centre stage; eight times he rode at his friend Charles Brandon, Duke of Suffolk, and each time he broke his spear. The field was then opened up to all contestants and the joust did not end until all the spears had been broken. Then, hungry after their exertions, everyone trooped off to supper. Afterwards, a dance was held; Charles seems to have taken genuine delight in watching the ladies dancing and when two groups of six noblemen irrupted into the chamber in disguise to dance there was unfeigned delight – no doubt! – when the most accomplished of all of them took off his mask to reveal himself as the King of England.

From jousting to a declaration of war: on Thursday 5 June, as Henry was arming himself for a jousting tournament a message arrived from the French ambassador and with great theatricality Henry invited Charles to read it with him. The Emperor-elect was delighted to do so and Henry informed him that on 21 May his king-of-arms had been received by Francis I at Lyons and had listed the grievances that Henry held against Francis, declaring that Henry now considered Francis to be his 'mortal enemy'. As the news seeped around the assembly a great clamour arose and the Englishmen shouted for war with France.[14] The first purpose of Charles V's visit to England had been accomplished. The jousting tournament that now took place might well have seemed to be a joyous rehearsal for the new war on France. Within weeks, Henry despatched his fleet under Sir Thomas Howard to patrol off the French coast.[15]

On Friday 6 June, the two allies rode to the capital city. They were welcomed a mile outside London at a tent of cloth of gold which contained two lodgings in which they dressed for their joyous entry into the capital. The allusion to the celebratory tents that Henry VIII and Francis I had used at the Field of the Cloth of Gold in 1520 was unmistakable, as too was the direct inference to be drawn – that Charles V had replaced Francis I as the ally of the King of England. Inside their tents, the two monarchs dressed in identical suits of cloth of gold lined with silver decoration and as they processed into London their clothing again identified them as equal partners. They were preceded by courtiers carrying their unsheathed swords and followed by their noblemen and courtiers, riding in pairs with the imperial party on the right: once again the two monarchs and their courts were identified as partners in a common enterprise. Sir Thomas More greeted them with a speech in praise of the two princes and of the love and peace that they enjoyed and which gave such joy to their subjects: he quite failed to mention that they were about to go to war together. At Southwark, Charles and Henry were welcomed by the representatives of the clergy as they passed by the Marshalsea, and at the King's Bench the Emperor-elect generously asked Henry VIII to pardon as many prisoners as he could: Henry duly did so.

There now began a series of nine pageants which were designed to impress Charles, who, as Duke of Burgundy and Grand Master of the Order of the Golden Fleece, was of course the pre-eminent practitioner of the genre in Europe.[16] The pageants were not as grand as those which had celebrated the marriage of Arthur and Katharine in 1501 (above, chapter 6) but they very self-consciously displayed the sophistication of the English court, emphasising that it was in the mainstream of European cultural development. More important still, they emphasised insistently the political (and therefore military) alliance between the two monarchs. That this was no alliance of mere convenience was made manifest by the detailed genealogies of the two houses which stressed the enduring historical bonds between them – Charles V and Henry VIII were both (like Katharine herself) descendants of John of Gaunt and of Alfonso

X ('the Wise') of Castile. More than this, the pageants demonstrated that Charles and Henry were figures of truly historic – and indeed of mythical – import: for instance, at the Drawbridge there were emblems of the territories ruled by Charles and two giants representing Hercules and Samson held a great table in which Charles's lands were listed. No one could have missed the significance of the emblem, for in the flags and banners carried by Charles's entourage the Pillars of Hercules stood as a central expression of his power. As Charles was Hercules, so Henry was Samson: how profoundly gratifying this symbolism must have seemed to him! Similarly, the pageant in the middle of London Bridge celebrating the figure of Jason with the Golden Fleece in front of him could not but have reminded everyone present that Charles was a modern Jason, the Grand Master of the Order of the Golden Fleece. The last element of the Emperor's duties was as the defender of Christendom against the Turkish infidel – a very contemporaneous observation at the moment that the Turk was besieging the Knights of St John on the island of Rhodes. Insistently, therefore, the pageants emphasised not merely the friendship between the monarchs and the equality that they enjoyed with each other but how historically important their alliance against France was: enveloped in pageantry and mythology, Henry and Charles were now intent on a holy war against France.[17]

As in 1501, the religious was mixed with the secular and the familial; when after the monarchs had seen all the pageants they passed to St Paul's where a *Te Deum* was sung, uniting the two crowns in their pursuit of the glory of God.[18] It was an extraordinary triumph for Henry VIII and Wolsey that the Holy Roman Emperor-elect should have entered England's capital city in such magnificence and with such evident joy, for Charles generously recorded how impressed he had been: on 7 June he wrote to the Abbot of Nájera (who was an unlikely commissary of Charles's army in Lombardy) of the 'magnificent reception' that he had received in London and of the 'solemn and costly pageants' that had been presented in his honour. Charles also wrote of the deep enthusiasm with which Henry had committed himself to war with France and itemised the forces that would be brought to bear; his and Henry's combined fleets would carry 18,000 armed men and would begin operations in eight days time when the English fleet would go to sea to seek and destroy as many French ships as possible. Once the French fleet had been incapacitated the two armies would go to war on land. However, it had obviously not yet been agreed exactly where they would do this: Charles observed that the armies would be disembarked either in Flanders or Gascony or Normandy according to circumstances. But wherever they sailed to, he was hopeful that the war would be carried on with sufficient vigour to oblige the French to withdraw from Italy to defend their north-eastern frontier. As for himself, Charles informed Nájera that he would leave London for Southampton within a few days to embark for Spain, where he would immediately begin a campaign against France on the northern frontiers. He would then put his affairs in Spain in order and go to Italy for his coronation as Emperor.[19] The Emperor-elect was in hearty good humour: his schedule was as clear-cut as his victories would be inevitable and overwhelming.

In fact, Charles's visit had not yet run one-quarter of its course. Henry took him to see Richmond Palace and Hampton Court (9–10 June) and then on to Windsor Castle, where they stayed for just over a week (11–20 June) and where, at last, they turned their attention to the main business of the Emperor-elect's visit. True, they spent two days there hunting (13–14 June) and enjoyed a 'disguising' in the Great Hall which seemed to serve as a reminder of what they were about: a proud horse would not be tamed and so 'amitie' sent 'prudence' and 'policie' which then tamed and bridled him. The allegory was obvious: the untamed horse was Francis I and 'amitie' represented Charles V and Henry VIII. For the next three days (16–18 June), Hall tells us, 'the princes and their councils sat for the most part in counsell'. The result of their deliberations were the two 'Treaties of Windsor' (16 June; secret provisions, 19th).

These treaties restated the terms that had been agreed at Bruges in 1521, promising English support for Charles in his war against France and providing him with an important loan. In the preamble to the treaty of 16 June Henry formally renounced his alliance with Francis because the King of France had created dissension within Christendom which made it impossible for the nations to unite under the leadership of the Papacy against the Turk. Since Charles V and himself were duty-bound to defend the Catholic Church they had concluded this perpetual treaty. More prosaically, Henry justified his action by accusing Francis I of supporting Albany's invasion of England and by claiming that the French invasion of Navarre was a breach of the Treaty of London. War would be declared on France if Francis I refused to make peace and it would be fought with the utmost vigour until both parties had recovered possessions seized from them by the French crown – the territories of the old Duchy of Burgundy for Charles, Gascony and Normandy for Henry.

In 1523, Charles would invade France from Spain while Henry would do so from Calais, each at the head of 40,000 men. The English navy would ensure that the Channel was kept open for Charles. The Emperor agreed to compensate Henry VIII and Wolsey for the French pensions that they would lose. When France was defeated it would be dismembered and divided between the allies.[20] By happy chance, the 50,000 ducats that Henry had sent to fund the imperial army in Italy reached Rome within a couple of days of the signing of the treaty: war with France could now be pursued more vigorously in Italy.[21]

The terms of the treaty of 16 June were published but three days later Charles and Henry signed a second treaty at Windsor, and this one was to remain secret for it committed them to the marriage of Charles to Princess Mary within eight years. The day chosen for this secret treaty was deeply symbolic, for it was Corpus Christi Day, one of the emblematic feast days of the Catholic Church. The implications of this marriage – should it ever come about – were explosive for two reasons: firstly, if Henry and Katharine produced no son (as was now all but certain) the eldest son of Charles and Mary would inherit Henry's crowns; secondly, Mary was already betrothed to the Dauphin of France, and for Charles to take the bride of the son of the King of France was certainly provocative and might even be seen as a declaration of war in its own right. Charles promised that he would not contract marriage with any other woman while Mary was underage and that as soon as she completed her twelfth year (which would be in 1528) he would send a proxy to London to contract his marriage with her *per verba de praesenti*. Since the Emperor-elect was related to his fiancée in the second degree of affinity, he and Henry would ask the Pope to issue the appropriate dispensation whenever the marriage was publicly announced. Mary's dowry would consist of 400,000 crowns, half of which was to be paid on the day of the wedding or within eight days of it and the remainder within the following calendar year. If Henry VIII and Katharine had a son and heir this dowry would be increased to 600,000 crowns as if in compensation for the loss of the immediate heritable rights to the Crown of England.

Charles and Henry were generously pleased to recognise the importance they attached to Wolsey's role in preparing their agreements. The cardinal received a substitute for his French pension and the promise of Charles's support at the next papal election. The agreement was to be kept secret until November (when another instalment of the French 'pension' to Henry VIII would be paid).[22]

Later on Corpus Christi Day, Charles signed a declaration of his obligations to Henry VIII (whom he described as his 'uncle'): the document in which he did so was endorsed '*obligatio Caesaris*'. He noted that Henry had declared war on Francis I because the King of France was an enemy of Charles himself and because he had during the last year stopped paying Henry's pension. The Emperor-elect now bound himself to compensate Henry by paying him the 133,305 gold crowns that Francis owed him – 66,801 crowns on 1 November 1522 and the same amount six months later, on 1 May 1523. Both payments would be made at Calais. Charles undertook to continue paying the pension every six months until Henry was entirely indemnified for his losses or until he conquered French towns to the value of 133,305 gold crowns: if the towns that Henry took were not valued at that amount Charles would make up the difference. If Henry made peace with Francis, Charles's payments would cease.[23] But Charles had still not finished reckoning the debts that he owed to Henry VIII: on 20 June he signed a document affirming that Henry had lent him 150,000 escudos to assist him in the pacification of Spain. He committed himself to repaying this money in the City of London within one year and again pledged his property and that of his subjects as surety.[24]

In the late afternoon of Corpus Christi Day, the alliance was sealed in a profoundly symbolic manner when Henry invested Charles with the Order of the Garter in Windsor Palace; Charles was presented with his own stall in St George's Chapel and received the sacrament with Henry. After Mass, both swore to keep the promises that they had made to each other and in the evening Henry laid on one of the very grandest of even his feasts to honour the new Knight of the Garter.[25]

To further emphasise the solemnity of the agreements between Henry and Charles, on 20 June Wolsey convened a legatine court and as papal legate *a latere* received the declarations of the Emperor-elect and the King of England that they had sworn to in their (secret) treaty of 19 June and that if either of them broke it he would automatically incur the dreaded penalty of excommunication. This was no routine act and it was solemnly witnessed by men of the highest seniority and rank – for Charles, Henry Count of Nassau; Gattinara, Imperial Chancellor; Pedro Ruiz de la Mota, Bishop of Palencia: for Henry, Thomas Ruthall, Bishop of Durham; George Talbot, Earl of Shrewsbury; Charles Percy, Earl of Worcester; Cuthbert Tunstal, Bishop-elect of London. A final signature probably attracted little attention among such exalted luminaries – Sir Thomas Boleyn.[26]

Even now that the main business of the visit had been accomplished, Charles did not hurry to return to Castile. True, on 21 June he began the journey to Southampton but he stayed at Farnham and Alresford before reaching Winchester, where he rested for a further two nights. Between 26 June and 3 July he then stayed in Wolsey's palace at Bishop's Waltham, and there on 2 July he and Henry agreed to one last treaty in which they itemised the forces that they would employ against France. Henry undertook to send 10,000 well-armed and equipped footsoldiers and arquebusiers under well-qualified captains to Calais before 1 August 1523 and to assemble a strong train of artillery to support them. Meanwhile, Charles would send 250 men-at-arms from his own household and 1,000 good horse and 3,000 German infantry to Tournehem. He would support these with twelve pieces of field artillery. More substantially, he promised to assemble 10,000–12,000 soldiers in the Low Countries to reinforce Henry's troops in any battle they undertook. The armies were to be commanded by Floris of Egmont, Count of Buren (Charles's Captain General in the Low Countries) and by Thomas Howard, Earl of Surrey, and once they were fully assembled they were to march on Boulogne and besiege it if they believed that they could force it to submit. If they considered this to be impracticable they were then to formulate another plan to do the greatest damage to the King of France. Whatever course of action Buren and Surrey chose, they were to stay in the field for three months and carry on the war without interruption.[27] On 3 July Charles said an affectionate farewell to Henry, and it was a profitable one for Hall records that he 'had great gifts given to him and much money lent to him' by Henry.[28]

Charles and his entourage travelled to Southampton on 4 July. The fleet of 180 or so ships which was to take them back to Spain had arrived on the previous day and it took two days in scenes of welling chaos to embark. Salinas – miserable to the last – noted that the embarkation of the troops was badly mismanaged while a great number of Charles's courtiers were obliged to leave their horses behind them because there was no room for them on the ships.[29] The fleet set sail at daybreak on 7 July and – unusually for a Spanish fleet carrying members of the royal family – it found the Bay of Biscay calm. Charles disembarked at Santander on the evening of 16 July.

For Charles, the weeks in England had been brilliantly successful: he had forged an alliance with Henry in which both parties were solemnly bound to go to war with France in 1523 and he had made the commitment to marry Mary Tudor in the hope that England would in the next generation join the multitude of countries already within his dynasty. And – it was no small matter – for six weeks he and his great entourage had lived for free at the expense of the King of England. He had, too, the means with which to deal with the aftermath of the revolt of the *comuneros* since he was accompanied by 4,000 German mercenaries and a substantial artillery train. Already defeated, Castile was now cowed and Charles was presented with no significant difficulties in meting out justice to those rebels who had not already been executed or punished.[30]

As for Henry VIII, he (and Wolsey) had abandoned their principle of neutrality: they were now fully in the imperial camp, and the marriage of Charles V and Mary Tudor would – if it took place – consolidate their alliance, ultimately by producing an heir. What power and influence England would enjoy then! But for these long-term gains, Henry and Wolsey had committed England to a war on mainland Europe that would be on an immeasurably greater scale than in 1513. They did so knowing that they no longer had Henry VII's treasure with which to wage it and that no substantial English interests were involved. It was an act of folly and was exceeded only by their failure to actually fight a war when they had given their binding pledge to the Emperor-elect that they would do so. In doing so they incurred the deeply bitter and unforgiving resentment of Charles V, who was a man to cherish the wounds done to him and to repay them with interest.

The responsibility for this decision has normally been laid at Wolsey's door. It used to be suggested that he was seduced by the promise of Charles's support for his papal ambitions but this is no longer taken seriously and it is recognised that Wolsey's policies had a much firmer basis than his egoism and greed. In fine, for all his grandeur and magnificence, Wolsey remained a royal servant, and – although he had differences of emphasis and sometimes even of policy with the king – he would never have committed Henry to such extraordinary expenses over such a long period as would have been involved in taking England to war to satisfy his personal ambitions.[31]

It was Henry VIII who made the decision and, as Bruce Wernham demonstrated, he did so because he was already deeply anxious that Katharine would not provide him with any more children and fearful of having to leave his throne to a daughter. Katharine's last pregnancy had ended in 1518 with yet another stillborn child and after twelve years of marriage – and with a wife who was already thirty-six years of age

– the succession to the throne lay with Mary, who was only six years old in 1522. If Henry did not live until Mary reached adulthood the country would have to be ruled by a nobleman or by a regency council in which senior noblemen would play prominent roles: this was anathema to Henry (who indeed as recently as 1521 had executed his leading nobleman, the Duke of Buckingham, for daring even to talk loosely about the succession).[32] Moreover, even if Mary reached adulthood, it was unlikely that she would be able to rule effectively: although there was no legal prohibition on female rule it was axiomatic that the throne of England could not be entrusted to a woman, and the only precedent, in the twelfth century, had been unambiguously disastrous.

Henry sought resolution for this dreadful dilemma in the agreement made at Windsor with the Emperor-elect in 1522. Probably they had discussed the matter in their two meetings in 1520 and it is certain that Wolsey and Charles had done so at Bruges in 1522. In 1521 Henry had gone to some lengths to persuade Charles of the dangers that would arise for him if the marriage of Mary with the Dauphin went ahead: the Dauphin would in time succeed to the French throne and would also become king-consort of England. A male child born to the couple would then inherit and unite both monarchies. Further, the combined navies of England and France would be able to close the Channel to Charles and the security of the Low Countries – and of the Burgundian heritage of Charles – would be in grave danger. If, on the other hand, Mary married Charles, their descendants would have an unchallengeable hegemony in Europe.[33]

We have seen that Charles had already been engaged to three French princesses before he committed himself to Mary Tudor. It is curious that this greatest of dynasts was careless about his own marital prospects, and there remains a strong suspicion that for personal reasons he did not really wish to marry. Most certainly, he was in no hurry to do so – although, as we will see, once he met the last of his fiancées, Isabella of Portugal, he rushed her with unseemly haste through the marriage ceremony and into the bedroom (below, chapter 12). Certainly, he was in no way behind Francis I and Henry VIII in enjoying the right of a Renaissance monarch to an active sex life: already by the end of 1522 he had a daughter by one mistress.[34] Charles also never lost sight of a fundamental political and dynastic imperative: once he chose his bride he would cut off all other diplomatic options. But mostly, he was in no hurry to be married; perhaps this was why he was content to be engaged to one lady (or child) after another.[35]

The Campaign of 1523 & the Treachery of the Duke of Bourbon

Neither Henry nor Charles were able to make good the lavish commitments to which they signed up at Windsor and Bishop's Waltham. Certainly, Henry did what he could; in 1522 Thomas Howard led a fleet against Morlaix in Brittany which resulted in the capture of three galleons and then – transforming himself from an admiral into a general – he commanded raiding parties from Calais into Picardy and Artois. But he achieved nothing other than to spend money that Wolsey had raised by forced loans.[36] Reluctantly – and for the only time in his ministry – Wolsey was obliged to persuade Henry to summon a Parliament. Henry demanded a massive subsidy and the opposition was so intense that the Parliament lasted for seventeen weeks, from April until October; in the event the Crown benefited not by the £800,000 that it had demanded but by about £150,000 and even that amount was to be spread over the years 1523–27. It was far from clear that Henry could fight a serious campaign in France with such minimal resources. In any event, there were those among his advisers who argued that the money could much better be used in protecting the frontier with Scotland. In September 1522, Albany took advantage of the English campaign in France to lead one of the largest Scottish armies ever to invade England but his soldiers had not forgotten the terrible lessons of Flodden Field a decade earlier and when at the end of November Lord Darcy offered them a truce, they abandoned their commander. Albany fled in disgrace to the Continent in October. Not for the last time, one of Albany's campaigns was a fiasco, but it was a salutary reminder to Henry and Wolsey of the vulnerability of the northern frontier.[37]

Henry's difficulties paled before those confronted by Charles as he came to understand the dreadful range of problems confronting him in Castile. It soon became evident that while the revolt of the *comuneros* had been occasioned by the grotesque mistakes made by Charles's advisers in the years 1517–20 and by what Ramón Carande has called the king's 'calamitous' absence of 1520–22, it was also the expression of wide-ranging problems that had been festering since Isabella's death in 1504.[38] Above all, in 1522 Charles had to establish firm government. He took a number of important measures – for instance in 1523 he established new councils of State, War and Finance on the Burgundian model – but he appreciated that, above all, he had now to stay in Spain and address himself seriously to resolving the major issues of governance confronting the country.

Charles understood full well – as did his Spanish subjects – that the range of his commitments would mean that he was destined to be a largely absentee monarch in Spain, and so it proved: in the forty years of his kingship in Spain (1516–56) Charles spent a total of only fifteen years and twenty-seven days in the country, but no less than half of that period belonged to the 1520s: on his return in 1522 he stayed in Spain for seven years and eighteen days (16 July 1522–2 August 1529) – three times more than the second-longest residence (21 April 1533–30 May 1535). But if Charles's concentration was now perforce on Spain, he had to recognise that he did not have the financial resources for major wars: on 12 January 1523 an adviser urged him to seek a truce in Lombardy for a year because he could not afford to fight a war there. And there was a war very close to home that demanded his attention, for in October 1521 the French, under Admiral Bonnivet, had captured the key frontier fortress of Fuenterrabía and had thereby opened up the road into Navarre and, beyond it, into Castile itself. The recovery of Fuenterrabía stood as a test of the seriousness of his kingship in Spain.

By the summer of 1523, therefore, both Henry VIII and Charles V had good reasons to renegotiate the treaties of Windsor and Bishop's Waltham. Dr Richard Sampson, Dean of the Royal Chapel, and Sir Richard Jerningham, Privy Councillor, travelled to Valladolid where on 2 July they agreed a treaty with Gattinara and other senior ministers which effectively postponed 'the Great Enterprise' until May 1525. Nevertheless, it was agreed that the two monarchs would assemble large armies on or before 17 August 1523 to fight what was described as a preparatory campaign against 'the French' but which was in fact a face-saving operation: Charles would send 20,000 men through Bayonne to conquer Gascony while Henry would send 15,000 foot and horse into Picardy or Artois and – as a first step – conquer Boulogne. The Archduchess Margaret would support the English effort with 3,000 foot from the Low Countries.[39] In truth, these would not be campaigns to destroy French power but rather to do no more than – hopefully – divert it from Italy: the 'Great Enterprise' of which Charles and Henry had dreamed at Windsor and Bishop's Waltham had been reduced now to two very unambitious and limited projects.

The ink was barely dry on the Treaty of Valladolid before all plans had to be rewritten when the astounding news reached Charles and Henry that France's leading nobleman, Charles III, Duke of Bourbon and Constable of France, was offering to serve them against Francis I.[40] Bourbon owned an enormous swathe of land in the Auvergne in the heartland of France and was wealthy enough to employ more than 1,000 people in his household. Certainly, as an accomplished military leader – he had led the vanguard at Marignano – he could raise an army of his own. Of course, as a subject of the French crown he owed his primary loyalty to Francis I but since he also held some lands in fief from Charles V he qualified as his vassal. It was here that Charles found his justification for agreeing to countenance Bourbon's treachery against his lawful sovereign, for under feudal law a vassal of two lords who was mistreated by one of them could lawfully appeal to the other for support. Almost disbelieving of his good fortune, in July Charles undertook to provide Bourbon with 10,000 German soldiers and even to marry one of his sisters to him when their war had been successfully brought to a conclusion.[41]

Bourbon now offered his services to Henry VIII: on 4 August 1523 he pledged to Henry's agent that he would shortly declare himself an enemy of the King of France and then help Henry to recover all of his territories in France that had been occupied by 'the French king'. As soon as Francis had marched into the Alps Bourbon would lead an army of his own troops and those given him by Charles V to tie Francis down in Italy. Galvanised by a prospect that was surely beyond his wildest dreams, Henry readily agreed to pay 100,000 crowns towards the cost of Bourbon's German mercenaries but it is not entirely clear how much thought if any he gave to the practicalities of finding this money; like Charles V, he could not conceive of rejecting Bourbon's offer and pushed forward in thoughtless exhilaration at the prospect of being able to win the Crown of France with the support of the most powerful nobleman in France.[42]

Bourbon's treacherous offer did really seem to offer the prospect of a genuine 'Great Enterprise' such as Charles and Henry had planned in 1522 and it dramatically reinvigorated the alliance between them. A three-pronged assault on France would be launched to take advantage of Francis's absence in Italy: Charles would invade Gascony from Spain and the English would march from Calais to take Boulogne while Bourbon – still undeclared in his treason – would wait for Francis to cross the Alps before attacking him from the rear. With Francis and his army isolated in Italy, France would be dismembered and divided between the three allies: Henry VIII would be crowned King of France in Paris.

Francis I was making his final preparations to depart for Italy when on or around 16 August he was warned that his most powerful nobleman was plotting treason against him. He confronted Bourbon, who coolly denied the allegations and asked for a week in which to make his preparations to march into Italy with him. However, Bourbon then met with Henry's ambassador, Sir John Russell, and ratified his agreement with Henry VIII, agreeing on 6 September that Henry's claim on the throne of France should be submitted to Charles V for a decision. On the following day he renounced his allegiance to his sovereign.

Francis knew well enough what was happening and, having stripped Bourbon of his titles and lands, handed command of his army to Bonnivet and remained in Lyons to deal with Bourbon. Bonnivet's campaign was a disaster; he failed to take Milan was then defeated by Colonna at the Battle of the Sesia and had to bring his army home in disgrace. Francis had suffered a first military humiliation in Italy but at least he had retained his crown.

Henry entrusted his campaign to Suffolk, ordering him to take Boulogne and thereby provide England with a second Channel port. It was a realistic if limited ambition and in September Suffolk marched out of Calais at the head of 11,000 men. It was then decided – probably on Wolsey's insistence – that it would be very expensive to tie the English army down in a protracted and costly siege of Boulogne: better by far to march on Paris itself! Suffolk made remarkable progress and came within 50 miles of the capital before his supplies were exhausted and the weather turned against him. With panic in the capital, Suffolk turned back on 30 October; in foul weather it took him until mid-December to reach Calais. His extemporised and ad hoc invasion of France had come tantalisingly near to bringing Henry glory such as none of his ancestors had won and when the king heard that Suffolk had turned away from Paris he was incandescent with rage. He would not, after all, be crowned in Paris.[43] His own favourite – a man who owed so much to him, not least for having been forgiven for marrying his sister without permission – had deprived him of the greatest ambition he had ever held.

Bourbon was in even greater disgrace. Having grasped the dagger, he was rendered impotent by his own anxieties and failed even to begin the campaign that had cost him everything; he lost his nerve and failed to march against Francis. His German mercenaries deserted him and Bourbon fled for safety into Italy. As for Charles: he sent an army into Gascony but it was easily contained and achieved nothing save to waste money. The golden opportunity presented by Bourbon's treachery had turned to dross: the three-pronged assault to dismember France in 1523 had become a three-pronged fiasco.

The Papal Election of 1523: Giulio de' Medici, Pope Clement VII (1523–34)

The invasion of Italy by Bonnivet's army cost Francis I the neutrality of Adrian VI, who now joined the imperial alliance against France.[44] But having at last committed himself to the cause of his former tutee, Adrian VI did not live to go to war alongside him; he died on 14 September 1523 after a pontificate of only twenty months. He had been unable to maintain the independence of the papacy in the face of the growing tensions between Charles V and Francis I and had failed to unite Christendom against the Turk while in Rome itself his austere honesty was held contemptuously against him: he was despised as an ungenerous and parsimonious pontiff.

Once again, Wolsey allowed himself to be beguiled, if only tentatively, by the prospect of being elected to the papacy. He reminded the imperial ambassador, de Praet, that at Windsor in 1522 Charles had assured him that he would do all he could to further his candidature.[45] Charles in turn itemised to de Praet the efforts he had (allegedly) made to facilitate Wolsey's election:

> The principal point is concerning the advancement of the Cardinal to the papal dignity. We have always desired, and with most sincere good feeling and intention have wished to promote this to the utmost of our power, having a full recollection of how we, and the king our good father and brother, being at [Windsor], opened to him our minds on his subject, exhorting him to think of it, and promising our best services in his assistance, because it appeared to us that his promotion and election would be attended with great good to Christendom, and advantage to our common interest ... and that you may be aware with what zeal and diligence we have taken up this affair in favour of the lord Legate, we send copies of letters in his behalf to the Duke of Sessa our Ambassador at the Court of Rome ... as well as of others afterwards sent to the sacred College, and to some of the Cardinals. You will show and read all these copies to the said lords the king and the Cardinal, apprising them, how we promptly sent off a special courier to Rome as the bearer of them, which the ambassadors here present can testify ... We firmly believe that the Cardinal of Medici will give his assistance to the lord Legate, from the little chance, as we are informed, of his own success ... We entertain a good hope therefore that all these efforts will prosper...[46]

Whatever the true intentions of Charles V, it was already too late: the conclave had on 19 November chosen Guilio de' Medici to succeed Adrian. The new pontiff was forty-five years of age and took the name of Clement VII in recognition of his determination to act as a moderating force between the great powers.[47]

It was to fall to Clement to play a decisive – or, perhaps more correctly, an indecisive – role in the resolution of the marital difficulties of Henry VIII and Katharine, and his career should therefore be briefly remarked upon. In truth, his beginnings were inauspicious enough: Giulio was born out of wedlock on 26 May 1478, a month after his father, Giuliano de' Medici, was murdered in 'the Pazzi Conspiracy'; he was christened as Giulio Zenobio and was brought up in the household of his uncle, Lorenzo the Magnificent. Among his friends and companions was his cousin Giovanni, the future Pope Leo X. After the fall of the Medici in 1494, Giulio and Giovanni travelled extensively together – to Venice, Bavaria, Flanders, France. When the cardinal was captured by the French at the Battle of Ravenna in 1512, Guilio took refuge in the rock of Cesena; it would not be the last time that an invading army forced him to find safety in a fortress.

On 9 March 1513 Giovanni was elected Pope, as Leo X. He immediately lavished his patronage on his cousin, and in doing so obliged him to abandon his intention to spend his life as a soldier and to become a high churchman: on 9 May, Leo named Giulio as Archbishop of Florence, notwithstanding that he was not a priest. He also legitimised him by declaring that his father had secretly admitted that he had intended to marry his mother, Fioretta Gorini – that, in canonical terms, they had been betrothed *per sponsalia de presenti*. That this betrothal had taken place may well have been known to Leo X alone. On 23 September 1513 Giulio was named as cardinal deacon and six days later he received his red hat. Curiously, his first advancement in his new dignity gave him office in England, when within days of his elevation he was named – with what irony! – as 'Protector of England'. On 6 December he received minor orders and on the 17th the diaconate.

Giulio served as Leo X's most trusted adviser. He organised the negotiations between Leo X and Francis I which in 1516 led to the Concordat of Bologna and was rewarded by Francis I with the title of 'Protector of France'. Francis's gesture was probably inspired by his rivalry with Henry VIII for he insisted that in taking on his new position Giulio should renounce his title as Protector of England. Supported no doubt by his cousin, he refused to do so and thus enjoyed both protectorates simultaneously – a typically Medicean act.

On 9 March 1517 Leo X recognised Giulio's pre-eminence in the Curia by naming him as Vice-Chancellor of the Holy Roman Church. It was clearly impossible for him to pursue his dazzling ecclesiastical career without entering the priesthood and on 19 December 1517, as he approached his fortieth birthday, he at last received holy orders. He performed one last act for Leo X, arranging his alliance with Charles V in 1521. Leo X died on 1 December 1521 and Giulio was a candidate in the lengthy conclave that eventually elected Adrian VI on 9 January 1522. When on 19 November 1523 he was in turn elected to succeed Adrian, the Spanish made the best of a bad job: Sessa informed Charles that he himself was now so powerful that he could 'convert stones into obedient sons' while Charles wrote unenthusiastically that the election of Giulio de' Medici was the best that he could have hoped for.[48] The Emperor-elect was soon to be disabused of even the limited confidence he had in the new Pope, for Giulio de' Medici was afflicted by terminal indecisiveness; he simply could not make decisions and hold to them. Perhaps he had to sway too often in the face of adversity; probably, too, he had been softened by the privileges that came with being born into the Medici family. His pontificate was to be among the most disastrous endured by the See of St Peter.

12

THE TURNING-POINT, 1524–1527

The Breakdown of the Marriage – and of the Imperial Alliance
1524: The End of the Marriage?

During 1524 Henry stopped sleeping with Katharine. This did not necessarily suggest that he had decided that his marriage was at an end; probably it indicated no more than that he was disenchanted with a wife who was evidently not going to provide him with a son and who was no longer physically attractive to him. Certainly, there was no denying that as Katharine entered her fortieth year she had lost her beauty and become stout as successive pregnancies and deliveries took their toll on her: as early as May 1515 a Venetian had ungallantly reported that 'she is rather ugly' and contrasted her appearance with that of her ladies-in-waiting.[1] By 1519, another Venetian praised her as best he could: 'she was … not handsome, though she had a very beautiful complexion. She was religious, and as virtuous as words could express.'[2]

Henry did not reject Katharine in favour of a rival, nor was he – as yet – questioning the validity of his marriage, much less seeking to find a way out of it: he did not begin that quest until 1526–27. Nor was Katharine confronted by a long-term rival. True, Henry had enjoyed a serious relationship with Elizabeth Blount (niece of Lord Mountjoy) since about 1514 and in 1519 had a son by her, who was christened Henry Fitzroy. But there could be no question of Henry marrying his mistress and their child was normally kept discreetly away from court.

In 1524 Henry VIII remained a deeply conservative and orthodox son of the Catholic Church and would probably have regarded the prospect of breaking with it as unimaginable. He believed that marriage was entered into for life and he never really changed that position (although his definition of what constituted a true marriage was refined somewhat over the years). However, the long, slow, process to which he so tentatively began to commit himself in 1524 cannot be understood simply as a personal or even as a regnal crisis, for it was played out against the ferocious war being fought in Italy between Charles V and Francis I: in 1524–27 this contest reached a new and defining intensity. As it did so it brought tumultuous consequences for Henry and for Katharine.

Imperial Triumph: The Battle of Pavia (24 February 1525)

Henry and Wolsey have often been criticised for playing their hand badly in the European crisis in the mid- to late 1520s but in reality the welling ferocity of the struggle between Charles V and Francis I probably made their task impossible: England could not balance the two great powers and much less could she commit large enough land forces to the Continent to make any substantial military difference between them. Ultimately, Henry and Wolsey had only one choice to make – whether to ally with Charles V or with Francis I – but since the balance between the two rivals swung violently, first in favour of Charles and then of Francis, English policy had constantly to adjust itself to dramatic changes in its terms of reference. The war would grow in savagery and endure (with a few brief pauses) until it was brought to an end by the Treaty of Cateau-Cambrèsis in 1559: it therefore outlasted Francis I and Henry, both of whom died in 1547, and Charles V, who abdicated as ruler of the Low Countries in 1555 and as King of Spain in 1556 and who then died in 1558 (retaining the imperial title to the last).

The dreadful human costs of the struggle were described in the 1560s by Blaise de Monluc, a distinguished French soldier who had fought in many of its battles. Monluc analysed the causes of the war as both a contest for mastery in Italy and as a highly personalised duel between Charles V and Francis I. Unusually for the period, the figures that he employed to describe the devastation that the war caused were thoroughly realistic:

> At this time the war between Francis the First and the Emperor Charles the Fifth broke out again with greater fury than before, the latter to drive us out of Italy, and we to maintain our footing there, though it was only to make it a place of sepulchre to a world of brave and valiant French.

God Almighty raised up these two great princes sworn enemies to one another, and envious of one another's greatness; an envy that has cost the lives of 200,000 persons, and brought a million families to utter ruin; when after all neither the one nor the other obtained any advantage by the dispute other than the bare repentance of having been the causes of so many miseries, and of the spilling of so much Christian blood.[3]

Charles's campaigns in the early months of 1524 were successful enough for him to feel that he had fulfilled his part of the 'Great Enterprise' to which he and Henry had committed themselves in 1522. He earned the laurels of military triumph by leading the army that recaptured Fuenterrabía (27 February) but was diverted from advancing into France by yet another French invasion of Italy when at the end of 1523 Francis sent Admiral Bonnivet into Italy with a powerful army. However, fortune favoured Charles, for the winter of 1523–24 was especially severe in northern Italy and the French exhausted themselves without achieving anything. When they then confronted the imperial forces at Sesia they were roundly defeated (30 April 1524). Charles followed up this fortuitous victory by sending his army into Provençe in July to begin the dismemberment of France.

By contrast, Henry achieved nothing. On 24 May he and Bourbon agreed that they would each invade France in the summer and Bourbon undertook – if only with the greatest reluctance – to pay homage to Henry as King of France. On 25 June 1524 he did so: 'I promise unto you upon my faith that I will by the help of my friends, put the Crown of France upon the king our common master's head, or else my days shall be cut off.'[4] Unfortunately, Bourbon's rhetoric again outstripped his resolve: he led his forces to join the imperial army that was besieging Marseilles but when Francis I arrived at Avignon he promptly retreated into the safety of Italy. Henry contributed financial support for this débâcle but did not commit any men to action in France in 1524. Not unreasonably, Charles was scornful of Henry's contribution to the war to which he had promised so much.

Francis I was equally dismissive of the threat posed to him by Bourbon, and in October 1524 again led his army across the Alps, seeking to restore the reputation of French arms and to replicate his success at Marignano in 1515. He had chosen his moment well, for Charles's army in Lombardy was exhausted (and unpaid) and as the French army entered Milan by one gate on 26 October 1524 the imperial army fled by another. Francis now proclaimed that his second conquest of Milan was no more than a prelude to a much greater campaign: 'I have not crossed the Alps in person or invaded Italy with 30,000 good infantry and the support of a fleet with 6,000 or 7,000 troops on board to stop now. I want nothing less than the entire state of Milan and the Kingdom of Naples.'[5] Confidently, he despatched an army under the Duke of Albany to conquer Naples. Italy would be his, north and south.

The renewal of major warfare in Italy had the most serious implications for the papacy. Clement cowered before the French invader as his predecessors had done in 1494 and 1499: on 12 December 1524 he agreed to ally with Francis, Venice and Florence against Charles V. In doing so Clement followed the Medicean tradition of placing his family's affairs above those of the papacy itself: Francis agreed to continue to allow Medici rule in Florence and to cede Parma and Piacenza to the papacy. Abandoned by his allies, fearful of his enemies and unable to pay his own troops, Charles sank into despair: 'My friends have forsaken me in my evil hour, all are equally determined to prevent me from growing more powerful and to keep me in my present distressed state.'[6]

Charles was saved by Francis's overweening pride in committing himself to besieging the imperial troops in the fortress of Pavia; the siege dragged on for eight months but Francis refused to withdraw into the safety of Milan, boasting that no French monarch had ever laid siege to a town and not captured it.[7] In doing so, he squandered his military strength and on 24 February 1525 paid a dreadful price for his arrogance: at the Battle of Pavia the French army, debilitated yet again by an unnecessarily long campaign, was slaughtered by the imperial force commanded by Fernando d'Ávalos, Marquis of Pescara: Bonnivet was among the 10,000 or so of Francis's soldiers who were killed. But worst – most unimaginable – of all, Francis himself was taken prisoner. The Battle of Pavia lasted only for a few hours but it utterly transformed the balance of power in Europe.[8]

The news of the astonishing victory reached Charles in Toledo on 10 March; he showed no triumphalism, merely acknowledging that 'the victory I acknowledge from none but God alone, who knowing my good will, rewards me far beyond my deserts'.[9] His restraint made a profound impression on those who witnessed it, as it was meant to do. But as Charles absorbed the tumultuous news, he must have been tempted to agree privately with the assessment of his brother Ferdinand – 'Your Majesty is now Monarch of the whole world.' Moreover, as Charles reflected that the great battle had taken place on his own birthday he may well have been reassured that he was indeed especially favoured by the Almighty.[10]

Henry VIII heard the news one day before Charles and was delightfully untrammelled by doubts or inhibitions: with exuberant innocence he proclaimed that he would travel at once to Paris to be crowned as King of France and would then divide France with his allies.[11] He despatched Cuthbert Tunstal, Bishop of London, and Sir Richard Wingfield to Spain to plan the next stage of the campaign with Charles and his ministers.[12] The two emissaries were to remind Charles that one of the major purposes of the alliance 'hath always been to expel the French King from his usurped occupation of the Crown of France', which belonged of course to Henry 'by just title of inheritance'.[13]

Henry's ambassadors were also to emphasise to Charles how his enormous power would be yet further extended by his marriage to Princess Mary, for in Paris after Henry had been crowned King of France he would hand his daughter over to Charles for their marriage and then accompany Charles to Rome for his coronation as Holy Roman Emperor. Charles's power would in time surely be further bolstered by the inheritance to a son by Mary of the thrones of Henry VIII himself. Remarkably, in Henry's prospectus, the imperial alliance would resolve the difficulties of the succession to the English throne but at the expense of ultimately alienating the throne itself to the Habsburg family.[14] Obliged to acknowledge that he would not have a son by Katharine, Henry seems to have drawn real consolation from the recognition that a grandson might become Holy Roman Emperor: the imperial alliance still held him in thrall. Beyond this, Henry's shopping list ranged from the epic to the prosaic; he hoped that he would have the Crown of France but if this proved impossible he would settle for the restoration to him of the old Angevin empire; if that was too much to ask, he would take Picardy, Normandy and Brittany; if that was not possible, he would settle for either Normandy or Picardy and Boulogne and a few other towns.

Charles encountered two problems with Henry's fulsome analysis of the benefits that would accrue to him from his triumph at Pavia – that Henry had contributed not a penny nor a man towards the great victory and that during 1524 Wolsey had become increasingly hostile to him. Not surprisingly, Henry's ambassadors reported back that Charles intended 'little or nothing … to your … profit or benefit'.[15] Indeed, Charles's own response was ruthlessly to the point: on 4 July 1525 he demanded that

Henry should either send Mary to Spain to prepare for her marriage to him or that he should absolve Charles from his promise to marry her: it was an ultimatum and Charles knew that it would be rejected.[16] Certainly, if Charles was going to take advantage of Pavia he would do so not by going to Paris to crown Henry VIII as King of France but by making his long-awaited journey to Italy to be crowned as Holy Roman Emperor.

However, in the grandeur of a victory without precedent the Emperor-elect was restrained by his own impoverishment: the war of 1524–25 had broken his finances and he could not afford to wage another campaign. Pavia had been one of the great military triumphs of its age but Charles was unable to pay the army that had won it for him.[17] A crucial part of the victory had been owed to the firepower of the 7,000 German mercenaries (landsknechts) led by Georg von Frundsberg, Prince of Mindelheim; Charles now played on their loyalty to him by sending them home with the promise of future payment for their services. He secured 100,000 ducats from Clement VII to help pay the Spanish and Italian forces and dismissed the latter, leaving the Spaniards to garrison Milan.[18] Charles was now taking dangerous risks with his own soldiers: if he could not pay them, would they remain loyal to him?

Henry's finances were similarly distressed. In his enthusiasm after Pavia he had despatched commissions on 21 March 1525 to raise an 'Amicable Grant' of about £500,000 with which he could fight the new campaign. Unfortunately, the demand provoked such hostility that it had to be abandoned. With it went also, in effect, the possibility of fighting a significant campaign in France: in 1525 as in 1523, Henry's subjects had failed to satisfy his demands for a war chest with which to fight against France – and for the second time Wolsey had not been able to provide the resources for Henry to lead his soldiers into battle against the French.[19]

Henry's plans – military and diplomatic – had come crashing down and he was furious with the world at large – with Charles for rejecting his daughter; and with his own subjects and with his cardinal-minister for failing to provide the resources to fight a triumphant war in France. He would not, after all, be crowned in Paris. He had lost – thrown away – his alliance with Charles of Habsburg at the very moment of Charles's greatest victory over Francis I and precisely as he himself began to ponder on the need to separate himself from Charles's aunt. Henry had, moreover, contrived to achieve all this exactly as Charles was reaching the decision to abandon his marriage to Mary Tudor in favour of one to Isabella of Portugal. The 'Great Enterprise' had ended as a multiple and resounding failure for the king's polity. On 30 August 1525 the war with France was brought to an end by the Treaty of the More: Louise of Savoy compensated Henry for his expenses in the war with a lavish pension and agreed not to meddle in Scotland. In return, Henry undertook not to invade France. The imperial alliance was at an end and England was allied with France at a time when her king was imprisoned in Madrid.

The Imprisonment of Francis I & the Breach Between Emperor-elect & the Pope

While Charles and his advisers discussed how to respond to the triumph at Pavia, Carlos de Lannoy, Viceroy of Naples, decided – apparently on his own initiative and without informing Charles of what he was doing – to send Francis to Spain.[20] To Charles's deep embarrassment the captive king reached Madrid on 11–12 August; he had him incarcerated in the Torre de Lujanes in the heart of the city. But Francis would not give up territories that he regarded as being lawfully his: on 16 August he secretly took an oath in the presence of the French ambassador that he would never cede Burgundy of his own volition and that if ever he was obliged to do so his action was to be regarded as null and void. However, weakened by his failure to eat properly and – not unnaturally – subjected to acute depression, Francis became so ill that by 11 September serious concerns had arisen of the possibility of him dying.[21]

Fearful of the shame that would envelop him if the King of France died in his custody, Charles deigned to meet Francis: he embraced him and assured him that he was not a slave but a free friend and brother (18 September). On the following day, Francis's sister Margaret, Duchess of Alençon, arrived to lead the negotiations for his release but on 22 September Francis collapsed into a semi-coma. Talks were suspended but Francis recovered some resilience and made a foolish attempt to escape disguised as one of his own black slaves; he managed only a few yards before being recaptured.

Charles's ministers divided over the response to be made to Francis's defeat and capture. Gattinara insisted that Charles should claim the whole of the Burgundian inheritance and oblige Francis to renounce his claims on Naples and Milan and refrain from helping Charles's enemies in Italy and the Low Countries. Charles's Castilian ministers had a different set of priorities. The two most senior of them – Charles's secretary Francisco de los Cobos and the Primate of the Spanish Church, Juan Pardo de Tavera, Archbishop of Toledo – argued strongly that Charles should now revert to the traditional Castilian policy of forging a marital alliance with

Portugal and that as an expression of this he should marry Isabella of Portugal rather than Mary of England. Cobos, who managed the finances of Castile, insisted that the kingdom was bankrupt and begged Charles to remember the lessons of the revolt of the *comuneros* – that he should not place financial burdens on his subjects that might drive them to rebellion. In this 'Castilian' view, Charles did not have the financial resources for any grand adventures in Italy or elsewhere and should consolidate his position within the Iberian peninsula by marrying Isabella of Portugal. Within the grand staterooms of the Alcázar of Toledo, therefore, a debate was beginning to take place with some force about the nature and purpose of Charles's monarchy and its future direction. A substantial part of the discussions centred on whether Charles should make the English match or abandon it in favour of a Portuguese marriage: it was a defining question for the future of Charles's monarchy in Spain.

Negotiations between Charles's ministers and Francis's led to the Treaty of Madrid (14 January 1526).[22] Francis renounced the Duchy of Burgundy and his claims to Naples, Milan and Arras. He agreed to return Bourbon's lands and titles but adamantly refused to allow him to return to court. Francis's two young sons would be brought to Madrid as hostages for his good behaviour on his release and he would seal the agreement by marrying Leonor, elder sister of Charles V. Gattinara scathingly insisted that Francis's pledges were worthless: remarkably, the Imperial Chancellor refused to dignify the Treaty of Madrid with his signature.

On 20 January, Francis was betrothed by proxy to Leonor. Charles came to Madrid on 13 February and spent a few days with Francis and then took him to Illescas to meet his fiancée. The monarchs then separated – Charles to travel to Seville for his own wedding, Francis to return home. On 17 March, Francis crossed the River Bidassoa into France; on passing his sons in midstream, with tears in his eyes he blessed them as they entered into captivity in Spain. He rode fast to Bayonne where his mother and court were waiting for him.[23] It took only weeks for Francis to renounce the agreement: on 16 May Lannoy wrote to Charles from Paris that ministers had declared that the Treaty of Madrid was invalid because it had been signed under duress and that under no circumstances would Francis give up Burgundy. Gattinara had been proved correct about the perfidy of the King of France.

Europe trembled before the new power of Charles V and a natural balancing of power now began to operate against him. Most importantly, the Pope confirmed publicly that he had turned against the Emperor-elect. It was not simply terror that inspired Clement's action: in daring to declare against the victor of Pavia Clement was holding firm to two principles that he held throughout his life – that the papacy could never endure the junction of Milan and Naples under the same ruler and that Milan had always to be independent of both Spain and France. He was also fearful that Charles would celebrate his triumph by coming to Italy to be crowned and by then forcing him to summon a General Council of the Church. In the late summer of 1525 he committed himself to an egregious act of folly, encouraging a conspiracy against Charles in Milan ('the Morone Conspiracy'), but Pescara dealt easily enough with it. A few months later, Clement formalised his opposition to Charles's supremacy in Italy by joining in a 'Holy League' with France, Venice, Florence and Milan ('League of Cognac', 22 May 1526). Somewhat optimistically the new allies committed themselves to expelling the imperial army from Italy, and to re-establishing Francesco Sforza as Duke of Milan.

Charles had already decided to break with the Pope. On 6 June – before he heard of the 'Holy League' – he wrote to the College of Cardinals insisting that if Clement failed to summon a General Council to reform the Church he himself would do so. He also ordered one of his senior generals in Italy, Don Hugo de Moncada, to inform the Pope that if he did not accommodate himself to Charles the Spanish forces in Italy would unite with those of the dissident Cardinal Pompeio Colonna to raise rebellion against Clement in Rome itself. Colonna loathed Clement, not least for defeating him at the conclave of 1523, and was consumed by the determination to overthrow him. Moncada arrived in Rome on 16 June 1526 but he could not persuade Clement to back down. On 13 June the College of Cardinals had unanimously approved the establishment of the Holy League and after three days of fruitless negotiation with Clement Moncada left Rome on the 19th to liaise with Colonna. On 23 June Clement issued a brief declaring that it was legitimate for the powers of Italy to go to war with Charles V.[24] The irresolute Pope had crossed his rubicon and the furious Emperor-elect now joined in alliance with a rebel cardinal against him.[25] The Eternal City would pay a dreadful price for Clement's miscalculations – and for his unwonted attempt at acting decisively.

Charles's Rupture with England, 1526: The Portuguese Marriage

Thomas Wolsey was among those who were deeply anxious about the growth of imperial power and after Pavia he urged Henry to ally himself with Francis I because there was so much more to be had from France than from the triumphant Emperor-elect. Wolsey recognised that the Anglo-imperial alliance had run its course and knew well enough that Charles was considering renouncing the marriage with Princess Mary in favour of one with Isabella of Portugal. Henry did not join the League of Cognac but gave it his tacit support, insisting that Charles should release the French princes and re-establish Francesco Sforza as Duke of Milan to guarantee the independence of the duchy. Henry hoped that the League would do his work for him in forcing Charles to come to terms with France – and perhaps in re-creating the situation in which England held a balancing of power. Wolsey sought to soften the blow by beguiling Henry with the range of opportunities that the dramatic reversal of his policy might provide for him.[26]

There was, indeed, an inevitability about Charles's decision to marry Isabella of Portugal. The marriage was well grounded in both family traditions and political realities; in his appreciation of the need to secure a Portuguese alliance as a precondition of his foreign policy Charles was truly the heir of Ferdinand and Isabella. Indeed, he had already demonstrated that forging an alliance with Portugal was a priority for him by marrying two of his sisters into the Portuguese royal family – Leonor to Manuel I (1518) and Catalina to John III (1524). Leonor had been widowed in 1521 and was therefore once again available for use in diplomatic negotiations.

Isabella of Portugal had been born in 1503 and brought Charles several advantages over Mary Tudor, most notably that as she was already well into her childbearing years Charles would not have to wait to marry and begin a family. As importantly, Isabella also carried a dowry of 1 million ducats – enough money to enable Charles to make serious preparations for his journey to Italy. By contrast, Mary's dowry was effectively non-existent for it would consist in practice of Henry writing off the 500,000 or so ducats that Charles owed him. Finally, Charles knew that he would shortly have to travel to Italy for his coronation and appreciated that he would be able to leave Isabella as his regent in Spain. Indeed, as early as the summer of 1525 Charles had explained his reasoning to his brother Ferdinand, emphasising that the Cortes of Castile was urging him to make the Portuguese marriage:

In order to leave these kingdoms under good order and government,
I see no other remedy than to marry Princess Isabella of Portugal,

since the Cortes [of Castile] have required me to propose myself for such a union; and ... on his part the King of Portugal offers me a million of ducats, most of them to be paid at once, in order to assist in defraying the expenses of our said journey into Italy. Were this marriage to take place, I could leave the Government here in the person of the said Princess, who should be provided with a good council, so that there would be no apparent cause to fear any new movement [*sc.* rebellion]...[27]

The negotiations with Portugal were conducted readily enough and the agreements were signed on 17 and 24 October 1525. Charles's mother and Isabella's – Juana and María – were sisters and so a papal dispensation from the impediment of affinity was promptly obtained.[28] Isabella made her solemn entry into Seville on 3 March 1526. Charles arrived a week later and was so enthralled by the beauty of his bride that he ordered that the marriage should take place at once: the ceremony was rushed through in the palace of the Archbishop of Seville around midnight on 10–11 March and the couple were immediately bedded. On the following morning their bedsheets were publicly paraded through the streets of Seville.[29]

Charles's rejection of the English marriage in 1525–26 proved to have the most profound implications. Bruce Wernham rightly described this as the 'turning-point' in the reign of Henry VIII. His analysis cannot be bettered:

This rejection of Mary by Charles did matter, mattered very greatly. For Henry VIII it was the unkindest cut of all. His subjects had shattered his dreams of conquering France. Now his nephew and ally had shattered the one apparently workable scheme which he had been able to devise for securing a peaceable succession to the throne of England. Charles had failed him in 1525 even more disastrously than Ferdinand had failed him in 1514. Now, as then, the immediate result was a sharp revulsion against the Spanish alliance and a turn towards friendship with England's ancient enemy, France. But this time Henry's resentment went much deeper and carried him into revolutionary courses whose effects were to prove far more lasting and wide-reaching ... The jilting of Princess Mary by Charles V in 1525 marked the great turning-point in Henry VIII's reign ... In the summer of 1525 [Henry] began to cast off the ties which so long had bound him to Spain and to Katharine.[30]

Henry's first expression of the 'revolutionary' change that he now began to make was brilliantly economical: on 7 June he installed Henry Fitzroy as a Knight of the Garter and on 15th broke with his practice by ostentatiously parading him at court. This was grievous enough an insult to Katharine – a reminder to her and the court that the king was capable of siring a son – and Henry compounded it three days later by raising the child to the Dukedom of Richmond and conferring upon him the dignity of Lieutenant-General of the North, an office that was customarily endowed upon on a prince of the realm. Susan Doran has reminded us of the deeply symbolic significance of the Dukedom of Richmond for the family that we invariably refer to as 'the Tudors': Henry VII had been Duke of Richmond before he became King of England and he and his successors preferred to use this title rather than the name of 'Tudor', which carried connotations of illegitimacy (and Welsh-ness).[31] But Henry VIII did more than raise his natural son to the title that his father had held: he also gave him precedence over all the peers of the realm and even over Princess Mary herself. Was Henry about to legitimise his bastard – and to renounce his Spanish alliance, perhaps even his Spanish wife and half-Spanish daughter?

Katharine took the point: she was so angry that for some weeks she refused even to speak to her husband. But Henry's cruelty had only just begun: in what must have been an excruciatingly painful gesture for Katharine, he despatched Mary to Ludlow Castle, ostensibly so that she could govern the Principality of Wales for him but in practice to deny her mother the comfort of her company. Moreover, Henry refused to confer upon his daughter the title of 'Princess of Wales' precisely because he did not wish to acknowledge her as the heiress to his throne.[32] Mary's status was thus dramatically diminished: from having been the fiancée of the Holy Roman Emperor-elect she was now not even certain that she was the heiress to her father's crowns although she was his only legitimate child. Katharine found the humiliation of her daughter insupportable: Henry had abandoned her marital bed and was now turning vindictively upon Mary.

Worse followed (although Katharine was not informed of this): early in 1526 Henry began to take discreet soundings from theologians and ecclesiastics about the canonical legitimacy of his marriage. It would shortly become evident that he had begun to agonise as to whether Katharine's failure to present him with a son represented a divine punishment on him for having married his brother's widow. Moreover, the first whispers began to circulate at court about Henry's affection for a young lady of Katharine's household, Anne Boleyn. When Henry appeared in the guise of a tortured lover bearing the legend 'Declare I not' at the Shrove Tuesday tournament in 1526 the more perceptive observers at court must have wondered whether his guise carried any serious significance.[33]

Anne Boleyn had been born in 1499 or 1500. She was the second daughter of Sir Thomas Boleyn and his wife Elizabeth Howard, daughter of the 2nd Duke of Norfolk. She had two siblings – Mary, who was a year or so older, and George, three or four years her junior. Both girls travelled with their father when he served as ambassador to Margaret of Austria in 1512–13, but while Mary apparently returned home Anne seems to have stayed in the Low Countries until 1514, then going (whether directly or not) to Paris, where she lived at the French court until 1521. Certainly, Anne was back in England by March 1522. She was not considered to be a great beauty but her years in Brussels and Paris had made her into a sophisticate, fluent in French and familiar with all the subtleties of life in great courts.

Apocalypse: The Destruction of Rome, September 1526–May 1527
When Charles ordered Moncada to liaise with Cardinal Colonna against Clement VII he could not have conceived just how devastating the consequences of his decision would be, for it led directly to a dreadful pillaging of the city in September 1526 and then to its near-destruction in May 1527.[34] Indeed, while Charles was determined to revenge himself upon Clement VII his more immediate thoughts in the late autumn of 1526 probably lay farther east, for on 28–29 August 1526 the janissaries of Suleiman the Magnificent had destroyed the Hungarian army at the Battle of Mohácz, killing King Louis II and breaking up his ancient kingdom. Charles would have to rethink all of his priorities in foreign affairs, for the Turk stood now at the very gates of Christendom and the patrimonial territories of the House of Habsburg: several senior councillors urged Charles to withdraw his army from Italy and despatch it to fight against Suleiman. It would have been better for his historical reputation had he followed their advice.

For three days (20–22 September) the forces of Cardinal Colonna pillaged Rome and they did so with the active connivance of Moncada.

Clement fled into the safety of the Castel Sant'Angelo and from there was able to observe the plundering of the city: only what followed a few months later deprived these days of the title of the 'Sack of Rome'. An observer recorded that

> the papal palace was almost completely stripped even to the bedroom and wardrobe of the Pope. The great and private sacristy of St Peter's, that of the palace, the apartments of the prelates and members of the household, even the horse-stalls were emptied, their doors and windows shattered; chalices, crosses, pastoral staffs, ornaments of great value, all that fell into their hands, was carried off as plunder by this rabble; persons of distinction were taken prisoner ...[35]

The first sack of Clement VII's Rome fulfilled its immediate purposes: Clement paid the Spanish infantry 30,000 ducats in gold to leave the city and duly declared that he was a faithful friend and ally of Charles V. Recognising that he was unable to effectively fund the defence of Rome, on 12 December 1526 Clement issued a brief excommunicating any soldier who henceforth violated the lands of the Holy See. It happened that on that same day, Antonio Pérez, Charles's representative in the city, presented Charles's reply to the papal letter of 23 June to the Consistory itself demanding that a General Council should be summoned to reform the Church.[36]

And still, Charles stepped up the pressure: he summoned von Frundsberg back to Italy and on 30 January 1527 his force of 10,000 landsknechts joined the Spanish infantry army outside Milan. The army, numbering probably over 25,000 men, decided to march on Rome to demand that the Pope make good their arrears of pay. Towards the end of February they were joined by Bourbon's troops. Italy was convulsed by fear of the raging monster in its midst, and when against all expectations it bypassed Florence it was evident that it was indeed headed for Rome. On 5-6 March, the enormous mob – it could no longer be called an army – crossed into the Papal States: unpaid, famished and furious with its commanders, it sought vengeance on the Pope whom it blamed for all its troubles.

While the tragedy unfolded in Italy, Charles made a belated effort to resolve his difficulties with England; he named Don Iñigo López de Mendoza y Zúñiga as ambassador to Henry VIII. Don Iñigo was a cleric, a younger son of one of the leading families of Castile – his father was the 2nd Count of Miranda – and a trusted confidant of Charles.[37] From the outset, his embassy was blighted by ill fortune: he left Spain without carrying his formal instructions and was then held prisoner in France for several months because he could not prove that he was an accredited ambassador. When he finally reached London he had to send to Spain for fresh accreditation. Such was the tension between Henry and Charles that López de Mendoza was forbidden access to Katharine and when he eventually met her it was in Wolsey's intimidating presence. Anglo–Spanish relations were indeed at a low-point, and when in January 1527 Wolsey gave a lavish banquet to celebrate the agreement to marry Mary into the French royal house, López de Mendoza was not even invited.[38] Henry would use his daughter to revenge himself on Charles.

On 30 April England and France signed an offensive alliance against Charles V (Treaty of Westminster). Mary would be betrothed either to Francis I or to his second son (Henri, Duke of Orleans) and Francis would supplement Henry's pension with a further 15,000 crowns a year. The two monarchs would jointly demand that Charles pay his debts to England and release the princes: if he refused to do so they would declare war on him. Mary's fate depended on Charles's decision; if he did not reach a settlement with England she would marry Francis I, but if Charles chose peace, she would marry Francis's second son and Francis would marry Eleanor. On 5 May, Henry took the oath to observe the treaty, celebrating his commitment with the customary tournaments and banquets.[39] He was now the ally of France against the Emperor-elect.

Once again, Henry's timing was truly awful. On 4 May Bourbon reached the outskirts of Rome. He was in command of a multinational force which had been reduced by losses on the road to about 23,000 men. Bourbon's intentions were probably not clear even to himself; probably he hoped for no more than to be able to capture Clement VII and force him to pay the arrears owing to his troops. But his army was now well beyond his control; desperate for pay, the soldiers fully appreciated that the Eternal City lay prostrate before them and they were not to be denied the pleasures of plundering it. At daybreak on 6 May the attack began. Bourbon himself was killed in the initial assault as his men flooded into Rome. Foolishly, Clement had refused to believe that the imperial army would assault Rome and was convinced that relieving allied forces were only a few days away. He was disabused of his confidence with such haste that it was observed that had he delayed to say three more *credos* before fleeing into the safety of Castel Sant'Angelo he would have been captured.[40] The Colonnas arrived on 10 May with 8,000 troops to add to the pillaging.

The slaughter was unrestrained: Francisco de Salazar sent an account to court in Valladolid in which he referred to the 'unparalleled atrocities' committed by the Spanish soldiers and the 'unimaginable' amount of treasure that they had pillaged. Perhaps as many as 20,000 people died; it has been estimated that by the end of the year the population of Rome had been halved. Throughout Rome, churches, religious houses and hospitals were destroyed and women were raped, many nuns among them. St Peter's was completely sacked and even its tombs were violated to find buried treasure, among them that of Julius II; bones and skulls were scattered on the floor. Only the churches of the Spanish and German nations survived intact and by a mystery the Vatican Library was spared. The initial onslaught on Rome lasted until on 17 May Clement agreed to hand over 100,000 ducats at once and as much again within the next two months. Final agreement was reached on 7 June and on that day the papal garrison was able to leave Castel Sant'Angelo. The imperial army remained in Rome until 10 July. Despondently, Salazar advised Charles V and his ministers that the city stank with thousands of unburied corpses and that it would take over 500 years for it to recover.

And still, Charles's mind wandered away from Rome, for exactly as the news of the Sack reached Valladolid his wife went into labour; on 21 May Isabella presented Charles with a son and heir, whom he named Philip for his own father.[41] So joyous was he that he refused to cancel or curtail the lavish festivities for the birth of his son and he took part in every joust and tournament; indeed, Charles let it be known that the celebrations would carry on for another month so that the Empress could join in them after her 'churching'. His senior Spanish advisers were outraged, both at the destruction of Rome by his army and by his apparent indifference to it: Navagero reported that the Archbishop of Toledo and the Duke of Alba were among those who spoke 'with exceptional freedom' to him about his responsibilities. Prince Philip was baptised on 5 June; Leonor, Queen of France, and the dukes of Alba, Frias and Béjar stood as godparents.[42] Rome was in ruins, but Charles was the master of Italy and his dynasty was secure in possession of its Spanish thrones. He had been unable to profit from the brilliant military triumph at Pavia but the destruction of Rome conferred – as appeared – unrivalled power upon him.

Annulment, 1527? Leviticus, Deuteronomy – and the Bull of Julius II
The Books of Leviticus & Deuteronomy

When Charles V's troops sacked Rome they severely jeopardised, if they did not completely shatter, the likelihood of the King of England ending his marriage to the Emperor-elect's aunt by agreement with the Pope. They did so, moreover, exactly as Henry and Wolsey – with excruciatingly unfortunate timing – committed England to an alliance with France against Charles V. Henry's attempt to end his marriage is often described as having been the pursuit of a 'divorce' but it was not originally that: what Henry sought from the Pope in the years immediately after 1527 was an *annulment* of his marriage to Katharine, a formal recognition by the papacy that the marriage had never existed because it had been canonically invalid despite (or because of) the dispensation granted in 1503 by Julius II. If Pope Clement agreed to issue an annulment he would thereby free Henry to marry Anne Boleyn *as if she were his first wife*. But as Henry's quest for an annulment became deeply rooted in theological complexities, the drama that it created was played out against the brutal realities of European politics – and the central reality, as far as Henry was concerned, was that Katharine's nephew controlled the papacy after his troops had sacked the Eternal City.

Henry VII's marital history has become proverbially celebrated but it is vital to any understanding of it to appreciate that he was deeply conservative in his theological and moral views, at least during the first half of his reign. Curiously, it may be affirmed that Henry believed deeply in the sanctity of marriage and although he came to believe even more profoundly in his own right to dispense with his wives – whether by annulment/divorce or by executing or merely abandoning them – he was (at least until the late 1520s) every bit as papal as the Pope in believing in the indissolubility of marriage. He has often been accused of hypocrisy in arguing *exactly as he fell in love with a younger woman* that a marriage with which he had been more or less content for well over a decade was canonically invalid. It is, however, very difficult to escape the conclusion that although the annulment of Henry's marriage to Katharine brought him some substantial personal and political (and sexual) advantages, the king was, by the later 1520s, genuinely sincere in his conviction that the marriage had been theologically invalid. Katharine was of course equally adamant that it was a true and vital marriage that defined her integrity as a woman and as a queen – and in any event she did not recognise the possibility of divorce any more than did her husband.

In seeking a papal annulment of his marriage in the years after 1527, Henry was driven by three impulses – the overarching importance of his obligation to produce a male heir to succeed him; his theological scruples about the legitimacy of his marriage to Katharine; and his love (or lust) for Anne Boleyn.

There can be no knowing when Henry began to develop his theological doubts about the legitimacy of his marriage to Katharine. A great deal of effort has gone into understanding this; some have suggested that the French Bishop of Tarbes first proposed it; others that it was Henry's own confessor who raised the problem with him.[43] Bishop John Stokesley (who played a prominent role in ending Henry's marriage) has also been identified as an instigator of the process. Certainly, Katharine herself believed that it was Wolsey who prodded Henry into his doubts and here at least there can be some certainty: Katharine was wrong. In many ways the search for the instigator of Henry's quest for an annulment resembles the medieval debates about the number of angels who could pivot on a pin's head – an interesting but ultimately unprofitable exercise of the imagination. More relevant, perhaps, has been the ongoing discussion among historians of Tudor England about the division of responsibility between the king and his ministers. In recent years, historians such as John Scarisbrick and George Bernard have argued that the man who was primarily responsible for instigating Henry VIII's policies was ... Henry VIII himself. This seems an eminently sensible position: Henry VIII was a man to choose his own wives – and to choose, too, how to rid himself of them.

Henry regarded himself as a theologian of European stature and at some time in the mid-1520s he had begun to worry that his lack of a male heir represented a divine punishment for having married his brother's widow. In particular, these anxieties derived from his understanding of two passages in the Book of Leviticus in the Old Testament which seemed not merely pertinent to his case but explicative of it.

The Book of Leviticus was, according to both Jewish and Christian tradition, dictated by God to Moses and its central purpose was to lay down the code of conduct that was to govern the lives of individuals and of society as a whole. Exegetically, it developed from the Books of Genesis and Exodus. It had many practical implications for sixteenth-century Europeans; for instance, it laid down the practice of excluding new mothers from civic and religious ceremonies until they had been 'purified' (or 'churched') forty days after giving birth. When Henry began to agonise over its teaching he was therefore dealing with a text that was believed to be very current and contemporaneous. Chapter 18 defined the various degrees of kinship within which marriage was forbidden: 'No man shall approach to her that is near of kin to him.' A man could not – under any circumstances – marry a spouse or sibling of his parents or children. Moreover, two passages explicitly prohibited a man from marrying a woman who had herself been married to his brother, and the second laid down a dreadful penalty:

> You shall not uncover the nakedness of your brother's wife: because it is the nakedness of your brother [18:16]

> If a man shall take his brother's wife, it is an unclean thing: he has uncovered his brother's nakedness. They shall be childless [20:21]

By contrast, another Old Testament text, the Book of Deuteronomy seemed to *require* that a brother should marry a dead brother's widow:

> When brothers live together, and one of them dies without children, the wife of the deceased shall not marry to another: but his brother shall take her, and raise up seed for his brother [20:6]

Leviticus and Deuteronomy therefore offered diametrically opposed teachings and it was to the former that Henry looked with most anxiety, and for two reasons – theologically, because Catholic canon law accepted that Leviticus had precedence over Deuteronomy; personally, because the death of Prince Henry in 1511 suggested to him that he and Katharine were indeed being punished for having contracted their marriage.

There was, however, an obvious difficulty: Katharine had conceived and borne live children, notably with the birth (and survival) of Princess Mary in 1516. It was altogether within the realms of royal scruples – but also perhaps of Renaissance translation principles – that one or more of Henry's advisers should have suggested to him that the Levitical text could be properly translated to fit his case by replacing 'children' with 'sons' – that someone who married his brother's wife would not have *male* children. This interpretation fitted the case perfectly.[44]

The first discussion that Henry is known to have had about his theological difficulties over his marriage took place when at the end of 1526 he raised the question with John Colet, Dean of St Paul's. He then seems to have shared his doubts with Wolsey early in 1527; Wolsey would later claim that he was so shocked by the implications of what he was being told that he knelt before Henry for 'an hour or two' to dissuade him from proceeding with his quest for an annulment.[45] Henry's doubts placed Wolsey in an agonising dilemma. As Henry's chief minister he would obviously have to accommodate himself to the king's determination to end his marriage and he could have had no doubts that if he failed to do so Henry would in all probability dispense with him. On the other hand, Wolsey knew only too well that if he was able to free Henry to marry Anne Boleyn and she became queen in Katharine's place his own position would become untenable, so deep was Anne's hostility to him.

The first attempt to end the royal marriage bore all the hallmarks of Wolsey's fertile imagination. He and William Warham, as the two English archbishops (and with Wolsey doubling up as papal legate), summoned Henry to appear before them in a series of meetings to justify his marriage to his brother's widow. The circumstances of this extraordinary project are shrouded in mystery but it is likely that Henry and Wolsey concocted the drama between them, for even a minister who was as senior – and as self-confident – as Wolsey would surely not have dared to insinuate to Henry that he had doubts about the legitimacy of his marriage unless Henry himself was privy to the plot.

The opening session took place in the greatest secrecy in Wolsey's residence at Westminster on 17 May 1527 and other meetings followed on 20, 23 and 31 May. Wolsey charged the king with having lived unlawfully for eighteen years with his dead brother's widow. For the first time, Henry raised the text in Leviticus 18:16 to claim that his marriage was invalid. Helpfully, Wolsey brought forward a series of arguments to suggest that the dispensation given by Julius II in 1503 was itself invalid. There was, accordingly, a two-tier approach – theological and ecclesiastical – which centred upon doubts raised by the teachings in Leviticus and about the validity of the dispensation of 1503. The strategy was certainly solid, for Henry's marriage to Katharine could have been canonically invalidated on either of the two grounds. However, Wolsey lost his nerve. Instead of proceeding to judgement, he decided that the matter was so grave that it needed to be considered by senior theologians and lawyers: evidently, he did not wish to take the primary responsibility for the dreadful decision that now had to be made. Wolsey also had to confront the grievous coincidence that on the very day after the last meeting of his court the news reached London that Rome had been sacked by imperial troops and that the Pope was effectively imprisoned.

In abandoning his own court, Wolsey threw away the king's best chance of securing an annulment of his marriage: had he and Warham declared at the turn of May–June 1527 on their own authority – and in the circumstances under which the Pope was a prisoner in Rome – that the king's marriage was canonically invalid they would almost certainly have carried the day, obliging Clement VII to accept after his release the de facto separation of Henry from Katharine. In the horror that engulfed Europe with the Sack of Rome, the grant of an annulment to Henry VIII would have gone comparatively unnoticed and Charles V would scarcely have been in a position to do more than berate Henry for his actions. But the moment was lost – and it was lost because Henry did not appreciate that Wolsey knew better than he how his marriage could be ended and because the cardinal himself lost his nerve at the critical moment. Wolsey's failure to act decisively (and unilaterally) in May 1525 was to change the history of England.

Julius II's Bull, 1503–27

As a churchman who was schooled in canon law and practised in the complexities of dealing with Rome, Wolsey understood perfectly well that great ecclesiastical or theological problems could be resolved by picking away at minute details. He appreciated that Julius II's bull of 1503 was a *pièce d'occasion*, a political rather than a theological document, designed to produce an outcome that was convenient to the three parties involved – the papacy and the monarchs of England and Spain. As Wolsey examined the bull in detail he came to understand that it provided substantial opportunities to him, for it was badly constructed and poorly phrased. Worse, it was designed to obfuscate because as we have seen Ferdinand of Aragon had made concessions to cover English legal anxieties about the implications for Katharine's remarriage if her first marriage had been consummated: accordingly he asked the Pope for a dispensation that covered both contingencies. Papal canon lawyers resolved the dilemma by allowing that 'perhaps' the marriage had been consummated while also stating as something akin to a fact of canon law that it had not been – and thereby satisfied Julius himself and the monarchs of Spain and England (above, chapter 7).

Moreover, as a *pièce d'occasion*, Julius's dispensation was soon outdated by events. The Pope justified his dispensation on the distinctly un-canonical grounds that its purpose was to stimulate peace between the English and Spanish monarchies. Two objections arose here – that the Crowns were already at peace and that it was no business of the papacy to issue a dispensation for marriage in order to facilitate a political arrangement. Moreover, since both Henry VII and Isabella had died before the marriage took place between Henry VIII and Katharine the document invalidated itself by referring to the wrong principals.[46] Pope Julius's bull was, in fine, a mess.

In any event, since Katharine resolutely and unalterably insisted that her marriage to Arthur had not been consummated, little progress could be made by way of proving that the impediment of affinity should have prevented her from marrying Henry VIII. Wolsey knew well enough if Katharine's word was accepted then no degree of affinity existed between herself and Henry or between their families – and Pope Julius's bull was, in this regard, therefore irrelevant.

The impediment of 'public honesty' was a very different matter. It will be recalled that canon law had insisted since the thirteenth century that a betrothal which had been fully and freely entered into by consenting adults carried virtually as definitive an effect in the canon law of the Church as did the consummation of marriage itself (above, chapter 5). Wolsey was among the first to recognise that Henry VIII might find considerably more room for manoeuvre in pursuing the difficulties raised by 'public honesty'. There could, after all, be no doubt that the betrothal of Arthur and Katharine had been widely publicised in both England and Spain; that their vows of marriage had been twice taken by Arthur and the Spanish ambassador standing as proxy for Katharine; and that as adults of fourteen and sixteen years of age, they had taken their vows personally in the grandeur of Westminster Abbey in front of the political and ecclesiastical nation. Moreover, they had then been publicly bedded and had – it was assumed – lived together as man and wife for four months before Arthur died. These circumstances should have created a powerful (and multiple) diriment impediment to any marriage taking place between Henry VIII and Katharine, *even if the marriage between Arthur and Katharine had not been consummated*. In other words, Henry VIII was not free to marry Katharine precisely because it was so widely known that she had already married Arthur: 'public honesty' would be deeply offended by his having done so.

All this was of course almost of little more than academic interest after the Sack of Rome: there was no way in which Pope Clement VII could have defied Charles V to annul the marriage of his aunt with Henry VIII.

But Wolsey knew that it might have been possible to make some headway, if not immediately then in a new political context at some time in the future. He was undone in the first instance by Henry's determination to pursue the argument through 'the Levitical Prohibition'.[47] This would suggest that the king was genuinely more convinced by the Biblical text than has sometimes been assumed – that perhaps he was more genuinely fearful of having committed grave sin than he was genuinely lustful for a life of sexual satisfaction with Anne Boleyn. We should at least consider the possibility that Henry VIII's conscience was a more formidable – and less pliable – instrument than has sometimes been suggested. Certainly, in pursuing the 'Levitical' argument he gravely damaged his own chances of success at Rome: to secure his annulment he really should have listened to his cardinal-minister.

Wolsey was prepared to attempt to coerce the Pope into complying with Henry's will. He insistently reminded Clement of Henry's services to the papacy, most notably in defending it against Luther. He was determined that Clement should understand the depths of Henry's determination to regularise his marital situation and to secure the succession to his throne. Insistently, too, Wolsey urged Clement to understand that the king would not allow a foreign jurisdiction to hold sway over his own regal powers within his kingdom. But Clement could not bring himself to act upon Wolsey's advice: Charles V – and his army – were much closer to him than was the King of England. Moreover, Clement understood well enough that he had one powerful weapon in his struggle with Henry – that he could excommunicate him and release his subjects from their obedience to him.

Henry was doubtless encouraged in his approach to Rome by his appreciation of the readiness with which the papacy had in recent years scattered dispensations from royal marital problems as if they were confetti. Most notably of course was this true of Alexander VI, but better and more honourable popes than he had lavished dispensations upon crowned heads in return for political favours. We have seen how the monarchs of Spain, Portugal, France and England all benefited substantially from the grant of such dispensations (above, chapter 5).

Nor was it merely the kings and queens of Europe who benefited: their siblings, uncles and aunts also did so. Most especially, Henry's confidence that the Pope would grant him his dispensation must have been powerfully reinforced by the dispensations which had facilitated marriages for his own sisters, Margaret and Mary. In February 1527 Clement allowed

Margaret Tudor an annulment of her marriage to Archibald Douglas, 6th Earl of Angus, on the grounds of 'public honesty' – that Angus had previously entered into a commitment to marry Lady Jane of Traquair and was therefore not free to pledge himself to Margaret. When Mary married Charles Brandon, Duke of Suffolk, in May 1515 Brandon had already had one marriage annulled (1507) and another dissolved (1513).[48] Henry certainly had every reason to anticipate that Pope Clement would find good reasons to favour him.

The King's Lawful Wife?

On 22 June 1527, Henry summoned Katharine to his chambers and informed her that their marriage was invalid and that for eighteen years they had been living in sin. Not surprisingly, Katharine collapsed into tears. She rallied sufficiently to insist that she had never consummated her marriage with Arthur and that she was – and would remain – Henry's lawful wife: to the end of her life this remained the bedrock of her case and she seems never to have addressed herself seriously to the difficulties raised by the questions of 'public honesty'. When Henry showed her his book arguing his case in canon law, she declared that she would rather accept the verdict of the Church: again, this would remain her central argument. The coherence with which Katharine responded to Henry's bombshell (despite her tears) strongly suggests that she had been warned in advance of what was coming.

Wolsey had by now reached his own considered conclusions and urged Henry to focus his appeal to the Pope on the insistence that the arguments that Henry VII and Ferdinand of Aragon had put to Pope Julius in 1502–03 had been canonically faulty; in granting his ambiguous dispensation, Julius II had merely complied with what the kings of England and Spain had asked of him, and if Clement now declared that the marriage of Henry and Katharine was invalid because Julius had been asked to give the wrong dispensation, *this carried no aspersions on papal competence or integrity*. Pope Clement could happily dispense with the dispensation that had been given so erroneously by his predecessor. Wolsey's analysis had driven to the very heart of the matter and provided Clement with the opportunity to reverse his predecessor's decision without damaging the reputation of the papacy.

Why Henry did not jump at the opportunity that the cardinal opened up for him is a mystery; Professor Scarisbrick (whose argument is closely followed here) has suggested that it was precisely because Henry was committed to the 'Levitical' principle that he made his fundamental error: 'it was not the wrong end of the stick that Henry grasped but the wrong stick'. Perhaps, too, Henry was beginning to doubt Wolsey's determination to secure an annulment for him. For whatever reason, Henry persevered in his insistence that he could not have a male child by Katharine *because* their marriage was invalid and should accordingly have been forbidden under Biblical precept.[49] In managing the theology of his approach to Rome, Henry contrived to destroy his own case – but in the circumstances that obtained after the Sack of Rome and the imprisonment of Clement VII it is doubtful whether anything could have secured him a papal annulment of his marriage in 1527.

Katharine realised that she had to let Charles V know what was happening and sent a servant to inform him of Henry's decision to abandon her. The Emperor responded at once to assure Katharine of his fullest support. He also despatched a favoured churchman, Bishop Francisco de los Ángeles de Quiñones, to the Pope, urging him to cancel Wolsey's status as legate *a latere* and to revoke the case to Rome. Charles also wrote to Henry, insisting that he should abandon the quest for an annulment. Europe now learned of Henry's intention to abandon his wife.[50]

Wolsey recognised that the imprisonment of Pope Clement provided him with the possibility of using an alternative approach to resolving Henry's marital difficulty – that he could take advantage of the Pope's inability to fulfil his functions by abrogating to himself a primary position in defending the Church. He was, after all, a cardinal who had seniority and prestige and who was accustomed to working with the crowned heads of Europe and he remained papal legate *a latere* in England. In July he crossed the Channel to meet Francis I to decide how the Treaty of Westminster of April 1527 could be implemented; he was accompanied by a cavalcade of nearly 1,000 horsemen. Wolsey suggested that Francis should invite all 'independent' cardinals to a council in Avignon which would then appoint Wolsey himself as Papal Vicar-General, with full powers to act for the imprisoned Pope. Professor Scarisbrick has rightly termed this plan 'audacious almost beyond belief and with few rivals, if any, in English history'.[51] Gossip and rumour circulated wildly around Europe about the realities of Wolsey's ambitions: in Valladolid, Navagero heard from imperial councillors that Wolsey intended to separate the Church of England from Rome, making himself de facto head of the Church during the Pope's imprisonment.[52] Not the least of the advantages of Wolsey assuming the powers of the Pope was that he would be able to settle the king's 'Great Matter' without even informing Clement of what he was doing. Such prompt action might even pre-empt a war with the Emperor. Wolsey was greeted by Francis at Amiens (9 August) and on the 18th the treaties were ratified: Princess Mary would marry Orleans.[53] England's alliance with Charles V had been abandoned.

While Wolsey was in France, Henry gave an extraordinary indication that he no longer had the fullest confidence in his ability to secure an annulment for him: on 10 September Wolsey was visited at Compiègne by William Knight, who was en route to Rome. Knight was an experienced diplomat who had served Henry on many embassies and Wolsey was appalled to find that Knight carried with him a document for Clement to sign which would allow the king to remarry *even if his first marriage had not been annulled*. Moreover, Knight was also to seek permission from the Pope for Henry *to marry a woman with whose sister he had already had sexual intercourse* or indeed *one with whom he had himself had sexual intercourse*. Anne Boleyn thus made her first – if anonymous – appearance on the international stage but so, too, of course, did her sister Mary, with whom Henry had enjoyed a long sexual relationship. Now it was Henry who had lost his nerve.

Knight was also to challenge the legitimacy of Julius II's bull by claiming that it had been obtained under false pretences. This brainstorm was the fullest recognition Henry ever gave of the right of the Pope to annul his marriage and to authorise his remarriage – but it also made it clear to the Pope that Henry was motivated, at least in part, by his passion for another woman and that he had sexually known both her sister and herself and so had established a double diriment impediment of affinity that should have prevented him from marrying her. Of course, Clement knew this well enough already and must have been astonished that Henry should have volunteered the information.

It has traditionally been believed that Anne Boleyn refused to engage in sexual intercourse with Henry until she was assured that he would divorce Katharine and marry her – that she tormented and enticed Henry into giving way to her determination to become Queen of England by not giving way to him in the bedroom. Professor George Bernard has daringly challenged this view, suggesting that Henry and Anne probably engaged in intercourse at the beginning of their relationship in (1525–6?) but that by the summer of 1527 were abstaining from it precisely because Henry dared not risk Anne becoming pregnant while he was appealing to Rome for an annulment of his marriage to Katharine. Bernard's remarkable *bouleversement* carries conviction for Henry knew that he dared not allow his opponents in the papal and imperial courts to suggest that he was merely asking the Pope to ratify and validate his own carnal indulgence.[54] It is amusing to think of Henry VIII restricting himself, as if he was a lovelorn teenager, to petting with his beloved so as not to damage his reputation for marital fidelity.

Wolsey forbade Knight to proceed to Rome but on the following day a letter arrived from Henry ordering him to do so. Wolsey wrote to Henry protesting that securing the annulment was his 'most inward desire' and he signed himself 'with a rude and shaking hand of your most humble subject, servant and chaplain'.[55] But Wolsey's General Council of the Church was a dismal failure: only four cardinals turned up at Compiègne to support Wolsey. He returned to London in September 1527: he had failed his king.

The King's Search for Support – and the First Missions to Rome

In the autumn of 1527 Henry began to seek a broad base of support from among England's courtly and ecclesiastical elites. In October he invited Thomas More to reflect upon the legitimacy of his marriage, opening a Bible to show him the Levitical injunction.[56] Henry had long held More in the highest personal and intellectual regard, recognising him as a man of high moral principle: if he could secure his support it would do much to legitimise his own position.[57] More, of course, was a deeply reflective man and he gave no commitment to the king other than that he would consider the matter, warily insisting that he was not sufficiently conversant with Scripture to make a judgement on the king's case. Henry accepted More's diffidence but suggested that he 'commune further' with Edward Foxe, who was compiling a book for him presenting his arguments. More did so but contrived still not to commit himself to an opinion and – for the moment – Henry apparently accepted More's position.

In November 1527 Henry summoned a number of scholars to Hampton Court and had a book read to them in the presence of some bishops and theologians. It was the beginning of his commitment to public discussion about his marriage and Henry doubtless understood that once he had opened the gates to public discussion of the subject his marriage could not survive – and especially so since it was known that he himself was deeply active in the process.

In London, Henry ratified his treaty with France and in affirmation of the new alliance was invested with the Order of St Michel on 10 November; the tournaments, feasts and masks were as dazzling as ever.

Princess Mary danced with the Lord Steward in anticipation of her marriage to the Dauphin. A play was staged in which the King of England and his cardinal were represented as the saviours of Church and Pope. St Peter himself appeared, conferring authority on Wolsey to save the Church and free the Pope. Wolsey then persuaded the kings of England and France to act jointly to liberate Pope Clement. But this was not enough: Francis I's two children then made their entrance, begging Henry and Wolsey to secure their freedom from the perfidious Emperor. Henry VIII and Wolsey were thus presented as central figures in re-ordering the affairs of Europe after the Sack of Rome. The Spanish were described as 'barbarians' while Charles himself was insulted as a 'tyrant' and it was even inferred that he may have been tainted with heresy. In fine, the performance could not have been more calculated to insult the Emperor-elect and all that he stood for.[58]

Wolsey also sent a mission to Rome to ask the Pope to confer authority upon him to judge the king's case. It consisted of three Italian churchmen who were experienced in English affairs – Girolamo Ghinucci, Bishop of Worcester since 1522; Uberto Gambara, who had been appointed papal nuncio in England earlier in 1527; and Gregory Casale, who held no post in England but who was experienced in church diplomacy and had served Henry on ecclesiastical matters. Casale's instructions (which were dated 5 and 27 December 1527) ordered him to persuade Clement to recognise the manifest invalidity of Henry's marriage and the canonical deficiencies of Julius II's bull and to establish a court to sit in England and issue a decretal commission instructing the judges to examine the facts of the case and to proceed to judgement on it. Wolsey himself would obviously sit on the commission, which could publish a decision which the Pope would (on his release) then ratify. The Curia was astonished to receive the request, believing that in reality Wolsey already had sufficient authority to try the case and to issue a verdict that would enable Henry to marry again.[59]

Charles V more than trumped the violence of the propaganda against him by releasing Pope Clement in December 1527, allowing him some controlled freedom in return for 300,000 ducats. Clement left Rome for Orvieto. The Pope's liberation meant that there was obviously now no need for a Papal Vicar General. Nevertheless, Clement VII immediately handed a dispensation to William Knight enabling Henry to marry again while neglecting to rule on whether the marriage with Katharine had been valid: in a truly extraordinary judgement he cravenly gave Henry VIII permission to marry bigamously. Knight was also given a commission for Wolsey to judge Katharine's case in England, but since the brief allowed Katharine to appeal to Rome against any decision given by the cardinal it was of no use to Henry. While apparently giving way to Henry in the most craven manner, Clement had in fact conceded nothing. Knight arrived back in London in February 1528 to inform the king that he had failed in his mission.

The news of Clement's 'escape' reached London on 3 January 1528. Two days later Wolsey marked the event with a pontifical High Mass at St Paul's. He then went on to the steps of the Cathedral to announce that the Pope had been freed. On 7 January 1528 he invited all the ambassadors at court to a great feast, and afterwards plays were presented in which Wolsey's role as the *Cardinalis Pacificus* was celebrated and three maidens dressed as Religion, Peace and Justice complained that they had been expelled from the whole of Europe by heresy, war and ambition.[60] The cardinal was, as appeared, at the very height of his power. But in reality he had failed his king. It only remained for Henry to work out how to dispense with both wife and minister – and to find councillors who could replace Wolsey and show him how he could replace Katharine with Anne.

13

1528–1529: THE 'MYSTERIOUS DARKNESS OF THE POPE'S MIND' & THE LEGATINE COURT

Italy 1527–28: French Invasion, Imperial Triumph
The Sack of Rome inevitably led to yet another re-balancing of the powers of Europe against Charles V. Eagerly, Francis I took the lead: at the beginning of August 1527 he despatched Lautrec with an army of over 30,000 men into Italy. He had three chief reasons for doing so – to take advantage of the weakness of Charles's power in Italy following the disintegration of the larger part of his army after the Sack of Rome; to revenge himself upon Charles V for his humiliations in Madrid; and to affirm to the princes of Europe that France's power was re-established and vigorous after his own release from imprisonment. Certainly, Francis chose his moment well, for the imperial army in Lombardy was in no condition to resist him and hurriedly took refuge in the fortress in Milan.[1]

Lautrec's march into and through Italy proved to be eerily reminiscent – in initial triumph and subsequent catastrophe – of Charles VIII's march in 1494–95. Lautrec used part of his army to invest Milan and Pavia, thereby tying down the Spanish forces in Lombardy, and marched south: on 9 February 1528 he crossed into the Kingdom of Naples. He then laid siege to the city of Naples while his ally the Genoese admiral Andrea Doria invested it by sea. Lautrec's arrival in Naples obliged the Spanish and German forces to leave Rome to reinforce the imperial army in 'the Kingdom' (16–17 February).[2] When Doria defeated the imperial forces

272

in a stunning naval victory off Cape d'Orso (28 May 1528) it seemed probable that Spain would lose control of the Kingdom of Naples and with it its hegemony in Italy. It was only one year since the Sack of Rome.

Francis I had indeed acted so promptly in launching his latest invasion of Italy that he had not found time to declare war on Charles V and on 22 January 1528, in Valladolid, the heralds of France and England formally did so.[3] Charles was indignant that Francis had broken his word to him and contemptuous of Henry VIII for allying with him. His response astonished those who witnessed it and appalled the princes and diplomats of Europe – on that same day, 22 January, he ordered the arrest of the ambassadors of France, Venice and Florence and had them led through the streets of Burgos as if they were common criminals; the people of the city duly hurled insults at them as they were taken off to confinement in the remote fortress of Poza in the mountains north of Burgos. In the hope that he could break the alliance between England and France, Charles did not initially arrest the English ambassadors in Spain – Edward Lee and Girolamo Ghinucci – but when they maintained their solidarity with their French allies he had them transported to Poza; they remained there under strict house arrest for four months.

Charles's decision to arrest the ambassadors severely damaged his reputation. Seven months after his troops had virtually destroyed Rome he seemed now determined to tear up the diplomatic conventions which had been the chief means of conducting European politics for the last fifty years: from Paris the Florentine ambassador wrote that Charles had violated not only the laws of God but his own honour.[4] In going to war with him, Francis I and Henry VIII could legitimately present themselves as the champions of the Pope and as the defenders of honesty and integrity in the conduct of international relations.

Open war with France in Italy once again obliged Charles to seek a reconciliation with England: for all that he regarded Katharine's cause as his own (as he put it to López de Mendoza) he was determined to do everything that he could to prevent England joining with France in military action against him. He therefore chose to blame Henry's dishonourable ministers rather than the king himself for the breakdown in relations, permitting himself to suggest that if Wolsey sought a reconciliation he would be prepared to forget how badly he had behaved towards him.[5]

Once again, Charles's military position in Italy was saved, as appeared, by an Act of Providence. As he had been redeemed in 1525 by Francis I's arrogance at Pavia, so now he was saved by perhaps the most astonishing diplomatic and military *bouleversement* of the sixteenth century: in July 1528 Doria transferred to the imperial side. This was no mere personal defection of short-term significance (as Bourbon's had proven to be in 1523) for Doria brought with him the galley fleet of Genoa and the enormous credit and banking resources of the Republic, and he did so for the simplest of reasons: Francis I had not kept his financial promises to him.[6] The defection of Genoa to Charles was to be a landmark in the development of Spanish power in Italy and well beyond, for Genoa became now a military ally of the Spanish monarchy and a major paymaster of the Crown: it remained so for a century. Starved of reinforcements by Doria's actions and once again committed to a prolonged siege, the French army was ravaged by plague and typhoid: Lautrec himself was among the thousands who died (15 August). Italy was again Spanish. The implications for Henry were stark: once more, Pope Clement was overwhelmed by the power – and the proximity – of the army of Charles V. And for all that Henry could pose as the defender of the Pope, he had again chosen the very worst of moments to declare war on the Emperor-elect.

Hiatus: Lorenzo Campeggio & the Establishment of the Legatine Court, April 1528–May 1529

In February 1528 Henry despatched Edward Foxe and Stephen Gardiner to Rome to urge Clement VII to issue a 'decretal commission' that would allow two papal legates sitting in England to decide the truth about his 'Great Matter' and issue a sentence to resolve it against which there could be no right of appeal. Foxe and Gardiner were among Henry's most trusted senior administrators and they formed the third English mission to Rome in less than a year, after William Knight in the late summer of 1527 and Gregory Casale and his two Italian colleagues at the turn of 1527–28. It will be recalled that Knight had secured no more than a bull allowing Henry to marry again if his marriage to Katharine was proven to have been unlawful while Casale had been given only a 'general commission' which allowed for judges merely to establish what the facts of the case were (chapter 12). In seeking a decretal commission, Foxe and Gardiner were to insist that Pope Clement undertook to be bound by the decision of the legatine court, thereby depriving Katharine of the right of appeal to him against any verdict that was unfavourable to her. They were also charged with convincing the Pope that the king's appeal was not being placed before him because Henry was in love with another woman: they may not have felt entirely confident that they would carry conviction in this, especially after what Knight had told Clement. They arrived in Orvieto on 21 March.[7]

The cascade of emissaries from England bemused Clement and his senior advisers, who appear to have believed that Wolsey could and should have resolved the matter himself by using his authority as papal legate in England; certainly, they had no wish to be involved in the marital difficulties of the King of England for they were confronted by much more serious (and dangerous) difficulties in Italy. Nevertheless, Henry seemed at first to have chosen his moment well, for Lautrec's triumphal march into Naples bade fair to liberate Clement from his dependence upon Charles V. Certainly, the Pope was very accommodating to the latest English delegates: at least one of his meetings with Foxe and Gardiner lasted for twenty hours. On 13 April – with Lautrec besieging the city of Naples – Clement duly issued a brief establishing a decretal commission but he did not specifically prohibit Katharine from appealing to him against the verdict of the two legates: when Foxe and Gardiner told him that it would not satisfy Henry, Clement dismissed their objections with the reply that he was terrified of the Emperor. Nevertheless, keen to do whatever he could not to make an enemy of Henry, Clement eventually sent Foxe back with three briefs – a dispensation for Henry VIII to marry Anne Boleyn while awaiting the verdict on the legitimacy of his first marriage; the authorisation for Wolsey to sit with Archbishop Warham or another English bishop to judge the case according to Church law and practice; and the authorisation for Wolsey and an as-yet unnamed papal legate to judge the legitimacy of the marriage of Henry and Katharine and issue a verdict on its status in Church law.

When Foxe returned to Greenwich early in May Henry listened to him joyously, believing that he had brought him everything that he wanted. Wolsey soon realised that Clement had in reality given the king much less than he needed: urgent messages were sent to Gardiner in Rome to secure a decretal commission that would explicitly prohibit any appeal to Rome. On 8 June, Clement again obliged, issuing a decretal commission in which he named Cardinal Lorenzo Campeggio to sit with Wolsey to judge the case and to issue a binding verdict.

Clement VII's ability to sway with political winds confused and often infuriated those who had to deal with him, most notably the princes of Europe and their agents: the Spanish ambassador at Rome in June

1529 referred despairingly to his obligation 'to peer into that mysterious darkness of the Pope's mind'.[8] It is true that Clement always exhibited a Medicean facility to adapt himself to prevailing circumstances even when this involved him in contradicting or countermanding decisions and judgements that he had previously made. But the manner in which he conducted his pontificate – at least after May 1527 – cannot be understood without reference to the extraordinary trauma that he suffered in witnessing the Sack of Rome from the Castel Sant'Angelo. Watching the butchery and destruction wrought on Rome by Charles V's barbarous troops changed him as a Pope and as a man. He gave expression to his agony by growing a beard in mourning for Rome; not surprisingly, his beard was grey and it grew down almost to his waist. The beard was an outward expression of inward trauma and Clement, who was so indecisive in so many of his actions, became determined that he would not allow the authority of the papacy to be further damaged. This was the more true because the years since Clement's elevation to the See of St Peter in 1523 had seen much of Germany abandon its fealty to the papacy. In dealing with Henry VIII's demands for an annulment of his marriage with Katharine, Clement fully understood that the king might renounce his (and England's) loyalty to Rome but he was nevertheless determined to meet his primary duty of defending the authority of the papacy itself. If Wolsey had taken the initiative in 1525–27 in annulling the marriage of Henry and Katharine Clement would almost certainly have accommodated himself to the new situation; if Wolsey and Campeggio had found a solution for him in 1529 Clement would undoubtedly have accepted it. But he himself would not take the responsibility for inflicting further damage upon the reputation of the papacy. Using whatever means he could find, Clement would spin out the process, but in the final analysis he would not abandon papal claims to authority over the customs and practices of the Church. And he was – as he so often reminded Henry's emissaries – terrified of Charles V's soldiers.[9]

Campeggio's journey to London was arduous and painful. Surprisingly for a man so given to prevarication and delay, he left Rome on the very day that he was presented with his commission (8 June) but he then caught a fever and had to rest constantly. He reached Paris on 17–18 September but was so ill that he then had to be carried to Calais in a litter. He rested for two days before embarking and – inevitably! – suffered a stormy crossing. It then took him eight painful days to travel from Dover to London, where he arrived on 9 October.

The slowness of Campeggio's journey towards London served to heighten tensions at court. Henry and Anne firmly hoped that Campeggio would shortly free them to marry; indeed, when Henry heard that Campeggio had reached Paris he tactfully sent Anne away from court, believing that he could present his case more effectively if the legate did not have to openly confront the reality of his relationship with his mistress.[10] Campeggio's colleague in the legatine court was less optimistic: Wolsey feared that if Henry won his case and married Anne his position as Henry's chief minister would become untenable while if Campeggio refused to grant an annulment Henry would inevitably punish Wolsey himself as the instigator of a failed policy. By contrast, Katharine could do little more than hope that Campeggio would recognise the justice of her case and that Charles V would find the means to intimidate the Pope and (through him) Campeggio.[11]

Charles did what he could to bolster the courage of his 'dearest and most beloved aunt'. Early in 1528 he sent López de Mendoza a copy of Julius II's brief of dispensation allowing Katharine to marry Henry; the ambassador presented it to Katharine in April and she then secreted it among her most private possessions. The implications of her possession of the document were to prove to be enormous, for as George Bernard has reminded us its very existence could well be taken to invalidate all that Clement VII had ordered Campeggio to achieve – and of course, Henry VIII and Wolsey had no idea that Katharine had the copy.[12]

Even Charles's avowed support could not console the queen in her increasing sense of abandonment and isolation. On 21 October the majority of the theologians of the prestigious Faculty of Theology at Paris declared in Henry's favour after an acrimonious debate.[13] When Henry then organised a meeting of senior lawyers in London on 15 November to advise him whether Katharine was indeed his lawful wife the queen wrote in despair to Charles begging him to ensure that Pope Clement did not undo the work of his predecessors who had authorised her marriage to the king.[14]

Katharine's fear that the world was closing in on her was deepened by the gloomy advice given her by the imperial ambassador. López de Mendoza, who was himself a canon lawyer, emphasised that Katharine had been badly advised to insist that she had been a virgin when she married Henry since virginity could not be proven except by personal oath. He also reminded the queen that Julius II's brief had expressly provided for the possibility that she and Arthur had not consummated their marriage; accordingly, he insisted that it was imperative that Katharine should demonstrate that Julius II's dispensation was canonically defective by virtue of a juridical or factual flaw.[15] The imperial ambassador had reached the same conclusion as Cardinal Wolsey.

Wolsey himself greeted Campeggio when he arrived in London and Henry and Katharine came from Greenwich to Bridewell to meet the two cardinal-legates. Henry took Campeggio and Wolsey into a large room where the foreign ambassadors (other than López de Mendoza, who had not been invited) were assembled. In opening speeches, Campeggio's orator spoke of the damage that the Church had suffered in recent years, most notably in the Sack of Rome. He urged Henry VIII as a peaceful monarch and as the Defender of the Faith to work for the peace of Europe, clearly implying that he should not push his claim for an annulment of his marriage. Henry's orator then replied, pointedly emphasizing that it had been imperial troops who had pillaged Rome and that Henry had only joined the League of Cognac because his best efforts to make peace between Charles V and Francis I had failed and because it was necessary to resist 'the tyrant'. After this pointed indictment of the Emperor, Henry took the two cardinals into a side room where Campeggio formally presented his credentials. It is probable that it was now that Campeggio showed Henry the decretal commission that he had brought from Rome.

Two days later (24 October) Campeggio and Wolsey visited Katharine in her private apartments. Campeggio presented the queen with his credentials and threw a bombshell directly at her by suggesting that the most appropriate solution to the difficulties confronting all parties would be for Katharine to retire into a convent and take vows of perpetual chastity – a device that had been often used to resolve royal marital difficulties and which could now be the more readily employed because the queen had reached 'the third stage' of her life and was no longer able to have children.[16]

It is not known whether Katharine had any intimation that Campeggio would make this devastatingly hurtful proposal. Furiously, she turned on Wolsey, accusing him of being the instigator of all her troubles. As she recovered her composure she curtly informed Campeggio that she held her husband's conscience and honour in greater esteem than anything in this world. Since, therefore, she had no scruples at all about her marriage to him she considered herself to be Henry's 'true and lawful wife'. She was confident that the Pope would never have put forward such a proposal had he been in possession of the truth. For her part, as a faithful and obedient daughter of the Church she asked nothing more than that she should not be judged before her case was heard. She spoke of the existence of papal bulls in Spain which removed all diriment impediments to her remarriage and threatened to produce them.

It was a heroic moment: like Martin Luther in front of Charles V at Worms, Katharine had stood alone to proclaim that there was a line that she would not cross, however painful it proved to be for her and whatever pressure was put on her. Flummoxed, Campeggio assured the queen that her case would be properly heard and that he would indeed do the fullest justice to her. The legate's opening gambit had failed – but he did, in the event, do justice to her.

On the following day Henry visited Campeggio, doubtless in the hope of hearing that Katharine had agreed to enter a nunnery. A witness who claimed to have overheard the conversation from an adjoining room reported that Henry urged Campeggio to take a decision and angrily raised his voice whenever the legate resisted him. The king then stormed into the room of Campeggio's secretary and vehemently demanded that a prompt decision be given. The cardinal-legate could have no doubt now about the determination of the two principal parties to the case he was supposed to resolve. On 27 October, Henry tried to intimidate Katharine. Brutally, he told her that she was not his wife: mendaciously, he informed her that the Pope had already decided against her and that Campeggio had come to England merely to implement a sentence that had already been given. But Katharine was not to be cowed: she enquired calmly of her husband how the Pope could condemn her without a hearing. Again, Henry lied to her: Charles V had made her case for her and the Pope had decided against her. Henry implored Katharine to enter the religious life and threatened that he would force her to do so if she refused. Tearful but unbroken, Katharine insisted that she could not act against her conscience and her own honour; she was convinced that no judge could hear her arguments and then decide against her and demanded that she be allowed to plead her case. Henry gave way: counsel would be appointed for her and he gave permission for Katharine to send to the Low Countries for a canon lawyer to guide her. On the following day counsel were named and they were men of distinction and independence – Archbishop Warham of Canterbury, Bishop Tunstall of London and Bishop Fisher of Rochester. Three canon lawyers were named to advise them together with the Spaniards Vives and Jorge Athequa (Katharine's confessor). Katharine would be well represented by men of high expertise and independence.

Wolsey was horrified by the potential of the trial that he was to co-judge; on 1 November he wrote to Casale to urge the Pope to understand what might happen if Rome did not give way to Henry – 'I throw myself at the Holy Father's feet ... I beg him to look on his royal majesty's holy and unchangeable desire ... his most just, most holy, most upright desire.' Wolsey clearly foresaw the ruin of the Church in England if Clement did not give way to Henry.[17]

At some time over the next few days, Katharine asked Henry for permission to meet Campeggio again, and he agreed. This time, she would apply the pressure. She did so on three fronts with a sophistication and a directness that must have profoundly shaken the cardinal. She started by asking him to receive her confession – a request that no priest could refuse. The sacrament of Confession involved the confessee in unburdening himself or herself of each and every sin he or she had committed, and the confessor was bound under the most serious penalties never to divulge to anyone what he had been told. Katharine affirmed that she had been a virgin when she had married Henry and when she then insisted that the dispensation of Julius II was valid she was in effect telling Campeggio that *as a matter of record* Rome had already decided in her favour. She subsequently maintained that she had told Campeggio that she and Arthur had only slept together on seven nights: was it now that she told him this? Did she specify whether those nights had been passed in London or in Ludlow? We cannot know.

It is also not clear whether it was during the Act of Confession or after it that Katharine presented the legate with the copy of Julius's brief of dispensation – what became known as 'the Spanish brief' – that she had held since April. In that moment, Campeggio surely understood that his mission in England was hopeless: he could not reconcile Henry and Katharine and dared not decide between them.

Still, Katharine had not finished with the cardinal: it was almost certainly now that she gave Campeggio permission to break the seal of the confessional – as she was fully entitled to do under canon law – to convey to the Pope precisely what she had told him. She had now hurled three bombshells at the cardinal-legate, at the Pope and the Curia. Above all, she had shown them how ruthlessly – and how skilfully – she would fight for her marriage and for her honour. She truly was the daughter of Isabella the Catholic.

Katharine was also deeply popular among the people of England and most especially among the citizens of London. Henry had good reason to be wary of her popularity and on 8 November he summoned senior courtiers and administrators so that he could explain his position to them. Without any apparent shame, he admitted his admiration and love for his wife and his decision not to share a bed with her again: 'If I were to marry again [and] if the marriage might be good, I would surely choose her above all women.' But he was driven irresistibly to conclude that for twenty years he had lived 'to God's great displeasure'.[18]

Henry and Wolsey were deeply shaken when they learned of the existence of 'the Spanish brief' and – much more – of its presence in London. They appreciated that they would have to begin their case again from scratch and did the best they could by denouncing the brief as a forgery and demanding that they should have sight of the original: on 19 November López de Mendoza reported that Henry's lawyers had told Katharine that the papal brief of dispensation was not a faithful copy and had not been logged into the papal register in time.[19] Five days later, Katharine again wrote despairingly to her nephew urging that 'after God, no one but your Majesty can help me' and she appealed to him as the Samaritan woman had done to Jesus when surrounded by people who were mocking her.[20] But even before he received her letter Charles had acted: on 12 December, from Toledo, he sent López de Mendoza copies of all the documents that had been located in Spain that might be useful in the queen's defence.[21]

In London, king and minister now turned the fullest pressure on Katharine. They despatched Warham and Tunstall and two other senior men to confront Katharine with the accusation that her defiance was raising such hostility to the king himself and to Campeggio that Henry feared that an assassination attempt might be made on one or both of them. If this did happen Henry – in life or in death – would hold Katharine responsible. Warham and Tunstall were instructed to advise Katharine that Henry believed that she now so hated him that he could no longer allow Princess Mary to come into contact with her: Katharine was to be separated from her beloved daughter. The king's delegates also complained that Katharine had dishonestly secreted the copy of Julius II's brief of dispensation and that she should have made it known to them that she had it.

Katharine furiously rejected the 'abominable' suggestion that she could ever seek to have Henry killed and professed herself convinced that Henry could not have been party to this suggestion for he knew that she valued his life above her own. As to the copy of the brief, she had not made its existence known because she had never believed that it would be necessary for her to make use of it. She did, however, confirm that López de Mendoza had given it to her six months ago although she did not make it clear whether he had done so in person.

While Katharine stood with rock-like immovability, Henry was fraying. He had been shaken not only by Katharine's determination and intransigence but also by the warmth of the reception given to the queen when she had appeared in public: he ordered that the populace should henceforth be kept out of the palace. He broadened his attack on his wife's conduct by opening up the implications of his marital crisis for his dealings with fellow monarchs: he summoned the Lord Mayor and aldermen of the City of London to inform them that Francis I had asked for Princess Mary's hand for the Duke of Orleans but had insisted on a categorical assurance that she was of legitimate birth, quite forgetting that it was he himself who was raising the question of Mary's legitimacy. Early in December, Henry sent Katharine away from Greenwich, to Hampton Court: Anne Boleyn moved into her rooms next to Henry's and was the central figure at the courtly celebrations over the Christmas period.[22] The pace was quickening.

Accordingly, in the last days of 1528 both Henry and Katharine made further appeals to Clement VII and to Charles V. Katharine readily agreed to Henry's suggestion that she should ask Charles V to send the original papal bull to England, believing that it could only serve to provide protection for her daughter and herself. Her letter to Charles was carried by Thomas Abel, a trusted servant, but when Abel arrived at the Spanish court he duly informed Charles that Katharine wished him to ignore the letter he was carrying to him and gave a verbal account of what had happened to her, passing on her insistence that Charles should oblige Clement VII to halt the proceedings against her. Charles accordingly agreed only to provide a verified copy of the papal bull and to have it read to the English ambassador but insisted that he would never allow the original to leave Spain. Once again, Katharine had outwitted her husband.[23]

Katharine also wrote to Clement VII asking him to take the case away from England and to try it himself arrived in Rome; her letter reached him on 6 March 1529. Support promptly came from her nephew: at the end of April, Charles V's ambassador in Rome insisted again that Clement should revoke the case to Rome.[24] At about the same time Henry and Wolsey had decided that they needed to make yet another appeal to Rome and despatched an embassy of no fewer than four men to support Lee and Ghinucci in persuading Clement grant the annulment – William Knight (again!), Francis Bryan, Peter Vannes and William Benet. They were received by the Pope at the end of March 1529.[25]

In Valladolid on 3 April 1529, in the presence of notaries and witnesses, one of Charles's senior ministers, Nicolas Perrenot de Granvelle, informed ambassadors Lee and Ghinucci that they would be allowed to inspect and read the original brief of Julius II providing dispensation for the marriage of Henry and Katharine. He handed them the brief to study and suggested that an attested copy could be sent to England. They rejected his offer on the grounds that the case had been referred to the Pope. Granvelle then had the document read aloud by two bishops in front of several senior advisers of Charles V.[26] The Emperor-elect's position was now that he had done everything that he could to accommodate the English request to study the papal brief: he would do no more.

Charles now turned his attention to his journey to Italy. He informed his Council of State that he would be travelling as a peacemaker rather than as a conqueror but he took the precaution of ordering the leading nobles in Spain to travel with him: he would not risk having them free to make trouble at home while he was in Italy.[27] He named his Empress as his Regent and established a renewed Council of State to advise her; Isabella (who was pregnant) was furious with her husband for leaving her and became ill. Nevertheless, on 8 April 1529 Charles left Toledo and set out for Barcelona, where he would embark for Italy.[28] On 23 April, as he neared the border of Catalonia, he wrote to Katharine (his 'dearest and most beloved aunt') informing her that he had urged the Pope to judge the case at Rome and assuring her that he would not fail in his duty to her. When at the end of June he reached Barcelona he wrote again to Katharine reiterating the strength of his support.[29] Shortly after his arrival in the Catalan capital Charles heard that Antonio de Leyva had crushed the French army at the Battle of Landriano, near Pavia (20–21 June 1529). When, therefore, on 27 July he sailed for Genoa he knew that he was once again the master of Italy and that he could impose his own settlement on the princes of Italy and – most importantly of all – on the Pope himself. He sailed with 9,000 infantry and 1,000 cavalry: despite his assurance to his Council of State in Toledo, Charles would arrive in Italy as a conqueror.[30]

The Legatine Court, Blackfriars, 31 May–31 July 1529[31]

The legatine court opened at Blackfriars on 31 May 1529 and the first public session took place on 16 June. On that day, Katharine presented herself to the cardinals and promptly followed the Spanish legal practice of *recusación*, arguing that her judges were disqualified from judging her case because of their close associations with King Henry – Wolsey because he had received many promotions and awards from the king over a decade and Campeggio because Henry had raised him to a bishopric in England. She insisted that her case should be heard by impartial judges and, having delivered her demand in writing, left the court.

The cardinal-legates opened the formal proceedings on 21 June: Henry and Katharine were waiting for them when they entered the chamber, Henry on the right under a canopy of gold brocade and Katharine on the left. The king and the queen were summoned to appear before the court one week later, on 28 June.

On 22 June Bishops Fisher of Rochester and Clerk of Bath and Wells appeared before the legates as Katharine's lawyers. They were a formidable team: although Fisher was a severe and ascetic churchman he was an experienced political operator who had served at court for two decades while Bishop Clerk had a wealth of legal, political and courtly experience, having served as Master of the Rolls (1522–23) and Dean of Windsor (1519–23) before being appointed to Bath and Wells in 1523. Fisher and Clerk defined their brief with provocative simplicity: they intended to prevent King Henry from falling into mortal sin by demonstrating that Katharine was indeed his lawful wife. They followed the queen's lead in the manner in which they opened their arguments: they rejected the right of Campeggio and Wolsey to sit in judgement on the case.

John Fisher was to be Katharine's first and greatest defender. He was a Yorkshireman (from Beverley) who had a brilliant academic career, rising to be Vice-Chancellor of Cambridge University (1501): a modern authority has said of him that he 'bestrode [the university] like a colossus'.[32] He had also become chaplain and confessor to Henry VII's mother, Margaret Beaufort, and it was probably with his encouragement that Lady Margaret founded St John's and Christ's Colleges in Cambridge and the 'Lady Margaret' professorships of divinity at Oxford and Cambridge. Fisher may even have served briefly as a tutor to the young Prince Henry, although the evidence on this is ambivalent. He was appointed as Bishop of Rochester in 1504 and held the position until his death. His status at court was such that in 1509 he was chosen to preach the homilies on the deaths of both Henry VII and Lady Margaret. Fisher was a modern intellectual, numbering Thomas More and Erasmus among his close friends, but he was – much more importantly – a deeply conservative churchman, profoundly anxious about the spread of heresy; it was no accident that he had preached the sermon at St Paul's Cross when Luther's books were burned in 1521, for he would spend his life fighting belligerently against those whom he perceived to be the enemies of the Church.[33] John Fisher was a Catholic traditionalist *par excellence*.

Although Fisher was intensely loyal to Katharine his primary purpose in leading her defence was therefore to protect the doctrines and practices of the Catholic Church. He perceived with utter clarity that Henry's attack on the legitimacy of his marriage could well develop into a wide-ranging assault upon the Church, its doctrines and its discipline and he foresaw – perhaps before anyone else – that it might well lead ultimately to an attack on the authority of the papacy itself in England. When he addressed a later session of the court he opened his defence of the queen in language that was provocatively blunt, declaring that he was prepared to die as if he was John the Baptist in maintaining the principle of the indissolubility of marriage: the allusion was unmistakable, for if Fisher was John the Baptist Henry VIII in killing him would be King Herod. It was a brutal dismissal of the king that Henry never forgot or forgave. In time he would indeed have Fisher's head, and he would take vindictive pleasure in doing so.[34]

On 28 June the royal couple appeared before the court. Henry made a powerful statement in which he asserted that he could no longer remain in the state of mortal sin that he had occupied now for twenty years and urged the two cardinals to find peace for him by resolving his case. Wolsey tacitly acknowledged the legitimacy of Katharine's hostility to him by promising that he would try the case to the best of his ability even though he had received many favours from Henry.

Then it was Katharine's turn. She proclaimed that she had rejected the legality of the court and sought a judgement in Rome. She then threw herself on her knees before her husband. Several accounts of her action exist, the most pithy of them from the Venetian observer, Ludovico Falier:

> The queen then rose, and throwing herself on her knees before the king, said aloud that she had lived for twenty years with his Majesty as his lawful wife, keeping her faith to him, and that she did not

deserve to be repudiated and thus put to shame without any cause; and she begged the judges to show in her favour.[35]

A much fuller (and more florid) account is given by George Cavendish in his *Life of Wolsey*:

She took pain to go about unto the king, kneeling down at his feet in the sight of all the court and assembly, to whom she said in effect, in broken English, as follows:

'Sir,' she said, 'I beseech you for all the love that there has been between us, and for the love of God, let me have justice and right, take of me some pity and compassion, for I am a poor woman and a stranger born out of your dominions, I have here no assured friend, and much less indifferent counsel: I appeal to you as to the head of justice within this realm. Alas! Sir, wherein have I offended you, or what occasion of displeasure [have I given you]? Have I acted against your will and pleasure, so that you should intend (as I perceive) to put me from you?

I take God and all the world to witness that I have been to you a true humble and obedient wife, ever conformable to your will and pleasure, that never said or did anything to the contrary thereof, being always well pleased and contented with all things wherein you had any delight or dalliance, whether it were in little or much, I never grudged in word or countenance, or showed a glimpse or spark of discontentment. I loved all those whom you loved only for your sake, whether I had cause or not and whether they were my friends or my enemies.

These twenty years I have been your lawful wife and more, and by me you have had diverse children, although it has pleased God to call them out of this world, which has been no fault in me.

When you had me at the first, I take God to be my judge I was a true maid without touch of man; and whether it be true or no, I put it to your conscience if there be any just cause by the law that you can allege against me, either of dishonesty or any other impediment, to banish me and send me away from you, I will happily go to my great shame and dishonour; but if there be none, then here I most humbly beg you to let me remain in my former estate and receive justice at your hands...'

And with that she rose up, making a low curtsey to the king and departed from thence...[36]

Three times the crier summoned Katharine to return but without a backward glance she marched away from the scene of her humiliation.

Katharine had once more demonstrated that she knew how to play politics, within the Church and within the legatine court. She had again intimidated her husband: Henry summoned his Privy Councillors for an urgent discussion while the legates suspended the court for the day. Wolsey recognised the power of Katharine's performance when on the following day he threw himself on his knees in front of her, begging her to give way to Henry. Shortly afterwards, a delegation of English bishops visited her with the same request but they received the same answer. Katharine had identified her case with the Law of God, and the cardinal-legates declared her to be in contempt of their court.

The Fall of Wolsey[37]

The disintegration of the French army in Italy after the death of Lautrec in August 1528 inevitably led to the re-establishment of Charles's military primacy in Italy. By the time that his army crushed the remnants of the French force at Landriano and restored his control of the Milanese (20–21 June 1529) the settlement was already made. Pope Clement was the first to come to heel. Terrified that Charles was at last leaving for Italy – and that he was bringing a large army with him – Clement hurriedly accommodated himself to him and once again he did so to the benefit of his own family: on 29 June by the Treaty of Barcelona, Charles and Clement agreed to restore the Medici to power in Florence and then to create a Medici dukedom in Florence which would be sealed by the marriage of Alessandro de' Medici with Charles's illegitimate daughter Margaret. The arrangement was bound to scandalise the people of Florence for Alessandro was himself the illegitimate son of Lorenzo II de' Medici, Duke of Urbino. Even though Alessandro was cousin to the Pope, the new dukes of Florence would be doubly tainted by bastardy.[38]

The peace treaty which brought the war in Italy to an end was signed at Cambrai on 5 August and became known as 'the Ladies' Peace' because it was negotiated by three formidable women – Margaret of Austria, aunt of Charles V and Governess of the Low Countries; Louise of Savoy, mother of Francis I and Marguerite of Navarre, sister of Francis I. It ratified the terms agreed in the Treaty of Madrid but with the exception that Charles V renounced his claims on Burgundy and Francis reciprocated by abandoning his pretensions to Milan, Genoa and Naples and the *señorío* of Flanders – so that Charles was no longer his vassal. The two French princes were to be freed in return for a payment of 2 million ducats and it was agreed that Francis would marry Leonor.[39]

Katharine's appeal against the legitimacy of the legatine court reached Rome in the first days of July. On 13 July, Clement agreed to suspend the court and three days later had the formal announcement made in Consistory; it was published on 23 July. In London, on 31 July, Campeggio prorogued the court for the summer on the pretext that ecclesiastical and legal jurisdictions in Rome did not conduct business during these months: he would reconvene the court at the beginning of the new legal term in October. Henry was furious: Katharine was triumphant: and Wolsey was terrified.[40] The Duke of Suffolk angrily remarked, in an observation that was to resonate through political and courtly society, that 'I see now the truth of what I have heard many people say; never at any time did a Papal legate do anything to the profit of England: they have always been and will hereafter be a calamity and a sore to this country'.[41]

The Pope's decision meant that the question of the legitimacy or otherwise of the legatine court would be judged in the first instance by the 'Sacred Roman Rota'. The Rota (as it was commonly called) was composed of judges ('auditors') who were ordained priests with doctorates in theology and canon law and their position was so valued in the Vatican that they were honoured *ex-officio* with the rank of bishops. It was their responsibility to define canon law in contentious cases of major importance and then to advise the Pope, who himself then prepared his own definitive judgement. What Katharine had won by rejecting the authority of the legatine court was precisely this: that Pope Clement (advised by the Consistory of Cardinals and the Rota) would now be the judge of whether or not she was the lawful wife of Henry VIII.

Clement did not apparently offer a public justification in 1529 for his decision to advoke the case to Rome but at the turn of 1530–31 he was engaged in a bitterly angry exchange of letters which was sparked off by Henry's letter to him of 6 December 1530 (which we will shortly consider): on 7 January 1531 Clement replied to Henry and his letter should be discussed here because it provides the broadest account of his thinking in advoking the case to Rome for his own judgement. Clement began by assuring Henry that he would never forget their long friendship despite the anger that had informed the king's letter to him:

We sent a legate to England at the king's own request, to judge the cause in conjunction with the English legate, and did not revoke him till the queen had complained frequently that she, as a stranger, was obliged to submit to judicial proceedings at the will of the king, whose word was law. She appealed to us, put in an oath of fear; and we, in a matter of such great scandal, which could not otherwise be expunged, undertook to judge the case ourselves, as by our office we were bound to do. By the unanimous decision of the [Consistory of] Cardinals we committed the cause to the Rota for judgement and agreed to abide by their decision.

What otherwise would your Highness have done, if you had been in our place? How could we refuse to admit the appeal? You say there was no ground for suspicion. We think so too: but the other party thinks and swears otherwise. Therefore we could not refuse [her].

You say the controversy is to be decided where it has arisen. True, but not where a suspicion exists on either side, whether it be just and reasonable or not.

If you believe that we lean more to one side than the other, how much greater must be the fear which the queen has in regard to yourself in your own kingdom, especially as the Archbishop of Canterbury, to whom you would have the affair committed, has already written on your behalf against the queen.

We say this not out of any suspicion of the integrity of your judgement but in justification of our conduct with regard to the queen's appeal.

We will speak with you as a friend and beg of you to put away the false suspicion you have conceived of us. There are many things in your letters in which we miss your usual wisdom and even your modesty, especially in that reiterated taunt that we are governed by the Emperor. As we would grant nothing that was unjust for him, you must not require us to do what is unjust for you, especially as the Emperor has always said that if the Queen failed in her cause he would acquiesce...

We say nothing of the principal business, as we have not heard both sides. When we have done so, we shall act impartially: but we must request of you not to demand in this more than duty allows us to grant. If you persist, we shall be sorry, but even if we do not give you satisfaction in the matter of law, we shall diminish nothing of our affection for you.[42]

The 'principal business' to which Clement alluded was of course the question of the legitimacy or otherwise of the marriage and central to this was the status of Julius II's brief of dispensation.

The revocation of Katharine's case to Rome (23 July 1529), the prorogation of the legatine court (31 July) and the signing of the Treaty of Cambrai (3–5 August) marked the definitive failure of Wolsey's foreign policy. Foreign ambassadors were denied access to him. On 19 September he accompanied Campeggio to Grafton so that Campeggio could bid farewell to the king before returning to Rome. No room had been reserved for Wolsey but Henry astonished observers – and probably Wolsey himself – by greeting the Cardinal with real warmth, raising him from his knees and entering into an intense discussion with him. Henry evidently found some real difficulty in dismissing the man who had been his senior minister for so long. Unable to confront Wolsey himself, Henry had the dukes of Norfolk and Suffolk demand that he surrender the Great Seal and that he leave court (21 September). But even now, Henry wavered: he urged Wolsey to trust in his good will and sent him a ring as a testament of his favour. Wolsey reciprocated by sending Henry his own most valued possession, a crucifix with a relic of the True Cross. He went to Esher to wait for what he hoped would be the summons to return to court.[43]

On 8 October, Henry paid a sudden visit to London and had a series of meetings with senior ministers, among them Norfolk and Suffolk. On the following day – the beginning of the legal term; the day on which the legatine court should have reassembled at Blackfriars – Wolsey was indicted in the King's Bench for illegally exercising the office of papal legate in contravention of the Statute of Praemunire. Nine days later he was dismissed from the Royal Council. He was also deprived of the Bishopric of Winchester and abbacy of St Albans. Perhaps more painful still, York Place in London was taken from him and his School at Ipswich was closed down. For some weeks his household had no goods and he had to borrow money from his chaplains to pay his servants.

Wolsey's immediate successors – Norfolk and Suffolk in particular – were not men of his calibre and abilities but one figure of truly international reputation did now join the government: on 25 October, Sir Thomas More was presented with the Great Seal as Lord Chancellor of England and he took the oath on the following day. There has been as much debate as to why Henry VIII chose him as to why More accepted.[44] Certainly, the king had both affection and admiration for More, whom he had known at least since he himself was eight years old. He respected More's intellect and perhaps, too, he was intrigued by More's reluctance to serve at court. More initially resisted Henry's requirement that he succeed Wolsey as Lord Chancellor but finally agreed to serve the office on what he understood to be Henry's guarantee that he would not be obliged to involve himself in the polemics surrounding the king's 'Great Matter'.

Within a few days of accepting the Great Seal, Sir Thomas once again found Henry pressing him for help over his marital difficulties: he subsequently recorded that Henry urged him in the name of their friendship to 'look and consider his great matter again' in the hope that More would be able to support him. But, More insisted, Henry 'graciously declared unto me' that he would be allowed to follow his own conscience. A committee of four of Henry's senior advisers then visited More to put pressure on him – Foxe; Thomas Cranmer, a chaplain to the Boleyn family; Nicolas de Burgo, an Italian Franciscan; and Edward Lee – but More was not persuaded and Henry once again agreed not to force the issue with him, saying (as More recorded) that he would never 'put any man in ruffle or trouble of his conscience'.[45]

More determined to retain the strictest neutrality rather than involving himself in the king's 'Great Matter'. Indeed, he refused even to read the cascade of tracts in favour of Katharine written by his friend John Fisher, preferring instead (as John Guy has noted) to follow the advice that he had set out in *Utopia* sixteen years ago: 'Don't give up the ship in a storm because you cannot hold back the winds … Instead, by an indirect approach you must strive and struggle as best you can to handle everything tactfully. What you cannot make wholly good, you may at least make as little bad as possible.'[46]

Whether More would be able to steer his course would be a severe test of his political skills as much as his strength of character for he was about to confront a dreadful conflict of his loyalties to Church and king.

At the end of April 1530, Thomas Wolsey set foot for the first time in the extensive territories of the Archbishopric of York. Foolishly, he continued to deal with the French and imperial ambassadors, unaware that Henry knew what he was doing. On 4 November he was arrested on a charge of high treason. It was said that the chambers in the Tower of London that the Duke of Buckingham had occupied were being prepared for him: the inference was obviously that Wolsey would follow Buckingham to the block. This sent out an intimidating message to churchmen: if a man who had served as Lord Chancellor and papal legate *a latere* and who was still Archbishop of York was not safe, then which churchman was? Wolsey was travelling south to London when he died at Leicester Abbey on 29 November.[47]

A New Imperial Ambassador: Eustace Chapuys

In July 1529 Charles appointed the Savoyard Eustace Chapuys to replace López de Mendoza: he reached in London in September.[48] Certainly, Katharine was relieved and gratified by his arrival. Recognising that she would find a strong ally in Chapuys, she immediately sent her physician, Fernando de Victoria, to bring the ambassador up to date on the progress of her case.[49]

Henry received Chapuys at Grafton. The two men fenced as they measured themselves against each other, calculating how far each intended to go in the conflict upon which they were about to engage. Henry had no qualms about threatening the Emperor-elect and when Chapuys defended the Pope's decision to advoke the case to Rome Henry spoke witheringly of Clement: 'Enough about that Pope, this is not the first time that he has changed his mind; I have long known his versatile and fickle nature.'[50] Henry complained that the case had been advoked to Rome purely as a result of the pressure placed on the Pope by the Emperor-elect. He protested that as a secular prince, Charles should never have involved himself in such matters and was 'extremely annoyed' that Charles had not sent him Pope Julius's brief of dispensation when he had requested it, for had he done this the issues would have been resolved and by now he and Katharine would have been free to marry again. Henry vehemently insisted that the papal dispensation was his property and should have been given to him.

Henry contemptuously dismissed the possibility that he and Katharine should be summoned to appear in Rome, swearing that he would never leave his kingdom and reminding Chapuys that the laws of England forbade Englishmen to appear before a foreign court under pain of confiscation of their property and imprisonment. Unstated was the obvious question: if a subject of the Crown could not lawfully seek judgement before a foreign court, how much less so could the King of England? Warming to his theme, Henry allowed himself to wonder whether it was even safe for anyone to travel to Rome in view of the violence of the imperial army which had sacked Rome in 1527. It was, however, for the Pope himself that his most withering scorn was reserved: Clement had solemnly promised that he would never revoke the case to Rome but had changed his mind out of fear of Charles V. Without any embarrassment, Henry even jumped to the defence of cardinals Campeggio and Wolsey, claiming that Clement's advocation of the case to Rome reflected on their honesty. As for his own integrity:

> I am a conscientious prince, who prefers his own salvation to all the goods and advantages of this world, as appears sufficiently from my conduct in this affair, for had I been differently situated and not prone to obey the voice of conscience, nobody should have hindered me from adopting other measures, which I have not taken and never will take.[51]

Henry readily agreed that Chapuys could meet Katharine. When the ambassador arrived Katharine spoke very quietly to him so that her comments should not be overheard by members of her household. She insisted that there was no need for Henry to be given the papal brief since people who knew the case understood well enough where justice lay. She urged Chapuys to thank Cardinal Campeggio in her name and in that of the Emperor 'for his honest and rightful behaviour, and the trouble he has taken in this affair. As to me, I am so grateful for what he has done that I should hardly know how to repay his services.'[52]

As Katharine reflected on her interview with Chapuys she decided that there was more to be said, and what she subsequently told him was stated so bluntly that the ambassador felt obliged to report it to Charles in cipher: Katharine recorded her deepening resentment at her husband's duplicity and her conviction that he was motivated primarily not by theological scruples but by his lust for a woman whom she could not bring herself even to name:

> The queen has sent me word expressly to warn Your Imperial Majesty against any attempts, past or future, made by the king or his ambassadors to persuade Your Majesty that the divorce case had been merely instituted for the discharge of his conscience. That is not the fact: the idea of the separation originated entirely in his own iniquity and malice.[53]

For Chapuys, too, Henry's primary motive was the sexual attraction of 'the Lady' (whom he, too, refused to name):

As far as I can hear and judge, this king's obstinacy and his passion for the Lady are such that there is no chance of recalling him by mildness or fair words to a sense of his duty. Things having come to such a pitch, there can be no security or repose [for the queen] unless the case be tried and decided [at Rome], and the sooner the better, for many reasons and political considerations, whereof Your Majesty is the best judge.[54]

Chapuys reported that the Duke of Norfolk was assuming control of the government of England.[55] He noted that when Henry visited York Place he was accompanied by Anne Boleyn, her mother and a gentleman of his chamber. As for Campeggio, Chapuys reported that when the cardinal-legate arrived at Dover his trunks were broken open by royal agents seeking to find the decretal bull that he had brought with him a year earlier. It was not to be found, for the legate had burned it.[56]

On the last day of 1529, Chapuys informed Charles V that Henry had recently shown more consideration to Katharine than hitherto and that Anne Boleyn had not lately appeared at court celebrations. In reality, Katharine was in despair, losing hope that Henry would return to her as he had done after other affairs and relying upon Charles V to wield his power over Pope Clement to resolve her difficulties. The ambassador also confidently reported that the majority of the bishops and canon lawyers had supported Katharine; no one, he reported, other than Stokesely had written in defence of Henry's case.[57] As Henry began to rack up the pressure on Pope and Emperor-elect (and on Katharine herself), Charles was represented in London by an ambassador who was as uninformed of English political realities as he was blithely optimistic about the capacity that his master wielded to change or even influence affairs in England. And Chapuys was a man who was already deeply set in his ways and in his view of the world: he did not get any better – or any better informed.

14

DESPAIR, 1530–1531: THE APPEALS TO ROME & THE ATTACKS ON THE CHURCH

Conjuncture: The Reformation Parliament & the Coronations of Charles V – and the Papal Bull of 30 March 1530

The first session of what has become known as 'the Reformation Parliament' opened at Blackfriars on 3 November 1529. It happened that on the very following day, Charles V arrived in Bologna to prepare for his coronations as King of Lombardy and Holy Roman Emperor. The juxtaposition of the two events – English Parliament; dual coronations – was coincidental but nevertheless carries deep symbolism, for while Henry still hoped that his 'Great Matter' could be resolved by agreement with the Pope the restoration of the power of Charles V in Italy (which was to be definitively expressed in his coronations) made that impossible; as Henry came to realise that this was the case so he turned to his own Parliament to find the means with which to separate himself from Katharine.

Charles would have much preferred to have been crowned at Rome (as Charlemagne had been) but the devastation of the city by his troops made this as impractical as it was impolitic and so he was obliged to organise his coronations in Bologna. He made a leisurely progress through northern Italy before arriving in the city.[1] Pope Clement had been humbly – and no doubt, apprehensively – waiting for him there since 25 October. The two men then remained together for four months until early March: the coronations were celebrated on 22 and 24 February 1530.[2]

It was against this background that the opening sessions of the new Parliament took place in London. It fell to Sir Thomas More, as Lord Chancellor, to open the Parliament and he defined its purposes as being to address the problems created by the growth of religious dissent and by the discovery of Wolsey's corruption. But even More was unable to avoid the conclusion that the king's 'Great Matter' would inevitably become part of the Parliament's business. For all that, the initial proceedings of the Parliament seemed innocuous enough. Thomas Audley, More's successor as Speaker, established committees to look into vexatious questions such as the levying by the clergy of mortuary fees for burying the dead.[3] These were often small issues but taken together they soon began to amount to a significant political programme which was designed to intimidate the Church in general and those churchmen in particular who opposed Henry over his remarriage.[4] Certainly, the Parliament that opened with such modest beginnings was to have the most momentous consequences; by the time that it closed in April 1536 Katharine had been divorced by Henry and England had detached itself from communion with the Roman Catholic Church – and both Katharine and Anne Boleyn were dead.

The fears that Clement had as to Charles's intentions were surely confirmed when at 10.00 p.m. on Friday 5 November the Emperor-elect made his formal entry into Bologna. Charles had arranged for the city to be splendidly decorated with triumphal arches and equestrian statues of classical soldiers and of Constantine and Charlemagne, the iconic forbears upon whom he modelled himself. Charles was accompanied by an enormous entourage that included hundreds of councillors, courtiers, and leading nobles from his different realms. However, courtly glitter was overwhelmed by the very bluntest manifestation of Charles's military power – 4,000 footsoldiers (among them contingents of Spanish infantry and the dreaded landsknechts who had sacked Rome), 800 cavalry and the baggage-train of an army, including ten pieces of artillery, followed the Emperor-elect. Charles himself was mounted on a dapple-grey horse and was dressed in full armour saving only that he wore a black cloth cap on his head instead of his helmet and carried a sceptre in his hand. No one present – least of all Pope Clement – could have misunderstood the belligerent symbolism of Charles's representation of self: he had come to Bologna as a military conqueror, judge and ruler.[5]

Clement, wearing his papal tiara, greeted Charles in front of the church of San Petronio and the Emperor-elect dismounted, knelt and kissed the

Pope's foot and then his hand. Clement reciprocated by kissing Charles on the cheek. Charles then made a short address, to which Clement replied and they entered the Church where they prayed together. They left hand in hand: they had affected their public reconciliation.

It had been Charles's intention to stay in Italy for only a few weeks before travelling to Germany to help his brother Ferdinand resist the Turkish advance and deal with the problems of the Reformation. But as he and Clement settled down in Bologna they heard that the Turkish siege of Vienna had been lifted. The news freed Charles to prolong his stay in Italy: that, too, had implications for Henry VIII.

Charles now imposed settlements on the rulers of Florence, Venice and Milan. Florence had entered the League of Cognac against Charles and had assisted the French invasion of Naples in 1528. Charles fully intended to punish the city and it will be recalled that under the terms of the Treaty of Barcelona of June 1529 he had agreed with Clement VII that the Medici should be restored to control of Florence as dukes of the city. For ten months, Florence held out against a siege by the imperial army but was obliged to capitulate in August 1530: at the insistence of the Pope, the great city was spared the horrors of a sack. The Medici were duly returned to power as Alessandro de' Medici became Duke of Florence. At the same time, Charles made a settlement with Venice and agreed to restore Francesco Sforza as Duke of Milan and to invest him with the dukedom. There was no doubt now that the Medici in Florence and the Sforza in Milan owed their titles to Charles V. He truly was the master of Italy.

Charles had received the first of his imperial crowns as King of the Romans at Aachen in October 1520. On 22 February 1530 (the feast of the Throne of St Peter) Clement VII celebrated Mass in the church of San Petronio, which was dressed in imitation of St Peter's itself; Charles knelt before the Pope as the iron crown of the ancient Kingdom of Lombardy was placed on his head and he was presented with a ring to symbolise his marriage to the Kingdom. To the curiously appropriate chorus of trumpet blasts and the thunderous crashing of artillery Charles was then publicly proclaimed King of Lombardy.

Two days later Clement VII conferred the imperial crown upon Charles, again in the church of San Petronio. The day was chosen with fastidious care: it was at once Charles's thirtieth birthday and the fifth anniversary of the Battle of Pavia. Once again, the air was heavy with the presence of military power: Charles's Spanish and Germany infantry were drawn up in battle formation outside the church. Inside, twenty-four cardinals lent their tremulous support to the Pope. After Clement had celebrated Mass he presented Charles with a sword, sceptre and orb and consecrated him with oil.[6] It had been eleven years since Charles had been elected to the imperial throne but only now could he lawfully assume the title of Holy Roman Emperor and nominate his successor as King of the Romans. Charles left Bologna on 21 March 1530 to travel to Germany, where on 5 January 1531 Ferdinand was duly elected as King of the Romans; he was crowned at Aachen on 11 January.[7]

Charles's coronations at Bologna in 1530 and Ferdinand's at Aachen in 1531 reshaped the structure of European politics, making it evident that the two great inheritances that Charles had received of the Spanish crowns (1516) and the imperial crown (1519) would be separated in the next generation; the former would pass through Charles's male line while the latter would descend through Ferdinand's. As for Charles: he was profoundly satisfied that he was at last the Holy Roman Emperor. He was now unambiguously the leading statesman of Europe and the heir to the Caesars: henceforth he styled himself 'Caesar'.[8] But while his status as Emperor endured his power did not, for it was always the case that as Charles's power grew the rival princes of Europe princes allied against him to reduce his strength.

While Charles gloried in his overdue coronations and made his plans to reshape Europe he had also to deal with an embassy from Henry VIII whose composition was so extraordinary as to be almost literally unbelievable. It was natural enough that Henry should have sent a diplomatic mission to Bologna to congratulate Charles on his coronations and it made good sense for the English diplomats to urge Clement and Charles to find a settlement for Henry's 'Great Matter'. So far, so good: but it quite transcended any diplomatic sense to entrust the mission to the father of Anne Boleyn! This, however, is what Henry did: his reasoning is frankly inexplicable. Thomas Boleyn, newly ennobled as Earl of Wiltshire was, in truth, a reasonably experienced diplomat; he had served on missions to the Low Countries and France (1512, 1518, 1521 and 1527). But on 20 January 1530 – the day before his departure from England – Henry raised him to the dignity of Lord Privy Seal to make it evident that he was now his senior minister. Charles and Clement could only have been profoundly insulted by being required to negotiate with the father of the woman with whom Henry intended to replace Katharine. In the event it did not matter overmuch, for Wiltshire arrived in Bologna on

14 March, three weeks after Charles had been crowned as Holy Roman Emperor and one week after Pope Clement had taken what appeared to be a decisive decision in his dispute with Henry VIII.

Wiltshire brought with him his own son, George, Viscount Rochford; Edward Lee, a crown lawyer and classical scholar who had helped Erasmus in revising his New Testament; Thomas Cranmer, who was to go on to Rome to liaise with Edward Carne and Girolamo Ghinucci (who were resident in the city as Henry's agents) to press Henry's case. Carne, as *excusator*, was charged with arguing that Henry could under no circumstances be summoned to Rome while Ghinucci served – as so often – as a general factotum, liaising between Englishmen and Italians.[9]

On 7 March 1530 Clement at last acted in the case of Henry and Katharine: true, he was not yet ready to announce his verdict on the legitimacy or otherwise of the marriage between them but he now authorised a papal bull which commanded Henry not to marry another woman until that sentence was pronounced and enjoined him to continue to treat Katharine with all the rights and privileges due to his lawful wife. This was a most solemn command by Pope Clement, for if Henry failed to do as instructed, he and his councillors were to be excommunicated and England was to be placed under interdict, thereby freeing all Englishmen from their loyalty to the king. Appreciating that Henry might well be able to prevent the bull from being brought into England, the Pope ordered that it was to be affixed to church doors in Rome and in three towns near England (Dunkirk, Bruges, Tournai) and on all the church doors of the diocese of Thérouanne: in this way it would undoubtedly become known in England. A second brief was drawn up at the same time, and this one was authorised by the Pope and his cardinals; it appears to have restated the injunctions and the penalties but it seems to have been buried by the papal bureaucracy and was apparently never despatched.[10]

A fortnight after Clement had drawn up the bull of 7 March he authorised another bull which was aimed at nullifying the pan-European debate about the legitimacy of Henry's marriage: on 21 March he informed Katharine that he had that day issued a bull which forbade all churchmen, notaries and advocates from speaking or writing against the validity of her marriage to Henry until he had issued his verdict. Anyone doing so was to be excommunicated.[11] Between 7 and 21 March 1530, therefore, Pope Clement at last took some positive actions in Henry VIII's 'Great Matter'. Or so it appeared. On 21 March, Charles V left Bologna, content no doubt that he had kept his promise to his aunt that he would oblige the Pope to act decisively in support of her.

It can have surprised none of the parties that Wiltshire's negotiations in Bologna were unproductive. Gloomily, he reported to Henry that the Pope 'is led by the Emperor, so that he neither will nor dare displease him'. Charles was openly contemptuous of the earl and had several angry exchanges with him but his most important words were pristine enough, for they bound him to support whatever decision Clement made – 'if the marriage with his aunt be found to be null, he will not maintain it, but if it is pronounced valid, he will'. But Charles also added that if the Pope decided against Henry he would be prepared to take such actions as he could to enforce his decision. The implication was clear: the Emperor would, if necessary, go to war with Henry to defend his aunt's honour.[12] Time would show that this was a promise that would be more readily made than acted upon – more empty words in support of Katharine.

Worse still for Henry: in Bologna, Katharine's representative had the exquisite audacity to serve a summons on Wiltshire which obliged Henry to appear at Rome for the trial of his marriage. Henry had thus far contrived to avoid being served with such papers and Wiltshire's guard evidently slipped in allowing himself to be presented with the writ. He complained to the Pope that his king should not have been summoned in this manner and it was reluctantly agreed – yet another timewasting device by Clement! – that a moratorium of six months should take place before the injunction became operative.[13]

Clement then conjured up yet another delay. Mindful no doubt of the inadequacies of Julius II's brief of 1503 he set up a commission of four senior churchmen to check his own bulls word by word to ensure that they were canonically and legally watertight before he despatched them. Tellingly, he included Cardinal Campeggio among the judges.[14] It is not known what recommendations the four men made but Clement decided not to despatch the bulls. He had not, after all, taken any action in Henry VIII's 'Great Matter'.

It may have been as an alternative to sending his bulls that Clement appointed a new nuncio to represent him in England: Antonio de Pulleo, Baron del Borgho in Sicily, arrived at London on 14 September 1530 but did not bring the papal bulls with him.[15] He met the king two days later and proposed that the case should be resolved by two judges named by Henry and Katharine. Henry was not satisfied and they discussed whether each side in the dispute might more properly nominate two judges. Del Borgho then suggested that the Pope should appoint a fifth judge, but knowing that this would give Katharine an in-built advantage Henry suggested that his good friend and ally Francis I should make the fifth nomination. While Henry and del Borgho argued over theoretical abstractions, the papal bull of 7 March effectively ceased to exist.

One other decision was taken (or confirmed) at Bologna by Charles and Clement: the two French princes were released from their imprisonment in Madrid. They crossed back into France on 1 July and – another coincidence! – on the following day the Faculty of Theology of the Sorbonne declared in favour of Henry VIII and against the Pope. Francis's leading diplomat, Jean du Bellay, had in April foreseen the significance of the dual events for Henry: 'If the King of England sees the princes [arrive] in France and ... has [the verdict] of the University of Paris ... I think he will marry immediately.'[16] That did not prove to be the case but the two events did foreshadow the creation of a new Anglo–French alliance against Charles V.

Henry did the best he could to apply pressure on Clement VII. He fastidiously demonstrated both his religious orthodoxy and his political power within England in a co-ordinated attempt to convince the Pope that he should come to terms with him: in May 1530 he summoned several bishops and representatives of Oxford and Cambridge universities to Westminster to discuss the nature of heresy and at the same time convened a meeting of the great men of his realm, lay and clerical, ordering them to bring their seals of office with them to London.

The notables of church and state arrived in Westminster on 12 June to find a draft letter to the Pope awaiting their signatures: it urged Clement to recognise the justice of Henry's claim that his marriage was unlawful and to allow the case to be judged in England. Attached to it already were the seals of both archbishops, four bishops, twenty-five abbots, two dukes, forty other lay peers and a dozen less important men. Many were outraged by the contents of the letter and a delay of a few days took place while it was redrafted to accommodate the more obvious objections. It was then taken round to the house of each notable and they were invited to sign it and attach their seals to it. By 13 July the great missive was ready for despatch.[17] The document must indeed have been as heavy as it was splendid for it carried the seals of all the signatories. It was divided into thirteen columns by rank and was in effect a roll-call of England's courtly and ecclesiastical elite. It was headed by the two archbishops, so that somewhat enigmatically Thomas Wolsey took the leading place; the archiepiscopal signatures were followed by those of the dukes of Norfolk and Suffolk and the marquises, bishops, barons and abbots and doctors of law of the realm. Impressive though the great clanking document was, Clement remained unmoved: he insisted that he would do his duty and that the threats in the letter addressed to him were unworthy of the seals attached to it.[18]

Royal Rages: The Responses of Henry & Katharine to Clement's Bulls of March 1530

Both Henry and Katharine were furious with Pope Clement as they learned of the existence of his three bulls of March 1530. Henry led the way in rebuking the Pope but when Katharine learned towards the end of 1530 that the Pope had not despatched his bulls her response was immeasurably more aggressive than Henry's had been: indeed, it was as contemptuous of the Pope as it was ferocious.

Henry wrote first, on 6 December.[19] He professed himself unable to believe that Clement had denied his request to have the case tried in England and learnedly quoted saints Cyprian and Bernard to support his argument that a dispute should be resolved in its place of origin. He complained that Clement had rejected the reasonable requests made to him by himself and his nobility and had ignored the mediatory efforts of Francis I. For good measure, Henry insulted Clement by insisting that he was wholly devoted to the Emperor's will. As for himself, Henry wrote that he 'abhorred' contention but that he would not 'brook denial'.

It is not clear how or when Katharine heard that the Pope had issued a bull enjoining her husband to return to her but had failed to despatch it. Certainly, once she learned of the existence of the bull of 7 March she must have hoped that Henry would obey the Pope but as she realised that the precious document had not even been sent her pent-up resentment of Clement VII turned to fury: on 17 December 1530 she wrote a letter to him that burned with almost uncontainable rage, accusing the pontiff of dereliction of duty and demanding that he fulfil the obligations that his office placed upon him of giving sentence in her case. But even as Katharine gave the fullest expression of her rage at the way in which she had been treated by the Pope she wrote, too, of her conviction that she could yet win Henry back if only he could be persuaded to live with her again:

Most Holy Father

The great need in which my troubled affairs stand require Your Holiness's redress and help (upon which the service of God and my own repose and the salvation of my soul, as well as that of the king, my Lord, depend). This obliges me to implore Your Holiness that I may be heard on that very account.

Even had I an ordinary claim to ask what I have so long and so fervently prayed for, and so frequently urged, how much more is it now evident that the justice of my cause is so great before God, who knows my perfect sincerity and innocence. I trust that Your Holiness will see that God, in His great mercy, wishes that the decision be published.

I believe that Your Holiness well understands that there is no learned or conscientious person acknowledging the power and authority of the Apostolic See who does not agree and maintain that the marriage between the King, my Lord, and me is indissoluble, since God alone can separate us. I cannot then do less than complain that my petitions ... should have been so long disregarded by Your Holiness.

One thing alone that comforts me in the midst of my tribulations, is to believe that God wishes to punish me for my sins in this world, and that therefore Your Holiness, His vicar on earth, will not forgive me. I humbly beg Your Holiness to have pity on me and accept as though I had been in Purgatory the penance I have already endured for so many years, thus delivering me from the pains, torments and sudden fears to which I am daily exposed and which are so great and so numerous that I could not possibly bear them had not God given me strength to endure ... I am convinced that God, in whom all my hopes are concentrated, will not abandon me in this cause in which justice is so obviously with me.

The remedy lies in [issuing] the sentence and determination of my case without any delay. Any other course short of that will do more harm than good, as appears quite evident from the evils which the delay has already produced. Should the sentence be further deferred, Your Holiness will appreciate that the delay will be the cause of a new hell [upon earth], the remedy for which will entail more disastrous measures than have ever yet been tried.

I have been informed that my enemies demand a new delay. I beg Your Holiness not to grant it to them, for in doing so, the greatest possible injury will be done to me, convinced as I am that everything proposed [by those people] is for the worst, as it might come to pass justice would suffer through it, and that from the Purgatory in which I now find myself I should be cast down into a temporal hell, from the bottom of which I should be continually raising my voice to God and complaining of the tiny amount of pity and mercy that Your Holiness has granted me.

Again I beg and entreat Your Holiness not to allow any further delays in this trial but immediately to pronounce full sentence in the most expeditious way. Until this is done I shall not cease begging Your Holiness, as did the Samaritan woman to Jesus Christ, on whom her remedy depended.

Some days ago Miçer [Miguel] Mai, the ambassador of his Imperial Majesty [in Rome] and my solicitor in this case wrote to say that Your Holiness had promised him to renew the brief which Your Holiness issued at Bologna and another one commanding the king my Lord to dismiss and cast away from him this woman with whom he lives. On hearing this, these 'good people' who have placed and still keep the King, my Lord, in this awkward position, began to give way, considering themselves lost. May God forgive whoever it was who was the cause of the briefs not being delivered, for the news of the preparation alone introduced a most marked improvement in my case; besides which, had the potion, though disagreeable to their mouths, been administered at the right time, that which I hope Your Holiness keeps in store for them would have been comparatively sweet.

I am, therefore, deeply grieved at the injury which was inflicted upon me by the withdrawal of the promised briefs but I bear all this with patience waiting for the remedy to the evils of which I complain. This can be no other, I repeat, than the sentence that I am expecting every day and hour.

One thing I should like Your Highness to be aware of, namely that my plea is not against the king, my Lord, but against the inventors and abettors of this cause. I trust so much in the natural goodness and virtues of the king, my Lord, that if I could only have him two months with me, as he used to be, I alone should be powerful enough to make him forget the past; but as they know this to be true they do not let him live with me.

These are my real enemies who wage such constant war against me; some of them [intending] that the bad advice they gave the king should not become public, though they have already been well paid for it, and others that they may rob and plunder as much as they can, thus endangering the estate of the king, my Lord, to the risk of his honour and the eternal perdition of his soul. These are the people from whom spring the threats and bravadoes preferred against Your Holiness, they are the sole inventors of them, not the king, my Lord. It is, therefore, urgent that Your Holiness put a very strong bit in their mouths, which is no other than the sentence.

With that the tongues of the bad counsellors will be stopped and their hope of mischief vanish; the greedy thieves will no longer devour him on whom they have been feeding all this time; they will set him at liberty, and he will become as dutiful a son of Your Holiness as he was in former times. This to me would be the greatest charity that ever Your Holiness bestowed on a human being; it will restore peace and happiness among the Christian princes, and set a good example to the whole of Christendom.[20]

Unknown to Katharine, Rome was already responding with unwonted alacrity. Henry's letter of 6 December clearly travelled at express speed for it reached the Vatican in time to be among the items considered in a secret Consistory of Cardinals on 23 December, together with four petitions put forward by Katharine's proctor.[21] Katharine had asked that a papal inhibition be issued forbidding the Archbishop of Canterbury from sitting in judgement on her marriage because it had already been expressly reserved for the decision of the College of Cardinals. She had also invited Clement to restate all the inhibitions directed to the bishops of England so that they too were forbidden to judge her case. Katharine also urged Clement to prohibit any woman 'and especially a certain Lady Anne' from contracting marriage with Henry. After long deliberations the Consistory of Cardinals decided that all of her petitions were justifiable in law and that the briefs should be granted: the English bishops were not to sit in judgement and Anne Boleyn was not to go through a marriage ceremony with Henry VIII. As we have seen, Clement responded on 7 January 1531 to Henry's letter of 6 December, rejecting his insistence that the case be tried in England (chapter 13).[22]

Almost before his letter had reached London, Clement had cause to write to Henry again, on 25 January.[23] Now it was his turn to express incredulity, for he had learned that Henry had sent Katharine away from court and was living openly with Anne. Clement professed that he simply could not believe this news and urged Henry to understand how scandalous his conduct was. Reminding Henry that he had previously regarded him as the Church's most zealous defender, Clement remonstrated with him as 'a loving father', urging him to take Katharine back and send Anne away from court: if he did not do so, he would be obliged issue a judgement against him. No doubt the pontiff reflected privately on his failure to despatch the bull of 7 March which had required Henry under threat of the dread penalties of excommunication and interdict to renounce Anne and take Katharine back as his lawful wife while awaiting his final sentence. The Pope had let the king off the hook.

The Royal Family: Henry, Katharine & Princess Mary, 1530–32
Continuing Affection

It was poignant that in the summer of 1530 Henry could still conduct his relations with Katharine with some residual affection, at least in public. In June Agustino Scarpinello, a Venetian resident in London, reported on the painful ambiguities of the positions in which Henry and Katharine found themselves:

> The queen also is with his Majesty, and they pay each other reciprocally the greatest possible attention, or compliments, in the Spanish fashion with the utmost mental tranquillity, as if there had never been any dispute whatever between them; yet has the affair not slackened in the least, although at this present but little is being done here, as both parties are collecting votes, in France, Italy, and several other places but it is not yet known with what success.
>
> At any rate, this most virtuous queen maintains strenuously, that all her king and lord does, is done by him for true and pure conscience's sake, and not from any wanton appetite.[24]

At the end of the year Scarpinello sent a very similar report:

> His Majesty is still at Hampton Court, enjoying his usual sports and royal exercises, and the queen remains constantly with him, nor does she at all omit to follow her lord and husband, so much reciprocal courtesy being displayed in public that anyone acquainted with the controversy cannot but consider their conduct more than human.[25]

Henry also allowed Katharine and Mary to spend five or six days together at Richmond and even gave Chapuys permission to visit them. But while he continued to display warmth to his wife in public he was indulging Anne more than ever, even indeed beginning to flaunt her at court: Anne had recently ridden pillion on his horse when they came to London from Windsor – an explicit public display of their closeness that drew much adverse comment.[26] Katharine did the best she could, urging Chapuys to have Charles persuade the Pope to insist that Henry separate himself from Anne while the case was being judged (not knowing of course that on 7 March Pope Clement had drawn up his brief for that purpose). Sadly, Katharine continued to assert that if Henry and Anne were kept apart for only a month she could win the king back.[27]

For her part, Anne was by the turn of 1530–31 becoming confident enough of the strength of her position to become more strident: in November 1530 she even dared to threaten that she would leave Henry and in an intriguingly ambiguous outburst regretted 'her lost time': was this an allusion to the passing of her childbearing opportunities – a suggestion that (as George Bernard has argued) Anne and Henry were currently abstaining from sexual intercourse precisely so that she should not become pregnant and destroy the king's reputation at Rome – or risk producing a child whose illegitimacy would necessarily disbar him or her from succeeding to the throne?[28] On New Year's Day 1531 Chapuys reported that he had heard that Henry and Anne would marry during the current Parliament and recorded her expressing sentiments that in others might have been taken as treasonable:

> The Lady feels assured of it. She is braver than a lion. She said to one of the queen's ladies that she wished all the Spaniards in the world were in the sea; and on the other replying that, for the honour of the queen she should not say this, she said that she did not care anything for the queen, and would rather see her hanged than acknowledge her as her mistress.[29]

Anne's welling self-confidence was of course devastating for Katharine and observers at court noted that the queen was beginning to crumble under the pressure with which she had now lived for years; in April 1531 Scarpinello reported that she was very ill 'from what the physicians call hysteria'.[30] Lodovico Falier, the Venetian ambassador in London, was more generous; in November 1531 he wrote descriptions of the royal couple in which he portrayed a king who was at the height of his physical and intellectual powers and a queen who, although showing the signs of age, remained greatly loved by the people of England. He did not comment on any signs of mental fragility in the queen:

In this eighth Henry, God combined such corporal and mental beauty, as not merely to surprise but to astound all men. Who could fail to be struck with admiration on perceiving the lofty position of so glorious a Prince to be in such accordance with his stature, giving manifest proof of that intrinsic mental superiority which is inherent to him.

His face is angelic rather than handsome; his head imperial and bald, and he wears a beard, contrary to English custom. Who would not be amazed when contemplating such singular corporal beauty, coupled with such bold address, adapting itself with the greatest ease to every manly exercise.

He sits his horse well, and manages him yet better; he jousts and wields his spear, throws the quoit, and draws the bow, admirably; plays at tennis most dexterously; and nature having endowed him in youth with such gifts, he was not slow to enhance, preserve, and augment them with all industry and labour. It seeming to him monstrous for a prince not to cultivate moral and intellectual excellence, so from childhood he applied himself to grammatical studies, and then to philosophy and holy writ, thus obtaining the reputation of a lettered and excellent prince. Besides Latin and his native tongue, he learned Spanish, French, and Italian. He is kind and affable, full of graciousness and courtesy and liberal; particularly so to men of knowledge, whom he is never weary of obliging.

Although always intelligent and judicious, he nevertheless allowed himself to be so allured by his pleasures, that, accustomed to ease, he for many years left the administration of the government to his ministers, well nigh until the persecution [*sc.* dismissal] of Cardinal Wolsey; but from that time forth he took such delight in his own rule, that from liberal he became avaricious, and whereas heretofore no one departed from his majesty without being well rewarded, so now all quit his presence dissatisfied.

He appears to be religious; he usually hears two daily masses, and on holy days [he hears] high mass likewise. He gives many alms, relieving paupers, orphans, widows and cripples; his almoner disburses annually 10,000 golden ducats for this purpose.

The queen is of low stature, rather stout, with a modest countenance; she is virtuous, just, replete with goodness and religion; she speaks Spanish, Flemish, French, and English; she is beloved by the islanders more than any queen that ever reigned; she is about forty-five years old, having lived thirty years in England, from the time of her first marriage...

[Princess Mary] is sixteen years old; a handsome, amiable, and very accomplished princess, in no respect inferior to her mother.[31]

Mario Savorgnano, an Italian naval commander who was visiting England, also wrote lengthy descriptions of Henry and Katharine and their daughter in the late summer of 1531:[32]

I saw the king twice, and kissed his hand; he is glad to see foreigners, and especially Italians; [he] embraced me joyously, and then went out to hunt with forty to fifty horsemen. He is tall of stature, very well formed, and of very handsome presence, beyond measure affable, and I never saw a prince better disposed than this one.

He is also learned and accomplished, and most generous and kind, and were it not that he now seeks to repudiate his wife, after having lived with her for twenty-two years, he would be no less perfectly good, and equally prudent. But this thing detracts greatly from his merits, as there is now living with him a young woman of noble birth, though many say of bad character, whose will is law to him, and he is expected to marry her, should the divorce take place, which it is supposed will not be brought about, as the peers of the realm, both spiritual and temporal, and the people are opposed to it; nor during the present queen's life will they have any other queen in the kingdom.

Her Majesty is prudent and good; and during these differences with the king she has evinced constancy and resolution, never being disheartened or depressed ... Her Majesty is not of tall stature, rather small. If not handsome she is not ugly; she is somewhat stout, and has always a smile on her countenance.

This princess is not very tall, has a pretty face, and is well proportioned, with a very beautiful complexion, and is fifteen years old. She speaks Spanish, French, and Latin, besides her own mother-

English tongue, is well grounded in Greek, and understands Italian, but does not venture to speak it. She sings excellently, and plays on several instruments, so that she combines every accomplishment.

The princess is much loved by her father, who does not make any demonstration against the queen – and always treats her with respect, and occasionally dines with her.

Henry and Katharine had traditionally sent each other messages every third day. In late July 1531, Katharine enquired of the king's health and expressed her regret at not having been able to see him before he left for the country; she would have hoped to have accompanied him or at least to have been allowed to have wished him farewell on his departure. Henry replied angrily that he cared not for Katharine's farewells and was indifferent as to whether she enquired after his health or not, complaining that she had caused him so much annoyance and sorrow in a thousand ways, most especially by having him summoned to Rome. She was in future to refrain from sending him messages or emissaries. Katharine responded that she had done nothing to deserve the king's anger and that everything she had undertaken had been with his approval and permission.

Henry consulted with members of the Privy Council before he composed his reply. He rejected Katharine's claim that she had not known Arthur carnally and insisted that he would be able to prove this by bringing witnesses (although he did not apparently make it evident what these witnesses had seen). Accordingly, Julius II had had no right to approve of their marriage. Katharine would do better to find people who could prove her alleged virginity at the time of her marriage to him rather than of simply talking about it to whoever would listen to her and sending messages and letters to him. He strongly advised her to discontinue the practice. Intriguingly, the letter bore no address because even after the king and his senior councillors had spent three days discussing the matter they were unable to formulate a title by which Katharine was to be addressed: was Katharine still 'Queen of England'?[33]

*

As Mario Savorgnano wrote, Princess Mary was, at the age of fifteen, a highly educated young woman.[34] Henry and Katharine had both taken a keen interest in her education and had ensured that she was guided by experienced and trustworthy people. In May 1520 Margaret Pole was appointed as governess to the princess and although she was removed in 1521 when her sons were suspected of involvement with the treason of the Duke of Buckingham, she was reinstated in 1525. Katharine, who had known Margaret since her arrival in England, trusted her completely and it is reasonable to assume that hers was the decisive influence in her appointment for Henry was inveterately suspicious of the Pole family.[35]

Henry and Katharine also took joint responsibility for appointing Thomas Linacre and Juan Luis Vives as the princess's tutors. The two men were from very contrasting backgrounds but both were imbued with humanist principles of educational theory; indeed both were friends of Erasmus and More. Linacre was a polymath who had earned a doctorate in Medicine at the University of Padua and become physician to Henry VIII and Thomas Wolsey. He used some of the wealth that he earned through his medical practice to establish chairs in Greek Medicine at Oxford and Cambridge Universities and to become co-founder of the Royal College of Physicians.[36] Vives was a Valencian intellectual of *converso* blood who may have fled Spain to escape the Inquisition; he had studied at the universities of Paris and Louvain and was presented by Wolsey with a lectureship in Latin, Greek and Rhetoric at Corpus Christi College, Oxford. In 1523, Henry and Katharine invited him to spend Christmas with them at Windsor Castle and it was presumably with their encouragement that he produced with Richard Fetherstone, a Cambridge academic, a manual for the teaching of young children (*De ratione studii puerilis*, 'A Plan of Childish Studies'). This encouraged the princess to undertake Biblical exegetical and patristic studies and to master classical languages. Mary was an enthusiastic and able student: it was said that by the time she was twelve she could translate any Latin text into English.

Like many royal siblings Mary went through a series of engagements to be married; it will be recalled that she was successively betrothed to Francis I's heir (October 1518) and to Charles V (September 1521). When Charles rejected her in 1525–26 in favour of Isabella of Portugal she was sent to Ludlow, ostensibly to supervise the government of the Marches and Wales but in reality to separate her from her mother as a punishment for Katharine for opposing Henry over his remarriage (chapter 13). In 1527 she was reinstated into her father's favour and engaged once again to a Frenchman, although it was uncertain whether it was to be Francis I or his son Henri that she would marry.

*Intimidation – and the Breach Between Henry & Katharine, Summer–
Autumn 1531*[37]

At the beginning of June 1531 a delegation of no fewer than thirty
senior servants of the king arrived at Katharine's temporary home in
Easthampstead at about nine in the evening just as the queen was going
to bed. The delegation was led by the dukes of Norfolk and Suffolk, the
Marquis of Dorset and the earls of Northumberland, Wiltshire and several
other noblemen. They were accompanied by an array of churchmen –
John Langland bishop of Lincoln and John Stokesley, Bishop of London
and Doctors Lee, Sampson and Stephen Gardiner. The power of State and
Church was to be brought to bear on the queen: the delegation numbered
senior courtiers who were close to the king as well as canon and civil
lawyers. Their intention was simple enough – to overwhelm Katharine in
her isolation and tiredness by bringing the fullest range of arguments in
canon law and national law and polity as to why she should give way to
Henry and facilitate his annulment of their marriage. They brought two
specific complaints from Henry – that Katharine had lived with Arthur as
his wife and had sexual relations with him; and that she had humiliated
Henry by having him summoned to appear at court in Rome.

Katharine was indeed weary but it is evident that she had been informed
in advance of arrival of the ministers and of their purposes. Once again,
a scene that had been carefully created to intimidate the queen served
only to provide her with a platform on which she performed with – as
appeared – utter fearlessness. Henry should have learned at Blackfriars
in 1529 that Katharine was a master-player of set-piece drama: alone,
without counsel, and weary at the end of the day she faced down the
grand royal delegation as, two years earlier, she had faced down Henry,
Campeggio and Wolsey at the legatine court.

Norfolk opened proceedings by informing Katharine that he and his
colleagues had come from the king on matters of great importance to
him and his kingdom and that they had brought with them the verdicts
of European universities: he did not need to remind Katharine that
these had gone against her. The king was deeply angered at having been
summoned to appear in Rome; nothing would induce him to leave his
kingdom unless he chose to do so, especially because he was supreme
and sovereign in his own realm in matters temporal and spiritual, as had
recently been recognized by Parliament and the clergy. Accordingly, in
the name of the king, the delegation formally required that Katharine
should abandon the appeal to Rome and allow impartial judges to hear

her case in England: if she did not do so, the Kingdom of England itself might be at risk. Norfolk reminded Katharine that she had always been treated as honourably as any Queen of England and could have no cause for complaint, adding – not altogether relevantly – that England had even helped her father to conquer Navarre and her nephew to defeat the *comuneros*.

Katharine's response was rooted in a matter of which her visitors could know nothing – 'I say I am his lawful wife and to him lawfully married' – and that the king himself well knew that she had come to him a virgin. She insisted that no one regretted more than she the situation into which the king had been placed but he himself was the chief cause of it. She could not believe that her proctors in Rome asked for unjust terms and insisted that the Pope was the only legitimate judge in a case such as her's. She did not expect any favours from the Pope, who had indeed been much more partial to the king than to her and had done her many injuries. But then Katharine drew back in her criticism of the Pope: remembering how carefully she had to speak, she added that she had no reason to complain of His Holiness. It was the king who had in the first case appealed to the Pope; for her part, she had followed the path of truth and justice. Those who had led the king astray should look to their consciences. She knew that Charles V was Henry's good and sincere friend and for her own part she acknowledged the king as her sovereign and was ready to serve and obey him. But the Pope was the Vicar of Christ, and he alone could judge her case.

In what was clearly a co-ordinated strategy individual members of the delegation then addressed the issues involved in the case as the king saw them. Dr Lee, Henry's almoner, stated that since Katharine had been known carnally by Arthur her marriage to his brother was a detestable and abominable act: he thereby made it evident that Henry retained his belief that he was being punished by God with childlessness because he had married his brother's widow – that Henry held steadfastly to his interpretation of the teaching in the Book of Leviticus. Katharine witheringly dismissed Lee as a man who was flattering the king rather than concerning himself with the truth. She declared that she had never had carnal relations with Arthur and was not prepared to discuss the matter further: if Dr Lee wished to do so he should go to Rome, where he would deal not with a woman but with learned men who would demonstrate to him that he had not even read everything on the subject.

Dr Sampson, Dean of the Royal Chapel, accused the queen in effect of *lèse-majesté* in insisting that the case be tried in Rome. He pointed out that even if Katharine won her case, the verdict would be overturned on appeal and so it was sensible to have the case tried outside Rome. Katharine contemptuously dismissed Simpson's arguments, noting that he had no knowledge of the sufferings that she had endured since the beginning of the process and suggesting that had he done so he would have tried to secure the verdict in the way that she had done. As for the theological technicalities of the case, she imperiously suggested that Sampson could profitably travel to Rome with Dr Lee and there discuss the matter to his heart's content with people who knew what they were talking about.

John Longland, Bishop of Lincoln, struck nearer home, reminding Katharine that proof existed that she had indeed slept with Arthur and therefore had in effect subsequently lived in concubinage – he did not mention with whom! – and had been punished by God for her sins with sterility. Katharine reminded the bishop that she had taken an oath under the seal of the confessional in front of Cardinal Campeggio that she had never had sexual relations with Arthur. She went on to affirm that she loved and esteemed King Henry as much as any woman could love a man and would never have lived one moment with him against her conscience: she knew perfectly well that she was his true and lawful wife and that evidence to the contrary was forged.

Dr Stokesley spoke in general terms and his accusation was properly rooted in canon law, stating – quite correctly – that the fact that Katharine had lived for a length of time under the same roof as the prince and shared his bed would be sufficient in a court of law to establish that she had been fully and properly married to him. This advice was very close to the position taken by the imperial ambassadors López de Mendoza and Chapuys but Katharine again swept the charge aside, insisting that she was concerned only with truth. As to his understanding of the laws of the Church: Dr Stokesley too could go to Rome and submit his allegations there to the judgement of men who knew what they were talking about. Was the queen enjoying herself at the expense of her inquisitors?

Katharine then rebuked her visitors as a group, saying how surprised she was that so many men of such power and influence should have called unannounced on her at such an hour. She was a poor woman without friends or counsel. Norfolk replied that, to the contrary, she had the most able counsel in all England – the Archbishop of Canterbury, the bishops of Durham and Rochester and others. Katharine scornfully waved the objection aside: when she asked the archbishop's advice he insisted that he wanted to have nothing to do with her case, while Durham insisted that he was the king's loyal subject and Rochester merely told her to be brave and hope for the best. The other lawyers appointed to argue her case had been equally bland and so she had to send to Flanders for lawyers as no one in England would dare act on her behalf.

The Earl of Wiltshire, father of Anne Boleyn, objected – naturally enough in the circumstances! – that the king had been summoned to appear personally in Rome. Katharine insisted that she had never asked for this to happen and that if it was a necessary by-product of the appeal being heard in Rome then the responsibility was not hers. When the delegation left, Katharine could feel that she had overwhelmed the ministers: their mission had been an abject failure.

Norfolk and Suffolk drew up an account of the interview for Henry and reported that Katharine was prepared to obey in him all things but that she owed prior obligations to two persons. Henry imagined that they meant the Pope and Emperor and Norfolk replied that 'God was the first; the second her soul and conscience, which the queen said she would not lose for anything in this world': Henry made no reply.

The king was, however, furious with the ministers who had failed him and the wife who had resisted him: he summoned Katharine back to court so that he could make one last personal effort to persuade her of the legitimacy of his case where his great delegation had failed. The couple met in an atmosphere of mutual rage on 14 July 1531. Henry complained that Katharine had offended in him a thousand or more ways, most especially by humiliating him in the eyes of Europe by having him summoned to appear at Rome. Somewhat more prosaically, Katharine protested that he had refused to see her before he left on his summer's hunting trip. Henry suggested that they should abandon their habit of communicating with each other every third day and stormed off to go on his summer's hunting progress. He and Katharine almost certainly never met again.[38]

About a fortnight later, Henry ordered Katharine and her daughter away from court and into internal exile: Katharine was to live at Wolsey's old house of the More, near St Albans, and Princess Mary at Richmond. Henry was of course entitled to exclude from his court anyone he wished – such was, indeed, one of the points of definition of life at court. But to exile his wife from his presence was a deeply serious matter in canon law that was likely to call ecclesiastical sanction down on the king's head, for it was in effect to bring about a quasi-divorce, breaking the vows of fidelity that Henry had taken to Katharine in 1509. Moreover, everyone knew that Henry was dismissing Katharine from his presence in order to free him to develop his relationship with Anne Boleyn. And most people at court knew what Pope Clement and his inner circle knew – that Henry was doing all this so that he could have a sexual relationship with a woman with whose sister he had already had a long sexual relationship. And so sending Katharine away from court raised a number of serious canonical issues for the king, not the least of them being that he was openly defying Clement VII's injunction in his letter of 25 January to renounce Anne. He was indeed beginning to burn his bridges.

Katharine was of course humiliated and outraged at being exiled from her husband: she loudly proclaimed that she was being sent to one of the worst houses in England and would have preferred to have been lodged in the Tower of London. Moreover, the move to the More cost her several of her advisers, who resigned because they no longer dared involve themselves in her affairs.[39] When Mario Savorgnano visited her in August he found that she was still being served with dignity although he obviously exaggerated the size of her entourage: 'I ... arrived at a palace called the More, where the queen resides. In the morning we saw her Majesty dine; she had some thirty maids of honour standing round the table, and about fifty who performed its services. Her Court consists of about 200 persons, but she is not so much visited as heretofore, on account of the king.'[40]

It is not clear whether Henry intended that Katharine's exile from court was to be permanent. Probably that was the case but in October he sent yet another delegation of ministers to urge her to settle her case against him by agreement rather than by insisting that it be heard in Rome. This commission was led by the redoubtable – and much travelled – Dr Lee, now Archbishop-elect of York in succession to Wolsey, the Earl of Sussex, Treasurer Fitzwilliam and Dr Sampson.[41] They insisted that there was not the slightest justification for the appeal to Rome, where the Pope would not dare do justice out of fear of Charles V and offered to have a judge elected from among the English bishops and lawyers to try the case. Katharine answered calmly: she had initially believed that the king was indeed pursuing an annulment or divorce out of genuine scruples of conscience and had urged him to convene the bishops of the realm to make a decision which she undertook to accept. The king refused to do this, claiming that he would only accept a verdict based on justice and law. He thereby committed them both to the course which led through the legatine court to the position in which they currently found themselves. Katharine was now convinced that Henry was troubled not by his conscience but by 'passion pure and simple': it was a defining change in her position.

It was probably in despair that the four men went on their knees before the queen and begged her for the sake of the king's honour, the princess's welfare, the good of the kingdom and her own peace of mind to agree to have the case tried in England. In return, Henry promised to treat her better than hitherto. Katharine out-acted them: she now knelt down and prayed that each and everyone present would use their good offices to persuade Henry to return to her since he well knew that she was his true and lawful wife. She insisted that if the king retained any scruple, he should submit it to judgement at Rome where justice would be fairly done. While the royal officials addressed her in low voices, she spoke loudly so that her servants in the next room could hear what she said.

When the deputies were about to leave they informed her that Henry gave her the choice between staying where she was or going to another small royal house or retiring into an abbey. The queen refused to choose, saying that she would go wherever the king commanded, even to a fiery stake if need be. The queen would move house for she had no choice but to obey her husband – but she would not budge an inch in her defence of her honour, and indeed that of her daughter.

The King's Case

The king's case at last began in the Rota early in June 1530. Henry had sent William Benet, Edward Carne and Thomas Cranmer to represent him. The key role was that of Carne, who as *excusator* was charged with ensuring that Henry was not summoned to be judged in person in Rome. Carne was ideally suited to the task, for he dealt in tiny details and found loopholes where even Clement's finest canonists thought none existed. Probably Carne was a pedant, but if so he was a pedant with eagle eyes and he drove his opponents in the Rota and Curia to distraction as, week after week, he found technical flaws or deficiencies in the documents they submitted to him.

But Edward Carne was far from alone in seeking to delay affairs in Rome, for Clement and his own canon lawyers were determined for very different reasons to prevent the case reaching a point at which the Pope was obliged to hand down his sentence. Who, after all, caused or accentuated more delays than did the Pope himself? In the spring of 1530

Clement had drawn up two briefs ordering Henry to abandon Anne and restore Katharine to her rightful place alongside him – and had then found reasons for not sending them to England. Now, in the summer, he protested that the case could not proceed in the Rota because Henry was not represented by accredited proctors while Katharine's were already in Rome. And so once again that classic and most infuriating of papal device was employed – as it had been in 1529 – of adjourning a case over the long summer of the Roman legal vacation in the hope that Henry would send men to argue his case in the court. Between them, Carne, the Pope and his lawyers ensured that Henry's case went nowhere in the summer of 1530.

In England, Henry waxed angrily about the illegality of a foreign potentate summoning him to appear before his court and began to develop the idea (which he had long favoured) that he was not merely a king but an emperor, possessed of the fullest powers over both state and church in his realms.[42] And at the More, Katharine waited for the papal briefs to arrive and trusted in her nephew to rescue her from humiliation, not least by obliging Pope Clement to proceed to judgement.

Far from being neatly resolved by a papal decision, Henry's 'Great Matter' now became something of a Europe-wide entertainment; certainly it provided many academics with useful employment – it has been estimated that twenty-three universities and 160 scholars made their contributions to the great debate that now unfolded.[43] In the spring of 1530 the universities of Oxford and Cambridge issued judgements in support of the king, albeit with dissenting minorities. In the summer a range of verdicts began to arrive from universities in France, Italy, Spain and the Empire. Those that were favourable to the king were printed in the *Censurae academiarum* ('Determinations of the Universities'). At the same time, English theologians published their own anthology – the *Collectanea satis copiosa* ('Sufficiently Abundant Collections') – which argued that the King of England held supreme jurisdiction within his realm and could not be summoned to appear as a plaintiff in Rome. In March 1531 Thomas More presented to Parliament the opinion of foreign universities which had declared in favour of the divorce; he was associating himself in this strategically important area with Henry's policy.[44]

Tardily, in 1530 Charles instructed the leading universities in Spain to rebut Henry's claims. In September, the University of Salamanca issued a general judgement in support of Katharine and in December its elite College of San Bartolomé produced a more detailed argument in her defence.[45] Not to be outdone, the Complutense of Alcalá – the *arriviste* rival of Salamanca – summoned twenty doctors of theology to argue from both Old and New Testaments that a man could lawfully marry his brother's widow and that the Pope could legitimately provide a dispensation for him to do so.[46] At the same time, Miguel Mai, Spanish ambassador in Rome, collected sets of papers to be submitted in Rome.[47] But there was no escaping the reality: Charles was falling behind Henry in the academic war of words. In the theatre of the universities of Europe, Katharine's case was going by default.

In England, Henry insisted to Chapuys in September that several popes had ruled that cases which originated in England could never be advoked outside it; as evidence, he produced the signatures and seals of those leading men in his kingdom who had subscribed to his position.[48] He would therefore allow the Archbishop of Canterbury to give judgement or indeed would even be prepared to permit the body of English clergy to decide the case. But he would not give way to papal claims and would seek the support of both the King of France and his own Parliament in his conflict with the Pope:

Should the Pope refuse this just and lawful request of mine, I know well what I shall do, for having fulfilled my duty to God and my conscience, as well as [my obligations] to my own subjects, as can be proved by the seals and signatures of all the nobility of this realm, I can safely proceed to action.

I am now only awaiting the return of the messenger I have sent to Rome, to appeal to Parliament for a decision which that body cannot fail to give, as it will shortly re-assemble partly on this business, so that even if the Emperor threatened me with war on this ground, I hope to be able to defend myself well with the help of my brother and perpetual ally the King of France, even should the Pope assist the Emperor. In such an event I would demand [that] the Pope [impose] ecclesiastical censures upon His Imperial Majesty for breaking old and new alliances, to which he is so solemnly pledged, and in which he ought not, and should not, for the sake of a woman, fail towards so great a friend as I am.

If Henry's effrontery knew no bounds his understanding of irony was distinctly limited: he emphasised that he would not allow Charles V to act against him 'for the sake of a woman'.

'The Integrity of My Body': The Spanish Government's Search for Evidence

The question of whether Katharine had been a virgin when Arthur died vexed the imperial ambassador in London. Like López de Mendoza before him, Chapuys argued that it was extremely difficult to prove virginity except by personal testament; he recognised that even Katharine's oath would be insufficient in a court of law since there was evidence that she had slept with Arthur, and this would in itself in canon law be sufficient to establish that it was entirely reasonable to assume that consummation had taken place. In Chapuys's view it would be necessary to prove that Katharine was a woman of such exemplary character as to be incapable of telling an untruth – and of perjuring herself. It is certain that Chapuys believed Katharine's version of her marriage to Arthur: he simply did not believe that it would stand up in a court of law, be it in Rome or in London.

For her part, Katharine was shocked and distressed to hear that discussions were taking place in the Vatican about transferring her case from Rome to a northern city near England such as Cambrai. She was convinced that Clement showed no favour towards her and that if the case was taken away from Rome all sorts of bribes and bullying would take place and that her solemn word would not be believed. She begged Charles to insist that the case remain at Rome. She continued, too, to urge him to seek out evidence from those who were qualified to give it: in March 1531 she wrote to him requiring that the Spanish government should seek out witnesses to verify her account of her relationship with Arthur.[49] In April she repeated the request, asking that evidence be collected in Spain as to 'the integrity of my body' when she married Henry.[50] In July she used the same formula, imploring Charles to have his servants find the witnesses in Spain who could testify as to the 'the integrity of my body' at the time of her second marriage.[51]

With painful tardiness, the Spanish crown took up Katharine's fight: in October 1531, the Empress Isabella, as regent for her absent husband, ordered that a search to be made in the Crown archives for papers in the case. It had long been known that when secretaries of Ferdinand and Isabella retired from office they had often taken their papers with them, regarding them as their private property rather than as state papers which belonged properly to the Crown. These men had scattered the length and breadth of Spain and even beyond it. Accordingly Isabella despatched agents to Calatayud, Zaragoza, Tarazona, Valencia and Sardinia to seek out their heirs and find if they had any relevant state papers in their possession: they were to collect all original documents or at the very least to make copies of them.[52] It was a hopeless cause, like looking for a needle in the proverbial haystack, but it was the best possibility now open to the Spanish crown if it was to support Katharine with hard evidence.

The Empress also sent out agents to locate the surviving members of Katharine's household at the time of her marriage to Arthur.[53] She provided a questionnaire for them to respond to. Unfortunately, the questions that they were now to be asked were those that should have been asked under stringent legal conditions in 1502: were the councillors of Henry VII of the opinion that the marriage of Arthur and Katharine had not been consummated because of the extreme weakness of the prince? Was it was true that Arthur was so weak that he was 'unfit for a woman' and 'whether he looked as if he were impotent for marriage'? Had the servants of Katharine (both Spanish and English) believed that Arthur had failed to consummate his marriage? Had Katharine's collapse after Arthur's death had been due to the marriage not having been consummated? Had Katharine been a virgin when she married Henry VIII and was she able to promptly consummate her marriage to him? Was it true that it was Henry himself who had proposed that he should marry Katharine – and that he had overruled his own mother and councillors in deciding to marry Katharine rather than a French princess?

The witnesses whom the Crown now sought to track down were not members of the social elite, did not live in palaces and had not left forwarding addresses: on their departure from court most of them simply disappeared from view. Moreover, some had reasons to hide from the Crown (and from the dreaded Inquisition), among them Katharine's own namesake and slave, who was married to a *morisco* crossbow-maker: *moriscos* had every motive to avoid the gaze of the central government. Among those who might reasonably be traced to give support to Katharine were Catalina Fortes, who was a nun in Toledo; María de Rojas, who now lived in northern Spain (and who had slept in Katharine's bedroom after Arthur's death); Fray Diego Fernández, Katharine's confessor, who was to be asked for the identity of the notary who signed the contract for Katharine's marriage to Henry.[54] The ponderous task of locating them now began.

The incompetence of the Spanish government was as much a concern for Ambassador Mai in Rome as was the prevarication of the Pope and the insolence of the English emissaries. At least Clement dismissed the English request for cardinalates for Ghinucci (Auditor of the Apostolic Chamber) and Protonotary Casale. Henry's letter of 6 December 1530 was read in Consistory and was received with indignation as being deeply insulting to the Pope and the Rota. The Pope himself introduced the application by the imperial ambassadors for a new brief of inhibition forbidding Henry VIII to marry again until the suit was resolved; he also forbade the Convocations of the Church in England to judge the affair. But at least one thing went Henry's way: on the curious grounds that no proof had been produced at Rome of Henry's adultery the cardinals refused to direct him to separate himself from Anne Boleyn.[55]

A Two-Pronged Attack on the Church: Parliament & Convocation

At the turn of September–October 1530 Henry began the process of intimidating the English clergy, and – most especially – those who had supported Katharine. His approach was apparently ambivalent as he swayed between the coarsest bullying and the most gentle compromising. He opened his campaign by having fifteen clerics indicted for offences against the Statute of Praemunire: eight of them were bishops and it was no accident that they included John Fisher and John Clerk, Katharine's lawyers in the legatine court. The fifteen were charged with lesser treason and their goods and possessions (but not their lives) were manifestly at risk. It was perhaps because Henry now felt more confident of his strength that he immediately broadened the attack: in January 1531 the whole clerical estate was indicted under praemunire for having acknowledged Wolsey's legatine authority and the jurisdictional claims of the papacy within England: that the charge was manifestly absurd did not lessen the terror that its threat carried to those who were vulnerable to it.

It was not surprising, therefore, that both Convocations came quickly to heel and that Henry allowed them to buy him off: the Convocation of Canterbury was granted royal pardon in return for fine of £100,000 and Northern Convocation – which was much less affluent – followed suit by promising £18,000 (February 1531). Henry was less successful in his effort to persuade Convocation to accept that the Archbishop of Canterbury could legitimately judge the divorce case: Convocation found strength enough to refuse the demand. Notwithstanding that failure, on 7 February 1531, Henry moved to his greatest (and most insidious) claim, insisting that churchmen should formally recognise him as their 'supreme head'. John Fisher led the resistance but found few who were brave enough to follow him although the Convocation of Canterbury at least had the spine to acknowledge Henry's claim 'as far as the law of Christ allows'.[56]

While Henry belligerently attacked the clergy of England he trod more carefully in his dealings with Rome: in February 1531 he assured the nuncio that 'there was never a question of any measure that could affect His Holiness. I have always upheld the authority of the Church in this my kingdom and fully intend to do so in the future.'[57] Henry had good reason to be careful, for he had learned that Clement VII was on the point of issuing mandatory briefs against him: in reporting this, Chapuys informed Charles V that he had heard that Henry and Anne were not sleeping well.[58] Perhaps Chapuys was reassured when Norfolk insisted to him in February 1531 that Katharine had nothing to fear from Parliament and that no proceedings would be taken against her there. But Katharine herself was deeply worried that after Henry was declared Head of the Church some 'outrageous act' might be taken against her: Katharine knew Henry better than anyone else – and most certainly better than did Charles V's ambassador.[59]

In June 1531, Henry protested in an interview with the papal nuncio that he would never allow the Pope to judge his case even if he was excommunicated ('I care not a fig for all his excommunications'). The Pope could do what he liked in Rome: Henry would do the same in England. Henry added, 'I take the Pope to be upon the whole a worthy man, but ever since the last wars he has been so awfully afraid of the Emperor that he dares not act against his wishes.' Then he added, 'Yet as I know him to be a thoroughly good man, and of great natural tact I will send him a newly printed book on condition that he will not show it to any living soul for some time to come. In this manner will I try to make him lean to the side of justice.' Henry then gave the nuncio a copy of a book which argued his case: it is not clear whether this was the collection of tracts that were supportive of his case that his ministers had compiled.[60]

The king was holding the line with his courtly and ecclesiastical elite – but only just. Most importantly, Sir Thomas More had not moved into opposition; although he was not actively supportive of the king's case he was not yet openly opposed to it and he resolutely did whatever he could to push the Crown's parliamentary business forward. On 30

March 1531, the day before Parliament was prorogued, More insisted in the House of Lords that the rumours that Henry wanted a divorce 'out of love for some lady' were untrue and suggested that the king's actions derived only from his own scruples at the realisation that he had unlawfully married. He led a deputation from the Lords to the Lower House and announced that Henry had asked 'the chief universities of all Christendom' to judge whether his marriage was licit or not and then invited the Clerk of Parliament to read out the favourable verdicts given by foreign universities in support of the king's position. More emphasised that Henry was only motivated by 'the discharge of his conscience and surety of the succession of his realm'.[61] In recognising the significance of the views of the great universities of Europe, More was acting as a Christian humanist; in paying due regard to the dynastic imperative facing his sovereign he was acting as a loyal servant of the Crown. It was for this reason that he refused Chapuys's request to visit him to discuss the king's 'Great Matter': Sir Thomas fully recognised that, both as Lord Chancellor and as an individual, he could not allow any suspicion to rear its head as to his loyalty to his sovereign.

John Fisher was altogether a different case. He sent Chapuys word that the king had attempted to suborn him and others who stood up to support the queen; Fisher claimed that Henry had told them a thousand lies – that the Pope would favour the English; that he was a bitter enemy of Charles V because of his insistence on summoning a General Council of the Church. Henry then summoned the bishop to interrogate him: Fisher assured him that there was little that was new except that the Pope was irritated at having to convene a General Council and wanted support to resist this. Henry took the precaution of interviewing the nuncio to corroborate what the bishop had told him.

In April 1531, Fisher believed that an attempt had been made to poison him. Henry reacted with savagery, intent on demonstrating that he was not involved:

Some of the servants of the Bishop of Rochester died lately, he being considered in that kingdom a very religious and worthy man; and although he had always publicly advocated the queen's cause, the king nevertheless invariably showed him great respect; and there being a suspicion of poison [that was aimed at] the bishop himself, he made a strong complaint about this to the king, who ordered the arrest of a cook who was suspected of the crime, he being in the bishop's service; and after racking him severely [the cook] was put to a cruel death, though it is said that he made no confession, save that as a jest he put some purgative powder in certain meats.[62]

In what was perhaps an early example of the savagery that came naturally to Henry when his own deepest interests were involved, the cook was boiled alive.

Anne Boleyn was more fearful of Rochester than anyone else. It may have been at her behest that Henry ordered Fisher not to come to London to attend Parliament, ostensibly out of fear that he would contract a fever as he had done in the previous year. But Fisher was not a man to be deterred: he insisted that even if he was to meet 100,000 deaths he would journey to London to speak in the queen's favour and that he would do so more openly than he had ever done.[63]

Katharine's prayers appeared to have been answered in the most spectacular fashion when in May 1531 a letter from Ferdinand the Catholic to his ambassador in Rome (Francisco de Rojas) was found which affirmed that Arthur had not consummated his marriage and that accordingly Rojas was to apply for a dispensation; this was not necessary but Ferdinand needed to satisfy the English.[64] Unfortunately, when the letter was shown to two lawyers they advised him that it would not be of much value in Katharine's defence but asked for more time to consider it: as we have seen (chapter 5) Ferdinand was merely covering all his options.[65]

In the last two months of 1531 Katharine sent at least two letters to Charles V, pleading with him for support. On 6 November she wrote that she was suffering an agony such as no Christian had ever endured. She had always obeyed Henry as his true wife and was unaware that she had ever done anything in this affair against his will. She could only call on God and Charles himself; she implored Charles to oblige the Pope to issue his verdict and thereby bring her agony to an end. She permitted herself to hope that God would forgive the Pope for the delays he had granted. She was all alone: her advisers were afraid of the king and dared not speak for her while her enemies were like falcons who swooped down on food that was put out for her supporters.[66]

Two weeks later, Katharine wrote to Chapuys; she was now living in Bugden, probably on a temporary basis. She reminded the ambassador that she had been appealing to Rome for nearly six years and urged that the imperial ambassadors at Rome insist that the sentence be issued as soon as possible. She feared that during the next session of Parliament it would be decided that she and her daughter were to be put to death and insisted that she would accept this fate for both of them to secure the joy and pleasures of heaven.[67]

By mid-December Katharine was back at the More. Again, she wrote scathingly to Charles V of the indifference of the Pope. She still hoped that Henry would – by God's grace – return to her. She used the metaphor of the bullfight to suggest that those who had prompted Henry to act against her had goaded him with lances like the bull in the arena, giving him false hopes and advancing malicious arguments. It was a pity that a person so good and virtuous should be thus deceived and misled every day. For her own part, Katharine would never cease praying that God enlightened Henry's mind. She signed her letter from the More, 'Separated from my husband without having ever offended him.'[68]

15

'THE POOREST WOMAN IN THE WORLD', 1532–1533: THE BREACH WITH ROME & THE DIVORCE

A Final Warning? Clement VII's Admonitory Brief, 25 January 1532
On New Year's Day 1532, Katharine sent Henry an exquisitely wrought gold cup. It was customary for married couples to exchange gifts at New Year but the gold cup touched a raw nerve in Henry for it pointedly emphasized Katharine's conviction that she remained his lawful wife: he was furious with her presumption. He had himself symbolically expressed the breach with Katharine and Mary by failing for the first time to give them presents to mark the New Year and so he returned the cup to Katharine (although not before he had carefully examined it). But while Henry spurned Katharine and Mary he sent splendid gifts to Anne and graciously accepted those that she sent him. Anne was now lodged in Katharine's former apartments and served by as many ladies as the queen had been: it was as if she was already queen.[1] The king's rejection of Katharine's New Year gift was to prove a turning-point in the disintegration of his relationship with her: Henry would thereafter show no kindness or consideration to Katharine as he had done in recent years (chapter 14). Henceforth, his treatment of her – and of Princess Mary – was to be increasingly characterised by vindictive and welling hostility. Henry was unforgiving of Katharine for what he regarded as her 'obstinacy' in refusing to give way to him: as he had recently informed the Pope, he was indeed not a man to brook opposition.

At the same time, Henry altered his approach at Rome, ordering Carne to emphasise to Clement VII that if Katharine's marriage to Arthur had not been consummated then no impediment of affinity existed between himself and Katharine and in consequence there had been no need for Julius II to have issued a dispensation permitting them to marry. Henry urged Carne to persuade Clement that in effect the celebrated document was irrelevant since there was nothing for Pope Julius to dispense from: it followed, in Henry's somewhat curious reasoning, that his marriage to Katharine was *ipso facto* unlawful.[2] He also maintained that the marriage should have been invalidated on the grounds of 'public honesty' – that it had been universally known that Katharine had married Prince Arthur and lived (and slept) with him as man and wife, if only for the briefest of periods (chapter 6). Did the king now reflect on the damage that he had done to his own case by insisting for so many years on 'the Levitical Principle'? There is no evidence that he did so. At last, after five years of furious, disorganised, egocentric and chaotic effort, Henry had arrived at the theological kernel which would probably have secured him an annulment of his marriage to Katharine – at another time; under another Pope, and with different political and military circumstances in Italy. Indeed, Henry had reached pretty much the conclusion that Wolsey had urged on him in the mid-1520s – that he was best advised to seek an annulment of his marriage by attacking Julius II's dispensation. But by 1532 it was, of course, far too late.

And perhaps, too, there is a further conclusion that we can draw from this latest example of Henry's impulsive and capricious approach to Rome – that it was indeed the king himself rather than any of his ministers who was responsible for the wilful and ever-changing demands made of the Pope. Could ministers have survived who changed their policies so abruptly and so often?

Henry's change of tack could not, of course, take account of the situation that was developing in Rome, where the Rota and the Consistory of Cardinals were in the process of formulating two conclusions to present to the Pope for him to consider in reaching his decision. The first of these was favourable to Henry (and was to be deeply dismaying to Katharine): remarkably, the Consistory decided that it simply could not be proven one way or the other whether Arthur and Katharine had consummated their marriage. The cardinals reached the same conclusion, therefore, as ambassadors López de Mendoza and Chapuys had done in London – that in terms of the rigours that necessarily governed the implementation of canon law, Katharine's strenuous affirmation that she had not consummated her marriage to Arthur was irrelevant simply because it could not be proven as a juridical fact whether what she was saying was true. The second conclusion of the Consistory was, however, much more damning to Henry: the cardinals accepted that because it was beyond doubt that Henry had chosen to marry Katharine of his own free will and had persisted in regarding her as his lawful wife for nearly twenty years and *had had children by her*, his marriage to her was fully valid and in consequence was indissoluble – he himself had made it so.

The advice being given to Clement in 1532 by his canonists and cardinals was therefore unequivocal – that even though it could not be proved whether Katharine's first marriage had been consummated, there was no doubt that her second was canonically valid on the grounds of the full and free commitment given to it by both Henry and Katharine over an extended period. In fine, Henry's own loyal dedication to the marriage therefore invalidated his arguments for ending it.

The Rota and the Consistory of Cardinals had not yet formulated these two principles in their entirety at the beginning of 1532 but the tide was already beginning to turn against Henry in Rome: on or about 12 January the Rota ruled that Carne was not to be admitted as *excusator* and in doing so effectively required that Henry himself should appear at Rome to plead his case in person. Dr Bonner promptly left Rome on 17 January to return to court to seek fresh instructions from the king.[3] And then on 25 January, Clement VII decided that he would issue Henry a final warning: he was to separate himself from Anne and to take Katharine back or be subject to the dreadful penalty of excommunication. But, as always with Pope Clement, taking a decision and implementing it were to prove to be two very different matters.

Not the least of the Pope's difficulties lay in his inability to deal successfully with the confrontational assault mounted on him by Dr Cristóbal Ortíz, the obscure Castilian lawyer who was Katharine's proctor in Rome. Ortíz was profoundly committed – professionally and personally – to arguing Katharine's case and despite his own humble background was no respecter of persons: he regularly wrote to Charles V telling him what he should do, and his bluntness in conversation eventually led Dr Miguel Mai, the imperial ambassador in Rome, to refuse to have anything to do with him.[4] That probably would have been the Pope's preferred option but Clement was too courteous and conscientious to follow Mai's lead.[5] He did the best he could: at the turn of 1531–32, when Ortíz demanded that Clement should immediately excommunicate Henry and Anne in accordance with the briefs that he had issued in 1530 and 1531, Clement suggested that Ortíz should draw up his own draft for a papal brief and submit it for consideration to his trusted adviser Pietro Accolti, Cardinal of Ancona. Ortíz enthusiastically did so but on 6 January Ancona rejected Ortíz's passage excommunicating Henry because it was not couched in 'proper Roman style' and needed to be refined by the Pope's secretary.

No whit dismayed, on the same day Ortíz had audience with the Pope. It was highly unusual for a Pope to receive visitors on a great feast day – 6 January was the Feast of the Epiphany – but Clement agreed to examine Ortíz's draft. It took the Pope only two days to give his verdict: he too found technical difficulties in the document, most notably that it allowed Henry only fifteen days from the publication of the briefs in the Low Countries to separate himself from Anne and recall Katharine. Clement ruled – quite correctly – that Henry could not properly be excommunicated within such a limited time-span since no previous notice of the imminence of the dreadful sentence had been given to him. It would accordingly be necessary to send Henry yet another brief warning him that he would be excommunicated if he did not obey the papal injunction – what was known as 'an admonitory brief'. Acting with undue alacrity, Clement had the brief drawn up, and signed it on 25 January. Exultant, Ortíz breathlessly claimed the credit: 'May God be praised. I have this moment persuaded his Holiness to send the brief.'[6]

Clement opened his brief by observing that ever since the beginning of his dispute with Katharine, Henry had continued to treat her as his queen but that he had recently expelled her from his court and 'cohabited openly with a certain Anne': he trusted that Henry would understand how unworthy his conduct was of a Christian prince and what a scandal it was causing to the Church. However, since Henry had hitherto been the 'most zealous' defender of the Church, Clement would do no more for the present than to rebuke him 'as a loving father' so that he would see the error of his ways and not oblige Clement to proceed to judgement in 'the principal cause' (*viz.*, the decision on the legality of Henry's marriage with Katharine). Withal, the Pope 'hoped' that Henry would take Katharine back as his wife and 'put away Anne'. Pope Clement had not only removed the fifteen-day clause that Ortíz had put in his own draft: he had taken away any reference to an impending excommunication. Far from being a papal bull or brief which solemnly obliged Henry to take

Katharine back under pain of excommunication, Clement's missive of 25 January 1532 was therefore little more than an anodyne and unspecified papal wish-list.[7] And even now Clement conjured up yet another delay: he informed Ortíz that he would not dispatch the brief until he had heard what proposals Dr Bonner was bringing back from Henry.[8] In despair, Ortíz clung desperately – as he was very careful to inform Charles V – to the conviction that the Vicar of Christ would not break his pledged word to him. He was soon to be disabused of his confidence in Pope Clement.

It is not known how or when Katharine was given the papal brief but she seems to have had sight of it before anyone else in England: on 14 April 1532 she wrote to Ortíz that she had seen it and that it was not strong enough. She urged her proctor to demand that the Pope should give sentence in the principal cause at once and again allowed herself to give the fullest expression to her anger and despair at Clement's behaviour: 'I know not what to say about his Holiness, but certainly when I see him holding this case in suspension, and Christendom swarming with heretics, it would seem to me as if he wanted their number to increase, and that whilst being, as he is, the supreme head and protector of the Church he yet wishes it to have this tremendous fall.'[9]

Ortíz readily agreed, for he concurrently informed Charles V that the brief was not strong enough and that in any event Henry would not obey it: he too insisted that the Pope should be prevailed upon to issue a stronger brief.[10]

The brief of 25 January 1532 was formally presented to Henry on 13 May by Nuncio del Borgho. The king was furious that the Pope should have commanded him to recall Katharine, claiming that it was his right to punish a woman whom the Pope claimed was his lawful wife and who was treating him so rudely. Vengefully, he gave orders for Katharine to be moved farther away from court. Reporting this to Charles V, Chapuys joined those who scorned the papal brief, noting that it would have been weak if it had been issued at the beginning of the process and now had only negative value.[11]

By July, Katharine's proctor had lost all patience with Clement and issued an astounding ultimatum to the Pontiff: Ortíz had the audacity to tell the Pope to his face that if he did not excommunicate Henry he himself would stand up on the Day of Judgement and accuse him before God of abandoning his duty. In anguish, the Pope replied that he had to be advised by lawyers in everything he did. Once again, Clement sent Ortíz away to discuss with Cardinal Ancona how best to proceed: Ancona merely told Ortíz that the case could not progress until Henry had mandated a proctor to represent him in Rome and that in consequence nothing could be done before the Vatican's legal summer vacation. When Ortíz pressed him, Ancona promised to study the case but then conveniently fell ill and was unable to meet the proctor. And then the Pope took to his sickbed. Illness and that hardy papal perennial – the legal vacation in the summer – were once again working against Katharine and her zealous proctor.[12] It would not be for the last time.

The King's New Ministers: Thomas Cranmer & Thomas Cromwell
While in Rome Pope Clement prevaricated and Ortíz raged, in London Henry began to allow free rein to the anti-clericalism that was so strongly represented among the Members of Parliament. Henry was indeed becoming increasingly convinced that he rightfully enjoyed within his realm the attributes of an Emperor – that he could properly control the Church as well as the State – and it suited his purposes in the spring of 1532 to encourage the House of Commons to attack the Church and its privileges: the king was indeed forming an alliance with his Commons against his churchmen. The House drew up a 'Supplication against the Ordinaries', listing a range of complaints against the operation of clerical courts and submitted it to the king. On 18 March Henry passed the 'Supplication' on to Convocation and required that it should formally acknowledge that all ecclesiastical legislation required the royal assent in order to be valid.[13] It was Henry's first major step to taking over control of the Church in England.

At the same time, Henry took direct action against the papacy by using Parliament to confiscate the papacy's chief source of income in England, the 'annates' which bishops paid to Rome on appointment to their sees (the 'Act in Conditional Restraint of Annates', 19 March). For good measure, the Act also proposed that if the Pope refused to issue bulls of consecration for bishops the authority of the Crown itself would suffice to validate such consecrations. An informed observer wrote that 'after this day the Bishop of Rome shall have no manner of authority within the realm of England'.[14] In order to apply extend the pressure upon Clement VII, Henry agreed that the provision was not to come into effect for a year.

On 15 May 1532, Convocation accepted that the king had the right to validate all legislation on the Church: the document by which it did so was properly – and cravenly – entitled 'The Submission of the Clergy', for by it Convocation abjectly surrendered its privileges and, with them, the independence of the Church in England.

Sir Thomas More recognised how significant the change of direction in royal policy was by resigning as Lord Chancellor on the following day. He did the best he could to blur his reasons for doing so by letting it be known that he was resigning because of the volume of the work involved in carrying out the office but everyone at court – not least Henry himself – appreciated that More's action represented a landmark in the development of the king's 'Great Matter'. Although More would do everything in his power to avoid breaking with the king, his resignation effectively made such a breach inevitable.[15] Henry was, after all, not a man to brook opposition, however discreetly it expressed itself.

As Henry lost the services of More he found other men who could develop his policies for him. During the course of 1532–33, he drew to himself two comparatively unknown men who would help free him from his marriage to Katharine and in doing so bring about revolutionary changes over the control of both Church and State: Thomas Cromwell began his ascent to the status of the king's leading minister in 1532 and in 1533 Thomas Cranmer was appointed Archbishop of Canterbury. Both were men of comparatively humble birth who were widely travelled in Western Europe and they shared a hostility to papal claims of suzerainty over the English Church. Both, too, were exceptionally clear-sighted in their aims and were possessed of administrative skills of a high order.

William Warham died on 22 August 1532: he was about eighty-two years of age and had been Archbishop of Canterbury since 1503 and Lord Chancellor from 1504. He had performed the marriage and coronations of Henry VIII and Katharine and had sat as Wolsey's assessor in the investigation in 1527 into the circumstances of the marriage to Katharine (chapter 12). Although he dropped hints about his opposition to royal policy Warham did not provide active leadership in opposing it until on 24 February 1532 he registered a protest against all Acts of Parliament which were injurious to papal power or to the prerogatives of the Archbishopric of Canterbury. It was already too late: although Warham made a serious effort to resist the 'Submission of the Clergy' in May he was too old and frail to be of account. He died three months later.

Thomas Cranmer was forty-three years old when he was appointed to succeed Warham in the primatial see.[16] A Cambridge academic, he was a modest but strong-willed man. He had made his career in 1529 when he had suggested to Gardiner and Foxe that Henry should seek the support of European universities in arguing that his marriage to Katharine could be declared illegal by English ecclesiastical courts without recourse to the Roman Curia. Henry instinctively recognised that Cranmer would be especially useful to him – 'this man, I swear, has got the right sow by the ear' – and ordered Cranmer to abandon all other work to study the issues in the case and advise him on how to deal with them. Cranmer threw himself into the task, visiting the universities of Oxford and Cambridge in the company of Gardiner and Foxe and travelling with the Earl of Wiltshire on his ill-starred mission to Bologna in 1530: ironically, in Rome in the summer of 1530, Clement appointed him 'Grand Penitentiary of England'. He returned to England in September and in January 1531 Henry despatched him as ambassador extraordinary to the Emperor, with a brief to forge a working alliance with Lutheran princes. At Nüremberg, he met Andreas Osiander, the celebrated Lutheran theologian; he became so close to him that in 1532 he married his niece Margaret.

It was traditional for the Crown to enjoy the revenues of the archiepiscopal see for one year before it was filled but Henry was so desperate to have Cranmer *in situ* that he advanced the money to Rome so that the papal bulls appointing him could be rushed through; foolishly, the Curia obliged him and issued them in February and March 1533. Cranmer was consecrated on 30 March. Cranmer took the oath of loyalty to the Pope with the defining caveat that he did so only insofar as his obligations to the Pope did not conflict with his duties to the king as Supreme Head: Diarmaid MacCullough has elegantly pointed out that 'Cranmer had formally benefited from papal bulls while equally formally rejecting their authority'.[17]

Thomas Cromwell had entered government service through the household of Wolsey. He seems to have been genuinely fond of the cardinal and certainly learned a great deal from him about the duties of the senior royal servant – and of the dangers of the service itself. He remained loyal to the cardinal after his fall from office. Cromwell was trained in the law and in 1523 and again in 1530 he was elected to the House of Commons. In that latter year he began his rise through the royal service when he was sworn in as king's councillor and by April 1533 had become Chancellor of the Exchequer. A year later he was the king's Principal Secretary.[18]

The Coming Out of Anne Boleyn: The Meeting of Henry VIII & Francis I (20–29 October 1532)
On 1 September 1532, at Windsor Castle, Anne Boleyn was created

Marchioness of Pembroke, and on the same day Henry concluded an alliance with France against Charles V: Henry thereby made very explicit the link between his commitment to Anne and the re-creation of the Anglo–French alliance.[19] Henry prepared now to take Anne with him to France for a meeting with Francis I at which he intended to renew their alliance against Charles V.[20] Henry and Francis knew that Charles V had arranged once again to meet with Clement VII at Bologna and were naturally anxious about their intentions: Henry, of course, was especially fearful that Clement was intent on persuading Charles to take military action against him. His decision to raise Anne to the nobility and to take her with him to meet Francis I was therefore designed at once as a gesture of open defiance to the Pope and the Emperor and as a commitment to the alliance with France which he saw as his best protection. It was also very pointed, for Henry also took with him his illegitimate son, the Duke of Richmond, who was now thirteen years old; in introducing Anne and Richmond to the King of France, Henry would announce to the world the new order that existed within his family and court. Having done so, it would be impossible for him to withdraw from his commitment to Anne and his rejection of Katharine (and of the imperial alliance).

With stark cruelty, Henry demanded that Katharine surrender all her jewels to him. Knowing full well that Henry intended to dress Anne in them, Katharine initially refused, adding that she would be sinning if she gave up her jewels to decorate a woman who was the scandal of Christendom and would thereby bring great infamy upon her husband. Nevertheless, she acknowledged that if Henry commanded her to hand her jewels over to him she would as a dutiful wife obey him: when Henry did so, Katharine duly sent him all her jewels.[21]

On 11 October Henry and Anne crossed to Calais.[22] Henry brought about 2,000 cavalrymen with him while Anne was accompanied by twenty ladies-in-waiting. Francis met Henry just outside Calais on 20 October. They then travelled to Boulogne where Francis introduced Henry to his sons, the Dauphin and the Duke of Angoulême, and Henry presented Richmond to Francis as a servant.

There was no repetition of the egregious splendour of 'The Field of the Cloth of Gold': Henry and Francis were now experienced and tested monarchs who had (mostly) dispensed with the fripperies of youth. True, there were the usual courtly festivals, including an afternoon of bull- and bear-baiting which seemed to have been enjoyed by all. But this was a business meeting, and over four days Henry and Francis held discussions about how best to oppose Charles V and to separate him from the Pope. Francis invested the dukes of Norfolk and Suffolk with the Order of S. Michel and Henry reciprocated by granting knighthoods of the Garter to two leading French noblemen. The first fruit of the *rapprochement* was that Francis sent cardinals Tournon and Grammont to Rome to intercede for Henry with the Pope and his cardinals and to insist that Clement should not ally himself with Charles.

Anne, who was of course very much at home in a French court, joined in the festivities with *élan*: she entered one of the dances wearing a mask and danced with Francis himself. When the king removed her mask he gallantly affected surprise on realising with whom he had been dancing. But not everyone was enchanted by Henry's mistress: an anonymous observer described her in unflattering terms: 'Madame Anne is not one of the handsomest women in the world; she is of middling stature, swarthy complexion, long neck, wide mouth, bosom not much raised, and in fact has nothing but the English king's great appetite, and her eyes, which are black and beautiful.'[23]

On 29 October the monarchs bade farewell to each other outside Calais. Storms in the Channel delayed the voyage home and Henry and Anne remained in Calais for twelve days: was it while they waited for the seas to calm that they consummated their relationship?

Prelude to Excommunication: Clement VII's Brief of 15 November 1532 & Henry's Marriage to Anne Boleyn (January 1533)
Before leaving Rome for Bologna, Clement sent a third brief to Henry: it was dated 15 November 1532.[24] Yet again he noted that he retained his affection for the king even though Henry's behaviour had deteriorated during the last two years and emphasised that he took the actions upon which he was now engaged with deep sadness. Was Clement mindful of Ortíz's savage rebuke to him when he affirmed that it was the responsibilities of his office that now obliged him to act against Henry? Certainly, he emphasised that he could not neglect the demands of justice and his obligation to do whatever he could to ensure the salvation of the king's soul. Accordingly, his actions now were motivated by the demands of honour and justice: he hoped that in time Henry would come to appreciate this.

Clement once again reminded Henry that it had been at his request that in 1529 he had committed the case to legates Campeggio and Wolsey even though it seemed to him 'rather unjust' to the queen that he should have done so and that he had subsequently advoked the case to Rome because he was obliged to do so by Katharine's appeal to him. Rather than waiting patiently for the verdict, Henry had sent Katharine away 'and publicly cohabited with a certain Anne': this was an offence against divine justice and so Clement had written to him on 25 January 1532, gently warning him against his behaviour. But still Henry continued in his disobedience and Clement now exhorted him under pain of excommunication to take Katharine back as his wife and reject Anne: he allowed him one month from the day on which he received the brief to do so. If at the end of that time Henry continued to live with Anne and isolate Katharine he was to be excommunicated. Clement forbade Henry to divorce himself from Katharine or to marry Anne while he waited for him to publish his final sentence. The Pope was very specific: if Henry married Anne, Clement would declare the marriage to be invalid and in consequence any children born of it would be illegitimate.

Having sent his brief to Henry, Clement travelled once again to Bologna to meet Charles V. Charles arrived in the city on 20 December 1532; once again, Clement was waiting for him, and they celebrated the Christmas and New Year festivities together. They then made two agreements. The first of them had momentous consequences for the Catholic Church: Clement agreed (after years of prevarication) to summon a General Council of the Church to address the problems of the Reformation and to reform the Church itself. When he wrote to Henry to inform him of this he expressed the hope that Henry would contribute to its proceedings.[25] Clement and Charles also signed a treaty of mutual defence against the Turk and in it they inserted a clause that had nothing whatever to do with the Turk: they agreed that the Pope would act on his brief of 17 November 1532 by taking action to oblige Henry to separate himself from Anne Boleyn.[26] There was talk of securing a compromise with Henry by moving the case away from Rome so that it could be judged at Cambrai, which lay in Charles's territories and was close to England.

Dr Ortíz was optimistic: he obtained a copy of the brief of 15 November and believed that in depriving Henry of his kingdom and absolving his subjects from their allegiance to him Pope Clement had provided Katharine with all that she could have wished for even in the final sentence itself. The proctor evidently believed, too, that Charles V would act to enforce the brief with military commitment.[27] By 22 February he had heard that the brief had been published in the Low Countries.[28]

Ortíz's spirits were lightened by the good news and he reported to the Empress that canon lawyers and diplomats in Rome were ridiculing Henry since the news had been maliciously leaked that as long ago as 1529 he had asked Clement for a dispensation to marry a woman with whose sister he had already had sexual intercourse:[29]

> The only new fact which has been ascertained is that there exists a greater degree of affinity between the king and this Anne Boleyn, his mistress, than even between him and his own legitimate wife; for it appears that he once had connection [*sc.* intercourse] with her sister, whereas his queen, as is well known, remained a virgin after her marriage with Prince Arthur. And yet, strange to say, it has now been proved that in order to marry this Anne he sent some time ago [to the Pope] to ask for a dispensation!
>
> Among other things, which His Holiness very wisely said to [Gregorio] Casale, the English ambassador, in answer to his application for [this] dispensation, pretending that in suing for a divorce from his queen, his master had listened only to his conscience, was this: 'How is it, then, that your master, the king, before the sentence was pronounced, and even before he had married this Anne, lived openly with her; and how can he conscientiously deny the validity of all former Papal dispensations when he presumes to ask for a similar one to marry this Anne notwithstanding his connection with her sister?'

But the time for irony and sarcasm was over: on 24 or 25 January 1533, Henry had secretly married Anne and it almost immediately became evident that she was pregnant.[30]

On 8 February, Henry summoned the nuncio to Greenwich so that he could accompany him in the royal barge to the opening of Parliament.[31] Chapuys noted with suspicion that Henry's generous courtesy to the nuncio was designed to demonstrate to his subjects just how friendly his relations were with the papacy at the very moment at which he had openly defied the Pope and married Anne. Certainly, del Borgho impressed upon the king that Clement was even more anxious than he was to be rid of the matter. But in private, the two men argued furiously: when del Borgho insisted that the Pope would shortly be obliged to pronounce sentence and that Henry should take Katharine back as his wife and treat her more cordially the king interrupted him – 'I will do nothing of the sort, and for this reason: her obstinacy, disobedience, and extreme rigour towards me have been such that a reconciliation is quite impossible.' Henry's insistence on Katharine's 'obstinacy' and 'disobedience' were to be a recurring theme: he would indeed brook no opposition.

Chapuys feared that Henry was playing for time, waiting for the right moment to secure a dispensation from Clement that would retrospectively validate his second marriage. Wrongly, he believed that the people of England would rise in revolt if Henry was excommunicated and emphasised how unpopular 'the Lady' was in the country. Rightly, he urged Charles to have Clement delay the expedition of the bulls for the Archbishopric of Canterbury until he had pronounced his verdict on the legitimacy of the marriage and insisted that the Pope should insert a clause into the Archbishop's oath forbidding him to involve himself in the divorce case. Chapuys believed that Cranmer was, in 'heart and soul' a Lutheran. The month stipulated in the papal brief had almost expired and there were no signs of Henry VIII obeying it: he would, in the ambassador's view, have to be forced to do so. This became the more true when Henry opened a new session of Parliament in February 1533 by having an act passed forbidding his subjects to appeal to Rome ('Act in Restraint of Appeals to Rome'). The pace was quickening.

Holy Week, 1533[32]

On 2 April the Convocation of Canterbury voted by 197 votes to 19 that the Pope did not have the authority to issue a dispensation which allowed a man to marry his brother's widow: he could not dispense with a provision of what was divine law. A committee of canon lawyers conveniently judged that the marriage of Arthur and Katharine had indeed been consummated.[33] Bishop Fisher was the only dissentient voice.

Armed with the support of Convocation, Henry committed himself to taking decisive action against Katharine and her supporters during Holy Week (6–13 April). This was of course a time when churchmen were preoccupied with the celebrations of the *triduum* of Easter weekend and it was probably no accident that Henry moved against Katharine during this time. On Palm Sunday, 6 April 1533, Bishop Fisher was arrested and placed under house arrest in the charge of Stephen Gardiner, Bishop of Winchester: the indefatigable bishop would no longer be free to speak publicly in support of Katharine. On the following Wednesday, 9 April, Henry sent yet another delegation of notables to Katharine to urge her to give up her appeal to Rome and allow the case to be tried in England: it was led by the dukes of Norfolk and Suffolk, the Marquis of Dorset and the Earl of Oxford. When Katharine refused they gave her the devastating news that Henry had married Anne Boleyn more than two months ago.[34]

Chapuys knew nothing of this when on Maundy Thursday (10 April) he was received by the king. Henry was in ebullient mood; when Chapuys rebuked him for his treatment of Katharine and told him that he should have respect for God, Henry replied that God and his conscience were on very good terms. When the ambassador then insisted that he had never heard of a man renouncing his wife after twenty-five years of marriage, Henry retorted that it was not as long as that and that the world found it strange that a Pope (*sc.* Julius II) had given a dispensation for his marriage to Katharine without having the power to do so. He insisted that he had to have a successor and Chapuys argued that he already had a daughter of childbearing age, waspishly reminding the king that his kingdom had come to him through the female line. Henry was obliged to agree with Chapuys that he had often said that Katharine had come to him as a virgin but claimed this was merely a 'manly jest', and that when jesting or feasting men said many things that they knew to be untrue. But it was in the fury of argument rather than in jest that Henry let slip – deliberately or otherwise – that Anne was pregnant.

Anne, too, took centre stage at court, perhaps because her pregnancy gave her even extra self-confidence: on Easter Saturday (12 April) she attended Mass as if she was already a member of the royal family, laden with Katharine's jewels and with an entourage of sixty young ladies. She now styled herself queen.[35]

But not all churchmen were cowed by royal power or preoccupied by the demands of Easter. A response did come to royal provocation and it arose in the very heart of the court. On Easter Sunday William Peto Provincial of the Minor Friars preached in front of the king at Greenwich and spoke of the difficulties that princes and their councillors sometimes found in understanding the truth. When Henry rebuked him the friar bluntly told the king that if he proceeded with his second marriage he would be in great danger of losing his kingdom since all his subjects were opposed to it.[36] Even Henry stepped back: the provincial had previously asked for permission to travel abroad on pilgrimage and the king now readily gave him it. Henry then insisted that a royal chaplain should preach another sermon in his presence but when the chaplain began to refute the arguments of the provincial, Henry Elston, the guardian of the friary angrily interrupted him, and volunteered to take the provincial's place. At the end of his sermon the chaplain claimed that all the universities and doctors had declared that the divorce was lawful: the guardian then said within the king's hearing that what the chaplain had said was a fabrication. When the provincial returned to Greenwich he refused Henry's order to deprive the guardian of his office in the order and punish him for his offence: furious, Henry ordered them both to be sent to prison until they changed their minds. Both men let Chapuys know that they would rather die than admit they were wrong.

In Rome, Clement VII lost his nerve yet again: on 11 April he informed the Emperor's advocate that he had decided to recall and modify the brief of 15 November 1532 because the English had complained that it contained errors. Enraged, Ortíz took the Emperor's proctor and advocate with him to confront the Pope: Ortíz insisted there were no errors in the brief and that it had been properly granted. As the great liturgical festivities of the Easter weekend – Good Friday, Easter Saturday and Easter Sunday (the *triduum*) – were imminent, Clement handed the matter to cardinals del Monte and Campeggio and auditors Simoneta and Paolo de Capizzuchi to consider. Del Monte told Ortíz that although he presumed that the brief was in order it was not fitting to deal with such matters during Holy Week and refused to examine it until after Easter. Campeggio accepted the commission and on Good Friday he sent Ortíz a copy of the objections made by the English. Unsurprisingly, Ortíz found them insubstantial.[37]

On 17 April, Fernando de Silva y Álvarez de Toledo, 4th Count of Cifuentes, arrived in Rome as imperial ambassador in place of Mai and immediately had an audience with the Pope who brought him up to date on events; Clement let Cifuentes understand that he knew of Anne Boleyn's pregnancy and that if Henry married her he could declare the marriage to be invalid. Cifuentes urged him to issue his sentence and thereby put an end to the dispute.[38] And there was a further problem: when Cifuentes called on Clement a few days later, the Pope made it clear that he would not proceed to judgement until he was certain that Charles would undertake to execute his sentence as the secular power – that, in effect, unless Charles agreed to wage war on England, the Pope would not even issue his sentence.[39]

Ortíz insisted that Henry had already been excommunicated and England placed under interdict by virtue of the papal briefs given at Bologna in 1530 and Rome in 1531, arguing that these briefs entitled any ecclesiastical judge to declare Henry, the members of his council and

Anne Boleyn to be excommunicated and the Kingdom of England placed under interdict. Fearful that Clement might secretly have sent absolution to Henry, Ortíz urged Charles to publish the briefs so that they could be known to everyone.[40]

Cranmer's Verdicts & the Coronation of Anne Boleyn[41]

Archbishop Cranmer opened his court at Dunstable Priory on 10 May: he held sessions on 10, 12, 16, 17 and 23 May.[42] Once again, Katharine refused to recognise the legitimacy of a court that was to sit in judgement on her marriage and would not appear in front of it. However, this suited Cranmer, who no doubt remembered Katharine's stunning performance at the legatine court in 1529 and was anxious that she should not appear in front of his tribunal lest she should find a way of undermining it or even of delaying his sentence.[43] Cranmer gave his verdict in what he described to Henry as 'your great and weighty cause' at 10.00 a.m. on 23 May: he ruled that the marriage of Henry and Katharine had been against the law of God and granted the king a divorce.[44] He further announced that he would give sentence on the legitimacy of the king's second marriage before the feast of Pentecost.[45]

Cranmer's first verdict cleared the way for the coronation of Anne as Queen of England. On Thursday 29 May Anne sailed from Greenwich to the Tower of London in a barge painted with her colours: she was accompanied by a fleet of 100–120 similar vessels: at the Tower, she was greeted by Henry, who gave her 'a loving kiss'. On Saturday afternoon, 31 May, Anne processed – as Katharine had done in 1509 – from the Tower of London to Whitehall Palace; she travelled in a litter covered with cloth of gold.[46] Notwithstanding that she was manifestly pregnant, Anne was dressed in white and her hair was loose over her shoulders, symbolising chastity. The 'greater part' of the nobility of England accompanied her. The people of London had gathered in enormous numbers to watch the spectacle and the streets were hung with tapestries and the floors were gravelled to prevent horses from sliding. The procession was led by a dozen of the French ambassador's men, indicating Francis I's support for the marriage. There were many pageants on the road: one of them may well have been designed by Hans Holbein. The litter was carried into Westminster Hall, where Anne thanked those who had attended her and withdrew to her chamber.

On Sunday at about 8.00 a.m. Anne was led on foot to the abbey by the Lord Mayor and aldermen of the City of London; the road was covered with precious cloth. It was normal for the populace to shout, 'God save the king! God save the queen!' but there was no public acclamation; when one of Anne's servants told the lord mayor to command the people to acclaim her he was told that this could not be produced by order even if the king gave the command. Many sneered at the 'H.A' painted in several places on the route.

Anne was led into the abbey by the archbishops of Canterbury and York and took up her position under the cloth of state. The Duke of Suffolk and the Lord Chamberlain served as the principal lay officers at the ceremony. At the high altar the Archbishop of Canterbury crowned her with the crown of St Edward, but since this was very heavy it was then taken off and a lighter crown made for her was put on her. She received the sacrament and then made a ceremonial offering at St Edward's shrine. The company returned to Westminster Hall for a sumptuous feast attended by 800 people: not inappropriately, Cranmer sat at Anne's right hand. The festivities were concluded with the creation of eighteen Knights of the Bath and with jousts in the new tilt-yard at Whitehall (2 June). On Wednesday 4th, Henry sent for the lord mayor to thank him and his colleagues. Henry had wrapped himself and his new marriage in the standards of Church, State and the City of London.

The Drawing of the Lines: Summer 1533

Before the news of Anne's coronation reached Rome, Ortíz wrote to Charles that someone – he did not say who but it was surely he himself – had asked the Pope to issue a new brief to confirm all previous briefs declaring that Henry and the Kingdom of England had incurred the censures of the Church so that no one could consider that Anne Boleyn's children were legitimate or claim that the previous briefs had been revoked. A new brief would also remind those in England who had supported the king that they were deprived of their offices and dignities, including bishoprics in the cases of churchmen.[47]

But still, Pope and Curia dallied. On 16 June, Rodrigo de Ávalos asked the Pope to give his sentence before the vacation (which would last from 8–10 July until the end of September).[48] On the following day, Clement reiterated to Cifuentes and Ávalos that while he hoped to proceed promptly to sentence he could not do so until he knew what Charles V's intentions were.[49] When, a few days later, Ávalos angrily told Clement that in a case of such importance there could be no such thing as vacations, the Pope replied that it was a very old custom and that he could not alter it.[50] The reading of depositions began on 23 June: since there were 150 of them it took two days to read them and when Cifuentes again urged Clement to expedite the process he showed no sign of being prepared to do so. In disgust, Ávalos reported to los Cobos that 'the case has been managed as if it concerned the poorest woman in the world'.[51]

On Thursday 3 July, Mountjoy visited Katharine at Ampthill. She was suffering from an injury to her foot which made it impossible for her to stand up, and her well-being was further blighted with a severe cold.[52] But she retained her spirit – when Mountjoy told her that she was henceforth to be known as the 'princess dowager', Katharine furiously responded that until her dying day she would maintain that she was the king's lawful wife and that her children were legitimate: when she was then told that Henry's marriage with Anne Boleyn had been judged to be lawful by the Lords, Commons and universities she insisted that this was a matter that only the Pope could judge: and when she was threatened with harm being done to her daughter and servants she replied that she would not damn her own soul for anything or for any threats that the king might make her. Rather, she would pray daily for the king and the preservation of his estate but would never abandon her title until the Pope gave the decision that she should do so. She asked to see Mountjoy's authorisation and wherever she found the name 'dowager princess' she furiously crossed it out. She insisted that if she admitted the king's claims it would be to acknowledge that she had been his harlot for twenty-four years. For good measure, Katharine scornfully dismissed the impartiality of the Archbishop of Canterbury.

On 5 July Henry issued a proclamation declaring that his marriage to Katharine was illegal and that it had been dissolved by the Primate of England. Accordingly, Katharine had been deprived of her dignity as 'Queen of England':[53]

Whereas the non-legitimate marriage between the king's highness and the Lady Katharine princess, relict-widow of Prince Arthur, has been legitimately dissolved by just ways and opinions, the divorce and separation having been made between his Highness and the Lady Katharine by the Right Reverend Father in God the Archbishop of Canterbury, Legate, Primate, and Metropolitan of all England.

Therefore the king's majesty has espoused, and taken for his wife, according to the laws of the Church, the truly high and excellent princess, the Lady Anne, now Queen of England, having had her solemnly crowned and anointed, as becoming the praise and glory and honour of the omnipotent God, the security of the succession and descent of the Crown, and to the great pleasure, comfort, and satisfaction of all the subjects of this realm.

All this [has been done] by the common consent of the Lords Spiritual and Temporal, and of the Commons of this realm, by authority of the Parliament, as in like manner by the assent and determination of the whole clergy in its constant convocations held and celebrated in both the provinces of this kingdom.

Anyone denying the validity of the divorce from Katharine or the marriage to Anne would be subject to the provisions of the Statute of Praemunire.

By reason whereof, and because the said divorce and separation is now made and finished, and the king's highness is legitimately married [*sc.* to Anne Boleyn] ... it is a thing therefore evident and manifest that the said Lady Katharine may not for the future have or use the name, style, or title, or dignity of queen of this realm, nor be in any guise reputed, taken, or inscribed, by the name of queen of this realm, but by the name, style, title, and dignity of princess dowager, which name it is fitting she should have, because she was legitimately and perfectly married and conjoined with the said Prince Arthur.

[Therefore] all the officials, ministers, bailiffs, receivers, factors, servants, keepers of parks or forests of the said princess dowager, or any other person or persons, of whatever state, grade, or condition, who, acting contrary to what is aforesaid, shall style, repute, acknowledge, and address, or in any guise obey the said Lady Katharine in virtue of any sort of security, or shall write to her, addressing her by the name of 'queen', or attempt to do or move any other act or acts, or any other thing or things to the impediment or derogation of such acts and processes as have been determined and completed, both by the celebration and confirmation of the said legitimate marriage, justly accomplished and concluded as [stated above] ... will clearly and manifestly incur the said great pains and penalties comprised and specified in the said Act.

'The Lady Katharine' was to be treated with the respect appropriate to her honour and noble lineage as the princess dowager; even her servants were to address her in this manner. After Carlo Capello had reflected on the king's proclamation he wrote to Venice that 'the queen will never act otherwise than as queen': he was correct in this.[54]

The Pope's Preliminary Sentences, 11 July & 8 August 1533

On Wednesday 9 July, a formal proposition was placed before a secret Consistory of Cardinals that Henry VIII should be excommunicated because he had defied the Pope and married his 'concubine'. The cardinals discussed the proposition for seven hours without reaching a consensus and it took them a further two days of debate before they could inform the Pope that they were in agreement: Henry's marriage with Katharine had *not* been prohibited by divine law. Armed with this verdict, on 11 July 1533 Clement VII decreed in the presence of his cardinals ('in Consistory') that the king's divorce from Katharine and his marriage to Anne Boleyn were null and void: accordingly, the king had incurred 'the greater excommunication': in effect, this meant that he was no longer to be regarded by his subjects and by the princes of Europe as the lawful monarch of England.[55] However, Clement suspended the implementation of this verdict until the end of September so that the king would have one final opportunity to reconsider his actions or to lodge an appeal against the decision.[56]

The verdict was unequivocal in every regard save that it did not concern itself with 'the principal cause'. It systematically rejected every aspect of the case put forward by Henry and his agents: even if the prohibition of marriage to a brother's widow did not derive from divine law; even if Henry had been a minor when the dispensation had been obtained from Julius II and even if he had protested on reaching puberty that he did not consider the dispensation to have been valid; even though there were no wars or even fears of war to justify the marriage – Clement declared that none of this was relevant, since Julius's dispensation had been granted 'to preserve peace' and this had been done. Clement therefore ruled that Julius's dispensation was valid: he had had the right to dispense Henry and Katharine from any diriment impediment of affinity.

Clement thereby validated Julius's brief even though he accepted the advice of the Consistory that it had not been proven that Katharine had been a virgin when she married Henry. What was decisive, in Clement's view, was that the marriage of Henry and Katharine had been 'public, notorious and consummated' and could therefore not be dissolved *even though the question of the consummation or otherwise of Katharine's marriage with Arthur could not be proven.* Clement followed the advice of his cardinals in emphasising that the decisive actions had been those of the king himself – that, for many years, Henry had acted upon the dispensation granted by Julius II and had lived with Katharine as man and wife. Accordingly, he had deprived himself of the right to protest against the validity (or relevance) of Julius II's dispensation. Clement therefore decreed that for these *and for many other reasons* he was entitled to proceed to judgement in 'the principal cause'.

On 11 July 1533, therefore, Pope Clement in Consistory pronounced sentence on these preliminary issues: Katharine was restored to her royal status and the marriage with 'Ana' was annulled and any children who were born from it were declared to be illegitimate. Henry himself was excommunicated and was given until 1 October to appeal against the Pope's decision. But still Clement had not proceeded to judge 'the principal cause' because he and his canonists in the Rota and the Consistory of Cardinals had found that there were deficiencies in the material presented by Katharine's agents. Nevertheless, on 17 July he informed Charles V that he expected him to provide assistance should he decide against Henry, for otherwise all his efforts would have been in vain.[57] On 8 August, Clement issued a papal bull formally commanding Henry to restore Katharine and separate himself from Anne within ten days on pain of excommunication. Moreover, the Pope required that Charles V and all other Christian princes and Henry's own subjects should assist in the execution of his command by force of arms.[58] Would the Emperor comply, for if he did not do so then surely no one else would? Reflecting in Rome on the developing crisis, the Spanish Cardinal of Jaén remarked that Henry was seeking a divorce not merely from his wife but from the Church. He thoroughly approved of the Pope's decision, noting that if it cost the Holy See the obedience of 'one unfruitful island', Clement would by his rigour gain the obedience of many kingdoms that were more important than England.[59]

16

UNDEFEATED: 'THE MOST OBSTINATE WOMAN THAT MAY BE'

The Years of Intimidation, 1553–54
The Birth of Princess Elizabeth, September 1533 & the Bastardisation of Princess Mary

The news of the papal bulls of 11 July and 8 August 1533 reached London in letters from Charles V to Chapuys at the end of August. They arrived at an especially distressing time for Katharine, for not only was she dreading the imminent birth of Anne's child but she had picked up rumours that Henry intended to confiscate the lands and goods that she retained from her marriage settlements: she regarded these as a defining part of her dignity as a queen. Her spirits rose when she heard of the contents of Charles's letters: she briefly hoped that they would oblige Henry to return to obedience to the papacy and evidently expected Charles to take military action immediately to execute Clement's VII's sentence.[1]

On Sunday 7 September, between 3.00 and 4.00 in the afternoon, Anne gave birth to a daughter: it was a shattering disappointment for both parents that their child was a girl, the more so because the king had been assured by a range of physicians, astrologers and even sorceresses that he would have a son.[2] There was talk at court that Henry would christen the child Mary, to emphasise that she was replacing Katharine's daughter, but instead he named her Elizabeth, presumably after his mother. The celebrations for the baptism were notably restrained: Chapuys was probably not being unduly hostile when he recorded that there had been no bonfires and public rejoicings and that the christening had been 'very cold and disagreeable both to the Court and the City'. However, Elizabeth's birth enabled the king to break another link with Katharine: he declared that Mary was no longer his heiress and was therefore not to be entitled 'Princess'.[3]

The king's announcement was a devastating blow for Katharine, for it invalidated all that she had done with her life. She fell into despair in what were to be her last years, isolated in a succession of small and uncomfortable houses and denied the comfort of having her daughter near her. Time would show that the hopes that she entertained of Charles V and Clement VII would never be realised.

Within weeks of Elizabeth's birth Henry despatched the earls of Oxford, Essex and Sussex to Beaulieu to demand that Mary renounce her title, promising that he would treat her generously if she did so.[4] Mary refused: she wrote to her father that while she would always obey him she could never relinquish the titles and prerogatives that had been given to her by God, nature and her parents and that as the daughter of a king and a queen she had the right to be styled 'Princess'.[5]

Katharine resolutely supported her daughter: in the autumn of 1533, she sent a deeply moving letter to Mary, who was now seventeen. The letter is undated but was almost certainly occasioned by the birth of Elizabeth for it contained Katharine's reflections upon the situation now confronting Mary and herself. She urged Mary to accept whatever God had planned for her while yet responding loyally to the demands of her father. Katharine sent Mary two devotional books in Latin to strengthen her faith and encouraged her to seek refuge from stress by continuing to play music. She urged her daughter to be steadfast and brave 'for we never come to the Kingdom of Heaven except through troubles'. She asked Mary to remember her to the Countess of Salisbury and signed her letter, 'Your loving mother, Katharine the queen.'[6] Certainly, Mary showed that she had her mother's determination: when at the turn of 1533–34 she was obliged to ask her father for new clothes she instructed her messenger that he was not to accept a cheque, for this would certainly not entitle her as 'Princess': he was only to take cash.[7]

Henry determined to reduce the households of both Katharine and Mary in order at once to make manifest their reduced status and to intimidate them. Absurdly, he claimed that Katharine's household was costing about £40,000 annually: in reality, Katharine had so few servants that the cost was only one-tenth of that figure.[8] Mary's household was much larger (as befitted her status as heiress to the throne until Elizabeth's birth): one account of its members listed no fewer than 162 people.⁹

In October 1533, the king ordered Baron Mountjoy, as Katharine's chamberlain, to identify the servants in her household who continued to address her as 'queen' rather than as 'princess dowager'. Mountjoy's inquisition was not severe and many of Katharine's servants did their best to support her loyally: some of her chaplains and ladies-in-waiting protested that they had taken oaths to her as 'queen' and so would be committing perjury if they now addressed her as 'princess dowager'. Mountjoy (who had been Katharine's chamberlain since 1512) found the task deeply distasteful and virtually asked Cromwell to have him relieved of his office:

> It is not therefore possible for me to be a reformer of other folks' tongues, or to accuse them, as I verily believe they are loyal to the king's grace; nor can I consent to vex and disquiet her, she keeping herself true to the king, as I know none other.
>
> If it be thought by the king that any other can serve him in this room better than I have done, as doubtless there are many, I beg you to be a means on my behalf that I may, without the king's displeasure, be discharged of the office of Chamberlain.¹⁰

Henry appears not to have acted on Mountjoy's request, perhaps because he had only a few months to live: when the baron died in 1534 he still held the title of Katharine's chamberlain. As for Henry, he would not again attempt to apply pressure on Katharine from within her own household. Future visitations would be much more intimidating.

The Last Chance: The Meeting of Clement VII & Francis I at Marseilles, October–November 1533

Once again, the rivalry of Charles and Francis in Italy – and most especially over the control of Milan – subsumed the king's 'Great Matter'. By the early 1530s it was evident that Francesco II Sforza had not long to live and both Charles V and Francis I claimed the right to name his successor as Duke of Milan. In his meeting with Clement VII at Bologna in 1532 Charles had tried to persuade the Pope to marry Sforza to his niece Catherine de' Medici but Clement had refused and subsequently accepted Francis I's offer of his second son, Henri, Duke of Orleans, as Catherine's husband. For Clement, the French marriage would have several advantages over an imperial alliance: it would raise the Medici to royal status and help to prevent the creation of an imperial bloc centred on Milan and intimidatingly adjacent to Florence; it would also help him to secure Francis's support against the convocation of a General Council of the Church.[11] For his part, Francis intended to push Clement for a reconciliation with Henry so as to separate him from Charles V and he persuaded Henry to attend the meeting to show his good faith. As his opening gambit in the preparations for his interview, Francis let Clement know that he would be asking him to extend to six months the period of grace allowed to Henry to take Katharine back. In his determination to oppose Charles V in Italy, Francis I now presented Henry with a marvellous opportunity: in the papal–French rapprochement against the Emperor lay Henry's greatest – and last? – hope of an agreed solution with the papacy to his 'Great Matter'.

Pope Clement fully demonstrated the importance that he attached to the alliance with Francis I by making the remarkable decision to travel to France to meet Francis and to allow Henry VIII to join them so that a solution could be found to his marital difficulties. On reflection, however, Henry decided that he dared not absent himself from England and so he sent Norfolk to represent him as head of a small delegation which included Rochford, brother of Queen Anne. As so often, Henry was his own worst enemy in his dealings with the papacy: having snubbed Pope Clement by not attending his meeting with Francis, he then gave great offence to him by once again inflicting a Boleyn upon him as a member of his delegation. On 18 August he then capped his dire performance and virtually ruled out any prospect of reaching an accommodation with Clement VII by instructing Dr Bonner to inform the Pope that he was lodging a formal appeal against his sentence to a General Council of the Church.[12] Did Henry VIII really want to resolve his 'Great Matter'?

Henry's strategy – such as it was – began to crumble even before Clement and Francis met. When Norfolk arrived in Lyons he learned that the Pope had announced that he intended to excommunicate Henry: he was so dumbfounded by the news that he nearly fainted and decided that he dared not be seen as a supplicant of the Pope at such a moment. He therefore left Bishop Gardiner of Winchester (who was ordinary ambassador to Francis I) and headed home for fresh instructions.[13] Meanwhile, the Pope decided en route to France that he could not agree to Francis's request that he provide an extension of six months for Henry to comply with his sentence, and at Pisa on 27 September – with only four days to go before his deadline for excommunicating Henry and

Anne expired – Clement proposed in Consistory that Henry should be allowed only one more month to obey him.[14] For the Pope, the dispute with Henry remained a theological rather than a diplomatic one.

Clement arrived in Marseilles on 12 October, accompanied by a dozen or so cardinals and thirty-two bishops. On the following day, Francis joined him: as a sign of their friendship they lodged in the same palace.[15] But even a newly blossoming friendship had its limitations: on 20 October, Clement formally refused the French request to rescind his order against Henry. Once again he insisted that he was obliged to judge the case because Katharine had specifically appealed to him and he refused even to discuss 'the principal matter' as he had not yet reached his decision on it.[16]

The marriage of Henri and Catherine was celebrated by the Pope on 28 October; the bridegroom was sixteen and the bride fourteen. Ungallantly, Francis I spent the night in the bedroom of the newly-weds to ensure that they consummated their marriage and then gaily announced that 'each had shown valour in the joust': was he mindful of the disaster that had followed for Henry VIII of Arthur's failure to consummate his marriage? Clement also evidently needed reassuring on this delicate subject for on the following morning he ceremonially visited the young couple in bed and happily noted that they both seemed satisfied.[17] Certainly, time would show that neither King nor Pope needed to have worried about the fecundity of the bride and groom: although the marriage was not always a happy one Catherine did her duty by Henri in presenting him with ten children, three of whom became kings of France.

On 7 November the English mission self-destructed when Bonner informed Clement that Henry had formally appealed to a future General Council of the Church against his sentence. Clement was outraged by Henry's effrontery: he hurriedly consulted with Giacomo Simoneta and Paolo Capizzuchi and when he met Bonner later in the day showed his anger by a gesture that was recognised by papal insiders as an expression of intense fury – by wrapping and unwrapping his handkerchief.[18] He reiterated that he was obliged as pontiff to judge the case because Katharine had appealed to him. It happened that Francis I entered the chamber at that moment and spent forty-five minutes in conversation with the Pope: he was appalled to learn what had happened, recognising that his efforts to reconcile Clement with Henry had been wrecked in front of his eyes by Henry's egregious appeal to a General Council. Clement duly consulted with his cardinals in Consistory before informing Bonner that Henry's appeal was frivolous and was rejected (10 November). On 20 November the Pope left for Rome, content that he had consolidated his alliance with France.[19] Henry had thrown away his last chance of a negotiated settlement of his 'Great Matter' with the Pope.

Francis I sent Bishop Jean du Bellay to inform Henry of the outcome of his meeting with Clement and to rebuke him for the manner in which he had conducted himself. Du Bellay was to remind Henry that at Calais in 1532 he and Francis had agreed to take a joint approach to Pope Clement to separate him from the Emperor and to oblige him to accommodate Henry. Most especially, they had agreed that Henry himself would be present at the meeting with Clement as the fullest public expression of his wish for a reconciliation with him. Francis was furious at the downgrading of the English mission as first Henry and then Norfolk absented themselves, regarding it as a grave slight on his reputation as convenor and host of the meeting. Moreover, Francis had secured a promise from the Pope that he would not take any new initiatives prior to their meeting on the understanding that Henry himself would not do so but Henry had then blithely proceeded with his belligerent programme against the English Church in Parliament. Du Bellay was to let Henry know that when Francis entered the papal chamber to learn that Dr Bonner was informing Clement of Henry's appeal to a General Council, the news 'put him in the greatest despair and anger' as he found that all the preparatory work that he had done on Henry's behalf had been undone by him in less than an hour. Du Bellay was to insist that a settlement of Henry's 'Great Matter' could have been reached if he had not made Clement so angry. In fine, du Bellay had the unenviable task of conveying to the King of England the contempt that the King of France had for the manner in which he conducted his business: 'The bishop may say here to Henry, as if of himself, that if he wishes to keep the friendship of the most powerful king and best friend in Christendom, he must not behave in this strange and suspicious way.'[20]

Francis thereby absolved himself of all guilt for the breakdown of discussions over Henry's 'Great Matter': Henry had undone the best efforts of Francis I to mediate with the Pope on his behalf and had wrecked his own case. It was to prove to have been his last chance to reconcile himself with the papacy.

Intimidation I: Suffolk's Mission to Katharine, December 1533

After Mountjoy's half-hearted failure to secure the oaths of loyalty to the Boleyn marriage (and its daughter) from Katharine and many of her servants, Henry in December 1533 entrusted his old friend Charles Brandon, Duke of Suffolk, to go to Kimbolton and force the oaths through. Now, too, there would be further punishment for Katharine and her servants: Suffolk was also charged to reduce the size of Katharine's household by dismissing her chancellor, almoner and receiver and other officials and of then moving her to a house in Somersham in East Anglia.[21] Like Mountjoy, Suffolk seems to have been deeply resentful of the task given him; his biographer, Steven Gunn, has suggested that he and his wife Mary (who was of course Henry's sister) probably sympathised with Katharine and that he had been distressed by having had to inform her in April 1533 that she was no longer queen. There was even a suggestion – admittedly conveyed through the dubious prism of the imperial ambassador – that Suffolk confessed and communicated before he set out for Kimbolton in the hope that some fateful accident might prevent him from carrying out the mission imposed upon him.[22]

Yet again, Katharine confronted a royal emissary with firmness: she courteously but emphatically told Suffolk that she would rather be 'hewn into pieces' than deny that she was the lawful wife of the king and refused even to countenance withdrawing her appeal to Rome. Katharine repeated that Henry had been the first to apply to the Pope and insisted that she would rather suffer a thousand deaths than consent to what was contrary to God's law, her own honour and the conscience of the king. As for moving to Somersham: she would only go to that unhealthy house if she was carried there by force. Nor would she tolerate the presence in her household of anyone who had taken an oath to her as 'princess dowager'.

Six of her servants refused outright to swear to recognise the Boleyn marriage. They were led by Bishop Athequa, her confessor, and Dr Miguel de la Sá, her physician, both of whom had been with Katharine since she came from Spain; the others were John Sotha and Philip Greenacre, her apothecaries, Anthony Rocke (whose position in the household is uncertain) and the Burgundian Bastian Hennyocke, gentleman-in-waiting.[23] Five men, all of whom appear to have been British, took the oath – William Mortimore, Thomas Payne, James Orme; and Thomas Jonson and Will Style, both of whom were servants of Bishop Athequa (and may therefore have been of Welsh origin). Suffolk believed that eight ladies might be persuaded to take the oath.[24]

Suffolk decided to dismiss Athequa but Katharine called his bluff by insisting that she was only able to confess in Spanish: the duke buckled, leaving Athequa with her. He dismissed Mountjoy together with the almoner and Master of the Horse, ordering them not to return to Katharine's service on pain of death, and imprisoned two chaplains (Abel and Barker) in the Tower of London: both would die there. Nothing is known of Barker but Abel cannot have been too surprised at his fate: as chaplain of Katharine he had published (in April 1532?) a defence of her marriage in which he argued 'that by no manner of law it may be lawful for King Henry to be divorced from the queen's grace, his lawful and very wife'. He was now imprisoned on the highly contrived charge of having disseminated the prophecies of 'the Nun of Kent' (below).[25]

Suffolk allowed Dr de la Sá to remain in place but sent away virtually all of Katharine's ladies of the chamber. When Katharine protested that she would not accept replacements for the servants who had been dismissed and would rather sleep in her clothes and lock the gate herself, Suffolk agreed that two ladies could remain with her. All the servants who remained, except the confessor, physician and apothecary (who could not speak English), were obliged to swear that they would not address her as queen. Still, Katharine would not budge: she protested that she would no longer regard these people as her servants but as her guards, and that she was a prisoner.

After six days the commissioners loaded Katharine's baggage onto carts and prepared a litter and horses for her journey to Somersham. Katharine's defiance was – as always – to the point: she locked herself in her chamber and challenged the commissioners to break the door down to take her away: this they dared not do. Katharine kept her chamber locked throughout the night in case an attempt was made to abduct her. Now she truly was a prisoner. Suffolk's mission was a fiasco and he was in despair: 'We find here the most obstinate woman that may be.'[26]

While Suffolk confronted Katharine the Duke of Norfolk was instructed to take Mary to Hatfield House, where – to her deep humiliation – she was to form part of the household of Princess Elizabeth.[27] The Countess of Shrewsbury begged to remain with Mary at her own expense but Henry refused to allow her to do so, dismissing her as an old fool.[28] Mary was shaken by the loss of her beloved governess but remained every whit as defiant as her mother: she continued to insist that the title of 'Princess' 'belonged to her and no other' and wrote a response to Norfolk and his colleagues that was apparently drafted by Chapuys:

My lords, as touching my removal to Hatfield, or to any other place his Grace may appoint me I will obey his Grace, as my duty is, but I protest before you, and all others present, that my conscience will in no wise suffer me to take any other than myself for princess, or for the king's daughter born in lawful matrimony; and that I will never wittingly or willingly say or do anything, whereby any person might take occasion to think that I agree to the contrary.

As God is my judge, I do not say this out of any ambition or proud mind. If I should do otherwise, I should slander the deed of my mother, and falsely confess myself a bastard, which God forbid that I should do, since the Pope has not so declared it by his definitive sentence: I submit myself to his final judgement.[29]

Mary was taken to Hatfield on 13 December 1533 and when a few weeks later Henry visited Elizabeth there she was confined to her rooms. Cromwell urged her to renounce her title but again she refused. When Henry departed she went onto a balcony to wave farewell to him: on seeing her Henry touched his cap and bowed. They did not see each other again for over two years. Despite the courtesy of his gesture, Henry was furious with his daughter: the French ambassador reported to Chapuys that the king had told him 'he would not see or speak to the princess on account of her stubborn and obstinate disobedience to his commands, which, he said, she had inherited with her Spanish blood'.[30] However, the king was not as icily hostile as he appeared: when he returned to court the French ambassador remarked to him how well educated Mary was and 'tears rushed to the king's eyes, and he could not help praising her many virtues and accomplishments'.[31]

Mary was unrelenting: when Anne visited Hatfield in March 1534 in the hope of a reconciliation she was bluntly rejected as Mary told her that 'she knew no other queen in England except her mother'. Furious, Anne followed Henry in reverting to national stereotyping, vowing that she would 'put down that proud Spanish blood'.[32]

The Day of Judgement, Rome & London, 23 March 1534: The Pope's Sentence & the First Act of Succession

In January 1534 Clement VII informed the Count of Cifuentes that he was ready to proceed to judgement.[33] Once again, Cifuentes insisted that the Pope should not issue his sentence until he had secured Charles's support but Clement would wait no longer: he ordered Giacomo Simoneta, auditor of the Rota, to undertake a final review all the documents in the case, and on Friday 27 February Simoneta duly presented his review to the Consistory of Cardinals.[34] A few days later the Pope ordered all the cardinals who were in Rome to stand ready to give their verdict in Consistory even though he admitted that he retained residual doubts about Katharine's case which he would require her lawyers to satisfy.[35]

On Monday 23 March, Clement VII and the Consistory of Cardinals spent more than six hours in discussion: it is probable that Clement had to convince some cardinals of the action that he was about to take. At all events, Clement on that day finally pronounced a definitive sentence in Katharine's favour: her marriage to Henry had indeed been lawful.[36] It had taken him five years to reach this conclusion – but still he was not yet ready to proceed to sentence in 'the principal cause'.

Dr Ortíz was exultant and proclaimed that the papal sentence represented the greatest of the Emperor's victories. He generously commended the support given to Katharine by cardinals Campeggio, Cayetano, Farnese and Sanctiquatro. He paid an especially intriguing compliment to Cardinal Campeggio: Ortíz recorded that Campeggio had maintained that if the case had turned on the proofs submitted by Katharine about her virginity when she married Henry VIII he would have had great doubts of the justice of her case, but that he nevertheless found in her favour because he believed that it had been established that the marriage was not prohibited by divine law. In other words, Campeggio recognised that even though he held doubts about the provenance of Katharine's virginity after her marriage to Arthur, he was yet convinced that her marriage to Henry was lawful in the eyes of the Church. Ortíz – who, we must always remember was a belligerently partisan observer – went even further: he informed Charles V that Campeggio had let it be known that he had *always* been certain that Katharine was in the right – presumably he meant by this that the cardinal had reached that conclusion during his ill-fated visit to London. Ortíz must surely have reflected that if Campeggio had made that view public in 1529–30 the years of agonised tumult over the king's 'Great Matter' would have been avoided.[37] Ortíz wrote to Katharine congratulating her on her victory without a single dissentient vote; he jubilantly informed her that even Cardinal Tribulcio, the representative of Francis I, had voted in her favour and that the Consistory had confirmed the judgement of the Rota in 1533 that her marriage was not unlawful. He urged Katharine and Mary to be brave and constant.[38]

Charles's Spanish advisers in Rome were divided as to the advice they should give him: the Cardinal of Jaén optimistically reported that

Clement would now be ready to join in a 'common enterprise' with the Emperor against Henry but Cifuentes refused to believe that Charles was obliged to take military action to execute the Pope's decision and doubted whether in practical terms the sentence would make any difference beyond saving Charles's honour and justifying Katharine's actions in appealing to Rome.[39] Indeed, when Cifuentes reflected on the papal sentence he advised Charles to bring pressure to bear on Henry by cutting English trade with all his dominions rather than by using force directly against him.[40]

While Clement was at last bringing himself to make a decision, Henry was beginning to make the fullest use of Parliament to break with Rome. The Parliamentary session that took place between January and March 1534 activated into law the 'Act in Absolute Restraint of Annates' and the 'Act for the Submission of the Clergy', both of which had been provisionally passed in 1532. These statutes cut off the Pope's supplies of revenue from episcopal and abbatial appointments and enabled the Crown to control nominations to these positions in the future.

Much more importantly, it happened that on the day that the Pope gave his sentence in Consistory – 23 March 1534 – Parliament declared in the (first) Act of Succession that Henry's marriage to Anne was lawful and that the succession to Henry's throne was to devolve upon her children. Princess Mary was thereby illegitimated in London on the very day of her mother's triumph in Rome.[41] The Act stipulated

> that the marriage heretofore solemnized between your highness
> and the Lady Katharine, being before lawful wife to Prince Arthur,
> your elder brother, which by him was carnally known, as does duly
> appear by sufficient proof in a lawful process had and made before
> Thomas, by the sufferance of God, now archbishop of Canterbury
> and metropolitan and primate of all this realm, shall be, by authority
> of this present Parliament, definitively, clearly, and absolutely
> declared, deemed, and adjudged to be against the laws of Almighty
> God, and also accepted, reputed, and taken of no value nor effect,
> but utterly void and annulled, and the separation thereof, made by
> the said archbishop, shall be good and effectual to all intents and
> purposes...
>
> And that the said Lady Katharine shall be from henceforth called
> and reputed only dowager to Prince Arthur, and not queen of this
> realm; and that the lawful matrimony had and solemnized between

your highness and your most dear and entirely beloved wife Queen Anne, shall be established, and taken for undoubtful, true, sincere, and perfect ever hereafter.

It was further enacted that anyone who, after 1 May 1534, in word, deed or act endangered the peace of the realm by questioning the validity of the king's marriage to Anne Boleyn was to be deemed guilty of high treason and subjected to the penalties appropriate to that offence. It was now the law of England that even to speak against Henry's second marriage and the legitimate right of its children to succeed to the throne was treasonable.[42]

The dramatic acceleration of events in London reflected the fact that Henry now had at his side the minister who would bring his case to a conclusion: Thomas Cromwell had began to cut Gordian knots in secular affairs in 1533 as Cranmer had done in ecclesiastical life. The first of these concerned the vexations created by the activities of Elizabeth Barton, 'the Nun of Kent', who had become a minor celebrity by experiencing visions years before the 'king's Great Matter' became widely known: in 1528 she was interviewed by Henry VIII and Wolsey and told them of her prophecies. In particular, she urged Wolsey to do what he could to protect the king's marriage to Katharine. Perhaps Elizabeth became beguiled by her own celebrity, for she soon stepped into perilous waters: when she subsequently learned that Henry was intending to replace Katharine with Anne Boleyn, she claimed to have had a divine revelation that if Henry married Anne he would not live for a further month, and when he then did so she conveniently had another vision in which God told her that He no longer accepted that Henry was King of England. She publicly proclaimed 'in the name and by the authority of God' that the marriage to Anne was illegal.

Cromwell appreciated that it would be easy enough to deal with the difficulties created by Elizabeth's rantings but he also recognised that she presented him with important opportunities, for she had done her best to involve Katharine and her supporters in intrigues: she had sent a message to Katharine that her descendants would reign in England and had actively solicited support from John Fisher and Thomas More in personal interviews that they had somewhat naively given to her. In striking at 'the Nun of Kent', Cromwell would be able to damage Katharine and target Fisher and More. The woman who had been known in and around Canterbury as a devoutly holy person – or a charlatan – now dramatically became a figure of national importance, providing Henry and Cromwell with a weapon with which to attack Katharine and her supporters.

Elizabeth and a few of her leading followers were arrested in September 1533. She confessed that she was herself the cause 'of all this mischief' and that all her visions were false. More prosaically, she acknowledged that a letter which she had claimed to have received directly from Mary Magdalen in heaven had in reality been written by a monk named Hawkeshurst of St Augustine's Canterbury.[43] On 23 November 1533 she and six followers (including two Friars Observant) stood on a scaffold at St Paul's Cross to endure the humiliation of hearing her confession read out and her claims denounced. Her trial before the Star Chamber in February 1534 was a formality: she and five of her supporters were found guilty of high treason and sentenced to death.

Two of these men were senior figures in religious orders – Dr Edward Bocking was a Benedictine and Dr Richard Risby a Franciscan. A further six, including Bishop Fisher and Thomas Abel, were convicted of lesser treason (misprision) and were sentenced to be imprisoned at the king's will and to have all their goods confiscated. The condemnation of Fisher was explicitly linked to his defence of Katharine – 'the obstinacy of the Bishop of Rochester against the marriage was confirmed and strengthened by [Barton's] revelation [sc. confession]'.[44] On 12 April Sir Thomas More was ordered to take the oath and when he refused he was committed to the Tower of London (17 April). On 20 April 1534 Elizabeth Barton and her five supporters were hanged at Tyburn and it was proclaimed that all prominent secular Londoners would now be obliged to take the oath. Henry would brook no opposition. More specifically, in executing Bocking and Risby the king had sent a chilling message to the religious orders that they were not exempt from royal justice.[45] It was but a prologue to what would now begin.

Intimidation II & III: The Delegations of Royal Ministers to Katharine, May–June 1534

At the turn of April–May 1534 Katharine was moved to a small house in Kimbolton. She was deeply despondent and wrote to Chapuys that she now believed that 'stronger' methods should be applied against Henry: there is little doubt that Katharine was inviting Charles to launch an invasion of England. Although she subsequently retreated from this position, she had in her despair crossed the line into disloyalty to her husband.

Mary remained resolute: 'God forbid that I should be so blinded by error or ambition as to confess that the king my father, and the queen my mother, have lived so long in adultery, or that I willingly contravene the ordinances and precepts of my holy Mother the Church by acknowledging myself illegitimate.' Mary feared that she might be poisoned but was at least consoled that if she was murdered she would go straight to heaven and be rid of the trials of the world: her only grief was for the tribulations of her mother.[46]

When Chapuys was summoned to meet the council in May Foxe told him that Henry's first marriage had been 'a detestable and abominable act' and that the king had married again for the peace of the kingdom in the hope that future male children would succeed to it: until that happened Princess Elizabeth was the heiress. Parliament had approved the statute detailing the succession to the throne and all of his subjects 'except two women, to wit Madame Katharine and Madame Mary as he called them' had refused to do take the oath: if they persisted in their obstinacy the king would be obliged to proceed against them according to the statute. There was a heated discussion and Chapuys informed the council of the Pope's sentences. He was told that Henry was sending Archbishop Lee of York; Cuthbert Tunstall, Bishop of Durham and Dr Foxe to exhort Katharine to acquiesce in the statute. Fearfully, Chapuys pondered whether Henry would send Katharine and Mary to the Tower.[47] Mountjoy and Suffolk – courtier and senior nobleman – had failed to intimidate Katharine: perhaps bishops carrying the threat of a death sentence would succeed.

In his instructions for this latest delegation, Henry once again 'marvelled' that Katharine continued to maintain that she had not consummated her marriage with Prince Arthur: he did not say – because he did not need to – that if the bishops could wring from Katharine an acknowledgement that she had not in fact been a virgin when Arthur died all his problems would disappear in a trice. And again, Henry insisted that 'the Bishop of Rome' had no jurisdiction in England over the succession to his throne and that in any event he had pre-empted and invalidated any possible papal sentence by appealing to a General Council of the Church. As for his treatment of Katharine: Henry would cut down on the number of Katharine's servants and insisted that they would have to take the oath to him. Moreover, he would not allow Katharine to enjoy the title of queen and promised that he would treat her well and allow her whatever company she chose if she agreed to abandon it. Did this imply that he would allow Katharine to have access to her daughter? But he would never allow any of his native subjects to refuse to take the oath that the Act of Succession required of them.[48]

Nothing is known of the degree of enthusiasm – or lack thereof – with which Bishops Lee and Tunstall set off for Kimbolton, and it appears that no direct account exists of the details of their mission. However, Katharine duly informed Chapuys that they had indeed threatened her with the penalties of statute, including death, if she refused to swear the oath. Her response, as always, was simple enough: she challenged anyone who wished to execute her to step forward, asking only that the sentence should be carried out in a public place and not in a secret chamber. That apart, nothing much seems to have happened: Katharine's confessor, physician, apothecary were forbidden to leave Kimbolton House and four servants were put in prison.[49] Another delegation had failed.

Infuriated by Katharine's resistance, Henry sent yet another delegation to Kimbolton in June. On Corpus Christi Day in the second week of June Sir Edmund Bedingfield told Katharine again that the king and his council refused to accept her insistence that she had not carnally known Prince Arthur and could not believe that she would persist in this. She protested that it was true and that she would not damn her soul to perdition by saying otherwise – not for the love of the king; not even for her daughter's well-being; not for honour or riches. She dismissed them scathingly as she had so many others before them: 'I do greatly marvel that any wise, noble or learned men (having a conscience) will take upon them to judge or determine any such act to be done betwixt prince Arthur and me; and Almighty God (from whom nothing can be hidden) knows that they speak untruly of me.'

She pointedly reminded them that Arthur had been only fifteen years, twenty-seven weeks and a few days old when he died and insisted that she had been a 'true maid' when she married Henry VIII: discreetly, she left them to draw their own conclusions as to why this should have been the case. Bedingfield then repeated Henry's insistence that her appeal to Rome had been invalidated by his appeal to a future General Council and that 'the Bishop of Rome' had no authority in England to define the succession of princes. Katharine wisely refused to be drawn into a discussion of the laws of England and insisted that she would await the Pope's decision and abide by it. She informed Bedingfield that she would allow her officials and servants to take an oath of loyalty to the king and to herself but to no other woman. Perplexed by Katharine's resolve, Bedingfield suggested that the king might allow Katharine's servants to swear to her as princess dowager. Katharine tartly replied that if her confessor, physician and apothecary took any such oath she would never trust them again.[50]

Some much-needed support came to Katharine when on 17 July Chapuys gallantly led a company of about sixty horsemen out of London on a journey which was ostensibly to be a pilgrimage to Walsingham but which would happen to pass by Kimbolton.[51] When a messenger from Katharine informed Chapuys that he would not be allowed to enter her house or to talk with her he permitted some of his men to ride within sight of the house: this greatly lifted the spirits of Katharine's ladies and, doubtless, of the queen herself. Convinced that he had done his duty, Chapuys proceeded to Walsingham: he had publicly demonstrated how badly Katharine was being treated – and that Charles V had not forgotten her.

John Fisher & Thomas More

John Fisher and Thomas More were both indicted in the Bill of Attainder that was presented in the House of Lords against Elizabeth Barton in February 1534. Fisher defended himself to the king by stating that he had only met Barton three times and had refused to offer her any encouragement. In any event, Fisher feared that he was terminally ill: 'Now my body is much weakened with many diseases and infirmities, and my soul is much inquieted by this trouble, so that my heart is more withdrawn from God and from the devotion of prayer than I would. And verily I think that my life may not long continue.' He asked Henry to free him of suspicion so that he could prepare for death – and indeed pray for the king himself.[52]

Fisher then presented his defence to the Privy Council, and in doing so demonstrated that he knew how to play courtly politics: he recalled that among those who had testified to him of Elizabeth Barton's holiness was no less an authority than William Warham, late Archbishop of Canterbury – whom he pointedly described as 'a man reputed of high wisdom and learning' – who had told him that many of Elizabeth's visions were authentic. Fisher dismissed the evidence brought against him with icy disdain: he insisted that he had never advised Elizabeth and did not see the need to report to the king what she had said to him since she herself had already told Henry of her visions.[53]

Sir Thomas More had an early success in defending himself: when he claimed in the Star Chamber that he had justified his position to the king himself, the judges perhaps lost their nerve and removed his name from the Bill of Attainder. More knew well enough that Cromwell would have a decisive voice in whether he lived or died and in two letters set out for him the defence that he would subsequently put forward at his trial. In the first of these he denied that in his brief association with 'the Nun' he had in any way compromised his loyalty to the king. He fastidiously set out the history of his discussions with Henry, insisting that it was the king himself who had first told him about Elizabeth Barton when, eight or nine years previously, he had asked him for advice on her prophecies. More had told Henry that he was sceptical about her visions, believing that she said nothing that might not have been said by any 'right simple woman': he dismissively refused even to become involved in judging whether a miracle had happened to her. He recorded that, around Christmastime 1532, Dr Risby had spoken highly to him of Elizabeth's holiness and informed him that Elizabeth had told Wolsey that God had put three swords into his hands and that he would be severely judged if he did not use them well: he was to reform spiritual life, to rule justly as Lord Chancellor and to resolve the difficulties over the king's marriage. Horrified that 'the Nun' was trespassing into political matters, More emphatically denied that he had entered into any discussions with her about the king's 'Great Matter' and insisted that on dismissing her he had done no more than give her money and ask her to pray for him and his family. He never spoke to her again and pointedly commended Cromwell for his vigilance in scrutinising her conduct.[54]

The date of this first letter of More's to Cromwell is uncertain but on 5 March 1534, he wrote again to him, setting out in precise detail his position over the king's 'Great Matter': his letter was a brilliant summing-up by a lawyer of the highest calibre – and More of course knew that it needed to be, for he was now fighting for his own life. Once again, he was careful to restate the assurances that he had received in person from the king, most notably that Henry had guaranteed that he would not oblige him to become involved in his 'Great Matter' to the prejudice of his own conscience.[55] More was now even more explicit about the details of his discussions with the king: he recorded that when he had met Henry at Hampton Court (in 1529) to report on a mission he had conducted abroad, the king took him for a walk in the garden and dramatically informed him that he now believed that his marriage to Katharine had not only been against the laws of the Church and of God but was so contrary to the law of nature that Pope Julius had not been entitled to have issued the dispensation permitting him to marry Katharine. Henry showed

More the text in Leviticus and asked him for his opinion of it. More naturally equivocated while he collected his thoughts and Henry urged him to speak to Foxe and to read with him a book that he was putting together to support the royal case. More emphasised to Cromwell that he had avoided becoming involved in the case during the period of the legatine court because he had no knowledge of ecclesiastical law: indeed, while the legates were sitting he was abroad, serving Henry on a mission in Cambrai to conclude the peace with the Emperor and Francis I. It was on his return in 1529 that he was made Chancellor. The implication of this concluding remark needed no emphasis: in appointing More to the highest judicial office in the land, the king self-evidently had the very fullest confidence in the way that he had conducted himself.

The king soon again invited More to consider his 'Great Matter' and repeated his promise that he would not require him to do or say anything against his conscience and that he should look first to God and then to himself: More well remembered the king's words and in time made an elegant play on them when he was brought to the block. He carefully stated as a matter of record that Henry had assured him that (as More summarised the king's words) he would 'never [be] willing to put any man in ruffle or trouble for his conscience'. For his part, he looked forward to serving the king in other matters. Moreover, he promised that he would never be drawn into speaking against the king's marriage to Anne (whom he described as 'this noble woman') and would pray for them and for their children.

More went further: he informed Cromwell that he had never believed that God had established the primacy of the papacy until he had become convinced of this by reading the king's book against Luther. Notwithstanding this remarkable revelation, More had firmly advised the king not even to touch upon the subject of papal primacy in his book since there might come a time when he was involved in a dispute with the Pope and be embarrassed by his own words. Henry refused. Intrigued (and deeply worried) by the difficulties that had thus been raised, over the next years More studied the writings of Church Fathers and the decrees of the General Councils of the Church. He duly became convinced that the primacy of the Bishop of Rome had been established by 'the Body of Christendom' to avoid schisms: he therefore drew the conclusion that no individual part of the Christian body could separate itself from the Pope as the common head of Christendom. This would be the conclusion that would govern all his future decisions in defending himself: he would stand simultaneously on his conscience and on his conviction that no single part of Christendom could stand out against papal primacy in Church affairs. But More's studies also convinced him that General Councils exercised God-given authority over the Church: accordingly, he was pleased to wish Henry a speedy resolution of his appeal to a General Council against the Pope's verdict.

More drew two further conclusions from his studies: he carefully but firmly advised Cromwell that the king should not make laws which appeared to derogate or diminish the authority of the Apostolic See and the General Councils. In doing so, More trod perilously close to treason in asserting that there were restrictions on Henry's powers in England. However, his second conclusion may well have brought comfort to king and minister: rather than defending the conduct of Pope Clement, More suggested that it was likely that the next General Council might depose him and replace him with a Pope who was acceptable to Henry. More therefore begged Cromwell to assure the king of his loyalty and insisted that in his dealings with Elizabeth Barton – 'that wicked woman' – he had intended nothing but good. But he also made it clear that he had drawn a line: he assured Cromwell that his guiding principle would always be to follow his conscience and that he would give up everything *except his soul* to spare himself from even one unpleasant glance from the king.

The crown, too, was drawing a line. In January 1535 Henry formally styled himself 'Henry VIII, by the Grace of God King of England and of France, Defender of the Faith and of Lord of Ireland and Supreme Head of the Church of England'.[56] His agents unleashed a whirlwind of anti-episcopal and anti-papal measures: Dr George Brown – who was rumoured to have officiated at the marriage of Henry and Anne – preached that all bishops who did not burn their papal bulls of appointment and secure replacements from the king should be severely punished; Cromwell solicitously took advice from bishops as to whether the king could make and unmake bishops at will;[57] Cranmer formally renounced the jurisdiction of the Bishop of Rome and several bishops followed his example.[58] In January 1535, Thomas Cromwell was appointed Vicar General over the Church. At once, he ordered that a survey be made of the land and possessions of the Church and that the monasteries of England should be visited so that each one of them could be assessed: he would show the king how to firmly establish his control over the Church in England – and how to profit mightily from doing so.

Pope & Emperor Triumphant: The Revival of the Catholic Crusade?
Clement VII died on 25 September 1534. There was only one candidate of
stature who was acceptable to both imperial and French parties and the
conclave required just one day to appoint Cardinal Alessandro Farnese
as his successor (13 October): he took the title of Paul III. Farnese was
sixty-eight years old and had been a cardinal for forty years. Like Charles
V and Francis I, Henry VIII had good reason to be gratified by Farnese's
election for the new Pope let it be known immediately upon his election
that he was favourably disposed to the King of England and anxious to
resolve his conflict with Rome.[59]

The election of Paul III coincided with a grave crisis in the Mediterranean
for in the summer of 1534 Suleiman's admiral Khair-ad-Din Barbarossa
attacked southern Italy and came close to the walls of Rome. He then
conquered Tunis in August and posed a grave and immediate threat
to Spain, Italy and the powers of the Western Mediterranean. Paul III
and Charles V responded with dramatic vigour: the Pope proclaimed a
crusade against the infidel and provided six galleys for a new imperial
fleet to attack Barbarossa. The crusading Knights of St John of Malta
committed another four galleys to the fleet and Charles brought together
all the men, ships and resources that he could muster from his various
realms. Moreover, Charles V undertook to lead the crusade in person.

When Christendom's great fleet assembled at Cagliari on 12 June it
consisted of seventy-four galleys and 300 transport ships and carried
30,000 soldiers. It disembarked at the derelict site of Carthage (16 June)
and within a month had taken La Goletta (14 July). It then turned on
Tunis, which submitted on 21 July. It was a victory of staggering import:
eighty-two galleys were added to the Christian fleet and some 20,000
Christians were freed from their captivity. For the first time, the forces
of Suleiman the Magnificent had been defeated in a major encounter by
a Christian force. Charles had reached one of the great pinnacles of his
career: he truly was the leader of Europe and the defender of Christendom
against the infidel. Most conveniently, in Naples he found documentary
evidence that the Most Christian King of France had secretly allied himself
with Suleiman and Barbarossa.[60] Charles's astounding triumph became
all the more delicious to him because it served to discredit his great rival.
And – as always – Charles knew how to celebrate in style: on 25 July, the
Emperor dressed himself in his cape as a Knight of St James to celebrate
the feast day of the patron of Spain, St James 'the killer of Moors': the
Emperor thereby proclaimed himself to Europe and (most especially) to

his Spanish subjects as the heir of St James. He had achieved the greatest ambition of his life: to be a crusading hero leading Christendom against the infidel.

Charles's victory reverberated around Europe. In London, Henry VIII and Cromwell feared that the Emperor might well now exultantly turn his triumphant forces on England.[61] At the end of January 1535 Chapuys had some heated discussions with Cromwell over the intentions of their respective monarchs: Chapuys denied that Charles V was intent on invading England but insisted that he would never accept the Boleyn marriage, while Cromwell vowed that Henry would not allow Mary to live with her mother and still had hopes that the Pope would retrospectively validate his marriage to Anne and declare that Elizabeth was legitimate.[62]

When Mary's health collapsed again early in 1535 Katharine urged Chapuys to do his best to win approval for Mary to live with her: she would nurse her in her own bed and look after her.[63] The ambassador was immediately given audience by the king and read Katharine's letter to him. Henry was concerned for his daughter's health but feared that if she lived with Katharine she might be able to flee abroad to the great detriment of his reputation. Moreover, he unremittingly blamed Katharine for having filled Mary's head with 'obstinacy and disobedience' and insisted that Mary would have to submit to his will. When Chapuys requested that Mary be placed under the charge of the Countess of Salisbury 'whom she regarded as her second mother' Henry replied that the Countess was a fool and not competent to look after his daughter while her present governess was an expert in female complaints. The interview did, however, yield an important success when Cromwell secured permission for Mary to be moved nearer to her mother.[64] On 1 April Mary took up residence at Hunsdon, 30 miles away from Kimbolton. Still not content, Chapuys asked for her to be placed even nearer to Katharine.[65]

From Intimidation to Terror: The Execution of the Carthusians, 4 May 1535

The crown's campaign against Katharine's supporters had thus far been comparatively low-key: prosecuting Elizabeth Barton did not require the fullest use of regal powers but it had enabled the Crown to isolate Fisher and More. In 1534, strengthened by the First Act of Succession (above) the government turned its attentions on two major major religious houses in London – the Friars Observant at Greenwich and the Carthusians of the Charterhouse. They were very different establishments: the house at

Greenwich had traditionally been very favoured by the royal family and its members often played vigorous (and controversial) roles in public life while the Carthusians separated themselves completely from the world, living a life of prayer behind their cloistered walls and receiving very few visitors. The members of both communities would now be required to take the oaths stipulated in the Act of Succession.

Henry VIII had been an enthusiastic patron of the 'Greyfriars' (as the Observants had become known after 1502). He had been baptised in their church, married Katharine there and had both of his daughters christened in its font. Katharine also had a special devotion to the friars and may even have been a member of the Third Order of St Francis. The 'Observants' – so called because they strictly observed the Rule of St Francis – gave generous support to Katharine; for instance, her chaplain, John Forest, organised opposition to the king in the Provincial Chapter of 1532 and a year later Cromwell's spies learned that two Observant friars had held secret communications with Katharine. On 21 December 1533 the leaders of the community were obliged to beg formally for royal forgiveness for having supported Katharine.

John Houghton, Prior of the London Charterhouse, originally asked in 1534 that he and his community should be exempted from taking the oaths required by the Act of Succession but by the end of May had accepted that he and his brothers could take the oath provided that they added the well-worn codicil 'as far as the law of Christ allows'. The compromise worked only for a brief moment, for in 1535 the whole community was called upon to take the oath without any qualifications. Houghton, with the heads of the other two English Carthusian houses (Robert Lawrence, Prior of Beavale and Augustine Webster, Prior of Axholme) pleaded for time but was arrested. On 28 April the three priors, together with Richard Reynolds, a Brigettine friar from Syon, and others were found guilty of high treason and sentenced to be hanged, drawn and quartered.

On 4 May 1535, More and his daughter Margaret watched the friars walk from the Tower to encounter their terrible fate. Five of them were hanged: thick ropes were used so that the men would suffer a prolonged agony. They were then cut down while still breathing, disembowelled and their bodies carved up for display in public places. They watched each other die one-by-one and continued to preach while the first executions were being carried out. Norfolk and other lords and courtiers were present and it was said that Henry's illegitimate son, the Duke of Richmond, witnessed the executions as a public sign of the king's approval.

Once the Terror had been unleashed, it fuelled itself remorselessly. Rumours were vigorously circulated at court that the same fate awaited Fisher, More and Dr Richard Fethersone if they did not recant within six weeks.[66] Cromwell interviewed More and urged him to accommodate himself to the king, promising that if he did so Henry would be generous with him.

By a terrible irony, it was not in London but in Rome that sentence was – in effect – pronounced on Fisher: on 22 May Paul III named Fisher as one of seven new cardinals. Dr Ortíz instinctively recognised that an honour which had been designed to protect Fisher would instead lead to his death.[67] So it proved: when Henry learned of Fisher's cardinalate he was incandescent, repeatedly proclaiming that he would cut off his head and send it to Rome so that the cardinal's hat could be fitted there. He also set a deadline for Fisher and More: unless they swore to the royal supremacy before St John's Day (24 June) they would be executed as traitors.[68] But the king did not wait for his deadline: Fisher was executed in the Tower on 22 June: he was so frail that he had to be virtually carried to the block. He was sixty-six years of age and had been a cardinal for a month.

Cromwell seems to have been genuinely admiring of More and may well have sought to save him from himself: twice – in April and May 1535 – he visited him in the Tower, perhaps in the hope of finding a compromise but More refused to budge. More was then subjected in June to an intense interrogation by Richard Rich, the Solicitor-General, who secured from him what he took to be a denial of Parliament's authority to confer ecclesiastical supremacy on the king: Rich was exultant, convinced that he had succeeded in trapping the brilliant lawyer where even Cromwell had failed.[69]

On 1 July 1535 More was indicted at Westminster Hall for high treason in that he had denied the king's title as 'Supreme Head' of the Church in England. He was tried by a bench consisting of Thomas Audley, the dukes of Norfolk and Suffolk, the Earl of Wiltshire, Rochford and Thomas Cromwell. He defended himself bravely and with elegance, denouncing the evidence of Richard Rich as perjury. Knowing full well that he was doomed he used his closing speech to defend the authority of the Pope and the Catholic Church. He was duly found guilty and sentenced to the hideous death of a traitor, by being hanged, drawn and quartered.[70] As More was taken to the waterfront to embark for the Tower with the executioner's axe symbolically turned towards him, Margaret pushed through the crowd to embrace him. It was perhaps because Henry was fearful of the damage that would be done to his own reputation by having More die in public as the Carthusians had done that he commuted his sentence to being beheaded: More had once joked that if his head could gain Henry a mere castle in France the king would take it from him. At least in taking his head now, Henry would spare him the dreadful agonies of a traitor's death.

On 5 July More wrote his famous last letter to his daughter and on the following day he was executed, dying with the courage and elegance that had marked his years of resistance to Henry. His words on the scaffold have passed into legend – he professed that he went to his death as 'the king's good servant but God's first' – but there may have been profound (and very characteristic) irony here: was Sir Thomas quoting the king's own words back at him, as recorded above?[71]

Fisher and More have been bracketed together by history, not least because the Catholic Church canonised them simultaneously (19 May 1935). In their very different ways both resolutely supported Katharine over many years, but they did not die in defence of her: each of them accepted the right of Elizabeth to succeed to the throne. They went to the block in defence of the Catholic Church and the primacy of the Pope – and because they would not allow Henry to replace the Pope as the head of their Church.

Rome reacted instantly to the execution of Fisher: at the end of July, Paul III declared that he was 'astounded' to hear of the execution of a Prince of the Church and announced that he would deprive Henry of his crown. He invited Charles V and Francis I to join together in a crusade to help him to do so.[72] On 30 August he proceeded to formally excommunicate Henry.[73] But Dr Ortíz knew that even now Rome would move cautiously; he reported that the publication of the documents authorising the dethronement (the 'executoriales') had been delayed.[74] At the end of September Chapuys reported the 'despair' felt by Katharine's supporters that the Pope did not act and urged that the trade embargo be used against England.[75] In November Dr Ortíz noted that the necessary papers had still not been despatched and that there would yet be a hiatus of one year before the papacy formally deprived Henry of his kingdom.[76] The Consistory tried to accelerate matters, stipulating that Henry should only be given two months to recant his heresy and schism and avoid being deprived of his kingdom.[77] As events whirled away from its control, Rome fiddled in its own inimitable way – and at its own pace.

Finale, 1536: The Deaths of Katharine & Anne
Katharine: Decline & Death

At some time during 1535, Katharine wrote to an unspecified friend who had tried to persuade Henry to allow Mary to visit her. It appears to have been the last long letter that she wrote and in it she set out her perspectives and principles as she neared what she knew would be the last days of her life. She so desperately wanted to have Mary visit her that she pledged that if Henry allowed Mary to live near her she would never encourage her to flee abroad, offering her own life as security for her promise. As for herself, she would die in England:

My special friend,
    You have greatly bound me with the pains that you have taken in speaking to the king my Lord concerning the coming of my daughter to visit me. You must await your reward from God, for (as you know) I have no power to reward what you have done with anything other than my good will.
    As touching the answer that has been given to you, that his Highness is content to send her to some place near me, so long as I do not see her, I pray you to give my great thanks to his Highness for the goodness which he shows to his daughter and myself, and for the comfort that I have received from this.
    As to my seeing her, you must inform [his Highness] that even if she came within one mile of me I would not travel to visit her for I am not able to move around and even if it were possible for me to do so I do not have the means with which to travel.
    But you must impress upon his Highness that what I asked for was that she be sent to where I am and assure him that the comfort and laughter which she would bring to me would undoubtedly be very healthy for her. I have experienced this because I have suffered from the same illness [of joylessness] and know how much good can come from [such a visit]. It was entirely just and reasonable of me to make this request, and it so greatly touched on the honour and conscience of the king my lord that I am very surprised that it has been denied to me.
    Do not, for love of me, fail to do this. I have heard here that [the king] has anxieties about trusting her to me, believing that I would flee from the country with her. I cannot believe that such a fear, which is so far from reason, should come from the royal heart of

his Highness and I cannot believe that he has so little trust in me. I beg you to insist to his Highness that I am – without any hesitation – determined to die in this kingdom and that I here pledge my own life as security that, if any such [escape] should be attempted, the king should do justice to me as the most evil woman who had ever been born.

Other matters I remit to your wisdom and judgement as a trusted friend, to whom I pray that God will give health.[78]

Katharine entered into her final decline at the turn of November–December 1535 when she suffered violent pains in her stomach and became unable to retain food. Chapuys received alarming reports from her physician about her decline and begged Cromwell to secure permission for him to visit her. When he met Henry he found the king anticipating Katharine's imminent death and looking forward to the new political situation that would follow from it. After the ambassador had left court Henry received further news of Katharine's decline and sent after him to emphasise that her death would remove all the difficulties between Charles V and himself: he even indicated to the ambassador that he might now be prepared to consider allowing Mary to visit her.[79] Whether or not the king was sincere in this intention, it was too late: on the last day of 1535 Sir Edmund Bedingfield wrote to Cromwell from Kimbolton that Katharine had not long to live.[80]

Chapuys rode hard to Kimbolton.[81] He met Katharine for fifteen minutes on 2 January but was only allowed to do so in the presence of one of Cromwell's agents: Katharine's chamberlain and her steward were also present. Katharine told the ambassador that she had been able to sleep for no more than two hours at a time in the previous six days; he begged her to conserve her strength. On the following day he spent an hour with her and in each of the next three days a further two hours or so.[82] Katharine showed some slight improvement; she began to sleep a little more comfortably and was able to retain some food. On the Tuesday evening Chapuys bade her farewell, believing that she was improving and in no imminent danger of death.

English law forbade a wife from making a will while her husband was alive and so Katharine had her physician write a short list of requests to be submitted to Henry in lieu of a will: she signed them and had them given to Chapuys.[83] She stipulated that she was to be buried in a house of the Observant Friars and that 500 masses were to be said for her soul.

She asked the king to make available the gold, silver and money that he owed her. Some of her servants were to go on pilgrimage to Walsingham to pray for her soul and to distribute money on the route. She itemised a number of bequests: the most important among them was a golden collar that she brought with her from Spain, which was to be given to her daughter. Four of her English ladies-in-waiting were to be rewarded for their fidelity: Mrs Darel was to be bequeathed £200 for her marriage and Mrs Blanche £100; Mrs Margery and Mrs Whyller were given £40 each while the latter was also to be paid her expenses for making Katharine's gown and a further £20. Her physician, goldsmith and lavender were to be given their wages for the coming year and Francisco Felipe was to be paid all that was owing to him and a further £40. Her gowns were to be cut up and made into ornaments which were to be presented to the convent in which she was buried.

On the morning of Friday 7 January 1536, Katharine wrote to Henry for the last time. The very title by which she addressed Henry made it evident that she remained his lawful wife and claimed the right to monitor his spiritual welfare:

My Lord and dear husband,

I commend myself to you. The hour of my death draws near, and my condition is such that, because of the tender love that I owe to you, and in only a few words, I put you in remembrance of the health and safeguard of your soul, which you ought to prefer before all worldly matters and before the care and tendering of your own body, for the which you have cast me into many miseries and yourself into many anxieties.

For my part I do pardon you all, yes, I do wish and devoutly pray to God that He will also pardon you.

For the rest, I commend unto you Mary, our daughter, beseeching you to be a good father to her, as I heretofore desired. I entreat you also, on behalf of my maids, to give them marriage-portions, which is not much, since there are only three of them. For all my other servants, I ask for one year's pay more than their due, lest they should be unprovided for.

Lastly, do I vow, that mine eyes desire you above all things[84]

Katharine heard Mass and received the sacrament. She begged the bystanders to pray both for her soul and that God would pardon the king and bring him back to the 'right road'. In mid-morning she received the last rites of the Church. She died at about 2.00 in the afternoon.[85] She was fifty-one years old.

At 10 o'clock or so in the evening, in conditions of great secrecy Katharine's body was opened up for disembowelling by one of her servants, who appears who have had scant experience of the practice: not even her physician was allowed to attend, presumably in case he might claim to have seen evidence of poisoning. The servant told Bishop Athequa in confidence that all of the queen's organs were sound except for her heart, which was black on the outside and within and did not alter at all in colour even when it was washed: if this unscientific analysis has any relevance it would suggest that Katharine died of a cancerous metastatic melanoma.[86] On 3 January Katharine's body was lain under a canopy of state in the Privy Chamber at Kimbolton.[87]

It seems evident that no thought had been given by the Crown as to how Katharine was to be buried until Henry made Sir William Paulet, his comptroller, responsible for her interment: no record exists for the date of the appointment. Certainly, Katharine was allowed little dignity even in death: by the time that her body was encased in a lead coffin on 15 January it must have begun to decompose very badly. It was then returned to the chapel, where it seems to have remained for a further twelve days or so. A succession of solemn masses were subsequently celebrated and they were attended by a variety of principal mourners – the Duchess of Suffolk, the Countess of Worcester, the countesses of Oxford and Surrey and some noble ladies of lesser rank. By Tuesday 25 January four chivalric banners were ready to display Katharine's various political roles: two of them bore Katharine's arms, one of them the crest of England and one jointly displayed the arms of England and Castile. Four golden standards celebrated her religious life – those of the Trinity, Our Lady, St George and St Katharine. But while the banners were prepared for the funeral the ladies of Katharine's suite were not: they had no suitable robes to wear in which to mourn her and for the first three weeks had to make do with old garments and use handkerchiefs to cover their heads. Not until 26 January were they provided with suitable new robes. On that evening a formal dinner was held at which the Countess of Surrey presided as chief mourner.

After Mass on Thursday 27 January the coffin was loaded onto a wagon for Katharine's final journey. A crucifer marched ahead of the procession carrying his cross; he was followed by sixteen priests and the gentlemen. Katharine's two senior male servants – her chamberlain and her steward – carried their rods of office and were accompanied by ten or so heralds with mourning hoods. Thirty-six maids accompanied the wagon and fifty servants of the gentlemen carried torches. Seven ladies served as chief mourners and another nine who were wives of local knights also accompanied the cortège.

The procession moved 9 miles up the modern A1 to Sawtry, where it was formally received by William Angell, the abbot, and his monks and placed under a canopy in the choir of the church. The abbot did such honour to Katharine as he was able: he burned 408 candles throughout the vigil. On the following day, Thomas Goodrich, Bishop of Ely, celebrated Mass: forty-eight poor people of the parish were provided with mourning hoods and carried candles to add dignity to the occasion.

On the afternoon of Friday 28 January Katharine made her last journey, from Sawtry to the Benedictine abbey of Peterborough. She was received at the door of the abbey by the abbot (John Chambers) and the bishops of Lincoln, Ely and Rochester[88] with a number of local abbots in attendance. Once again, an abbot bravely did honour to her: the coffin was carried into the mourning chapel, which was lavishly hung with eighteen banners which emphasised Katharine's status in the royal families of England and Spain: among them were those of Charles V, Henry VIII, Queen Isabella and Prince Arthur; Katharine's sister, the Queen of Portugal; those of Castile, Aragon, Sicily and England; and that of John of Gaunt. In addition a number of pennants were displayed, including two which carried the arms of Katharine and her father. Great golden letters around the chapel displayed Katharine's motto, 'Humble and Loyal'. Masses were celebrated by the three English bishops in attendance and they allowed Bishop Athequa to serve at least one of them as deacon. Henry was represented by Sir William Paulet while Eleanour, daughter of the Duke of Suffolk, served as chief mourner. Fisher's replacement as Bishop of Rochester, John Hilsey, preached the homily, speaking against the power of 'the Bishop of Rome' and the marriage of Katharine and Henry VIII: uncharitably, he committed Katharine to her final resting place by insisting that she had never been Queen of England.

The news of Katharine's death was greeted with delight by the king: on Sunday 9 January, Henry dressed from head to toe in celebratory yellow with a white feather in his cap and had Princess Elizabeth triumphantly conducted to Mass to the sound of trumpets. After dinner he joined the ladies of the court for a dance and Chapuys recorded – whether from his own observation or not he did not make clear – that Henry danced as if transported with joy.[89] Unfortunately, the king's celebrations were curtailed when on 24 January he was knocked unconscious by a heavy fall in the tilt-yard at Greenwich; it took him two hours to regain consciousness. But a more profound and enduring disaster followed: on 29 January Anne miscarried of a boy whom she had borne for about sixteen weeks.

Anne's miscarriage took place, by the most extraordinary irony, on the day of Katharine's funeral. The loss of a another boy profoundly affected the king and he began to question the validity of his second marriage as he had the first: as Diarmaid MacCullough had written, 'once more he was pulled back to the nightmare of divine prohibitions'. Was God again punishing him for having married a woman with whom he had been in a relationship of affinity? Anne's enemies gathered: most ominously, they were led by Thomas Cromwell, who within a month or so was actively intriguing against her.[90]

And still, Clement VII prevaricated. When he heard of Katharine's death he needed to rethink the whole of his strategy towards England, for he doubtless recognised that Henry's marriage to Anne had instantly acquired a sort of legitimacy. And so Clement did what he always did: he temporised. On 11 February Ortíz reported that the Pope had decided to allow Henry three further months during which he could recant his 'great sins' against the Church and the Papal See before he deprived him of his kingdom.[91]

Charles V reacted to Katharine's death with real animation, recognising that it liberated him to make new arrangements in foreign policy. The Emperor was in Naples when the news reached him and he duly wrote to Chapuys that he was grieved at the manner of her death but that he looked forward to an improvement in relations with England to counter the power of France.[92] As he reflected further, Charles made an impressive list of the advantages that could flow to him at once from a reconciliation with Henry: he could wean Henry away from his alliance with France and 'get the better of the King of France' (whom he described as the source of all his troubles); he could release Henry from his theological 'error' and relieve Mary from danger. Chapuys was to remind Henry that the House of Habsburg's treaties with England were 'more ancient and binding' than those that England had with France and that in any event the Treaty of Cambrai obliged Henry to take military action against France on Charles's side.

And – as always with Charles – there were advantages to be sought for his dynasty: he ordered Chapuys to suggest to Henry that Mary might marry Dom Luis of Portugal, the Emperor's brother-in-law. Such a marriage would make it feasible to remove Mary from England and make it possible for her in time to return – with her military allies? – to secure her rightful inheritance. Chapuys was also to suggest to Henry that he could profitably invest some of the goods that he had despoiled from the Church in joining Charles in a crusade against the Turk.[93]

Still, the Emperor pondered: a fortnight later (after he had reached Rome) he wrote to Chapuys that he was to inform Henry that it was Charles himself who had persuaded Clement VII not to proceed with the declaration of Henry's privation of his throne. More substantial, still, 'we are much inclined to promote it [*sc.* friendship with England] frankly, and show the king that we desire his amity above all things'.[94] As Charles developed his theme that he wanted to efface 'all that is past to the disadvantage of our amity' he revealed much more of himself than was his custom:

And in truth, it seems to us that, everything considered, we could not do more for the king even if he were another father, as hitherto we have esteemed him, and shall, if he pleases, continue to do so; for, although we know his great prudence, magnanimity, and virtue, and [appreciate] that he can well understand by himself where his interests lie in regard both to the princess our cousin and his kingdom, as he has said to you...

Yet he ought to observe that what we have said to him through you was not with a view to our own interests, but rather, since it is a question of establishing amity between us, to clear away the things which might involve occasion of distrust hereafter, and, as it seems to us, for his good and quiet. Indeed it seems to us that if we did not urge it he might justly conceive that we had not such good will towards him as we have [in reality] but that we dissembled in order to keep him and his affairs in trouble, and so hold him in greater restraint, as we know that others [*sc.* Francis I] have done and still do. As he is clear-sighted we cannot think how he does not perceive and remedy it.[95]

The grandson of Ferdinand II – 'the Fox of Aragon' – was himself a Machiavellian.

Incest, Treason & Plot: The Fall & Execution of Anne Boleyn

If Anne had delivered a healthy boy in January 1536 her future would have been secured with her status as the mother of a male heir to the throne. Her failure left her vulnerable not only to the vagaries of Henry's scruples about affinity – Leviticus again! – but to the machinations of her enemies, and it did so against the background of the appearance of a new lover for the King: by the end of February rumours were beginning to circulate at court that the king's favours were being directed to one of Anne's ladies-in-waiting, Jane Seymour. Chapuys cheerfully regaled Charles V with the story that Henry had not spoken to Anne more than ten times in the last three months. If he ambassador exaggerated – as so often – he yet understood a basic truth: the king had tired of his queen, and was unforgiving of her second miscarriage.[96]

Thomas Cromwell seized the wind. The circumstances under which he and Anne had fallen out are shrouded in fogs that are unusually thick even for Henry VIII's court.[97] It appears that they disagreed over the uses to which the profits from the dissolution of the monasteries were to be put as also whether England should seek to renew the imperial alliance (Cromwell) or stay with France (Anne). Certainly, Cromwell by the turn of 1535–36 had decided with his customary clarity that he could not survive in office if Anne remained as queen.

Cromwell organised the dénouement with brutal efficiency: on 30 April Mark Smeaton, a court musician, was arrested and charged that he had committed adultery with the queen. Over the next days a number of men were taken to the Tower for interrogation: three of them were figures of significance at court as gentlemen of the king's Privy Chamber – Henry Norris, William Brereton and Sir Francis Weston. Whether through terror or torture – or both – they all confessed and enabled the Crown to draw up a list of dates on which each had committed adultery with the queen. Nor had they been alone: Anne's own brother George confessed that he had committed incest with her.

George Bernard has summarised the details of the indictment, and it is interesting to note that Henry became convinced that Anne seems often to have betrayed him by having two lovers simultaneously. This was no simple or isolated case of adultery, and it is significant that the dates of adultery that were established in the torture chambers and courtroom of the Tower all post-dated the birth of Princess Elizabeth in September 1533: there could be no questions raised as to her legitimacy: 'Having married Henry VIII in early 1533, Anne Boleyn had then allegedly had sexual relationships with Henry Norris in October or November 1533, with William Brereton in November or December 1533; with Mark Smeaton in April or May 1534; with Sir Francis Weston in May or June 1534; and with her brother in November and December 1534.'

But multiple adultery – incest, even – was not sufficient to discredit the queen for whom Henry had risked so much: to put his queen to death, Henry needed to establish that Anne had committed the very highest of treasons and his agents duly discovered that she had conspired with her sexual partners to have him assassinated, and that she had promised to marry one of her co-conspirators after the deed was done.[98]

Weston, Norris and others were tried at Westminster by a bench led by Audley and including the dukes of Norfolk and Suffolk, the earls of Oxford, Westmoreland, Wiltshire and Sussex and Cromwell himself. Smeaton pleaded guilty to having had carnal knowledge of the queen and threw himself on the king's mercy. Norris, Brereton and Weston all pleaded not guilty but the jury rejected their pleas: on 12 May, they were sentenced to be executed at Tyburn.[99]

On 2 May Anne herself and her brother George, Viscount Rochford, were arrested. They were charged with having committed incest – a crime so abhorrent that conviction for it would justify any treatment. Their trial took place – conveniently enough! – in the Tower of London in front of the Duke of Norfolk, making full use of his rank as well as of his positions as Treasurer, Earl Marshal and Lord High Steward to judge the Queen of England. Anne was charged that

> despising her marriage, and entertaining malice against the king, and following daily her frail and carnal lust, [she] did falsely and traitorously procure by base conversations and kisses, touching, gifts, and other infamous incitations, divers of the king's daily and familiar servants to be her adulterers and concubines, so that several of the king's servants yielded to her vile provocations.

Dates were provided of the adultery with each individual. Rochford was found guilty that, 'despising the commands of God and all human laws', he had 'violated and carnally knew the said queen' on 5 November and on various other days.

The verdicts, on 15 May, were inevitable: both were found guilty. Anne was sentenced to be burned or beheaded in the Tower, at the king's pleasure, while her brother was to be drawn, hanged and quartered for high treason.[100] The executions of Anne's alleged lovers took place on 17 May and on that day Cranmer declared that the marriage of Henry and Anne had been null and void because of the affinity created by Henry's relationship with Mary Boleyn.[101] Of course the logic of this was that if Anne had not been lawfully married to Henry she could not have committed adultery, but no one commented on this anomaly – or at least not in England: in Rome, the Curia (which had known about Henry's relationships with Mary and Anne Boleyn for years) may well have guffawed.

Anne's successor was already in place: on 18 May, Jane Seymour's brother Edward was given rooms in the palace at Greenwich precisely so that Jane could have ready access to Henry. Jane Seymour was in her mid-twenties and was distantly related to Henry VIII, being a descendant of Edward III. She had served as a lady-in-waiting to both Katharine and Anne. On that day, Chapuys was able to send a detailed characterisation of the king's new mistress to Charles V: she had neither beauty nor wit and was inclined to be haughty but the ambassador was delighted to record that she held Mary in great affection.[102]

Henry commuted Anne's terrible sentence as he had More's and even went so far as to spare the cumbersome (and often brutal) axe: on 19 May, Anne Boleyn was beheaded in the Tower by a French swordsman. Cromwell and other leading ministers were present at the execution together with a crowd that was said to number 2,000 people. Anne died bravely and without making any confession of guilt: she thereby greatly improved her daughter's chances of succeeding to the throne one day.[103] Anne was thirty-five years old, and had survived Katharine by only four months.

Later in the day, Cranmer (who had received Anne's confession in the Tower) issued dispensations for Henry and Jane Seymour from their affinity with each other as fifth cousins. On the following day – 20 May – they were married in Whitehall: for the third time Henry VIII married in secret. On 4 June Jane was proclaimed Queen of England. A fortnight later, on 18 June, Thomas Cromwell succeeded Anne's father as Lord Privy Seal. For the first time since Henry had begun to worry about 'the Levitical Prohibition' some dozen or so years earlier, he was at last free of the problems that it had created for him – saving, that is, what he was to do with his obstinate elder daughter.

The Submission of Princess Mary

As Katharine's death had changed everything between Henry VIII and

Charles V, so that of Anne Boleyn transformed Henry's relationship with Princess Mary. Since Anne had committed multiple adulteries Henry could not be certain that Elizabeth was his daughter. There were even discussions at court as to whether the Duke of Richmond should now have precedence over Mary because while both of them were illegitimate it was undeniable that both were the king's children and at least Richmond was a male. Cromwell told Chapuys that in the next Parliament Henry would declare that Mary was his heir. It was, however, necessary for Mary to write an exculpatory letter to her father begging for his forgiveness, and Cromwell obligingly sketched out a draft for her to consider.

As always, the secretary had an agenda, and he now carefully orchestrated the reconciliation between Henry and Mary. Chapuys was given audience with Henry at 8.00 a.m. on 25 May and their discussions proved to be both friendly and fruitful. It was either at that meeting or one that Cromwell held with Chapuys four days later that it was agreed that Mary would write a letter to Henry seeking reconciliation and that the ambassador could vet it before it was sent. Cromwell informed Chapuys that Henry would shortly marry Jane Seymour and to the ambassador's astonishment let it slip – accidentally or otherwise – that princes often did things so extravagant and dishonest that he himself would rather lose one of his arms than think of acting thus.[104]

Mary duly wrote to her father on 1 June, begging for his blessing and forgiveness and acknowledging all her offences against him, 'humbly beseeching your Highness to consider that I am but a woman and your child'. She rejoiced to hear of the marriage with Jane Seymour, offered to wait upon the new queen and prayed that God would send Henry a prince to succeed him.[105]

On 10 June Mary wrote further letters to Henry VIII and Cromwell. She again begged her father's forgiveness and looked forward to receiving from him some token or message of reconciliation. She 'fervently' desired to see him again and prayed for himself and the queen.[106] In her letter to Cromwell she assured him that she would continue to follow his advice because he was 'one of my chief friends [after] his Grace and the queen'. She would rather lose her life than displease Henry VIII but she could go no further than she had already done.[107]

What happened next is not certain. It appears that Cromwell was furious with Mary, perhaps over what she had *not* written in her letter: was it that she had refused to explicitly acknowledge that her parents' marriage had been invalid? At all events, Cromwell wrote a letter to Mary in which he declared that he was ashamed of having supported her and rebuked her that 'with your folly you undo yourself', declaring that 'I think you the most obstinate woman that ever was'. He had sent her a book of articles to sign, and if she did so and sent him a letter of repentance he would again intercede for her with the king. Otherwise, he would have no further dealings with her: 'If not, I take leave of you for ever more and want you never to write to me again for I will never think you other than the most ungrate, unnatural, and most obstinate person living, both to God and your most dear and benign father.'[108]

Mary wrote yet again to her father on 14 and 15 June. In her first letter she told Henry how dismayed she was that he had not accepted her repentance in her previous letters.[109] On 15 June she was more explicit, declaring that she was

> most humbly prostrate before the feet of your most excellent Majesty, your most humble, faithful, and obedient subject, which hath so extremely offended your most gracious Highness that mine heavy and fearful heart dare not presume to call you father … saving [that] the benignity of your most blessed nature doth surmount all evils, offences, and trespasses, and is ever merciful and ready to accept the penitent, calling for grace in any convenient time.

Mary acknowledged that she had 'most unkindly and unnaturally' offended the king by not submitting to his just laws, an offence that was a thousand-fold more grievous in her than it would have been in any other person. She accepted that she deserved to be punished and promised that she would never again seek her father's forgiveness if she offended him. She threw herself – soul and body – onto his 'fatherly pity' and would do whatever he commanded her.[110] Probably the letter was enough to reconcile Mary with Henry. Certainly, on 22 June, she capitulated, formally accepting the royal supremacy. In doing so, she recognised that the marriage of her parents had been illegal and that she herself was illegitimate:

> The confession of me, the lady Mary, made upon certain points and articles under written, in the which, as I do now plainly and with all mine heart confess and declare mine inward sentence, belief, and judgement, with a due conformity of obedience to the laws of the realm; so minding for ever to persist and continue in this determination, without change, alteration, or variance, I do

most humbly beseech the king's Highness, my father, whom I have obstinately and inobediently offended in the denial of the same heretofore, to forgive mine offences therein, and to take me to his most gracious mercy.

Mary acknowledged the king as her sovereign and submitted to all his laws like a true subject and repudiated 'the pretended authority of the Bishop of Rome'. More, she acknowledged that the marriage between the king and her mother, the late princess dowager, had been 'by God's law and man's law incestuous and unlawful'.[111] Two weeks later, Henry and his queen paid Mary the courtesy of visiting her at Mary at Hunsdon. The king subsequently allowed Mary to return to court, if only briefly.

POSTSCRIPT

When Katharine died in 1536 she was already, in a very real sense, a figure from the past, for the Reformation which began with Luther's publication of his theses in 1517 – the year after the birth of Mary Tudor - had now gathered such momentum as to be irreversible while at the same time the Catholic Church was beginning to reform and renew itself to confront the threat from Protestantism: it did so definitively in the great Council of Trent (1545–63), which redefined the structure, doctrine and practices of the Church. In a brilliant essay, Pierre Chaunu has emphasised the significance of the years 1517 and 1536 for the development of the Reformation – the first as 'a point of departure' and the second as 'a point of arrival'.[1] By 1536 Europe was beginning to divide into a Catholic south and a Protestant north and despite the brutal 'religious wars' of the next century or so that would remain substantially the case. Katharine had foreseen much of this: insistently she had demanded of the papacy that it support her in order to save Catholicism in England, and if in the event there was so much more to the Reformation in England than the fate of this one extraordinary woman, time was to prove her analysis was correct. Pope Clement VII's refusal or inability to act over Henry VIII's 'Great Matter' until it was too late did as much damage to the papacy as the Sack of Rome had done: England was lost to Rome, and Mary I's endeavours to turn back the tide only resulted in that tide running the more powerfully and enduringly against the Church to which she and her mother were so profoundly committed.

Within months of Katharine's death, widespread disturbances arose in Northern England against the religious changes being introduced by

Henry and his government, most especially against the Dissolution of the Monasteries. The Dissolution provided a focal-point that had hitherto been lacking for those who, in the North of England, were most firmly attached to the old religion. Rebellion began in rural Lincolnshire in October 1536, when a force of perhaps 40,000 marched on the county capital. As the Duke of Suffolk led a royal army to suppress them an even more dangerous rebellion arose in Yorkshire and, under the able leadership of Robert Aske, it presented itself as a religious and spiritual rebellion against the changes introduced by the king's evil ministers. It became known as the 'Pilgrimage of Grace' and so widespread was it that the name soon applied generically to all the rebellions against the Crown, as in the last three months of 1536 the North was convulsed by revolt. When Pontefract Castle surrendered to the rebels (31 October), it seemed as if the North might be lost to the Crown. The rebellion was put down with a savagery (and a duplicity) that was typical of the last years of Henry's reign: the Tudor dynasty survived and was indeed strengthened by its brush with disaster.

As Henry re-established his control in the North, his third wife presented him with the male heir for whom he had so longed: on 12 October 1537, Jane Seymour gave birth to a son, who was named Edward. Three days later, Mary and Elizabeth stood as godmothers at the child's christening. But still calamity dogged Henry and his wives: Jane's labour lasted into its third day and it killed her – she died on 24 October.

In the years 1540–43, Henry married a further three times but had no more children.[2] In 1540 Thomas Cromwell arranged for him to marry Anne, daughter of the Duke of Cleves, who ruled a tiny but strategically important territory on the Lower Rhine. Henry was much taken by Anne's appearance as portrayed by Hans Holbein, but when she arrived in England found her physically and socially repulsive: the great painter had flattered to deceive. The marriage was apparently never consummated and was annulled by Cranmer after six months (9 July 1540), while Cromwell paid with his head in a badly botched execution (23 July). Anne was pensioned off but treated honourably as 'the king's sister': she outlived Henry by a decade, dying peacefully on 16 July 1557.

For his fifth wife, Henry once again turned to a young woman who was well connected at court (as Anne Boleyn and Jane Seymour had been): Catherine Howard's father was Lord Edmund Howard, the younger brother of Thomas, Duke of Norfolk, and she was the first cousin of Anne Boleyn. Like Anne, Catherine attracted the king's eye while serving as a lady-in-waiting to the queen (Jane Seymour). Henry duly married her on 28 July 1540, but when Cranmer produced evidence of Catherine's adultery the new queen was doomed. Catherine was executed on the same spot as Anne Boleyn (13 February 1542): she was nineteen years of age. Henry's sixth and last marriage was apparently for companionship rather than for procreation: on 12 July 1543 he married Catherine Parr, who had already been twice widowed. Catherine nursed Henry tenderly in his old age and may have been responsible for persuading him to legitimise his two daughters: certainly, shortly before the king died (28 January 1547) he signed his will stipulating that the throne was to pass to Edward and that if he died without heirs it was to go in turn to his two half-sisters, Mary and Elizabeth. Widowed for a third time, Catherine Parr married Sir Thomas Seymour and presented him with a daughter on 30 August 1548, but she died from the ravages of the birth (7 September 1548).

Henry's last years were marked by a dreadful physical decline and they were characterised, too, by an increasingly wilful and brutal polity. Two of Katharine's staunchest supporters died in effect for their commitment to her – Fr Forest was burned at Smithfield (22 May 1538) and Margaret Pole was executed at the Tower (27 May 1541). In reality Margaret went to her death because she and her family had a claim on the throne, but Henry never forgot or forgave her lifelong commitment to Katharine. Certainly, the execution was among the cruellest of its era; it was said that an incompetent executioner required a dozen or so strokes to despatch the elderly lady.[3] In addition, fifteen or so Carthusians went to their deaths in remembrance of their opposition to Henry and their support of Katharine.

The king who had so mismanaged his marriages at least got his testamentary provisions right, for Henry was indeed succeeded in turn by each of his children. But the curse on the Tudor family persisted, for none of the children had heirs of their own – Edward VI (1547–53); Mary I (1553–58) and Elizabeth I (1558–1603), the first and third of them without marrying.

Edward's government established a fully autonomous and radical Church of England while Mary's then restored Catholicism as the national religion and returned the country to its allegiance to the papacy.[4] But Mary's reign proved to be disastrous for Catholicism and for the relationship with Spain upon which she and her mother had set so much store: in 1554 she married Charles V's only son, the future Philip II of Spain, but at thirty-eight was already too old to have children and suffered only false pregnancies which embarrassed her husband and drove him from her. Mary's restoration of Catholicism provoked as much anger as it did support, but when she committed herself to a programme of burning heretics – over 260 men and women died at the stake and many more died in prison – she lost much of her legitimacy in the eyes of her subjects and few mourned her when she died. Many laid the blame for the burnings at the feet of her Spanish husband and so contributed to the development of that increasingly virulent anti-Spanish sentiment that characterised much of English life over succeeding generations: in reality, Philip seems to have counselled Mary against the burning of heretics.

As with Spain, so with the Pope: Mary's reign validated a welling hostility to the papacy and so justified and facilitated the anti-Catholic legislation that Elizabeth introduced as she consolidated her grip on the Crown in her first decade in power. How much the ferocious intensity that Mary showed in pushing forward her religious reforms owed to her bitterness at the treatment that she and her mother had endured at Henry VIII's hands must remain a matter for speculation.

Mary's disastrous reign had seemed proof enough to many of the proverbial truth that a woman could not reign in her own right. Elizabeth then demonstrated an acute political genius by ruling without marrying: she thus neatly bypassed the problems that would have arisen for her as a female ruler while keeping the world in suspense as to when and with whom she would marry. As she did so she showed that she had all the political qualities of both her father and her mother and she became in time a truly national leader, to whom even the dwindling community of English Catholics remained (on the whole) loyal. When Elizabeth died in 1603 the throne passed without serious challenge to James VI of Scotland, the descendant of Henry VIII's sister Margaret: the new king thus united the thrones of England and Scotland.

Henry survived Katharine by eleven years. His death coincided almost exactly with that of Francis I (31 March 1547), while by 1547 Charles V was in a state of physical and psychological decline that led him to plan his own abandonment of power: he duly abdicated as ruler of the Low Countries and Spain in 1555–56. However, Charles could not bring himself to abandon his imperial title and retained it until his death in 1558: he was then succeeded by his brother Ferdinand, and so the union of Spain and the Holy Roman Empire was undone. Only after Charles's death were the wars that he had fought with Francis I and his successor Henry II brought to a conclusion by the Peace of Cateau-Cambrèsis in 1559.[5]

Henry's last decade or so was marked by progressive and debilitating illnesses, the nature of which have been much debated. It was once thought that the king's physical decline was due to the effects of syphilis, but this is generally discounted and it has recently been suggested that he may have been afflicted with a blood disease which in itself could have been equally responsible for his failure to produce a male heir and for his psychological decline in his last decade or so: Drs Whitley and Kramer, in putting forward this argument, have thereby freed Henry's first two wives of their 'guilt' for failing to present him with a male heir and offered a tantalisingly suggestive explanation of Henry's moral disintegration in the 1540s.[6]

This new research raises tantalising possibilities which might be properly tested if Henry's remains were subjected to DNA testing. But even in the unlikely event of permission being given for such an exhumation and testing it is doubtful whether anything could be achieved by it, for there are good reasons for suspecting that when Mary became queen she had her father secretly disinterred and his bones burned as being those of a heretic. If this really did happen then Henry himself became one of the victims of the queen who is known in English history as 'Bloody Mary'.[7] Did Mary's quest for revenge for her mother and herself truly follow Henry even into the grave?

NOTES

1 Europe & its World, 1500: Recovery & Expansion
1. There is a voluminous literature on the map. See Arthur Davies, 'The Date of Juan de la Cosa's World Map and its Implications for American Discovery', *The Geographical Journal*, I, no. 142, 1976, pp. 111–116; Fernando Silió Cervera, *La carta de Juan de la Cosa (1500): Análisis cartográfico*, Santander: Fundación Botín, 1995; Hugo O'Donnell Duque de Estrada, 'El Mapamundi denominado Carta de Juan de la Cosa y su verdadera naturaleza', *Revista General de Marina*, Sept. 1991, pp. 161–181. See also Luis a Robles Macías, 'Juan de la Cosa's Projection: A Fresh Analysis of the Earliest Preserved Map of the Americas', http://www.stonybrook.edu/libmap/coordinates/seriesa/no9/a9.htm.
2. John Hatcher, 'England in the aftermath of the Black Death', *Past and Present*, 144 (Aug. 1994), pp. 3–35.
3. Samuel K. Cohn Jr, 'The Black Death, Tragedy, and Transformation', in John Jeffries Martin (ed.), *The Renaissance World*, New York and London, 2007, pp. 69–83, at p. 69.
4. Braudel, *The Mediterranean [and the Mediterranean World in the Age of Philip II]*, 2 vols, London, 1973, i, pp. 402–3.
5. David Cressy, *Birth Marriage & Death: Ritual, Religion and the Life-Cycle in Tudor and Stuart England*, Oxford University Press, 1999; see especially the detailed section on 'Birth', pp. 15–94; and Ralph A. Houlbrooke, *The English Family 1450–1700*, Longman, London and New York, 1985, especially chapter 6, 'Parents and children: infancy and childhood', pp. 127–65.
6. See the valuable website, 'The Cardinals of the Holy Roman Church', http://www2.fiu.edu/~mirandas/cardinals.htm.

7. Ingrid Rowland, 'Rome at the Center of a Civilization', in Martin, *The Renaissance World*, pp. 31–50, at p. 31.

8. Eamon Duffy, *Saints and Sinners: A History of the Popes*, Yale University Press, New Haven and London, 2006, p. 178.

9. *Memoirs of a Renaissance Pope: The Commentaries of Pius II: An Abridgment*, Leona C. Gabel (ed.), Capricorn Books, New York, 1962, p. 357.

10. Hubert Jedin, *A History of the Council of Trent*, 2 vols, London, Edinburgh and New York, 1961; see especially book two, 'Why so late? The antecedents of the Council of Trent 1517–1545'.

11. The prince-archbishops of Mainz, Trier and Cologne; the King of Bohemia, the Count Palatine, Duke of Saxony and Margrave of Brandenburg.

12. Friedrich Heer, *The Holy Roman Empire*, London, 1968, pp. 122–47.

13. Janine Garrisson, *A History of Sixteenth-Century France, 1483–1598: Renaissance, Reformation and Rebellion*, Macmillan Press, Basingstoke, 1995, pp. 3, 9–10.

14. M. J. Rodríguez-Salgado, 'Obeying the Ten Commandments: The First War between Charles V and Francis I, 1520–1529', in Blockmans and Mout, *The World of Emperor Charles V*, pp. 15–67, at p. 32, n. 47.

15. Braudel, *Mediterranean*, I, pp. 408–10.

16. Milan was ruled by the Visconti family until 1447 when the last ruler, Filippo María, named Alfonso of Aragon, King of Naples, as his heir. This accentuated the instability because the other powers of Italy – and most especially the papacy – feared the juncture of Milan and Naples. There then followed a brief republican period ('The Ambrosian Republic') before Francesco Sforza won Milan in 1450, claiming that he was the legitimate heir to the Visconti by virtue of his marriage to Bianca Maria Visconti, daughter of Filippo Maria.

17. In 1264 Pope Clement IV conferred the kingdom upon Charles of Anjou, Count of Provence and brother to King Saint Louis of France, but after 'the Sicilian Vespers' (1282) the kingdom split into two: the island of Sicily formed a kingdom under the Crown of Aragon while Naples remained in the Angevin family. The two kingdoms were briefly united during the reign of Alfonso of Aragon (1435–58) but on his death Sicily passed to his uncle Juan. The Angevins hung on in Naples until 1481 when Charles of Maine bequeathed the kingdom to Louis XII. Alfonso's bastard, Ferrante of Aragon (1458–94), was debarred by his illegitimacy

from ruling Sicily but Pius II invested him with the Crown to secure his support for the crusade against the Turk. The uncertainties over the legal title to the kingdom created systemic vulnerability, while the Crowns of France and Aragon could claim that they had the right to rule the two parts of the ancient kingdom; as with Milan in the north, control over Naples in the south therefore brought France and the Spanish monarchy into conflict with each other. See Denys Hay and John E. Law, *Italy in the Age of the Renaissance 1380–1530*, chapter 4, 'The South and the Islands', pp. 169–97.

18. On the court of Burgundy, C. A. J. Armstrong, 'The Golden Age of Burgundy Dukes that Outdid Kings', in A. G. Dickens (ed.), *The Courts of Europe Politics, Patronage and Royalty 1400–1800*, Thames and Hudson, London, 1977, pp. 55–75. Biographies by Richard Vaughan, *Philip the Good: The Apogee of Burgundy* and *Charles the Bold: The Last Valois Duke of Burgundy*, Longmans, London, 1970 and 1973 and by Christine Weightman, *Margaret of York: The Diabolical Duchess*, Amberley Publishing, 2009 are especially valuable.

19. Philippe de Commynes, *Memoirs: The Reign of Louis XI 1468–83*, ed. and trans. Michael Jones, Penguin Classics, Harmondsworth, 1972, pp. 64–5.

20. *The Emperor Charles V: The Growth and Destiny of a Man and of a World-Empire*, trans. C. V. Wedgwood, Jonathan Cape, London 1963, at p. 31.

21. Vaughan, *Charles the Bold*, pp. 45–53.

22. Weightman, *Margaret of York*, p. 62.

23. Heer, *Holy Roman Empire*, pp. 122–8.

24. Mary had to endure an unpleasant – but not untypical – piece of play-acting when she met her fiancé; Margaret of York told him that his bride had hidden a carnation on her person and invited him to find it. The Archbishop of Trier (who was an imperial elector) suggested that he might 'Open the lady's bodice', and on doing so, Maximilian located the flower. Heer, *The Holy Roman Empire*, pp. 133–47.

25. Jean-Marie Cauchies, 'Un príncipe para los Países Bajos, para España, para Europa', in Miguel Ángel Zalama and Paul Vandenbroeck, *Felipe I el Hermoso La Belleza y la Locura*, Madrid, 2006, p. 74.

26. Commynes, *Louis XI*, pp. 64–5.

27. Cauchies, 'Un príncipe para los Países Bajos', p. 74.

2 *Spain: The Catholic Kings: A Question of Legitimacy?*

1. Luis Súarez Fernández, *Los Reyes Católicos*, Barcelona, 2005, pp. 19–24; Tarsicio de Azcona, *Isabel la Católica: Vida y reinado*, Madrid, 2004, pp. 67–8; Peggy K. Liss, *Isabel the Queen: Life and Times*, Oxford University Press, 1992 pp. 45–8.

2. *Los Reyes Católicos*, I, p. 5; see also Suárez, *Los Reyes Católicos*, pp. 24, 28.

3. Azcona, *Isabel la Católica*, p. 109; Liss, *Isabel the Queen*, p. 68.

4. Henry had repeatedly tried to marry her off in an attempt to exercise some control over her and in 1466 betrothed her to Don Pedro Girón, Master of the Military Order of Santiago, a violent nobleman who had been recently widowed. Isabella was distraught, and in April 1466 as Girón headed to court she spent a night in tearful prayer, begging that God kill either her or Girón before the nuptials took place: Girón dutifully died before he reached court. The incident bolstered Isabella in that sense of providential destiny that was to become so much a part of her personality. Liss, *Isabel the Queen*, pp. 62–3.

5. Juan I of Castile had two sons, Enrique III of Castile and Fernando I of Aragon; Isabella was the granddaughter of Enrique III by his marriage to Catalina de Lancaster and Ferdinand was the grandson of Fernando and Leonor de Alburquerque.

6. Ernest Belenguer, *Fernando el Católico Un Monarca Decisivo en las Encrucijadas de su Época*, Barcelona, 2000, pp. 74–81; Suárez, *Los Reyes Católicos*, pp. 64–73; Liss, *Isabel the Queen*, pp. 78–81.

7. There is a voluminous (and rapidly growing) literature on the reign of Ferdinand and Isabella. The 500th anniversary of Isabella's death in 2004 stimulated some important writing; see especially, Pedro Navascués Palacio, *Isabel la Católica Reina de Castilla*, Lunwerg, Barcelona and Madrid, 2002; Julio Valdeón Baruque (ed.), three volumes of essays on *Isabel la Católica*, Instituto de Historia Simancas (see Bibliography for individual titles); *Isabel La Católica La Magnificencia De Un Reinado*, Sociedad Estatal de Conmemoraciones Culturales Junta de Castilla y León, Valladolid, 2004. This literature is best approached in English through Liss, *Isabel the Queen*, John Edwards, *Ferdinand and Isabella*, Longmans, Edinburgh, 2005 and David A. Boruchoff, *Isabel la Católica, Queen of Castile: Critical Essays*, Palgrave Macmillan, 2003.

8. Azcona, *Isabel la Católica*, p. 125.

9. On Borja's family and career, the articles in *Diccionario de Historia Eclesiástica de España*, 5 vols, ed. Quintin Aldea Vaquero *et al.*, Madrid,

1972–89 [henceforth *DHEE*], I, pp. 275–80; 'Rodrigo de Borja y Borja' in the website 'The Cardinals of the Holy Roman Church', http://www2.fiu. edu/~mirandas/bios1456.htm. A brilliant study of the Borgias, Michael Mallet, *The Borgias: The Rise and Fall of a Renaissance Dynasty*, Paladin, London, 1972.

10. Suárez, *Los Reyes Católicos*, pp. 90–92

11. Pulgar, *Los Reyes Católicos*, I, pp. 65–70.

12. Glyn Redworth and Fernando Checa, 'The Courts of the Spanish Habsburgs 1500–1700', in John Adamson (ed.), *The Princely Courts of Europe 1500–1750*, pp. 43–65. The essays in this excellent volume can be supplemented by those in A. G. Dickens, *The Courts of Europe Politics, Patronage and Royalty 1400–1800*, London, 1977.

13. On the agreement that governed their joint rule (the 'Concordia de Segovia', 15 January 1475), Azcona, *Isabel la Católica*, pp. 146–9 and Liss, *Isabel the Queen*, pp. 110–11.

14. An exceptional itinerary, Antonio Rumeu de Armas, *Itinerario de los Reyes Católicos, 1474–1516*, Madrid, 1974.

15. Joseph Pérez, 'Fernando el Católico y Felipe I el Hermoso', in Benjamín González Alonso (ed.) *Las Cortes y las Leyes de Toro de 1505*, Cortes de Castilla y León, Salamanca, 2006, pp. 159–72, at p. 169.

16. Helen Rawlings, *The Spanish Inquisition*, Oxford, Blackwell, 2006.

17. Miguel-Ángel Ladero Quesada, 'Isabel la Católica: perfil politico de un reinado decisivo', in *Isabel La Católica*, pp. 33–48.

18. Edwards, *Ferdinand and Isabella*; see especially chapter 3, 'The War against Islam', pp. 48–67; a graphic description of the assault on Málaga, pp. 58–64.

19. The conquest had begun in 711 but the northern parts of Spain had not been occupied for long. Toledo was recovered in 1084 and in the early thirteenth century the 'reconquest' had reached the Guadalquivir valley: the gates to Andalucía were opened in 1212 with the victory at Las Navas de Tolosa; Córdoba fell in 1236 and Seville in 1248. Thereafter, the reconquest paused for two and a half centuries until in 1482 Isabella embarked upon the final push against the mountain kingdom of Granada.

20. On confirmation of the title, 19 December 1496, Suárez Fernández, *PIIC* IV, p. 167.

21. His 'Relación del Viaje' is published in J. García Mercadal, *Viajes de Extranjeros por España*, 6 vols, Junta de Castilla y León, Valladolid, 1999, I, pp. 305–90, at p. 380.

22. *Los Reyes Católicos*, I, pp. 75–8.

23. Suárez Fernández, *Los Reyes Católicos*, pp. 139–40.

24. 'This pregnancy was greatly desired by everyone in the kingdom, because they only had Princess Isabella, who was seven years old, and in those [seven] years the queen had not become pregnant. And with great penances, prayers and sacrifices and [patronised] holy works, she prayed to God that she should conceive and she gave birth [in Seville] to a son, who was named Prince Don Juan; he was born on the twenty-ninth day of June of this year of 1479. Because of the birth of this prince, great celebrations took place throughout the cities and towns of the kingdoms of Castile and Leon and Sicily and all the other lordships of the king and the queen in thanks to God for having given them a male heir for them', Pulgar, *Crónica de los Reyes Católicos*, 2 vols, Granada 2008, ed. Juan de la Mata Carriazo, I, pp. 324–5.

25. Vicenta Márquez de la Plata, *El Trágico Destino de los Hijos de los Reyes Católicos*, Madrid, 2008, pp. 18–21.

26. Pulgar, *Los Reyes Católicos*, I, p. 404 and II, p. 40; Márquez de la Plata, *El Trágico Destino*, pp. 92, 164.

27. Pulgar predated the birth by a day, ascribing it to 15 December, *Los Reyes Católicos*, II, p. 204.

28. Joseph Pérez, 'Los hijos de la Reina. La política de alianzas', in Navascués Palacio, *Isabel la Católica Reina de Castilla*, pp. 53–82.

29. Catalina Montes Mozo, *A Renaissance Princess: The Court of Catherine of Aragón*, University of Portsmouth, 2000; Marquez de la Plata, *El Trágico Destino*, p. 94.

30. Münzer, 'Relación del Viaje', pp. 380–81.

31. Pérez, 'Los Hijos de la Reina', p. 43.

32. Rodríguez-Salgado, 'Obeying the Ten Commandments', pp. 40–42.

33. 'The wedding took place in a monastery near Évora: according to popular rumour, the princes consummated their marriage in the monastery itself, to the scandal of the monks ...', Pérez, 'Los Hijos de la Reina', p. 60; Suárez, *PIIC* III, p. 15.

3 England: 'A King to be Obeyed': Henry VII

1. González de Puebla to Ferdinand and Isabella, London 15 July 1488, *CSPS* I, no. 21, at p. 7.

2. Doran, *Tudor Chronicles*, pp. 6–7.

3. Michael K. Jones and Malcolm G. Underwood, *The King's Mother Lady Margaret Beaufort, Countess of Richmond and Derby*, Cambridge University Press, 1992.

4. The following account is based upon an anonymous document drawn up for submission to Henry VII and his advisers for their approval prior to the ceremony, 'Device for the coronation of King Henry VII', printed by W. Jerden (ed.), *Rutland Papers*, Camden Society 1842, pp. 1–24. For a modern analysis, the brilliant study of court ceremonies by Sydney Anglo, *Spectacle Pageantry, and Early Tudor Policy*, Oxford, Clarendon Press, 1969, pp. 8–11.

5. He swore, 'I shall keep the privileges of canon law and of holy Church ... and I shall in as much as I may by reason and right by God's grace defend you, and enrich you, bishops and abbots throughout my realms, and all the churches to you and them committed', 'Device for the coronation of King Henry VII', printed by W. Jerden (ed.), *Rutland Papers*, Camden Society 1842, pp. 1–24, at p. 15.

6. 'Device', pp. 2 and 6.

7. Anglo, *Spectacle, Pageantry*, pp. 16–18.

8. Emma Cavell, 'Henry VII, the North of England, and the First Provincial Progress of 1486', *Northern History*, XXXIX, 2, September 2002, pp. 187–207, quotation at p. 198.

9. Indeed, while he was in Lincoln he heard that Viscount Lovell and Humphrey Stafford had fled from house arrest. It was likely that Lovell was attempting to raise a general rebellion in the North and the Stafford brothers in the West Midlands. Henry seems to have sent men to deal with what became local difficulties but there was no rebellion.

10. Anglo, *Spectacle, Pageantry*, pp. 22–3.

11. Unfortunately, foul weather delayed the arrival of some of the dignitaries, notably the Earl of Oxford, the Lord Chancellor; the guests had to wait three hours for him to arrive. No doubt there were many wry jokes about the forty days of rain that proverbially came when it rained on St Swithun's Day (15 July).

12. Frederick Hepburn, 'Arthur, Prince of Wales and his training for kingship', *The Historian*, 55, 1997, pp. 4–9.

13. Suárez, *Los Reyes Católicos*, pp. 708–9.

14. Ana Echevarria, 'Catalina of Lancaster, the Castilian Monarchy and Coexistence', in Roger Collins and Anthony Goodman (eds), *Medieval Spain Culture, Conflict and Coexistence: Studies in Honour of Angust Mackay*, Palgrave, Macmillan, Basingstoke, 2002, pp. 79–122.

15. Suárez, *Los Reyes Católicos*, p. 705.

16. Henry VII to John Weston and others, Westminster, 10 March 1488, *CSPS* I, no. 13, p. 3; Suárez, *Los Reyes Católicos*, p. 705.

17. Ferdinand and Isabella to González de Puebla and Sepúlveda, no date; and two despatches from Murcia, 30 April 1488, *CSPS* I, nos 14–16, p. 3.

18. González de Puebla to Ferdinand and Isabella, London, 15 July 1488, *CSPS* I, no. 21, pp. 5–12, at p. 7.

19. 'Indenture between [González de Puebla] and [Juan de] Sepúlveda, ambassadors of Ferdinand and Isabella ... and Richard, Bishop of Exeter, and Giles Daubeney, commissioners of Henry VII', *CSPS* I, no. 20, p. 5, and González de Puebla to Ferdinand and Isabella, London, 15 July 1488, *op. cit.*

20. González de Puebla to Ferdinand and Isabella, London, 15 July 1488, *op. cit.*

21. Ferdinand and Isabella to González de Puebla, no date but entered into *CSPS* I as 'mid-July' 1488, no. 22, pp. 12–14 and González de Puebla to Ferdinand and Isabella, London (?), 30 Oct. 1488, *CSPS* I, no. 26, p. 16.

22. Suárez, *Los Reyes Católicos*, p. 708.

23. Valladolid, 17 Dec. 1488, *CSPS* I, no. 29, pp. 17–19.

24. 'Journals of Roger Machado. Embassy to Spain and Portugal A.D. 1488', printed in James Gairdner (ed.), *Historia Regis Henrici Septimi a Bernardo Andrea Tholosate*, London, 1858, at pp. 328–68, henceforth 'Journals of Roger Machado'. An important Spanish edition of the text, Juan Manuel Bello León and Beatriz Hernández Pérez, 'Una embajada inglesa a la corte de los Reyes Católicos y su descripción en el "Diario" de Roger Machado. Año 1489', in *España Medieval*, 2006, 26, pp. 167–202.

25. 'Journals of Roger Machado', pp. 340–42.

26. *Ibid.* pp. 350–51. It was of course Juana not María who was engaged to the Archduke Philip while Katharine was 'Princess of Wales' and not 'of England'.

27. 'Treaty between Spain and England, 27–28 March 1489', *PIIC* III, no. 12, pp. 124–47; [*CSPS* I, no. 34, pp. 21–24]; Suárez, *Los Reyes Católicos*, p. 709.

28. R. B. Wernham, *Before the Armada, the Growth of English Foreign Policy 1485–1588*, Oxford University Press, 1966, p. 71.

29. A promise of marriage *per verba de futuro* meant that the parties consented to marry in the future (and to consummate the marriage); it did not necessarily have to be a marriage by proxy but in the case of Arthur and Katharine this was the case while they were minors and

resident in their separate countries – thus the provision that they would subsequently commit themselves *per verba de praesenti* (*viz.*, to declare in the present tense) to marry. This taking of vows *per verba de praesenti* ordinarily – but not always – implied that the vows would be taken when the parties involved had reached adulthood. I am obliged to Fr Phillip Harris for advice on this distinction. See Catholic Encyclopedia, 'Civil Marriage', http://www.newadvent.org/cathen/09691b.htm.

30. J. Scarisbrick, *Henry VIII*, London, 1968, pp. 3–20; David Starkey, *Henry: Virtuous Prince*, Harper, London, 2008, pp. 59–99; on the festivities, Anglo, *Pageantry, Spectacle*, pp. 53–4.

31. On the Britanny crisis, Berenguer, *Fernando el Católico*, pp. 179–84.

32. On Warbeck, Ian Arthurson, *The Perkin Warbeck Conspiracy, 1491–1499*, Stroud, 2009.

33. Henry VII: articles respecting a war with France, Westminster 22 Nov 1491, *CSPS* I, no. 63, p. 39.

34. Treaty between Henry VII and Ferdinand and Isabella, Westminster, 8 March 1492, *CSPS* I, no. 81, pp. 48–9.

35. He wrote to Isabella from Andermund on 8 September 1493 setting out a history of his career, BL. Egerton 616, f. 3.

36. Treaty of Ferdinand and Isabella with Charles VIII, King of France, Narbonne, 8 Jan. 1493 and Barcelona, 19 Jan. 1493; Spanish version, *PIIC* III, no. 115, pp. 368–83; summary of French version, *CSPS* I, no. 78, p. 43.

4 Betrothal, 1494–1497: The Promise of a Marriage: French War, Spanish Diplomacy

1. On Ferrante's extraordinary brutality (which encouraged his opponents to welcome the French invaders), David Abulafia, 'Ferrante of Naples. The Statecraft of a Renaissance Prince', *History Today*, 45, 2, 1995.

2. Quoted by Garrisson, *Sixteenth-Century France*, p. 112.

3. On the following, the essays in David Abulafia, *The French Descent into Renaissance Italy 1494–95*, Variorum, Aldershot, 1995; see particularly Abulafia's 'Introduction: from Ferrante I to Charles VIII', pp. 1–25 and Georges Peyronnet, 'The distant origins of the Italian wars: political relations between France and Italy in the fourteenth and fifteenth centuries', pp. 29–53.

4. Two graphic descriptions: Francesco Guicciardini, *The History of Italy*, ed. and trans. Sidney Alexander, New York and London, 1969, pp. 69–75 and Johann Burchard, *At the Court of the Borgia*, ed. and trans. Geoffrey

Parker, Folio Society, London, 1963, pp. 98–106. On Alexander, Mallett, *The Borgias*, chapters 6 and 7.

5. Guicciardini, *The History of Italy*, p. 75.

6. 'Tratado de alianza, conocido bajo el nombre de Liga Santa…', Venice, 31 March 1495, *PIIC* IV, pp. 327–47, [*CSPS* I, no. 96, pp. 55–6].

7. Belenguer, *Fernando el Católico*, pp. 188–90. A succinct analysis of Ferdinand's dynastic policy, Edwards, *Ferdinand and Isabella*, chapter 7, 'Dynasty and Legacy', pp. 146–70.

8. Suárez Fernández, 'Estudio', *PIIC* IV, pp. 105–21.

9. 'Capitulaciones para el matrimonio de Felipe de Austria y Juana de Castilla, el príncipe Juan y Margarita de Habsburgo', Antwerp, 20 June 1595, *PIIC* IV, no. 51, pp. 263–5.

10. Brandi, *The Emperor Charles V*, p. 41.

11. Anon., 'Relación de los aparejos y gastos para la flota que ha de conducir a Flandes a Doña Juana', July (?) 1496, *PIIC* IV, pp. 469–89.

12. Fernández Álvarez, *Carlos V*, p. 16; Súarez Fernández dated the marriage ceremony and consummation to 18 October, *PIIC* IV, p. 145.

13. Márquez de la Plata, *El Tragic Destino de los Hijos de los Reyes Católicos*, p. 151.

14. Suárez, *Los Reyes Católicos*, p. 809.

15. González de Palencia to Ferdinand and Isabella, London, 19 July 1495, *CSPS* I, no. 98, pp. 57–60.

16. Ferdinand and Isabella to Jofre de Sasiola, 'Instrucciones para la embajada en Inglaterra…', Madrid, 3 Nov. 1494, *PIIC* IV, no. 51, pp. 263–5; see also, *ibid.*, pp. 91–2 [*CSPS* I, no. 90, pp. 51–2]. It is likely that Sasiola, for reasons that are not known, was unacceptable to the English.

17. Ferdinand and Isabella to Dr Rodrigo González de Puebla, 'Instrucciones … para su negociación con el rey de Inglaterra', Madrid, 25 Feb. 1495, *PIIC* IV, no. 67, pp. 304–6 [*CSPS* I, no. 93, pp. 53–4].

18. González de Puebla to Ferdinand and Isabella, London, 19 July 1495, *PIIC* IV, no. 98, pp. 396–9; [*CSPS* I, no. 98, pp. 59–60].

19. 'And you are to say to the King of England that he should greatly consider whether the King of France might not make himself much more powerful [than he is] because his friendship is so unreliable and he looks after his friends so badly and does not fulfil what he promises', Ferdinand and Isabella to González de Puebla, Tarazona, 22–24 Aug. 1495, *PIIC* IV, no. 102, pp. 411–16, at p. 413; [*CSPS* I, no. 103, pp. 67–9].

20. 'Firstly, that the marriage of our daughter the Princess Katharine with the Prince of England should be arranged jointly with an alliance of

friendship between the King of England and ourselves; the one must not be arranged without the other and the King of the Romans, our brother and the Archduke our son are also to be included ...', *ibid.*, pp. 481–2.

21. 'We order you to work greatly with all your forces so that the King of England should assist the Pope in his need. In addition to other reasons, all Christian princes are obliged to help him and [it would be insufferable] if the King of France, having seized the Pope's lands and held them against his will as he is doing today should then inflict even greater damage on the Pope than the Turks themselves could do ...', *ibid.*, p. 479

22. 'The French house is the old enemy of the House of England', *ibid.* p. 483.

23. Ferdinand and Isabella to González de Puebla, Tortosa, 30 Jan. 1496, *PIIC* IV, no. 130, pp. 478–88 and powers given to González de Puebla, same place and date, *ibid.*, no. 132, pp. 489–93; [*CSPS* I, no. 80, pp. 80–86].

24. Suárez, *Los Reyes Católicos*, pp. 793–5.

25. Ferdinand and Isabella to González de Puebla, Almazán, 26 April 1496, *PIIC* IV, no. 150, pp. 529–37 [*CSPS* I, 132, pp. 93–8].

26. Same to same, Almazán, 27 April 1496, *ibid.*, no. 152, pp. 538–9 [*CSPS* I, 133, pp. 98–9].

27. Henry VII, 'Treaty with the Pope, the King of the Romans, Ferdinand and Isabella of Spain and the Dukes of Venice and Milan', papal copy, Rome, 18 July 1496; [*CSPS I*, no. 146, pp. 113–14]; Wernham, *Before the Armada*, p. 45.

28. Isabella to González de Puebla, no place and Oña, 12 and 15 Sept. 1496, *PIIC* IV, nos 183–4, pp. 620–29; [*CSPS* I, nos 158 and 160, pp. 123–8].

29. Henry VII, Treaty with Ferdinand and Isabella, London, 1 Oct. 1496, *CSPS* I, no. 163, pp. 129–30; Ratification by Ferdinand and Isabella, Burgos, 1 Jan. 1497, *PIIC* V, no. 4, pp. 128–42; Katharine's instructions, Burgos, 1 Jan. 1497, *ibid.*, no. 5, pp. 142–4.

30. Undated decree of Henry VII, *PIIC* V, no. 8, pp. 151–2.

31. 'Tregua entre los Reyes Católicos y Carlos VIII', Lyon, 25 Feb. 1497, *PIIC* V, pp. 158–65.

32. Ferdinand and Isabella to González de Puebla, Burgos, 28 March and 8 April 1497, *PIIC* V, nos 16 and 18, pp. 169–75.

33. Doran, *Tudor Chronicles*, p. 47.

34. Suárez Fernández, 'Estudio', *PIIC* V, pp. 43–4; Hepburn, 'Arthur, Prince of Wales', p. 4.

35. Thomas P. Doyle, O. P., 'Marriage', in *The Code of Canon Law: A Text and Commentary*, ed. James A. Coriden *et al.*, The Canon Law Society of America, London, 1985, p. 737. See also J. Neuner S. J. Dupuis, S. J. *The Christian Faith in the Doctrinal Documents of the Catholic Church*, ed. Jacques Dupuis, New York, 1996, p. 714: 'Alexander III [declared] that mutual consent makes the marriage, but the bond is perfected and becomes absolutely indissoluble through consummation. Previous to consummation, marriage can be dissolved by solemn religious profession.' I am obliged to Fr Phillip Harris for introducing me to these texts and guiding me through them.

5 *1497–1501: The Renegotiation of a Marriage – and the Condition of Prince Arthur*

1. Marquez de la Plata, *El Trágico Destino de los Hijos de los Reyes Católicos*, pp. 54–6.
2. Suárez, *Los Reyes Católicos*, pp. 821–3 and 848–51.
3. Andrés Bernáldez, *Historia de los Reyes Católicos*, Seville, 1870, pp. 51.
4. Pedro de Ayala to [Ferdinand and Isabella?], London, 6 May 1498, *CSP Milan* I, no. 558, pp. 342–3.
5. Ferdinand and Isabella, 'Instrucciones al comendador Sancho de Londoño a su paso por Inglaterra', Alcalá de Henares, 7 March 1498, *PIIC* V, no. 45, pp. 210–12; 'Complemento' of same date, *ibid.*, no. 46, pp. 212–13; 'Memorial para la embajada en Inglaterra y Flandes para Sancho de Londoño y el subprior de Santa Cruz', *ibid.*, no. 47, pp. 213–15 and 'Instrucciones complementarias ... a Sancho de Londoño', *ibid.*, no. 51, pp. 219–20; *CSPS* I, nos 191–2, pp. 147–9.
6. Londoño and Matienzo to Ferdinand and Isabella, London, 18 Jul. 1498, *PIIC* V, pp. 230–7; [*CSPS* I no. 204, pp. 159–164].
7. González de Puebla to Ferdinand and Isabella, London, 15 July with a postscript of 19 July 1498, *PIIC* V, no. 67, pp. 246–54; *CSPS* I, no. 202, pp. 153–67.
8. 'The Queen of England and the mother of the king were present at the discussions on this day and to hear what they said about your Highnesses and the Princess of Wales was to [give cause] to praise God', *ibid.*, letter of 15 July, at pp. 247–8.
9. 'The Queen of England and his mother told me to write to your Highnesses that since the Lady Margaret was there [in Spain] she should continue to speak in her French language with the Princess of Wales so

that she could better learn that language, and that when she came here, with the blessing of God, these ladies could talk to each other [in French] because they do not understand Latin and much less Spanish. They also said to me that your Highnesses could henceforth have [Katharine] drink wine because the waters here do not allow any alternative...', *ibid.*, postscript of 19 July, p. 250.

10. Londoño and the sub-prior wrote on 18 July how badly they had been received by González de Puebla; he had been very hostile to them and was very favourable towards Henry VII. He was widely disliked and they launched into an extensive diatribe against him that was probably anti-Semitic in its roots, *PIIC* V, pp. 230–7, [*CSPS* I, no. 204, pp. 159–64, especially pp. 162–3.

11. Matienzo (Sub-Prior of Santa Cruz) to Ferdinand and Isabella, 16 Aug. 1498, *PIIC* V, no. 72, pp. 279–80; *CSPS* I, no. 217, p. 182.

12. Guicciardini, *History of Italy*, p. 132.

13. 'Tratado de paz entre Louis XII y los Reyes Católicos', Marcoussis, 5 Aug. 1498, *PIIC* V, no. 73, pp. 280–88.

14. González de Puebla to Ferdinand and Isabella, London, 25 Aug 1498, *PIIC* V, no. 79, pp. 296–309, [*CSPS* I, no. 221, pp. 185–92].

15. Hepburn, 'Arthur, Prince of Wales', pp. 4–9.

16. The following is based upon Juan de Tamayo (secretary of González de Puebla), 'Ceremonia del matrimonio de Catalina con Arturo', Bewdley, 19 May 1499, *PIIC* V, no. 111, pp. 390–94 [*CSPS* I, no. 241, pp. 209–10].

17. *CSPS* I, no. 246.

18. Suárez, *Los Reyes Católicos*, pp. 97–9; [*CSPS* I, no. 244, pp. 210–12].

19. Ferdinand II had returned to Naples after fleeing in 1494 but died immediately, allegedly of excessive sexual activity, *PIIC*, *iii*, p. 167.

20. Burchard, *The Court of the Borgia*, pp. 142–7; Suárez, 'Estudio', *PIIC* V, pp. 36–8. The best account, Mallet, *The Borgias*, pp. 139–43.

21. 'So having summed up all that the duke did, I cannot possibly censure him. Rather, I think I have been right in putting him forward as an example for all those who have acquired power through good fortune and the arms of others', Niccolò Machiavelli, *The Prince*, ed. and trans. George Bull, Penguin Classics, Harmondsworth, 1964, p. 60.

22. Suárez Fernández, *Los Reyes Católicos*, pp. 833–4; the articles on the Borja family in *Diccionario de historia eclesiástica de España*, 5 vols, (ed. Q. Aldea Vaquero *et al.*), Madrid, 1972–89, I, pp. 275–80; 'Rodrigo de

Borja y Borja', 'The Cardinals of the Holy Roman Church', http://www2. fiu.edu/~mirandas/cardinals.htm.

23. Suárez Fernández, 'Estudio', *PIIC* V, pp. 102–5.

24. This was certainly the view of Guicciardini, *History of Italy*, pp. 158–9.

25. Ferdinand and Isabella had allowed Margaret to return to the Low Countries in March 1500.

26. Cauchies, 'Un príncipe para los Países Bajos...', p. 76.

27. Enrique García Hernán (ed.), *Monumenta Borgia VI (1478–1551)*, Valencia–Rome, 2003, especially pp. 17–23.

28. A list of her entourage, *PIIC* VI, no. 13, pp. 108–9; Suárez, *Los Reyes Católicos*, pp. 846–7.

29. González de Puebla to Ferdinand and Isabella, London, 11 Jan. 1500, *CSPS* I, no. 249, pp. 213–14.

30. Same to same, London, 16 June 1500, *PIIC* VI, no. 22, pp. 118–29, [*CSPS* I, no. 268, pp. 222–9].

31. His correspondence – sometimes more referred to than read – *Correspondencia de Gutierre Gómez de Fuensalida, embajador en Alemania, Flandes e Inglaterra (1496–1509)*, Madrid 1907.

32. Ferdinand and Isabella to Gómez de Fuensalida, Seville, 5 May 1500, *ibid.*, pp. 115–16.

33. Ferdinand and Isabella to González de Puebla, Granada, 6 June 1500, *PIIC* VI, no. 19, pp. 115–7, [*CSPS* I, no. 266, pp. 220–22].

34. González de Puebla to Ferdinand and Isabella, Canterbury, 27 June 1500, *PIIC* VI, no. 26, pp. 135–6; [*CSPS* I, no. 280, pp. 233–4].

35. Gómez de Fuensalida to Ferdinand and Isabella, London, 29 June 1500, *Correspondencia de ... Gómez de Fuensalida*, pp. 116–19.

36. Same to same, London, 6 July 1500, *ibid.*, pp. 119–24.

37. Same to same, London, 8 July 1500, *ibid.*, pp. 125–9.

38. 'He sabido de persona çierta quel Rey tyene determinado quel Prínçipe conosca a su muger el dia de la velaçion, y apartarsela despues por dos o tres años, porque en alguna manera diz que el Prínçipe es flaço, y el Rey me dixo que los queria tener consigo los tres años primeros hasta quel Prínçipe supiese governarse por sy; y asymismo supe de buen lugar que con la Prínçesa se hara lo que con el Archiduque se haze, que es quel Prínçipe cunpla todo lo que avra menester, y que no terna casa aparte, ni cosa conoçida en vida del Prínçipe, porque desta manera esta la Reyna, avnque nunca se vso en Inglaterra syno agora', Fuensalida to Ferdinand and Isabella, from St Omer, 25 July 1500, p. 132. The reference to the

Archduke Philip is again tautologous, but when he married Juana in 1497 Burgundian household etiquette was instituted for the first time in the household of a Castilian princess – *viz.*, that the households of the two spouses were joined together. I am obliged to Dr Santiago Martínez Hernández for guidance on the historical context of this passage and to my colleagues Begoña Rodríguez and Miguel Arrebola for clarifying its linguistic complexities.

39. Gómez de Fuensalida to Ferdinand and Isabella, St Omer, 25 July 1500, *Correspondencia de … Fuensalida*, pp. 130–37.

40. Henry VII to Ferdinand and Isabella, 24 July 1500; [*CSPS* I, no. 283, p. 239].

41. Ferdinand and Isabella to González de Palencia, Granada, 25 July 1500, *PIIC* VI, no. 29, pp. 141–3; [*CSPS* I, no. 284, pp. 239–41].

42. Same to same, Granada, 13 Aug 1500, *PIIC* VI, no. 33, pp. 146–7; [*CSPS* I, no. 285, pp. 241–2].

43. Ferdinand and Isabella, 'Instrucciones a Puebla sobre reiteración del matrimonio y dote', no place, 3 Oct. 1500, AGS PR 52, f. 120 [*PIIC* VI, no. 39, pp. 164–6]

44. Katharine to González de Puebla, Granada, 20 Dec. 1500, *PIIC* VI, no. 45, pp. 183–5; [*CSPS* I, nos 290 and 291, p. 248].

45. González de Palencia to Ferdinand and Isabella, Abingdon, 27 Dec. 1500, *PIIC* VI, no. 46, pp. 185–92; [*CSPS* I, no. 292, pp. 248–53].

46. Isabella to González de Palencia, Granada, 23 March 1501, *PIIC* VI, no. 52, pp. 208–10; [*CSPS* I, no. 293, pp. 253–4].

47. Same to same, Granada, 8 April 1501, *CSPS* I, no. 296, pp. 256–7.

48. Isabella to Henry VII, Granada, 8 April 1501, *CSPS* I, no. 297, p. 257.

49. 'Isabella to González de Puebla, Granada, 21 May 1501 and Ferdinand and Isabella to same, Granada, 5 July 1501, *PIIC* VI nos. 58 and 63, pp. 216 and 248.

6 1501–1502: *Marriage to the Frail Prince*

1. Ferdinand and Isabella to González de Puebla, Santa Fé, 21 May and Granada, 5 July 1501, *CSPS* I, nos 299 and 302, pp. 258–9.

2. Lic. Alcaraz to Queen Isabella, (Plymouth?), 4 Oct. 1501, *PIIC* VI, no. 79, p. 278–9.

3. Miguel Pérez de Almaçan, 'Sequito de Catalina destinado a permanecer en Inglaterra', no date, *PIIC* VI, no. 60, pp. 218–19; [*CSPS* I, no. 288, pp. 246–7].

4. The following account draws on the anonymous history of the arrival of Katharine; the festivities with which she was welcomed; the wedding;

and the death of Arthur, *The Receyt of the Ladie Kateryne*, published with an important introduction by Gordon Kipling for The Early English Text Society by Oxford University Press, 1990. See also, *Hall's Chronicle*, London, 1809, pp. 493–7 and the anonymous *Chronicle of the Grey Friars of London*, ed. John Gough Nicholas, Camden Society, London, 1852, p. 27. A brilliant analysis of the festivities, Sydney Anglo, *Spectacle, Pageantry, and Early Tudor Policy*, Oxford, Clarendon Press, 1969, pp. 98–103; a valuable doctoral thesis by Jessica Erin Riddell, 'A Mirror of Men': *Sovereignty, Performance, and Textuality in Tudor England, 1501–1559*, Queen's University, Kingston, Ontario, Canada, 2009.

5. *The Receyt of the Ladie Kateryne*, p. 7.

6. Henry was accompanied by Edward Stafford, 3rd Duke of Buckingham, the most important nobleman in England; Buckingham brought an entourage of 400 men – an indication at once of his power but also perhaps of his tactlessness.

7. Anglo, *Spectacle Pageantry*, pp. 56–97, quotations at pp. 58, 97.

8. Kipling, 'General Introduction' to *The Receyt of the Ladie Kateryne*, pp. xv–xvi.

9. *The Receyt of the Ladie Kateryne*, p. 13.

10. *Ibid.*, pp. 39–51.

11. *Ibid.*, p. 42.

12. 'And then the Lord Prince and His Grace and nobles, after the goodly celebrations and dances, with pleasure and myrth … departed to his chamber and bed, wherein the princess had already been reverently laid down and rested before his arrival. Then, after the appropriate practices and customs in marriages of persons of noble blood, their bed and room were blessed with the pouring of certain oils … by the bishops … who were present; first they were courteously refreshed with wine and spices and then they were required and urged to leave. And so these worthy persons concluded and consummated the effect and end of the sacrament of matrimony. The day thus with joy, mirth and gladness reached its end', *The Receyt of the Ladie Kateryne*, pp. 46–7.

13. *Ibid.*, p. 47.

14. Anglo, *Spectacle, Pageantry*, pp. 98–103.

15. *The Receyt of the Ladie Kateryne*, pp. 50–51.

16. *Ibid.*, pp. 52–79.

17. *Ibid.*, pp. 34–5.

18. *Ibid.*, p. 35.

19. *Ibid.*, p. 58.

20. *Ibid.*, pp. 77–8.

21. Richmond, 28 Nov. 1501, *CSPS* I, no. 311, pp. 264–5.

22. Richmond, 30 Nov. 1501, *ibid.*, no. 312, p. 265.

23. Above, pp. 101.

24. Ayala to Ferdinand and Isabella, no place, *CSPS Supplement to Volumes 1 and 2*, London, 1868, pp. 1–12.

25. *The Receyt of the Ladie Kateryne*, pp. 78–9.

26. *Ibid.*, pp. 81–93 and Ralph Houlebrooke, 'Prince Arthur's Funeral', *Arthur Tudor*, pp. 64–76. See also Leland, *Collectanaea*, v, pp. 373–4.

27. See Houlebrooke, 'Prince Arthur's Funeral'; on the re-enactment of the funeral in 2002, Julian W. S. Litten, 'The Re-enactment of the Funeral of Prince Arthur', *Arthur Tudor*, pp. 167–80.

28. *The Receyt of the Ladie Kateryne*, pp. 80–81.

29. Wernham, *Before the Armada*, p. 51.

7 Widowhood – and the Papal Dispensation to Remarry

1. Antonio de Lalaing, Señor de Montigny, 'Primer Viaje de Felipe el Hermoso a España en 1501', printed in García Mercadal, I, pp. 402–517, at p. 425–8.

2. Ferdinand and Isabella to Fernan Duque de Estrada, Toledo, 10 May 1502, *PIIC* VI, no. 95, pp. 312–14; Suarez, *Los Reyes Catolicos*, pp. 861–4. The ambassador's name has led to much confusion; he is often described as the 'Duke of Estrada' but in fact 'Duque de Estrada' was his family name and he was not a duke.

3. Montigny, 'Primer Viaje de Felipe el Hermoso', pp. 403–17.

4. María Isabel de Val Valdivieso, 'Juana, retrato de una heredera', in Benjamín González Alonso (ed.), *Las Cortes y las Leyes de Toro de 1505*, Junta de Castilla y León, Salamanca, 2006, pp. 141–58, at p. 149; Cauchies, 'Un príncipe para los Países Bajos …', pp. 78–80.

5. 'She entered into rigorous mourning for the departure of her husband', Montigny, 'Primer Viaje', p. 465.

6. Val Valdivieso, 'Juana, Retrato de una Heredera', pp. 152–4; for a detailed account, Suárez, *Los Reyes Católicos*, cap. 18, 'Madre de Loca', pp. 455–85.

7. Val Valdivieso, 'Juana, Retrato de una Heredera', p. 152.

8. 'The duke [of York], suspecting that his brother's wife was with child, as was thought possible by the expert and wise men of the prince's council, was by a month or more delayed from his title, name and pre-eminence, in which time the truth might easily appear to women', *Hall's Chronicle*, p. 497.

9. Ferdinand and Isabella to González de Puebla, Toledo, 10, 21 and 29 May 1502; and to Duque de Estrada, Toledo, 10 May, nos 93–5 and 98–99, pp. 312–19; [*CSPS* I, nos 318–21, pp. 267–9].

10. Same to Duque de Estrada, Toledo, 14 and 16 June 1502, *ibid.*, nos 102 and 104, pp. 322–24; [*CSPS* I, nos 322, 325, pp. 269–71].

11. Isabella to Duque de Estrada, 12 July and 10 and 25 August; and same to González de Puebla, 18 July and 10 August, all from Toledo, *PIIC* VI, nos 107–11, pp. 329–41; [*CSPS* I, nos 327, 342, 343, pp. 272–4 and 276–282].

12. Isabella to Duque de Estrada, Toledo 12 July 1502, *PIIC* VI, no. 107, quotations at p. 329; [*CSPS* I, no. 327, pp. 272–4].

13. Isabella to Duque de Estrada, Toledo, 25 Aug. 1502, *PIIC* VI, no. 111, pp. 336–41; see especially p. 357.

14. Two letters of Ferdinand to Duque de Estrada, Zaragoza, 1 Sept. 1502, *PIIC* VI, nos 112–13, pp. 341–4; [*CSPS* I, nos 347, and 349, pp. 286–90].

15. See pp. 38, 77–8, 85, 96–7, 127–8.

16. On the bedsheets, *LP* iv III 5774 (1, 3.13).

17. Catholic Encyclopedia, 'Sacraments', http://www.newadvent.org/cathen/13295a.htm.

18. All discussion of the canonical legality of the marriage must start with the sustained excellence of the account by Scarisbrick, *Henry VIII,* especially chapter 7, 'The Canon Law of the Divorce', pp. 163–97.

19. Catholic Encyclopedia, 'Sacrament of Marriage', http://www.newadvent.org/cathen/09707a.htm

20. Isabella to González de Puebla, Alcalá de Henares, 11 April 1503, *PIIC*, no. 125, pp. 361–3; quotation at p. 362; [*CSPS* I, no. 359, pp. 294–5].

21. Same to Duque de Estrada, Alcalá de Henares, 11 and 12 April 1503, *PIIC* VI, no. 126, pp. 363–71, quotation at p. 363; *CSPS* I, no. 360, pp. 295–304].

22. *Ibid.*, p. 364.

23. *Ibid.*, pp. 365–6.

24. *Ibid.*, p. 369.

25. *Ibid.*, p. 367.

26. *Ibid.*, p. 368.

27. Treaty between Ferdinand and Isabella and Henry VII, Richmond, 23 June 1503, *CSPS* I, no. 364, pp. 306–8.

28. Ferdinand to Francisco de Rojas, Barcelona, 23 Aug. 1503, *PIIC* VI, no. 143, pp. 390–2; [*CSPS* I, no. 379, pp. 309–10].

29. In addition to the Archbishopric of Avignon (1474–1503) and the See of Bologna (1483–1502 he held the following: Carpentras (1471–2); Lausanne (1472–6); Catania (1473–4); Coutances (1576–7; Viviers (1477–9); Mende (1478–83); Sabina (1479–83); Ostia (1483–1503); Lodeve (1488–9); Savona (1489–1502) and Vercelli (1502–03). The Cardinals of the Holy Roman Church, 'Guiliano della Rovere', http://www2.fiu.edu/~mirandas/bios1471.htm#Dellarovere.

30. It may be indeed that the meeting did not even qualify as a 'conclave' since the cardinals appear not to have been locked away while they made their decision.

31. Ratification of the treaty by Ferdinand and Isabella, Barcelona, 24 Sept. 1503, *PIIC* VI, no. 148, pp. 415–32; two letters of Ferdinand to Henry VII, Barcelona, 24 September, *ibid.*, nos 150–151, pp. 434–6; [*CSPS* I, nos 372–6, pp. 313–17].

32. Two letters Isabella to Duque de Estrada, 3 October 1503, *PIIC* VI, nos 155–6, pp. 440–44; [*CSPS* I, nos 380 and 385, pp. 317–22].

33. Suárez, *Los Reyes Católicos*, pp. 869–70. At the moment of triumph, king and general fell out. Gonzalo Fernández de Cordoba offered asylum in Naples to Cesare Borgia when he arrived in Naples on 28 April 1504. Ferdinand insisted he be sent to Spain as a prisoner. This offended the Great Captain's sense of honour and led to an irreparable breach between the two men.

34. Joseph Pérez, 'Fernando el Católico y Felipe I el Hermoso', *Cortes de Toro 1505*, pp. 159–72, at p. 163.

35. Suárez, *Los Reyes Católicos*, p. 881.

36. The papal dispensation, 23 Dec. 1503, AGS PR 53, no. 89; [*CSPS* I, no. 389, p. 322].

37. Ferdinand and Isabella to Duque de Estrada, Medina del Campo, 26 June 1504, *PIIC* VI, no. 171, pp. 478–80; [*CSPS* I, no. 394, pp. 325–7].

38. 'Partido de Granuche como tengo dicho vinole este breve del Papa y luego el mismo dia me le enbio para que le viese y mostrase a la señora prinçesa', Duque de Estrada to Isabel, London, 10 August 1504, *PIIC* VI, no. 176, pp. 484–7, at p. 487; [*CSPS* I, no 398, pp. 329–30].

39. Ferdinand to Henry VII, Medina del Campo, 24 Nov. 1504, *PIIC* VI, no. 184, pp. 503–4.

40. Bishop of Worcester to Henry VII, Rome, 17 March 1505, *CSPS* I, no. 426, pp. 349–50.

41. Scarisbrick, *Henry VIII*, pp. 187–97.
42. 'It therefore seems possible to conclude that, since Katharine's first marriage was not consummated, and since a diriment impediment had been set up between her and Henry and not dispensed by the bull of 1503, her second marriage may well have been invalid in the eyes of the Church', *ibid.*, p. 189.

8 *1504–1509: The End of the Anglo-Spanish Alliance?*
1. Quoted by Pérez, 'Fernando el Católico y Felipe el Hermoso', p. 163.
2. Montigny, 'Primer Viaje de Felipe el Hermoso a España', p. 455; Ferdinand to Henry VII, Medina del Campo, 24 Nov. 1504, *PIIC* VI, no. 184, pp. 503–4; [*CSPS* I, no. 409, p. 339].
3. Bernáldez, *Historia de los Reyes Católicos*, cap. CCII.
4. Scarisbrick, *Henry VIII*, p. 192–3.
5. A very important collection of essays, Benjamín González Alonso (ed.), *Las Cortes y las Leyes de Toro de 1505*, Cortes de Castilla y León, Salamanca, 2006; see especially Juan Manuel Carretero Zamora, 'Las Cortes de Toro de 1505', pp. 269–96.
6. Gómez de Fuensalida, Gutierre, *Correspondencia de Gutierre Gómez de Fuensalida, embajador en Alemania, Flandes e Inglaterra (1496–1509)*, Madrid 1907, pp. 351, 359, 375, 394.
7. Pérez, 'Fernando el Católico y Felipe el Hermoso', p. 164.
8. Two important studies, Bethany Aram, *Juana la Loca, Queen of Castile, 1479–1555*, John Hopkins University Press, Baltimore and London, *c.* 2005 and Miguel Ángel Zalama, *Vida Cotidiana y arte en el palacio de la Reina Juana I en Tordesillas*, Universidad de Valladolid, 2003, chapter 1, 'Doña Juana antes de Tordesillas', pp. 23–82; two articles – María Isabel del Val Valdivieso, 'Juana, Retrato de una Heredera', in González Alonso, *Las Cortes y las Leyes de Toro 1505*, pp. 141–58 and Joseph Pérez, 'Los Hijos de la Reina: La Política de Alianzas', in Navascués Palacio (ed.), *Isabel la Católica Reina de Castilla*, pp. 53–82, at pp. 80–82.
9. Suárez, *Los Reyes Católicos*, pp. 892–4.
10. Ferdinand to González de Puebla, Segovia, 22 June 1505, AGS PR 54, no. 27 [*CSPS* I, no. 432, pp. 354–7].
11. Montigny, 'Segundo Viaje de Felipe el Hermoso a España en 1506', pp. 517–65, at pp. 517–19; I have adopted the traditional ascription of this essay to Montigny.
12. Cauchies, 'Un príncipe para los Países Bajos...', pp. 83–4.
13. For detailed discussions, Suárez, *Los Reyes Católicos*, pp. 894–5 and Belenguer, *Fernando el Católico*, pp. 245–9.

14. Katharine to González de Puebla, Richmond, 24 March 1505, *CSPS* I, no. 427, p. 340.

15. González de Puebla to Ferdinand, London, 11 Aug. 1505, AGS PR 54, no. 27 [*CSPS* I, no. 439, pp. 368–9].

16. Ferdinand to González de Puebla, Segovia, 22 June 1505, *ibid.*, no. 27a [*CSPS* I, no. 431, p. 354].

17. 'Protestation' of Henry, Prince of Wales, Richmond, 27 June 1505, *CSPS* I, no. 435, pp. 353–61.

18. González de Puebla to Ferdinand and Isabella, London, 23 Oct. 1504, *PIIC* VI, no. 179, pp. 490–96; [*CSPS* I, no. 402, pp. 331–6].

19. Henry VII to Katharine, Lewes, 27 Aug. 1504, *PIIC* VI, no. 178, pp. 490–91; [*CSPS* I, no. 400, pp. 330–31].

20. González de Puebla to Ferdinand, London, 17 Aug. 1505, AGS PR 54, no. 15; [*CSPS* I, no. 440, pp. 371–3].

21. Katharine to Henry VII, Durham House, 28 Aug. 1505, AGS PR 54, no. 32; [*CSPS* I, no. 441, pp. 373].

22. Scarisbrick, *Henry VIII*, p. 9.

23. Copy, Katharine to Ferdinand, Richmond, 11 December 1501 British Library, Cotton Manuscripts Vespasian CXII, f. 250. Part of the original printed (but misdated, 5 Dec. 1501), Gómez de Fuensalida, *Correspondencia*, pp. LXIV–LXVI.

24. Katharine to Ferdinand, Richmond, 15 Dec. 1505, AGS PR 54, no. 36; [*CSPS* I, no. 449, p. 373].

25. Suárez, *Los Reyes Católicos*, p. 896; see also Belenguer, *Fernando el Católico*, pp. 250–51.

26. Doran, *Tudor Chronicles*, p. 66.

27. The account of the voyage are based upon Montigny, 'Segundo Viaje de Felipe el Hermoso a España', pp. 531–4 and 'A narrative of the reception of King Philip of Castile in England in 1506', *CSPS* I, no. 451, p. 379.

28. Steven Gunn, 'Henry VII (1457–1509), King of England and Lord of Ireland' in *Oxford Dictionary of National Biography*, http://www.oxforddnb.com/view/article/12954?docPos=1.

29. 'El Segundo Viaje de Felipe el Hermoso ...', p. 535; Henry VII, 'Treaty of Alliance with Philip King of Castile', Windsor, 9 Feb. 1506, *CSPS* I, no. 452, pp. 380–81.

30. Margaret's matrimonial history was typical of the age and is worthy of remark. In 1482 she was betrothed to the French dauphin and went to live in France, but in December 1491 was repudiated by the dauphin

in favour of Anne of Brittany. She returned to the Low Countries in June 1493 and was betrothed to the *infante* of Spain, Don Juan. In 1497 Margaret travelled to Spain to marry Juan but he died shortly after the marriage and she then miscarried his child (who would have been the heir to Castile). In 1501 she married Philibert, Duke of Savoy, but when he died in September 1504 they were childless and Margaret determined to remain unmarried.

31. Quoted by Montigny, 'El Segundo Viaje de Felipe el Hermoso', pp. 537–8.

32. *Ibid.*, p. 538.

33. The Count of Miranda made an even more extraordinary gesture; when he heard of the storm that dispersed Philip's fleet he organised a relief expedition to find him and bring him back. He learned that Philip was staying in England and returned home.

34. Suárez, *Los Reyes Católicos*, pp. 901–9.

35. Cauchies, 'Un príncipe para los Paises Bajos...', pp. 84–5.

36. Pérez, 'Fernando el Católico y Felipe el Hermoso', p. 169.

37. Montigny, 'El Segundo Viaje de Felipe el Hermoso', p. 551.

38. A detailed and sensitive account, Zalama, *Vida Cotidiana ... de la Reina Juana I*, pp. 54–82.

39. Belenguer, *Fernando el Católico*, pp. 257–81.

40. Ferdinand to González de Puebla, Valencia, 20 July 1507, CSPS I, no. 528, pp. 420–21.

41. Two letters of same to same, Valencia, 20 July 1507, CSPS I, nos 528–9, pp. 420–22.

42. In 1521 Juana was briefly freed by the *comuneros*; Zalama, *Vida cotidiana ... de la Reina Juana I*, pp. 75–6.

43. Perry, *Sisters to the King*, pp. 37–54.

44. 'The Solempnities & Triumphies doon & made at the Spousells and Mariage of the Kynges doughter, the Ladye Marye to the Prince of Castile, Archduke of Austria', James Gairdner (ed.), *Camden Miscellany*, vol. 9, London, 1893, at p. 32. Two important accounts, Anglo, *Spectacle, Pageantry*, p. 104 and Perry, *Sisters to the King*, chapter 3, 'Princess of Castile'.

45. From Richmond, BL Egerton 616, f. 17.

46. Juan López to Ferdinand, Valladolid, 28 Aug. 1506, AGS PR 54, no. 3, [CSPS I, no. 484, pp. 397–8].

47. Letters of Ferdinand to Henry VII and to Katharine, Naples, 15 March 1507, AGS PR 54, 79; [CSPS I, nos 501 and 504, pp. 403–6].

48. González de Puebla to Ferdinand, London, 15 April 1507, [*CSPS* I, no. 511, pp. 408–10].

49. Two letters of Katharine to Ferdinand and one to Miguel Pérez de Almazán, Richmond, 15 April 1507, AGS PR 54, nos 10, 41 and 39; [*CSPS* I, no. 513, pp. 410–12].

50. Katharine to Ferdinand, Richmond, 8 August 1507, AGS PR 54, no. 43; see also same to same, Ewel, 15 Aug. 1507, AGS PR 54, no. 44; [*CSPS* I, no. 532, pp. 422–3.

51. Two letters of González de Puebla to Ferdinand and Miguel Pérez de Almazán, Woodstock, 7 Sept. 1507, AGS PR 54, no. 24 and un-numbered; [*CSPS* I, nos 543 and 545, pp. 428–31].

52. Katharine to Ferdinand, Woodstock, 7 Sept. 1507, AGS PR 54, no. 47; [*CSPS* I, no. 541, pp. 426–7].

53. Same to same, Ewell (?), 4 Oct. 1507, AGS PR 54, no. 48; [*CSPS* I, no. 551, pp. 433–6].

54. Same to Juana, Richmond, 25 Oct. 1507, *CSPS* I, no. 553, pp. 439–41.

55. Ferdinand to González de Puebla, no date, Jan. (?) 1508, *CSPS* I, no. 577, pp. 452–4.

56. Same to Gutierre Gómez de Fuensalida, Burgos, 7 Jan. 1508, *Correspondencia de … Gómez de Fuensalida*, pp. 407–13.

57. Gómez de Fuensalida to Ferdinand, London, 1 March 1508, *ibid.*, pp. 414–16.

58. Same to same, Richmond, 11 March 1508, *ibid.*, pp. 416–23, quotation at p. 418.

59. Same to same, Greenwich, 21 March 1508 with postscript of 2 April, *ibid.*, pp. 427–32.

60. Same to same, London, 17 April 1508, pp. 432–5, quotations at p. 435.

61. Ferdinand to Gómez de Fuensalida, Burgos, 18 April 1508, *ibid.* pp. 435–40.

62. Gómez de Fuensalida to Ferdinand, London, 22 April 1508, *ibid.*, pp. 442–4.

63. Same to same, London, 9 May 1508, *ibid.*, pp. 445–52; on Prince Henry, p. 449. Gómez de Fuensalida added a gloss: 'Those of his council told me yesterday that he had some weakness and that he did not eat any meat and was very thirsty and that his stomach was so weak that he could not digest anything and that he had no temperature and was bitterly ill but did not want to obey his physicians', p. 451.

64. Same to same, London, 17 June 1508, *ibid.*, pp. 453–5.

65. Same to same, London, 5 July 1508, *ibid.*, pp. 457–65.

66. Same to same, London, 24 July 1508, *ibid.*, pp. 467–9.

67. Same to same, London, 26 July 1508, *ibid.*, pp. 469–72.

68. Same to same, Valladolid, 7 Aug. 1508, *CSPS* I, no. 588, pp. 461–4.

69. Same to same, London, 2 Sept., 1508, *ibid.*, pp. 477–8, at p. 477.

70. Same to same, London, 11 Sept. 1508, *ibid.*, pp. 478–86; the quotations, p. 482 (Henry VII to Katharine and the descriptions of Henry VII's responses); p. 483 (Henry's rejection of Ferdinand's power and wealth).

71. Suárez, *Los Reyes Católicos*, pp. 922–3 and 931.

72. Katharine to Ferdinand, Richmond, 9 March 1509, *CSPS* I, no. 603, pp. 469–71 and Gómez de Fuensalida's account of this dispute, in undated letter to Ferdinand, *Correspondencia de … Gómez de Fuensalida*, pp. 533–40.

73. Same to same, Richmond, 20 March 1509, *ibid.*, no. 604, pp. 471.

74. S. J. Gunn, 'The Accession of Henry VIII', *Historical Journal*, 64, 1991, pp. 278–87 and DNB.

75. J. Wickham Legge, 'The Gift of the Papal Cap and Sword to Henry VII, *Archaeological Journal*, lvii, 1900, pp. 183–203.

76. Ferdinand to Fuensalida, Valladolid, 12 May 1509, AGS PR 54, no. 93.

77. Same to Henry VIII, Valladolid, 11 May 1509, *ibid.*, no. 94.

78. Same to same, no date, *ibid.*, no. 8. When the news of Henry's death was confirmed Ferdinand and Secretary Almazán wrote a series of letters on 18 May to Fuensalida and to Katharine urging that they should do all they could to ensure that the marriage with Prince Henry took place as soon as possible, *CSPS* II, nos 12–15, pp. 3.

9 Wife to Bluff King Hal: The Childbearing Years

1. On Henry at the beginning of his reign, Scarisbrick, *Henry VIII*, chapter 1, 'The New King', pp. 3–20; David Starkey, *Henry: Virtuous Prince*, London, 2008 and David Loades, *Henry VIII*, Amberley Publishing Publishing, Stroud, 2011, chapter 1, 'The Prince', pp. 29–49.

2. Commynes's description of Edward IV might be applied to Henry VIII: by 1470 'he was already … accustomed … to more luxuries and pleasures than any prince of his day because he thought of nothing else but women (far more than is reasonable), hunting, and looking after himself. During the hunting season he would have several tents brought along for the

ladies. All in all he had made a great show of this and also he had a personality as well suited to these pursuits as any I have ever seen. He was young and more handsome than any man then alive. I say he was at the time of this adventure because later he became very fat', *The Reign of Louis XI*, p. 188.

3. Steven Gunn, 'The French Wars of Henry VIII', in Black, *The Origins of War in Early Modern Europe*, John Donald Publishers, Edinburgh, 1987, pp. 28–51.

4. 'This was the biggest army with which any king of England had invaded France. All the army was mounted, and it was the best turned-out and the best armed that had ever gone to France, for most if not all the nobles of England were in it', Commynes, *The Reign of Louis XI*, p. 237.

5. Scarisbrick, *Henry VIII*, pp. 24, 26–7.

6. Hall, *Chronicles*, p. 515.

7. Andrea Badoer, Sebastian Giustinian, and Pietro Pasqualigo, Venetian ambassadors in England, to the Signory, *CSPV* II, no. 614, p. 242.

8. Francesco Chieregato, Apostolic Nuncio in England, to Isabella d'Este, Marchioness of Mantual, *ibid.*, no. 918, p. 400.

9. Sebastian Giustinian, Venetian Ambassador in England, 'Report of England', (Venice?), 10 Sept. 1519, *ibid.*, no. 1287, pp. 557–63, at p. 559.

10. Hieronimo Moriano, Secretary of Lodovico Falier, Venetian ambassador in England, to (?), London, 2 Jan. 1529, *CSPV* II, no. 386, pp. 185–6.

11. Gómez de Fuensalida to Ferdinand, London, 8 May 1509, *Correspondencia de … Gómez de Fuensalida*, pp. 517–25.

12. David Starkey, *Six Wives: The Queens of Henry VIII*, London, 2003, pp. 4–5 and Scarisbrick, *Henry VIII*, pp. 12–13.

13. The fullest account of the coronation and festivities, Hall, *Chronicles*, pp. 507–14.

14. Quoted by John Guy, *A Daughter's Love: Thomas and Margaret More*, Fourth Estate, London, 2008, p. 27.

15. Two important analyses of the ceremonies: Alice Hunt, 'The coronation of Henry VIII and Katharine', in *The Drama of Coronation: Medieval Ceremony in Early Modern England*, Cambridge University Press, 2008, pp. 22–38 and Jennifer Loach, 'The Function of Ceremonial in the Reign of Henry VIII', *Past and Present*, 1994, pp. 43–68.

16. Jennifer Loach points out that there were some interesting perquisites for office-holders at the coronation; for instance, as Earl Marshal, Surrey

could claim the horses and trappings used by the king and queen on their procession from the Tower to Westminster, the cloth from the king's table at the coronation banquet and the handing spread out behind him. Other officers enjoyed similar rights, 'The Function of Ceremonial in the reign of Henry VIII', pp. 46–7.

17. Quoted by Hunt, 'The coronation of Henry VIII and Katharine', p. 35.

18. Guy, *A Daughter's Love*, p. 28.

19. See especially, Hunt, 'The coronation of Henry VIII and Katharine', pp. 25–33.

20. Hall, *Chronicles*, pp. 510–12.

21. Henry VIII to Ferdinand, Greenwich Palace, 17 July 1509, AGS PR 54, nos 100 and 100b, [*CSPS* II, no. 19, p. 20].

22. Ferdinand to Katharine, Valladolid, 13 Sept. 1509, *CSPS* II, no. 22, pp. 21–2.

23. Simon Thurley, *The Royal Palaces of Tudor England: Architecture and court life*, Yale University Press, New Haven and London, 1993, p. 13.

24. The extensive literature on courts in this period is best approached through two collections of essays: John Adamson (ed.), *The Princely Courts of Europe 1500–1750*, Weidenfeld & Nicolson, London, 1999 and A. G. Dickens (ed.) *The Courts of Europe Politics, Patronage and Royalty 1400–1800*, London, 1977. On the Henrician court, David Starkey (ed.), *Henry VIII A European Court in England*, BCS, London, 1991 and Neville Williams, *Henry VIII and his Court*, London, 1971.

25. See the stimulating essay by John Adamson, 'The Making of the Ancien-Régime Court 1500–1700' in *The Princely Courts of Europe 1500–1750*, pp. 7–41.

26. See the accounts in *CSPV* II, nos 942, 944, 945 (quotation), 987, 996, 1000, 1052.

27. Mario Savorgnano to (?), Brussels, 25 Aug. 1531, *CSPV* IV, no. 682, pp. 285–9.

28. The following draws on Shirley, *The Royal Palaces of Tudor England*, pp. 27–36 and Neville Williams, *Henry VIII and his Court*, London, 1971, pp. 15–26.

29. Thurley, *Royal Palaces of Tudor England*, p. 39.

30. Sebastian Giustinian to the Signory, London, 30 Sept. 1516, *CSPV* II, no. 780, pp. 324–5.

31. Anglo, *Spectacle, Pageantry*, p. 108.

32. Luis Caroz de Villaragut, Spanish ambassador in England to Ferdinand, London, 29 May 1510, *CSPS* II, no. 45, p. 44; see Steven Gunn, 'The Early Tudor Tournament', in Starkey (ed.), *Henry VIII: A European Court in England*, pp. 47–8.

33. Henry VIII to Ferdinand, Greenwich, 1 Nov. 1509, *CSPS* II, no. 23, pp. 23–4.

34. Ferdinand to Katharine, no place or date, 28 (?) Nov. 1509, *CSPS* II, no. 28, p. 29.

35. David Cressy, *Birth, Marriage & Death: Ritual, Religion and the Life-Cycle in Tudor and Stuart England*, Oxford University Press, 1999; see especially 'Birth', pp. 15–94; see also, Olwen Hufton, *The Prospect Before Her: A History of Women in Western Europe, volume 1, 1500–1800*, London 1995, especially chapters 4 ('On Being a Wife') and 5 ('Motherhood'), pp. 134–216.

36. Anna Whitelock, *Mary Tudor England's First Queen*, Bloomsbury, London, Berlin and New York, 2010, pp. 9–10.

37. Diego Fernández to Ferdinand, Greenwich, 25 May 1510, AGS PR 54 no. 122; [*CSPS Supplement to vols I and II*, no. 7, p. 34]

38. Katharine to Ferdinand, Greenwich, 27 May 1510, AGS PR 54 no. 52 [*CSPS* II, no. 43, p. 38].

39. This was understood at the time: 'Some have them (*sc.* menstrual periods) when they be with child', quoted by Cressy, *Birth, Marriage and Death*, p. 42 and p. 489, n. 18. Part of the problem confronting modern historians has lain in the obscure and misleading translation of key passages into Latin by an editor of the *Calendar of State Papers, Supplement*... who was clearly embarrassed by the subject, Luis Caroz to Miguel Pérez de Almazán, London, 28 May 1510, *CSPS Supplement to vols I and II*, no. 8, pp. 36–44.

40. Andrea Badoer, 'Reading in the Senate of letters from the ambassador in London', London, 15th January...', *CSPV* II, no. 95, p. 43.

41. Hall, *Chronicles*, pp. 517–19; Anglo, *Spectacle, Pageantry*, pp. 111–12.

42. Katharine to Ferdinand, Greenwich, 25 May 1510, AGS PR 54 no. 122b; [*CSPS* II, no. 43, p. 38].

43. 'A male heir was born to the King of England and will inherit the crown, the other son having died', *CSPV* II, no. 329, p. 140.

44. Badoer to the State, London (?), 8 Jan. 1515, *CSPV* II, no. 555, p. 223.

45. Sebastian Giustinian, Venetian Ambassador in England to the Council of Ten, London 24 Feb. 1516, *ibid.*, no. 691, p. 285.

46. 'Advices from England', 13 Dec. 1518, *CSPV* II, no. 1123, p. 480.

47. Sebastian Giustinian, Venetian Ambassador in London, to the Signory, Lambeth, 10 Nov. 1518, *CSPV* II, no. 1103, p. 474.

48. John Dewhurst, 'The alleged miscarriages of Catherine of Aragon and Anne Boleyn', *Medical History*, 1984, 28, pp. 49–56. In September 1511 Wolsey thought that the queen might have been pregnant, p. 52.

49. Sebastian Giustinian to the Signory, London, 20 Feb. 1516, *CSPV* II, no. 690, p. 285.

50. Nicolò Sagudino, Secretary of Sebastian Giustinian, Venetian ambassador in England, to Alvise Foscari, London, 3 May 1515, *ibid.*, no. 624, pp. 246–9.

51. Andrea Badoer and Sebastian Giustinian, Venetian ambassadors in England, to the Signory, London, 29 Oct. 1515, *ibid.*, no. 659, pp. 267–8.

52. Scarisbrick, *Henry VIII*, p. 74.

53. For graphic accounts, *CSPV* II, nos 879, 881, 887, 910.

54. Anderson, *Origins of the Modern European States System*, p. 85.

55. League between Henry VIII and Ferdinand, London, 24 May 1510, AGS PR 54, no. 108; Juana was included in the treaty as Queen of Castile; ratification of the treaty, London, 20 Nov. 1510, *ibid.*, no. 107.

56. *Hall's Chronicle*, pp. 521–2; Cruickshank, *Henry VIII and the Invasion of France*, pp. 4–5.

57. On Henry's foreign policy in the early years, Scarisbrick's splendid chapter 2 'The Renewal of the Hundred Years War', *Henry VIII*, pp. 21–40.

58. Wernham, *Before the Armada*, pp. 82–3.

59. Garrisson, *A History of Sixteenth-Century France*, p. 129.

60. Moorhouse, *Great Harry's Navy*, pp. 71–87.

61. Anderson, *Origin of Modern European State System*, pp. 86–7.

62. *Hall's Chronicle*, pp. 527–32; Scarisbrick, *Henry VIII*, p. 29–31.

63. Anderson, *Modern European States System*, p. 87.

64. 'Confederación del Rey Católico y Enrique VIII de Inglaterra', London, 18 April 1513, AGS PR 55, no. 2.

65. Suárez, *Los Reyes Católicos*, pp. 942–6.

66. Ferdinand to Luis Caroz de Villaragut, no place, end of March 1513, *CSPS* II, no. 89, pp. 98–103.

67. On the campaign, Charles Cruickshank, *Henry VIII and the Invasion of France*, Allan Sutton Publishing, 1994; size of army, p. 18.

68. Katharine to Cardinal Bainbridge, London, 18 Sept. 1512, *CSPV* II, no. 203, p. 83.

69. See *CSPV* II, nos 239, 268, 283, 288, 294, 341.

70. To Wolsey, 25 August, quoted by Cruickshank, *Henry VIII and the Invasion of France*, p. 107.

71. Katharine to Henry VIII, Woburn, 16 Sept. 1513, printed by Polydore Vergil, *The Anglica Historia*, Camden Society, London, lxxiv, 1950, p. 221.

72. Cruickshank, *Henry VIII and the Invasion of France*, p. 163.

73. 'Confederación' between the representatives of Maximilian, Henry VIII and Ferdinand of Aragon, Lille, 17 Oct. 1513, AGS PR 55, nos 1 and 3; Wernham, p. 85.

74. Elton's voluminous writings are best approached through his *Studies in Tudor and Stuart Politics and Government*, Cambridge University Press, 1974–92; Scarisbrick, chapter 3, 'The Coming of Wolsey', *Henry VIII*, pp. 41–66; Peter Gwyn, *The King's Cardinal: The Rise and Fall of Thomas Wolsey*, Pimlico 2002; G. W. Bernard, *The King's Reformation Henry VIII and the Remaking of the English Church*, Yale University Press, New Haven and London, especially chapter 1, 'The Divorce', pp. 1–72. Two excellent collections of essays – Diarmaid MacCulloch (ed.), *The Reign of Henry VIII: Politics, Policy and Piety*, Palgrave, Basingstoke, 1995 and John Guy (ed.), *The Tudor Monarchy*, Arnold, London, 1997.

75. George Cavendish, *The Life of Cardinal Wolsey*, George Routledge and Sons, Glasgow, Manchester and New York, 1890, p. 24.

76. Sebastian Giustinian to the Signory, London, 17 July 1516, *CSPV* II, no. 750, p. 310. On Wolsey's rise, Gwyn, *The King's Cardinal*, chapter 1, 'From Butcher's Cur to Lordly Prelate', pp. 1–32.

77. The list of bishoprics that he held simultaneously is retailed with gusto by Gwyn, *The King's Cardinal*, pp. 4–5; for instance in 1518 he was given that of Bath and Wells, and in 1523 exchanged this for Durham; in 1529 he swapped Durham for Winchester.

78. Sebastian Giustinian, retiring Venetian ambassador in England, to Doge and Senate, (Venice?), 10 Sept. 1519, *CSPV* II, no. 1287, pp. 557–63, at pp. 560–61; see other accounts, nos 750, 894, 944, 951, 953.

79. Scarisbrick, *Henry VIII*, p. 54.

80. Wernham, *Before the Armada*, p. 87.

81. Scarisbrick, *Henry VIII*, pp. 51–5.

82. Treaty between Louis XII and Henry VIII, St Germain en Laye, 9 July and 7 Aug. 1514, *CSPS* II, nos 178, 183, pp. 224–8 and 229–36; see also, *ibid.*, nos 193–200 for the pensions paid by France to English courtiers and ministers.

83. Lorenzo Pasqualigo, merchant of Venice, to his brothers Alvise and Francesco, Sanuto Diaries, *CSPV* II, no. 500, p. 198 and Nicolò di Favri of Treviso, attached to the Venetian embassy in England, to Francesco Gradenigo, London, 24 Sept. 1514, *ibid.*, no. 505, pp. 198–202; see Perry, *Sisters to the King*, chapter 7, 'A Nymph from Heaven', pp. 116–133.
84. *CSPV* II, nos 508–11, pp. 203–12.
85. Perry, *Sisters to the King*, pp. 111–15.
86. Caroz to Fray Juan de Zúñiga (Juan de Eztuniga), Provincial of Aragon, London (?), 6 Dec. 1514, *CSPS* II, no. 201, pp. 248–9.

10 *The Great Rivals, 1515–1521: Charles of Habsburg & Francis of Valois*
1. Francis was the son of Charles, Count of Angoulême, and Louise of Savoy; Louis XII reluctantly acknowledged him as his heir and married him to his daughter Claude (18 May 1514); to do so he had to break the promise that Claude would marry Charles of Burgundy. A splendid biography, R. J. Knecht, *Renaissance Warrior and Patron: The Reign of Francis I*, Cambridge University Press, 1994.
2. Marco Antonio Contarini to Mafio Liom, Paris, 29 March 1515, *CSPV* II, no. 600, pp. 236–7.
3. A fine characterisation of him, Alonso de Santa Cruz, *Crónica del Emperador Carlos V*, 5 vols, Madrid, 1920–25, in III, pp. 37–40.
4. Fernández Álvarez, *Carlos V*, p. 62.
5. Parker, 'The Political World of Charles V', in Blockmans and Mout (eds), *The World of the Emperor Charles V*, pp. 113–226, at p. 113; Patrick Williams, *Philip II*, Palgrave Macmillan, Basingstoke, 2001, pp. 9–10.
6. See, for example, Manuel Fernández Álvarez, *Corpus Documental de Carlos V*, 4 vols, University of Salamanca, 1973–79.
7. A detailed analysis of the complexities of the rivalry between Charles and Francis in the early years of Charles's reign, M. J. Rodríguez-Salgado, 'Obeying the Ten Commandments: The First War between Charles V and Francis I, 1520–1529', in Blockmans and Mout, *The World of Emperor Charles V*, pp. 15–67, at p. 19.
8. Prudencio de Sandoval, *Historia de [la Vida y Hechos del Emperador] Carlos V*, 3 vols, Biblioteca de Autores Españoles, vols 80–82, Madrid, 1955–6, I, pp. 105–6; Sebastian Giustinian, Pietro Pasqualigo and Marco Dandolo, Ambassadors in France, to the Signory, Paris, 25 March 1515, *CSPV* II, no. 592, pp. 233–4.

9. A detailed discussion of the French pensions, David Potter, 'Foreign Policy', in MacCulloch (ed.), *The Reign of Henry VIII Politics, Policy and Piety*, pp. 101–133, at pp. 125–8.

10. Garrisson, *Sixteenth-Century France*, pp. 137–9.

11. Quoted by Andrea Badoer, Venetian ambassador in England, to Signory, London, 6 March 1515, *CSPV* II, no. 594, pp. 234–5.

12. 'Confederación y Liga', London, 19 Oct. 1515, AGS PR 55, no. 4; Ratification of the Treaty, Westminster, 27 Oct. 1515, *ibid.*, no. 23; Henry swore to observe it in Greenwich, 27 Oct. and Ferdinand in an unnamed place, 11 Dec. 1515, *ibid.*, no. 21.

13. A full analysis, Gunn, *Charles Brandon, Duke of Suffolk*, pp. 35–8.

14. Ferdinand to Prince Charles, Madrigalejo, 22 Jan. 1516, *CODOIN*, xiv, pp. 353–5. On Germaine and her daughter Isabel, Fernández Álvarez, *Carlos V*, pp. 97–9.

15. 'Fernando el Católico y Felipe el Hermoso', p. 171.

16. Parker, 'The Political World of Charles V', at pp. 117–18; Rodríguez-Salgado, 'Obeying the Ten Commandments...', p. 20.

17. Charles, King of Spain, Middelburgh, 18 July 1517, *CSPS* II, no. 256, p. 287; on the negotiations for the loan, Sebastian Giustinian to the Signory, London, 19 July 1517, *CSPV* II, no. 930, p. 406.

18. Charles, King of Spain, Middelburgh, 22 July 1517, *CSPS* II, no. 259, p. 288.

19. Detailed accounts of Charles's visit to Spain, Santa Cruz, *Crónica de Emperador Carlos V*, III, p. 15–36; and Lorenzo Vital, 'Relación del Primer Viaje de Carlos V a España', in García Mercadal, *Viajes de Extranjeros*, I, pp. 589–746; see also, Fernández Álvarez, *Carlos V*, pp. 78–83.

20. Sandoval, *Historia de ... Carlos V*, I, pp. 121–2; Fernández Álvarez, *Carlos V*, pp. 89–91.

21. *Cortes de los Antiguos Reinos de León y Castilla*, Real Academía de Historia, vol. IV, Madrid, 1882, pp. 260–84.

22. Sandoval, *Historia de ... Carlos V*, I, pp. 118–19; Vitali, 'Relación del Primer Viaje de Carlos V', pp. 725, 729–36.

23. Fernández Álvarez, *Carlos V*, p. 101.

24. The fullest treatment, Gwyn, *The King's Cardinal*, chapter 3 'The Making of the Treaty of London', pp. 58–103.

25. Hoyle's important essay 'War and Public Finance', in Diarmaid MacCulloch (ed.), *The Reign of Henry VIII Politics, Policy and Piety*, Palgrave Macmillan, Basingstoke, 1995, pp. 75–99, at p. 85.

26. On the celebrated opposition of John Colet, Dean of St Paul's, Scarisbrick, *Henry VIII*, pp. 32–3.

27. E. V. Cardinal, *Cardinal Lorenzo Campeggio Legate to the Courts of Henry VIII and Charles V*, Chapman and Grimes, Boston, 1935, pp. 15–56.

28. Sebastian Giustinian, Venetian Ambassador, to the Signory, London, 5 Oct. 1522, *CSPV* II, no. 1085, p. 462.

29. 'Anonymous account of the entertainments made in England when the French ambassadors went there to conclude the marriage of the Dauphin of France with the Lady Mary', no place, 9 Oct. 1518, no. 1088, pp. 464–9, at p. 465. On Mary's education, Whitelock, *Mary Tudor*, pp. 25–9 and John Edwards, *Mary I: England's Catholic Queen*, Yale University Press, New Haven and London, 2011, pp. 1–17.

30. Giustinian to the Signory, London, 5 Oct. 1518, *op. cit.*; Anglo, *Spectacle, Pageantry*, pp. 128–9.

31. On the structure of the Empire, Heer, *The Holy Roman Empire*, pp. 122–47 and Michael Hughes, *Early Modern Germany, 1477–1806*, Macmillan, Hong Kong, 1992, pp. 10–29.

32. J. Strieder, *Jacob Fugger the Rich Merchant and Banker of Augsburg, 1459–1525*, Archon Books, no place, 1966, pp. 153–5 and Ramón Carande, *Carlos V y sus Banqueros*, 3 vols, Crítica, Barcelona, 1983, II, pp. 13–20.

33. Rodríguez-Salgado, 'Obeying the Ten Commandments', p. 22.

34. *Ibid.*, p. 60.

35. Fernández Álvarez, *Carlos V*, pp. 116–19.

36. Pedro Girón, *Crónica del Emperador Carlos V*, Madrid, 1964, p. 137.

37. *Cortes de los Antiguos Reinos de León y Castilla*, IV, pp. 285–334.

38. *Ibid.*, pp. 293–8.

39. On the revolt, Joseph Pérez, *Los comuneros*, Madrid: La Esfera de los Libros, 2006.

40. On the detailed arrangements for the meeting, Treaty between Charles V and Henry VIII, London, 11 April 1520, *CSPS* II, no. 274, pp. 296–9.

41. Anglo, *Spectacle, Pageantry*, pp. 138–9; Itinerary of Charles V, http://bib.cervantesvirtual.com/historia/CarlosV/presentacion.shtml

42. An important collection of letters and papers on the Field of the Cloth of Gold, *CSPV* III, nos 58–98, pp. 38–79. An important analysis, Joycelyn G. Russell, *The Field of the Cloth of Gold: Men and Manners in 1520*, Routledge, London, 1969.

43. Anglo, *Spectacle, Pageantry*, pp. 139–58.

44. Charles V and Henry VIII, Treaty, no place, 14 July 1520, *CSPS* II, no. 287, p. 312.

45. Pérez, *Los Comuneros, passim*.

46. Fernández Álvarez, *Carlos V*, pp. 130–2.

47. Scarisbrick, *Henry VIII*, pp. 115–17.

48. Rodríguez-Salgado, 'Obeying the Ten Commandments', pp. 30–32.

49. Brandi, *Charles V*, pp. 153

50. Gwyn, *The King's Cardinal*, chapter 5, 'Peace or War: The Calais Conference of 1521', pp. 144–58.

51. On Wolsey's purposes, Scarisbrick, *Henry VIII*, pp. 82–94.

52. Wernham, *Before the Armadas*, pp. 96–7.

53. Whitelock, *Mary Tudor*, p. 22.

54. Mario Sanudo, [*Venice Cità Excelentíssima: Selections from the] Renaissance Diaries of Marin Sanudo*, ed. Patricia H. Labalme and Laura Sanguineti White, John Hopkins University Press, Baltimore, 2008, pp. 180–1.

55. Bernard de Mezza, imperial ambassador to England, to Charles V, London, 19 Dec. 1521, printed by Bradford, *Correspondence of Charles V*, pp. 14–20; at p. 19.

56. Charles V to Mezza, Ghent, 16 Dec 1521, *ibid.*, pp. 21–25, at p. 22.

57. Mezza to Charles V, (London?), 24 Dec. 1521, *ibid.*, pp. 26–7.

58. Charles V to Henry VIII, Ghent, 27 Dec. 1521, *ibid.*, pp. 27–9, at p. 28.

59. Same to Wolsey, Ghent, 27 Dec. 1521, *ibid.*, p. 30.

60. The conclave lasted from 27 December 1521 until 9 January 1522. Adrian's election proved to be of historic significance; it was the last time that a cardinal became Pope without attending the conclave and he became the last non-Italian to be elected until John Paul II in 1978; 'The cardinals of the Holy Roman Church', http://www2.fiu.edu/~mirandas/cardinals.htm, 'Conclave of December 27 1521 to 9 January 1522'.

61. Same to same, Brussels, 5 Feb. 1522, Bradford, *Correspondence of Charles V*, pp. 34–5.

11 *Katharine's Salvation? 1522–1523: The Emperor's Visit & the Sealing of the Imperial Alliance*

1. Itinerary of Charles V, http://bib.cervantesvirtual.com/historia/CarlosV/presentacion.shtml; seventeen anonymous papers, mostly of preparations for the visit, printed by William Jerdan (ed.), 'The visit of

the Emperor Charles V to England, A. D. 1522', *Rutland Papers XXI: Original Documents Illustrative of the Courts and Times of Henry VII and Henry VIII*, Camden Society, London, 1842, pp. 59–100; *Hall's Chronicle*, pp. 634–42; Anglo, *Spectacle, Pageantry, and Early Tudor Policy*, chapter V, 'The Imperial Alliance and the Entry of the Emperor Charles V into London June 1522', pp. 170–206; Stewart Mottram, *Empire and Nation in Early English Renaissance Literature*, Cambridge 2008, chapter 3, 'England's Empire Apart: The Entry of Charles V and Henry VIII (1522)', pp. 37–66.

2. See M. J. Rodríguez-Salgado, *The Changing Face of Empire: Charles V, Philip II and Habsburg Authority, 1551–1559*, Cambridge University Press, 1988, especially pp. 1–50.

3. 'Ceulx que lempereur entend mener avecques luy en Angleterre, le nombre des serviteurs et des chevaulx', *Rutland Papers*, pp. 60–65.

4. Untitled paper, *ibid*., pp. 65–6.

5. Anon., 'Ceulx que lempereur entend mener avecques luy en Angleterre, le nombre des serviteurs et des chevaulx', *Rutland Papers*, pp. 60–65.

6. Anon., 'Lodgings appointed for themperour and his retinue, etc.', *ibid*., pp. 86–93.

7. Anon., 'Remembraunces as touching themperors comyng', *ibid*., pp. 78–9.

8. Anon, 'Anno xiijmo Regis Henrici viij. Wynes remenyng the xxvj day of Marche …', *ibid*., pp. 68–9.

9. Anon., 'Lodgings appointed for themperour and his retinue, etc…', *ibid*., p, 86.

10. Anon., 'Lodegyngs appouynted for themperors noblemen in London at the Kyngs coming theder', *ibid*., pp. 93–5.

11. *Hall's Chronicle*, pp. 633–4.

12. *Ibid*., p. 635.

13. Martín de Salinas to Treasurer Salamanca, Greenwich, 5 June 1522, *El Emperador Carlos V y su corte según las cartas de Don Martin de Salinas, embajador del infante Don Fernando (1522–1539)*, Madrid, 1903–05, pp. 30–4.

14. Hall, *Chronicles*, pp. 635–7.

15. Geoffrey Moorhouse, *Great Harry's Navy: How Henry VIII Gave England Sea Power*, Phoenix, London, pp. 180–82.

16. On these, Anglo, 'The Imperial Alliance and the entry of the Emperor Charles V into London June 1522', chapter V of *Spectacle, Pageantry and Early Tudor Policy*, pp. 170–206 and Stewart Mottram, 'England's

Empire Apart: The Entry of Charles V and Henry VIII', chapter 3 of *Empire and Nation in Early English Renaissance Literature*, Cambridge, 2008, pp. 37–66.

17. See Mottram, *Empire and Nation*, pp. 39, 48.

18. Anglo, *Spectacle Pageantry*, pp. 191–202.

19. Charles V to Abbot of Nájera, London, 7 June 1522, *CSPS* II, no. 423, pp. 430–1; Mottram, *Empire and Nation*, p. 39. Salinas recorded on 7 June that Charles intended to hasten his departure from England, to Treasurer Salamanca, London, 7 June 1522, *CSPS* II, no. 424, pp. 431–2.

20. Charles V and Henry VIII, Treaty of Windsor, 16 June 1522, AGS PR 55, no. 6 (1), [*CSPS* II, no. 427, pp. 434–5].

21. Juan Manuel to Charles V, Rome, 18 June 1522, *CSPS* II, no. 428, p. 436–7.

22. Charles V and Henry VIII, Secret Treaty of Windsor, 19 June 1522, AGS PR 55, no. 10, [*CSPS* II, no. 430, pp. 438–40]; Henry's oath to observe the treaty, no date or month, 1522, AGS PR 55, no. 9; Rodríguez-Salgado, *The Face of Empire*, p. 64.

23. Charles V, Windsor Castle, 19 June 1522, *CSPS* II, no. 433, p. 441.

24. The same, Windsor Castle, 20 June 1522, *ibid.*, no. 434, p. 442.

25. *Hall's Chronicle*, p. 641.

26. Cardinal Wolsey, Windsor Castle, 20 June 1522, AGS PR 55, no. 12; [*CSPS* II, no. 435, p. 442].

27. Treaty of Bishop's Waltham, 2 July 1522, AGS PR 55, no. 5; [*CSPS* II, no. 442, pp. 449–51].

28. *Hall's Chronicle*, pp. 641–2.

29. To Treasurer Salamanca, Southampton, 6 July 1522, *El Emperador Carlos V y su Corte*, pp. 48–52; [*CSPS* II, no. 443, p. 451].

30. The three leaders of the *comuneros* revolt – Juan Padilla, Juan Bravo and Francisco Maldonado – had already been executed and a further score or more followed them to the scaffold while as many again died in prison. Charles established his court in Valladolid and visited Juana three times during the course of 1523; he was taking no chances with her. A general pardon was issued to cover 293 people (on payments of fines in many cases), Joseph Pérez, *Los Comuneros*, Madrid, 2006, pp. 134–5.

31. An extended discussion, Gwyn, *The King's Cardinal*, chapter 9, 'The Great Enterprise', pp. 354–410.

32. *Ibid.*, pp. 159–72.

33. Wernham, *Before the Armadas*, pp. 100–103.

34. On 28 December 1522 Johanna van der Gheyst gave birth to the child who became known as Margaret of Parma.

35. For a full discussion of Charles's purposes, Rodríguez-Salgado, 'Obeying the Ten Commandments'.

36. On the financing of war, Richard Hoyle's important essay 'War and Public Finance', in Diarmaid MacCulloch (ed.), *The Reign of Henry VIII: Politics, Policy and Piety*, Palgrave Macmillan, Basingstoke, 1995, pp. 75–99.

37. Wernham, *Before the Armada*, pp. 104–5; Gwyn, *The King's Cardinal*, pp. 369–70.

38. *Carlos V y sus Banqueros*, II, Cap. I 'Años de aprendizaje (1520–1532)'.

39. Charles's commission, Valladolid, 28 June and Henry's, London 17 May 1523, Treaty between Charles V and Henry VIII, Valladolid 2 July 1523, AGS PR 55, no. 11 (1), [*CSPS* II, no. 561, pp. 555–7].

40. Bourbon had served Francis with distinction at Marignano and been rewarded by being named on the battlefield as Constable of France. The reasons for Francis's developing hostility to him are not at all clear – perhaps the king feared both the extent and centrality of his landed territories which formed an enormous bloc south of Paris; perhaps, too, Francis envied Bourbon's military reputation. Whatever the reason, the king took advantage of Bourbon's family difficulties to fill his own war chest. The constable owed his ducal title to his wife Suzanne, Duchess of Bourbon, and when she died childless in 1521 she bequeathed all her lands and titles to him. However, Louise of Savoy, mother of the king, claimed both territories and titles through her own kinship with Suzanne. Strong-minded as Louise was, it is highly doubtful that she would have presumed to have made such a claim without the active encouragement of her son. Certainly, Francis naturally sided with her. In doing so he drove Bourbon to rebellion – as perhaps he had always intended to do. In August 1522, Bourbon made approaches to Charles V, offering to rebel against Francis if Charles supported him with men and money, Knecht, *Renaissance Warrior*, pp. 210–11.

41. Although Bourbon had made an agreement with Henry VIII, England was not included in the treaty. The reason was not some Machiavellian sleight of hand, but rather that Henry's ambassador failed to arrive in time, *ibid.*, p. 206.

42. Articles proposed to Henry VIII by Charles, Duke of Bourbon, no place, 4 Aug. 1523, *CSPS* II, no. 583, pp. 575–6.

43. Gunn, *Charles Brandon*, pp. 75–8. See also Gunn's 'The Duke of Suffolk's March on Paris in 1523', *EHR* 101, 1986, pp. 596–634.

44. Knecht, *Renaissance Warrior*, p. 201.

45. De Praet to Charles V, London, 6 October 1523, printed by Bradford, *Correspondence of Charles V*, pp. 83–7.

46. Minute of letter from Charles V to de Praet, Pamplona, 27 November 1523, *ibid.*, pp. 88–9

47. For the details of the voting in the election, Duke of Sessa to Charles V, Rome, 28 Oct. 1523, *CSPS* II, no. 606, pp. 589–91; Sessa recorded that Wolsey's candidature collapsed with the decision among the cardinals that they would not elect an absentee candidate (as they had done in the previous election). See also Hook, *The Sack of Rome 1527*, pp. 19–22.

48. Sessa to Charles V, Rome, 18 Nov 1523 and Charles to Lope Hurtado de Mendoza, Vitoria, 2 March 1524, *CSPS* II, nos 610 and 622, pp. 591 and 606.

12 The Turning-Point, 1524–1527

1. Nicolò Sagudino, secretary of Sebastian Giustinian, Venetian ambassador in England, to Alvise Foscari, London, 3 May 1515, *CSPV* II, no. 624, pp. 246–9.

2. Report of England by Sebastian Giustinian, on his retirement as Venetian ambassador, to Signory, (Venice ?), 10 Sept. 1519, *ibid.*, no. 1287, pp. 557, at p. 560.

3. Blaise de Monluc, *The Habsburg-Valois Wars and the French Wars of Religion*, ed. Ian Roy, Longman, London, 1971, p. 37.

4. Quoted by Knecht, *Renaissance Warrior*, p. 214.

5. *Ibid.*, p. 218.

6. Rodríguez-Salgado, 'Obeying the Ten Commandments', p. 41.

7. A graphic description, Monluc, *The Habsburg-Valois Wars*, pp. 48–50

8. A full account, Sandoval, *Historia de ... Carlos V*, II, pp. 65–94.

9. Gasparo Contarini to the Signory, Madrid, 12 March 1525, *CSPV* III, no. 956, pp. 413–14.

10. Quoted by Rodríguez-Salgado, 'Obeying the Ten Commandments', pp. 42–3.

11. Anglo, *Spectacle Pageantry*, pp. 207–8. It added to Henry's joy that Richard de la Pole was among those killed at Pavia.

12. Contarini to the Council of Ten, Madrid, 19 April 1525, *CSPV* III, no. 987, pp. 420–8.

13. Wernham, *Before the Armadas*, pp. 106–7.

14. 'Is like to ensue unto the Emperor, the whole monarchy of Christendom. For of his own inheritance he hath the realm of Spain and a great part of Germany, the realms of Sicily and Naples, with Flanders, Holland, Zeeland, Brabant, and Hainault and his other Low Countries; by election he hath the Empire, whereunto appertaineth all the rest of Italy and many imperial towns in Germany and elsewhere; by the possibility apparent to come by my lady Princess [Mary] he should hereafter have England and Ireland, with the title to the superiority of Scotland, and in this case all France with the dependencies', quoted by Wernham, *Before the Armadas*, p. 107.

15. Scarisbrick, *Henry VIII*, pp. 137–8.

16. Gasparo Contarini, Andrea Navagero and Lorenzo Priuli to the Senate, Toledo, 4 July 1525, *CSPV* III, no. 1057, p. 456.

17. Carande, *Los Banqueros de Carlos V*, II, pp. 37–42.

18. Hook, *The Sack of Rome*, pp. 44–8.

19. Scarisbrick, *Henry VIII*, pp. 138–9.

20. Knecht, *Renaissance Warrior*, pp. 240–45.

21. Santa Cruz, *Crónica del Emperador Carlos V*, II, pp. 173–7.

22. Sandoval, *Historia de … Carlos V*, II, pp. 138–60 and Santa Cruz, *Crónica del Emperador Carlos V*, II, pp. 180–220; there are slight differences in the transcriptions.

23. Eleanor remained in Spain until the princes had crossed into the country and then travelled to join Francis I, Knecht, *Renaissance Warrior*, pp. 246–8.

24. Hook, *The Sack of Rome*, pp. 49–92.

25. The task of presenting the papal brief of 23 June to Charles V was entrusted to Baldassare Castiglione, the celebrated Mantuan nobleman who had served as papal nuncio at the Spanish court since 1524: Castiglione handed it to Charles on 18 September at Santa Fé, just outside Granada. The two men greatly admired each other and their interview was a painful one. Charles left Castiglione in no doubt that he was now committed to going to war with the Pope, Fernández Álvarez, *Carlos V*, pp. 371–6.

26. 'Your Grace shall have the high and notable thanks of the Pope's holiness, the French king, the Venetians, and all the League ; you shall not be driven to expose any treasure more than this exile sum; Your Grace shall conserve your amity with the Emperor, acquiring, with God's grace, great thanks of him for concluding the peace; and finally the glory and honour thereof, and of all the good successes, shall principally be ascribed

unto Your Highness by whose counsel this league has been begun and, God willing, shall take this virtuous and honourable end', Scarisbrick, *Henry VIII*, p. 144.

27. Extract of letter from Charles V to Archduke Ferdinand, King of Bohemia, Toledo, 25 July 1525, printed by Bradford, *The Correspondence of the Emperor*, pp. 132–9.

28. *CDCV* I, pp. 100-15; Fernández-Álvarez, *Carlos V*, pp. 328–9.

29. Sandoval, *Historia de ... Carlos V*, II, pp. 163-6; Santa Cruz, *Crónica del Emperador Carlos V*, II, pp. 226–30 and 240–44; Fernández-Álvarez, *Carlos V*, pp. 325–43.

30. Wernham, *Before the Armadas*, pp. 110–11.

31. Doran, *Tudor Chronicles*, pp. 6–7.

32. Whitelock, *Mary Tudor*, pp. 32–5.

33. The following paragraphs follow G. W. Bernard, *Anne Boleyn Fatal Attractions*, Yale University Press, New Haven and London, 2010, especially chapter 3 '"Whose pretty dukkys I trust shortly to kiss": Henry's infatuation with Anne', pp. 19–36.

34. An authoritative analysis of the events of 1527, Rodríguez-Salgado, 'Obeying the Ten Commandments', pp. 55–7.

35. Account of Girolamo Negri, a Secretary to Cardinal Cornero, quoted by Hook, *The Sack of Rome*, p. 98.

36. Hook, *The Sack of Rome*, p. 115.

37. He had been one of the first Spanish aristocrats to attach himself to Charles, when in 1506 on the death of Philip of Burgundy he travelled to Brussels to commit himself to him, 'The Cardinals of the Holy Roman Church', *Biographical Dictionary*, http://www2.flu.edu/mirandas.

38. Marco Antonio Venier, Venetian ambassador in England, to Doge and Signory, two letters from London, 4 Jan. 1527, *CSPV* IV, nos 3 and 4, pp. 2–3.

39. Anglo, *Spectacle, Pageantry*, pp. 211–12; Scarisbrick, *Henry VIII*, p. 145.

40. Letters of Francisco de Salazar to (Gattinara?), Rome, 18 May and 11 June 1527, AGS E 847, ff. 180–1 [*CSPS* III–II, nos 70 and 87, pp. 195–201 and 238–45]. A full account, Sandoval, *Historia de ... Carlos V*, II, pp. 235–43.

41. Navagero to Doge and Signory, Valladolid, 21 May 1527, *CSPV* IV, no. 115, p. 66.

42. Same to same, Valladolid, 17 June 1527, *CSPV* IV, no. 124, pp. 68–9. Detailed accounts of the celebrations for the baptism, Sandoval, *Historia de ... Carlos V*, II, pp. 246–50.

43. A lucid analysis, Virginia Murphy, 'The Literature and Propaganda of Henry VIII's First Divorce', in MacCulloch, *The Reign of Henry VIII*, pp.135–58.

44. A brilliant discussion, Bernard, *The King's Reformation*, pp. 3, 17; Bernard suggests that it was probably Robert Wakefield or John Stokesley who suggested the re-translation.

45. Scarisbrick, *Henry VIII*, p. 154.

46. Bernard, *The King's Reformation*, pp. 17–30.

47. Gwyn, *The King's Cardinal*, pp. 386–402.

48. Perry, *Sisters to the King*, pp. 120–22, 231–4 and 160–78.

49. Scarisbrick, *Henry VIII*, pp. 194–7; quotation at pp. 196–7.

50. *Ibid.*, p. 157.

51. *Ibid.*, pp. 146–7.

52. Navagero to Signory, Valladolid, 27 July 1527, *CSPV* IV, no. 143, p. 78.

53. Anglo, *Spectacle, Pageantry*, pp. 225–30.

54. Bernard, *Anne Boleyn*, pp. 19–36; see also Bernard's, *The King's Reformation*, pp. 8–9.

55. Scarisbrick, *Henry VIII*, pp. 158–9.

56. Bernard, *The King's Reformation*, p. 128.

57. On their relationship, Guy, *A Daughter's Love*, p. 58.

58. Marco Antonio Venier, Venetian ambassador in England, to Doge and Signory, London, 20 and 23 Oct. 1,8, 11 and 27 Nov. 1527, *CSPV* IV, nos 188, 192, 201, 205, 208, 210, pp. 100–109; Anglo, *Spectacle, Pageantry*, pp. 230–35.

59. Scarisbrick, *Henry VIII*, pp. 202–6.

60. Gasparo Spinelli, Secretary of the Venetian Ambassador in London, to (?), London, 8 Jan. 1528m, *CSPV* IV, no. 225, pp. 115–16; on the festivities, Anglo, *Spectacle, Pageantry*, pp. 235–7.

13 1528–1529: The 'Mysterious Darkness of the Pope's Mind' & the Legatine Court

1. It happened that a few days before Lautrec marched the Spanish commander in Lombardy, Antonio de Leyva, wrote to Charles V that 'I haven't a farthing, and very few troops' and that he could only preserve his army by retreating into the safety of Milan, Kenneth M. Setton, *The Papacy and the Levant (1204–1571)*, 4 vols, The American Philosophical Society, Philadelphia, vol. III, *The Sixteenth Century to the Reign of Julius III*, p. 285.

2. Hook, *The Sack of Rome*, pp. 228–31.

3. The following is based on Navagero's letter to the Signory summarising the events of the last six months and Zuam Negro (Secretary of Navagero) to his father, Antonio Negro, both from Bayonne, 1 June 1528, *CSPV* IV, nos 290–91, pp. 141–51. The ambassadors were allowed to leave Poza on 19 May and crossed into France on 30th.

4. Juliano Soderini, Florentine ambassador to France, to Signory of Florence, Poissy, 7 February 1528, *ibid.*, no. 234, pp. 119–20; see also, 'Advices from France...', 10 Feb. 1528, *ibid.*, no. 236, pp. 121–2.

5. Charles V to Iñigo López de Mendoza, Monzón, 5 July 1528, *CSPS* III–II, no. 483 pp. 728–31.

6. Santa Cruz, *Chrónica del Emperador Carlos V*, II, pp. 408–15; Sandoval, *Historia de ... Carlos V*, II, pp. 316–17; Gasparo Contarini, Venetian Agent in England, to the Signory, Viterbo, 30 July and 11 Aug. 1528 and Antonio Suriano, Venetian ambassador in Florence, to the same, Florence, 7 Aug. 1528, *CSPV* IV, nos 327, 331 and 333, pp. 162–4.

7. Scarisbrick, *Henry VIII*, pp. 207–8; Bernard, *The King's Reformation*, pp. 9–11.

8. Miguel Mai to Charles V, Rome, 7 June 1529, *CSPS* IV–I, no. 35, pp. 69–72, at p. 70.

9. Francesco Guicciardini provided a fascinating gloss on Clement's grant of the decretal commission, which may well suggest how the Pope presented his action to insiders in Rome: 'For since that King was insisting on a declaration of nullity of his first marriage, the Pope, who had spoken many words about it with Henry's ministers (inasmuch as, finding that other princes did not trust him very much, the pontiff made every effort to keep himself under the king's protection), had most secretly drawn up a decretal bull in which the marriage was declared invalid. This was told to ... Cardinal Campeggio, and he was commissioned to show it to the king and the Cardinal of York, saying that he had a commission to publish it if acknowledgement of the king's case should not succeed prosperously in the court, so that they might more easily consent to have the case juridically debated, and tolerate with a more equitable soul the long drawn-out proceedings (which he had enjoined Cardinal Campeggio to retard as much as he could), and not to promulgate the bull unless first he had received a new commission from the Pope. Cardinal Campeggio tried to convince the king that the Pope's intention was to grant the divorce, which he felt he would have to do and which it is believable he had already in mind to do ... For the Emperor's power and interests having

grown in Italy, the Pope not only did not wish to offend him any further, but also wanted to revoke the offence which he had already given him. Therefore, even before he became ill, he had decided to refer the divorce case to the higher court, and had sent Francesco Campana to England to Cardinal Campeggio, pretending to the king that he was sent for other reasons, although related to that case, but actually with a commission to Campeggio to burn the bull. And although Campeggio delayed in carrying this out because the Pope's illness intervened, after the pontiff had recovered, he carried out his orders. Hence the Pope, freed of this fear, referred the matter to the higher court to the greatest indignation of the king, especially when demanding the bull of the cardinal, he learned what had happened to it', *History of Italy*, pp. 405–7.

10. López de Mendoza to Charles V, London, 18 Sept. 1528, *CSPS* III–II, no. 550, pp. 788–90.

11. Same to same, London, 30 Sept. 1528, *ibid.*, no. 562, pp. 803–5.

12. Bernard's magisterial discussion of the issues in the divorce, chapter 1 'The Divorce', *The King's Reformation*, pp. 1–72; on 'the Spanish brief', pp. 10–11.

13. Fr Ambrosio de la Serna to Katharine's physician, Paris, 8 Nov. 1528, *CSPS* III–II, no. 578, pp. 829–32.

14. Katharine to Charles V and the Empress Isabella, Greenwich, 19 Oct. 1528, *ibid.*, no. 571, pp. 822–3.

15. López de Mendoza to Charles V, London, 13–16 Oct. 1528, *ibid.*, no. 570, pp. 818–22.

16. The fullest discussion of Katharine's response, Bernard, *The King's Reformation*, pp. 73–87; see also Scarisbrick, *Henry VIII*, pp. 213–16 and Gwyn, *The King's Cardinal*, chapter 12 'The King's Great Matter', pp. 501–48. John Edwards reminds us that Katharine's mother had solved the problem of la Beltraneja by despatching her into a convent in Lisbon, *Mary I*, pp. 30–31.

17. Scarisbrick, *Henry VIII*, pp. 215–16.

18. *Ibid.*, pp. 216–17.

19. López de Mendoza to Charles V, London, 19 Nov. 1528, *CSPS* III–II, no. 587, pp. 849–50.

20. Hampton Court, 24 Nov. 1528, *ibid.*, no. 593, pp. 855–6.

21. Charles V to López de Mendoza, Toledo, 12 Dec. 1528, *ibid.*, no. 602, pp. 863–4.

22. Scarisbrick, *Henry VIII*, p. 218.

23. López de Mendoza insisted that the brief should under no

circumstances be shown to the English ambassadors; he urged Charles to persuade Clement VII to abandon the legatine court and advoke the case to Rome, to Charles V, London, 16 Jan. 1529, *CSPS* III–II, no. 614, pp. 877–9. A week later, the ambassador insisted even more strongly that the Pope should not allow the case to be heard in England; the queen's case was entirely dependent upon the original of Julius II's dispensation and an attested copy should be made of it to be sent to London, López de Mendoza to (Secretary) Muxetula, London, 25 Jan. 1529, *ibid.*, no. 618, pp. 881–3.

24. Scarisbrick, *Henry VIII*, pp. 222–3.

25. Bernard, *The King's Reformation*, pp. 10–12, 32–4.

26. 'Act of the Exhibition of the Dispensation Brief to the English Ambassadors', 3 April 1529 *CSPS* III–II, no. 662, pp. 967–8.

27. Fernández Álvarez, *Carlos V*, pp. 389–413.

28. The documents are printed in *CDCV* I, pp. 137–54; see also, Sandoval, *Carlos V*, II, p. 328.

29. Charles V to Katharine, Fraga, 23 April and Barcelona, 27 June 1529, *CSPS* III, no. 674, pp. 989–90 and IV–I, no. 54, p. 115. Shortly before Charles left Toledo, López de Mendoza departed from England; on the details, his letters to Charles, London, 15 March 1529, AGS E 553, f. 308 [*CSPS* III no. 650, pp. 926–7] and Gravelines 3 June, 1529, *CSPS* IV–I, no. 27, p. 55.

30. Guicciardini, *History of Italy*, p. 414.

31. The following is based upon Lodovico Falier, Venetian Ambassador in England to (the Signory?), London 22, 23 and 29 June 1529, *CSPV* IV, no. 482, pp. 219–20; Cavendish, *The Life of Wolsey*, pp. 114–29; *Hall's Chronicle*, pp. 753–56; a modern analysis, Scarisbrick, *Henry VIII*, pp. 224–5.

32. MacCullough, *Thomas Cranmer*, p. 24.

33. On Fisher's career and his attitude to Katharine's case, Bernard, *The King's Reformation*, pp. 101–25; for Professor Bernard's extended analysis of the defenders of Katharine, *ibid.*, pp. 73–224; two succinct biographies, Richard Rex, *DNB* and http://www2.fiu.edu/~mirandas/bios1535.htm#Fisher.

34. Scarisbrick, *Henry VIII*, p. 225.

35. Falier to Signory, *op. cit.*, p. 219.

36. Cavendish, *The Life of Cardinal Wolsey*, pp. 116–18.

37. The fullest treatment of Wolsey's fall, Gwyn, *The King's Cardinal*, chapter 13 'Wolsey's Downfall', pp. 549–98.

38. Hook, *The Sack of Rome*, pp. 248–9.

39. Treaty of Cambrai printed by Sandoval, *Carlos V*, II, pp. 38–60; Fernández Álvarez, *Carlos V*, pp. 384–5.

40. Scarisbrick, *Henry VIII*, p. 226 and Bernard, *The King's Reformation*, p. 35.

41. As reported by Chapuys to Charles V, London, 21 Sept. 1529, *CSPS* IV–I, no. 160, pp. 235–6.

42. Clement VII to Henry VIII, Rome, 7 Jan. 1531, *LP* V, no. 31, pp. 12–13.

43. Scarisbrick, *Henry VIII*, p. 235.

44. On More, John Guy, *A Daughter's Love: Thomas and Margaret More*, Harper Collins, London, 2008; an extended essay on More, Bernard, *The King's Reformation*, pp. 125–51; see also, Scarisbrick, *Henry VIII*, pp. 236–7.

45. Guy, *A Daughter's Love*, pp. 185–6; see also Scarisbrick, *Henry VIII*, p. 236.

46. Guy, *A Daughter's Love*, p. 186.

47. Agustino Scarpinello to Francesco Sforza, Duke of Milan, London, 2 Dec. 1530, *CSPV* IV, no. 637, pp. 266–8.

48. Charles V to Katharine, Barcelona, 6 July 1529, *CSPS* IV–I, no. 57, pp. 116–17.

49. The following is based upon Chapuys to Charles V, London, 21 Sept. 1529, *ibid.*, no. 160, pp. 220–39.

50. *Ibid.*, p. 229.

51. *Ibid.*, p. 225.

52. *Ibid.*, p. 232.

53. *Ibid.*, pp. 236–7.

54. *Ibid.*, p. 237.

55. Same to same, London, 25 Oct. 1529, *ibid.*, no. 194, pp. 292–306.

56. Piero Francesco de Bardi to Maffio Bernardo, London, 24 Oct. 1529, *CSPV* IV, no. 519, pp. 232–3.

57. London, 31 Dec. 1529, *CSPS* IV–I, no. 241, pp. 381–95, at p. 385.

14 Despair, 1530–1531: The Appeals to Rome & the Attacks on the Church

1. Arriving in Genoa (where he stayed 19–29 August), he travelled to Piacenza (6 September–30 October) and Parma (28–30 October), 'Los viajes de Carlos V', http://bib.cervantesvirtual.com/historia/CarlosV/presentacion.shtml.

2. Doge and Senate to Lodovico Falier, Venetian Ambassador in England, Venice, 27 March 1530, *CSPV* IV, no. 570, p. 240.

3. Stanford E. Lehmberg, *The Reformation Parliament 1529–1536*, Cambridge University Press, 1970, pp. 76–104; Guy, *A Daughter's Love*, pp. 189–91.

4. Scarisbrick, *Henry VIII*, pp. 247–8.

5. The following is based upon 'Los viajes de Carlos V', http://bib. cervantesvirtual.com/historia/CarlosV/presentacion.shtml; Gasparo Contarini to the Signory, Bologna, 5 Nov. 1529, *CSPV* IV, no. 524, pp. 234–6; 'Diarium Consistorium et Conclavorum, MDXXVIII', *CSPS* IV–I, no. 210, pp. 321–2; an important essay, Peter Burke, 'Presenting and Representing Charles V', in *Carlos V*, pp. 293–475, especially p. 432.

6. Fernández Álvarez, *Carlos V*, pp. 413–20.

7. *Ibid.*, p. 440.

8. Rodríguez-Salgado, 'The Ten Commandments...', pp. 84–6.

9. On this mission, Starkey, *Six Wives*, pp. 400–07, which is closely followed here; see also MacCullough, *Cranmer*, pp. 48–53. Articles in *DNB* by Joseph S. Block on George Boleyn; Claire Cross on Lee; L. E. Hunt on Carne; and Cecil H. Clough on Ghinucci. Lee and Ghinucci had of course been Henry's ambassadors in Spain who had been arrested and briefly imprisoned in Poza in 1528.

10. 'Report from Rome on the Matrimonial Cause of England', no day, Feb. 1533, *CSPS* IV–II, no. 1045, pp. 588–92; the original bull has not apparently survived but the inhibitory bull published on the same day has been published: 'Clement VII. Bull, notifying that on the appeal of Queen Katharine from the judgement of the Legates, who had declared her contumacious for refusing their jurisdiction as being not impartial, the Pope had committed the cause, at her request, to Master Paolo Capisucio [*sc.* Pucci], the Pope's chaplain and Auditor of the Apostolic palace, with power to cite the king and others; that the said Auditor, ascertaining that access was not safe, caused the said citation, with an inhibition under censures, and a penalty of 10,000 ducats, to be posted on the doors of the churches in Rome, at Bruges, Tournai and Dunkirk, and the towns of the diocese of Thérouanne. The queen, however, having complained that the king had boasted notwithstanding the inhibition and mandate against him, that he would proceed to a second marriage, the Pope issues this inhibition, to be fixed on the doors of the churches as before, under the penalty of the greater excommunication, and interdict to be laid upon the kingdom', Bull of Clement VII, Bologna, 7 March 1530, *LP* IV–III, no. 6256, pp. 2815–6.

11. Clement VII to Katharine of Aragon, no place, 21 March 1530, *LP* IV–III, no. 6279, p. 2822.

12. 'The Divorce', 25 March 1530, *LP* IV–III, 6285, pp. 2824–5. See also, Bishop of Tarbes to [Francis I], Bologna, 27 March 1530, and same to Montmorency, 28 March, *ibid.*, nos 6290 and 6293, pp. 2826–9; quotation from Charles V, Starkey, *Six Wives*, pp. 404–5.

13. Starkey, *Six Wives*, pp. 404–05.

14. The others being Cardinal del Monte, Bishop Simoneta and Paolo Pucci, 'Report from Rome on the Matrimonial Cause of England', *op. cit.*

15. Chapuys to Charles V, London, 14 Sept. 1530, *CSPS* IV–I, no. 425, p. 712.

16. Quoted by Starkey, *Six Wives*, p. 411.

17. The Spiritual and Temporal Lords of England to Clement VII, 13 July 1530, *LP* IV–III, no. 6513, pp. 2923–30.

18. Clement VII to the English Nobility Rome, 27 Sept. 1530, *ibid.*, no. 6638, p. 2991.

19. Hampton Court, *ibid.*, no. 6759, pp. 3055–6.

20. Katharine to the Pope, no place, [17] Dec. 1530, *CSPS* IV–I, no. 548, pp. 855–7.

21. 'Secret Consistory of the Cardinals', 23 Dec. 1530, *LP* IV–III, no. 6772, p. 3060.

22. Clement VII to Henry VIII, Rome, 7 Jan. 1531, *LP* V, no. 31, pp. 12–13.

23. Same to same, Rome, 25 Jan. 1531, *ibid.*, no. 750, p. 358.

24. Agustino Scarpinello to Francesco Sforza, Duke of Milan, London, 28 June 1530, *CSPV* IV, no. 584, pp. 245–6.

25. Same to same, London, 16 Dec. 1530, *ibid.*, no. 642, pp. 270–2, at p. 271.

26. Chapuys to Charles V, London, 10 May 1530, *CSPS* IV–I, no. 302, pp. 530–6, at pp. 535–6.

27. Same to same, London, 10 June 1530, *ibid.*, no. 345, pp. 585–7.

28. Same to same, no place, 27 Nov 1530, *ibid.*, no. 509, pp. 817–22, quotation at p. 819.

29. Same to same, London, 1 Jan. 1531, *LP* V, no. 24, pp. 10–11.

30. Scarpinello to Francesco Sforza, Duke of Milan, London, 19 April 1531, *CSPV* IV, no. 664, p. 279.

31. Lodovico Falier, Venetian Ambassador to England, Report to the Senate, no place, Nov. 1531, *ibid.*, no. 694, pp. 292–301.

32. Mario Savorgnano to (?), Brussels, 25 Aug. 1531, *ibid.*, no. 682, pp. 285–9.

33. Chapuys to Charles V, London, 31 July 1531, *CSPS* IV–III, no. 775, pp. 222–7.

34. On the following, John Edwards, *Mary I: England's Catholic Queen*, Yale University Press, New Haven and London, 2011, especially pp. 1–37.

35. Hazel Pierce, 'Margaret Pole', *DNB*.

36. Vivian Nutton, *DNB* and 'Thomas Linacre', The Catholic Encyclopedia, http://www.newadvent.org/cathen/09265b.htm.

37. The following is based upon the accounts in *Hall's Chronicle*, pp. 781–2; Chapuys to Charles V, London, 6 June 1531, *CSPS* IV–II, no. 739, pp. 169–78; Bernard, *The King's Reformation*, pp. 74–5.

38. 'The king after Whitsuntide and the queen removed to Windsor, and there continued until the 14 day of July, on which day the king removed to Woodstock and left her at Windsor, where she lay a while and after removed to the More and afterwards to Easthamstead: and after this day, the king and she never saw together', *Hall's Chronicle*, p. 781; Bernard, *The King's Reformation*, p. 75.

39. Chapuys to Charles V, London 4 Nov. 1531, *CSPS* IV–II, no. 818, pp. 277–8.

40. Savorgnano to (?), Brussels, 25 Aug. 1531, *CSPV* IV, no. 682, pp. 285–9.

41. Same to same, London, 16 Oct. 1531, *ibid.*, no. 808, pp. 263–6 and *LP* V no 478, pp. 226–7; Bernard, *The King's Reformation*, pp. 75–6.

42. A vigorous account of the discussions, Scarisbrick, *Henry VIII*, pp. 259–70.

43. MacCullough, *Cranmer*, p. 41.

44. Bernard, *The King's Reformation*, p. 134.

45. 'Juicio de la Universidad de Salamanca en la causa del matrimonio del Rey de Inglaterra Enrique VIII y la Reina D[oñ]a Catalina', Salamanca, 19 Sept. 1530 and 'Juicio emitido por el Colegio de San Bartolomé en la causa matrimonial existente entre Enrique VIII y D[onñ]a Catalina, Reyes de Inglaterra', Salamanca, Capilla de San Bartolomé, 7 Dec. 1530, AGS PR 43, nos 90 and 108.

46. 'Testimonio en que veinte Doctores Teólogos de la Universidad Complutense sientan cinco proposiciones sobre que no es contrario al derecho natural tomar por esposa la viuda del hermano, ni contra el derecho del Antiguo ni del Nuevo Testamento; y solo son prohibidos

tales matrimonios por ley positive y humana, y el Papa puede dispensar tal impedimento', Alcalá de Henares, Colegio de San Ildefonso, 21 Sept. 1531, AGS PR 53, no. 95.

47. 'Carta de Micer Mai, Embajador en Roma, enviando y pidiendo al Arzobispo de Santiago, Presidente del Consejo de Castilla, papeles relativos a la causa de Inglaterra, y dando cuenta de la marcha que ésta lleva', Rome, 20 Jan. 1531, *ibid.*, no. 114.

48. Chapuys to Charles V, London, 20 Sept. 1530, *CSPS* IV–I, no. 433, pp. 720–7, quotations and pp. 723 and 727.

49. Same to same, London, 8 March 1531, *ibid.*, no. 648, pp. 82–3.

50. Katharine to same, London, 5 April 1531, AGS E 22, f. 14; [*ibid.*, no. 681, pp. 112–13].

51. Same to same, Windsor, 28 July 1531, *ibid.*, no fol.; [*ibid.*, no. 772, pp. 220–21].

52. 'The Empress's instructions to search for the treaty of marriage between Queen Katharine of Aragon and Henry VIII and other papers relating thereto', Ocaña, [Oct.] 1531, *CSPS* IV–I, no. 570, pp. 879–81.

53. 'Interrogatory of questions to be addressed to various persons of the household of the Queen of England', no place or date, *ibid.*, no. 572, no. 572, pp. 883–4.

54. 'List of persons likely to give information or evidence on the first and second marriages of the Queen of England', *ibid.*, no. 573, p. 885; see also, *ibid.*, nos 574–7, pp. 886–7.

55. Miguel Mai to Charles V, no place, 10 Jan. 1531, *CSPS* IV–II, no. 588, pp. 7–11.

56. Scarisbrick, *Henry VIII*, pp. 273–81.

57. Chapuys to Charles V, London, 31 Jan. 1531, *CSPS* IV–II, no. 619, pp. 43–5; Scarisbrick, *Henry VIII*, pp. 280–81; Russell, *The Crisis of Parliaments*, p. 93.

58. Same to same, London, 13 Jan. [1531], *ibid.*, no. 598, pp. 22–8.

59. Same to same, London, 14 Feb. 1531, *ibid.*, no. 635, pp. 61–4.

60. Same to same, London, 6 June 1531, *ibid.*, no. 739, pp. 169–78.

61. Guy, *A Daughter's Love*, p. 210.

62. 'English Intelligence received at the Imperial Court. Anonymous letter and unaddressed letter from Ghent', 29 April 1531, *CSPV* IV, no. 668, pp. 280–81; see also Chapuys to Charles V, London, 1 March 1531 *CSPS* IV–II, no. 646, pp. 78–81.

63. Chapuys to Charles V, London, 9 Oct. 1531, *ibid.*, no. 805, pp. 260–1.

64. Archbishop Juan Pardo de Tavera of Toledo to Charles V, Toledo, 30 April 1531 AGS E 22, no fol.; [*CSPS* IV–II, no. 710, pp. 145–6].
65. Same to same, Illescas, 21 May 1531, *ibid.*, f. 36; [*CSPS* IV–II, no. 728, pp. 160–1].
66. Katharine to Charles V, The More, 6 Nov. 1531, *ibid.*, no fol.; [*CSPS* IV–II, no. 819, pp. 279–80].
67. Same to Chapuys, Bugden, 22 Nov. 1531. AGS E 22, f. 228; [*CSPS* IV–II, no. 833, pp. 291–2].
68. Same to Charles V, The More, 15 Dec 1531, AGS E 853, f. 22; [*CSPS* IV–II, no. 860, pp. 331–2]; see also her letter to Charles, The More, 31 Dec. 1531, *ibid.*, f. 149; [*CSPS* IV–II, no. 877, p. 348].

15 'The Poorest Woman in the World', 1532–1533: The Breach with Rome & the Divorce

1. Chapuys to Charles V, London, 4 Jan. 1532, *CSPS* IV–II, no. 880, pp. 352–5.
2. Scarisbrick, *Henry VIII*, p. 286. See the detailed analysis of Henry's policy in Virginia Murphy, 'The Literature and Propaganda of Henry VIII's First Divorce', in MacCullough (ed.), *The Reign of Henry VIII Politics, Policy and Piety*, pp. 135–58.
3. Mai to Charles V, Rome, 15 Jan. 1532, AGS E 857, f. 58; [*CSPS* IV–II, no. 884, pp. 360–2].
4. On Ortíz's relationship with Charles V, see especially his letter to him, Rome, 21 Aug. 1532, *CDCV* I, pp. 383–7.
5. The following is based upon Ortíz's letters to Charles V, Rome, 22–25 Jan. 1532 and to los Cobos, 25 Jan, *ibid.*, nos 893 and 887, pp. 371–5 and 363–6 [AGS E 858, f. 146].
6. Ortíz to los Cobos, *ibid.*, at p. 365.
7. Clement VII to Henry VIII, Rome, 25 January 1532, *LP* V, no. 750, p. 358.
8. Ortíz to Charles V, Rome, 25 Jan. 1532, *ibid.*, no. 893, pp. 371–5.
9. Katharine to Ortíz, Ampthill (?) 14 April 1532, *ibid.*, no. 931, pp. 422–3; quotation at p. 423.
10. Ortíz to Charles V, [Rome], April 1532, *LP* V, no. 933, p. 439.
11. Chapuys to Charles V, London, 22 May 1532, *ibid.*, no. 952, pp. 447–9.
12. Ortíz to Charles V, Rome, 28 July 1532, AGS E 858, f. 157; [*CSPS* IV–II, no. 979, pp. 485–7].
13. Brigden, *New Worlds, Lost Worlds*, pp. 118–20.

14. John Greville, quoted by MacCullough, *Cranmer*, p. 116.

15. *Hall's Chronicle*, p. 789; a detailed analysis of More's position, Bernard, *The King's Reformation*, pp. 125–51.

16. On his career, MacCullough, *Cranmer*.

17. Chapuys to Charles V, London, 27 Jan. 1533, *LP* VI, no. 89, pp. 34–6; see MacCullough, *Cranmer*, pp. 83–9, quotation at p. 89.

18. Cromwell's career was studied in intense detail by G. R. Elton, originally in *Tudor Revolution in Government: Administrative Changes in the Reign of Henry VIII*, Cambridge University Press, 1953; see also his *Reform and Renewal: Thomas Cromwell and the Common Weal*, Cambridge, 1973; John Guy, 'Thomas Wolsey, Thomas Cromwell and the Reform of Henrician Government', in MacCullough (ed.), *The Reign of Henry VIII*, pp. 35–57.

19. 'On Sunday ... the first of September [at Windsor], he created the lady Anne Boleyn Marchioness of Pembroke, and gave to her one thousand pounds land by the year, and that solemnity finished he rode to the College to Mass, and when the Mass was ended, a new league was concluded and sworn between the king and the French king...', *Hall's Chronicle*, p. 790.

20. 'Creacion of lady Anne, doughter to therle of Wilteshier, marquesse of Penbroke', 1 Sept. 1532, and Chapuys to Charles V, London, 5 Sept. 1532, *LP* V, nos 1274 and 1292, pp. 552 and 562–3.

21. Chapuys to Charles V, London, 1 Oct. 1532, *CSPS* IV–II, no. 1003, pp. 523–30. It is not made clear whether the jewels included those that Katharine brought with her from Spain.

22. *Hall's Chronicle*, pp. 789–94 and two accounts of the meetings, 29 Oct. 1532, *LP* V, nos 1484–5, pp. 623–5. See also Zuam Antonio Venier to Signory, Abbeville, 31 Oct. 1532, *CSPV* IV, no. 822 (wrongly numbered in text), pp. 361–4; Carlo Capello to the Signory, and anonymous 'Summary of the Interview between the Kings of England and France', London, 31 Oct. 1532, *ibid.*, nos 823 and 824, pp. 364–8.

23. Anon., 'Summary of the Interview between the Kings of England and France', Boulogne (?), 31 Oct. 1532, *ibid.*, no. 824, pp. 365–8.

24. Clement VII to Henry VIII, Rome, 15 Nov. 1532, *LP* V, no. 1545, pp. 649–50.

25. Same to same, Bologna, 2 January 1533, *LP* VI, no. 11, p. 6.

26. Clement VII and Charles V, Bologna, 24 February 1533, *ibid.*, no. 182, p. 83.

27. Ortíz to the Empress Isabella, Bologna, 19 Jan. 1533, *ibid.*, no. 53, p. 21.

28. Same to same, Bologna, 24 Feb. 1533, *ibid.*, no. 178, p. 82.
29. Same to same, Rome, 7 Feb. 1533, *CSPS* IV–II, *ibid.*, no. 1044, pp. 587–8 and *LP* VI, no. 134, p. 57.
30. On the marriage, MacCullough, 'The Date of Henry VIII's marriage to Anne Boleyn', in *Cranmer*, Appendix II, pp. 637–8; see also Bernard, *Anne Boleyn*, pp. 66–7.
31. The following paragraphs are based upon Chapuys to Charles V, London (?), 9 Feb. 1533, *CSPS* IV–II, no. 1047, pp. 592–600; quotation from Henry at p. 594.
32. Same to same, London, 10 and 15 April 1533, *LP* VI, nos 324 and 351, pp. 149–51 and 163–9 and *CSPS* IV–II, nos 1058 and 1061, pp. 628–32 and 635–45.
33. 'The Divorce', 5 April 1533, *LP* VI, no. 311, pp. 145–6; Carlo Capello to the Signory, London, 12 April 1533, *CSPV* IV, no. 870, pp. 392–3; Bernard, *The King's Reformation*, p. 67.
34. Chapuys to Charles V, London, 10 April 1533, *LP* VI, no. 324, pp. 149–51.
35. Same to same, London 15–16 April 1533, *ibid.*, no. 351, pp. 163–9.
36. Same to same, V, London, 16 April 1532, *ibid.*, no. 934, pp. 424–9.
37. Ortíz to Charles V, Rome, 14 April 1533, *ibid.*, no. 341, pp. 159–61.
38. Cifuentes to Charles V, Rome, 21 April 1533, *ibid.*, no. 365, pp. 171–2.
39. Same to same, Rome, 7 May 1533, *ibid.*, no. 454, pp. 203–4.
40. Ortíz to Charles V, Rome, 3 May 14533, *ibid.*, no. 436, p. 198.
41. 'Coronation of Anne Boleyn', *ibid.*, nos 561–3, 584–5 and 601, pp. 245–51, 264–6 and 276–8; see also Carlo Capello to the Signory of Venice, London, 7 June 1533, *CSPV* IV, no. 912, pp. 418–19.
42. Bernard, *Anne Boleyn*, pp. 67–8.
43. Cranmer to [Cromwell], 17 May 1533, *LP* VI, no. 496, p. 219.
44. Thomas Bedyll to Cromwell, Dunstable, 23 May after 10.00 a.m., *ibid.*, no. 526, pp. 230–1.
45. Same to Henry VIII, Dunstable, 23 May 1533, *ibid.*, no. 528, p. 231; see also '*ibid.*, no. 529, pp. 231–2.
46. Carlo Capello to the Signory, London, 7 June 1533, *CSPV* IV, no. 912, pp. 418–19.
47. Ortíz to Charles V, Rome, 16 June 1533, *LP* VI, no. 654, pp. 296–7.
48. Rodrigo de Ávalos to Charles V, Rome 16 June, 1533, *ibid.*, no. 656 p. 298.
49. Cifuentes to Charles V, Rome, 17 June 1533, *ibid.*, no. 663, p. 301.

50. Ávalos to Charles V, Rome, 24 June 1533, *ibid.*, no. 699, p. 312.

51. Rome, 30 Jun. 1533, *ibid.*, no. 725, p. 322.

52. 'The Divorce, 3–4 July 1533', *ibid.*, nos 760, 765, pp. 339–41.

53. 'Proclamation by Henry VIII', London, 5 July 1533, *CSPV* IV, no. 933, pp. 430–2; quotations at pp. 430–1.

54. Carlo Capello to the Signory, London, 12 July 1533, *ibid.*, no. 943, pp. 435–6.

55. There were two types of excommunication – 'minor', which merely excluded the named person from receiving the sacraments and 'major' which deprived him of all contact with the Church until he had been absolved; in Henry's case, 'the greater excommunication' clearly implied that he was no longer to be regarded as the lawful monarch of England and entitled to the obedience of his subjects or recognition as such by Christian princes, 'Excommunication', Catholic Encylopedia, http://www.newadvent.org/cathen/05678a.htm

56. 'The Pope's Sentence', Rome, 11 July 1533, and 'Relacion de lo que ha pasado sobre la causa de la Serenísima Reyna de Ynglaterra', [11 July], *LP* VI, nos 807–8, pp. 357–8.

57. Clement VII to Charles V, Rome, 17 July 1533, *ibid.*, no. 853, p. 375.

58. Bull of Clement VII, [Rome], 8 Aug. 1533, *ibid.*, no. 953, p. 413; the document is dated 6 August in 'The Papal Sentence', *LP* VI, no. 1447, p. 578.

59. [Esteban Gabriel Merino], Cardinal of Jaén to Francisco de los Cobos Rome, 14 Aug. 1533, *ibid.*, no. 980, p. 423.

16 Undefeated: 'The Most Obstinate Woman That May Be'

1. Chapuys to Charles V, London, 3 Sept 1533, *LP* VI, no. 1069, pp. 451–3.

2. Anonymous account of the birth, 'The Princess Elizabeth', Sept. 1533, *ibid.*, no. 1111, p. 464 and Chapuys to Charles V, London, 10 Sept. 1533, *ibid.*, no. 1112, p. 465.

3. Chapuys to Charles V, London, 15 Sept. 1533, *ibid.*, no. 1125, pp. 468–72.

4. The Princess Mary, 'Articles to be proposed and showed on our behalf unto our daughter lady Mary …', no date, Sept. 1533 (?), *ibid.*, no. 1186, pp. 491–2.

5. Whitelock, *Mary Tudor*, pp. 55–6.

6. Katharine to Mary, Buckden (?), no date [Sept. 1533?], *LP* VI, no. 1126, p. 472.

7. Chapuys to Charles V, London, 21 Feb. 1534, *CSPS* V-I, no. 17, p. 57.

8. A list of the monies expended on wages and food exists for the period from 19 December 1533 to 30 September 1534: it came to £2951.14.6.5 which would have meant that the household cost about £4,000 annually, anonymous account, 'Katharine of Aragon, expenses', 30 Sept 1534, *LP* VII, no. 1208, p. 468.

9. 'The Princess Mary', 1 Oct. 1533, *ibid.*, no. 1199, p. 498.

10. Mountjoy to Cromwell, Stondon, 10 Oct. 1533, *ibid.*, no. 1252, pp. 512–13; on Mountjoy, James P. Carley, *Dictionary of National Biography*.

11. Guicciardini, *History of Italy*, pp. 437–8.

12. Henry VIII to Dr Bonner, Windsor, 18 Aug. 1533, *LP* VII, no. 998, p. 430.

13. Scarisbrick, *Henry VIII*, p. 318.

14. Cifuentes to Charles V, Pisa, 28 September 1533, *LP* VI, no. 1166, p. 487.

15. On the meeting, Francisco López de Gómara, *Guerras de mar del Emperador Carlos V*, Madrid, 2000, pp. 152–4; The Pope's visit to Marseilles, letters of 13 Oct. 1533, and Francis I to the Bailly of Troyes, Marseilles, 14 Oct. 1533, *LP* VI, nos 1280 and 1288, pp. 518–21; see also, 'Interview of the Pope and Francis I', no date, Oct. 1533, *ibid.*, no. 1373, p. 546; see Knecht, *Renaissance Warrior*, pp. 299–304.

16. Cifuentes to Charles V, Marseilles, 23 Oct. 1533, *LP* VI, no. 1331, pp. 534–6.

17. Knecht, *Renaissance Warrior*, p. 300; Frieda, *Catherine de Medici*, p. 46.

18. Simoneta was raised to a cardinalate on 21 May 1535, presumably as a reward for his services over the case, 'Cardinals of the Holy Roman Church', http://www2.fiu.edu/~mirandas/bios1535.htm#Simoneta.

19. Bonner to Henry VIII, Marseilles, 13 Nov. 1533, *LP* VI, no. 1425, pp. 566–9.

20. Francis I and Clement VII, no date, *ibid.*, no. 1426, pp. 569–71 (Oct. 1533); quotation at p. 571.

21. Chapuys to Charles V, London, 9 and 27 Dec. 1533, *ibid.*, nos 1510 and 1571, pp. 610–12 and 632–4.

22. Gunn, *Charles Brandon*, pp. 118–19.

23. 'List of Katharine of Aragon's household who refused to swear and of those who swore', n.d. (Jan 1534?), *LP* VII, no. 135, p. 51. The paper records no writer or recipient; it is my supposition that it was sent by Suffolk to Cromwell.

24. Correctly or otherwise, four of these were given the Christian name of Elizabeth (Darrell, Fynes, Otwell and Lawrence); Emma Browne; Margery Otwell; Dorothy Wheler and Blanche Twyforde.

25. Catholic Encyclopedia, http://www.newadvent.org/cathen/14659b.htm

26. Duke of Suffolk and others to Henry VIII and same to Norfolk, Bugden, Friday 19 Dec. 1533, *LP* VI, nos 1541–2, p. 622. In a letter to Cromwell of the same place and date, Suffolk and his colleagues recorded that 'we find this woman more obstinate than we can express' and that they despaired of being able to persuade even one servant to take the oath, *ibid.*, no. 1543, pp. 622–3; further details from Chapuys to Charles V, London, 23 and 27 Dec. 1533, *ibid.*, nos 1558 and 1571, pp. 627–9 and 632–4.

27. The King's Council, 2 Dec 1533, *ibid.*, no. 1486, p. 599 and Chapuys to Charles V, London, 9 Dec. 1533, *ibid.*, nos 1486 and 1510, pp. 599 and 610–12.

28. Chapuys to Charles V, London, 16 Dec. 1533, *ibid.*, no. 1528, pp. 617–19.

29. Whitelock, *Mary Tudor*, pp. 57–8; see also Edwards, *Mary I*, pp. 18–37.

30. Chapuys to Charles V, London, 11 Feb. 1534, *CSPS* V–I, no. 10, pp. 31–7.

31. Same to same, London, 17 Jan. 1534, *ibid.*, no. 4, pp. 11–15; Whitelock, *Mary Tudor*, p. 59–62.

32. Same to same, London, 7 March 1534, *CSPS* V–I, no. 22, pp. 72–6; quotation at p. 72.

33. Cifuentes to Charles V, Rome, 12 and 23 Jan. 1534, *LP* VII, nos 39 and 96, pp. 17–18 and 37 [*CSPS* V–I, no. 2, pp. 5–9].

34. Ortíz to Charles V, Rome, 25 Feb. 1534, *ibid.*, no. 230, pp. 90–1.

35. Cifuentes to Charles V, Rome, 10 March 1534, *ibid.*, no. 311, p. 134.

36. Same to same, Rome, 24 March 1534, *CSPS* V–I, no. 27, pp. 84–6; Cifuentes was mistaken in believing that Clement had given sentence in 'the principal cause'.

37. Ortíz to Charles V, Rome, 24 March 1534, *LP* VII, no. 370, pp. 152–3 and *CSPS* V–I, nos 29–30, pp. 88–90.

38. Same to Katharine, Rome, 24 March 1534, *LP* VII, no. 371, pp. 153–4 and *CSPS* V–I, no. 30, p. 91.

39. Cardinal of Jaén to [Francisco de los Cobos], Comendador Mayor [of León] and Cifuentes to Charles V, both from Rome, 24 March 1534, *LP* VII, nos 368–9, p. 152.

40. Cifuentes to Charles V, Rome, 14 April 1534, *ibid.*, no. 484, p. 197.

41. Chapuys to Charles V, London, 30 March 1534, *CSPS* V-I, no. 32, pp. 95-7; on the statutes, Scarisbrick, *Henry VIII*, chapter 10, 'The Royal Supremacy', pp. 305-54.

42. 'The First Act of Succession', http://www.luminarium.org/encyclopedia/firstactofsuccession.htm, printed from Henry Gee and William J. Harvey (eds), *Documents illustrative of English Church History*, London, 1914, pp. 232.

43. Undated papers on 'the Nun of Kent', *LP* VII, nos 70, 72, pp. 28-9.

44. *Ibid.*, no. 72.

45. Alan Neame, *The Holy Maid of Kent: The Life of Elizabeth Barton 1506-1534*, London, 1971; Catholic Encyclopedia, http://www.newadvent.org/cathen/02319b.htm.

46. Chapuys to Charles V, London 14 May 1534, *LP* VII, no. 662, pp. 253-5 and *CSPS* V-I, no. 57, pp. 151-5.

47. Same to same, London, 19 May 1534, *ibid.*, no. 690, pp. 263-8; *CSPS* V-I, no. 58, pp. 155-66.

48. [Instructions to persons sent to Katharine of Aragon], no date, 1534, *LP* VII, no. 696, pp. 271-2.

49. Chapuys to Charles V, London, 29 May 1534, *ibid.*, no. 726, pp. 281-2 [*CSPS* V-1, no. 60, pp. 169-73.

50. 'Katharine of Aragon', 4 June 1534, *LP* VII, no. 786, pp. 301-2.

51. Chapuys to Charles V, London, 27 July 1534, *ibid.*, no. 1013, pp. 386-9; *CSPS* V-I, no. 75, pp. 219-26.

52. John Fisher, Bishop of Rochester, to Henry VIII, Rochester, 27 Feb. 1534, *LP* VII, no. 239, pp. 98-9.

53. Same to the Lords of the Parliament, no place or date, *ibid.*, no. 240, pp. 99-100.

54. More to Cromwell, no place or date, *ibid.*, no. 287, pp. 118-21.

55. Same to same, Chelchithe 5 March [1534], *ibid.*, no. 289, pp. 122-5.

56. 'The King's Style', 15 Jan. 1535, *ibid.*, no. 52, p. 18.

57. Chapuys to Charles V, London, 28 Jan. 1535, *ibid.*, no. 121, p. 38.

58. 'The Royal Supremacy', 10 Feb. 1535, *ibid.*, no. 190, p. 74; Sir Gregorio de Casale to Cromwell, Rome, 12 Oct. 1534 and to Duke of Norfolk, Rome, 15 Oct. 1534, *LP* VII, nos 1255 and 1262, pp. 484-6; Setton, *The Papacy and the Levant*, III, p. 394-6. On the war in the Mediterranean, Phillip Williams, *Empire and Holy War in the Mediterranean: The Galley and Maritime Conflict between the Habsburgs and Ottomans*, I. B.

Taurus, London, 2013: I am obliged to Phillip for his guidance on this complex subject.

59. Sir Gregorio de Casale to Cromwell, Rome, 12 Oct. 1534 and to Duke of Norfolk, Rome, 15 Oct. 1534, *LP* VII, nos 1255 and 1262, pp. 484–6; Setton, *The Papacy and the Levant*, III, p. 394–6. On the war in the Mediterranean, Phillip Williams, *Empire and Holy War in the Mediterranean: The Galley and Maritime Conflict between the Habsburgs and Ottomans*, I. B. Taurus, London, 2013: I am obliged to Phillip for his guidance on this complex subject.

60. Charles's accounts of the campaign, letters to Lope de Soria, Cagliari, 12 June, and La Goleta, 29 and 30 June, 14 and 25 July and 16 Aug. 1535, *CDCV*, I, pp. 424–44; see also, López de Gómara, *Guerras de Mar del Emperador Carlos V*, pp. 163–81 and Sandoval, *Historia de … Carlos V*, II, pp. 546–67; a detailed modern account, Fernández Álvarez, *Carlos V*, cap. V, 'El último cruzada: Túnez', pp. 487–513; see also, Setton, *The Papacy and the Levant*, III, pp. 396–8.

61. Chapuys to Charles V, London, 13 Oct. 1535, *LP* IX, no. 594, pp. 196–9.

62. Same to same, London, 9 Feb. 1535, *LP* VIII, no. 189, pp. 66–74.

63. Katharine to Chapuys, Kimbolton [12 Feb. 1535], *ibid.*, no. 200, pp. 76–7.

64. Chapuys to Charles V, [London?], 4 March 1535, *ibid.*, no. 327, pp. 129–31.

65. Same to same, London, 7 March 1535, *ibid.*, no. 355, pp. 141–5.

66. 'The Carthusians', no place or date, *ibid.*, no. 661, pp. 247–9; Chapuys to Charles V, London, 5–8 May 1535, *ibid.*, no. 666, pp. 250–8. A detailed account, 'The Charterhouse Monks', [19 June 1535], *ibid.*, no. 895, p. 354 records that eighteen Carthusians were condemned to death and that seven were hanged, drawn and quartered and another three were chained upright for thirteen days; two others were left hanging on the rope and were apparently not drawn and quartered and others died in prison, allegedly smothered to death. The sequence of the account is not always clear.

67. Dr Ortíz to the Empress Isabella, Rome, 31 May 1535, *ibid.*, no. 786, p. 294.

68. Chapuys to Charles V, London, 16 June 1535, *ibid.*, no. 876, pp. 345–6.

69. More to Margaret Roper, [The Tower], 2 or 3 May 1535, *ibid.*, no. 659, pp. 246–7. More's imprisonment, trial and execution are best followed in Guy, *A Daughter's Love*, pp. 219–74.

70. 'Trial of Thomas More', *ibid.*, no. 974, pp. 384–6.

71. More to Margaret Roper, The Tower, 5 July 1535 and 'Summary of trial and execution of Sir Thomas More', 6 July 1535, *ibid.*, nos 988 and 996, pp. 391 and 394–5.

72. Paul III to Francis I, Rome, 26 July 1535, *LP* VIII, no. 1117, p. 437.

73. Paul III, 'Excommunication of Henry VIII', Rome, 30 Aug. 1535, *LP* IX, no. 207, p. 67.

74. Dr Ortíz to the Empress Isabella, Rome, 1 Sept. 1535, *ibid.*, no. 249, pp. 84–5.

75. Chapuys to Granvelle, London, 25 Sept. 1535, *ibid.*, no. 435, pp. 141–2.

76. Dr Ortíz to Charles V, Rome, 4 Nov. 1535, *ibid.*, no. 770, pp. 260–1; see also, Cifuentes to Charles V, Rome, 5 Nov. 1535, *ibid.*, no. 774, pp. 261–2.

77. Same to the Empress Isabella, Rome, 16 Dec. 1535, *ibid.*, no. 983, p. 331.

78. Printed by Sanders, *Intimate Letters of England's Queens*, pp. 9–10.

79. Chapuys to Charles V, London, 30 Dec. 1535, *LP* IX, no. 1036, pp. 356–8.

80. Sir Edmund Bedingfield to Cromwell, Kimbolton, 31 Dec. 1535, *ibid.*, no. 1050, p. 362.

81. His account of her final days, to Charles V, London, 9 Jan. 1536, *LP* X, no. 59, pp. 20–2.

82. Bedingfield to Cromwell, Kimbolton, 5 Jan. 1536, *ibid.*, no. 28, p. 11.

83. Will of Katharine of Aragon, Jan. 1536, *ibid.*, no. 40, p. 15; a detailed account of Katharine's last days, Chapuys to Charles V, London, 21 Jan. 1536, *ibid.*, no. 141, pp. 47–54.

84. Sanders, *Intimate Letters*, p. 12.

85. Sir Edward Chamberlain and Sir Edmund Bedingfield to Cromwell, [Kimbolton], 7 Jan. 1536, *LP* X, no. 37, p. 14.

86. Chapuys to Charles V, London, 21 Jan. 1536, *op. cit.* I am obliged to Dr Veronica Sprott for advice on these symptoms.

87. The following paragraphs are based upon 'Death and burial of Katharine of Aragon', no date, *LP* X, no. 284, pp. 104–6.

88. John Hilsey had replaced Fisher when he was dispossessed of the bishopric in 1535.

89. Chapuys to Charles V, London, 21 Jan. 1536, *op. cit.*

90. *Thomas Cranmer*, p. 149.

91. Ortíz to Empress Isabella, Rome, 11 Jan. 1536, *LP* X, no. 82, p. 29.

92. Charles V to Chapuys, Naples, 29 Feb. 1536, *ibid.*, no. 373, pp. 148-9.

93. Same to same, Gaeta, 28 March 1536, *ibid.*, no. 575, pp. 224-8.

94. Same to same, Rome, 13 April 1536, *ibid.*, no. 666, p. 264.

95. Charles V to Chapuys, Pontremulo, 15 May 1536, *ibid.*, no 887, pp. 367-9; see also same to same, Borgo St Domino, 18 May 1536, *ibid.*, no. 907, p. 376.

96. Chapuys to Charles V, London, 25 Feb. 1536, *ibid.*, no. 351, pp. 131-5.

97. On the following, MacCullough, *Cranmer*, pp. 154-9.

98. *Anne Boleyn*, pp. 2-7.

99. 'Trial of Weston, Norris and others', Westminster, 12 May 1536, *LP* X, no. 848, p. 351.

100. 'Trial of Anne Boleyn and Lord Rochford', 15 May 1536, *ibid.*, no. 876, pp. 361-3.

101. 'Anne Boleyn', 17 May 1536, *ibid.*, no. 896, p. 373.

102. Chapuys to Antoine Perrenot, lord of Granvelle, London, 18 May 1536, *ibid.*, no. 901, pp. 373-4.

103. Same to Charles V, London, 19 May 1536, *ibid.*, no. 908, pp. 376-80.

104. Same to same, London, 6 June, *ibid.*, no. 1069, pp. 440-52.

105. Mary to [Henry VIII], Hunsdon, 1 June 1536, *LP* X, no. 1022, p. 424.

106. Same to same, Hundsdon, 10 June 1536, *ibid.*, no. 1109, p. 467.

107. Same to Cromwell, Hundson, 10 June 1536, *ibid.*, no. 1108, pp. 466-7.

108. Cromwell to Mary, no place or date, *ibid.*, no. 1110, pp. 467-8.

109. Mary to Henry VIII, Hunsdon, 14 June 1536, *ibid.*, no. 1133, p. 475.

110. Same to same, Hunsdon, 15 June [?] 1536, *ibid.*, no. 1136, pp. 477-8.

111. 'The Princess Mary's Submission', undated, *LP* X, no. 1137, p. 478.

Postscript

1. See the brilliant essay by Pierre Chaunu, 'Foreword' in the collection of essays that he edited, *The Reformation*, Gloucester, 1989, pp. 11-15.

2. For full accounts of these marriages, see Starkey, *Six Wives*, 'Part Three: The Later Queens', pp. 611-765.

3. Hazel Pierce, 'Margaret Pole' and Peter Marshal, 'John Forest', *Dictionary of National Biography*.
4. Susan Brigden, 'Rebuilding the Temple', *New Worlds, Lost Worlds*, pp. 179–212.
5. Williams, *Philip II*, pp. 21–42.
6. Drs Whitley and Kramer have suggested that Henry may carried the 'Kell antigen' in his blood, which may have explained the miscarriages suffered by Katharine and Anne Boleyn if their blood was Kell positive. They further suggest that Henry may have suffered from 'the Macleod Syndrome', a genetic disease which led to physical and psychological deterioration in middle age, Catrina Banks Whitley and Kyra Kramer, 'A new explanation for the reproductive woes and mid-life decline of Henry VIII', *The Historical Journal*, 53, 4, 2010, pp. 827–848.
7. Scarisbrick, *Henry VIII*, p. 497.

BIBLIOGRAPHY

Internet Sites

Act of Succession, 1534, http://www.luminarium.org/encyclopedia/
firstactofsuccession.htm

Calendar of State Papers, Spain, http://ihr-history.blogspot.co.uk/2009/03/
calendar-of-state-papers-pain.html#!/2009/03/calendar-of-state-papers-
spain.html.

Calendar of State Papers, Venice, http://www.british-history.ac.uk/
catalogue.aspx?gid=140.

Catholic Encyclopedia, http://www.newadvent.org/cathen/.

Chronicle of King Henry VIII of England, ed. M. A. S. Hume, G. Bell and
Sons, 1889, http://archive.org/details/chroniclekingheoohumegoog.

Chronicle of the Grey Friars of London, ed. John Gough Nicholas,
Camden Society, London, 1852, http://archive.org/details/chronicleofgre
yfoolondrich.

Itinerary of Charles V, Biblioteca Virtual Miguel de Cervantes, http://bib.
cervantesvirtual.com/historia/CarlosV/presentacion.shtml.

Oxford Dictionary of National Biography, http://www.oxforddnb.com/.

Polydore Vergil, *Anglica Historia*, http://www.philological.bham.ac.uk/
polverg/27eng.html.

Portal de Archivos Españoles [Spanish archival documents online], http://
pares.mcu.es/.

The Cardinals of the Holy Roman Church, compiled by Salvador Miranda
for Florida International University, http://www2.fiu.edu/~mirandas/
cardinals.htm.

Original Printed Material

Anglería, Pedro Mártir de, 'Epistolario', ed. Juan López de Toro, Madrid, *Colección de Documentos Inéditos para la Historia de España*, vols VIII and IX, Madrid, 1953.

Bello León, Juan Manuel and Hernández Pérez, Beatriz, 'Una embajada inglesa a la corte de los Reyes Católicos y su descripción en el "Diario" de Roger Machado. Año 1489', *España Medieval*, 26, 2006, pp. 167–202.

Bernáldez, Andrés, *Historia de los Reyes Católicos*, Seville, 1870.

Burchard, Johann, *At the Court of the Borgia: Being an Account of the Reign of Pope Alexander VI Written by his Master of Ceremonies Johann Burchard*, ed. and trans. Geoffrey Parker, Folio Society, London, 1963.

Calendar of State Papers, Spain: see internet sources.

Calendar of State Papers, Venice: see internet sources.

Cavendish, George, *The Life of Cardinal Wolsey*, London, 1890.

Charles V, *Correspondence of the Emperor Charles V and his Ambassadors at the Courts of England and France from the original letters in the Imperial Family Archives at Vienna*, ed. William Bradford, London, 1850.

Commynes, Philippe de, *Memoirs: The Reign of Louis XI 1468–83*, ed and trans. Michael Jones, Penguin Classics, Harmondsworth, 1972.

'Cortes de los Antiguos Reinos de León y Castilla', *Real Academía de Historia*, vol. IV, Madrid, 1882.

De la Torre, A. and de la Torre, E., *Cuentas de Gonzalo de Baena, Tesorero de Isabel la Católica (1477–1491)*, Madrid, 1955.

Doran, Susan (ed.), *The Tudor Chronicles 1485–1603*, London, Quercus, 2008.

Fernández Álvarez, Manuel (ed.), *Corpus Documental de Carlos V*, 4 vols, Universidad de Salamanca, 1973–9.

Fernández de Oviedo, Gonçalo, *Carro de las donas*, Valladolid, 1542 (lib. II).

Galíndez de Carvajal, Lorenzo, 'Anales breves del reinado de los Reyes Católicos D. Fernando y Doña Isabel ...' in R. Cayetano Rosell, *Crónicas de los Reyes de Castilla, Biblioteca de Autores Españoles*, LXX, Madrid, 1878.

García Mercadal, J., *Viajes de Extranjeros por España y Portugal desde los tiempos más remotos hasta comienzos del Siglo XX*, 6 vols, Junta de Castilla y León, Salamanca, 1999.

Gee, Henry and William John Harvey, *Documents Illustrative of English Church History*, London, 1914.

Girón, Pedro, *Crónica del Emperador Carlos V*, Madrid, 1964.

Gómez de Fuensalida, Gutierre, *Correspondencia de Gutierre Gómez de Fuensalida, embajador en Alemania, Flandes e Inglaterra (1496–1509)*, Madrid 1907.

Guicciardini, Francesco, *The History of Italy*, ed. and trans. Sidney Alexander, New York and London, 1969.

Hall, Edward, *Hall's Chronicle; Containing the history of England, during the reign of Henry the Fourth, and the succeeding monarchs, to the end of the reign of Henry the Eighth...*, ed. J. Johnson *et al.*, London, 1809.

Hallam, Elizabeth (ed.), *The Chronicles of the Wars of the Roses*, Guild Publishing, London, 1988.

Henry VIII, *Letters of Henry VIII 1526–29*, London, 2001.

Jerdan, William (ed.), *Rutland Papers: Original documents illustrative of the courts and times of Henry VII and Henry VIII*, Camden Society, London, 1842.

Katharine of Aragon, *The Receyt of the Ladie Kateryne*, ed. Gordon Kipling, Oxford University Press, for the Early English Text Society, no. 296, 1996.

Letters and Papers Foreign and Domestic of the Reign of Henry VIII, eds Brewer, J. S., J. Gairdner *et al.*, vols 1–9, London, 1882–1920.

Machiavelli, Niccolò, *The Prince*, trans. George Bull, Penguin Classics, Harmondsworth, 1964.

Marineo Sículo, L., *De rebus Hispaniae Memorabílis*, Alcalá de Henares, 1533.

Marineo Sículo, L., *Epistolarum familiarum*, Valladolid, 1514.

Monluc, Blaise de, *The Habsburg-Valois Wars and the French Wars of Religion*, ed. Ian Roy, Longman, London, 1971.

Montigny, Antoine de Lalaing, Señor de, 'Primer viaje de Felipe el Hermoso a España en 1501' and 'Segundo viaje de Felipe el Hermoso a España en 1506', in García Mercadal, J. (ed.), *Viajes de Extranjeros por España y Portugal*, I, pp. 402–517 and 517–565.

More, Thomas, *The Yale Edition of the Complete Works of St Thomas More*, 15 volumes (1963–97).

Pius II, *Memoirs of a Renaissance Pope: The Commentaries of Pius II*, ed. Leona C. Gabel, Capricorn Books, New York, 1962.

Pulgar, Fernando del, *Crónica de los Reyes Católicos*, ed. Juan de Mata Carriazo, 2 vols, Granada, 2008.

Salinas, Martín de, *El Emperador Carlos V y su corte según las cartas* de Don Martin de Salinas, embajador del infante Don Fernando (1522–1539): Con introducción, notas é indices por A. Rodríguez Villa, Madrid, 1903–05.

Sandoval, Prudencio de, *Historia de la Vida y Hechos del Emperador Carlos V*, 3 vols, Biblioteca de Autores Españoles vols 80–82, Madrid, 1955–6.

Santa Cruz, Alonso de, *Crónica del Emperador Carlos V*, 5 vols, Madrid, 1920–25.

Sanudo, Mario, *Venice Cità Excelentíssima: Selections from the Renaissance Diaries of Marin Sanudo*, ed. Patricia H. Labalme and Laura Sanguineti White, John Hopkins University Press, Baltimore, 2008.

Saunders, Margaret (ed.), *Intimate Letters of England's Queens*, Amberley Publishing, Stroud, 2009.

Suárez Fernández, Luis, *Política internacional de Isabel la Católica: estudios y documentos*, 6 vols, Universidad de Valladolid, 1965–2002.

'The Solempnities & Triumphies doon & made at the Spousells and Mariage of the Kynges doughter, the Ladye Marye to the Prince of Castile, Archduke of Austria. A. D. 1508', James Gairdner (ed.), *Camden Miscellany*, vol. 9, London, 1893.

Valera, Diego de, *Crónica de los Reyes Católicos*, Madrid, 1927.

Secondary Works

Abulafia, David (ed.), *The French Descent into Renaissance Italy 1494–95*, Variorum, Aldershot, 1995.

Abulafia, David, 'Ferrante of Naples: The Statecraft of a Renaissance Prince', *History Today*, 45, 2, 1995.

Abulafia, David, 'Introduction: from Ferrante I to Charles VIII', in Abulafia, David, *The French Descent into Renaissance Italy 1494–95*, pp. 1–25.

Adamson, John (ed.), *The Princely Courts of Europe: Ritual, Politics and Culture under the Ancien Régime 1500–1750*, Weidenfeld and Nicolson, London, 1999.

Álcala, Ángel and Sanz Hermida, Jacobo, *Vida y Muerte del Príncipe Don Juan, hijo de los Reyes Católicos*, Junta de Castilla y León, Valladolid, 1999.

Anderson, M. S., *The Rise of Modern Diplomacy, 1450–1919*, London, 1993.

Anglo, Sydney, *Spectacle Pageantry, and Early Tudor Policy*, Clarendon Press, Oxford, 1969.

Aram, Bethany, *Juana la Loca, Queen of Castile, 1479–1555*, John Hopkins University Press, Baltimore and London, *c.* 2005.

Armstrong, C. A. J., 'The Golden Age of Burgundy Dukes that Outdid Kings' in A. G. Dickens (ed.), *The Courts of Europe Politics, Patronage and Royalty 1400–1800*, London, 1977, pp. 55–75.

Arthurson, Ian, *The Perkin Warbeck Conspiracy 1491–1499*, The History Press, Stroud, 2009.

Azcona, Tarsicio de, *Isabel la Católica: Vida y reinado*, Madrid, 2004.

Banks Whitley, Catrina and Kramer, Kyra, 'A new explanation for the reproductive woes and midlife decline of Henry VIII', *The Historical Journal*, 53, 4, Dec. 2010, pp. 827–848.

Bell, A. F., *Luis de León*, Oxford, 1925.

Bernard, G. W., *Anne Boleyn: Fatal Attractions*, Yale University Press, New Haven and London, 2010.

Bernard, G. W., *The King's Reformation Henry VIII and the Remaking of the English Church*, Yale University Press, New Haven and London, 2005.

Black, Jeremy (ed.), *The Origins of War in Early Modern Europe*, John Donald Publishers, Edinburgh, 1987.

Blockmans, Wim and Mout, Nicolette (eds), *The World of the Emperor Charles V [Proceedings of the Colloquium, Amsterdam 2001]*, Amsterdam, 2004.

Blockmans, Wim, *Emperor Charles V, 1500–1558*, London, 2002.

Bonney, Richard, *The European Dynastic States 1494–1660*, Oxford University Press, 1991.

Boruchoff, David A. (ed.), *Isabel la Católica, Queen of Castile: Critical Essays*, Palgrave Macmillan, Basingstoke, 2003.

Brandi, Karl, *The Emperor Charles V: The growth and destiny of a man and of a world-empire*, trans. C. V. Wedgwood, Jonathan Cape, London 1963.

Brigden, Susan, *New Worlds, Lost Worlds The Rule of the Tudors 1485–1603*, Penguin Books, London, 2001.

Camón Aznar, J., *Sobre la muerte del príncipe Don Juan*, Real Academia de la Historia, Madrid, 1953.

Carande, Ramón, *Carlos V y sus Banqueros*, 3 vols, Barcelona, 1983.

Carretero Zamora, Juan Manuel, 'Las Cortes de Toro de 1505', in González Alonso (ed.), *Las Cortes y las Leyes de Toro de 1505*, Cortes de Castilla y León, Salamanca, 2006, pp. 269–96.

Cauchies, Jean-Marie, 'Un príncipe para los Países Bajos, para España para Europa', in Zalama and Vandenbroeck, *Felipe el Hermoso*, pp. 71–86.

Charles V, *El Mundo de Carlos V: De la España Medieval al Siglo de Oro*, Sociedad Estatal para la Conmemoración de los Centenarios de Felipe II y Carlos V, Madrid, 2000.

Chaunu, Pierre (ed.), *The Reformation*, Palgrave Macmillan, 1990.

Cohn, Samuel K., 'The Black Death, tragedy, and transformation', in J. J. Martin, *The Renaissance World*, pp. 69–83.

Cressy, David, *Birth Marriage, and Death: Ritual, Religion, and the Life-Cycle in Tudor and Stuart England*, Oxford University Press, 1999.

Cruickshank, Charles, *Henry VIII and the Invasion of France*, Alan Sutton, Bath, 1994.

Dewhurst, John, 'The alleged miscarriages of Catherine of Aragon and Anne Boleyn', *Medical History*, 1984, 28, pp. 49–56.

Dickens, A. G., *The Courts of Europe Politics, Patronage and Royalty 1400–1800*, London, 1977.

Doran, Susan (ed.), *Henry VIII: Man and Monarch*, British Library, London, 2009.

Duffy, Eamon, *The Stripping of the Altars Traditional Religion in England c. 1400-c. 1580*, Yale University Press, New Haven and London, 1992.

Edwards, John, *Mary I: England's Catholic Queen*, Yale University Press, New Haven and London, 2011.

Elton, G. R., *Reform and Renewal: Thomas Cromwell and the Common Weal*, Cambridge University Press, 1973.

Elton, G. R., *Studies in Tudor and Stuart Politics and Government*, Cambridge University Press, 4 vols, 1974–92.

Elton, G. R., *Tudor Revolution in Government: Administrative Changes in the Reign of Henry VIII*, Cambridge University Press, 1953.

Fernández Álvarez, Manuel, *Carlos V, El César y el Hombre*, Madrid, 2006.

Garrisson, Janine, *A History of Sixteenth-Century France, 1483–1598: Renaissance, Reformation and Rebellion*, Macmillan Press, Basingstoke, 1995.

González Alonso, Benjamín, *Las Cortes y las Leyes de Toro de 1505*, Cortes de Castilla y León, Salamanca, 2006.

Gunn, S. and Monckton, Linda (eds), *Arthur Tudor, Prince of Wales: Life, Death & Commemoration*, The Boydell Press, Woodbridge, 2009.

Gunn, Steven, 'The Early Tudor Tournament', in Starkey (ed.), *Henry VIII: A European Court in England*, pp. 47–8.

Gunn, Steven, 'The French Wars of Henry VIII', in Black, *The Origins of*

War in Early Modern Europe, pp. 28–51.

Gunn, Steven, *Charles Brandon, Duke of Suffolk c. 1484–1545*, Basil Blackwell, Oxford, 1988.

Guy, John (ed.), *The Tudor Monarchy*, London, 1997.

Guy, John, 'Thomas Wolsey, Thomas Cromwell and the Reform of Henrician Government', in MacCullough (ed.), *The Reign of Henry VIII*, pp. 35–57.

Guy, John, *A Daughter's Love: Thomas and Margaret More*, Fourth Estate, London, 2008.

Gwyn, Peter, *The King's Cardinal: The Rise and Fall of Thomas Wolsey*, Pimlico, 2002.

Hatcher, John, 'England in the Aftermath of the Black Death', *Past and Present*, 144 (Aug. 1994), pp. 3–35.

Hay, Denys and Law, John E., *Italy in the Age of the Renaissance 1380–1530*, London, 1989.

Hook, Judith, *The Sack of Rome 1527*, Palgrave Macmillan, Basingstoke, 2004.

Houlbrooke, Ralph A., *The English Family 1450–1700*, Longman, London and New York, 1984.

Hoyle, Richard, 'War and Public Finance', in MacCulloch (ed.), *The Reign of Henry VIII: Politics, Policy and Piety*, pp. 75–99.

Hufton, Olwen, *The Prospect Before Her: A History of Women in Western Europe, Volume 1: 1500–1800*, London, 1995.

Hughes, Michael, *Early Modern Germany, 1477–1806*, Macmillan, Hong Kong, 1992.

Ives, E. W., *Anne Boleyn*, Oxford, 1986.

Jedin, Hubert, *A History of the Council of Trent*, 2 vols, London, Edinburgh and New York, 1961.

Jones, Michael K. and Underwood, Malcolm G., *The King's Mother Lady Margaret Beaufort, Countess of Richmond and Derby*, Cambridge University Press, 1992.

Knecht, R. J., *Renaissance Warrior and Patron: The Reign of Francis I*, Cambridge University Press, 1994.

Lehmberg, Stanford E., *The Reformation Parliament 1529–1536*, Cambridge University Press, 1970.

Liss, Peggy K., *Isabel the Queen: Life and Times*, Oxford University Press, 1992.

Loach, Jennifer, 'The function of ceremonial in the reign of Henry VIII', *Past and Present*, 142 (Feb. 1994), pp. 43–68.

Loades, David, *Henry VIII*, Amberley Publishing, Stroud, 2011.

Lynn, Caro, *A College Professor of the Renaissance: Lucas Marineo Sículo among the Spanish Humanists*, University of Chicago Press, 1937.

MacCulloch, Diarmaid (ed.), *The Reign of Henry VIII Politics, Policy and Piety*, Palgrave, Basingstoke, 1995.

MacCulloch, Diarmaid, *Thomas Cranmer*, Yale University Press, New Haven and London, 1996.

Mallett, Michael, *The Borgias: The Rise and Fall of a Renaissance Dynasty*, Paladin Books, London, 1972.

Márquez de la Plata, Vicenta, *El Trágico Destino de los Hijos de los Reyes Católicos*, Madrid, 2008.

Martin, John Jeffries (ed.), *The Renaissance World*, New York and London, 2007.

Montes Mozo, Catalina, *A Renaissance Princess: The Court of Catherine of Aragón*, University of Portsmouth, 2000.

Moorhouse, Geoffrey, *Great Harry's Navy: How Henry VIII Gave England Sea Power*, Phoenix, London, 2005.

Mottram, Stewart, *Empire and Nation in Early English Renaissance Literature*, D. S. Brewer, Cambridge, 2008.

Navascués Palacio, Pedro (ed.), *Isabel la Católica Reina de Castilla*, Lunwerg, Barcelona and Madrid, 2002.

Neame, Alan, *The Holy Maid of Kent: The Life of Elizabeth Barton 1506–1534*, London, 1971.

Parker, Geoffrey, 'The Political World of Charles V', in Soly (ed.), *Charles V: 1500–1558*, pp. 113–226.

Parry, J. H., *The Spanish Seaborne Empire*, Harmondsworth, 1966.

Pérez Bustamante, Rogelio (ed.), *Don Juan: Principe de las Españas (1478–1497): Colección Diplomatica*, Madrid, 1999.

Pérez, Joseph, 'Fernando el Católico y Felipe I el Hermoso', in González Alonso, *Las Cortes y las Leyes de Toro de 1505*, pp. 159–72, at pp. 164–5.

Pérez, Joseph, 'Los Hijos de la Reina. La Política de Alianzas', in Navascués Palacio (ed.), *Isabel la Católica: Reina de Castilla*, pp. 53–82.

Pérez, Joseph, *La revolución de las Comunidades de Castilla (1520–1521)*, 7th ed., Madrid, 1999.

Perry, Maria, *Sisters to the King*, Chatham, 2002.

Peyronnet, George, 'The distant origins of the Italian wars: political relations between France and Italy in the fourteenth and fifteenth centuries', in Abulafia, David (ed.), *The French Descent into Renaissance Italy 1494–95*, pp. 29–53.

Potter, David, 'Foreign Policy', in MacCulloch (ed.), *The Reign of Henry VIII: Politics, Policy and Piety*, pp. 101–33.

Redworth, Glyn and Checa, Fernando, 'The Courts of the Spanish Habsburgs 1500–1700', in John Adamson (ed.), *The Princely Courts of Europe*, pp. 43–65.

Riddell, Jessica Erin, '*A Mirror of Men': Sovereignty, Performance, and Textuality in Tudor England, 1501–1559*, unpublished doctoral thesis, Queen's University, Kingston, 2009.

Rodríguez de Maribona y Dávila, M., *Historia de los Príncipes de Asturias*, Madrid 1996.

Rodríguez-Salgado, M. J., 'Obeying the Ten Commandments: The First War between Charles V and Francis I, 1520–1529', in Blockmans and Mout, *The World of Emperor Charles V*, pp. 15–67.

Rowlands, Ingrid, 'Rome at the Center of a Civilization', in Martin, *The Renaissance World*, pp. 31–50.

Rumeu de Armas, Antonio, *Itinerario de los Reyes Católicos, 1474–1516*, Madrid, 1974.

Russell, Joycelyne G., *The Field of the Cloth of Gold Men and Manners in 1520*, Routledge, London, 1969.

Scarisbrick, J. J., *Henry VIII*, London, 1968.

Schilling, H., 'The Reformation and the Rise of the Early Modern State', in James D. Tracey (ed.), *Luther and the Modern State in Germany*, Kirksville, 1986.

Setton, Kenneth M., *The Papacy and the Levant (1204–1571)*, 4 vols, The American Philosophical Society, Philadelphia, vol. III, *The Sixteenth Century to the Reign of Julius III*, 1984.

Soly, Hugo (ed.), *Charles V 1500–1558: The Emperor and his Time*, Mercatorlonds, Antwerp, 1999.

Starkey, D. and Coleman, C. (eds), *Revolution Reassessed: Revisions in the History of Tudor Government and Administration*, Oxford, 1986.

Starkey, David (ed.), *Henry VIII: A European Court in England*, BCA, London, 1991.

Starkey, David, *Henry: Virtuous Prince*, London, 2008.

Starkey, David, *Six Wives: The Queens of Henry VIII*, London, 2003.

Strieder, J., *Jacob Fugger: The Rich Merchant and Banker of Augsburg, 1459–1525*, Archon Books, 1966.

Suárez Fernández, Luis, *La España de los Reyes Católicos*, Barcelona, 2005.

Thurley, Simon, *The Royal Palaces of Tudor England: Architecture and*

Court Life 1460–1547, Yale University Press, New Haven and London, 1993.

Val Valdivieso, María Isabel del, 'Juana, Retrato de una Heredera', in González Alonso, Benjamín, *Las Cortes y las Leyes de Toro 1505*, pp. 141–58.

Valdeón Barique, Julio (ed.), *Visión del Reinado de Isabel la Católica*, Instituto Universitario de Historia Simancas, Valladolid, 2004.

Valdeón Baruque, Julio (ed.), *Isabel la Católica y la Política*, Instituto Universitario de Historia Simancas, Valladolid, 2001.

Valdeón Baruque, Julio (ed.), *Sociedad y Economía en Tiempos de Isabel la Católica*, Instituto Universitario de Historia Simancas, Valladolid, 2002.

Weightman, Christine B., *Margaret of York: The Diabolical Duchess*, Amberley Publishing, 2009.

Wernham, R. B., *Before the Armada: The Growth of English Foreign Policy 1485–1588*, London, 1966.

Whitelock, Anna, *Mary Tudor: England's First Queen*, Bloomsbury, London, Berlin and New York, 2010.

Williams, Neville, *Henry VIII and his Court*, Weidenfeld & Nicholson, London, 1971.

Williams, Patrick, *Philip II*, Palgrave Macmillan, Basingstoke, 2001.

Williams, Phillip, *Empire and Holy War in the Mediterranean: The Galley and Maritime Conflict Between the Habsburgs and Ottomans*, I. B. Taurus, London, 2013.

Zalama, Miguel Ángel and Vandenbroeck, Paul, *Felipe el Hermoso La Belleza y la Locura*, Madrid, 2006.

Zalama, Miguel Ángel, 'El rey ha muerto, el rey continúa presente: El interminable viaje de Felipe I de Burgos a Granada', in Zalama and Vandenbroeck, *Felipe el Hermoso*, pp.195–210.

Zalama, Miguel Ángel, *Vida Cotidiana y Arte en el Palacio de la Reina Juana en Tordesillas*, Universidad de Valladolid, 2003.

ACKNOWLEDGEMENTS

I am deeply obliged to Jonathan Reeve for inviting me to write this book and for seeing it through the press with incomparable patience and good humour. My interest in the study of history was stimulated by the inspirational teaching of John Tobias, and the book is dedicated to him in recognition of the enduring debt that I (like so many others) owe him: great teachers really do change lives. It is dedicated, too, to Isabella, the first grandchild of Margaret and myself: Isabella has brought such joy into our lives, and is truly a princess.

I am very grateful to Dr Santiago Martínez Hernández for his advice on courtly and linguistic matters, to Fr Phillip Harris of St John's Roman Catholic Cathedral in Portsmouth for his patience in guiding me through the complexities of canon law and for directing me to the appropriate sources to study it properly, and to Dr Veronica Sprott for interpreting for me the symptoms from which Katharine died.

At Portsmouth, I am obliged to friends and colleagues whose generosity and support have made it such a pleasure to spend a working lifetime (and more) at the university: Miguel Arrebola-Sánchez, Bill Brierley, Rebecca Bunting, Elizabeth Clifford, Professor and Vice-Chancellor John Craven, Rob Hobbs, Maria Hooper, Claire Hutchinson, Margaret Kemble, Anne Matear, John Naysmith, Bob Osborne, Lorraine Randall, Begoña Rodríguez, Dave Russell and Christine Woollins. Special thanks to Professor Tony Chafer and the Centre for European and International Research for their support over many years. Special thanks also to Gillian Ferrett and John Steadman of the History Centre, Portsmouth City Library, and editor Alex Bennett of Amberley Publishing, for their generous help.

My greatest debt, as always, is to Margaret, who illuminates every day of my life.

School of Languages and Area Studies, University of Portsmouth
11 February 2013

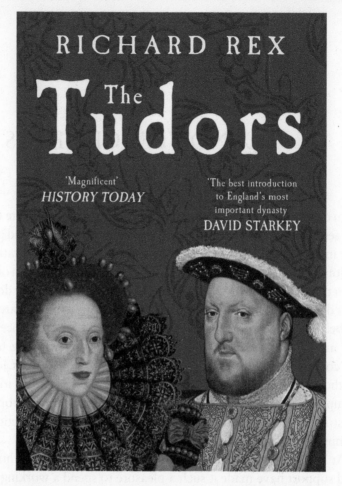

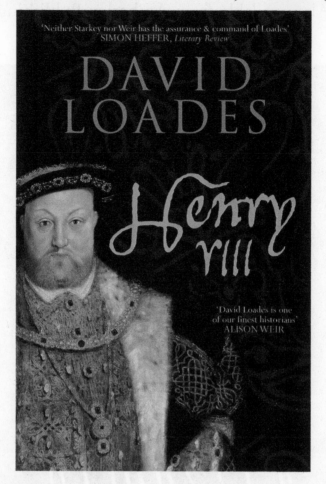

Also available from Amberley Publishing

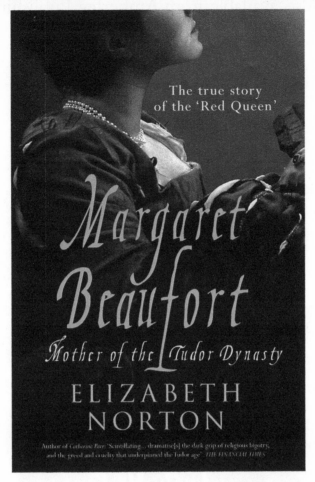

The true story
of the 'Red Queen'

Margaret
Beaufort
Mother of the Tudor Dynasty

ELIZABETH
NORTON

Author of *Catherine Parr*: 'Scintillating... dramatise[s] the dark grip of religious bigotry,
and the greed and cruelty that underpinned the Tudor age'. *THE FINANCIAL TIMES*

Divorced at ten, a mother at thirteen & three times a widow.
The extraordinary true story of the 'Red Queen', Lady Margaret
Beaufort, matriarch of the Tudors

'Portrait of a medieval matriarch' THE INDEPENDENT

Born in the midst of the Wars of the Roses, Margaret Beaufort became the greatest heiress of her time.
She survived a turbulent life, marrying four times and enduring imprisonment before passing her claim
to the crown of England to her son, Henry VII, the first of the Tudor monarchs.

Henry VII gave his mother unparalleled prominence during his reign and she established herself as an
independent woman.

£9.99 Paperback
63 illustrations (39 col)
272 pages
978-1-4456-0578-4

Also available as an ebook
Available from all good bookshops or to order direct
Please call **01453-847-800**
www.amberleybooks.com

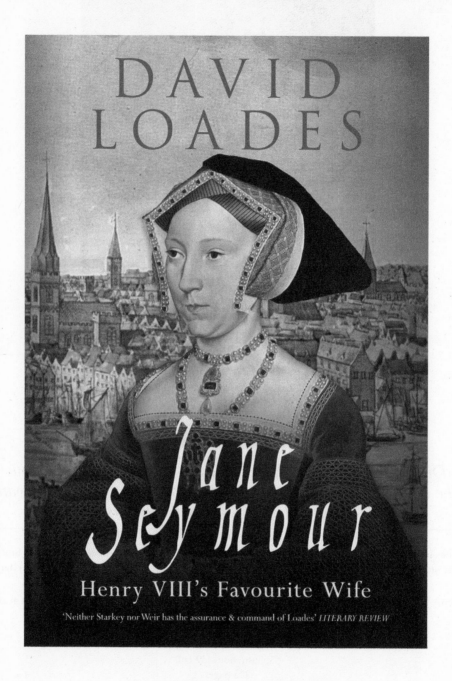

The Tudor femmes fatales
who changed English history

The Boleyn Women

ELIZABETH NORTON

Also available from Amberley Publishing

A biography of Henry VIII's fifth wife, beheaded for playing Henry at his own game – adultery

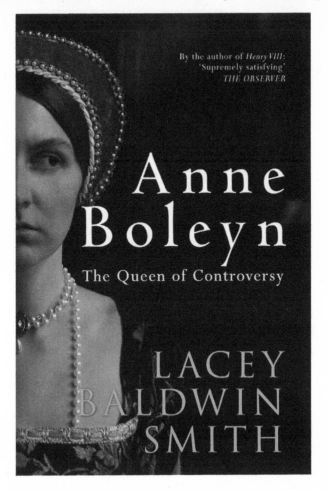

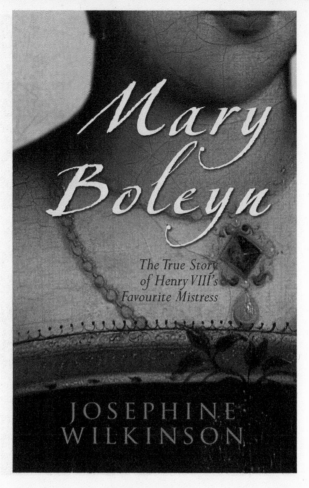

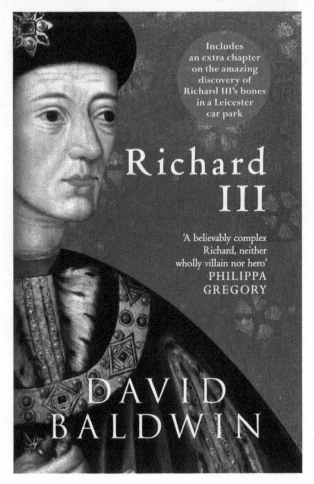

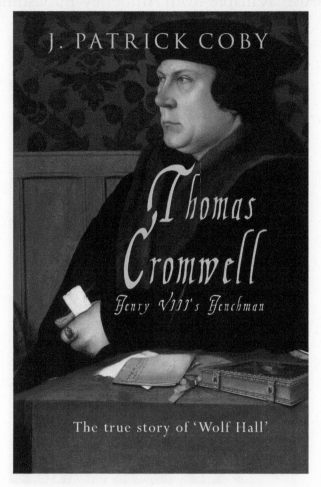

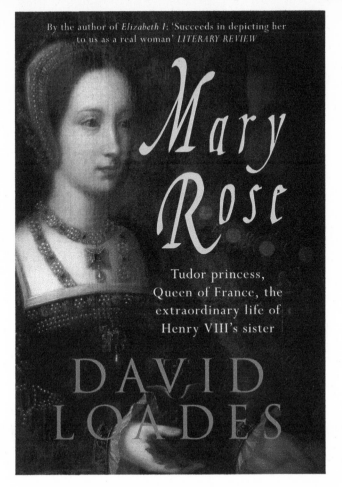

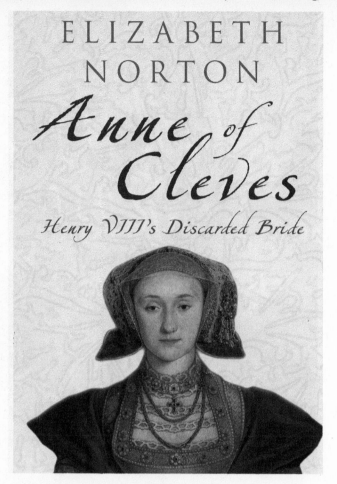

Also available from Amberley Publishing

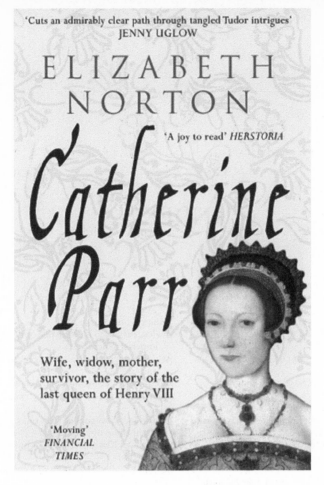

'Cuts an admirably clear path through tangled Tudor intrigues'
JENNY UGLOW

ELIZABETH
NORTON

'A joy to read' HERSTORIA

Catherine Parr

Wife, widow, mother,
survivor, the story of the
last queen of Henry VIII

'Moving'
*FINANCIAL
TIMES*

Wife, widow, mother, survivor, the story of the last queen of Henry VIII

'Scintillating' THE FINANCIAL TIMES
'Norton cuts an admirably clear path through the tangled Tudor intrigues' *JENNY UGLOW*
'Wonderful, an excellent book, a joy to read' HERSTORIA

The sixth wife of Henry VIII was also the most married queen of England, outliving three husbands
before finally marrying for love. Catherine Parr was enjoying her freedom after her first two arranged
marriages when she caught the attention of the elderly Henry VIII. She was the most reluctant of all
Henry's wives, offering to become his mistress rather than submit herself to the dangers of becoming
Henry's queen. This only served to increase Henry's enthusiasm for the young widow and Catherine
was forced to abandon her lover for the decrepit king.

£9.99 Paperback
49 illustrations (39 colour)
304 pages
978-1-4456-0383-4

Also available as an ebook
Available from all good bookshops or to order direct
Please call **01453-847-800**
www.amberleybooks.com

INDEX